THE THIRD WOMAN

HOUGHTON MIFFLIN COMPANY · BOSTON

Dallas   Geneva, Ill.   Hopewell, N.J.   Palo Alto   London

THE THIRD WOMAN

MINORITY WOMEN WRITERS

OF THE UNITED STATES

Edited by DEXTER FISHER

Director of English Programs,
Modern Language Association

Printed in the U.S.A.
Library of Congress Catalog Card Number: 79-87863
ISBN: 0-395-27707-8

AMERICAN INDIAN WOMEN WRITERS

PAULA GUNN ALLEN "Catching One Clear Thought Alive," "Grandmother," and "Moonshot: 1969." Copyright © 1977 by Paula Gunn Allen. By permission of the author. "Medicine Song" from *Four Indian Poets,* ed. John R. Milton (Dakota Press, 1974). Copyright © 1974 by John R. Milton. Reprinted by permission of John R. Milton.

KAY BENNETT "The Changing Woman Story" from *Kaibah: Recollections of a Navajo Girlhood* by Kay Bennett. Copyright © 1964 by Kay Bennett. Reprinted by permission of Westernlore Books.

JANET CAMPBELL "Aaron Nicholas, Almost Ten," "Desmet, Idaho, March 1969," and "On a Catholic Childhood" from *Voices of the Rainbow,* ed. Kenneth Rosen (Viking Press, 1974). Copyright © 1975 by Kenneth Rosen. Reprinted by permission of the author and Kenneth Rosen. "The Snow Keeps Falling" from *Time to Greez! Incantations from the Third World.* Copyright © 1975 by Janet Campbell Hale. Reprinted by permission of the author with grateful acknowledgment to Glide Publications.

"THE CHANGING WOMAN" from *Myth and Modern Man* by Barbara Dodds Stanford and Gene Stanford. Copyright © 1972 by Barbara Dodds Stanford and Gene Stanford. Reprinted by permission of Pocket Books, a Simon & Schuster division of Gulf & Western Corporation.

ELIZABETH COOK-LYNN "XXI," "Contradiction," "History of Unchi," and "Some of My Best Friends" from *Then Badger Said This* by Elizabeth Cook-Lynn (Vantage Press, 1977). Copyright © 1977 by Elizabeth Cook-Lynn. Reprinted by permission of the author.

ANITA ENDREZZE-DANIELSON "The Belly Dancer's Song," "Making Adjustments," "Shaman/Bear," "Still Life." Copyright © 1977 by Anita Endrezze-Danielson. By permission of the author.

NIA FRANCISCO "Friday Noon Feelings" and "Tomorrow Noon" originally appeared in *The Indian Historian,* 9, No. 2 (Spring 1976). Copyright © 1976 by *The Indian Historian.* Reprinted by permission of the author and Jeanette Henry, editor of *The Indian Historian.* "iridescent child" from *Southwest: A Contemporary Anthology,* ed. Karl and Jane Kopp. Copyright © 1977 by Nia Francisco. Reprinted by permission of the author and Karl Kopp. "she-bear" from *I Had Been Hungry All the Years,* ed. Glenna Luschei. Copyright © 1975 by Nia Francisco. Reprinted by permission of the author and the publishers of Solo Press.

ACKNOWLEDGMENTS

JOY HARJO " 'Are You Still There,' " "Conversations Between Here and Home," and "Watching Crow, Looking South Towards the Manzano Mountains" from *The Last Song* by Joy Harjo (Puerto del Sol Press, 1975). Copyright © 1975 by Joy Harjo. Reprinted by permission of the author. "There Was a Dance, Sweetheart." Copyright © 1977 by Joy Harjo. By permission of the author.

ROBERTA HILL "Conversation Overheard on Tamalpais Road" and "Leap in the Dark." Copyright © 1977 by Roberta Hill. By permission of the author.

MOURNING DOVE (Hum-ishu-ma) "The Great Spirit Names the Animal People: How Coyote Came by His Power" from *Tales of the Okanogans,* ed. Donald Hines. Copyright © 1976 by Donald Hines. Reprinted by permission of Donald Hines.

OPAL LEE POPKES "Zuma Chowt's Cave" from *The Man to Send Rain Clouds,* ed. Kenneth Rosen (Viking, 1974). Copyright © 1974 by Kenneth Rosen. Reprinted by permission of The Viking Press.

WENDY ROSE "For the White Poets Who Would Be Indian" and "I Expected My Skin and My Blood to Ripen" from *Academic Squaw: Reports to the World from the Ivory Tower* by Wendy Rose (Blue Cloud Press, 1977). Copyright © 1977 by Wendy Rose. Reprinted by permission of the author. "Long Division: A Tribal History" originally appeared in *Caliban: A Journal of New World Thought and Writing,* 1, No. 2 (Spring/Summer 1976), and in *Long Division: A Tribal History* by Wendy Rose (Strawberry Press, 1976). Copyright © 1977 by Wendy Rose. Reprinted by permission of the author and Roberto Marquez, editor of *Caliban.* "Vanishing Point: Urban Indian" has appeared in *The Next World,* ed. Joseph Bruchac, and *Long Division: A Tribal History* by Wendy Rose. Copyright © 1977 by Wendy Rose. Reprinted by permission of the author.

HELEN SEKAQUAPTEWA "Marriage" by permission from *Me and Mine: The Life Story of Helen Sekaquaptewa as Told to Louise Udall* (Tucson: University of Arizona Press), copyright © 1969.

LESLIE MARMON SILKO "Gallup, New Mexico—Indian Capital of the World" first appeared in *New America: A Review,* 2, No. 3 (Summer/Fall 1976). The selection presented here is from *Ceremony* by Leslie Marmon Silko (Viking, 1977). Copyright © 1977 by Leslie Silko. Reprinted by permission of the author and Richard Seaver. "Toe'osh: A Laguna Coyote Story" and "Where Mountain Lion Lay Down with Deer" from *Voices of the Rainbow,* ed. Kenneth Rosen (Viking, 1975). These poems first appeared in *Laguna Woman* by Leslie Silko. Copyright © 1974 by Leslie Silko. Reprinted by permission of the author, Kenneth Rosen, and Richard Seaver. "Stories and Their Tellers—A Conversation with Leslie Marmon Silko." Copyright © 1977 by Dexter Fisher. By permission of Dexter Fisher. "Storyteller" first appeared in *Puerto del Sol,* Fall 1975. Copyright © 1975 by Leslie Silko. Reprinted by permission of the author and Richard Seaver.

ELIZABETH SULLIVAN "Legend of the Trail of Tears" from *Indian Legends of the Trail of Tears and Other Stories* as told by Elizabeth Sullivan. Copyright © 1974 by Elizabeth Sullivan. Reprinted by permission of the author.

JUDITH IVALOO VOLBORTH "Black-Coat Meets Coyote (Three Conversations of the Absurd)" and "Three Songs to Mark the Night" from *Thunder-Root* by J. Ivaloo Volborth. Copyright © 1977 by J. Ivaloo Volborth. Reprinted by permission of the author.

MARNIE WALSH "Poets/Poems," "Thomas Iron-Eyes Born *circa* 1840. Died 1919, Rosebud Agency, S.D.," and "Vickie Loans-Arrow 1972" from *A Taste of the*

BLACK WOMEN WRITERS

NAOMI LONG MADGETT "Offspring," "Writing a Poem," and "Black Woman" from *Pink Ladies in the Afternoon* (Lotus Press, 1972) by Naomi Long Madgett. Copyright © 1972 by Naomi Long Madgett. Reprinted by permission of the author.

PAULE MARSHALL "Brooklyn" from *Soul Clap Hands and Sing* by Paule Marshall. Copyright © 1961 by Paule Marshall. Reprinted by permission of the author.

MAY MILLER "Death Is Not Master," "Place in the Morning," and "The Scream" from *Dust of Uncertain Journey* by May Miller. Copyright © 1975 by May Miller. Reprinted by permission of the author.

TONI MORRISON " 'Intimate Things in Place'—A Conversation with Toni Morrison" from *The Massachusetts Review*. Copyright © 1977 The Massachusetts Review, Inc. "1921" from *Sula* by Toni Morrison. Copyright © 1973 by Toni Morrison. Reprinted by permission of Alfred A. Knopf, Inc.

ANN PETRY "Doby's Gone" from *Miss Muriel and Other Stories* by Ann Petry. Copyright © 1944 Atlanta University. Reprinted from *Phylon: The Atlanta University Review of Race and Culture,* Vol. 5, Fourth Quarter (December 1944), 361–366, by permission of *Phylon.*

NTOZAKE SHANGE "Cypress-sassafras" from *Sassafras* (Shameless Hussy Press, 1977) by Ntozake Shange. Copyright © 1976, 1977 by Ntozake Shange. Reprinted by permission of Russell and Volkening as agents for the author.

ALICE WALKER "Burial." Copyright © 1972 by Alice Walker. Reprinted from *Revolutionary Petunias and Other Poems* by permission of Harcourt Brace Jovanovich, Inc. "Women." Copyright © 1970 by Alice Walker. Reprinted from *Revolutionary Petunias and Other Poems* by permission of Harcourt Brace Jovanovich, Inc. "The Revenge of Hannah Kemhuff." Copyright © 1973 by Alice Walker. Reprinted from *In Love and Trouble* by permission of Harcourt Brace Jovanovich, Inc. "Saving the Life That Is Your Own: The Importance of Models in the Artist's Life." Copyright © 1976 by Alice Walker. Reprinted by permission of the Julian Bach Literary Agency, Inc.

MARGARET WALKER "I Want to Write" and "For Gwen" from *October Journey*. Copyright © 1973 by Margaret Walker. Reprinted by permission of the author and Broadside Press.

SHERLEY WILLIAMS "Any Woman's Blues," "The Collateral Adjective," and "Say Hello to John." Copyright © 1975 by Sherley Williams. Reprinted from *The Peacock Poems* by permission of Wesleyan University Press. "generations:" has appeared in *Nimrod,* 21, No. 2, and 22, No. 1 (University of Tulsa). Copyright © 1978 by Sherley Williams. Reprinted by permission of the author and the editor of *Nimrod.*

YVONNE "Aunt Martha: Severance Pay" and "1936." Copyright © 1978 by Yvonne. By permission of the author.

CHICANA WRITERS

FABIOLA CABEZA DE BACA "The Women of New Mexico" from *We Fed Them Cactus* (University of New Mexico Press, 1954). Copyright © 1954 by the University of New Mexico Press. Reprinted by permission of the publishers of the University of New Mexico Press.

ANA CASTILLO "Napa, California," "1975," and "Our Tongue Was Nahuatl" originally appeared in *Revista Chicano-Riqueña,* 4, No. 4 (Autumn 1976). Copyright ©

CARMEN TAFOLLA "Bailar..." "...Repeating Chorus...," "Allí por la calle San Luís," and "San Antonio." Copyright © 1977 by Carmen Tafolla. By permission of the author.

CARMEN TOSCANO "La Llorona" from *La Llorona* by Carmen Toscano (1959). By permission of the Fondo de Cultura Economica.

INÉS HERNANDEZ TOVAR "Para un viejito desconocido que aun conozco," "Para Teresa," and "To other women who were ugly once" from *Con Razon, Corazon: Poetry* by Inés Hernandez Tovar. Copyright © 1977 by Inés Hernandez Tovar. Reprinted by permission of the author.

ESTELA PORTILLO TRAMBLEY "Pay the Criers" and "The Burning" from *Rain of Scorpions* (Tonatiuh Publications, 1975). Copyright © 1975 by Estela Portillo Trambley. Reprinted by permission of the author.

MARCELA CHRISTINE LUCERO-TRUJILLO "The Dilemma of the Modern Chicana Artist and Critic" was first published in *De Colores Journal*, 3, No. 3 (1977). Copyright © 1977 by *De Colores*. Reprinted by permission of the editor of *De Colores*. " 'Machismo Is Part of Our Culture,' " "No more cookies, please," "Roseville, Minn., U.S.A.," and "The Músicos from Capulín." Copyright © 1977 by Marcela Trujillo. By permission of the author. "The Advent of My Death" from *Time to Greez! Incantations from the Third World*. Copyright © 1975 by Third World Communications. Reprinted by permission of Glide Publications.

XELINA "Urban Life," "Witnesses," and "Nightmare." Copyright © 1977 by Xelina. By permission of the author.

ASIAN AMERICAN WOMEN WRITERS

AI "Twenty-Year Marriage," "The Anniversary," "The Country Midwife: A Day" from *Cruelty* by Ai (Houghton Mifflin, 1973). Copyright © 1973 by Ai. Reprinted by permission of the author.

MEI-MEI BERSSENBRUGGE "Ghost," "Old Man Let's Go Fishing in the Yellow Reeds of the Bay," "Chronicle" from *Summits Move with the Tide* by Mei-Mei Berssenbrugge (*The Greenfield Review*, 1974). Copyright © 1974 by Mei-Mei Berssenbrugge. Reprinted by permission of the author.

DIANA CHANG "Rhythms" and "What Matisse Is After" first appeared in *The Painted Bride Quarterly*, 2, No. 1 (Winter 1975). Copyright © 1975 by Diana Chang. Reprinted by permission of the author and *The Painted Bride Quarterly*. "Still Life" appeared in *Bridge: An Asian American Perspective*, 4, No. 4 (October 1976). Copyright © 1976 by Diana Chang. Reprinted by permission of the author and *Bridge*. "Cannibalism" appeared in *Confrontation*, No. 8 (Spring 1974). Copyright © 1974 by *Confrontation* Magazine. Reprinted by permission of Martin Tucker, editor of *Confrontation*. Excerpt from *Intimate Friends*. Copyright © 1977 by Diana Chang. By permission of the author. "Woolgathering, Ventriloquism and the Double Life" from *The American Pen*, 3, No. 1 (Winter 1970–1971). Copyright © 1970 by Diana Chang. Reprinted by permission of the author. "Allegory" appeared in *New York Quarterly*, Issue No. 4 (Fall 1970). Copyright © 1970 by Diana Chang. Reprinted by permission of the author.

FAY CHIANG "it was as if" appeared in *Sunbury*, 2, No. 1 (Spring 1976). Copyright © 1976 by Fay Chiang. Reprinted by permission of the author.

JESSICA HAGEDORN "Sometimes You Look Like Lady Day." Copyright © 1973, 1977 by Jessica Hagedorn. By permission of the author. "Song for My Father" originally appeared in the book *Dangerous Music* published by Momo's Press in San Francisco. Copyright © 1975 by Jessica Hagedorn. Reprinted by permission of the author.

TERU KANAZAWA "The Look of Success" and "Dumb Patronage." Copyright © 1977 by Teru Kanazawa. By permission of the author.

HELEN AOKI KANEKO "Enigma," "Wind," "Upon Seeing an Etching." Copyright © 1977 by Helen Aoki Kaneko. By permission of the author.

MAXINE HONG KINGSTON "No Name Woman" from *The Woman Warrior: Memoirs of a Girlhood Among Ghosts* by Maxine Hong Kingston. Copyright © 1975, 1976 by Maxine Hong Kingston. Reprinted by permission of Alfred A. Knopf, Inc.

GERALDINE KUDAKA "On Writing Asian-American Poetry" and "i shoulda told you." Copyright © 1977 by Geraldine Kudaka. By permission of the author.

SHIRLEY GEOK-LIN LIM "Modern Secrets," "Christmas in Exile," "Potions," and "I Would Like." Copyright © 1977 by Shirley Geok-Lin Lim. By permission of the author.

LAUREEN MAR "My Mother, Who Came from China, Where She Never Saw Snow" and "Chinatown 4." Copyright © 1977 by Laureen Mar. By permission of the author. "Chinatown 1" and "Chinatown 2" first appeared in *The Greenfield Review*, 6, 1 & 2, (Spring 1977). Copyright © 1976 by *The Greenfield Review*. Reprinted by permission of Joseph Bruchac, editor of *The Greenfield Review*.

JANICE MIRIKITANI "Sing with Your Body" and "Attack the Water" from *Asian American Heritage*, ed. David Wand (Washington Square Press, 1974). Copyright © 1973 by Janice Mirikitani. Reprinted by permission of the author.

GAIL MIYASAKI Grateful acknowledgment is made to *Asian Women* for permission to reprint "Obāchan" by Gail Miyasaki. Copyright © 1971 by *Asian Women's Journal*.

JOANNE HARUMI SECHI "Being Japanese-American Doesn't Mean 'Made in Japan.'" Reprinted with permission of P.E.N. American Center from *The American Pen*, 5, No. 3 (Late Summer 1973).

LAURA TOKUNAGA "Behind Locked Doors" appeared in *Bridge: An Asian American Perspective*, 4, No. 4 (October 1976). Copyright © 1978 by Laura Tokunaga. Reprinted by permission of the author. "Geography" and "Tiger Year" appeared in *Counterpoint* (Asian Studies Center, UCLA, 1976). Copyright © 1978 by Laura Tokunaga. Reprinted by permission of the author.

HISAYE YAMAMOTO "Las Vegas Charley" first appeared in *The Arizona Quarterly* 17, No. 4 (Winter 1961); it was subsequently published in *Asian American Heritage*, ed. David Wand (Washington Square Press, 1974). Copyright © 1961 by *The Arizona Quarterly*. Reprinted by permission of the author and the editor of *The Arizona Quarterly*. "Seventeen Syllables" from *Counterpoint* (Asian Studies Center, UCLA, 1976). Copyright © 1949 by *Partisan Review;* copyright © renewed 1976 by Hisaye Yamamoto DeSoto. Reprinted by permission of the author.

CONTENTS

CONTENTS

BLACK WOMEN

WRITERS

CONTENTS

CHICANA

WRITERS

ASIAN AMERICAN

WOMEN WRITERS

CONTENTS

PREFACE

Though twenty years have passed since the inception of the civil rights movement and more than a decade separates the women's movement from the present day, minority women writers have yet to be represented adequately in anthologies or to receive the critical attention their literature deserves. Usually the emphasis in black studies, or its equivalent, has been on male authors; similarly, the focus in women's studies has been on white women writers. I hope to begin, at least, to ameliorate the situation by demonstrating, with this anthology, not only that minority women have created and pursued a literary tradition of their own, but that their works represent some of the most exciting and creative innovations going on in contemporary literature. Just as the nations of the third world are "emerging" in the sense that the Euro-American world has "discovered" them, so is "the Third Woman" revealing herself to us, though she has always been present. Her hyphenated existence—as Asian American, black American, Mexican American, or American Indian—imbues her angle of vision with perceptions that revitalize our concepts of tradition and folklore, language and imagination.

The purpose of this anthology is to present the range, both in subject and style, of the best of the literature written by contemporary minority women in the United States. The volume may be used in introductory, multiethnic, or women's literature courses, as well as in survey courses in American literature. An introduction, providing a historical and cultural context for the literature, precedes each section. The four appendices at the end offer suggestions for discussion and topics for writing in the areas of folklore, contexts, storytelling, and poetry. The design of these appendices is cross cultural so that thematic, generic, and stylistic comparisons may be made among individual works from the four sections. At the end of each section is a selected reading list that includes anthologies and journals pertinent to minority women writers, as well as primary works by them. In addition, biographical information, when available, precedes the work of each author.

To the extent possible this anthology avoids the "shotgun" approach of including a single work by as many authors as possible. Rather, multiple selections demonstrate both the linguistic and artistic versatility of individual authors, as well as these authors' contributions to a developing literary tradition. Within reason, I have tried not to duplicate pieces that have been widely anthologized and have included a number of new works previously unpublished. By necessity some authors have been excluded, but the decision in most instances has been made because their work is readily accessible in other places.   •

Finally *The Third Woman* represents a collective effort to bring together in one place the best of the literature by minority women, and for their continuing encouragement and support, I wish to thank all of the contributors. I wish also to acknowledge the Modern Language Association's Commission on the Literatures and Languages of America for its work in redefining American literature by encouraging and promoting the study and teaching of America's "neglected" literatures. For their helpful comments at each stage in the development of the manuscript, I am indebted to all my readers, including G. E. Carter, University of Wisconsin, La Crosse; Mary Anne Ferguson, University of Massachusetts, Boston; Kai-yu Hsu, San Francisco State University; Mildred B. Munday, the Ohio State University; and Mary Helen Washington, University of Detroit. I wish especially to thank LaVonne Ruoff of the University of Illinois at Chicago Circle, and Michael Dorris of Dartmouth, to whom I owe the happy inspiration of the title of this book.

GENERAL INTRODUCTION

In 1773 Phillis Wheatley became the first African in America to publish a book of poetry in English. A century later, Sarah Winnemucca Hopkins wrote *Life Among the Piutes,* becoming one of the first American Indians to record the customs and rituals of her tribe. These two minority women are among the pioneer writers whose works mark the inception of a literary tradition that has begun to flower in the twentieth century. Gwendolyn Brooks, for example, received the 1949 Pulitzer Prize in poetry for *Annie Allen,* and became the first black to be so honored. In 1973 Alice Walker won the Rosenthal Award of the National Institute of Arts and Letters for *In Love and Trouble,* a collection of short stories about black women. And in 1976 the National Book Critics' Circle Award went to Maxine Hong Kingston for her inspired memoirs of a Chinese American childhood in *The Woman Warrior.* These are only three examples of the number of minority women included in this anthology who have received literary awards and creative writing fellowships.

Yet, despite these impressive achievements, most minority women writers remain virtually unknown to students of literature. Their works are isolated in small-press publications or regional journals; all too frequently, their books go out of print and become inaccessible; most are neglected by anthologists, while those few who are regularly anthologized suffer because the same works are selected over and over again. All of this results in a common assumption that there *is* no literature by minority women.

The purpose of *The Third Woman* is to demonstrate just the opposite— that there is, in fact, a rich body of literature by minority women that has developed within a historical and cultural framework. Such literature deserves our attention not only because it exists but because it has the resources for expanding our imaginative powers and deepening our appreciation of language and genre. In seeking to reflect the extraordinary range of subjects and linguistic styles that fall into the domain of minority women writers, I have avoided selecting only pieces that are exclusively "political" or "feminist." Rather, the political statement of this book derives from its existence as the first major collection of literature by American Indian, Afro-American, Chicana, and Asian American women. And although feminism informs a number of the selections here, it is but one of many subjects—including heritage, tradition, creativity, relationships, and identity—addressed by minority women writers in a variety of genres ranging from blues poetry to personal narratives, from sonnets and elegies to essays and fiction.

The Third Woman is organized by minority group for the sake of efficiently presenting the framework within which individual works should be read. This is not to say that the Asian American woman writer is confined by her ethnic background, but rather to suggest the historical and cultural conditions that may enrich her perspective. Why, for example, is Chicana poetry primarily bilingual? What has led American Indian writers to integrate the oral tradition into their literature? Why are folk sources so essential to black literature? Literature does occur in a context, and an understanding of the special and unique qualities of a given cultural landscape can greatly enhance our appreciation of individual works. For that reason, then, each part begins with "Contexts"—selections that illuminate the historical and cultural circumstances within which the fiction and poetry have been nurtured. Folklore, legends, personal narratives, interviews, and essays are included to indicate some of the impulses that lie behind the literature. The second division within each part—"Traditions, Narratives, and Fiction" —includes short stories, myths, and folktales that imaginatively amplify the dimensions of context, while the poetry of the third division illustrates the linguistic versatility of minority women writers. The four appendices at the end of the book—"Folklore and Literature," "Texts and Contexts," "Storytelling and Narratives," and "Poetry"—provide focused discussions of elements common to the literatures of all four groups and may be read in conjunction with the study of each literature. Because, with few exceptions, the majority of the selections are by contemporary writers, the introduction to each section discusses the historical and literary contributions of the earlier women writers.

Leslie Marmon Silko, a young Laguna writer, has said, "You don't have anything if you don't have the stories." It seems that the value of this anthology resides in the continuing power of literature to affirm the values by which we live, and, certainly, our vision of the world is incomplete without the "stories" offered here by minority women writers.

LONG DIVISION: A TRIBAL HISTORY

Our skin loosely lies across grass borders;
stones shooting up through the cells are loaded
down with placement sticks, a great tearing
and appearance of holes. We are bought and divided
into clay pots; we die in granite scaffolding
on the shape of the Sierras and lay down with lips open
thrusting songs on the world. Who are we

and do we still live? Our shamans sleep
saying no. So outside of eternity we struggle
til our blood has spread off our bodies and
frayed the sunset edges; it's our blood that

gives you those southwestern skies. Year after year
we give, harpooned with hope only to fall bouncing through
the canyons, our songs decreasing with distance.
I suckle coyotes and grieve.

Wendy Rose

It will take a long time, but the story must be told.
There must not be any lies.

Leslie Marmon Silko, Storyteller

AMERICAN INDIAN

WOMEN WRITERS

INTRODUCTION

HISTORICAL PERSPECTIVES

To study American Indian literature is to study the power of language to shape one's perception of human experience.* The word has power because it is the vehicle of the imagination and the means of clarifying relationships between individuals and their landscapes, communities, visions. As Paula Gunn Allen (Laguna) says,

> The tribes seek through song, ceremony, legend, sacred stories (myths), and tales to embody, articulate, and share reality, to bring the isolated self into harmony and balance with this reality, to verbalize the sense of the majesty and the reverent mystery of all things, and to actualize, in language, those truths of being and experience that give to humanity its greatest significance and dignity. The artistry of the tribes is married to the essence of language itself, for in language we seek to share our being with that of the community, and thus to share in the communal awareness of the tribes.[1]

Language is the means by which one "knows" the universe and shares that knowledge with the community.

In preliterate tribal communities, this regard for language is expressed within the oral tradition through storytelling—the means by which those stories and legends, myths and folklore, poetry and song that constitute the memory banks of tradition of a given culture are handed down from one generation to the next. In most tribal communities, storytelling takes place in the winter evenings when the tribe has settled into one area for the season and there is time to enjoy the individual talents of the various storytellers. Storytelling within the oral tradition is as much a form of entertainment as of education, and its context is one of performance. Voice intonations, gestures, facial expressions, verbal embellishment—all exhibit the particular gifts of the storyteller, whose audience can anticipate each sequence of events that is to come. Indeed, the audience is an integral part of the performance context of oral storytelling, often determining whether the stories to be shared will be sacred or secular, narratives of a mythic past or accounts of more recent historical events. Women as well as men may be storytellers; within some of

---

* Although "American Indian" is the term used most frequently in this section, some prefer "Native American" for historical accuracy; that is, Indians were America's first natives.

the Plains cultures and the matrilineal Pueblo cultures, for example, the grandmother is the supreme storyteller, passing on her knowledge of tradition to the young.

N. Scott Momaday (Kiowa) has said, "Storytelling is imaginative and creative in nature. . . . The possibilities of storytelling are precisely those of understanding the human experience."[2] And for Leslie Marmon Silko (Laguna), "You don't have anything if you don't have the stories."[3] Storytelling, then, is integral to the oral tradition because it is a way of storing knowledge, and as long as the tribe exists as a community, the word as spoken is sufficient. But what happens to storytelling and the oral tradition when the community begins to break down under the pressure of external conflicts, the advent of reservation life, and the introduction of English-based education? In short, what happens when a way of life that has existed for centuries suddenly undergoes cataclysmic and brutal changes, such as occurred for many American Indians during the nineteenth century?

While it is not the purpose here to examine all the historic odds against survival that Wendy Rose decries in "Long Division: A Tribal History" or to recount the calamities that have plagued American Indians—disease, Indian wars, broken treaties, relocation—the impact of certain events cannot be forgotten or overestimated. The Indian Removal Act of 1830, for example, under the direction of the Bureau of Indian Affairs (BIA) established in 1824, not only ordered the eviction of almost all Indians east of the Mississippi into the lands of the West but also led to the infamous Trail of Tears and the death of four thousand Cherokees in that forced midwinter march. The 1840 Gold Rush all but eliminated the Indians of California. By 1883 the southern and northern herds of buffalo, the very core of survival for the Plains Indians, had been destroyed, and the Sun dance—one of the most important rituals of the Siouan tribes—had been outlawed. Reservations were established in 1851, replacing the policy of removal, and in 1879 the first off-reservation school for Indians opened its doors in Carlisle, Pennsylvania. The Dawes Severalty Act of 1887, which provided for the assignment of small plots of land to individuals, reflected the assimilationist thrust of government Indian policy and was ultimately to reduce the remaining Indian land base from 132 to 32 million acres by 1928. In addition to loss of land, the act had disastrous consequences for those Plains Indians who found the shift from a nomadic hunting and warfare culture to a static agricultural economy almost impossible to make. Many of them turned to the newly found Ghost Dance religion, hoping to realize its promise of the return of the dead and the buffalo, but the massacre of Indians at Wounded Knee in 1890 shattered forever any dreams of recapturing an idyllic past.[4] Further resistance was futile. By 1910 the government estimated that 210 thousand Indians were left of the 10 to 15 million people who were natives of America when Europe first made contact with the New World at the end of the fifteenth century.

Dispossessed of their land and rights, threatened with the dissolution of their culture, and demoralized by confinement to reservations, American Indian men and women began writing down their life stories and recording tribal lore in an effort to preserve the traditions of the past. They adhered to the concept that it might take a long time, but "the story must be told. There must not be any lies." Writing became a means to perpetuate tradition in the face of cultural disintegration, and it also created new audiences and gave Native Americans a chance to tell their side of the story. By the end of the nineteenth century, a written tradition was beginning to emerge out of the oral tradition that would reach fruition in the 1960s and 1970s in the works of contemporary American Indians. The word continued to be equated with ways of knowing and of passing knowledge on.

American Indian women have been a part of the storytelling tradition—both oral and written—from its inception, passing on stories to their children and their children's children and using the word to advance those concepts crucial to cultural survival. One of the first narratives by a woman is *Life Among the Piutes,* written by Sarah Winnemucca Hopkins in 1883. Prompted by her desire to stir public opinion on behalf of the sad plight of her tribe, she depicts with vivid description her struggle to help the Paiutes in the face of Indian wars and broken treaties. The proceeds from the book helped finance a lecture tour to the East that eventually resulted in some legislation in favor of the Paiutes.[5]

In 1901 Zitkala-Sa, a Dakota Sioux woman, wrote *Old Indian Legends* and noted in the preface, "I have tried to transplant the native spirit of these tales—root and all—into the English language since America in the last few centuries has acquired a second tongue."[6] Written for children, her collection includes legends and trickster tales that she had learned as a young girl. She later published *American Indian Stories* in 1921; in this book she describes, among other things, the painful experience of being sent to boarding school without speaking English or knowing American customs.[7]

Another writer of the period is Marie McLaughlin, whose publication in 1916 of *Myths and Legends of the Sioux* reflects a growing trend among American Indians to establish a literary tradition based on the material of their culture. Hum-ishu-ma (Mourning Dove) is one of the first American Indian women, for example, to explore the significance of heritage through fiction. Born in 1888 in Idaho, Mourning Dove was reared for a time with her grandmother, who imbued in her a respect for ancestral customs and lore. Her first book, *Co-ge-wea—The Half Blood,* published in 1927, may well be the first American Indian novel by a woman.[8] A fictional account of events that occurred during the last great roundup of buffaloes on the Flathead Indian Reservation in Montana in 1908, the novel examines the complex sensibilities of the half-breed who is, in this case, a woman. Somewhat sentimental, the novel is nevertheless important because it combines elements of the oral tradition of the Okanogans (Mourning Dove's tribe) with a contemporary problem. While the narratives of these early authors may strike a modern reader as romanticized views of Indian life, they are invaluable for their insights into the conflicts surrounding the transition to reservation life.

During the early postreservation period, Indians began to feel a need to organize themselves politically, not only to protect their rights by treaty but also to present their point of view to the American public. The Society of the American Indian (SAI) was formally established in 1911, launching a Pan-Indian movement that would span the next two decades. Its purpose was to provide a collective forum for Indians who sought to redress the numerous inequities they had suffered. Zitkala-Sa (whose English name is Gertrude Bonnin) served as secretary-treasurer of the SAI for several years and was acting editor of its publication, *The American Indian Magazine*, from 1918 to 1919.[9] Often appearing in native dress, Bonnin lectured widely and campaigned for citizenship for American Indians, reforms and employment of Indians in the Bureau of Indian Affairs, and equitable settlements of tribal land claims.

When the SAI disintegrated under the pressure of internal politics, Bonnin went on to found the National Council of American Indians in 1926 and served as president until her death in 1938. Once called the most important member of the early Pan-Indian movement, Bonnin was instrumental in generating interest in Indian affairs among the members of the General Federation of Women's Clubs. The white women of that organization joined ranks with the Indian Rights Association to sponsor investigations into government treatment of Indian tribes. Eventually, the collective efforts of the various Pan-Indian organizations produced the Indian Citizenship Bill, which was passed in 1924, and the appointments for the first time of Native Americans to serve as commissioner and assistant commissioner of the Bureau of Indian Affairs.

The period from the 1890s to the 1930s may be called the period of transition, for Native Americans were compelled to make enormous adjustments to reservation life and boarding schools and to learn the customs and language of Anglo-American society. While a number of Indians, like Bonnin and Mourning Dove, were finding their own voices in literature and political movements, an even greater percentage of Native Americans remained on reservations, isolated from the mainstream of American society. Sought out by anthropologists intent on preserving as much information as possible about prereservation beliefs and customs, these Indians composed another type of story, the "as told to" narrative or "ethnographic autobiography." In response to questions posed by anthropologists, individuals told their life stories, usually with the aid of an interpreter.

A number of these "as told to" life stories were narrated by women. Organized to cover the major events in a woman's life—from early childhood through puberty ceremonies and education to marriage and child rearing—

these autobiographies provide important records of the woman's position in various tribal communities, reversing many of the stereotypes about Indian women. Examples of such autobiographies include Truman Michelson's *Autobiography of a Fox Woman* (1918); *Waheenee: An Indian Girl's Story,* recorded and published by Gilbert Wilson in 1921; *The Autobiography of a Papago Woman* (1936) by Ruth Underhill; and *Mountain Wolf Woman* (1961) as told to Nancy Lurie. (An excerpt from Helen Sekaquaptewa's life story [1969] begins on page 31.)

In most of the ethnographic autobiographies and early personal narratives, the authors concentrated on recording aspects of their heritage. Still acutely sensitive to the violent and rapid changes they underwent and convinced of the passing of the old way, they tried to preserve as much of their history as possible. Some Native Americans went on to become anthropologists and ethnographers themselves to insure the authenticity of what was recorded. A notable example is Ella Deloria, a Yankton Sioux, whose work with the Dakota storytellers, published as *Dakota Texts* in 1932, is still the classic authority in the field.

While the urge to perpetuate cultural traditions continues to be a predominant theme in the Native American literature of the last two decades, the emphasis has shifted from a description of the characteristics of heritage to an analysis of the relationship between individuals and their heritage. What does it mean to be an Indian or a "breed"? What is the significance of the oral tradition? Can the written word communicate as much as the spoken word?

With the publication of the Pulitzer Prize-winning *House Made of Dawn* by N. Scott Momaday in 1968, American Indian literature has come into its own. Intensely aware of the impending loss of culture through assimilation, authors such as Momaday yoke tradition with contemporary concerns as they examine the dilemma of the individual caught between two worlds and seek to resolve that conflict through storytelling and a revitalization of the traditions and rituals of their inherited past.

CONTEXTS AND NARRATIVES

Making significant contributions to current American Indian literature are a number of women whose work has its roots in the storytelling tradition of their grandmothers. Ever sensitive to the imperatives of their history, the authors in the first section, "Contexts," present different aspects of their heritage. In the opening interview, Leslie Marmon Silko discusses the importance of writers perpetuating certain stories and traditions within their culture. Each writer has stories to "protect" and by so doing insures the longevity of tradition. Elizabeth Cook-Lynn records one of the Sioux stories that explains the importance of sound to her culture, illustrating in the process the difference between an "Anglo" world view and a Sioux perspective. Elizabeth Sullivan's personal narrative is a poignant recounting of a young girl's observations of the horrors experienced on the Trail of Tears. And in "Marriage," Helen Sekaquaptewa narrates the Hopi customs surrounding that ceremony and offers insight into the conflict that often exists between Indian customs and American society.

In the next section, "Traditions, Narratives, and Fiction," there are several examples of the different ways Indian women writers draw on their heritage in their literature. In *Coyote Stories,* published in 1933, Mourning Dove imaginatively records the humorous stories of Coyote and his adventures. Of these stories, one of which is included here, Mourning Dove says:

> The Animal People were here first—before there were any real people.
>
> Coyote was the most important because, after he was put to work by the Spirit Chief, he did more than any of the others to make the world a good place in which to live. There were times, however, when Coyote was not busy for the Spirit Chief. Then he amused himself by getting into mischief and stirring up trouble. Frequently he got into trouble himself, and then everybody had a good laugh—. . .
>
> My people called Coyote *Sin-ka-lip,* which means Imitator. He delighted in mocking and imitating others, or in trying to, and, as he was a great one to play tricks, sometimes he is spoken of as "Trick Person."[10]

Coyote is one of the archetypal trickster figures in American Indian societies and may be seen as both a mirror and a mask of humanity. He is the transformer, bringing about change through his cunning in outwitting monsters and evil forces. At the same time, he is the overreacher who fails, sometimes with humiliation, when he extends beyond his limits. Mourning Dove has recorded the stories of Coyote in her tribe, the Okanogan, but he exists for many tribes and is the subject of several of the poems in the third section.

"The Changing Woman Story" has been excerpted from *Kaibah: Recollections of a Navajo Girlhood* by Kay Bennett and is an example of the way stories are passed down. It is a creation story, an account of how Navajo people were brought into existence, and it is told by a grandmother. When this version is compared to the traditional folklore account that is also included, it is clear that the grandmother is emphasizing aspects of the story that will remain with her pupils. She doesn't change the "facts," but she does couch them in a familiar context. Origin Stories or Creation Myths are part of the religious tradition of every tribe and are central to the position of women in Native American communities. According to John and Donna Terrell,

> The concept that woman was made from man is not found in Indian religion. Indians accept and adhere to the doctrine that the female of

their kind was created simultaneously with the male. For apparent reasons, each was endowed with peculiar qualities and sensibilities, neither was accorded supremacy, and each was made dependent upon the other for existence.[11]

The respect accorded women in the Creation Myths has been reflected historically in the position of women within tribal societies. Many tribes are matrilineal, passing both clan names and ownership of property through the female line. Navajos honor women in the construction of their traditional home, the hogan, which is built on four poles representing the four directions. Each pole is named after a female deity, so that the support of the home literally depends on the female. Before reservation life considerably changed traditional roles, women often held positions of importance in tribal government. Perhaps the most famous example of this importance comes from the Iroquois Great Law of Peace:

> The lineal descent of the people of the Five Nations shall run in the female line. Women shall be considered the progenitors of the nation. They shall own the land and the soil. Men and women shall follow the status of their mothers. You are what your mother is; the ways in which you see the world and all things in it are through your mother's eyes. What you learn from the father comes later and is of a different sort. The chain of culture is the chain of women linking the past with the future.
>
> As litany in every calling together of the Longhouse Iroquois people, these words are said in order to recall the original instructions given to humans at the time of our creation: "We turn our attention now to the senior women, the Clan Mothers. Each nation assigns them certain duties. For the People of the Longhouse, the Clan Mothers and their sisters select the chiefs and remove them from office when they fail the people. The Clan Mothers are the custodians of the land, and always think of the unborn generations. They represent life and the earth. Clan Mothers! You gave us life—continue now to place our feet on the right path." [12]

Among the Iroquois and the majority of the Pueblo tribes of the Southwest, the woman, as the progenitor of the kinship system, was respected and honored. But her role was no less important in the patrilineal cultures, such as the tribes of the Plains. For example, within the Sioux culture, the woman played an integral part in the Sun dance, the tribe's most important ritual. Selected for her virtue, she had the honor of chopping down the sacred cottonwood tree, the symbolic and mystical center of the Sun dance.

However, the woman's role began to change as the power of the tribes diminished in the nineteenth century, and reservation life replaced the freedom of mobility. Deprived of their ancestral roles as hunters and warriors, men began to move into areas that had previously been the province of women, adopting some of the white attitudes toward women and treating them as inferiors rather than equals. Indian women have continued in their traditional role as teachers, but as the old order has been inverted, they have begun to express their desire for change. Nia Francisco, a young Navajo woman, echoes the sentiments of many Indian women when she says, "It's time for women to become leaders again. The gods will grant them that honor very soon because man has abused the honor of taking care of the woman. There is a myth building up of the woman regaining the power she had traditionally."[13]

But for the time being, power resides within each woman's natural resources of wit, intelligence, and self-concept. In "Gallup, New Mexico— Indian Capital of the World," Leslie Marmon Silko examines the relationship between a prostitute and her son, challenging society's stereotype of the "fit" mother. "Storyteller" presents another view of the woman and her capacity for survival. The protagonist is a young Eskimo woman whose existence and search for meaning in the stark, lonely environment of Alaska become inextricably linked to the process of storytelling. Alienation is also the theme of "The Snow Keeps Falling" by Janet Campbell, in which she presents a brief sketch of the isolation a young Indian boy feels in a predominantly white school. And in "Zuma Chowt's Cave," Opal Lee Popkes places her character outside society to analyze the values that lie behind the categories of "primitive" and "civilized." With irony, she inverts the normal order of things.

POETRY

Continuing to explore the power of transformation inherent in the word, the poets of the last section draw on the oral tradition for symbols and images to express a range of ideas, feelings, and experiences in their poetry. A nostalgia for the old ways and for a past that seems to be changing all too rapidly is expressed in poems about revered grandparents, ancestral figures, and storytelling. Anna Lee Walters remembers what her grandfather has taught her in "Hartico," while Paula Gunn Allen poignantly captures the essence of her grandmother in these lines:

> From beyond time,
> beyond oak trees and bright clear water flow,
> she was given the work of weaving the strands
> of her body, her pain, her vision
> into creation, and the gift of having created,
> to disappear.

The grandmother is the storyteller, passing on what is vital, in "History of Unchi" by Elizabeth Cook-Lynn. And in "Thomas Iron-Eyes," Marnie Walsh bitterly contrasts the greatness of the past, when even death was confronted with nobility and ritual, with the squalid despair of the present, when one waits "for the wagon/ to bring the government box of pine."

If there is a yearning for the past, there is an equal resentment over the conditions of the present, and some of the women forcefully decry a society that would make artifacts out of its first inhabitants, confining them to reservations as showpieces for anthropologists or relocating them to alien urban ghettos.[14] Marnie Walsh focuses on the despair, alcoholism, and poverty of spirit that grow out of reservation life in her portrait of Vickie Loans-Arrow, a woman who would "like to die/but cant." Her story is told in a semiballad form by a friend whose verbal understatement contrasts sharply with the enormity of her anguish.

Wendy Rose repeatedly touches on the plight of both the reservation and the urban Indian, drawing on earth mother imagery to convey her own sense of helplessness in righting the situation. She ends "Long Division: A Tribal History," the poem that opens this section, with the line "I suckle coyotes and grieve." The woman, once so strong in Indian life, no longer has the power even of the trickster to transform the Indian's condition into a sane existence. In "I expected," she lashes out vehemently against collectors and artifact hunters who have literally killed both the body and the spirit of those whose possessions they covet. She likens their frenzied ravishing to the rape of a woman and, again, her instincts as a woman and mother to protect her own are rendered impotent; there is "not enough magic/to stop the collectors." Even the power of the Medicine Ones becomes ineffectual in the face of the unmitigated pressures on the urban Indian, who literally vanishes into anonymity.

For many of the poets, feminism is synonymous with heritage, and a search for one yields a concern with the other. Nia Francisco identifies herself in terms of the history of her people in "iridescent child," framing her poem in the form of a traditional Navajo prayer. In "she-bear," she combines feminine imagery with symbols of the bear, who represents luck and long life. The bear is also central to Anita Endrezze-Danielson's poem "Shaman/Bear," in which the shaman has been transformed into a bear and the woman becomes the foliage waiting to be devoured and made fertile. In "The Belly Dancer's Song," the poet compares the sensuality of the belly dancer's seductive dance to the tribal tradition of women dancing to earn their dowry.

In some of the poems, however, a more universal feminine voice is heard. Endrezze-Danielson's "Making Adjustments," for example, is a sardonic poem full of anger at the deadly compromises a woman makes in marriage. "Leap in the Dark" by Roberta Hill touches on the thoughts and feelings of a woman caught in the midst of her routine household chores who must seal "her nimble dreams with water from a murky bay." And in "Conversation Overheard on Tamalpais Road," Hill creates a moving portrait of a woman who dances with her imagination, though she is bound to a wheelchair.

As a symbol of all that has been lost, the land is another recurring image in Native American poetry. Landscapes become part of the imagery of feeling as well as the touchstone for memory in the poetry of Joy Harjo, while a yearning to regain the past—the forgotten songs and stories, her own origins —is expressed by Leslie Marmon Silko's description of a time and a place "Where Mountain Lion Lay Down with Deer." Changes in the land are painful reminders of what has irrevocably passed away.

For Paula Gunn Allen, this tension between a desire to retrieve the past and an awareness of the inevitability of change is expressed by journeys into the metaphysical underpinnings of tradition. "Medicine Song," for example, is a complex poem that applies symbols from Laguna culture to the healing of a soul. And in "Moonshot: 1969," she contrasts the technological significance of landing on the moon with the mythic place of the moon in the history of human sensibility.

The American Indian women writers in this section have inherited both the greatness of the remote past and the pain and conflict of the recent past. It remains to be seen what role they will ultimately take in tribal life, but their literature is testimony to their awareness that culture is dynamic and that change is not a negation of tradition. Nostalgia and a sense of loss haunt their landscapes, yet the predominant note is hopeful because their literature is an extension of an oral tradition based on the power of the word that has managed to survive and to maintain the American Indian community. In the words of Paula Gunn Allen,

> The key is in remembering, in what is chosen for the dream.
> In the silence of recovery we hold
> the rituals of the dawn
> now as then.

NOTES

1. Paula Gunn Allen, "The Sacred Hoop: A Contemporary Indian Perspective on American Indian Literature," in *Literature of the American Indians,* ed. Abraham Chapman (New York: New American Library, 1975), p. 113.
2. N. Scott Momaday, "The Man Made of Words," in *Literature of the American Indians,* ed. Abraham Chapman (New York: New American Library, 1975), p. 104.
3. Leslie Marmon Silko, *Ceremony* (New York: Viking Press, 1977), p. 2.
4. With the official closing of the frontiers in the late 1880s, the Ghost Dance religion began to spring up among various Indian tribes. Based on the visions of Wovoka, a Paiute seer, the religion promised a return to the idyllic time before the coming of the white man. The dead would return, along with the buffalo, and help bring an end to the white society. The Sioux

enthusiastically held Ghost Dances on their reservation, much to the consternation of local Indian agents, who did not understand the nature of the religion and feared possible insurrection. Through a series of misunderstandings, the BIA ordered that the dances be stopped, weapons removed from the tribe, and several leaders confined until the "messianic craze" died down. The disastrous result was the massacre at Wounded Knee on 29 December 1890. Several Indians refused to submit to searches for weapons, and within minutes the army had killed all the men and several hundred women and children fleeing for their lives. For a complete analysis of the religion and its outcome, see James Mooney, *The Ghost Dance Religion and the Sioux Outbreak of 1890* (Chicago: University of Chicago Press, 1965; originally published as Part 2 of the Fourteenth Annual Report of the Bureau of Ethnology to the Secretary of the Smithsonian Institution, 1892–1893).

5. For more information on Sarah Winnemucca Hopkins, see Marion E. Gridley, *American Indian Women* (New York: Hawthorn, 1974), pp. 54–60. Please note that "Paiute" has become the conventional spelling of her tribe.

6. Zitkala-Sa, *Old Indian Legends* (Boston: Ginn, 1901). Zitkala-Sa's statement is particularly significant because it is a reminder of the incredible linguistic diversity of American Indians. At the time of Columbus's first contact with the New World, Native Americans spoke over four hundred different languages, which derived from at least seven language families, each as complex as Indo-European. Each language represented a distinct culture, and while contact existed between tribes, there was no common linguistic denominator. A Hopi, for example, would not have been able to understand a Sioux any more than an English-speaking person could understand a Greek. It should be noted, though, that with few exceptions, the language of American Indian literature is English because this is the first written language that Indians learned.

7. Zitkala-Sa, *American Indian Stories* (Washington, D.C.: Hayworth Press, 1921). Along with reservations, the Bureau of Indian Affairs created boarding schools to educate Indians and help them become assimilated into American life and culture. Unfortunately, the schools were so far away from the reservations that children could be separated from their families for as much as twelve years, with the result that they were literally "deculturated," losing fluency in their own language and developing a profound sense of being an outsider to two cultures. Ironically, the efforts of the BIA schools to help Indians adapt to American society often backfired, as Zitkala-Sa describes when she recounts one of her own experiences. All of the Indian children were required to have their hair cut in the boarding school she attended, but she resisted because within the Sioux tradition, "short hair was worn by mourners, and shingled hair by cowards."

8. The first novel published by an Indian was *Queen of the Woods* by Chief Simon Pokagon, which appeared in 1899. For a discussion of other early works, see Charles R. Larson, *American Indian Fiction* (Albuquerque: University of New Mexico Press, 1978).

9. For information on the Pan-Indian movement, see Hazel Hertzberg, *The Search for an American Indian Identity* (Syracuse: Syracuse University Press, 1971). Biographical information on Gertrude Bonnin appears in

Marion E. Gridley, *American Indian Women* (New York: Hawthorn Books, 1974), pp. 81–93.

10. Mourning Dove, preface to *Coyote Stories* (Caldwell, Idaho: Caxton Printers, 1933), p. 7.

11. John and Donna Terrell, *Indian Women of the Western Morning: Their Life in Early America* (New York: Dial Press, 1974), p. 27.

12. Shirley Hill Witt, "The Brave-Hearted Women," *Civil Rights Digest,* 8, No. 4 (Summer 1976), 39. For more information on the role of Indian women in tribal life, see Valerie Shirer Mathes, "A New Look at the Role of Women in Indian Society," *American Indian Quarterly,* 2, No. 2 (Summer 1975), 131–139.

13. This comment is from an unpublished interview between Nia Francisco and Dexter Fisher, conducted at Navajo Community College on the Navajo Nation, 26 January 1977.

14. Relocation was a governmental policy adopted after World War II to help reservation Indians assimilate more readily into American society by urging them to move into urban areas. Unfortunately, the results were far from satisfactory, and many Indians returned to their communities at the first opportunity.

CONTEXTS

LESLIE MARMON SILKO

Born in Albuquerque in 1948, Leslie Marmon Silko grew up at the Laguna Pueblo Reservation, where she currently lives and writes. She graduated from the University of New Mexico and attended several semesters of law school before deciding to devote herself full time to writing. She has published *Laguna Woman* (1974), a collection of poems, and *Ceremony* (1977), her first novel. Her short stories and poems have been anthologized in many books, including *The Man to Send Rain Clouds* (1974), *Carriers of the Dream Wheel* (1975), *Voices of the Rainbow* (1975), *Yardbird Reader 5* (1976) and *The Remembered Earth* (1978). In 1974 she received the Award for Poetry from *The Chicago Review*. In 1975 her story "Lullaby" was selected as one of the twenty best short stories of the year and included in Martha Foley's *Best Short Stories of 1975*. Of mixed ancestry—Laguna, Mexican, and white—she says, "What I know is Laguna. This place I am from is everything I am as a writer and human being."

STORIES AND THEIR TELLERS—
A CONVERSATION WITH LESLIE MARMON SILKO*

[*Fisher*]: *What do you think is the relationship between traditional and contemporary Native American literature?*

[Silko]: Well, there are a number of relationships. One relationship that I see as a continuum, and it's a loose one, is that in Native American communities, especially the more rural ones, there has always been a tremendous concern with language. I think that growing up within a community that has this concern with language and storytelling is important because you get attuned to hearing stories. A person who is accustomed to listening, who knows what a story is, can glean out of all sorts of information the heart of the story. When I go to the Laguna Acoma High School to talk to Native American kids, I tell them that storytelling for Indians is like a natural resource. Some places have oil, some have a lot of water or timber or gold, but around here, it's the ear that has developed. You have it. In a sense, it's accidental just like uranium is accidental in a given region. But I want them to know that this potential exists. There's the possibility for telling stories. I think it has to do with community, with growing up in certain kinds of communities as opposed to others.

[*F*]: *You would relate your growing up in this community as essential?*

[*S*]: Yes, I think it's crucial. You can talk all day long about identity, census numbers, etc. You can be a full blood and grow up in Cincinnati and lose

* This interview was conducted at Laguna Pueblo, New Mexico, on 28 January 1977. The interviewer was Dexter Fisher.

touch. Their experience is different from the person who is in the community where there is constant concern for language. The community is tremendously important. That's where a person's identity has to come from, not from racial blood quantum levels.

[F]: *Did you grow up at Laguna primarily?*

[S]: All the way.

[F]: *Did you go through high school here?*

[S]: We didn't have a high school. I went to the Head Start school. I went through the third and fourth grade here at Laguna at the BIA [Bureau of Indian Affairs] school. After the fourth grade, everyone had to go to boarding school. Most of the kids went off to boarding school, but my dad had gone to Albuquerque Indian School and he hated it. He used to run away and he didn't want us to have to go, so we and some other families from Laguna used to drive in every day. That was a hundred-mile round trip. I did that until I was sixteen. At that time, my aunt in Albuquerque died and left my mother a house, so we moved into Albuquerque and came back to the pueblo on the weekends.

[F]: *Did you go to the University of New Mexico?*

[S]: Yes.

[F]: *Do you know the Laguna language?*

[S]: Very little. I know very little because we're mix-blooded. I know as much as Grandma knows to get along at the store, but there was an absolute value placed on speaking English. I grew up with my great-grandmother, so I understood a lot more when I was small.

[F]: *When did you first begin to write?*

[S]: I started writing when I was in the fifth grade. A teacher gave us a list of words to make sentences out of, and I just made it into a story automatically. I can just do stories.

[F]: *Why don't you talk a bit about your novel,* Ceremony. *How does the section on Gallup fit in?* ["Gallup, New Mexico—Indian Capital of the World" is included in "Traditions, Narratives, and Fiction"—ed.]

[S]: That piece works in a number of different ways in the overall structure of the novel. My character from Laguna, Tayo, is going with his uncle to Gallup to see a very strange, unpopular, and unorthodox medicine man who lives up in the hills in a very old place in the dumps above the Gallup ceremonial grounds. As they go into Gallup, this piece fits in, though it doesn't have anything directly to do with the story. The section is about the little child and his relationship to his mother. It also relates to Tayo because his mother comes and goes like the kid's mother. Tayo lost his mother when he was very young, so the child's mother becomes a metaphor for his mother and the mother of creation. The Laguna story that I follow is about the mother creator, and it's uncorrupted by Christianity. The mother in the Gallup section has her own kind of momentum and her own way and that goes without saying. But because she and the other mothers aren't conventional, the assumption is that they are unfit and their children should be taken from them. The idea I was trying to work with is that nobody has the conventional mother, really. If a mother is docile on the outside, she may be seething inside; no one really has the perfect mother. I became intrigued by this. Both Tayo and the child really know they are loved, and when the little boy is waiting for his mother to come back, he doesn't feel as rotten as the outward appearance of his life shows. He's been loved. It all comes together in the end, his being loved, the mother, the creator.

[F]: *Why did you entitle the novel* Ceremony?

[S]: That's what it is. Writing the novel was a ceremony for me to stay sane. My character in the beginning of the novel is very sick. He's been in the mental ward in Los Angeles, but he doesn't remember. He doesn't remember being a prisoner of war in the Philippines. A lot of my cousins, a lot of people from this area, were in the same position during the war. They got caught. So my character is very sick, and I was very sick when I was writing the novel. I was having migraine headaches all the time and horrible nausea that went on and on. I kept writing and all of a sudden it occurred to me that he was very sick and I was wondering if he was going to get well, because of those who came back, some made it and some didn't. My dad and uncle were in the war and they did okay, but some didn't. So here I was in my novel working on my character every day, and I was trying to figure out how some stay sane and some don't, and then I realized that the one thing that was keeping me going at all was writing. And as Tayo got better, I felt better. But then he had lapses. These weren't one for one though. I was just telling my creative writing class the other day that when you're writing and trying to describe something you go to your own experience to see how you have felt in similar situations, because that's all you can describe.

[F]: *Have you studied writing formally?*

[S]: I took a couple of classes. I was an English major, but at that time they didn't have a creative writing major, and they didn't have very many teachers. Now, I'm part of a whole fleet of creative writing teachers. I never could get too much out of the classes except discipline. I had to have papers in on time, but with my fiction, I just sort of did it. I couldn't just change one section because then the whole thing would unravel.

[F]: *What do you like to read?*

[S]: Everything! I love Milton and Shakespeare, especially the tragedies. I don't have much patience with a lot of contemporary literature, because there's a lot of crap going around.

[F]: *Has there been any one major influence on your writing?*

[S]: The major influence has been growing up around here and listening to people and to the way the stories just keep coming.

[F]: *Let's go back for a minute to the notion of context. It is obvious from your short stories that environment, particularly the landscape here at Laguna, is important. What do you think people should know about context before they read your stories?*

[S]: Well, nothing really. I don't know. Maybe if there are words like *arroyo* that aren't clear, those could be explained. That's irritating. I used to get irritated with T. S. Eliot and all his Greek. I would wish that people would have a little bit better understanding of place, that in geography classes they would teach how people live in Bethel, Alaska, and Laguna, New Mexico, or Iowa City, etc. It's as if what you see on television takes the place of a geography class. Instead, in Bethel, people live without indoor plumbing, and there's one truck that comes around to deliver water and another one to pick up the waste products. What I would ideally wish for is that people had just a general familiarity, a sense of the history, when the Spaniards came in, just American history, for Christ's sake, but they don't. It can be turned around on us; for example, I don't think people here know much about New York subways. I think what's horrifying is that we're made to believe that the television lifestyle and geography are one, and we're really so diverse. It's sad. Anyway, that's all my stories really need. Included in geography should be the way people live, some of their attitudes, their point of view, so if you have even just a smattering of Pueblo point of view, that helps. It's not much.

[F]: *Is there such a thing as a "Native American" perspective? Or would you say there's a tribal perspective?*

[S]: As far as perspective goes, there's mine. Leslie Marmon. And insofar as I've grown up here and learned things here and loved people from here, the perspective I have involves very definitely Laguna and Laguna people and Laguna culture. What I write about and what I'm concerned about are relationships. To that I bring so many personal things that have been affected by where I come from, but I don't think one should oversimplify and say this is a Laguna point of view. It's my point of view, coming from a certain kind of background and place.

[F]: *Would you distinguish Native American literature from other literatures, like black literature or Jewish literature, for example?*

[S]: Those definitions are okay, if you have to begin to break things up into groups. It's better than talking about Group 1, Group 2, Group 3. If everyone wants to talk about the same thing, it's useful to say that this will be the group that's to talk about Ezra Pound, but I think what writers, storytellers, and poets have to say necessarily goes beyond such trivial boundaries as origin. There's also the danger of demeaning literature when you label certain books by saying this is black, this is Native American, and then, this is just writing. That's what's going on now, and I don't like it.

[F]: *The other side of that coin, equally insidious, is the whole notion of universals, that literature is good only if it is universal. What do you think?*

[S]: I would say that good literature has to be accessible. It's incredibly narcissistic to be otherwise. Artists can't work with a chip on their shoulders, and that's what has happened to a lot of feminists. Politics can ruin anything. It will ruin a picnic. Politics in the most crass sense—rally around the banner kind. I'm political, but I'm political in my stories. That's different. I think the work should be accessible, and that's always the challenge and task of the teller—to make accessible perceptions that the people need. Sometimes, it's not even that clear. Sometimes, it's just the storyteller uncontrolled. There are these stories that just have to be told in the same way the wind goes blowing across the mesa. That's what the teller used to have to do anyway, make accessible certain ways of seeing things. This is the beauty of the old way. You can stop the storyteller and ask questions and have things explained. And what's going on is an experience or perception being made accessible to those people. And it isn't too difficult to move from that setting into a wider and wider audience. That's why I like to talk about accessibility. That doesn't mean that you won't learn more and more as you go on, and that takes us back to the context—depending on how familiar you are with the context, you'll get more or less. Like with Hopi country. I'm from Laguna and I know a fair amount about Laguna and Acoma things. I have good friends up at Hopi, and the more I go up and hang around the more I can get into it.

[F]: *What would you say are some of the things you want to make accessible to people?*

[S]: Things about relationships. That's all there really is. There's your relationship with the dust that just blew in your face, or with the person who just kicked you end over end. That's all I'm interested in. You have to come to terms, to some kind of equilibrium with those people around you, those people who care for you, your environment. I notice things about feeling good about meeting a certain animal when I'm out walking around the hills. I'll come back after a wonderful day, and someone will say that place is full of snakes. And I just had the feeling there wouldn't be any problem with snakes and there wasn't. As a matter of fact, snakes know when people are afraid of them and when to get upset. It's just like a horse. And people are the same. If you come into a room all mad and upset, pretty soon you get everyone else all mad and upset. Relationships are not just limited to man-woman, parent-child, insider-outsider; they spread beyond that. What finally happens in the novel, for example, is that I get way out of the Southwest in a sense and get into the kind of destructive powers and sadism that the Second World War brought out. Yet, it is all related back to Laguna in terms of witchcraft.

[F]: *What is your favorite piece of the things you've written?*

[S]: My favorite story is one that isn't set in the Southwest, but I love my characters in it. It's called "Storyteller," and it's set in the tundra of Bethel, Alaska. It's a long short story, and it sets out what the relationship of the storyteller to people is. The story is interesting to me and I like it, perhaps because the landscape is different, because I find a common point where I can relate to the land, regardless of whether it's land I'm from or not. That's a big step for me, to go to a completely alien landscape. I managed. What I did in that story finally was to get the interior landscapes of the characters, and yet they are still related to the tundra and the river because that's how she does the guy in. I love that story just because I like the characters and how she does the guy in.

[F]: *How does humor fit in with your own writing?*

[S]: It's generally double-edged. It seems with humor, there's always something beyond just the laughing—that when you're laughing, you have to think beyond to greater considerations. I think of a lot of the stories that happen around here. Something happens to someone and you just laugh and laugh, but generally while you're laughing, you have an awareness of something great. You get a sense of history insofar as you remember all the other stories like that. Sometimes they were funnier, and sometimes they weren't so funny at all. My next novel is going to be about the function of humor. I got to thinking about funny stories. Whatever just happened, it would be related to other things that had happened, and finally the function of the stories would be to keep you from feeling that God had just dropped a rock on your head alone or that you had been singled out in some way, which is really dangerous, because the stories remind you that this isn't the first time. Or if you feel everyone is laughing at you, someone can always tell a story where something worse happened. So pretty soon, after the whole thing is over with, things are back in perspective. The function of humor is very serious and very complex.

[F]: *Do you think there are any contemporary myths emerging?*

[S]: I don't see that there has ever been any end to the stories. They just keep going on and on. So far, I haven't seen that there are any new ones. There's a need to have a multiplicity of perspectives and tellers. I tell some stories. Simon Ortiz tells others. We need certain tellers to look after certain myths. The ones I'm looking after have always been around. It's part of a continuum. I see it more as a matter that certain people come along and work with the myths that have always been there.

[F]: *How do you relate to the women's movement?*

[S]: I feel I've benefited by it just generally in the sense that anything that undermines the stereotypes perpetrated on all of us by white men is helpful. What it does is take some of the pressure off those of us who have never lived very close to the stereotypes. I've always been the way I was. Here at Laguna, a lot more is expected of women; women are expected to be strong, to manage the property. Children belong to women and to their families. Women do the plastering. It's a relief to have the stereotypes knocked down. It's just made it easier for me to do what I want to do.

[F]: *How would you characterize your literature?*

[S]: I would say that a good story is really important and that's what I work for because with a good story there is no end to the possibilities. . . .

ELIZABETH COOK-LYNN

A member of the Crow Creek Sioux tribe, Elizabeth Cook-Lynn was born in 1930 at Fort Thompson, South Dakota. She is currently an assistant professor of English at Eastern Washington State College. She has published literary criticism in *CCCC Journal* and *The Indian Historian* and poetry in *The South Dakota Review* and *Prairie Schooner*. Her book, *Then Badger Said This*, was published in 1977.

FROM THEN BADGER SAID THIS

XXI

Literal history has had its special way of describing the tragedy of the American Indian, and it has taken on a substance of its own as all histories do. In one sense that kind of history is valid and real, of course, but in another it is a cruel distortion, like concentrating in sorrow on the traceless disappearance of winter snow beneath the sun without the telling of nourishment for early spring fertility. This distortion comes about, I believe, because the traditions of literal men suffer a weakness, a flaw—a silence, if you will, which makes them seem deaf. Literal history, you see, has no sound. Yet, sound, however faint and fickle, is essential to identity and survival. There are many ancient stories told in various contexts throughout all oral cultures emphasizing the importance of sound. This is one told by the Sioux:

> Swan was a young Sioux boy who liked to study tracks and signs and other things a warrior must know to become famous as a scout in his tribe. His interests became known to the headman who then asked him to scout the location of an enemy and bring back news of their strength both in horses and warriors.
>
> Swan traveled without stopping for food and he watched every sign in the air, on the ground and in the bushes and trees. At nightfall he was very tired and so he set his tipi and started to prepare his arrows for whatever might befall him in enemy country.
>
> Sitting by his fire, Swan carefully ground the edges of an arrow be-

tween two flat stones to make the point sharper. He was so intent upon his work that when an owl in the tree over his tent softly spoke, "who-o-o, whooo-oo-o," it seemed so close that he was startled and he dropped his arrow. As he bent over to pick up the arrow, his eyes rested on the surface of a bowl of water he had placed near his fire when he was getting his evening meal. He saw reflected in the water the face of an enemy looking down at him through the smoke hole in the top of his tipi.

Showing no sign of having heard the owl nor of having seen the enemy face, Swan continued to sharpen his bow, turning this way and that, sighting its accuracy. Then with a quick twist of the wrist, he shot an arrow straight up through the face looking down at him. The enemy scout fell over dead.

In native cultures the story is told with varying events and settings, but the message is essentially the same. The "whoo-oo-o" of the owl is a significant statement, however ambiguous, and if it is your belief that creative and spontaneous acts can bridge the gap between what is known and what is not, the gathering of sensory data available to you gives the process of language and, ultimately, history, a credence scorned by literal men. The response to sound is evident in all Sioux art forms, and in historical recitation it is profound and complete. Accountably, then, Swan's history remained his own and when he returned to the camp and told his people that the owl spoke to him, they knew it to be true.

ELIZABETH SULLIVAN

Born in Oklahoma, Elizabeth Sullivan, a full-blood Creek, has devoted much of her time to preserving the stories and oral histories of her tribe. She recorded *Indian Legends of the Trail of Tears and Other Creek Stories* in 1974. In the preface to that collection, she says, "All the legends and stories of tragedies were told to me by my great-grandmother and other elder members of the Creek Indians living in various parts of the old Creek Nation. I am a full-blood Creek and reared in and around full-blood traditions."

LEGEND OF THE TRAIL OF TEARS

Annakee observed the beauty around her. It was a beautiful day. The fruit tree blossoms were in bloom, corn and tobacco had been planted and the cottonwood leaves were like glass. She noticed the huge trunk of older trees whose rough scars showed where the medicine man had stripped the bark for his use for the sick Indians who were dependent on his knowledge and mercy. The south wind sprang up. The clouds became very dark and it began to rain. Annakee ran in the house to her grandmother's arms. She was cuddled and soon her fears were forgotten.

Little did she know that before too long, General Andrew Jackson's army would abuse them and remove all of the comforts of home life. There would be no blossoms in bloom; their crops would be destroyed and they would be driven out to go West to Indian Territory—a cruel and death journey.

When the removal began Annakee could not understand all the changes taking place. She only knew her grandmother's eyes were bloodshot, her cheeks sunken, her lips cracked. Annakee held closely to her grandmother's hand as they walked on with so many Indians. Some she did not know. Everyone appeared fearful and sad. She saw many crying. Annakee began to suffer from irritating mosquito bites. She would scratch mercilessly until she bled. Her little legs were so tired and her feet ached.

At night, she saw the stars in the sky that used to twinkle and shine like dew drops in the rainbow as her grandmother's tales had told about the mystery of the heavenly bodies. But tonight the stars appeared dim and seemed to be hiding from her as she looked up in the sky.

Annakee remembered her home. The corn crib was full of corn. They had plenty of dried fruit and meat. Her father and mother saw to that. Her two older brothers were hunting all of the time. They even knew how to shoot with bow and arrow to kill fish when they came up for air after shoe string roots had been pounded and put into the river up stream and a dam was made.

One comfort she had and held tightly was a doll her grandmother had made from a corncob. She had long sleeves and a skirt, even had an apron on with cross stitch at the bottom just like grandmother's dress.

Along the journey they would camp for three or four days and then go on. The soldiers were mean and hateful. She began to notice, if a baby cried and cried from thirst or the fatigue in the cradle on the back of the mother, the man on the horse would say something that she could not understand and jerk the baby and take it by the legs and whip it against the trunk of the tree until it went limp and then would throw it aside.

Once she saw a mother cry and run to her dead baby. The soldier then whipped her with a long whip that would pop loud. The mother would not let go of the bleeding broken body of her child. She was whipped to death and left as they went on.

Annakee shivered and thought it was a bad dream. It appeared to her that her grandmother took command and would converse with the women at night during camp out. She told the women who had babies still suckling, "If the soldiers get your baby, let it go. Some have to look after the older children. Never look back; just march on." After that, it became a common practice.

"God lives, Creator of all things, be fearful and pray." They sang songs in whispers not audible to the soldiers who would camp nearby. The aroma of the soldier's food reached them and hunger became almost unbearable.

Her grandmother was very stern and told her—"Learn never to cry, even if you are hurt or hungry. Never look back to see what is going on in the back." This, she learned very quickly.

The soldiers saw a white man with two boys and a beautiful Indian wife helping and walking along with this band of Indians. They came up to a village that had been deserted. They found a corn crib with corn in it. They took this white man, put him in the crib, nailed it up and set fire to it. The journey continued. The Medicine Man said, "Someday, we will see him." Of course, no one believed him. He stated that the soldiers hated the Indians so much. They would burn their own kind alive—a good honest man who had only been guilty of helping them. This man's name was Galahead.

Annakee had mixed emotions. She had grown up for she had suffered so much for a child of seven years.

Some of the men folks tried to make a break. They were shot to death. Those who escaped in the forest were caught by the big dogs and in no time were destroyed by the vicious dogs. The tragedy in the wilderness was unforgettable, yet so true. Sometimes, as weeks went by these soldiers would tear the clothing off young girls twelve years of age and older or young mothers and molest them. She always turned her head the other way when these things happened. When the journey grew into weeks and months they were allowed to camp by the body of water. They would stay at camp as long as two weeks. They were well patrolled but men were allowed to hunt nearby as food was getting low.

In the dense forest Annakee saw strange birds, different-shaped leaves than she had ever seen. She asked her grandmother about it. Her grandmother held her very close by the campfire and told her that they had come far far away from home and they would never see their homeland and advised her to be brave and never cry.

The worst part of the trip was a time when hundreds of men, women and old women and children disappeared in a huge mean-looking river which was swift, deep and muddy—the mighty Mississippi River. Rowboats were available from the army but there were not near enough. While they camped by the river the men were allowed to make rafts six to nine feet in length. Animal skins were used for tying the rafts together. They were dangerous but a person could hold on to the log to keep from sinking. Some who were physically able swam across—other rafts capsized. Two men used feather mattresses for boats. The Big House fire was preserved and saved across the Mississippi River by three men. The three men held the container of hot coals with each hand and used only one hand to swim across this swift river. The coals were finally safely carried across to the other side. The fire was the redman's friend—significant of closeness, togetherness and cooked meals. Wild beasts feared fire so they stayed away from campfires.

To add to the misery of the trail, snow descended. It remained very cold and the trip became almost unbearable. One cold morning, they started to travel. The snow was coming down but Annakee did not cry. She noticed that grandmother was getting so thin and was getting sick. She never smiled anymore. All the army men rode horses and were in wagons. One soldier kept looking behind her. He got so close that she thought he was trying to run over her with the horse. So she looked behind her.

Her little moccasins were worn out and her little feet had been wrapped up with cloth. Suddenly each step she took left footprints of bright blood. She looked down to her feet. They did not hurt any more because her feet were numb. The soldier took her by her little thin arm and put her in the saddle in front of him. His body was warm and she snuggled next to him and was soon fast asleep.

That night when they camped she had a chill and fever followed. She was aware that she would be left behind to die alone in this dense forest. She also remembered her grandmother had told her that death was beautiful—a person drifted off to sleep without pain. She asked her grandmother that very night, "Will I get to see the man they killed and hung on the tree if I go to sleep in death?" The grandmother said, "Yes, but you are not going to die."

Each day when they traveled the kind soldier wrapped her up and carried her on the horse—Annakee did not remember much when she was so sick. Food began to be short. One day she noticed two men take one bean and divide it, so that women and children could have just a little more to eat. Somehow there were less soldiers. Some began to get sick and die.

Spring came and the weather was warm. Sometimes they would come up to a camp. Those who went ahead of them had camped there. Each band of Indians was assigned to a group of soldiers. One main food was corn. The women folks had saved some corn back in case of extra need.

Months later, Annakee became stronger and was able to play with other children. This had not been allowed before. It appeared the mean soldiers became friendly and kind. The Indians were allowed to have council meeting at camp when the Medicine Man would give them a talk. He told them surely they would get to their destination and they would be left alone to start all over again. The Medicine Man noticed also that the soldiers were running out of their supplies.

The soldiers began to get sick. Some of the horses died, so some had to walk.

The Chief said, "This is our time to rebel. We need our food. We shall not give one grain of corn to them. We have suffered so much. Our loved ones they killed, they would not let us bury our dead. We will show no mercy."

They camped for a long time near a river to hunt and fish, not patrolled as before.

Regardless of what horrible scenes Annakee saw, she observed and saw the beauty in the trees and small animal life. She pretended she had to protect her doll. She talked to the doll every day. This made her almost forget the reality that was about her.

At one time all they had for food was parched corn boiled in water. One sick soldier came to the campfire and held a tin cup for broth.

The grandmother was dishing out the broth. She looked up to him in surprise. The Chief spoke up and said, "Let him starve." Annakee looked over and saw it was the soldier who had held her and let her ride the horse months and months ago. She ran up and told her grandmother to give him the broth. After that she became a symbol of mercy and took away the hate, fear and somehow helped all those who saw her. They all had to travel together in harmony. The missionaries had taught her what love was—how you felt—forgiveness.

The Medicine Man told the tales about the little people who could confuse you, emotionally upset a person, even make you run away into the forest where they would hide you. They would make fun of you and hide behind the leaves or side of a trunk of a tree and you became frightened with dreams and began to hallucinate. The Medicine Man was sympathetic and understanding to his patients who were emotionally disturbed. It was real to Annakee and the myth about the little people, she accepted.

She saw the Medicine Man take a large kettle, fill it with water, put roots in it and chant and blow into the kettle. The fire kept the water boiling or to simmer at times. This lasted twelve hours. Then the sick man was given only four sips. The sick man got up as if he had been in a dream and returned to normal behavior.

Annakee began to think about the large steamboat she was on, when crossing the Mississippi River and how a very large steamboat with soldiers aboard had hailed for them to stop. Most of the Indians had been paid gold pieces for their land. These were very small amounts yet it was the only choice they had. The captain of the steamboat talked with the captain and they were told to remain still. The large steamboat backed far away and with a launch, rushed the small boat and split it in two pieces. Nearly all were drowned. The gold was taken from all the Indians aboard. Somehow Annakee was saved by someone helping her to the shore. Most of the women who could not swim were drowned.

Years later after settling in Indian Territory, Annakee would gather her grandchildren around the campfire and tell them the story of her removal and she would say, "If it was not for the soldier who picked me up and cuddled me during my illness, you all would not be here."

The Indians knew how to camouflage themselves. They would hide behind trees and capture a lone soldier and slay him and put him up the fork of a tree. They began to seek revenge as there was no way they could survive anyway. They became warlike as the soldiers began to weaken. Some soldiers, after arriving at their destination, remained with the Indians and intermarried with them. Becoming deserters, it was necessary to change their names.

Galahead arrived, joined his wife and two sons and changed his name to Watson.

The author is a descendant of Watson being the daughter of Fanny Watson Konard on Creek Roll 6526, daughter of Josiah Watson, Creek Roll 4557.

HELEN SEKAQUAPTEWA

When Louise Udall approached Helen Sekaquaptewa, a Hopi, and asked her to record her life story, her answer was, "I have thought of doing it, but I didn't think I was capable." When asked by the trader at Oraibi about the book, Helen replied, "I am talking. She is writing." The result is *Me and Mine: The Life Story of Helen Sekaquaptewa* (1969). The author was born in 1898 in the Hopi village of Old Oraibi in Arizona.

MARRIAGE

The home of the bridegroom is the center of activity in a Hopi wedding. When a couple decides to marry, the father of the groom takes over. He furnishes everything—cotton for the weaving and food to feed the workers during the time the weaving is in progress. Each household keeps a supply of cotton on hand against the time when a son may marry.

In Emory's case there was a problem. His parents had separated years before and his mother had remarried and lived in Oraibi. Emory lived with his mother during his childhood; Wickvaya, Emory's grandfather, also lived in the same household. This is why Wickvaya took his grandson to school at Keams Canyon and brought him back in the spring. Emory's father was among the men sent to the Indian School at Carlisle in Pennsylvania for five years, in 1906. When he returned he went to Hotevilla to live, and in due time remarried. Emory had never lived with his father.

Emory's mother wanted us to come to her home in Oraibi, but Emory had been away at school so many years that it wasn't really home to him. As he grew older he had lived in Bacabi, with his cousin Susie and her husband, who was his godfather, during the summers that he was home, helping in whatever way he could. Susie invited us to come to her home, and Emory's uncles and cousins all helped put in for the cotton and food and were the hosts for us.

After we decided to get married, I spent every minute that I could grinding in preparation for feeding the wedding guests. Women and girls of my relatives who wanted to help started grinding too. When my sister Verlie walked with me to Bacabi to Susie's house, I carried a big pan full of fine white cornmeal. I never left Susie's house for the entire period (about a month) and was under her watchful care, even slept with her the first three nights.

As a bride I was considered sacred the first few days, being in a room with the shades on the windows, talking to no one. All this time I was steadily grinding corn which was brought in by Emory's kinswomen. Each brought, say, a quart of corn in a basket or on a plaque to be passed in to me to be ground, each lot separately. After the first grinding I handed the corn out and waited while it was roasted and passed back to me to be ground real fine. As each lot was finished, I put it back into its own container, lining it up along the wall with others. When the aunts came back in the evening to get their corn there was food on the table and they ate. White corn was the grist the first day, blue corn on the second and third days. At the end of each day Susie gave me a relaxing rubdown.

Early each morning of the first three days, Cousin Susie went with me to the east edge of the mesa, and there, facing the rising sun, we bowed our heads and each offered a silent prayer for a happy married life. Our days began with the rising of the sun and ended with its setting, because there was no artificial light for night working.

The fourth day is the actual wedding day. Everyone of the relatives is up when the cock crows, to participate in the marriage ritual, the hair washing. Suds are made from the tuber of the yucca root, pounded into a pulp, put into two basins of water, and worked with the hands until the pan is filled with foamy suds.

Two pans were placed side by side on the floor, where Susie and my sister Verlie prepared the suds. Usually the mothers of the bride and groom do this. Susie and Verlie acted for our mothers. While Susie washed my hair, Verlie washed Emory's. Then each took a strand of hair and twisted them together hard and tight as a symbol of acceptance of the new in-law into the clan (family) and also to bind the marriage contract, as they said, "Now you are united, never to go apart."

Next Emory was taken outside and stripped to the waist by the women of my family. Each had brought her small container of water which she poured over his shoulders as he knelt over a tub. They splashed the water over him with their hands. It was still dark, so they could not see him; they put a blanket around him, and he came back into the house to get warm from that icy bath.

Now, with our hair still wet and hanging loose, Emory and I walked together to the eastern edge of the village and once more faced the rising sun, and with bowed heads we prayed in silence for a long time; for a good life together, for children, and to be together all of our lives and never stray from each other.

After my hair was dry on this day, they combed it up like a married woman, never to be worn in maiden style again. Married women parted their hair from the center in the front to the nape of the neck. Each side was folded over the hand until it reached nearly to the ear where it was bound with a cord made from hair and a little yarn, leaving a soft puff at the ends. The hair in front of the ears was cut into sideburns about two inches long.

The making of the robes begins on the morning of the nuptial hair washing. The father or uncle of the groom (in our case Susie's father) took a bag of cotton and, passing through the village, stopped at each house. He was expected, and each housewife opened her door and extended a plaque to receive some cotton (everyone was required to wash his hands before touching the cotton). Immediately all hands went to work cleaning the cotton of seeds, burrs, and little sticks. It was all cleaned that same day.

In the evening the uncles, godfather, and men who wished to help, gathered at the groom's house to card the cotton. The cards were a pair of flat, wire-toothed brushes, four by twelve inches, with wooden handles at a slight angle, on the long side. They were bought from the trader and used for both wool and cotton. I watched my father and my grandfather use them in my time. A small handful of cotton was spread over all the teeth of one card; with the second card, the cotton was combed back and forth until all the lumps were out and it became fluffy. Another motion made it into a strip as long as the card, which strip was put aside and another one started. The men worked late carding big piles of white cotton. Coal-oil lamps lighted their work. During this time the men told stories, with the bride sitting nearby, along with the kinswomen. From time to time the bride thanked the workers for their service. Everyone enjoyed the stories, and before they realized it, it was midnight and quitting time. The men were served refreshments and everyone went home to bed. It took several nights to do the carding.

All the men in the village worked to spin this cotton into thread in one day. Food was obtained and prepared to feed the whole village. Ten or fifteen sheep were required. If the host didn't have sheep of his own, he bought them. One or two might be donated by someone. Wood had to be brought in for the cooking and to heat the kivas.

At sunrise on spinning day the custodian of each kiva* went early to clean up his kiva and start the fire and get it warm. The women were busy too, putting the big kettles on the fire and adding ingredients for the stew, making ready every plaque and basket.

After his breakfast, each man went to his kiva, taking his spindle (every adult male owns one). Emory's uncle came around early to deliver to each kiva the carded cotton to be spun. In Bacabi there were three kivas. Soon all spindles were humming away. Emory's uncle checked the kivas from

* The underground ceremonial chamber of the Hopi and other Pueblo people.

time to time to keep them all supplied with carded cotton. Dinner would be late, so they were served a snack at noon in the kiva. The spun cotton was made into skeins; the warp thread was finer than the woof. The pile of light, fluffy hanks of warp and woof thread was beautiful.

In the meantime the women were getting the food and tables ready. My relatives and myself were served earlier so we could be free to serve the community dinner. However, the bride did not serve but mingled with the other women. They teased me as all made merry and had a happy time. The men were served at the tables in Susie's house and neighboring houses as needed, and then the women and children of the village ate. Whatever food was left, especially the stew, was divided among the people.

The weaving took about two weeks, and it began a few days after the spinning was finished. One sheep was butchered this time, and the other foods were made ready for the first day of the weaving. At dawn and before breakfast the three special looms used in wedding weaving were brought out from their storage place to the kiva (one kiva) where they were untied and spread out on the floor. Two or three men at a time worked at the long and tedious job of stringing each loom, rolling the warp back and forth to each other, over the notches close together on the two end poles.

The bridal clothing consisted of a robe six by eight feet, a second one about four by six feet to cover the shoulders, and a girdle about ten inches wide and eight feet long, which is tied around the waist. The moccasins had leggings made of white buckskin. Then there is the reed roll, which is a sort of suitcase in which to wrap and carry extra gifts. Emory gathered the reeds from the edge of the wash, cut them into uniform lengths and tied them together with cord like a bamboo window blind.

The threaded looms were hung from loops in the ceiling beams and fastened to loops on the floor and stretched tight, and the weaving began, the best weavers taking turns during the day. The belt is braided rather than woven.

At noon, food was brought to the kiva by relatives. After dinner a man took his place at each loom and worked until evening. The host did not weave all the time, but he stayed with them at all times. In the evening each man carried the loom he had worked on to Susie's house, where I received them and put them away in a back room for safekeeping. The men sat down to eat of piki* and beans and leftover food from dinner and somviki, which is tamales made from finely ground blue corn, sweetened and wrapped in corn husks, and tied with yucca strips and then boiled, and made by the bride every evening. As the weavers left after supper, I gave each of them a few tamales on top of a folded piki. Each morning the weaving continued. Only one man could work on each loom at a time, but the best weavers came and took turns during the day. Other men came, bringing

* Paper-thin bread, shaped into conical rolls while still warm.

their spinning or knitting, or just sat and visited and listened as the older men retold the traditional stories. Sometimes they all sang together.

About halfway through the rites, our consciences troubled us, because we felt the Hopi way was not quite right. We decided to get a license and be married legally. Emory told his folks what we wanted to do. He made application to the agency at Keams Canyon, and a marriage license was obtained by mail from Holbrook, the nearest county seat. It took about a week. In the afternoon that the license came, I went to my father's house in Hotevilla; Emory went with me. I just walked in and told my father that I was going to be married by license that night and had come to get my clothes. I could feel the disapproval of my father and my sister as I gathered the things I was going to wear. I just could not stay there and get dressed. I took my clothes and went to one of the school teachers, and she let me dress in her house.

I was married in a white batiste dress, which was my pride and joy. I had earned the money and bought the material and made the dress in domestic art class in the Phoenix school. It had lace insertion set in bow knots around the gathered skirt, on the flared sleeves, and on the collar. My teacher had entered it in the State Fair, and I got second prize on it. I wore it once to a party and then decided it was too nice to wear and put it away in a box.

Later I made this dress into two little dresses for my first baby, our little girl "Joy." About the second time that I hung these dresses out on the clothesline to dry, one of them disappeared. Two years later I was getting water at the spring one day, and there was a little two-year-old girl playing around, wearing that dress. I took her by the hand, led her to my house, and took off the dress (it was too little for her anyway). I put a nice colorful gingham dress on her, and gave her some bread and jam. She was pleased with it all, as I opened the door and sent her home. I heard no more on that. My babies wore out those dresses.

We were married in the evening on February 14, 1919, in the living room of the home of Mr. Anderson, principal of the school in Hotevilla, by Reverend Dirkson of the Mennonite Mission. Emory's people, including some of his cousins, came to the ceremony. The teachers served some refreshments and gave us some little presents and a room where we could spend the night. In the morning they served a wedding breakfast, and then we went back to finish the tribal wedding rites at Bacabi.

Emory was working at the school and had to be on the job, so he wasn't able to participate in the weaving during the daytime. The activity died down after the first few days anyway, the weavers carrying on until everything was done. I helped with the grinding and cooking until the outfit was completed.

When the weaving was finished the men took the robes from the looms and brought them into the house to be tried on. A border of sixteen running stitches in red was embroidered in the two corners, suggesting a limit of sixteen children, the most a person should have, and four stitches in each of the other two corners in orange, suggesting a minimum number of children. The white moccasins with leggings in one piece were finished just in time to be put on with the rest of the outfit. It was by then evening; food was placed before the guests and everyone ate again. (Hopis do not invite you to eat. They set the food before you, and the food invites.)

The next morning before sunup, Susie led the others in clothing me, first washing my hair. Everyone admired the bride, and I was now ready to go back to my father's house. A line of white cornmeal was sprinkled on the ground, pointing the way. There was a lot of snow on the ground, so they wrapped rags over my white moccasins so I wouldn't get them wet or muddy. Emory's people went with me out of the village and over the little hill back to my home in Hotevilla. Emory did not go with me this time. How I wished that my own dear mother could be there to meet me. The sun was just coming up when we got to my father's house. Verlie opened the door, and my father thanked them for the beautiful bridal apparel that would make his daughter eligible to enter the world of the hereafter. Thus ends the wedding ritual.

I went inside and removed the wedding apparel and spread it out on the bed. Then all the clan women came in and admired and tried on the robes. Then everything was rolled up and stored away. After a period of time these may be used as needed, even cut into kilts for men to wear or to make bags to carry packs on burros.

A bride of the village who has been married in the preceding year should dress in her complete bridal attire and go into the plaza at the time of the Home Dance, accompanied by her mother-in-law, and show herself to the kachinas* during their last round of the day, thus establishing her status as a married woman in their eyes. We had gone to Idaho but were back by the Home Dance in July. My father had shown his disapproval of me by cutting up my big robe and making little kilts out of it. I had taken the small robe with me. I had my moccasins and did make this appearance, accompanied by Susie.

Miss Abbott came to see me once during the thirty days of the tribal ceremony. She said she did not want to embarrass me, but she whispered in my ear, "You have never looked better in your life. You look healthy and happy. You have rosy cheeks. This has done you good."

The groom may follow the bride to her home as soon as he likes. Some go right away, some wait a long time before claiming their brides. Emory

* Supernatural beings who are the rainmakers. Members of the Kachina cult dress up to impersonate the various beings at ritual rainmaking dances. Kachina dolls are wood carvings that represent the supernatural spirits.

came over after a few days and stayed a couple of nights, but I could see that the tension and hostility was hard on him; too many children, too little room, not even a room to ourselves. After my going through all that ceremony just to please my family, my sister was still so hostile that I felt neither wanted nor welcome.

One day, about a month after we were married, when no one was at home, I felt that I could not stand it another minute. I gathered and packed my belongings, as many as I could carry, returning later for the rest of them, and went to the house where Emory lived near the school. He was at his work teaching shop when I got there. I cleaned up the house and had a meal cooked when he came home, and we were real happy. Soon afterward I got a job teaching beginners in the school. It was hard to get teachers there because it was so isolated.

TRADITIONS, NARRATIVES, AND FICTION

MOURNING DOVE

Mourning Dove (Hum-ishu-ma) was born in a canoe near Bonner's Ferry, Idaho, in 1888. A member of the Okanogan tribe, she lived most of her life in and around the Okanogan section of the Colville Reservation in Washington. Though she and her husband were migrant laborers, she took with her everywhere an old typewriter and managed to write at night after long hours in the fields during the day. Her first book, *Cogewea—The Half Blood,* was published in 1927 and may well be the first novel by an American Indian woman. Though she aspired to write romantic novels, she was encouraged by her lifelong friend and mentor, Lucullus V. McWhorter, to collect and record the traditional tales of her tribe for future generations. The result was *Coyote Tales* published in 1933. She died in 1936 at the age of 49.

THE GREAT SPIRIT NAMES THE
ANIMAL PEOPLE: HOW COYOTE CAME BY HIS POWER

The Great Spirit[1] called all his people together from all over the earth. There was to be a change. He would give names to the people, and the Animal World was to rule. The naming was to begin at the break of day, each one having the right to choose his or her name according to who came first to the Spirit Chief's lodge. The Spirit Chief would also give each one their duty to perform in the changed conditions.

It was the night before the New World. Excitement was among the people. Each one desired a great name of note. All wished to be awake and first at the lodge of the Great Spirit Chief. Everyone wanted power to rule some tribe, some kingdom of the Animal World.

Coyote was of a degraded nature, a vulgar type of life. He was an imitator of everything that he saw or heard. When he asked a question, when he asked for information and it was given him, he would always say, "I knew that before! I did not have to be told." That was Coyote's way. He was hated by all the people for his ways. No one liked him. He boasted too much about his wisdom, about everything. Coyote went among the anxious people, bragging to everyone how early he was going to rise, how he would be the first one at the Spirit Chief's lodge. He bragged of the great name he would choose. He said, "I will have three big names to select from: there is Grizzly Bear [*Kee-lau'-naw*], who will be ruler over all running, four-footed animals; Eagle[2] [*Milka-noups*], who will lead all the flying birds; Salmon [*En'-tee-tuek*], who will be chief over all the fish of every kind."

Coyote's twin brother, who took the name of Fox [*Why-ay'-looh*], said to him, "Do not be too sure. Maybe no one will be given his choice of names. Maybe you will have to retain your own name, Coyote. Because it is a degraded name, no one among the tribes will want to take it."

This angered Coyote. He answered back to his brother, "I am tired of that name! I do not want to take it! Let someone else carry it. Let some old man or some old woman take it who cannot win in war as I can. I am going to be a great warrior in the New World. My brother, I will make you beg me when I am called Grizzly Bear, Eagle, or Salmon."

Fox laughed. He said to his brother, "Go back to your lodge! Go get your sleep, or you will not wake in time in the morning to select your name."

Coyote went to his tepee in anger. He determined not to sleep that night. He would remain awake so as to be the first at the Spirit Chief's lodge for the name he wanted. As Coyote stooped to enter his tepee, his five children all called in one voice: "*Le-a'-whn* (father)!" [3] Their hungry and eager little faces were filled with the expectation that he had brought something home to eat. Coyote had no food. The children, their hair combed back and tied in a hard knot on the top of their heads with strips of buckskin, were disappointed. The mother, Coyote's wife (afterwards Mole), sat on her feet at the side of the doorway, a good woman, always loyal to her husband in his mischief-making and troubles. Never jealous, she was always useful in his adventures. From her place at the doorway, she looked up at Coyote and said in a disappointed tone, "Have you no food for the children? They are starving! I can find no roots to dig."

"*Eh-ha!*" grunted Coyote sarcastically. He answered his wife, "I am no common person to be spoken to in that fashion by a mere woman. Do you know that I am going to be a great Chief at daybreak tomorrow? I shall be Grizzly Bear. I will devour my enemies with ease. I will take other men's wives. I will need you no longer. You are growing too old, too ugly to be the wife of a great warrior, of a big Chief as I will be."

Coyote's wife, accustomed to his abusive language, turned to her corner of the lodge, took some old bones, and placed them with water in the *la-ah'-chin* (cooking basket). With two sticks she lifted hot rocks from the fire and dropped them in the *la-ah'-chin*. The water boiled and there was poor soup for the hungry children.

Coyote ordered his wife to gather plenty of wood for the tepee fire where he would sit without sleep all night. Half of the night passed; Coyote grew sleepy. His eyes would close however hard he tried to keep them open. Then he thought what to do. He took two small sticks and braced his eyelids apart. He must not sleep! But before Coyote knew it, he was fast asleep. He was awakened by his wife, Mole [*Pul'-laqu-whu*], when she returned from the Spirit Chief's lodge, when the sun was high in the morning sky. (Mole loved her husband and did not want to lose him. She wished him to remain Coyote, did not want him to become a great chief only to leave her for younger and more handsome women. This is why she did not call him at early morn.)

Coyote jumped up from where he lay. He hurried to the lodge of the Chief Spirit. Nobody was there, and Coyote thought that he was first. He did not know that the people had all chosen their names and had scattered everywhere over the earth. He went into the lodge and spoke, "I am going to be Grizzly Bear!"

The Chief answered, "Grizzly Bear was taken at daybreak!"

Coyote said, "Then I shall be called Eagle!"

The Chief answered Coyote, "Eagle has chosen his name. He flew away long ago."

Coyote then said, "I think that I will be called Salmon."

The Spirit Chief informed Coyote, "Salmon has also been taken. All the names have been used except your own: Coyote. No one wished to steal your name from you."

Poor Coyote's knees grew weak. He sank down by the fire in that great tepee. The heart of the Spirit Chief was touched when he saw the lowered head of Coyote, the mischief-maker. After a silence the Chief spoke, "You are Coyote! You are the hated among all the tribes, among all the people. I have chosen you from among all others to make you sleep, to go to the land of the dream visions. I make a purpose for you, a big work for you to do before another change comes to the people. You are to be father for all the tribes, for all the new kind of people who are to come. Because you are so hated, degraded and despised, you will be known as the Trickperson. You will have power to change yourself into anything, any object you wish when in danger or distress. There are man-eating monsters on the earth who are destroying the people. The tribes cannot increase and grow as I wish. These monsters must all be vanquished before the new people come. This is your work to do. I give you *squ-stenk'* powers to kill these monsters. I have given your twin brother, Fox, *shoo'-mesh*[4] power to help you, to restore you to life should you be killed. Your bones may be scattered; but if there is one hair left on your body, Fox can bring you back to life. Now go, despised Coyote! Begin the work laid out for your trail. Do good for the benefit of your people."

Thus, Coyote of the Animal People was sent about the earth to fight and destroy the people-devouring monsters, to prepare the land for the coming of the new people, the Indians. Coyote's eyes grew slant from the effects of the sticks with which he braced them open that night when waiting for the dawn of the name-giving day. From this, the Indians have inherited their slightly slant eyes as descendants from Coyote.

After Coyote had left the lodge of the Spirit Chief, the Chief decided to give to the Animal World and to the coming new people the benefit of the spiritual works of the Sweat-house.[5] But there was no one left to take the name, so the wife of the Spirit Chief felt pity for the animals and people, and she took the name of the Sweat-house. A spirit, she cannot be seen. But she is there! The pole-ribs of the sweat-house represent the wife of the Chief Spirit. Her songs are still sung by the present generation. She still hears the sorrows, the woes of her people, in the chant which goes up from the cone-shaped structure.

NOTES

1. *Hah-ah', or Hwa-hwa'*—Spirit. *Eel-me'-whem*—Chief. While the Okanogan, Colville, and other Salishan stock tribes of the interior paid homage to a great variety of minor "powers" or deities (as many members of the tribes still do), they firmly believed in a Spirit Chief, or Chief Spirit, an all-powerful Man Above. This belief was theirs before they ever heard of Christianity, notwithstanding statements made to the contrary.
2. *Milka-noups*—the "War Eagle," or "Man Eagle" (golden eagle) whose white plumes with black or brown tips are prized for decorative and ceremonial purposes, particularly for war bonnets and other headgear, dance bustles, coup sticks, and shields. The tail feathers of the bald eagle, *Pak-la-kin* (White-headed-bird) are not valued so highly. In the old days the use of eagle feathers was restricted to the men. Except in rare instances, women were not privileged to wear them.
3. *Le-a'-whn, or La-ee-whoo*. This form of address is employed only by males. A daughter calls her father *Mes'-tem,* and her mother *Toom.* A son calls his mother *Se-goo'-ey*.
4. *Shoo'-mesh*. With the exception of Coyote's "power," all "medicine" is spoken of as *shoo'-mesh* (or Manitou), which is regarded as definite aid communicated by the Spirit Chief through various mediums, inanimate objects as well as living creatures. Not infrequently an Indian will seek to test the potency of his medicine over that of another. Some present day medicine-men and medicine-women are reputed to possess magic power strong enough to cause the sickness or even the death of enemies, of anyone incurring their displeasure. When Fox steps over Coyote to bring him to life, he generally steps over him three times before he finishes rebuilding the scattered remains. Three is a mystic number to the Indians.
5. *Quil'-sten*—Sweat-house. A mystic shrine for both temporal and spiritual cleansing, the sweat-house is one of the most venerated institutions. Its use is governed by strict rules, said to have originated with Coyote, the great "law-giver." To break any of the rules is to invite misfortune, if not disaster.
   Sweat-houses, or lodges, are mound-shaped, round, or oval at the base, three to four or five feet high at the center, and four to six feet in diameter, accommodating three to four persons. In some sweat-houses there is room but for one bather. Pliant branches—usually willow or fir, depending upon the locality and growth available—are planted like interlocking croquet

wickets to make the frame. Where these "ribs" cross, they are tied together with strips of bark. There are never less than eight ribs. The frame is covered with swamp tule mats, blankets, or canvas. In primitive times sheets of cottonwood bark, top-dressed with earth, frequently formed the covering. Where a permanent residence is established, a framework is covered with tule mats, top-dressed with three or more inches of soil that is well packed and smoothed. The floor is carpeted with matting, grass, ferns, or fir boughs. The last are regarded as "strong medicine," and always are used if obtainable. They give the bather strength, and they are liked, besides, for their aromatic odor. The Indians rub their bodies with the soft tips of the fir boughs, both for the purpose of deriving power and for the scent imparted.

Just within and at one side of the lodge entrance, a small hole serves as a receptacle for the stones that are heated in a brisk fire a few steps from the structure. The stones, large as a man's fist, are smooth, unchipped, "dry land" stones—never river-bed rocks. The latter crack and explode too easily when subjected to a combination of intense heat and cold water. By means of stout sticks, the heated stones are rolled from the fire into the sweat-house. Then the entrance is curtained tightly with mat or blanket, and the bather sprinkles cold water on the little pile of stones, creating a dense steam.

To the novice, five minutes spent in the sweltering, midnight blackness of the cramping structure seem an eternity and almost unendurable.

Several "sweats," each followed by a dip in a nearby stream or pool, properly constitute one sweat-bath. The customary period for a single sweat is ten to twenty minutes; although votaries from rival bands or tribes often crouch together in the steam for twice or thrice that time. Thus they display to one another their virility and hardihood. To further show their strength and their contempt for the discomfort of such protracted sweating, they will blow on their arms and chests. The forcing of the breath against the superheated skin produces a painful, burning sensation. Hours, even days, may be spent in "sweat-housing."

The stones used are saved and piled outside the sweat-lodge, where they remain undisturbed. For services rendered they are held in a regard bordering on reverence. An Indian would not think of spitting or stepping on these stones or of "desecrating" them in any way.

Old-time warriors and hunters always "sweat-housed" before starting on their expeditions or for rewards in racing, gambling and love. Many of the modern, school-educated Indian men and women often resort to the sweat-house to pray for good fortune and health.

THE CHANGING WOMAN
Navajo Origin Myth

In the great desert of multicolored sand stood the Mountain-Around-Which-Moving-Was-Done, and at the foot of this great mountain was found a baby girl.

First Man and First Woman found the child when the earth was still unformed and incomplete. They took her home with them and raised her carefully, and the gods smiled on her and loved her. As she grew into womanhood, the world itself reached maturity as the mountains and valleys were all put into the proper places.

At last she was grown and the world was complete, and to celebrate her becoming a woman, the gods gave her a Blessing Way, Walking-into-Beauty. Songs and chants were sung to her, and her body was shaped with a sacred stick so that it would grow strong and beautiful. Each morning of the ceremony, she ran to greet the sun as it arose. The sacred ceremony was preserved and it is now given to all Navajo girls when they reach adulthood.

But the young girl did not stay the same. Each winter she became withered and white-haired, just as the earth became bare and snow-covered. But each spring as the colors of life grew back on the land, the colors of youth and beauty appeared in her cheeks and in her hair. So she is called Changing Woman, or "A Woman She Becomes Time and Again."

The sun fell in love with Changing Woman, but she did not know what to do with him. So she went to First Woman for advice. On the advice of First Woman, she met the sun and he made love to her. Nine months later, twin sons were born to her and she raised them with love and care. For monsters had now appeared in the world, and the people were being destroyed. Changing Woman hoped her sons could save the world from the monsters.

When the twin boys were grown, Changing Woman sent them to the sun, their father, to get power from him so that they could fight the monsters. After undergoing severe tests by their father, the boys returned and destroyed all of the monsters.

Now the world was complete and the monsters were dead. It was a perfect place for people, but there were very few left. Changing Woman pondered over this problem, and at last she took two baskets of corn. One was of white corn and one was of yellow corn. From the white cornmeal she shaped a man and from the yellow cornmeal she shaped a woman.

And so the earth was populated again, a changing world and a beautiful world—the world of Changing Woman.

KAY BENNETT

The following excerpt is from *Kaibah: Recollections of a Navajo Girlhood* (1964), which is "a true story of an average Navajo family and an average Navajo girl as lived by the author during the period from 1928–1935."

THE CHANGING WOMAN STORY

Sometimes Grandma would tell the children stories of the days when she was a girl, or repeat the tribal legends of how the gods would come to visit the people when the tribe was young. One day, while she was working at her loom, the girls begged her to tell them again of the Changing Woman.

"Very well," she said. "Sit still, and listen." She thought for a while, then said: "In the beginning a man and his wife lived at the Mountain Which Moves, just east of here. One morning the man looked up at the mountain and saw a small cloud over it. The cloud stayed over the mountain for four days, and the man told his wife he must go to see what was the matter.

"He climbed the mountain and, under the cloud, he found a small pond. He saw that a basket was floating in the middle of it. He waded out to the basket. Inside of it he found the most beautiful baby girl he had ever seen.

"He took the baby in the basket home to his wife, and she fed her, and wrapped her in a warm blanket. The baby grew up to be a young woman in four days. She had long black hair, which was always brushed, so that it shone in the sun. She had beautiful brown eyes, which sparkled like the stars on a clear night. Her body was straight and strong, and she walked erect, with her head held high and proud.

"One day she was gathering wood in the forest to take to her mother's hogan. She gathered a large pile, and tied it together with an old scarf she had brought with her for that purpose. But as she knelt down, taking hold of the scarf to swing the bundle to her shoulder, she felt someone pressing down so strongly that she could not lift it. She looked around, but saw no one, so she tried again to lift it, but without success. For someone was pressing down too strongly. Four times she tried. The fourth time, when she looked around, she saw a stranger, splendidly dressed. A light was all around him, making his beads and silver shine so brightly that she could scarcely look at him.

" 'Woman,' he said, 'the God of the Sun has been watching you. He is pleased with you, and will take you to be his wife. Go home, and tell your father to build you a shelter from the boughs of the pine tree, and in four days go to this shelter. There the God of the Sun will come to you.'

"She went home and told her parents what the stranger had said to her, and her father went to work and completed the hogan in four days. The young woman moved into the shelter, and that night the God of the Sun came to her. Four days later she gave birth to a son. She was very proud of the beautiful baby and waited for the God of the Sun to come, so she might show him the boy. But the god did not return.

"She waited four days. Then, leaving her baby with her parents, she started out to look for the god's home. She walked for four days, until she came to a great hogan made of turquoise and silver, built on the shore of the east ocean. The young woman walked up to the door and knocked four times. A voice told her to enter. She opened the door, and stepped into the hogan, and stood looking around in amazement. The polished turquoise walls were nearly covered with beautiful clothing, bear skins, deer skins, buffalo hides, and jewelry. The floor was spread with buffalo hides and fine sheep skins. Two women were sitting at one side, sewing. The older woman asked, 'What do you want?' The young woman answered, 'I seek the God of the Sun. Is this his home?' The older woman said, 'Yes, this is the home of the God of the Sun. He is my husband. What do you want from him?'

"The young woman cried, 'He spoke of no wife when I married him and bore him a son!' The wife of the Sun God said, 'I have been his wife for many years, and this girl is his daughter.' As she spoke, she laid her hand on her beautiful daughter's arm, and stroked it gently. 'I will wait for him to return,' said the young woman.

"Finally the God of the Sun returned to his home and was surprised and a little embarrassed to see the young woman sitting opposite his wife. The young woman asked, 'Am I your wife?' He said, 'I have never seen you before.' She said, 'I have borne a son for you. He is a beautiful boy.'

"The God denied her four times before his first wife spoke. 'Why do you deny that you have taken a second wife? What are you going to do with her? She cannot live here with me. You must build her a hogan in another place.'

"The God of the Sun took his new wife outside, and said, 'You should not have come here and embarrassed me before my wife.' She answered, 'I am also your wife, but I would not have come if you had told me you had another wife. Now what will you do for me and for our son?' The

Sun God told her he would build her a hogan in the middle of the west ocean. He said, 'Go now, and when you arrive, it will be completed. I will come to you every evening, but I must return here every morning to carry the sun across the sky.'

"She started off on the long journey to the ocean in the west, and by morning had reached the home of her parents. Her son, who had grown into a strong young man, came to greet her. 'Did you find my father?' he asked. 'Yes, my son,' she answered, 'he is building us a hogan in the west. I must go there today. You must stay here, and make a place for our people. You must destroy the giants, the great scaled lizards, the snakes, and the flying beasts who would eat our people. Your father will give you the power to destroy them.'

"She bade her son goodbye, and resumed her journey across the prairie toward the western ocean. She was very thirsty by the time she reached the foot of the Turquoise Mountains, so, taking a stick, she dug a hole and it filled with water. She scooped a little out with her hand, drank, and started climbing the mountain. When she reached the top she sat down to rest and eat, but as she looked into a small pool formed by a mountain spring, she saw her own reflection in the pool. She was shocked to see that she had become old and ugly. She sat and cried, but soon she felt the wind on her cheek, and the God of the Wind spoke to her. 'Wash your face in the pool, and give corn pollen to the gods,' he said, 'and you will regain your youth and your beauty.'

"She did as she was told, washed her face, then faced the east. She threw a little pollen into the air and cried, 'Oh, God of the Morning, give me back my youth and beauty, so I will not lose the love of my husband.' Then she turned to the south, and gave pollen as she prayed to the gods who lived there. Then she prayed to the gods in the west, and finally to the great gods of the north. The gods pitied her, and thought the God of the Sun should not have punished her so severely for embarrassing him before his wife.

"They told her that she must follow the sun as he moved across the sky, but she must always stop and renew her youth in the little pool. They gave her the name of Changing Woman. She cooked some corn dumplings, and, feeling strong and refreshed, started off again for her new home. When she reached the middle of the western ocean she saw a beautiful hogan all built of mother-of-pearl. It stood on top of a mountain, in the middle of a small island, and shone with all the colors of the rainbow in the evening sun. She climbed the mountain and entered the hogan, and a warm feeling swept over her, for the inside was even more beautiful. The walls and roof were of mother-of-pearl, which gave off a soft blue light, and the floor was covered with buffalo hides. There were shelves of bright red coral, and on the walls hung beautiful dresses, rainbow-colored blankets, and the skins of animals from the four corners of the world. The God of the Sun had seen what happened on the top of Turqouise Mountain, and he was ashamed. He had decided to give the Changing Woman everything she could wish for and had sent his helpers to build a hogan that would please her.

"Now every day as the Changing Woman follows her husband across the world, she stops to renew her youth at the little pool, and to give corn pollen to the gods who helped her. The God of the Sun divides his time between his wife in the turquoise hogan in the east, and the Changing Woman in the mother-of-pearl hogan in the west."

LESLIE MARMON SILKO

Born in Albuquerque in 1948, Leslie Marmon Silko grew up at the Laguna Pueblo Reservation, where she currently lives and writes. She graduated from the University of New Mexico and attended several semesters of law school before deciding to devote herself full time to writing. She has published *Laguna Woman* (1974), a collection of poems, and *Ceremony* (1977), her first novel. Her short stories and poems have been anthologized in many books, including *The Man to Send Rain Clouds* (1974), *Carriers of the Dream Wheel* (1975), *Voices of the Rainbow* (1975), *Yardbird Reader 5* (1976), and *The Remembered Earth* (1978). In 1974 she received the Award for Poetry from *The Chicago Review*. In 1975 her story "Lullaby" was selected as one of the twenty best short stories of the year and included in Martha Foley's *Best Short Stories of 1975*. Of mixed ancestry—Laguna, Mexican, and white—she says, "What I know is Laguna. This place I am from is everything I am as a writer and human being."

GALLUP, NEW MEXICO—
INDIAN CAPITAL OF THE WORLD

"The travelling made me tired. But I remember when we drove through Gallup. I saw Navajos in torn old jackets, standing outside the bars. There were Zunis and Hopis there too, even a few Lagunas. All of them slouched down against the dirty walls of the bars along hiway 66, their eyes staring at the ground like they had forgotten the sun in the sky; or maybe that was the way they dreamed for wine, looking for it somewhere in the mud on the sidewalk. This is us too, I was thinking to myself, these people crouching outside bars like cold flies stuck to the wall."

They parked the truck by the Trailways bus station and walked across the railroad tracks. It was still early in the morning, and the shadows around the warehouses and buildings were long. The streets and sidewalks were empty, and on a Saturday morning in Gallup, Tayo knew what they would see. From the doorway of a second-hand store he could see feet, toes poking through holes in the socks. Someone sleeping off the night before, but without his boots now, because somebody had taken them to trade for a bottle of cheap wine. The guy had his head against the door; his brown face was peaceful and he was snoring loud. Tayo smiled. Gallup was that kind of place, interesting, even funny as long as you were just passing through, the way the white tourists did driving down 66, stopping to buy Indian souvenirs. But if you were an Indian, you attended to business and then left; and you never stayed in that town after dark. That was the warning the old

Zunis and Hopis and Navajos gave about Gallup. The safest way is to avoid bad places after dark.

The best time to see them was at dawn because after the sun came up they would be hiding or sleeping inside shelters of old tin, cardboard and scrap wood. The shelters were scattered along the banks of the river. Some of them were in the wide arroyo which the creek cut through Gallup, but the others were in the salt cedar and willow thickets which grew along the stream banks. Twice or three times a year the police and the welfare people made a sweep along the river, arresting the men and women for vagrancy and being drunk in public, and taking the children away to the Home. They were on the Northside of town anyway, Little Africa, where Blacks, Mexicans and Indians lived; and the only white people over there were Slav storekeepers. They came at Gallup Ceremonial time to clean up before the tourists came to town. They talked about sanitation and safety as they dragged the people to the paddy wagons; in July and August, sudden cloudbursts could fill the arroyos with flood water, and wash the shelters away.

They had been born in Gallup. They were the ones with light-colored hair or light eyes; bushy hair and thick lips—the ones the women were ashamed to send home for their families to raise. Those who did not die, grew up by the river, watching their mothers leave at sundown. They learned to listen in the darkness, to the sounds of footsteps and loud laughing, to voices and sounds of wine; to know when the mother was returning with a man. They learned to stand at a distance and see if she would throw them food—so they would go away to eat and not peek through the holes in the rusting tin, at the man spilling wine on himself as he unbuttoned his pants to crawl on top of her.

They found their own places to sleep because the men stayed until dawn. Before they knew how to walk, they learned how to avoid fists and feet.

When she woke up at noontime she would call him to bring her water. The lard pail was almost empty; the water looked rusty. He waited until she crawled to the opening. He watched her throat moving up and down as she drank; he tried to look inside to see if she had brought food, but the sun was high now and the inside of the shelter was in shadow. She dropped the pail when it was empty and crawled back inside. "Muh!" he called to her, because he was hungry and he had found no food that morning. The woman with the reddish color hair, the one who used to feed him, was gone. Her shelter was already torn down, taken away in pieces by others in the arroyo. He had prowled for garbage in the alleys behind the houses, but the older children had already been there. He turned away from the shelter and looked up at the traffic on the bridge. Once he had crawled up there and stood on the bridge, looking down at the shelter, and then around at the street where it crossed the tracks; he could even see downtown. She had taken him with her when he was very small. He remembered the brightness of the sun, the heat, and all the smells of cars and food cooking, the noise, and the people. He remembered the inside, the dark, the coolness, and the music. He laid on his belly with his chin on the wooden floor, and watched the legs and the shoes under the tables, the legs moving across the floor; some moved slowly, some stumbled. He searched the floor until he found a plastic bar straw, and then he played with piles of cigarette butts he had gathered. When he found chewing gum stuck beneath the tables he put it in his mouth and tried to keep it, but he always swallowed it. He could not remember when he first knew that cigarettes would make him vomit if he ate them. He played for hours under the tables, quiet, watching for someone to drop a potato chip bag or a wad of gum. He learned about coins, and searched for them, putting them in his mouth when he found them. Once they had lived somewhere else, a place full of food. He dreamed about that place in the past, and about a red blanket which was warm, and moved rhythmically like breathing.

He got used to her leaving the bar with men, giving somebody a dollar to buy the boy food while she was out. After he ate, he slept under the tables and waited for her to come back. The first time she did not come back, the man who swept floors found him. He did not cry when the man woke him; he did not cry when the police came and tried to ask him his name. He clutched the last piece of bread in his hand and crouched in the corner; he closed his eyes when they reached for him. After a long time, she came for him. She smelled good when she carried him and she spoke softly. But the last time, he remembered the white walls and the rows of cribs. He cried for a long time, standing up in the bed with his chin resting on the top rail. He chewed the paint from the top rail, still crying, but gradually becoming interested in the way the paint peeled off the metal and clung to his front teeth.

When she came for him she smelled different. She smelled like the floors of the room full of cribs, and her long hair had been cut. But she came back for him, and she held him very close.

They stayed in the arroyo after that. The woman with the reddish hair helped them drag twisted pieces of old roof tin from the dump, down the banks of the river to the place the other shacks were, in sight of the bridge. They leaned the tin against the crumbly gray sides of the arroyo. His mother rolled big bricks up from the river bed to hold the pieces of cardboard in place. It was cold then, and when the sun went down they built small fires from broken crates they found in the alleys and with branches they tore from the tamarack and willow. The willows and tamaracks were almost bare then, except for the branches higher than a man could reach. One of the men brought an axe with a broken handle, and the drunks who lived in the arroyo chopped down the tamaracks and willows, laughing and passing a bottle around as they took turns with the axe. The only trees they left were where all the people went. A strong, stinging smell that came from that place. He learned to watch out for shit and in the winter, when it was frozen, he played with it—flipping it around with a willow stick. He did not play with the other children; he ran from them when they approached. They belonged to the woman who stayed under the bridge, with low tin walls to block the west wind. That winter he heard a strange crying sound coming from under the bridge, and he saw the children standing outside the low sides of the shelter, watching. He listened for a long time and watched. The next day it was quiet, and the woman carried a bundle of bloody rags away from the bridge, far away, north toward the hills. Later on he walked the way she had gone, following the arroyo east and then north, where it wound into the pale yellow hills. He found the place, near the side of the arroyo where she had buried the rags in the yellow sand. The sand she had dug with her hands was still damp on the mound. He circled the mound and stared at a faded blue rag partially uncovered, quivering in the wind. It was stiff with a reddish-brown stain. He left that place and he never went back; and late at night when his mother was gone, he cried because he saw the mound of pale yellow sand in a dream.

Damp yellow sand choking him, filling his nostrils first, and then his eyes as he struggled against it, fought to keep his eyes open to see. Sand rippled and swirled in his dream, enclosing his head, yellow sand and shadows filling his mouth, until his body was full and still. He woke up crying, in a shallow hole beside the clay bank, where his mother had thrown the old quilt.

He slept alone while his mother was with the men—the white men with necks and faces bright red from the summertime, Mexican men who came from the section gang boxcars at the railroad, looking for the women who waited around the bridge—the ones who would go down for a half bottle of wine. The black men came from the railroad tracks too, standing on the bridge looking down at them. He did not know if they looked at him or if they were only looking at his mother and the women who lined up beside her, to smile and wave and yell "hey honey" up to the men. The white people who drove by looked straight ahead. But late one afternoon some white men came and called, until the women came out of the lean-tos and then the men yelled at them and threw empty bottles, trying to hit them. The woman with reddish hair threw the bottles back at them, and screamed their own words back to them. The police came. They dragged the people out of their shelters—and they pulled the pieces of tin and cardboard down. The police handcuffed the skinny men with swollen faces; they pushed and kicked them up the crumbling clay sides of the arroyo. They held the women in a circle, while they tried to catch the children who had scattered in all directions when they saw the police coming. The men and the women who were too sickdrunk to stand up were dragged away, one cop on each arm. He hid in the tamaracks, breathing hard, his heart pounding, smelling the shit on his bare feet. The summer heat descended as the sun went higher in the sky, and he watched them lying flat on his belly in the dry leaves of tamarisk that began to itch, and he moved cautiously to scratch his arm and his neck. He watched them tear down the last of the shelters, and they piled the rags and coats they found and sprinkled them with kerosene. Thick black smoke climbed furiously into the cloudless blue sky, hot and windless. He could feel the flies buzzing and crawling around his legs and feet, and he was afraid that the men searching would hear them and find him. But the smell in the remaining grove of tamarack and willow was strong enough to keep them away. The men in dark green coveralls came with steel cannisters on their backs and they sprayed the places where the shelters had been; and in the burnt smell of cloth and wood, he could smell the long white halls of the place they kept children. At sundown he woke up and caught sight of the headlights on the traffic across the bridge. He stood up slowly and looked restlessly toward the arroyo banks, thinking about food. -

It was a warm night and he wandered for a long time, in the alleys behind the houses, where the dogs barked when he reached into the tin cans. He ate as he made his way back to the arroyo, chewing the soft bone cartilage of pork ribs he found. He saved the bones and sucked them to sleep in the tamaracks and willows. Late in the night he heard voices, men stumbling and falling down the steep crumbling bank into the arroyo, and he could hear bottles rattle together and the sound of corks being pulled from the bottles. They talked loudly in the language his mother spoke to him, and one man sat with his back against the bank and sang songs until the wine was gone.

He crawled deeper into the tamarack bushes, and pulled his knees up to his belly. He looked up at the stars, through the top branches of the willows. He would wait for her, and she would come back to him.

JANET CAMPBELL

"I was born on January 11, 1947, on the Coeur d'Alene Reservation in northern Idaho. When I was ten my family moved to Wapato, Washington, on the Yakima Reservation. I disliked school and did poorly in it. I didn't attend school at all the year I was supposed to have been in ninth grade, just began the next year in the tenth grade. I worked as a waitress, I picked cherries, apricots, peaches, stripped hops. I painted, wrote poetry, read serious books. In 1963, with a tenth-grade education, twenty dollars in my pocket, and a youthful optimism I now find amazing, I went to San Francisco to seek my fortune. Times were hard for a long, long time." * Janet Campbell is now a law student at Berkeley. Her first novel, *The Owl's Song,* was published in 1974. Her poems and short stories have been widely anthologized and published in various journals and magazines. She is currently working on a second novel.

THE SNOW KEEPS FALLING

The theme of the seventh, eighth, and ninth grade dance is "Winter Wonderland," the committee decided, and it'll be semi-formal. That's what it says on the blackboard behind Miss Jenkins. And right under the announcement is a drawing in colored chalk of a high-steepled little church. The bell is ringing and there's bright green pine trees all around and there's snow falling and old-fashioned people, women in hoop skirts and bonnets, men in top hats and long overcoats, are walking toward the church. Alan Christenson did it. He's the eighth grade class artist and every month or so he does a new colored chalk drawing.

Miss Jenkins always wears bell-bottomed pants suits in winter and you can see the outline of her girdle seams through the pants and the place where the garters fasten onto her stockings. She's talking about the defeat of the Spanish armada. She's sitting on the edge of her desk, casual like, one knee drawn up a little. She has greasy, thin hair, blond in places, grey-brown in places, hanging loose and stringy around her face. Little raw-looking, red pimples dot her chin and forehead. She has a cold and her nose is red and runny and she has to keep taking kleenexes from the box on her desk and wiping her nose. Alan Christenson told her his mother wanted her to come to dinner sometime this week and she said okay tell her how about Friday. He asked her right in class after the eight o'clock

* From *Voices of the Rainbow,* ed. Kenneth Rosen (New York: Viking Press, 1974), pp. 226–227.

bell. That's the way the people are in Bradley, I mean the white people, the Suyappi. They're very tight, like a family. Only two-hundred people live in Bradley.

Outside it's begun to snow. For a long time there's been dark skies and grey, sunless days. Winds run fast and hard and the cold is so sharp it bites right through my clothes and skin and it feels like my bones are freezing. But no snow for weeks. Too cold for snow.

I'm trying not to listen to Miss Jenkins. I watch the snow falling. It's coming down harder. I can't help but hear a little of what Miss Jenkins is saying. I'd like to ask a question about a certain document. I try concentrating on the falling snow. I haven't asked questions in class in two years, none of us, the five Indians still left in school by eighth grade, have. We know they'll either ignore our questions or make a joke out of them. It used not to be like that when we were little kids. We had Suyappi friends then, school friends I mean, not the kind that stays overnight or you go any place with. Many Indian kids dropped out in sixth grade and I wanted to too but Dad wouldn't let me. He said, do like the law says. Them and their dances and parties, their class officers and basketball games. They don't even see us most of the time. They seem to be looking right through us just like we weren't here. Or else they look at us with that *look*, like we're dirty, you know, *vile* somehow. There's Levi and Hank and Tony, besides me, and Teresa Louis. My buddies are Levi and Hank and like me they're just living for the day eighth grade is over with and we're free at last. Tony is going away to BIA school and Teresa's going on right here. She's the daughter of tribal councilman Louis and wears good clothes and gets good grades and is so quiet you hardly notice her. She doesn't talk to anyone, Suyappi or Indian. Just sticks to herself.

The snow is *really* coming down now, and the wind is blowing hard. It's not just me looking out the window now. Everyone is. Miss Jenkins goes over to the windows and looks down.

"Any buses, Miss Jenkins?" someone asks. She turns and shakes her head, "No, not yet," she says. She goes back to her desk, sits down at her chair and reads from our history text.

About half the students that go to the school don't live in town. They live out in the country and there are five buses going five different routes. When the snow storms start getting bad during school hours then the buses come and everyone is sent home. Then the school is closed until the blizzards are over and the snow plows clear the roads. The trouble with that is any time that's lost because of the weather has to be made up in the spring. Last year it was two weeks. It's getting close to the 11:30 lunch break. I can tell without looking at the clock by the smell of food coming up from the cafeteria. My stomach growls. No breakfast this morning. The lunch sure smells good.

I'm looking out the window at the snow storm getting worse and smelling the food cooking when Miss Jenkins' droning voice stops. I turn my head and see that Dad's standing in the doorway. He said he might be coming into town today looking for work but he has a pretty bad chest cold so I didn't think he would.

He's wearing the patch over his blind eye. He doesn't usually, just for special things, like funerals and going into the city to see a movie. And he's holding his floppy, shapeless, wide-brimmed hat with both hands in front of him.

"I come for my boy," he says, nodding his head toward me. I get up from my desk and go with him. We don't talk until we get out of the school building.

"You find work?" I ask.

"No," he says, "I didn't come looking for work today. I was going to stay in bed, then I saw the storm coming up and thought I'd better come and get you."

We get into the truck, an old Ford pick-up. It's black with the words: JOE'S REPAIR AND HAULING painted in white. The engine sputters and groans awhile before finally turning over. We sit and wait a few minutes letting the motor warm·up. The truck makes a lot of shaking, clattering noise as we take off. We pass the first bus on its way to the school. We go through Bradley's main street, past the Cafe-Motel, the post office, the service station, the drygoods store and the Big Bear saloon, on out of town. About a mile out we have to stop the truck and get out and remove the snow from the windshield. It's coming too hard and heavy for the wipers to take care of it all.

Our place is about fifteen miles out on the reservation from town. The first few miles are hard. The road is narrow with sharp turns and on one side is sheer cliff. Dad lost the sight of his eye a long time ago when he was a young man fighting the Germans in France. He won't let me drive though, says I'm too young and likely to be reckless. He's known these roads, he says, since they were made and could drive over them even if he was blind in *both* eyes. There are pine trees growing tall and close together on either side of the road, up along the cliff, and you can't see but a little ways ahead.

Then the road becomes straight and comes out of the wooded area and we're making better time. We have to stop again to brush the snow away. In the north and the west are big dark mountains rising high. It's hard to see them through the snow. We're going through miles of small, rolling hills. The hills have been covered with snow for a long time and the old snow has gotten dry and hard and dirty-looking. The new snow falls on top of the old. It covers it and makes it clean and pure white again.

We come to our road and turn off the straight, paved highway. He stops the truck. I get out and check the mailbox. Dad's check is there, the one he gets each month from the government for having lost his eye. The house is more than a mile down the dirt road from the highway. We travel slowly, rattling and bumping along. The house is white and hard to see with all the white snow on the ground around it. The dogs, there are three of them now because one died last summer, are out in front barking at us. Dad drives the truck into the yard, parks it, covers it with two canvases. I help him. We go inside.

There's plenty of canned food in the pantry and flour and macaroni, plenty of wood in the shed and packed behind the stove, plenty of kerosene for our lamps. The blizzard can go on as long as it wants and we'll be okay. Dad takes off his shoes and socks and puts them in front of the stove. He has a new detective magazine. He's going to go lay down and read, he says. I take off my boots and socks too. Outside the blizzard is so bad you can't see but a few feet away. I light a lamp and go let the dogs in. The two older ones settle down near the stove and sleep. The younger one runs nervously from room to room looking around.

The wind is howling and moaning. I go get my flute from up on top of the closet. I carved it myself so it isn't a real flute and it only makes five different notes. I sit down in the big lumpy chair and blow on my flute. Them and their Winter Wonderland! Them and their 4-H club! When school lets out in the spring, oh, man, is it going to be great. Levi and Hank and me just taking it easy, I'll work with Dad cleaning and hauling for money. We'll booze it up and go to all the big celebrations and it'll be just great.

The younger dog has settled down by the stove too, but every once in awhile he lifts his head up and makes a little whimpering sound.

OPAL LEE POPKES

Opal Lee Popkes is a Choctaw, born in New Mexico in 1920. Besides her short stories which have been anthologized in *The Man to Send Rain Clouds* (1974), she has written eleven unpublished novels and is currently researching a project on pre-Columbian trade routes. She lives with her family in Columbia, Missouri, where she works at Stephens College. Of her childhood, she comments, "The most poignant pain to bear is the ill will of society. Full bloods were totally banished; those with less than full blood were allowed to live within the community but were ostracized. While ostracism is more painful, it is preferred to banishment because we can still observe and learn how to be a citizen, though the rights of citizenship are forbidden.... Society makes observers of Indians.... I taught myself to find the advantages of ostracism, and I engaged in community activities vicariously, learning through reading, pursuing the goal of learning everything in the world out of a book, by myself."

ZUMA CHOWT'S CAVE

In 1903 an Indian named Chowt followed a pack of rats through Dume Canyon, north of Santa Monica. To Chowt, the wind-scarred canyon was not Dume Canyon (a white-man name) but was called Huyat, something white people would have laughed at had they known its meaning.

But the white man chasing Chowt was less interested in the terrain than in proving his superiority to a fleeing Indian. Chowt had learned devious methods of avoiding capture. He tried to tell them the truth. He was following a rat, which was the truth. The white man stopped chasing, and sat down to laugh so long and hard that Chowt escaped and continued to follow the trail of the rat.

Chowt did not particularly care for his diet of small animals unless he was near starvation, but at that moment he was. He was also thirsty.

1903 was a dry year, when rats in prolific numbers left their haunts in search of water. In fact, the year was so dry they said even that a rat with an itch could start a fire with the shine of his eyes. Rubbing two blades of grass sparked a conflagration.

The rats searched for water. Chowt hungered for the fresh coolness of spring water. So he followed the rats through Dume Canyon, along the split-rock cliffs beside the Pacific Ocean. There was plenty of ocean to drink, but the rats knew as well as Chowt to scamper down the ocean edge, to other places, darting back and forth. Chowt sat down on a rock and waited for them to make up their minds. The little water wands didn't seem to be in any great hurry.

Chowt was a little man, small even as Indians go, and appeared to be a large bird poised on the 'rock, with his tiny legs drawn up under him.

The rats angled up a burned slope. Chowt followed. They ignored him. He was too far away to be attacked, but close enough to see the hundreds of gray bits of coarse fur, slipping in and out among the rocks, clinging with long tails and claw feet, always upward on the smooth slope, bypassing the boulders, going around the steep upward crags, speckling the side of the hill. They angled back and forth, but their general direction was to the north, from where even Chowt could smell water.

It took them two days to reach the top of the hill. They drank the meager dew at night, ate the same wild oats Chowt ate, and chewed on the same berry bushes. Chowt's body craved meat, but he waited patiently for them to find water before he would devour the water wands.

Chowt could see higher hills, even a few mountains to the north, but the rats seemed to prefer this particular hill, which climbed abruptly toward the ocean, ending in a sharp, high cliff facing the Pacific. Chowt knew the hill also ended in an abrupt cliff on the north side. The south slope was covered with gray vegetation, burned by wind, salt, and sun. Toward the east, the hills meandered into other, taller hills. But the rats went north, where a five-hundred-foot drop awaited them.

They continued onto a rock jutting out ten feet or so above the northeast canyon floor and disappeared. Others traveled over the top until all the rats had disappeared. None fell into the canyon, therefore Chowt knew they had found their gold.

Chowt waited patiently, in case the rats came out. During the night he heard them scurrying about, eating grass seeds, and then hiding again before the sun lightened the sky.

Chowt waited for the sun to come up, to evaporate any dew that might make the rocks slick. Then he walked casually to the top of the boulder, squatted, leaned over to see a small cave entrance large enough for any midget Indian named Zuma Chowt.

Slowly he swung himself down, with nothing but a half thousand feet of air below him, and clung to the rock with lichen tenacity, hanging by the sweat of his fingers. His feet swung blindly toward the rocky lip below the cave entrance. With a mighty swing he heaved himself feetfirst into the cave.

He crawled backward, listening, hearing the gush of liquid echoing in the silent cave. Every few feet he swept his short arms above him, judging the ever-increasing height of the cave ceiling. Then he stood erect in the damp stillness.

Dark encircled him completely as he felt along the side of the cave until water splashed onto his hand. He smelled the water before he drank, then felt with his feet to find where the spring splashed from the cave wall; he stood under the cold water and murmured pleasures. On hands and knees he followed the stream to its outlet in the rocks.

The next few weeks Chowt spent trying to get out of the cave. He made the inside of the mountain into a molehill in his desperate struggle for survival. He pounded the walls, listening for the dull, flat sound that said dirt instead of rock, a place to dig for an opening, an escape.

Using his strong, thin fingers, he clawed and dug at the dirt that faced the ocean, because a deep cleft in the rock floor indicated that at one time the water had emptied into the ocean through a waterfall which had been shunted aside during some past earthquake. Somewhere in that rocky cliff there must still be an opening.

When hunger gnawed at him, he sat quietly, waiting for the rats to attack. Then he pounced and came out the victorious diner. But the supply of rats was rapidly becoming exhausted, and still he had not found an exit.

Then one day Chowt's raw and bleeding hands dug into dirt and returned filled with nothing but salty ocean air. He peeked through the hole to see the sun setting on a brilliant ocean. He ripped his clothing apart, made a rope, and swung down.

In the months that followed, Chowt decided that the better part of valor— eluding the white man—would be to make the cave his home. He stole ropes and spades from nearby villages and returned to the cave.

He would sit on the top of the hill and contemplate his home and stare for long hours at the ocean which crashed against the cliff below. Then one day he shoved a few stones here and there, placing them carefully at the top of the hill where the cracked stone layered beneath the thin vegetation. Then he swung down to the bottom of the cliff and stood in the surf, looking upward. Carefully he shoved stones here and about. Though the rocks appeared to be shoved at random, he had a plan.

When he went topside again, he broke small stones loose from beside and beneath the larger ones, and suddenly it seemed that the whole cliff was tumbling into the ocean.

He waited until the dust had subsided, then looked down at the debris he had created. The top of the hill was now reasonably flat, and as the stones and boulders had fallen they had crashed into the smaller ones he'd placed so carefully, thus changing the course of the stones so they landed in a haphazard V in the ocean.

He sat for a long time in the cliff opening, waiting for the tide to come in, and when it did the water roared into his inlet with a vengeance. He tossed out a long piece of twine with a fishhook on the end.

But along with the man-made fishing hole came an unexpected problem. The tide rushed into the V-shaped inlet and, with nowhere else to go, rose with a roar, splashing water halfway up the cliff. During storms the waves would expend themselves, with a mighty heave, into the cave itself.

Luckily, however, storms were infrequent, and with his stolen spade he dug dirt from inside his new home, moved rocks, chiseled, and finally fashioned a commodious place which, though dark and cool, was periodically washed by ocean storms.

He dug out the other veins of the cave. He stopped fighting the white man long enough to settle peaceably in Dume Canyon.

Once or twice a year he walked to Oxnard to earn or steal oddments of clothing. He was past the time when the pecking between races excited him, and, too, the white man had become bored and embarrassed by the continual harassment of the remnants of Indian bands.

His female Indian acquaintances wanted nothing to do with itinerant Indians. They had jobs as servants, or returned to the reservations.

During the hot California summers he walked throughout the state, wherever he pleased, looking not unlike a tiny Mexican—except for the fold of skin across his eyelids and his thin mouth—dressed in a pair of boy's overalls. In winter he improved his quarters.

Dume Canyon, squatting halfway between Santa Monica and Oxnard, improved with the help of Chowt. He trimmed dead branches for firewood, used the dead brush for bedding, trapped the wild animals that harassed the ranchers, cleaned the cliffs of dangerous rock that might fall on him, or unsuspecting cowboys, and developed the water source in the cave. He learned to harness the black gold which dripped and disappeared between the rocks inside his cave—and in the discovery, made quite by accident, he almost buried himself alive.

Few people knew that Chowt lived in a cave in Dume Canyon. After two white men fell off the cliff trying to get to him, they decided he was a monument to the judiciousness of the new laws that said Indians hurt nobody.

A few years after Chowt arrived, the state built a road along the ocean, cutting through the rocks at the foot of his cliff home. The builders never realized Chowt was watching them from behind the dead branches that camouflaged his cave opening.

Civilization closed in on Chowt after that first road was built. It hurt him to see a wagon and team of mules, then eventually a car or two, drive past, filled with people. Though he mellowed and became like a bonsai—tiny, pruned, seeming to live forever as an unseen gray ghost—civilization hurt him. When there had been no one, it had been easier; now he felt an ache, like a missing leg, a missing arm; he longed for human laughter, a human voice.

One day he returned to the cave with a friend, a fellow Indian, but after a year or two the friend couldn't stand the solitude and loneliness, and left. Chowt tried bringing a squaw to live with him, but she couldn't stand him. So he built, and struggled on, until loneliness overwhelmed him again.

One day when Chowt was seventy-five, he raided the home of an Oxnard banker, kidnaped the Indian servant girl, and took her for a wife. The older people in Oxnard remembered him then and laughed at the romance of such an old codger. Newspaper people searched old files and reprinted the old stories about him. A master's thesis was written about the one remaining Indian in the area, the goat of the hills. One doctor's dissertation was begun, but when the doctor-to-be tried to climb up to Chowt's cave for an interview, he fell off, after which people decided to leave Chowt alone. Indians were no longer being punished for white men's clumsiness.

And much to everyone's surprise, including Chowt's, the Indian girl stayed with him.

By 1944 he was completely forgotten by the younger generation. He was ninety years old, but still active and well. He had learned a few English phrases from his wife and still made a few trips into Oxnard, but most of his time was spent happily with his wife and daughter, whom he taught to survive in the best way he knew how—through his old Indian ways. His fortress was inaccessible, his life was secure, and he saw no reason to change his ways for himself or his little family. His cave was situated on public land, so no person harassed him about it.

Once a scoutmaster shepherding his troop through the area thought he saw a gray ghost of a woman swinging across the cliffs on a rope, but he refused to admit it to his scouts, and instead told them about Tarzan. A motorist swore he heard a mermaid singing off key, but the motorist had liquor on his breath. An intrepid teen-age rock hound told people how he caught his foot in a trap and a dark woman with a hairy body opened the trap and set him free. But the teen-ager gave up rock collecting and did not return for a second look.

A man named Leo Corrillo offered to finance a public park out of the area, but nobody wanted useless rocks and a cruel surf.

Also in 1944, Chowt's daughter turned fifteen. Her brown skin blackened from the sun, she was a thin shadow climbing over rocks and through bushes, with wild, uncombed black hair and a bloodcurdling scream that practiced peculiar English to the Pacific Ocean. She would swing on a wet seaweed rope firmly anchored inside the cave, or use one Chowt had stolen at Oxnard. Any person seeing her thus move over the face of the rocky cliffs would have sworn he had seen a mountain goat skipping nimbly. And with good reason. She wore garments of fur or skins, having made them according to Chowt's instructions. She balanced herself with the agility of a mountain goat, having learned that from her father too. He taught her how to squat high up in the rocks in the sun, like a gray wildcat, to watch the ocean for food. He taught her everything he knew, and her mother taught her pidgin English.

The Indian girl squatted on a rock far up on the cliff to watch what appeared to her to be a log drifting in to shore. She spread her leather skirt about her legs, dug her toes against the rock, and pondered what she could do with that log.

It wasn't the same kind of log one chopped down green or picked up from a dead tree. Driftwood was hard and light.

"I want that log." In her mind she devised various uses for it. She could cut it in half and make two stools. She could burn out the center and make a dugout canoe. She could split it, burn it, make fence posts, a seat, or even a ladder out of it. No, it wasn't a scrubby pine or a limber sapling. It would be pretty, too. She could even float on it out into the ocean and catch fish.

She swung down the cliff on her rope, ran across the rutted road to the beach, and dived into the breakers, her leather skirt clinging to her body like a second skin. As she swam closer she saw a person clinging to the driftwood and as she came up to him he smiled wanly, thinking help was arriving. The girl slapped him across the side of the head, sending him tumbling into the breakers. With one hand grasping the log, she swiftly outdistanced the weary man.

He pleaded, but she was already nearing the beach. Salt water filled his mouth. He sputtered. He turned on his back to float, letting the surf carry him toward the beach, until finally he lay like a half-drowned rat amid the litter of rusty cans, half-buried old fire holes, broken bottles, soggy paper cartons. All with a stench to match.

"Fuckin' bastard!" He lay there shivering, the sand filtering over him in the strong wind, as he waited for his breath to return. He looked about for a place to hide in case the military was searching for him. Down the coast-line, shrouded in September heat, he could see the outlines of a military post. He judged the distance to be about five or ten miles. "Goddamn! I didn't desert just to be shot for a deserter!"

The entire beach was as silent as the day Chowt had first stepped upon it. Seagulls perched or stood at the water's edge, backing away when the surf nibbled at their feet. Then they followed the water as it went out again, leaving bits of smelly sewage. They clustered in groups that flew upward to avoid the incoming water, searching to find fish, because they had already picked the rusty cans clean or eaten the last bit of discarded meat. No sun-bathers came to this beach any more, because of the garbage and also because its surf dumped clumps of oil and tar from a sunken tanker a few miles offshore.

Sand whirled and dribbled over the rock, only to be captured by the water as the surf pounded forward. There was a smell of tar and oil everywhere.

When the man finally staggered to an upright position, the seagulls fled. "I wonder where that damn dame come from," he said aloud, but his words drifted into the wind and smashed on the red-rock canyon walls leaning in layers for miles down the deserted shoreline.

He could see the road clinging to the edge of the ocean. But there was no car in sight. "Gas rationing," he said, glad no civilian was about to intrude on his freedom. The eroded stone peaks stood defiantly against the ocean, with only the ribbon of road hanging between.

He stared at the cliffs. No vegetation except bunches of dead bushes dotting the cliffs. Nothing but broken rock—pocked, burned black by wind and sun, or bleached red. No life. To the south, through the haze, he could see what he thought was Santa Monica.

He crossed the road and stood beneath the canyon cliff, where the wind was less fierce. Breakers followed him obediently to the road, fell back. Huge boulders lay to either side of him.

He saw a car coming so he hid among the coarse rocks. There, warm, resting in a pocket of sun, he moaned, laid his head on a bunch of dry grass, and waited for the car to pass. Then he sighed, leaned more comfortably into the warm afternoon sun, closed his eyes, and went to sleep.

Several jeeps full of military police drove slowly back and forth, and had Private Nelson Winks been awake he would have heard them say, "Probably sharks got him." And, "Don't see how he had the strength to make it. Probably drowned."

The girl hid above in the cave, and when Private Winks awoke, the beach once more seemed vacant and captured in silence. He rummaged in his pockets for food, found nothing but a chewed wad of gum and a wet cigarette package. He laid the package of cigarettes on the rocks to dry and popped the gum into his mouth, chewing lint and gum together. The gum still contained its spearmint flavor.

He climbed up onto one of the boulders. Just as he reached the top he fell back, but not before he had seen a service station down the road. "Coupla miles. And I don't see no MPs." His intention was to walk to the service station, but he changed his mind when he heard a jeep nearing from the north.

"Damn, they ain't gonna find me!" He hid behind a boulder. "Thousand miles of water in front of me, and rocks behind me. No better than a cornered rat."

But the jeep drove by, and his confidence returned. He said aloud, "I can make it to the service station before dark."

Seagulls once more perched around him. Then he heard a noise above. Thinking it was a seagull, he looked up, preparing to duck, but he saw the figure of a girl dressed from head to foot in skins.

"Rat's ass!" he exclaimed, sheltering his head from the shower of rocks. "I know that's a girl," he muttered, "but she don't look like no broad I ever seen." He moved aside as a large rock bounced where his head had been a moment before. "That's the same priss that tried to bash my head in and stole my log. How the hell did she get way up there? She must be half mountain goat!"

She was brushing rocks off the ledge, and they fell like bullets around Winks. He clasped his hands together over his head. "Damn you, you she-ass. I ain't gonna take that!" He reached for a rock and slung it upward. She plucked a rock out of a crevice and threw it at him. He ducked. The rock missed his head but slammed into his leg, knocking him sideways, so that he hit his head against the cliff and crumpled down, unconscious, on a jagged seat.

She sat on the ledge, dangling her feet over the side, now and then non-chalantly peering down at his prone figure. She was very dark, and her long black hair was plaited into a pigtail that coiled like a snake beside her on the ledge.

She heard a call from above, and the face of a woman appeared out of the cave. Her mother said something in her native tongue to the girl and it was ignored as the girl casually swung her feet back and forth. The woman repeated her demand and the girl said, in English, defiantly, "I won't!" It wasn't the kind of flat, angry "won't" a white girl might have uttered, in that there was no stubbornness to her tone of speech. Rather, her voice was coarse and untrained, oddly singsong, as though she'd learned English that had been tuned in to the wind, moving up and down as though the notes had been blown across the top of a bottle. Actually, that was indeed why she spoke English that way—because it had come to her from across the cave entrance.

"You will!" said the older woman, in a softer English than the girl, for the mother had learned her English from people accustomed to speaking it.

"I won't!" said the girl. "Kill him." She picked up another rock, aimed it down at Winks.

The mother said patiently, "I tell you it is a man. A man like your father. It is a man like a husband. It is not an animal to be slaughtered for food. It is a man. A man!"

"White man?" she asked, and the words were strangely harsh against the cliff.

"White man," said the mother.

"Kill, kill, kill, kill," she singsonged. "Kill, kill, kill, kill."

The mother reverted to her native tongue. "*Ubayi na Chowt, na Chowt.*" Then she lowered a rope.

The girl pouted, muttered angrily, but climbed down the rope, barely touching the rocks as she swung in and out, shoving with her toes like a ballet dancer. Then she stood beside Winks, looked down at his limp figure, picked up a rock, and pulled back her·arm for a good hard aim.

The woman let loose a blistering string of words, clearly condemning the girl. She kept scolding her, chattering like an angry bird, while the reluctant girl tied the rope about Winks. Then the woman began pulling him up the side of the cliff to the cave above.

The girl made no attempt to move the soldier's limp, unconscious body out of the way of the sharp rocks which ripped into his flesh; his blood marked his ascent up the wall.

Then the girl shoved him into the mouth of the cave, tossed the rope in, and went away to sulk on the ledge hewn out of the wall inside the cave. She watched her mother take long thin leaves from a plant and lay them on Wink's bleeding back, on the open wounds the rocks had cut into his shoulders, and where his head had banged against the cliff. She tied the leaves on with green seaweed strings around his head, waist, and chest. She tied his hands together and his feet; then she too went to the ledge and sat down beside her daughter.

They argued, jabbered, chattered—first in their native tongue, then in sprinkles of Spanish, English, whatever language the woman had picked up in the kitchens of her past. There was even a *"mais oui."* However, English came more easily.

The old woman said, "When I came here there were no soldiers, no roads, nothing but water and rock and Henry's tree. Now we got dirty beach and rocks. Trash on beach."

"Trash on beach," echoed the girl. "Trash on beach."

"I sen' you to Mrs. Eli. She teach you white ways of white man," said the mother, not knowing the woman called Eli had been dead for ten years.

"But Dowdy says stay here where Henry only kill," argued the girl. "Henry" was the name they had deciphered from a cross Chowt had once stolen from a church. The cross now occupied a revered niche next to the drops of oil that fell continually onto a rock where, once lit, they burned steadily like a candle might—a spot where the family did its cooking and odd worshiping.

Winks opened his eyes, rolling them in an arc that took in the whole room with a quick glance. On seeing the two women, he yelled. They answered coolly, in quiet words that, even though spoken in English, had a wild quality, perhaps because they blended with the pounding surf. "Pray to Henry," the old woman was saying.

They watched Winks struggle with his seaweed bonds, screaming at them. They did not stir, even when he wriggled across the stone floor to the cave entrance and looked down at the road below. He moaned, inched himself backward, sliding, dragging a seaweed mat they had placed under him.

For a long time he stared at them, the gloom of the cave broken by a single shaft of light from the cave opening, then he whispered in an agonized voice through his pain. "You ain't niggers. You ain't got them flat noses or wide lips, and they ain't got your kind of hair. I know now. I'm on Guadalcanal, and you're natives, and I'm about to be dumped in a stew pot." He began to whimper. The two women did not move.

"Who are you?" he pleaded. They ignored him but continued their jabbering to each other while he tried to add them up to something. "Let me see. . . . I was near Santa Monica when I dove overboard. I know I wasn't rescued. I couldn't have drifted down to Old Mexico because I never lost sight of that string of mountains. But you can't be Americans, because people like you don't live in the U.S.A."

His head hurt, and he wondered if they had smashed it. His hands were tied. They had even knotted the seaweed between his fingers, spreading them until they felt like crabs. The rough weeds with which the old woman had treated his wounds felt like spikes. He looked toward the little oil flame beside the cross. The slow drip would fall on the rocky niche, burn furiously, then almost go out before another drop ignited it again, and the smoke curled up to disappear mysteriously.

"This is a cave," he argued to himself. "I must be near Santa Monica. I remember. I looked up and something knocked me down. You—dressed in skins. Skins! Indians! You Indians? I'll be damned. Indians!"

The old woman looked steadily at him and nodded as she picked up a flat, hollowed-out rock.

He said, "Well, you ain't friendly Indians. How in the hell did people like you keep from gettin' civilized? Where you been? Don't you know there's a world out there?"

The girl picked up another rock, a long flat one shaped like a fence picket.

He ducked, expecting to be smashed. "Cut me loose?" he asked.

The old woman got up and went over to him, her long black cotton skirt swishing. She reached over him and untied a few of the knots that held his hands and arms.

"She understands, I think," he murmured. He picked some of the leaves from his head, smelled them, muttered, and threw them on the floor. "Wonder what kind of junk they doused me with? They must have beat me up."

He sat up and could see more clearly that the cave was fairly well lighted from the large entrance, beside which was set a cross of wood on which were tied bushes, with their roots sticking out into the cave: a removable camouflaging door.

The room extended backward into darkness, but there appeared to be another source of light where the rocks jutted out to semienclose this particular large room, which was about fifteen feet wide and barely tall enough for a man of Wink's size to stand up. He wished he could.

The floor of the cave was covered intermittently with seaweed mats, tightly woven. Here and there throughout this front area, and in the semidarkness beyond, rocks jutted up two or three feet from the floor; they were hewn flat across the top and crudely made articles were set upon them.

His head began to pain him again. "Damn if that junk didn't have some kind of medicine in it." He felt the side of his face, covered with dried blood. It hurt, so he reached for the leaf he'd thrown away and reinserted it under the seaweed strings.

Here and there on the floor he could see reflections of light playing, as though reflected from water, and he wondered if escape would be possible. As his eyes became more accustomed to the gloom, he saw other things— a crude loom made of tree branches that leaned against a wall near the cliff entrance, bearskins and woven mats hanging neatly from wooden pegs in the rock walls.

The old woman slipped up behind him, grabbed his hands, and looped the seaweed around them so quickly Winks could not protest.

"Damn you to hell. If I wasn't aching in every bone I'd bat you one."

The girl walked away into the depth of the cave. The old woman sat down and silently watched him.

Then Winks became aware of the light sounds of tinkling water falling, bubbling, gurgling, dripping. Yet he saw nothing.

The girl returned, having taken off her wet leather skirt, and was wearing a very short, ragged skirt and a sleeveless cotton shirt. As she moved around he saw she wore no underclothing at all, and there was not a hair on her body. The soles of her feet were white and the palms of her hands were white, in contrast to the deep brown of the rest of her.

I hope they ain't cannibals, he thought. Then, expecting no answer, he said, "How long you lived here?"

The girl said nothing, but the old woman said, in her strange singsong voice that flirted up and down like a flute, "Chowt came here fifty years ago."

"Forty, Mowma," said the girl. Winks could scarcely understand either of them because of the way they trilled and spilled their words like water.

"I'll be damned. What do you want to live here for?" He could smell the salt in the air. Ocean air. "How come your old man picked this place to hole up in?"

The old woman turned to the girl, and they threw his words back and forth, trying to translate them. Then the girl said, in a surly manner, "He followed the rats."

"Rats follow water," explained the old woman.

After having listened to their meager conversation, he was beginning to make out their language. They acted as though their oldest friends were the sun, the wind, the stars. There was no human touch about them. They were people in name only.

"How far to Santa Monica?" he asked. "Why don't you live there? I'd go on relief before I'd live here."

They seemed to tire of him suddenly, because the girl walked away to the place where the little pool of oil burned and returned with what appeared to him to be pieces of tiny tree limbs, which she shared with her mother.

"I'm hungry," he said. He might as well have been one of the rocks protruding from the floor of the cave. "I'm hungry!" he shouted. "Is that a stove? What you got cookin'? I want something to eat." His fear of the woman waned as his pain eased, so he shouted, "You goin' to let me lay here and starve? Gimme one of them sprouts to eat."

The woman bit them off, chewing slowly, ignoring him. "Chowt come and you eat," said the old woman.

Winks thought about her words. "Shout come and you eat?" But he'd been shouting and nothing had happened.

Then the woman went to the kitchen niche again and by the light of the burning oil he could see her pick dishes from between the rocks in the wall. She returned with a tray made of seaweed, on which were a few chipped dishes and some coarse spoons whittled from wood.

She set the tray on one of the protruding floor-rocks near him. He could identify pepper-tree twigs among the woven seaweed of the tray. She set her table.

"You goin' to untie me?" asked Winks.

She returned to the niche for more dishes, this time of metal. She plucked more dishes from a woven bag hanging from a peg between two rocks on the wall. These dishes had the appearance of tarnished, unpolished silver.

Winks turned his attention again to his wounds, which were completely covered by the long strips of leaves and bark. "Whatever medicine man you got, he's better than what they gave me at the dispensary. I'll bet these leaves would even cure the clap!" He looked closely for a long time at his bandages. Then suddenly he said, "You got a bathroom?"

Surely they understood *that* word. The girl looked at her mother, then sat down at the crude table and bit off a piece of stick. She began to chew.

"I gotta go to the john," he repeated. The girl glared, picked up a smooth round stone from a basket filled with rocks, and threw it at him. It missed only because he ducked.

"I gotta go," he said, wondering how Robinson Crusoe had managed. In all his reading about shipwrecks or people abandoned on desert islands this basic bodily function had never been a problem.

He could feel the salt caking on his body, the dried blood. He grunted, imitating a bodily function, hoping. In answer the girl picked up a handful of stones and slammed them at him.

"You are the throwinest female," he muttered.

"I kill him?" the girl asked her mother.

"No. Mrs. Eli had white husband. You have white husband too, and I have grandbaby."

LESLIE MARMON SILKO

Born in Albuquerque in 1948, Leslie Marmon Silko grew up at the Laguna Pueblo Reservation, where she currently lives and writes. She graduated from the University of New Mexico and attended several semesters of law school before deciding to devote herself full time to writing. She has published *Laguna Woman* (1974), a collection of poems, and *Ceremony* (1977), her first novel. Her short stories and poems have been anthologized in many books, including *The Man to Send Rain Clouds* (1974), *Carriers of the Dream Wheel* (1975), *Voices of the Rainbow* (1975), *Yardbird Reader 5* (1976), and *The Remembered Earth* (1978). In 1974 she received the Award for Poetry from *The Chicago Review*. In 1975 her story "Lullaby" was selected as one of the twenty best short stories of the year and included in Martha Foley's *Best Short Stories of 1975*. Of mixed ancestry—Laguna, Mexican, and white—she says, "What I know is Laguna. This place I am from is everything I am as a writer and human being."

STORYTELLER

I

Every day the sun came up a little lower on the horizon, moving more slowly until one day she got excited and started calling the jailer. She realized she had been sitting there for many hours, yet the sun had not moved from the center of the sky. The color of the sky had not been good lately; it had been pale blue, almost white, even when there were no clouds. She told herself it wasn't a good sign for the sky to be indistinguishable from the river ice, frozen solid and white against the earth. The tundra rose up behind the river but all the boundaries between the river and hills and sky were lost in the density of the pale ice.

She yelled again, this time some English words which came randomly into her mouth, probably swear words she'd heard from the oil drilling crews last winter. The jailer was an Eskimo, but he would not speak Yupik to her. She had watched people in the other cells; when they spoke to him in Yupik he ignored them until they spoke English.

He came and stared at her. She didn't know if he understood what she was telling him until he glanced behind her at the small high window. He looked at the sun, and turned and walked away. She could hear the buckles on his heavy snowmobile boots jingle as he walked to the front of the building.

It was like the other buildings that white people, the Gussucks, brought with them: BIA and school buildings, portable buildings that arrived sliced in halves, on barges coming up the river. Squares of metal panelling bulged out with the layers of insulation stuffed inside. She had asked once what it was and someone told her it was to keep out the cold. She had not laughed then, but she did now. She walked over to the small double-pane window and she laughed out loud. They thought they could keep out the cold with stringy yellow wadding. Look at the sun. It wasn't moving; it was frozen, caught in the middle of the sky. Look at the sky, solid as the river with ice which had trapped the sun. It had not moved for a long time; in a few more hours it would be weak, and heavy frost would begin to appear on the edges and spread across the face of the sun like a mask. Its light was pale yellow, worn thin by the winter.

She could see people walking down the snow-packed roads, their breath steaming out from their parka hoods, faces hidden and protected by deep ruffs of fur. There were no cars or snowmobiles that day so she calculated it was fifty below zero, the temperature which silenced their machines. The metal froze; it split and shattered. Oil hardened and moving parts jammed solidly. She had seen it happen to their big yellow machines and the giant drill last winter when they came to drill their test holes. The cold stopped them, and they were helpless against it.

Her village was many miles upriver from this town, but in her mind she could see it clearly. Their house was not near the village houses. It stood alone on the bank upriver from the village. Snow had drifted to the eaves of the roof on the north side, but on the west side, by the door, the path was almost clear. She had nailed scraps of red tin over the logs last summer. She had done it for the bright red color, not for added warmth the way the village people had done. This final winter had been coming down even then; there had been signs of its approach for many years.

II

She went because she was curious about the big school where the Government sent all the other girls and boys. She had not played much with the village children while she was growing up because they were afraid of the old man, and they ran when her grandmother came. She went because she was tired of being alone with the old woman whose body had been stiffening for as long as the girl could remember. Her knees and knuckles were swollen grotesquely, and the pain had squeezed the brown skin of her face tight against the bones; it left her eyes hard like river stone. The girl asked once, what it was that did this to her body, and the old woman had raised up from sewing a sealskin boot, and stared at her.

"The joints," the old woman said in a low voice, whispering like wind across the roof, "the joints are swollen with anger."

Sometimes she did not answer and only stared at the girl. Each year she spoke less and less, but the old man talked more—all night sometimes, not to anyone but himself; in a soft deliberate voice, he told stories, moving his smooth brown hands above the blankets. He had not fished or hunted with the other men for many years although he was not crippled or sick. He stayed in his bed, smelling like dry fish and urine, telling stories all winter; and when warm weather came, he went to his place on the river bank. He sat with a long willow stick, poking at the smoldering moss he burned against the insects while he continued with the stories.

The trouble was that she had not recognized the warnings in time. She did not see what the Gussuck school would do to her until she walked into the dormitory and realized that the old man had not been lying about the place. She thought he had been trying to scare her as he used to when she was very small and her grandmother was outside cutting up fish. She hadn't believed what he told her about the school because she knew he wanted to keep her there in the log house with him. She knew what he wanted.

The dormitory matron pulled down her underpants and whipped her with a leather belt because she refused to speak English.

"Those backwards village people," the matron said, because she was an Eskimo who had worked for the BIA a long time, "they kept this one until she was too big to learn." The other girls whispered in English. They knew how to work the showers, and they washed and curled their hair at night. They ate Gussuck food. She laid on her bed and imagined what her grandmother might be sewing, and what the old man was eating in his bed. When summer came, they sent her home.

The way her grandmother had hugged her before she left for school had been a warning too, because the old woman had not hugged or touched her for many years. Not like the old man, whose hands were always hunting, like ravens circling lazily in the sky, ready to touch her. She was not surprised when the priest and the old man met her at the landing strip, to say that the old lady was gone. The priest asked her where she would like to stay. He referred to the old man as her grandfather, but she did not bother to correct him. She had already been thinking about it; if she went with the priest, he would send her away to a school. But the old man was different. She knew he wouldn't send her back to school. She knew he wanted to keep her.

III

He told her one time that she would get too old for him faster than he got too old for her; but again she had not believed him because sometimes he lied. He had lied about what he would do with her if she came into his bed. But as the years passed, she realized what he said was true. She was restless and strong. She had no patience with the old man who had never changed his slow smooth motions under the blankets.

The old man was in his bed for the winter; he did not leave it except to use the slop bucket in the corner. He was dozing with his mouth open slightly; his lips quivered and sometimes they moved like he was telling a story even while he dreamed. She pulled on the sealskin boots, the mukluks with the bright red flannel linings her grandmother had sewn for her, and she tied the braided red yarn tassels around her ankles over the gray wool pants. She zipped the wolfskin parka. Her grandmother had worn it for many years, but the old man said that before she died, she instructed him to bury her in an old black sweater, and to give the parka to the girl. The wolf pelts were creamy colored and silver, almost white in some places, and when the old lady had walked across the tundra in the winter, she disappeared into the snow.

She walked toward the village, breaking her own path through the deep snow. A team of sled dogs tied outside a house at the edge of the village leaped against their chains to bark at her. She kept walking, watching the dusky sky for the first evening stars. It was warm and the dogs were alert. When it got cold again, the dogs would lie curled and still, too drowsy from the cold to bark or pull at the chains. She laughed loudly because it made them howl and snarl. Once the old man had seen her tease the dogs and he shook his head. "So that's the kind of woman you are," he said, "in the wintertime the two of us are no different from those dogs. We wait in the cold for someone to bring us a few dry fish."

She laughed out loud again, and kept walking. She was thinking about the Gussuck oil drillers. They were strange; they watched her when she walked near their machines. She wondered what they looked like underneath their quilted goosedown trousers; she wanted to know how they moved. They would be something different from the old man.

The old man screamed at her. He shook her shoulders so violently that her head bumped against the log wall. "I smelled it!" he yelled, "as soon as I woke up! I am sure of it now. You can't fool me!" His thin legs were shaking inside the baggy wool trousers; he stumbled over her boots in his bare feet. His toe nails were long and yellow like bird claws; she had seen a gray crane last summer fighting another in the shallow water on the edge of the river. She laughed out loud and pulled her shoulder out of his grip. He stood in front of her. He was breathing hard and shaking; he looked weak. He would probably die next winter.

"I'm warning you," he said, "I'm warning you." He crawled back into his bunk then, and reached under the old soiled feather pillow for a piece of dry fish. He lay back on the pillow, staring at the ceiling and chewed dry strips of salmon. "I don't know what the old woman told you," he said, "but there will be trouble." He looked over to see if she was listening. His face suddenly relaxed into a smile, his dark slanty eyes were lost in wrinkles of brown skin. "I could tell you, but you are too good for warnings now. I can smell what you did all night with the Gussucks."

She did not understand why they came there, because the village was small and so far upriver that even some Eskimos who had been away to school would not come back. They stayed downriver in the town. They said the village was too quiet. They were used to the town where the boarding school was located, with electric lights and running water. After all those years away at school, they had forgotten how to set nets in the river and where to hunt seals in the fall. Those who left did not say it, but their confidence had been destroyed. When she asked the old man why the Gussucks bothered to come to the village, his narrow eyes got bright with excitement.

"They only come when there is something to steal. The fur animals are too difficult for them to get now, and the seals and fish are hard to find. Now they come for oil deep in the earth. But this is the last time for them." His breathing was wheezy and fast; his hands gestured at the sky. "It is approaching. As it comes, ice will push across the sky." His eyes were open wide and he stared at the low ceiling rafters for hours without blinking. She remembered all this clearly because he began the story that day, the story he told from that time on. It began with a giant bear which he described muscle by muscle, from the curve of the ivory claws to the whorls of hair at the top of the massive skull. And for eight days he did not sleep, but talked continuously of the giant bear whose color was pale blue glacier ice.

IV

The snow was dirty and worn down in a path to the door. On either side of the path, the snow was higher than her head. In front of the door there were jagged yellow stains melted into the snow where men had urinated. She stopped in the entry way and kicked the snow off her boots. The room was dim; a kerosene lantern by the cash register was burning low. The long wooden shelves were jammed with cans of beans and potted meats. On the bottom shelf a jar of mayonnaise was broken open, leaking oily white clots on the floor. There was no one in the room except the yellowish dog sleeping in front of the long glass display case. A reflection made it appear to be lying on the knives and ammunition inside the case. Gussucks kept dogs inside their houses with them; they did not seem to mind the odors which seeped out of the dogs. "They tell us we are dirty for the food we eat— raw fish and fermented meat. But we do not live with dogs," the old man once said. She heard voices in the back room, and the sound of bottles set down hard on tables.

They were always confident. The first year they waited for the ice to break up on the river, and then they brought their big yellow machines up river on barges. They planned to drill their test holes during the summer to avoid the freezing. But the imprints and graves of their machines were still there, on the edge of the tundra above the river, where the summer mud had swallowed them before they ever left sight of the river. The village people had gathered to watch the white men, and to laugh as they drove the giant machines, one by one, off the steel ramp into the bogs; as if sheer numbers of vehicles would somehow make the tundra solid. But the old man said they behaved like desperate people, and they would come back again. When the tundra was frozen solid, they returned.

Village women did not even look through the door to the back room. The priest had warned them. The storeman was watching her because he didn't let Eskimos or Indians sit down at the tables in the back room. But she knew he couldn't throw her out if one of his Gussuck customers invited her to sit with him. She walked across the room. They stared at her, but she had the feeling she was walking for someone else, not herself, so their eyes did not matter. The red-haired man pulled out a chair and motioned for her to sit down. She looked back at the storeman while the red-haired man poured her a glass of red sweet wine. She wanted to laugh at the storeman the way she laughed at the dogs, straining against their chains, howling at her.

The red-haired man kept talking to the other Gussucks sitting around the table, but he slid one hand off the top of the table to her thigh. She looked over at the storeman to see if he was still watching her. She laughed out loud at him and the red-haired man stopped talking and turned to her. He asked if she wanted to go. She nodded and stood up.

Someone in the village had been telling him things about her, he said as they walked down the road to his trailer. She understood that much of what he was saying, but the rest she did not hear. The whine of the big generators at the construction camp sucked away the sound of his words. But English was of no concern to her anymore, and neither was anything the Christians in the village might say about her or the old man. She smiled at the effect of the subzero air on the electric lights around the trailers; they did not shine. They left only flat yellow holes in the darkness.

It took him a long time to get ready, even after she had undressed for him. She waited in the bed with the blankets pulled close, watching him. He adjusted the thermostat and lit candles in the room, turning out the electric lights. He searched through a stack of record albums until he found the right one. She was not sure about the last thing he did: he taped something on the wall behind the bed where he could see it while he laid on top of her. He was shrivelled and white from the cold; he pushed against her body for warmth. He guided her hands to his thighs; he was shivering.

She had returned a last time because she wanted to know what it was he stuck on the wall above the bed. After he finished each time, he reached up and pulled it loose, folding it carefully so that she could not see it. But this time she was ready; she waited for his fast breathing and sudden collapse on top of her. She slid out from under him and stood up beside the bed. She looked at the picture while she got dressed. He did not raise his face from the pillow, and she thought she heard teeth rattling together as she left the room.

She heard the old man move when she came in. After the Gussuck's trailer, the log house felt cool. It smelled like dry fish and cured meat. The room was dark except for the blinking yellow flame in the mica window of the oil stove. She squatted in front of the stove and watched the flames for a long time before she walked to the bed where her grandmother had slept. The bed was covered with a mound of rags and fur scraps the old woman had saved. She reached into the mound until she felt something cold and solid wrapped in a wool blanket. She pushed her fingers around it until she felt smooth stone. Long ago, before the Gussucks came, they had burned whale oil in the big stone lamp which made light and heat as well. The old woman had saved everything they would need when the time came.

In the morning, the old man pulled a piece of dry caribou meat from under the blankets and offered it to her. While she was gone, men from the village had brought a bundle of dry meat. She chewed it slowly, thinking about the way they still came from the village to take care of the old man and his stories. But she had a story now, about the red-haired Gussuck. The old man knew what she was thinking, and his smile made his face seem more round than it was.

"Well," he said, "what was it?"

"A woman with a big dog on top of her."

He laughed softly to himself and walked over to the water barrel. He dipped the tin cup into the water.

"It doesn't surprise me," he said.

v

"Grandma," she said, "there was something red in the grass that morning. I remember." She had not asked about her parents before. The old woman stopped splitting the fish bellies open for the willow drying racks. Her jaw muscles pulled so tightly against her skull, the girl thought the old woman would not be able to speak.

"They bought a tin can full of it from the storeman. Late at night. He told them it was alcohol safe to drink. They traded a rifle for it." The old woman's voice sounded like each word stole strength from her. "It made no difference about the rifle. That year the Gussuck boats had come, firing big guns at the walrus and seals. There was nothing left to hunt after that anyway. So," the old lady said, in a low soft voice the girl had not heard for a long time, "I didn't say anything to them when they left that night."

"Right over there," she said, pointing at the fallen poles, half buried in the river sand and tall grass, "in the summer shelter. The sun was high half the night then. Early in the morning when it was still low, the policeman came around. I told the interpreter to tell him that the storeman had poisoned them." She made outlines in the air in front of her, showing how their bodies laid twisted on the sand; telling the story was like laboring to walk through deep snow; sweat shone in the white hair around her forehead. "I told the priest too, after he came. I told him the storeman lied." She turned away from the girl. She held her mouth even tighter, set solidly, not in sorrow or anger, but against the pain, which was all that remained. "I never believed," she said, "not much anyway. I wasn't surprised when the priest did nothing."

The wind came off the river and folded the tall grass into itself like river waves. She could feel the silence the story left, and she wanted to have the old woman go on.

"I heard sounds that night, grandma. Sounds like someone was singing. It was light outside. I could see something red on the ground." The old woman did not answer her; she moved to the tub full of fish on the ground beside the work bench. She stabbed her knife into the belly of a whitefish and lifted it onto the bench. "The Gussuck storeman left the village right after that," the old woman said as she pulled the entrails from the fish, "otherwise, I could tell you more." The old woman's voice flowed with the wind blowing off the river; they never spoke of it again.

When the willows got their leaves and the grass grew tall along the river banks and around the sloughs, she walked early in the morning. While the sun was still low on the horizon, she listened to the wind off the river; its sound was like the voice that day long ago. In the distance, she could hear the engines of the machinery the oil drillers had left the winter before, but she did not go near the village or the store. The sun never left the sky and the summer became the same long day, with only the winds to fan the sun into brightness or allow it to slip into twilight.

She sat beside the old man at his place on the river bank. She poked the smoky fire for him, and felt herself growing wide and thin in the sun as if she had been split from belly to throat and strung on the willow pole in preparation for the winter to come. The old man did not speak anymore. When men from the village brought him fresh fish he hid them deep in the river grass where it was cool. After he went inside, she split the fish open and spread them to dry on the willow frame the way the old woman had done. Inside, he dozed and talked to himself. He had talked all winter, softly and incessantly about the giant polar bear stalking a lone man across Bering Sea ice. After all the months the old man had been telling the story, the bear was within a hundred feet of the man; but the ice fog had closed in on them now and the man could only smell the sharp ammonia odor of the bear, and hear the edge of the snow crust crack under the giant paws.

One night she listened to the old man tell the story all night in his sleep, describing each crystal of ice and the slightly different sounds they made under each paw; first the left and then the right paw, then the hind feet. Her grandmother was there suddenly, a shadow around the stove. She spoke in her low wind voice and the girl was afraid to sit up to hear more clearly. Maybe what she said had been to the old man because he stopped telling the story and began to snore softly the way he had long ago when the old woman had scolded him for telling his stories while others in the house were trying to sleep. But the last words she heard clearly: "It will take a long time, but the story must be told. There must not be any lies." She pulled the blanket up around her chin, slowly, so that her movements would not be seen. She thought her grandmother was talking about the old man's bear story; she did not know about the other story then.

She left the old man wheezing and snoring in his bed. She walked through river grass glistening with frost; the bright green summer color was already fading. She watched the sun move across the sky, already lower on the horizon, already moving away from the village. She stopped by the fallen poles of the summer shelter where her parents had died. Frost glittered on the river sand too; in a few more weeks there would be snow. The predawn light would be the color of an old woman. An old woman sky full of snow. There had been something red lying on the ground the morning they died. She looked for it again, pushing aside the grass with her foot. She knelt in the sand and looked under the fallen structure for some trace of it. When she found it, she would know what the old woman had never told her. She squatted down close to the gray poles and leaned her back against them. The wind made her shiver.

The summer rain had washed the mud from between the logs; the sod blocks stacked as high as her belly next to the log walls had lost their square-cut shape and had grown into soft mounds of tundra moss and stiff-bladed grass bending with clusters of seed bristles. She looked at the northwest, in the direction of the Bering Sea. The cold would come down from there to find narrow slits in the mud, rainwater holes in the outer layer of sod which protected the log house. The dark green tundra stretched away flat and continuous. Somewhere the sea and the land met; she knew by their dark green colors there were no boundaries between them. That was how the cold would come: when the boundaries were gone the polar ice would range across the land into the sky. She watched the horizon for a long time.

She would stand in that place on the north side of the house and she would keep watch on the northwest horizon, and eventually she would see it come. She would watch for its approach in the stars, and hear it come with the wind. These preparations were unfamiliar, but gradually she recognized them as she did her own footprints in the snow.

She emptied the slop jar beside his bed twice a day and kept the barrel full of water melted from river ice. He did not recognize her anymore, and when he spoke to her, he called her by her grandmother's name and talked about people and events from long ago, before he went back to telling the story. The giant bear was creeping across the new snow on its belly, close enough now that the man could hear the rasp of its breathing. On and on in a soft singing voice, the old man caressed the story, repeating the words again and again like gentle strokes.

The sky was gray like a river crane's egg; its density curved into the thin crust of frost already covering the land. She looked at the bright red color of the tin against the ground and the sky and she told the village men to bring the pieces for the old man and her. To drill the test holes in the tundra, the Gussucks had used hundreds of barrels of fuel. The village people split open the empty barrels that were abandoned on the river bank, and pounded the red tin into flat sheets. The village people were using the strips of tin to mend walls and roofs for winter. But she nailed it on the log walls for its color. When she finished, she walked away with the hammer in her hand, not turning around until she was far away, on the ridge above the river banks, and then she looked back. She felt a chill when she saw how the sky and the land were already losing their boundaries, already becoming lost in each other. But the red tin penetrated the thick white color of earth and sky; it defined the boundaries like a wound revealing the ribs and heart of a great caribou about to bolt and be lost to the hunter forever. That night the wind howled and when she scratched a hole through the heavy frost on the inside of the window, she could see nothing but the impenetrable white; whether it was blowing snow or snow that had drifted as high as the house, she did not know.

It had come down suddenly, and she stood with her back to the wind looking at the river, its smoky water clotted with ice. The wind had blown the snow over the frozen river, hiding thin blue streaks where fast water ran under ice translucent and fragile as memory. But she could see shadows of boundaries, outlines of paths which were slender branches of solidity reaching out from the earth. She spent days walking on the river, watching the colors of ice that would safely hold her, kicking the heel of her boot into the snow crust, listening for a solid sound. When she could feel the paths through the soles of her feet, she went to the middle of the river where the fast gray water churned under a thin pane of ice. She looked back. On the river bank in the distance she could see the red tin nailed to the log house, something not swallowed up by the heavy white belly of the sky or caught in the folds of the frozen earth. It was time.

The wolverine fur around the hood of her parka was white with the frost from her breathing. The warmth inside the store melted it, and she felt tiny drops of water on her face. The storeman came in from the back room. She unzipped the parka and stood by the oil stove. She didn't look at him, but stared instead at the yellowish dog, covered with scabs of matted hair, sleeping in front of the stove. She thought of the Gussuck's picture, taped on the wall above the bed and she laughed out loud. The sound of her laughter was piercing; the yellow dog jumped to its feet and the hair bristled down its back. The storeman was watching her. She wanted to laugh again because he didn't know about the ice. He did not know that it was prowling the earth, or that it had already pushed its way into the sky to seize the sun. She sat down in the chair by the stove and shook her long hair loose. He was like a dog tied up all winter, watching while the others got fed. He remembered how she had gone with the oil drillers, and his blue eyes moved like flies crawling over her body. He held his thin pale lips like he wanted to spit on her. He hated the people because they had something of value, the old man said, something which the Gussucks could never have. They thought they could take it, suck it out of the earth or cut it from the mountains; but they were fools.

There was a matted hunk of dog hair on the floor by her foot. She thought of the yellow insulation coming unstuffed: their defense against the freezing going to pieces as it advanced on them. The ice was crouching on the northwest horizon like the old man's bear. She laughed out loud again. The sun would be down now; it was time.

The first time he spoke to her, she did not hear what he said, so she did not answer or even look up at him. He spoke to her again but his words were only noises coming from his pale mouth, trembling now as his anger began to unravel. He jerked her up and the chair fell over behind her. His arms were shaking and she could feel his hands tense up, pulling the edges of the parka tighter. He raised his fist to hit her, his thin body quivering with rage; but the fist collapsed with the desire he had for the valuable things, which, the old man had rightly said, was the only reason they came. She could hear his heart pounding as he held her close and arched his hips against her, groaning and breathing in spasms. She twisted away from him and ducked under his arms.

She ran with a mitten over her mouth, breathing through the fur to protect her lungs from the freezing air. She could hear him running behind her, his heavy breathing, the occasional sound of metal jingling against metal. But he ran without his parka or mittens, breathing the frozen air; its fire squeezed the lungs against the ribs and it was enough that he could not catch her near his store. On the river bank he realized how far he was from his stove, and the wads of yellow stuffing that held off the cold. But the girl was not able to run very fast through the deep drifts at the edge of the river. The twilight was luminous and he could still see clearly for a long distance; he knew he could catch her so he kept running.

When she neared the middle of the river she looked over her shoulder. He was not following her tracks; he went straight across the ice, running the shortest distance to reach her. He was close then; his face was twisted and scarlet from the exertion and the cold. There was satisfaction in his eyes; he was sure he could outrun her.

She was familiar with the river, down to the instant the ice flexed into hairline fractures, and the cracking bone-sliver sounds gathered momentum with the opening ice until the sound of the churning gray water was set free. She stopped and turned to the sound of the river and the rattle of swirling ice fragments where he fell through. She pulled off a mitten and zipped the parka to her throat. She was conscious then of her own rapid breathing.

She moved slowly, kicking the ice ahead with the heel of her boot, feeling for sinews of ice to hold her. She looked ahead and all around herself; in the twilight, the dense white sky had merged into the flat snow-covered tundra. In the frantic running she had lost her place on the river. She stood still. The east bank of the river was lost in the sky; the boundaries had been swallowed by the freezing white. And then, in the distance, she saw something red, and suddenly it was as she had remembered it all those years.

VI

She sat on her bed and while she waited, she listened to the old man. The man had found a small jagged knoll on the ice. He pulled his beaver fur cap off his head; the fur inside it steamed with his body heat and sweat. He left it upside down on the ice for the great bear to stalk, and he waited downwind on top of the ice knoll; he was holding the jade knife.

She thought she could see the end of his story in the way he wheezed out the words; but still he reached into his cache of dry fish and dribbled water into his mouth from the tin cup. All night she listened to him describe each breath the man took, each motion of the bear's head as it tried to catch the sound of the man's breathing, and tested the wind for his scent.

The state trooper asked her questions, and the woman who cleaned house for the priest translated them into Yupik. They wanted to know what happened to the storeman, the Gussuck who had been seen running after her down the road onto the river late last evening. He had not come back, and the Gussuck boss in Anchorage was concerned about him. She did not answer for a long time because the old man suddenly sat up in his bed and began to talk excitedly, looking at all of them—the trooper in his dark glasses and the housekeeper in her corduroy parka. He kept saying, "The story! The story! Eh-ya! The great bear! The hunter!"

They asked her again, what happened to the man from the Northern Commercial store. "He lied to them. He told them it was safe to drink. But I will not lie." She stood up and put on the gray wolfskin parka. "I killed him," she said, "but I don't lie."

The attorney came back again, and the jailer slid open the steel doors and opened the cell to let him in. He motioned for the jailer to stay to translate for him. She laughed when she saw how the jailer would be forced by this Gussuck to speak Yupik to her. She liked the Gussuck attorney for that, and for the thinning hair on his head. He was very tall, and she liked to think about the exposure of his head to the freezing; she wondered if he would feel the ice descending from the sky before the others did. He wanted to know why she told the state trooper she had killed the storeman. Some village children had seen it happen, he said, and it was an accident. "That's all you have to say to the judge: it was an accident." He kept repeating it over and over again to her, slowly in a loud but gentle voice: "It was an accident. He was running after you and he fell through the ice. That's all you have to say in court. That's all. And they will let you go home. Back to your village." The jailer translated the words sullenly, staring down at the floor. She shook her head. "I will not change the story, not even to escape this place and go home. I intended that he die. The story must be told as it is." The attorney exhaled loudly; his eyes looked tired. "Tell her that she could not have killed him that way. He was a white man. He ran after her without a parka or mittens. She could not have planned that." He paused and turned toward the cell door. "Tell her I will do all I can for her. I will explain to the judge that her mind is confused." She laughed out loud when the jailer translated what the attorney said. The Gussucks did not understand the story; they could not see the way it must be told, year after year as the old man had done, without lapse or silence.

She looked out the window at the frozen white sky. The sun had finally broken loose from the ice but it moved like a wounded caribou running on strength which only dying animals find, leaping and running on bullet-shattered lungs. Its light was weak and pale; it pushed dimly through the clouds. She turned and faced the Gussuck attorney.

"It began a long time ago," she intoned steadily, "in the summertime. Early in the morning, I remember, something red in the tall river grass. . . ."

The day after the old man died, men from the village came. She was sitting on the edge of her bed, across from the woman the trooper hired to watch her. They came into the room slowly and listened to her. At the foot of her bed they left a king salmon that had been split open wide and dried last summer. But she did not pause or hesitate; she went on with the story, and she never stopped not even when the woman got up to close the door behind the village men.

The old man would not change the story even when he knew the end was approaching. Lies could not stop what was coming. He thrashed around on the bed, pulling the blankets loose, knocking bundles of dried fish and meat on the floor. The man had been on the ice for many hours. The freezing winds on the ice knoll had numbed his hands in the mittens, and the cold had exhausted him. He felt a single muscle tremor in his hand that he could not suppress, and the jade knife fell; it shattered on the ice, and the blue glacier bear turned slowly to face him.

POETRY

WENDY ROSE

Wendy Rose, a Hopi, was born in California in 1948. Currently a doctoral student in anthropology at the University of California at Berkeley, she is also a professional artist and writer. Her books of poetry include *Hopi Roadrunner Dancing* (1973), *Long Division: A Tribal History* (1976), and *Academic Squaw: Reports to the World from the Ivory Tower* (1977). She comments, "It is my greatest but probably futile hope that someday those of us who are 'ethnic minorities' will not be segregated in the literature of America."

I EXPECTED MY SKIN AND MY BLOOD TO RIPEN

"When the blizzard subsided four days later (after the massacre), a burial party was sent to Wounded Knee. A long
trench was dug. Many of the bodies were stripped by whites
who went out in order to get the ghost shirts and other
accoutrements the Indians wore . . . the frozen bodies were
thrown into the trench stiff and naked . . . only a handful of
items remain in private hands . . . exposure to snow has stiffened the leggings and moccasins, and all the objects show
the effects of age and long use. . . ." There follows: moccasins
at $140, hide scraper at $350, buckskin shirt at $1200,
woman's leggings at $275, bone breastplate at $1000.
        Plains Indian Art: Sales Catalog by Kenneth Canfield, 1977

I expected my skin and my blood
to ripen
not be ripped from my bones;
like green fruit I am peeled
tasted, discarded; my seeds are stepped on
and crushed
as if there were no future. Now
there has been
no past.   My own body gave up the beads
my own arms handed the babies away
to be strung on bayonets, to be counted
one by one like rosary stones and then

to be tossed to each side of life
as if the pain of their borning
had never been.
My feet were frozen to the leather,
pried apart, left behind—bits of flesh
on the moccasins, bits of papery deerhide
on the bones. My back was stripped
of its cover, its quilling intact; was torn,
was taken away, was restored.
My leggings were taken like in a rape
and shriveled to the size of stick figures
like they had never felt
the push of my strong woman's body
walking in the hills.
It was my own baby whose cradleboard I held.
would've put her in my mouth
like a snake
if I could, would've turned her
into a bush or old rock
if there'd been enough magic
to work such changes. Not enough magic
even to stop the bullets.
Not enough magic
to stop the scientists.
Not enough magic
to stop the collectors.

FOR THE WHITE POETS
WHO WOULD BE INDIAN

just once. Just long enough
to snap up the words, fish-hooked
to your tongues: you think of us now
when you kneel on the earth, when
you turn holy in a temporary tourism
of our souls;
            with words you paint your faces,
            chew your doeskin, touch beast
            and tree as if sharing a mother
            were all it takes, could bring
instant and primal knowledge.
You think of us only when

your voice wants for roots,
when you have sat back on your heels
and   become   primitive.

You finish your poems
and go back.

VANISHING POINT: URBAN INDIAN

It is I in the cities, in the bars, in the
dustless reaches of cold eyes who
vanishes, who leans

underbalanced into nothing; it is I
without learning, I without song, who
dies & cries the death time, who

blows from place to place hanging onto
dandelion dust, dying over & over. It is I
who had to search & turn the stones,

half-dead crawl through the bones, let
tears dissolve the dry caves where
woman-ghosts roll piaki* & insects move
to keep this world alive.

It is I who hold the generous bowl that
flows over with shell & stone,
that is buried in blood, that places its
shape within rock carvings.

It is I who die bearing cracked turquoise
& making noise
so as to protect your fragile immortality
O Medicine Ones.

* Rolled cornwafers (Hopi).

JOY HARJO

Joy Harjo was born in Oklahoma in 1951 and is a member of the Creek tribe. She is a graduate student in the Writers' Workshop Program at the University of Iowa. She has published a book of poetry, *The Last Song* (1975), and has been anthologized in *Settling America* (1975), *Traveling America* (1977), and *Southwest: A Contemporary Anthology* (1977).

THERE WAS A DANCE, SWEETHEART

It was a dance.
Her back against the wall
at Carmen's party. He was alone
and he called to her—come here come here—
That was the first time
she saw him and she and Carmen
later drove him home and all the way
he talked to the moon to stars and to
other voices riding in the backseat
that Carmen didn't see.

And the next time was either a story
in one of his poems or what she had heard from crows
gathered before snow caught
in the wheels of traffic silent
up and down Central Avenue.
He was two thousand years old.
She ran the bars with him,
before the motion of snow
caught her too, and he moved in.
It was a dance.

In the dance were mesas winding
off the western horizon, the peak

of Mountain Taylor that burned up every
evening at dusk light.
And in rhythm were Sandia mountain curves
that she fell against every night looking up
looking up. She knew him then, or maybe it had been
the motion of crows against the white cold and power lines.
The voice that was him moved into her rocked
in her and then the child small and dark
in the dance dance dance of the dance.

There was no last time she saw him.
He returned with stars, a certain moon
and in other voices like last night.
She heard him first. Screen door slammed
against the wall. Crows outside the iced-tight windows.
Which dance. Locked and echoed and sucked
the cliffs of her belly in.
She picked up their baby from the crib,
more blankets to tuck them in.
Loud he called—come here come here—

It was a dance.

"ARE YOU STILL THERE"

there are sixty-five miles
of telephone wire
between acoma
                and albuquerque
i dial the number
and listen for the sound
of his low voice
                on the other side
"hello"
        is a gentle motion of a western wind
cradling tiny purple flowers
that grow near the road
                towards laguna
i smell them
as i near the rio puerco bridge
my voice stumbles
returning over sandstone
        as it passes the cañocito exit

"i have missed you"   he says
the rhythm circles the curve
of mesita cliffs
                to meet me

but my voice is caught
shredded on a barbed wire fence
at the side of the road
and flutters soundless
in the wind

CONVERSATIONS BETWEEN HERE AND HOME

Emma Lee's husband beat her up
this weekend
His government check was held
up, and he borrowed the money
to drink on.
Anna had to miss one week of work
because her youngest child
got sick,
she says, "It's hard sometime, but
easier than with a man."
"I haven't seen Jim for two weeks
now," his wife tells me on the phone
(I saw him Saturday with that Anadarko
woman)

angry women are building
houses of stones
they are grinding the mortar
between straw-thin teeth
and broken families

WATCHING CROW, LOOKING SOUTH
TOWARDS THE MANZANO MOUNTAINS

crow floats in winter sun
a black sliver
in a white ocean of sky

he is the horizon
drifting south of Albuquerque

the horizon dances
along the blue edge
of the Manzanos
wind is an arch
a curve
on the black wing of crow

a warm south wind
if it stays for a while
will keep a crow dancing for thirty years
on the ridge
of a blue mountain breeze.

LESLIE MARMON SILKO

Born in Albuquerque in 1948, Leslie Marmon Silko grew up at the Laguna Pueblo Reservation, where she currently lives and writes. She graduated from the University of New Mexico and attended several semesters of law school before deciding to devote herself full time to writing. She has published *Laguna Woman* (1974), a collection of poems, and *Ceremony* (1977), her first novel. Her short stories and poems have been anthologized in many books, including *The Man to Send Rain Clouds* (1974), *Carriers of the Dream Wheel* (1975), *Voices of the Rainbow* (1975), *Yardbird Reader 5* (1976), and *The Remembered Earth* (1978). In 1974 she received the Award for Poetry from *The Chicago Review*. In 1975 her story "Lullaby" was selected as one of the twenty best short stories of the year and included in Martha Foley's *Best Short Stories of 1975*. Of mixed ancestry—Laguna, Mexican, and white—she says, "What I know is Laguna. This place I am from is everything I am as a writer and human being."

WHERE MOUNTAIN LION LAY DOWN WITH DEER
February 1973

I climb the black rock mountain
  stepping from day to day
        silently.
I smell the wind for my ancestors
    pale blue leaves
    crushed wild mountain smell.
Returning
  up the gray stone cliff
  where I descended
        a thousand years ago.
Returning to faded black stone
  where mountain lion lay down with deer.
It is better to stay up here
        watching wind's reflection
        in tall yellow flowers.
The old ones who remember me are gone
    the old songs are all forgotten
and the story of my birth.
How I danced in snow-frost moonlight
  distant stars to the end of Earth,
How I swam away
      in freezing mountain water

                    narrow mossy canyon tumbling down
                            out of the mountain
                            out of deep canyon stone
                    down
                        the memory
                                spilling out
                                into the world.

TOE'OSH: A LAGUNA COYOTE STORY
For Simon Ortiz

    I

In the wintertime
at night
we tell coyote stories
                    and drink Spañada by the stove.
How coyote got his
ratty old fur coat
            bits of old fur
            the sparrows stuck on him
            with dabs of pitch
that was after he lost his proud original one in a poker game.
Anyhow, things like that
are always happening to him
that's what she said.

And it happened to him at Laguna
and Chinle
and at Lukachukai too,
because coyote
got too smart for his own good.

    II

But the Navajos say he won a contest once.
It was to see who could sleep out in a
snowstorm the longest
and coyote waited until chipmunk badger and skunk were all

curled up under the snow
and then he uncovered himself and slept all night
inside
and before morning he got up and went out again
and waited until the others got up before he came
in to take the prize.

III

Some white men came to Acoma and Laguna a hundred years ago
and they fought over Acoma land and Laguna women and
even now
some of their descendants are howling in
the hills southeast of Laguna.

IV

Charlie Coyote wanted to be governor
and he said that when he got elected
he would run the other men off
the reservation
and keep all the women for himself.

V

One year
the politicians got fancy
at Laguna.
They went door to door with hams and turkeys
and they gave them to anyone who promised
to vote for them.
On election day all the people
stayed home and ate turkey
and laughed.

VI

The Trans-Western pipeline vice president came
to discuss right-of-way.
The Lagunas let him wait all day long

because he is a busy and important man.
And late in the afternoon they told him
to come back again tomorrow.

VII

They were after the picnic food
that the special dancers left
down below the cliff.
And Toe'osh and his cousins hung themselves
down over the cliff
holding each other's tail in their mouth
making a coyote chain
until someone in the middle farted
and the guy behind him opened his
mouth to say, "What stinks?" and they
all went tumbling down, like that.

VIII

Howling and roaring
Toe'osh scattered white people
out of bars all over Wisconsin.
He bumped into them at the door
until they said,
                    "Excuse me"
And the way Simon meant it
was for 300 or maybe 400 years.

JUDITH IVALOO VOLBORTH

Judith Ivaloo Volborth, an Apache/Comanche, was born in 1950 in New York City. Her poems have been published in *Talking Leaf, Nishnawbe News, Poetry Review, Alcheringa, Westwind,* and *A Press.* She has also published a collection of poetry entitled *Thunder Root: Traditional and Contemporary Native American Verse* (1978).

BLACK-COAT MEETS COYOTE
(Three Conversations of the Absurd)

I

"Why do your People dance like that,"
Black-Coat demanded,
"out in the open, of all places?"
"Why do your People sit indoors,"
Coyote replied,
"with their heads covered and
their eyes cast downwards?"

I I

"What kind of a god inhabits a stone?"
Black-Coat asked of Coyote.
"What kind of a god inhabits a cross?"
Coyote replied.
"Why, the Holy Ghost,"
answered Black-Coat.
"But you see," Coyote explained,
"holy is not a class to us."

"You know," Black-Coat went on,
"Our Shepherd loves all lambs."
"Yes, but does he love Coyotes?"
"Why of course, Our Shepherd loves all,"
Black-Coat exclaimed,
"why Our Shepherd can even save *you*."
"Save me," Coyote laughed,
"save me from what,
a flock of sheep?"

THREE SONGS TO MARK THE NIGHT

I

On the Moon's rim
abalone horses
circling,
circling.
And here I stand
with an empty bridle.

II

On the green leaf
they are sleeping,
the beetles,
they are sleeping;
below them
a wet-nosed Coyote
about to sneeze.

III

Mist-filled Moon
rising,
rising.
The odor of sea-foam
meets the fog.
And Coyote out collecting
dream fragments along the shore.

NIA FRANCISCO

Born in 1952 on the Navajo Nation, Nia Francisco is currently working as an education specialist at the Bilingual/Bicultural Center of the Navajo Division of Education in Window Rock, Arizona. Her poetry has appeared in *The Indian Historian, Sun Tracks, New America, Southwest: A Contemporary Anthology* (1977) and *The Remembered Earth* (1978). Of herself, she says, "I am a full-blooded Dine-Navajo. I am born of the salt clan and I am of the red bottom/redside burn clan. I am blessed with two children. That is my identity, and to see myself as a writer is awkward. What I write is an extension of my clans, who we are. Our thoughts are personal, yet universal ... yet uniquely ours."

SHE-BEAR

Seeing tiny winter frost against cedar bough
She-bear conceives while walking on untold
                    sunset ground
Feelings drifting, later unthinking with falling snow
All the while walking North   across quiet sky

IRIDESCENT CHILD

call me dine asdzaani*
i am child of winter nights
        growing in rhythm of summer thaw
i am the one you will see walking before dawn
        and dancing after raindew has dried

call me
        southwest child

recently earth greeted us
        a hand shake   an earth tremor
near farmington NM and tsaile arizona

    * Navajo woman.

south of aneth utah and tawoac colorado
        She says, "it's been years since
            i stretched and yawned . . ."

            there is a rainbow surrounding
                    incircles my stomping ground
                    (like an embrace)
            the entrance from the east, from dawn's step
    `   a rainbow stands
            a rainbow with a face and limbs
            a rainbow   a proctor and my shield

call me
        decadent child

decades ago and every day now BIA
        devours my heart   they ripped out
of my ancestors   a hundred years ago
leaving our blood spots as legal documents
of victory reflecting distorted faces
in the subtle-blue shadows the Sun never sees
BIA   and ø'olt'a' † decapitates a thousand children
in the thickness of sage brush shrubs
leaving confused faces on the ground

call me
        artifact child

amongst native people
missionaries are trying to change
coyote stories to parables of recent times
but now indians are expected to act indians
        for the glamour and benigned donator
(it is foreign to be indian from india)
besides it is too damn expensive to buy
back our pawned jewelries
even our hand made jewelries, moccasins
and clothes   or   to rob those museums
(50¢ to xerox one sheet !!!)

call me
        child-bearing child

    † School.

i am a child of winter stories
    feet bundled with warmest rags
    born into a blizzard
named after surviving in a cradle board
now a grown woman touching
a man of experience
his experience of killing plants, animals
and VC people
his experience of raving
    about his male pride and manliness
    and i am making copies of him for him
    (carbon)
producing innocuous eyed males

call me
    incorrigible female

my body is curved and carefully carved
    at the touch of the wind
      sculptured like sexy mesas
      and sand stone cliffs
my hair black like storm clouds
    and you'll often see black birds
      flying through my thoughts
      and gestures
my breath is the rain essence
my finger nails are chips of abalone shell
    and i have a purple shadow
like a hedge hog cactus
i have been cured by the smoke of cedar bough

TOMORROW NOON

potent male rain
    clouds so fertile
his face black
as the face of a black man
    i sold him a story
a lifetime tale
which made him smile
if i stay near this thunder
and caress his blackbirds

flying through my hair
tomorrow noon
he will rise as red
as rusty as my
all so beautiful as when we begin
as when i first met him
among the rising cliffs of my hands

FRIDAY NOON FEELINGS

a desire to embrace you
        becomes a kiss of spring
        that sweeps across desert land
leaving sprinkles of rain pollen
        on my lips
and indian paintbrush flowers
        on my memories
(wanting . . . and waiting)

a desire to touch you
        becomes clouds caressing mountains
        in the highlands behind me
        while dew drops and deer trail melt
        on my palms
(wanting . . . and waiting)
        only
talking a weeping whisper
        to invisible rainbow people
        within myself.

RAMONA C. WILSON

Ramona C. Wilson, a member of the Colville tribe, was born in 1945 in Washington. Her poems have been published in *Voices from Wah-Kon-tah* (1974), *Voices of the Rainbow* (1975), *The First Skin Around Me* (1976), and *Dacotah Territory* #6.

EVENINGSONG 2

during one period I remember
you made poems all day
by breakfast one
and by evening enough to light our table.
anticipating the sun
we would leave our beds instantly
no regret
days to watch the lazy fish
the ever-singing birds
to crawl under vines an hour
for a handful of sweetness
to watch the river without melancholy
the deep green water slow
as the arch of the daily sun
to watch the evening come with only shouts
ticklish games behind grass.
now the crickets are monotonous
the fish have long since decayed.
twilight comes
we light all the lamps.

KEEPING HAIR

My grandmother had braids
at the thickest, pencil wide
held with bright wool
cut from her bed shawl.
No teeth left but white hair
combed and wet carefully
early each morning.
The small wild plants found among stones
on the windy and brown plateaus
revealed their secrets to her hand
and yielded to her cooking pots.
She made a sweet amber water
from willows,
boiling the life out
to pour onto her old head.
"It will keep your hair."
She bathed my head once
rain water not sweeter.
The thought that once
when I was so very young
her work-bent hands
very gently and smoothly
washed my hair in willows
may also keep my heart.

ELIZABETH COOK-LYNN

A member of the Crow Creek Sioux tribe, Elizabeth Cook-Lynn was born in 1930 at Fort Thompson, South Dakota. She is currently an assistant professor of English at Eastern Washington State College. She has published literary criticism in *CCCC Journal* and *The Indian Historian* and poetry in *The South Dakota Review* and *Prairie Schooner*. Her book, *Then Badger Said This,* was published in 1977.

CONTRADICTION

As one who does not mind
the transitory touch,
makes woman-song so breathless, blind;
She hears the wolves at night
prophetically: Put them behind,
the legends we have found,
care not a bit,
go make a night of it!

She wonders why you dress your eyes
in pulsing shades of Muscatel,
why wailing songs of what-the-hell
make essences to eulogize.

Sometimes she squints against the sun
that is your face, no place to run.

Yet, every time the beavers judge
the depth of dams for winter's grudge,
she knows the risk
that's in the ice
when women throw down bundles.

"Grandchild, I am an old woman
but I have nothing to tell about
myself. I will tell a story."

They say
that storytellers such as she
hold no knives of blood
no torch of truth
no song of death;
that when the old woman's bones
are wrapped and gone to dust
the sky won't talk and roar
and suns won't sear the fish beneath the sea.

They even say
that her love of what is past
is a terrible thing.
Hun-he . . .
What do they know
of glorious songs
and children?

SOME OF MY BEST FRIENDS

To get things straight
must your eyes see what my eyes see?
The Marabar Caves as womb?
Bear Butte as vision?

I have a funny feeling
that the universal spread of myths of men
is a put-up job, flyspecked and empty
that alliance will jam and thaw and flood
and Woolf will out.

We have walked away from history
and dallied with a repetition of things
to the end of the bar and booze
Like a time bomb it ticks as rapidly
for White Hawk as for Little Crow
or me.

JANET CAMPBELL

"I was born on January 11, 1947, on the Coeur d'Alene Reservation in northern Idaho. When I was ten my family moved to Wapato, Washington, on the Yakima Reservation. I disliked school and did poorly in it. I didn't attend school at all the year I was supposed to have been in ninth grade, just began the next year in the tenth grade. I worked as a waitress, I picked cherries, apricots, peaches, stripped hops. I painted, wrote poetry, read serious books. In 1963, with a tenth-grade education, twenty dollars in my pocket, and a youthful optimism I now find amazing, I went to San Francisco to seek my fortune. Times were hard for a long, long time." * Janet Campbell is now a law student at Berkeley. Her first novel, *The Owl's Song*, was published in 1974. Her poems and short stories have been widely anthologized and published in various journals and magazines. She is currently working on a second novel.

ON A CATHOLIC CHILDHOOD

Even after Confession,
Sister Mary Leonette told me
(I was six years old at the time)
My soul would be scarred by sin.
This was during catechism.
I had a question:
"Can't you make your guardian angel go away?
Not even while you're going to the toilet?"
Mary Leonette glared at me
And the children laughed.
She was from Vermont and didn't
Like it in grubby old Omak, Washington, all that much.
I thought guardian angels were creepy
And sermons boring,
And when I had to kneel during Mass
I prayed to God
To make it pass quickly
Because my knees ached.
Padre Nostros De En Chalis
Smelling incense
And having to look at a gory

* From *Voices of the Rainbow*, ed. Kenneth Rosen (New York: Viking Press, 1974), pp. 226–227.

life-sized painted statue of
the crucified Christ,
And think of
The poor souls
In purgatory
And a recent sin of my own
I'd never confess:
    I stole my sister's
          plastic glows-in-the-dark Virgin Mary
          And hid it deep within the lilac bush.
God would never understand.

DESMET, IDAHO, MARCH 1969

At my father's wake,
The old people
        Knew me,
    Though I
        Knew them not,
And spoke to me
In our tribe's
Ancient tongue,
Ignoring
The fact
That I
Don't speak
The language,
And so
I listened
As if I understood
What it was all about,
And,
Oh,
How it
Stirred me
To hear again
That strange,
    Softly
    Flowing
Native tongue,
So
Familiar to
My childhood ear.

He was once a tiny, helpless thing,
A being for whom
I was the very center of the universe,
And even later on,
Watching him as he learned
To walk and talk
And explore the world,
I knew all there was to know
About his sweet, limited life.

Now he has his own thing going,
Quite apart from me,
Interests that do not concern me,
Things I just wouldn't understand,
Secrets shared
With other little boys,
But not with me.

For only a while longer
I'll be able to
Hug his little boy body
And kiss his smooth, soft cheek
And tuck him in at night,
For only a while longer.
I am afraid.

ANNA LEE WALTERS

Born in Oklahoma in 1946, Anna Lee Walters, a Pawnee/Otoe, currently lives on the Navajo Nation with her husband and two sons. She is an educational consultant and curriculum specialist at Navajo Community College. She likes to paint as well as write, because "both allow consistent examination of oneself." Of Indian literature she says, "I wish there were a way to connect Indian literature and the oral tradition in talking about them, because so much of my writing comes from what I've heard." Her poetry and short stories have been anthologized in *The Man to Send Rain Clouds* (1974), *Voices of the Rainbow* (1975), and *The Remembered Earth* (1978), among other collections.

A TEACHER TAUGHT ME

I

a teacher taught me
more than she knew
patting me on the head
putting words in my hand
—"pretty little *Indian* girl!"
saving them—
going to give them
back to her one day . . .
show them around too
cousins and friends
laugh and say—"aye"

II

binding by sincerity
hating that kindness
eight years' worth
third graders heard her
putting words in my hand
—"we should bow our heads
in shame for what we did
to the American Indian"
saving them—
going to give them

III

in jr. hi
a boy no color
transparent skin
except sprinkled freckles
followed me around
putting words in my hand
—"squaw, squaw, squaw"
(not that it mattered,
hell, man, I didn't know
what squaw meant . . .)
saving them—
going to give them
back to him one day . . .
show them around too
cousins and friends
laugh and say—"aye"

back to her one day . . .
show them around too
cousins and friends
laugh and say—"aye"

IV

slapping open handed
transparent boy
across freckled face
knocking glasses down
he finally sees
recollect a red
handprint over minutes
faded from others
he wears it still
putting words in my hand
—"sorry, so sorry"
saving them—
going to give them
back to him one day
show them around too
cousins and friends
laugh and say—"aye"

HARTICO

Grandpa, I saw you die in the Indian hospital at Pawnee,
    twenty years ago, but look who is talking, you know
    of it all too well. . . .

    I can measure time. You, yourself, showed me how.
    But how does one count another man's loss? Do I count
    on my fingers the memories and think of the stars as
    my tears?

Grandpa, beautiful brown old Oto!
    At Red Rock, do you still cross the creek to walk

your rolling green hills? Has time, with her sense
of duty, covered your tracks with mine?

Then let me climb the hills for you.
My children shall follow me with theirs after them.
One day, we will be so many that we could hold hands,
form a circle and dance around the earth.

Grandpa, to you, I close my eyes from distractions
and open my heart. . . .

Remember when I was a rabbit?
It was the manner of a child who knew nothing but play.
You could not be but what you were. A handsome, but tired,
powerful old bear.

I saw you and know this to be true. You would pull yourself
upright and scan my horizon. Hands up as though you would
advise me some caution. In the early morning sun, I saw it
circle you with its brilliance. It seemed to me to be a
sign. Then down you relaxed, signaling me with your
spirit. Rabbit, be happy! Go with the morning!

Grandpa, I saw an old bear hold a rabbit
ever so gently in one huge hand. I heard him sing bear words
rabbit did not know but could understand.

The bear was sleepy. The rabbit could tell because the
bear would often yawn. . . .

Grandpa, the bear would then speak. This is what he said.
"Rabbits are fond of songs that sing about frybread!"

Old bear gave the song to the rabbit. They held it
between them to make it strong with laughter from
the rabbit and the bear.

There is not another one like it. My children have
searched for one. I brought the song here now
so you can look at it. We will sing it.

Grandpa, old bear has passed away but the rabbit remains.
For four nights, old bear lay alone, very cold
silently greeting people who came to warm him with their words.
All for you, they drummed and sang in Oto. It was to tell
the people of the world it would be wise to mourn as we were
one less, and therefore not so strong.

ANNA LEE WALTERS
111

On the fourth day, old bear left the rabbit far behind.
He began a lonesome journey, for which he was in no hurry,
but the next in line.

All the people gathered to bring old bear tears that pale day.
It made a simple rabbit very proud when you gracefully
accepted them, in the old way. . . .

Grandpa, I see the rabbit, now and then, in a water mirror.
He comes and goes. Years have shaped a bear around a jumpy
rabbit. The bear sings. I know it. Within himself,
he sings of rabbits and frybread.

Grandpa, I tell you this. It comes from memories of long ago.
It was something that you said.

MARNIE WALSH

Marnie Walsh is a Sioux.

THOMAS IRON-EYES
BORN *CIRCA* 1840.
DIED 1919, ROSEBUD AGENCY, S.D.

I

I woke before the day, when the night bird
Knocked three times upon my door
To warn the Other Sleep was coming.
By candlelight I painted the two broad stripes
Of white across my forehead, the three scarlet spots
Upon my cheek. I greased well my braids
With sour fat from the cooking pot, then tied them
With a bit of bright string saved for the occasion.
From the trunk I took the dress of ceremony,
The breechclout and the elkskin shirt,
The smoke of their breaths strong in my nose;
Smoke not of this time, this life or place,
But of my youth, of the many lodges I dwelt within;
The pony raids, the counting coup;
The smell of grass when it first was green,
And the smell of coming snows, when food was plentiful
Within the camp, and ice crept over the rivers.
Carefully I put on the dress, then the leggings with scalps,
As thin now and as colorless as the hair

Of sickly animals, sinew-tied along the seams;
And on my feet the red-beaded moccasins
Worn by none but the bravest of warriors.
I lie here, waiting, my dry bones and ancient skin
Holding my old heart.
The daystar finds me ready for my journey.

II

Another time, another life, another place,
My people would have wrapped me in deerskin,
Sewed me in the finest of furs;
Then borne me in honor to the cottonwood bier,
Laying at my right hand the sacred pipe,
And at my left the arrows and bow, the lance
I long ago bound with thongs and hung
With the feathers from the eagle's breast.
Below the scaffold of the dead
My pony of the speckled skin and fierce heart
Would be led, and with a blow of the stone ax
Upon his skull, lie down to wait my need.
I would know that far above
In the sacred hoop of the sky
Long-sighted hawks, hanging on silent wings,
Marked my passage.

III

When the Life-Giver hid from the night,
The dark wind would speak to my spirit
And I would arise, taking up my weapons.
Mounting my horse I would follow
The great path over the earth,
The road leading to the Old Grandfathers
Beyond the stars.
I would see the glow of their cooking fires
Bright as arrow tips across the northern sky;
Waiting for me, old friends dance and feast
And play the games of gambling.
Behind me drums would beat, and willow whistles cry
Like the doves of spring who nested
In the berry bushes near the river by my village.

I would pause to hear my sons in council
Speaking of my deeds in war, my strength and wisdom,
Praising me; knowing my women in their sorrow
Were tearing their clothing, their faces bloodied
And smeared with ashes.

IV

But I am Thomas. I am here,
Where no grass grows, no clear rivers run;
Where dirt and despair abound,
Where heat and rain alike rust out
The souls of my people, the roofs of tin;
Where hunger sits in the dooryards,
Where disease, like a serpent, slips from house to house.
I am Thomas, waiting for the wagon
To bring the government box of pine;
Waiting for the journey to the burying ground
Below sandy buttes where rattlesnakes
Stink in burrows, and the white man's wooden trinities
Stand in crooked rows.
There I shall be put beneath the earth.
There shall my spirit be sealed within
The planks of the coffin.
There I shall not hear the dark wind's cry
To come and ride the starry road
Across the holy circle of the sky.

POETS/POEMS

I am the chariot
rolling through alleys
on philosophic wheels.
Follow me and be blinded
in my fiery dust.

I am the bird
moulten with love,
wingless in the thicket.
Bend close and be bitten
by the snake beside me.

I am the box
within a box
within a box.
Open me and be deafened
by my shadow.

I am the unicorn
feeding in the forest
on leaves of glass.
Stalk me and be wounded
by a flowering arrow.

I am the eye
without a lid
looking at you.

VICKIE LOANS-ARROW
1972

I

this morning
me and my cousin
charlene lost-nation
are in to bobby simons bar
and charlene say
i tired of living
there aint nothing in it
and bobby simon
behind the bar
goes ha ha ha
when she fall off
the stool
im laughing too
she so drunk
she funny

II

i get her up
then she say
there aint nothing in it

to them old white farmers
drinking their beer
and talking crops
they dont listen
dont even look at her
and bobby simon say
i see your mama out front
so we go out
and the sun so yellow
burn my eyes
and make charlenes mama
shiver like shes made
out of water
but it only the wind
all gold color
moving everything in waves

III

she say goddam you
charlene them kids of yours
come over and i got to
take them in
while you drunk all the time
i aint going to do it
no more
it too damn hot
i watch her shoes all torn
and wrinkly
and her fat legs
floating on the yellow wind
then charlene say
there aint nothing in it
it all plain shit
and we go back in the bar

IV

we drink and she pulls
her face up tight
tells me it dont pay to think
theres something to it

cause there aint
and says wont nobody
never believe her
what she says
i just laugh
she so drunk
she funny

V

well me and bobby simon
drink some more
I seen charlene
when she gone to the can
she dont come back
pretty soon bobby simon
say i better check her out
so i go to see
i find her all right
sitting in a corner
theres blood on her mouth
and her chin
and down her dress

VI

she looks at me
and i see the knife
sticking out between her teeth
and remember what that means
and i know shed like to die
but cant
so she killed her tongue
instead
i leave her there
i go out the door
and down the street
and the yellow wind
make me shiver and sweat
because now i believe her
but wont never say so

ANITA ENDREZZE-DANIELSON

Born in California in 1952, Anita Endrezze-Danielson, a Yaqui, presently lives in Spokane, Washington. She completed her BA and MA degrees at Eastern Washington University and has taught English at various schools in the area. Her poetry has been anthologized in *Carriers of the Dream Wheel* (1975), *Voices of the Rainbow* (1975), and *The First Skin Around Me* (1976); it has also appeared in numerous journals, including *Poetry Northwest, Blue Cloud Quarterly, Indian Voice,* and *Dacotah Territory.* In 1977 she won first place for poetry at the Pacific Northwest Writers' Conference.

THE BELLY DANCER'S SONG

(Traditionally, women danced to earn their dowry)

Look at me, circles of silver
rising, dropping like stars! Around my waist
a string of rain. My hips shiver,

singing spells in your heart. Who will give me
coins, a dowry of pleasing?
These arms are beckoning you. See

my cymbals of suns! My eyes are the dark side
of the moon. These veils will cover us
in our private dance. What I reveal, wide

as the night's song, will be yours.
Is there a man who will put his hands
on my hips, and delight in my dance? Hours

of dance will not dull my grace.
Who is this dancer, you ask, who is she?
I wear coins engraved with face
of a beautiful woman. Ah! It is me!

STILL LIFE

It is the room around the bowl
of fruit, the man around the body
that I paint. The flat venetian blinds
send slats of ochre light, dust dancing
like ragged ballerinas. Oranges sleep,
lazy alley cats, curled in the heat.
With my knife, I slap thick oil on apples:
red knees streaked with grass stains.
Dried paint clots my nails;

Pearls of oil cling to my hair.
I consider my husband's skin in terms of light
lengths, as if shin to thigh were a mountain ridge,
last to keep the day's light. I carve
his cheekbones into winged plateaus,
model the air above the small of his back
with purplish dusk. In this still life,
my life is still-centered like the ruby bowl,
its cut glass dark as plums or fleshy shadows.

SHAMAN/BEAR

He sniffs the autumn air,
fur bristling, rippling, like a red robe
of falling leaves. He looks for me.
I am a tamarack   this time
my fingers yellow as meadow
grass   changing in the light:
now thick with pine-dark dew,
now frost black as his snout.   He rises
pawing stumps   slashed by lightning
before I was born.   He remembers
the hard heat   splitting   the air
clouds deep in his throat   summers ago
the sun smoking in a tree.
Now he eats ashes, making spells
in a tongue few Indians speak.

He knows I'm here, legs trembling, cheeks red
as kinnikinic berries. It is time.
The Moon of Popping Trees has darkened

the gold birches. I dream of the season
His spell will cause my belly to swell
child-heavy   my womb full
as a Salmonberry moon.

MAKING ADJUSTMENTS

Marry the man your parents want for a son.
Go to bed with him like clockwork.
Keep your poems in the stove,
your hands away from knives.

Sleep around with quick, ugly men.
Talk to yourself and let them answer for you.
Adjust your body to thieving hands;
count the times they come and subtract
them like years from your life.

When you've got it all swallowed,
when you've turned your bones into nothing
but someone else's sexual hardness,
men will damn you Medusa
and you'll long to burn their genitals
in your ritual fires. You'll want
to sit on your haunches devouring
your scabby skin, each lesion
a portrait of a lover, each howl
a memory of your last adjustment.

But you will wipe their feet
with your hair, light
their pipes with your burning,
betray your betrayal with the arch
of your back. You will need
no further announcement
of your death.

ROBERTA HILL

An Oneida of Wisconsin, Roberta Hill was born in 1947. She has published poems in numerous journals such as *The Northwest Review, Dacotah Territory, American Poetry Review,* and *Sun Tracks,* as well as in such anthologies as *Carriers of the Dream Wheel* (1975) and *Voices of the Rainbow* (1975). A recipient of a National Endowment Fellowship grant, she is currently working on a book of poems. She says of her writings, "I work as hard (consciously, unconsciously) as I can to hear the music of the voice that speaks through me. Perhaps it is my thoughts, perhaps it is the music of what I can perceive around me. . . . I sense that I am trying to regain an image of wholeness. Before that can occur, I feel one must be aware of what is left."

LEAP IN THE DARK

The experience of truth is indispensable for the experience of beauty and the sense of beauty is guided by a leap in the dark.

Arthur Koestler

I

Stoplights edged the licorice street with ribbon,
neon embroidering wet sidewalks. She turned

into the driveway and leaped in the dark. A blackbird
perched on the bouncing twig of a maple, heard

her whisper, "Stranger, lover, the lost days are over.
While I walk from car to door, something inward opens

like four o'clocks in rain. Earth, cold from autumn,
pulls me; I can't breathe the same

with dirt for marrow and mist for skin
blurring my vision, my vision's separate self.

I stand drunk in this glitter, under the sky's grey shelter.
The city maple, not half so bitter, hurls itself

in two directions, until both tips darken and disappear,
as I darken my reflection in the smoking mirror

of my home. How faint the sound of dry leaves,
like the clattering keys of another morning, another world."

II

She looked out the window at some inward greying door.
The maple held her glance, made ground fog from her cigarette.

Beyond uneven stairs, children screamed,
gunned each other down. Then she sealed her nimble dreams

with water from a murky bay. "For him I map
this galaxy of dust that turns without an answer.

When it rains, I remember his face in the corridor
of a past apartment and trace the anguish around his mouth,

his wrinkled forehead, unguarded eyes, the foreign fruit
of an intricate sadness. With the grace that remains,

I catch a glint around a door I cannot enter.
The clock echoes in dishtowels; I search love's center

and bang pans against the rubble of my day, the lucid
grandeur of wet ground, the strangeness of a fatal sun

that makes us mark on the margin of our loss,
trust in the gossamer of touch, trust in the late-plowed field."

III

When the sun opened clouds and walked into her mongrel soul,
she chopped celery into rocky remnants of the sea,

and heard fat sing up bread, a better dying.
The magnet in each seed of the green pepper kept her flying,

floating toward memories that throb like clustered stars:
the dark water laughter of ducks, a tangle of November oaks,

toward sudden music on a wheel of brilliant dust
where like a moon she must leap back and forth

from emptiness. "I remember the moon shimmering
loss and discovery along a water edge, and skirting

a slice of carrot, I welcome eternity in that eye of autumn.
Rare and real, I dance while vegetables sing in pairs.

I hug my death, my chorus of years, and search
and stretch and leap, for I will be apprentice to the blood

in spite of the mood of a world
that keeps rusting, rusting the wild throats of birds."

IV

In lamplight she saw the smoke of another's dream:
her daughter walk woods where snow weighs down the pine,

her son cry on a bridge that ends in deep-rooted dark,
her man, stalled on a lonely road, realize his torque

was alcohol and hatred. "Hungry for silence, I listen
to wind, the sound of water running down mountain,

my own raw breath. Between the sounds, a seaborn god
plays his reed in the caverns of my being.

I wear his amethyst, let go my dreams: millers, lacewings,
and junebugs scatter, widen and batter the dark,

brightening this loud dust with the fever of their eyes.
Oh crazy itch that grabs us beyond loss

and lets us forgive, so that we can answer birds and deer,
lightning and rain, shadow and hurricane.

Truth waits in the creek, cutting the winter brown hills:
it sings of its needles of ice, sings because of the scars."

CONVERSATION OVERHEARD ON TAMALPAIS ROAD

There wasn't a chill even underneath the pines.
The guests had gone to dance
and only two women remained.
The one in a wheelchair fingered the shawl
in her lap, listening to her sister's voice,
the distant music . . .

"Wind and wheels now gather your dress
under this muggy sun, Bernarda.

You were never punctual, except in elated sweat,
in the stomp sting of stepping
to the music of guitars. Your legs ache
in fraudulent sleep and night rubs
your back, quietly and forgivingly
as any man. Warm as a sparrow,
the castanet rests in the leaf of your palm.
Aren't you bitter? Beneath the eucalyptus,
they're playing the guitar again, Bernarda."

"I ride the webs of my chair and the wind
works one leaf into butterfly,
turns clouds from a purple west
into foam, billow, rainbowed beings.
Even starlings, too hungry to sing,
linger in the sun's final flash.
I have danced and it taught me well:
when we no longer care, we're no longer in rhythm.

Then a change comes and we change.
Peddling our light to live by sordid rivers,
we call each other tramp and claim the stars.
But I have fallen toward a death,
so strangely warm and healing;
the dark lap of earth has sent me forth,
a shoot bending brightly on the waves.
My legs and I now have a pact,
remembering that misery
is one lamp I live by.

I ride the webs of my chair and the sea
ebbs with each possibility a secret I accept—
that we are most alive when letting go;
then the light in common things
can glow: the mist melts
into eucalyptus; each downy seed wanders
faithful to its field; the sparrows
and the castanets greet winter's opal dawn,
while I dance on and on, gladdened
by a purling world. Can your guarded eyes
believe this reach of wind, this transparent sea?"

PAULA GUNN ALLEN

Paula Gunn Allen, a Laguna Pueblo, lives in Albuquerque, New Mexico, where she was born in 1939. A recipient of a National Endowment for the Humanities Creative Writing Fellowship, she is currently working on a family history. She has taught at San Francisco State University, University of New Mexico, and Ft. Lewis College. Her books of poetry include *The Blind Lion* (1975), *A Cannon Between My Knees* (1978), *Shadow Country* (forthcoming), and *Coyote's Daylight Trip* (forthcoming). A member of the Modern Language Association's Commission on the Literatures and Languages of America, she has also published numerous articles on Native American literature in various journals and books. She characterizes her writing as "intense, serious, metaphysical. . . . I write to articulate what has meaning and to record my own experience in order to create a kind of understanding as well as a kind of psychic space."

GRANDMOTHER   .

Out of her own body she pushed
silver thread, light, air
and carried it carefully on the dark, flying
where nothing moved.

Out of her body she extruded
shining wire, life, and wove the light
on the void.

From beyond time,
beyond oak* trees and bright clear water flow,
she was given the work of weaving the strands
of her body, her pain, her vision
into creation, and the gift of having created,
to disappear.

After her,
the women and the men weave blankets into tales of life,
memories of light and ladders,
infinity-eyes, and rain.
After her I sit on my laddered rain-bearing rug
and mend the tear with string.

   * I am a member of Oak Clan.

MOONSHOT: 1969

Had nothing to do on Wednesday
but watch the house grow hot and silent
in the heat. The dust on the t v and under the couch
looks muggy. The cat and I sleep, hot, waiting for dark.

The moon is still more imagination than rock. It is said
that two men have at last soared beyond the heat and noise—
blood no longer heavy
head, hands, heart
light
beyond our sight if not the subtle hearing of the grounded
quick-fingered machines.
But I love you.
How equate the moonlight falling
soft across your shoulders with ash and stone
so deceptively light, impossibly cohesive?
Where they are is not where we have been.

When I say moon
I do not mean that dark, pretty hulk
45,000 miles out there, but moon:
heart, a quiet cool house;
children breathing dreams,
whimpering sometimes to their visions;
moon: a light softly centering inside my eyes:
no one can land there where there is no land
and the air too vague
to provide footing to luminous ghosts;
moon: spirit of the spirit's strength;
moon: wandering pale forests,
springing out of undefinable lost impulse,
hunting through networks more complex than all
buzzing, humming technocracies of Washington, Houston, Flagstaff. . . .

The Source of that light was lost ages ago,
but still spreads toward me, trembling at the edges of my eyes
always threatening to break through.
Not 90 million miles outside of me, but inside,
that light,
frozen on
that moon,
that I do not see so much as remember
as a feeling is remembered: never touched or seen but
heard, in echoing, aching moon dreams.

PAULA GUNN ALLEN

The idea was not that gazing at the moon
    (now another base, the outer edge of our expansion,
      that moon that is cratered and carved
      volcanic rock, meteor pocked
      that circles predictably as our machines circle us)
would drive a woman insane. Gazing at an object,
however distant, cannot drive a woman anywhere,
certainly not over to the far reaches of visioning
where the real is incommunicable and so thought
by strangers
not to exist, but gazing into the moon reaches of the mind,
searching with careful fingers of sense-memory,
listening inside the ear for lost songs,
almost forgotten footfalls,
feeling gingerly with the tongue-tip of the heart—
this gazing, steady, frightened, is the scape of moon madness,
the certain consequence of remembering
what is best forgot.

On television I hear them say
that because man has landed on the moon
he has laid forever its tidal pull on the heart to rest.
Outside my bedroom window, late, I sleep and wake and sleep again,
feel the soft light fall on my face,
see its evanescent glow polish your shoulders, back, buttocks,
the lined and wrinkled bottom of your moonward sole
to a dull mysterious lustre;
I wake, sleep, dream.

CATCHING ONE CLEAR THOUGHT ALIVE

Second-hand platitudes like antique watches
engraved with unreadable scrolled initials of another time, tick,
carry you from present to another place
in abstraction tempo, unmetronomed, untimed, not
yesterday, not this second, not of anyone's doing, but
counted, like implicit truths, left-overs from last night's faith.

You carry the seconds (hard) in your pocket
rolling time around in your hand like spare change:
listening to the click of days, of hours, of walks,
unattached, down morning streets.
And this is how you spend it, waiting for hope (bearded
and gold-chained like grandfather) to come to you, to

roll your mornings in flavored papers from the past, to give
taste to someone else's meanings, someone's words,
unspeakable in this place, this ungraspable time.

And hungry like Coyote in a gopherless land
(gone crazy in no time) you stalk time and incidence
as though they were a herd of grazing sheep you are circling,
watching for the one that is too small, too
weak, too separate to be kept safe in the fostering circle,
the living matrix of what is known; you watch
for the one too slow to stop your leap, your
teeth in time.

MEDICINE SONG

I add my breath to your breath
That our days may be long on the Earth;
That the days of our people may be long;
That we shall be one person;
That we may finish our roads together.
May my father bless you with life;
May our Life Paths be fulfilled.

—Laguna

I (SHADOW WAY)

In this room where voices spin the light
making webs to catch forbidden visions (center
that cannot be grasped) climb
ladders that do not reach the Sky, hands
do not meet, glances unmet rise, fall
gracelessly against shadows that hold the song inside,
tongueless celebration of what is absurd.
Light follows dark (helpless voices climb)
as though precious life could be so stilled,
as though a flicker of mind could turn hurt
or terror into this night's entertainment.
The woman next to me clutches knees to chest,
shrinks into a corner of the room, as though she could
disappear, gracefully evade the web that grows around us.
The wall becomes a solid past, no unexpecteds here
her shoulders seem to say, and hurt that is not hers feels
out the room, voices climb, circle, spin toward finity, sing
obstinately.

II (THE DUCK-BILLED GOD)

On the webbed finger of a water dream swims
One who is named Child of the Lake,
Foolish emblem on the bare surface of the dream.
(Finger of time pointed at my face;
as though some unheard shame had dowsed my mind)
and this is unexpected. I have known my shadow lurked
just out of reach, but that it should confront my sight
in crystal clarity, turning into a shadowed burial place,
making of dream absurdity—ah, but I saw the duck-billed face
of Macibol turn toward me, I
heard his words, misunderstood their sounding and became,
as swift as waters bearing him from me,
plaything of a mind half-gone.

III (LAMENT)

Long (as song so stricken goes)
I've worn the crown of penitence on my tongue,
a layering of cloud familiar to my eyes
(that is the sign of Macibol)
and long have told the songs and tales of Ka-waik*
how I might make of wanderings a reason,
an image of a sacred ladder I might climb
as earth and water climb to help the wingless fish upstream.
But in a room of solid sounds, where shame is emblem
and fear its hopeless twin, the voices that climb upsong
can only make blank utterance that grows too blind to dream.

IV (THE DEAD SPIDER)

Child of water, desert mind
webbed and broken on the surface of the lake
body so small the damage barely shows
small thing, unable to spin, turn
in your death, shadow too stricken to flow,
find a place among some clutching reeds to rest.
Blow your dead breath over the surface of the lake,
dream in your silent shadow, celebrate.

* An Eastern Pueblo people usually called by the Spanish name of Laguna.

ADDITIONAL READINGS

Note: The books listed here primarily anthologize contemporary literature as opposed to traditional or precontact literature by American Indian writers.

Anthologies

Allen, Terry, ed. *The Whispering Wind.* Garden City, N.Y., Doubleday, 1972. A publication of the Institute of American Indian Arts, this book contains poetry by Liz Sohappy, Janet Campbell, Ramona Carden, Donna Whitewing, Patricia Irving, and Agnes Pratt.

Chapman, Abraham, ed. *Literature of the American Indians—Views and Interpretations.* New York, New American Library, 1975. Critical essays on Native American literature.

Dodge, Robert K., and Joseph B. McCullough, eds. *Voices from Wah-Kon-tah: Contemporary Poetry of Native Americans.* New York, International Publishers, 1974.

Faderman, Lillian, and Barbara Bradshaw, eds. *Speaking for Ourselves—American Ethnic Writing.* Glenview, Ill., Scott, Foresman, 1969; revised ed. 1975. The Native American section includes works by Juanita Platero, Siyowin Miller, Wendy Rose, and Liz Sohappy.

Hobson, Geary, ed. *The Remembered Earth: An Anthology of Contemporary Native American Literature.* Albuquerque, N.M., Red Earth Press, 1978. Over twenty-five women are included.

Katz, Jane B., ed. *I Am the Fire of Time — The Voices of Native American Women.* New York, E. P. Dutton, 1977. Arranged by theme—growing up, courtship, marriage, and so forth—this collection includes brief excerpts from autobiographies juxtaposed to poems and statements by contemporary writers.

Kopp, Janet and Karl, eds. *Southwest: A Contemporary Anthology.* Albuquerque, N.M., Red Earth Press, 1977. Includes Native American women writers.

Milton, John, ed. *Four Indian Poets.* Vermillion, S.D., Dakota Press, 1974. Includes poetry by Paula Gunn Allen.

Mirikitani, Janice, et al., eds. *Time to Greez! Incantations from the Third World.* San Francisco, Glide Publications, 1975. Includes works by Wendy Rose and Janet Campbell.

Momaday, Natachee Scott, ed. *American Indian Authors.* Boston, Houghton Mifflin, 1972. Contains a representative sampling of traditional, historical, and contemporary selections.

Niatum, Duane, ed. *Carriers of the Dream Wheel.* New York, Harper & Row, 1975. Includes poetry by Liz Sohappy, Gladys Cardiff, Roberta Hill, Dana Naone, Anita Endrezze-Probst(-Danielson), Wendy Rose, and Leslie Silko.

Reed, Ishmael, Al Young, eds. *Yardbird Lives.* New York, Grove Press, 1978. A multicultural anthology, including many works by women.

Rosen, Kenneth, ed. *The Man to Send Rain Clouds.* New York, Viking, 1974.

This collection includes seven stories by Leslie Silko, two by Anna Lee Walters, and one by Opal Lee Popkes.

————. *Voices of the Rainbow: Contemporary Poetry by American Indians.* New York, Viking, 1975. Includes works by Roberta Hill, Leslie Silko, Janet Campbell, Anna Lee Walters, Anita Endrezze-Probst(-Danielson), Ramona Wilson, and Patty Harjo.

Sanders, Thomas E., and Walter W. Peek, eds. *Literature of the American Indian.* Hollywood, Cal., Glencoe Press, 1973. Includes creation stories, trickster tales, historical material, and contemporary literature.

White, James L., ed. *The First Skin Around Me: Contemporary American Tribal Poetry.* Moorhead, Minn., The Territorial Press, 1976.

Journals and Periodicals

"A": A Journal of Contemporary Literature ("A" Press, c/o William Oandasan, Box 311, Laguna, N.M. 87026). Literature by and about Native Americans.

Alcheringa (Boston University)

American Indian Culture and Research Journal (UCLA)

American Indian Quarterly (P.O. Box 443, Hurst, Texas 76053)

ASAIL Newsletter (Association for the Study of American Indian Literature. c/o Karl Kroeber, Columbia University, N.Y.)

Blue Cloud Quarterly (Moorhead State College, Minn.)

Dacotah Territory—Issue #6 is a special Native American issue, edited by James L. White, c/o P.O. Box 775, Moorhead, Minn. 56560

Greenfield Review, particularly #3 (1973); c/o Greenfield Center, N.Y. 12833

The Indian Historian (San Francisco)

La Confluencia (P.O. Box 409, Albuquerque, N.M. 87103); multicultural.

Melus (University of Southern California)

New America, 2, No. 3 (1976), special Native American issue, c/o American Studies, University of New Mexico

Nimrod, 16 (1972), American Indian issue, c/o University of Tulsa

Shantih, 4, No. 2 (Summer–Fall 1979), special Native American issue, c/o P.O. Box 125, Bay Ridge Station, Brooklyn, N.Y. 11220

Sun Tracks: An American Indian Literary Magazine (University of Arizona, Tucson 85721)

Wambli Ho (Sinte Gleska College, Rosebud, S.D.)

Life Stories and Autobiographies

Abeita, Louise. *I Am a Pueblo Indian Girl.* New York, William Morrow, 1939.

Bennett, Kay. *Kaibah: Recollections of a Navajo Girlhood.* Los Angeles, Western Lore Press, 1964.

Hopkins, Sarah Winnemucca. *Life Among the Piutes: Their Wrongs and Claims.* Ed. Mrs. Horace Mann. New York, G. P. Putnam's Sons, 1883.

Kelley, Jane Holden. *Yaqui Women.* Lincoln: University of Nebraska, 1978.

Landes, Ruth. *The Ojibwa Woman.* New York, W. W. Norton, 1971.

Lone Dog, Louise. *Strange Journey: The Vision Quest of a Psychic Indian Woman.* Healdsburg, Calif., Naturegraph Co., 1964.

Marriott. Alice. *Maria, The Potter of San Ildefonso.* Norman, University of Oklahoma Press, 1948.

———. *The Ten Grandmothers.* Norman, University of Oklahoma Press, 1945.

Marriott, Alice, and Carol K. Rachlin. *Dance Around the Sun—The Life of Mary Little Bear Inkanish: Cheyenne.* New York, Thomas Y. Crowell, 1977.

Michelson, Truman. *The Autobiography of a Fox Woman.* 40th Annual Report of the Bureau of American Ethnology (Washington, D.C., Smithsonian Institution, 1925), pp. 303–307.

Mountain Wolf Woman—The Autobiography of a Winnebago Indian. Ed. Nancy Oestreich Lurie. Ann Arbor, University of Michigan Press, 1961.

Price, Anna (Her Eyes Grey). "Personal Narrative of Anna Price." In *Western Apache Raiding and WarFare,* Keith H. Basso (ed.), Tucson, University of Arizona Press, 1971.

Qoyawayma, Polingaysi. *No Turning Back.* Albuquerque, University of New Mexico Press, 1964.

Reichard, Gladys. *Dezba, Woman of the Desert.* Glorieta, N.M., Rio Grande Press, 1971.

Scott, Lola. *Karnee, A Paiute Narrative.* Greenwich, Conn., Fawcett, 1966.

Shipek, Florence C. *The Autobiography of Delphina Cuero: A Diegueño Indian.* Los Angeles, Dawson's Book Shop, 1968.

Smith, Dana Margaret. *Hopi Girl.* Palo Alto, Stanford University Press, 1931.

Udall, Louise. *Me and Mine: The Life Story of Helen Sekaquaptewa.* Tucson, University of Arizona Press, 1969.

Underhill, Ruth. *Autobiography of a Papago Woman. Memoirs of the American Anthropological Association,* 46 (1936).

Zitkala-Sa. "Impressions of an Indian Childhood." *Atlantic Monthly,* 85 (January 1900).

———. "The Schooldays of an Indian Girl." *Atlantic Monthly,* 85 (February 1900).

———. "An Indian Teacher Among Pagans." *Atlantic Monthly,* 85 (March 1900).

———. "Why I Am a Pagan." *Atlantic Monthly,* 90 (December 1902).

Primary Sources

Allen, Paula Gunn. *The Blind Lion*. Berkeley, Thorp Springs Press, 1975. Poetry.

————. *A Cannon Between My Knees*. New York, Strawberry Press, 1978. Poetry.

Campbell, Janet. *Custer Lives in Humboldt County*. Greenfield Center, N.Y., Greenfield Review Press, 1978. Poetry.

————. *The Owl's Song*. New York, Doubleday, 1974. Fiction.

Campbell, Maria. *Half-Breed*. New York, Saturday Review Press, 1973. Fiction.

Cook-Lynn, Elizabeth. *Then Badger Said This*. New York, Vantage, 1977. A collection of sketches, poems, and thoughts inspired by the Sioux oral tradition.

Deloria, Ella. *Speaking of Indians*. New York, Friendship Press, 1944. An ethnographic study of the Sioux.

Harjo, Joy. *The Last Song*. Las Cruces, N.M., Puerto del Sol Press, 1975. Poetry.

————. *What Moon Drove Me to This*. Berkeley, Reed and Cannon, 1979. Poetry.

Rose, Wendy. *Academic Squaw—Reports to the World from the Ivory Tower*. Marvin, S.D., *Blue Cloud Quarterly*, 1977. Poetry.

————. *Hopi Roadrunner Dancing*. Greenfield Center, N.Y., Greenfield Review Press, 1973. Poetry.

————. *Long Division: A Tribal History*. New York, Strawberry Press, 1976. Poetry.

Silko, Leslie Marmon. *Ceremony*. New York, Viking, 1977. Fiction.

————. *Laguna Woman*. Greenfield Center, N.Y., Greenfield Review Press, 1974. Poetry.

Sullivan, Elizabeth. *Indian Legends of the Trail of Tears and Other Creek Stories*. Tulsa, Okla., Giant Services, 1974.

Volborth, J. Ivaloo. *Thunder Root: Traditional and Contemporary Native American Verse*. UCLA, American Indian Culture and Research Center, 1978.

Walsh, Marnie. *A Taste of the Knife*. Boise, Ahsahta Press, 1976. Poetry.

We are a people. A people do not
throw their geniuses away. If they do,
it is our duty as witnesses for the future
to collect them again for the sake of our
children. If necessary, bone by bone.

Alice Walker

I am a black woman
the music of my song
some sweet arpeggio of tears
is written in a minor key
and I
can be heard humming in the night
can be heard
*   humming*
in the night

Mari Evans

BLACK WOMEN
WRITERS

INTRODUCTION

HISTORICAL PERSPECTIVES

The importance of continuity in a writer's life—of understanding one's historical and literary legacy—cannot be overestimated. History places experience in context, and literature provides the form for individual expression. In the development of black literature, history and literature have often been one: Achieving literacy before and during slavery was an extreme political act for a black person because slaves were prohibited from learning to read and write. The "quest for freedom" was synonymous with the "quest for literacy," and each act of writing became a political and historical event.[1] Indeed, one of the first literary forms to emerge in black literature, and one that has had a profound impact on its direction, is the slave narrative. As documentaries of life under slavery, these narratives are clearly important historical statements. To the student of literature, they are equally significant in their influence on the development of narrative and autobiography. While black literature is intimately related to black history, it is, perhaps, even more inextricably bound to the verbal traditions within black culture that became, during slavery, creative outlets for individual expression. These outlets served not only as entertainment but as safety valves for the intolerable conditions of bondage. Denied education and the opportunity to become literate, slaves turned their verbal skills to oral storytelling, sermons, proverbs, boasts, elaborate courtship rituals, toasts, work songs, and spirituals. From West Africa, according to Langston Hughes and Arno Bontemps, slaves brought with them the tradition of storytelling with its full slate of animal characters and slowly transformed these tales into the popular stories of Uncle Remus.[2] Verbal exchanges, such as the call and response pattern of field hands, became formalized in church sermons in which preacher and congregation urged each other on with vocal expressions of hope. Work songs and spirituals bound blacks into a community, as did folk sermons and stories. In some instances, spirituals served as coded messages for helping slaves to escape and as warnings of impending danger, while stories evolved into parables for explaining the intricate relationships between slaves and their owners.

Zora Neale Hurston has said that folklore is what blacks had before they knew there was art. Any number of people could tell the same story, and because the "facts" of the story were already known, the telling of the story became the art form. To render the complexity of the black experience, the slave became a consummate verbal artist, initiating and nurturing rich and vital oral traditions that continue to inform black culture and literature. Indeed, as Mary Berry and John Blassingame have demonstrated, "Twentieth-century blacks obviously inherited what folklorists call 'skill in the verbal arts' from the slaves. The slave was the quintessential folk poet. In his courtship rituals, toasts, and greetings he demonstrated those rhythmical patterns characteristic of twentieth-century black speech." [3] To read black literature strictly as history or sociology is to miss the wealth of this verbal complexity and the imaginative transformation of oral forms into literary art that is at the heart of so much of modern black literature.

As verbal artists and historians of their culture, black women have been as instrumental as men in linking one generation to the next by passing on stories, songs, folklore. As writers, their imperative is to shape their heritage into a literary tradition that builds on the past, and, in the process, creates a community of shared, yet particular, experience. The problem, as Alice Walker defines it in the opening essay of this section, is that accessible literary models for contemporary black women writers are rare and must be actively sought. What is not rare is the model of the black woman in her infinite varieties, and it is her personal history that shapes the narrative of contemporary literature. It is the black woman who hums the sorrow songs of slavery; she becomes the mute observer of violent travesties committed upon her race; she survives by crafting a mask that mirrors the faces others would give her. And though plagued by a multitude of stereotypes thrust on her by blacks and whites alike, the black woman persists in asserting her right to individuality and in seeking expression for her particular story.

The writers in this section are responding to that call from within themselves and from their social and historical counterparts. Their purpose is to authenticate the experience of black women, to establish a context for understanding the traditions of the past, and to create a sense of place and community, giving the community back to itself by elevating the commonplace to the artistic. As writers, they seek to render oral expression in written forms, to translate the minor key of the blues and the complexity of jazz into poetic diction, and to affirm the function of folklore in both literature and society. Above all, black women writers are conscious of their own role in becoming models who will establish continuity from the past to the present for future generations of writers.

Locating literary models among their predecessors is a challenge to contemporary black women writers because so little critical attention has been given to the earlier women writers. [4] Yet, women have contributed to each major period in the development of black literature from its inception, demonstrating a unique courage in overcoming the obstacles to literacy that confronted them. For example, Lucy Terry, a slave girl and author of "Bars Fight" (1746), is recognized as the first Afro-American to write poetry. In 1773 Phillis Wheatley became the first black to publish a book of poetry. Brought to America from Africa and sold to the Wheatley family, Phillis had a very unusual experience for a slave in that she was treated as a member of the family and taught to read. Writing soon followed, and Phillis became a minor celebrity in Boston, writing poems on a variety of subjects in the neoclassical style of the period.

In the nineteenth century, the struggle for freedom shaped the literature of many black writers who felt that the conditions of slavery precluded the possibility of writing on any other subject. Frances Ellen Watkins Harper (1825–1911) was one of the first black women to campaign for women's rights as well as against racial inequality. A free black, she became active in a variety of reform movements, writing essays and lecturing throughout the North and the South on antislavery and temperance issues. Among her works are four volumes of poetry, including *Sketches of Southern Life* (1872), and the first novel written by a black woman, *Iola Leroy; or Shadows Uplifted* (1893). Then as now, however, Afro-Americans were concerned that their literature should not be exclusively limited to racial themes. In a letter to the editor of *The Anglo African,* the first Negro literary magazine, Harper expresses this dilemma: "If our Negro talents are to be recognized we must write less of issues that are particular and more of feelings that are general. We are blessed with hearts and minds that compass more than ourselves in our present plight." [5]

Another pioneer writer of the period and a contemporary of Frances Harper, Charlotte Forten (1838–1914) was the first black woman to keep a journal of the times. From 1854 to 1864, she carefully recorded events of the day and detailed the injustices suffered by blacks under slavery. This impulse to keep a record of one's personal and social history manifested itself in autobiography and slave narratives as well. Spurred on by abolitionists, slaves and former slaves narrated events of their lives under slavery for white audiences eager to hear the sordid facts. Despite the tendency of some authors to indulge in melodramatic excesses, slave narratives are central to the development of Afro-American literature because they represent the tentative first efforts of blacks to find their own voices. Though most of the slave narratives were written by men, the most notable of which was the 1845 narrative by Frederick Douglass, women also contributed to this genre. In 1860 William and Ellen Craft published *Running a Thousand Miles for Freedom,* and in 1861 Linda Brent wrote *Incidents in the Life of a Slave Girl.* Also from this period comes Elizabeth Keckley's *Behind the Scenes; or, Thirty Years a Slave and Four Years in the White House,* which was published in 1868. As the dressmaker for Mrs. Lincoln, she offers interesting additions to the storehouse of memorabilia surrounding Lincoln. Her distance from her subject, particularly in light of her life as a former slave, raises provocative literary issues of irony and authorial control.

The decades after the Civil War were filled with the upheaval and anger occasioned by Reconstruction, which led to mass migrations by blacks from the South to the North to escape what was fast becoming institutionalized racism. Despite their efforts to "accommodate" to the demands of white society, blacks were disenfranchised, discriminated against, and finally relegated to inferior status. Many blacks, however, refused to accept the stereotypes of their "inferiority," symbolized by the minstrel tradition of the day, with the result that, by the turn of the century, a new movement in black consciousness was beginning to emerge. In 1903 W. E. B. Du Bois published *The Souls of Black Folk,* which countered the negative images of blacks with an incisive analysis of their dilemma:

> After the Egyptian and Indian, the Greek and Roman, the Teuton and Mongolian, the Negro is a sort of seventh son, born with a veil, and gifted with second-sight in this American world,—a world which yields him no true self-consciousness, but only lets him see himself through the revelation of the other world. It is a peculiar sensation, this double-consciousness, this sense of always looking at one's self through the eyes of others, of measuring one's soul by the tape of a world that looks on in amused contempt and pity. One ever feels his twoness,—an American, a Negro; two souls, two thoughts, two unreconciled strivings; two warring ideals in one dark body, whose dogged strength alone keeps it from being torn asunder.[6]

In a letter to Du Bois in 1903, Jessie Fauset, a woman novelist of the period, expresses the essence of his profound influence on black writers at that time: "I am glad *glad* you wrote it [*The Souls of Black Folk*]—we have needed someone to voice the intricacies of the blind maze of thought and action along which the modern, educated colored man or woman struggles." [7]

Du Bois opened the way for artists and writers to explore the intricacies of the black psyche and look "behind the veil" of double consciousness. The result was a renewed and invigorated interest in the black experience that reached its literary peak in the Harlem Renaissance (1910–1930). But few of the women writing during this period—women such as Angelina Grimké, Anne Spencer, Alice Dunbar Nelson, Gwendolyn Bennett, Jessie Fauset, and Nella Larsen—have received the critical attention they deserve, perhaps because of their departure from the literary mainstream of the twenties. For example, when black men were celebrating the rebirth of pride in black culture and affirming so actively the unique values of black life, many of the women writers, particularly the poets, seemed reticent to express a literary black nationalism. In part, their position as women may have isolated them from the literary coteries dominated by men, but it is also possible that they were conscious then of shaping a distinctively black female literary tradition. This is the kind of critical problem that needs to be addressed before the contributions of these earlier black women writers can be fully understood, recognized, and assessed, and those writers whose contributions have been substantial given their due attention. Despite the work that remains to be done to fill in the gaps of our understanding of the earlier black women writers, it is clear that the contemporary writers included here are making a conscious effort to shape a literary tradition that is distinctly black and female and that takes into account the legacies of the past.

CONTEXTS AND NARRATIVES

Zora Neale Hurston is perhaps the most dramatic example of a black woman writer who has been rescued from obscurity by careful scholarship and by younger women seeking literary models among their female predecessors. In the opening essay, Alice Walker describes how she literally discovered Hurston in a footnote when she was searching for material on black folklore to inform one of her short stories. As one of the first black anthropologists, Hurston did her field work among southern blacks, making an invaluable contribution to folklore, literature, and anthropology by gathering and recording songs, sayings, stories, histories, hexes—a wealth of material that she later wove into her fiction.[8] Of immense value to anyone with an interest in the black oral tradition and folklore is *Mules and Men,* from which the introduction and Section VII are included here in "Contexts." Not only did Hurston establish black folklore as a unique, creative art form, but she demonstrated in her own fiction how folklore could function as a literary device, illuminating the subtlety of relationships within black culture. Through research, the personal commitments of writers such as Alice Walker, and the contribution of Robert Hemenway's outstanding literary biography, Zora Neale Hurston is finally being granted her proper place in literature.[9] Her resurrection is important because she is a model, and without models, writers are disconnected from their past, denied the continuity that makes tradition a viable entity within culture.

Conscious of grounding their literature firmly in their history as a people, many contemporary black women writers turn to the past. Alice Walker looks to Zora Neale Hurston for her inspiration and for folk sources to inform "The Revenge of Hannah Kemhuff." Lucille Clifton records the oral histories of her family in *Generations.* Toni Morrison examines the history that links together three generations of women in *Sula.* Sherley Williams writes a series of poems entitled "Generations," and Yvonne sketches poetic portraits of her female ancestors. All of the writers create a sense of community that implicitly connects the individual to her history.

Unlike the male writers, who tend to focus their literature on the confrontation between the white and black worlds, black women writers concentrate more intensely on the black community alone and the human relationships within that community. This is not to say that black-white conflicts do not exist, as they certainly do in "The Revenge of Hannah Kemhuff," but the emphasis is different. In this story, for example, Walker is more interested in the limits of endurance of the black woman and the way she seeks revenge by entrusting her faith in certain beliefs of the community. The story is really a fictional account of how the folk tradition functions to affect behavior, becoming an artistic outlet for the oppressed. Even so, the action is still within the community. And that community must be located in a cultural space that can be defined by geography as well as by history and tradition.

Toni Morrison discusses the importance of place in the interview included here, stating that she feels a "very strong sense of place, not in terms of the country or the state, but in terms of the details, the feeling, the mood of the community, of the town." Stories do occur in places, but what the women writers emphasize is the importance of place and community as a character. By confining their landscapes of action to the community and examining the routines of daily life and feeling under a magnifying glass, black women writers accomplish two things: they highlight the art of daily living and give back to the community a mirror of itself; and in that mirror, they can correct the stereotypes about black life that seem to proliferate so irresponsibly in our society.

Black women, particularly, have been stereotyped over and over again as two-dimensional characters who fall into one of the many slots ranging from the superhuman matriarch driven by a mountain-moving faith to the pleasure-seeking, lascivious prostitute. As Mary Helen Washington has pointed out, it is no accident that "one of the main preoccupations of the black woman writer has been the black woman herself—her aspirations, her conflicts, her relationship to her men and her children, her creativity.[10] This does not mean that literature becomes sociology, but rather that it reveals the complexity of the black female sensibility.

The stories contained in "Traditions, Narratives, and Fiction" begin to complete our understanding of that sensibility. The world is seen from the angle of the child in "Doby's Gone" by Ann Petry and "Maggie of the Green Bottles" by Toni Cade Bambara. In both instances, the child reduces the reality of the world to manageable terms, at the same time ironically magnifying those realities. Doby is Sue Johnson's imaginary companion in her loneliness and a buffer zone against the color line in the outside world. While there is a social determinism present in the story in the clear color prejudice of the white world, Petry does not dwell on that determinism but rather on the psychology of the child who must experience discrimination without understanding it. There is a lyrical quality in her work and a humor that gives her characters some choices in a seemingly polarized world. Indeed, Sue Johnson finally fights the white children who are taunting her and, in so doing, establishes the beginning of a relationship where none has existed.

In Bambara's story, the narrator recalls her childhood infatuation with her great-grandmother who, to everyone else, is irascible, eccentric, and alcoholic. But to Peaches, Maggie is an enchantment, an inspiration to her imagination, a model of fortitude who rewrites the family history and gives her a wonderful sense of fresh possibilities. Both stories are touched by a tenderness that renders poignantly the innocence of childhood.

Kinship and the importance of oral history are the subjects of *Generations* by Lucille Clifton, from which "Lucy" is excerpted. It is not necessary to recite the horrors of slavery to know how totally the black family was threatened by extinction. Oral histories were, as we have seen, a way of preserving the links between past and future generations and essential to blacks who had been severed so violently from their African backgrounds. In "Lucy," Lucille Clifton not only captures the importance of "roots" to her own identity as a black woman, she also exemplifies the art of storytelling—that rare mixture of humor, repetition, and homily that keeps alive forever in a child's mind the significance of her heritage and her responsibility to that personal history.

History is also a subject of "1921" by Toni Morrison. In fact, through revealing the history of Eva Peace, her daughter Hannah, and her granddaughter Sula, Morrison reverses many of the common stereotypes about black women. Eva Peace is a bold challenge to the stereotype of the everenduring, strong-backed mother, and through her, Morrison exposes the holes in every mother's humanity. While Eva accepts her responsibility for taking care of her family after her husband leaves, she also comes face to face with her feelings for the first time and must decide how she feels. She settles on hatred for her shiftless husband, which allows her to assume a certain autocratic imperialism with other men and with her family. She does not question her decisions and is anything but peaceful. In fact, necessity elicits from her an almost primeval energy that she uses to bring things into existence and as quickly to destroy them. There is no question about her strength, but Morrison also suggests, almost satirically, that the price is great, although in Eva's case, she is richly remunerated for her sacrifice. With the community as a frame of reference, Morrison also turns inside out the stereotype of the "easy" woman in her portrayal of Hannah, exposing the hypocrisy of some members of the black community who would just as soon perpetuate stereotypes of women as deal with the real person behind the behavior.

Seeing behind the mask, though, can be dangerous, as Paule Marshall proposes in "Brooklyn," a story about a confrontation between an aging white French professor and a young black woman from the South. Marshall reveals the way in which some whites use black women to work out their own problems in feeling, but also suggests that black women can be accomplices to such manipulation through the habit of masking their feelings. Ultimately, the story centers on how one breaks out of an expected role to express authentic feelings, which must be done before a real relationship can be established.

POETRY

The poets in this section span a period of over thirty years. In 1941 Naomi Long Madgett published her first book of poetry, entitled *Songs to a Phantom Nightingale.* Margaret Walker won the Yale University Younger Poets Award in 1942 for her volume of poems, *For My People,* and Gwendolyn Brooks published her first collection of poems, *A Street in Bronzeville,* in 1945. In 1949 she was awarded the Pulitzer Prize for *Annie Allen,* the first black to receive that honor. May Miller, who has been writing for a number of years, published her first collection of poems, *Into the Clearing,* in 1959. What characterizes the poetry of these women and the younger poets in this section is their imaginative and innovative use of language. Black poetry is oral and auditory. It is meant to be heard, read aloud, shared. This is a poetry of the concrete, rich with imagery; it is also a poetry of subtlety, of shades of feeling. With few exceptions, the poetry included here centers on relationships—relationships with oneself, one's history, the family, society, politics—and what is *heard* are the different voices of women telling their stories.

Once a relationship does come into existence, particularly a love relationship, it is not always easy to sustain, and the despair of loneliness becomes a central theme in the literature of black women. While this theme is certainly prevalent in women's literature in general, its expression takes on an especially haunting quality in the poetry of black women in the transformation of the blues into poetic diction.[11] "Any Woman's Blues" by Sherley Williams clearly derives from the blues, with its repetition of phrases, the simple story line, and the rhythm of "worrying" a line through its minor key of feeling. The blues form implies a shared relationship: By following a certain formula of expression one is able both to communicate her own particular story, or "private blues," and at the same time convert it into "any woman's blues."

Even if the blues does not explicitly inform the structure of a poem, it can be present in the mood of a poem. Singing the blues is a way of establishing a relationship with one's pain. Mari Evans says, "The music of my song/some sweet arpeggio of tears/is written in a minor key." Feelings are controlled, compressed, and contained in an economy of expression that increases the magnitude of the experience. The "blues mood" in poetry becomes another way of masking experience, and it is this ambiguity that lends such richness to the poems of black women writers.

Ambiguity is also conveyed through poetic style, and of the contemporary poets, Ntozake Shange is, perhaps, the most experimental with language. Her play, *For Colored Girls Who Have Considered Suicide When the Rainbow Is Enuf,* which is a series of spoken poems, has been an unprecedented success on Broadway. The selection included here from *Sassafras* is characteristic of her style. It is an interior monologue of memory, a series of different voices recalled by the narrator, all of whom tell a part of "the story." Written in the stream-of-consciousness style with no stanza breaks and no punctuation, the poem almost demands to be read aloud and explored for emphasis. Shange's use of dialect endows each character with her own particular voice.

Alice Walker achieves the same effect in her poem "Burial," which is a narrative told in the first person. The attention to minute detail is that of the storyteller who recalls the past with deep emotion and lingers over every moment. These are oral histories rendered poetically, and what emerges is a profound respect for kinship and a recognition that one's personal identity depends on the continuity from past to present. Yvonne achieves a similar feeling of continuity in her portraits of her great-grandmother and her aunt, which are excerpts from a much longer poem on the history of the black woman. History is the key here. Whether one looks to the past, as Walker, Yvonne, and Williams do, or to the future, as is the case with Colleen McElroy in her poems to her children, history unifies experience and is a constant reminder that the individual is part of a group. Though loneliness may prevail, one is *not* alone. Kinship is the proof of a communal history.

June Jordan explores that history in the public arena in her portrait of a black woman and her memorial to Martin Luther King. She combines alliteration with verbs of destruction—"rip rape/ exacerbate despoil disfigure"— with such intensity that the language runs over itself until it explodes, as does the anger of the poem. In contrast, the poetry of Audre Lorde attains its power through control and irony. Hers is a poetry of reversal: "Rooming houses are old women/ rocking dark windows into their whens." By juxtaposing space and time with concrete objects, Lorde challenges the complacency of those who too easily forget that age does not diminish passion. No subject escapes her scrutiny, including the very personal one of her own creative endeavors. She writes, "All the poems I have ever written/ make a small book/ the shedding of my past in patched conceits/ moulted like snake skin, a book of leavings." With irony, she mocks the comfortable arrogance that goes with achievement.

Black literature has been termed a literature of oppositions, and certainly the poets here invert assumptions and topple stereotypes. In "They Clapped," Nikki Giovanni exposes the false expectations of those who would turn to Africa for answers. Gwendolyn Brooks ironically contrasts the luxury of dreams and personal visions with the reality of onion fumes and rent payments in "kitchenette building." Nor does she spare the white woman in "Bronzeville Woman in a Red Hat," who would sooner preserve her prejudice about blacks than come face to face with one. Yet social inequities do not prevent Brooks's anguished cry as a mother in "What shall I give my children?" She chooses the sonnet form for this poem almost as a way of putting limits on an emotion that could otherwise consume her.

The poetry of black women is largely a poetry of control; it is not a poetry of excess or indulgence. In part, that would be lifting the mask off too far and turning the blues into an elegy. But more importantly, to be totally centered on the self would be to forget one's history, the kinship of a shared community of experience, the crucial continuity between past and present that must be maintained in order to insure the future. When Margaret Walker writes, "I want to write the songs of my people/ . . . I want to frame their dreams into words, their souls into notes," she is describing what the women writers here, consciously or not, have superbly achieved.

NOTES

1. For a fuller discussion of the quest for freedom and literacy as the pregeneric myth underlying black literature, see Robert B. Stepto, "Teaching Afro-American Literature: Survey or Tradition; or The Reconstruction of Instruction," in *Afro-American Literature: The Reconstruction of Instruction,* eds. Dexter Fisher and Robert B. Stepto (New York: Modern Language Association, 1979).

2. Langston Hughes and Arno Bontemps, *The Book of Negro Folklore* (New York: Dodd, Mead, 1958).

3. Mary Berry and John Blassingame, "Africa, Slavery, & the Roots of Contemporary Black Culture," *Massachusetts Review,* 18, No. 3 (Autumn 1977), 512–513.

4. A notable exception is Jean Fagan Yellin, *Writings By and About Afro-American Women, 1800–1910* (Boston: G. K. Hall, 1980 expected publication).

5. *Cavalcade—Negro American Writing from the 1760's to the Present,* eds. Arthur P. Davis and Saunders Redding (Boston: Houghton Mifflin, 1971), p. 53.

6. W. E. B. Du Bois, *The Souls of Black Folk* in *Three Negro Classics* (New York: Avon Books, 1965), pp. 214–215.

7. Arnold Rampersad, *The Art and Imagination of W. E. B. Du Bois* (Cambridge, Mass.: Harvard University Press, 1976), p. 68.

8. Zora Neale Hurston's most popular novel is *Their Eyes Were Watching God* (Philadelphia: J. B. Lippincott, 1937; reprinted by the University of Illinois Press, 1978). She also wrote *Jonah's Gourd Vine* (Philadelphia: J. B. Lippincott, 1934; reprinted, 1971), *Mules and Men* (Philadelphia: J. B. Lippincott, 1935; reprinted by Harper & Row, 1970), *Moses, Man of the Mountain* (Philadelphia: J. B. Lippincott, 1939; reprinted by Chatham Bookseller, 1974), *Dust Tracks on the Road* (Philadelphia: J. B. Lippincott, 1942; reprinted, 1971), and *Seraph on the Suwanee* (New York: Charles Scribner's Sons, 1948; reprinted by AMS Press, 1974).

9. Robert E. Hemenway, *Zora Neale Hurston—A Literary Biography* (Urbana: University of Illinois Press, 1977).

10. Mary Helen Washington, *Black-Eyed Susans—Classic Stories By and About Black Women* (New York: Doubleday-Anchor Books, 1975), p. x.
11. For a full discussion of the blues, see Sherley Williams, "The Blues Roots of Contemporary Afro-American Poetry," *The Massachusetts Review,* 18, No. 3 (Autumn 1977), 542–554.

CONTEXTS

ALICE WALKER

Born in 1944 in Georgia, Alice Walker is a contributing editor to *MS* Magazine. Her books include *The Third Life of Grange Copeland* (1970) and *Meridian* (1976), both novels; *Once* (1968) and *Revolutionary Petunias and Other Poems* (1973), volumes of poetry; *In Love and Trouble* (1973), a collection of short stories; and *Langston Hughes, American Poet* (1974), a biography for children. Her essays and stories have appeared in numerous journals and magazines. She was awarded a Guggenheim in fiction for 1977–1978 and was the recipient of the Lillian Smith Award and a Creative Writing Award from the National Endowment for the Arts, among other fellowships. In 1974 *Revolutionary Petunias and Other Poems* was nominated for a National Book Award, and *In Love and Trouble* won the Rosenthal Award of the National Institute of Arts and Letters.

SAVING THE LIFE THAT IS YOUR OWN: THE IMPORTANCE OF MODELS IN THE ARTIST'S LIFE

There is a letter that Vincent Van Gogh wrote to Emile Bernard that is very meaningful to me. A year before he wrote the letter, Van Gogh had had a fight with his domineering friend, Gauguin, left his company, and cut off, in desperation and anguish, his own ear. The letter itself was written in Saint Remy, in the South of France, from a mental institution to which Van Gogh had voluntarily committed himself.

I imagine Van Gogh sitting at a rough desk too small for him, looking out at the lovely Southern light, and occasionally glancing critically next to him at his own paintings of the landscape he loved so much. The date of the letter is December, 1889. Van Gogh wrote:

> However hateful painting may be, and however cumbersome in the times we are living in, if anyone who has chosen this handicraft pursues it zealously, he is a man of duty, sound and faithful.
>
> Society makes our existence wretchedly difficult at times, hence our impotence and the imperfection of our work.
>
> . . . I myself am suffering under an absolute lack of models.
>
> But on the other hand, there are beautiful spots here. I have just done five size 30 canvases, olive trees. And the reason I am staying on here is that my health is improving a great deal.
>
> What I am doing is hard, dry, but that is because I am trying to gather new strength by doing some rough work, and I'm afraid abstractions would make me soft.

Six months later, Van Gogh—whose "health was improving a great deal"—committed suicide. He had sold one painting during his lifetime. Three times was his work noticed in the press. *But these are just details.*

The real Vincent Van Gogh is the man who "has just done five size 30 canvases, olive trees." To me, in context, one of the most moving and revealing descriptions of how a real artist thinks. And the knowledge that when he spoke of "suffering under an absolute lack of models" he spoke of that lack both in terms of the intensity of his commitment, and the quality and singularity of his work—which was frequently ridiculed in his day.

The absence of models, in literature as in life, to say nothing of in painting, is an occupational hazard for the artist, simply because models in art, in behavior, in growth of spirit and intellect—even if rejected—enrich and enlarge one's view of existence. *Deadlier still,* to the artist who lacks models, is the curse of ridicule, the bringing to bear on an artist's best work, especially his or her most original, most strikingly deviant, only a fund of ignorance, and the presumption that, as an artist's critic, one's judgment is free of the restrictions imposed by prejudice, and is well-informed, indeed, about all the art in the world that really matters.

What is always needed in the appreciation of art, or life, is the larger perspective. Connections made, or at least attempted, where none existed before, the straining to encompass in one's glance at the varied world the common thread, the unifying theme through immense diversity, a fearlessness of growth, of search, of look, that enlarges the private and the public world. And yet, in our particular society, it is the narrowed and narrowing view of life that often wins.

Recently, I read at a college and was asked by one of the audience what I considered the major difference between the literature written by black and white Americans. I had not spent a lot of time considering this question, since it is not the difference between them that interests me, but rather the way black writers and white writers seem to me to be writing one immense story—the same story, for the most part—with different parts of this immense story coming from a multitude of different perspectives. Until this is generally recognized, literature will always be broken into bits, black and white, and there will always be questions, wanting neat answers, such as this.

Still, I answered that I thought, for the most part, white American writers tended to end their books and their characters' lives as if there is no better existence for which to struggle. The gloom of defeat is thick.

By comparison, black writers seem always involved in a moral and/or physical struggle, the result of which is expected to be some kind of larger freedom. *Perhaps this is because* our literary tradition is based on the slave narratives, where escape for the body and freedom for the soul went hand in hand, or perhaps it is because black people have never felt themselves guilty of global, cosmic sins.

This comparison does not hold up in every case, of course, and perhaps does not really hold up at all. I am not a gatherer of statistics, only a curious reader, and this has been my impression from reading many books by black and white writers.

There are, however, two books by American women that illustrate what I am talking about: *The Awakening,* by Kate Chopin, and *Their Eyes Were Watching God,* by Zora Neale Hurston.

The plight of Mme Pontellier and that of Janie Crawford are quite similar. Each woman is married to a dull, society-conscious husband and living in a dull, propriety-conscious community. Each woman desires a life of her own and a man who loves her and makes her feel alive. Each woman finds such a man.

Mme Pontellier, overcome by the strictures of society and the existence of her children (along with the cowardice of her lover), kills herself rather than defying the one and abandoning the other. *Janie Crawford,* on the other hand, refuses to allow society to dictate behavior to her, enjoys the love of a much younger, freedom-loving man, and lives to tell others of her experience.

When I mentioned these two books to my audience, I was not surprised to learn that only one person, a young black poet in the first row, had ever heard of *Their Eyes Were Watching God* (*The Awakening* they had fortunately read in their "Women in Literature" class) primarily because it was written by a black woman, whose experience—in love and life—was apparently assumed to be unimportant to the students (and the teachers) of a predominantly white school.

Certainly, as a student, I was not directed toward this book which would have urged me more toward freedom and experience than toward comfort and security, but was directed instead toward a plethora of books by mainly white male writers who thought most women worthless if they didn't enjoy bullfighting or hadn't volunteered for the trenches in World War II.

Loving both these books, knowing each to be indispensable to my own growth, my own life, I chose the model, the example, of Janie Crawford. And yet this book, as necessary to me and to other women as air and water, is again out of print. But I have distilled as much as I could of its wisdom in this poem about its heroine, Janie Crawford:

> *Janie Crawford*
>
> *I love the way Janie Crawford*
> *left her husbands*
> *the one who wanted to change her*
> *into a mule*
> *and the other who tried to interest her*
> *in being a queen.*

A woman, unless she submits
is neither a mule
nor a queen
though like a mule she may suffer
and like a queen pace the floor.

It has been said that someone asked Toni Morrison why she writes the kinds of books she writes, and that she replied: because they are the kind of books I want to read.

This remains my favorite reply to that kind of question. As if anyone reading the magnificent, mysterious *Sula,* or the grim, poetic *The Bluest Eye* would require more of a reason for their existence than for the brooding, haunting *Wuthering Heights,* for example, or the melancholy, triumphant *Jane Eyre.* (I am not speaking here of the most famous short line of that book: "Reader, I married him" as the triumph, but rather of the triumph of Jane Eyre's control over her own sense of morality and her own stout will, which are but reflections of her creator's, Charlotte Brontë, who no doubt wished to write the sort of book *she* wished to read.)

Flannery O'Connor has written that more and more the serious novelist will write, not what other people want, and certainly not what other people expect, but whatever interests her or him. And that the direction taken, therefore, will be away from sociology, away from the "writing of explanation," of statistics, and further into mystery, into poetry and into prophecy. I believe this is true, *fortunately true; especially* for "Third World Writers"; Morrison, Marquez, Ahmadi, Camara Laye make good examples; and not only do I believe it is true for serious writers in general, but I believe, as firmly as did O'Connor, that this is our only hope—in a culture so in love with flash, with trendiness, with superficiality, as ours—of acquiring a sense of essence, of timelessness and of vision. Therefore, to write the books one wants to read is both to point the direction of vision at the same time as following it.

When Toni Morrison said she writes the kind of books she wants to read, she is acknowledging the fact that she must, in a society in which "accepted literature" is so often sexist and racist and otherwise irrelevant or offensive to so many lives, she must do the work of two. She must be her own model as well as the artist attending, creating, learning from, realizing the model, which is to say, herself.

(It should be remembered that, as a black person, one cannot completely identify with a Jane Eyre, or with her creator, no matter how much one admires them. And certainly, if one allows history to impinge on one's reading pleasure, one must cringe at the thought of how Heathcliff, in the New World far from Wuthering Heights, amassed his Cathy-dazzling fortune.)

I have often been asked why, in my own life and work, I have felt such a desperate need to know and assimilate the experiences of earlier black women writers, most of them unheard of by you and by me, until quite recently. Why I felt a need to study them and to teach them.

I don't recall the exact moment I set out to explore the works of black women, mainly those in the past, and certainly, in the beginning, I had no desire to teach them. Teaching being for me, at that time, less rewarding than star-gazing on a frigid night. *My discovery of them*—most of them out of print, abandoned, discredited, maligned, nearly lost—came about, as many things of value do, almost by accident. As it turned out—and this should not have surprised me—I found I was in need of something that only one of them could provide.

Mindful that throughout my four years at a prestigious black and then a prestigious white college I had heard not one word about early black women writers, one of my first tasks was simply to determine whether they had existed. After this, I could breathe easier, with more assurance about the profession I myself had chosen.

But the incident that started my search began several years ago: I sat down at my desk one day, in a room of my own, with key and lock, and began preparations for a story about voodoo, a subject that had always fascinated me. Many of the elements of this story I had gathered from a story that my mother several times told me. She had gone, during the Depression, into town to apply for some government surplus food at the local commissary, and had been turned down, in a particularly humiliating way, by the white woman in charge.

My mother always told this story with a most curious expression on her face. She automatically raised her head higher than ever—it was always high —and there was a look of righteousness, a kind of holy *heat* coming from her eyes. She said she had lived to see this same white woman grow old and senile and so badly crippled she had to get about on *two* sticks.

To her, this was clearly the working of God, who, as in the old spiritual, ". . . may not come when you want him, but he's right on time!" To me, hearing the story for about the 50th time, something else was discernible: the possibilities of the story, for fiction.

What, I asked myself, would have happened, if, after the crippled old lady died, it was discovered that someone, my mother perhaps (who would have been mortified at the thought, Christian lady that she is), had voodooed her?

Then, my thoughts sweeping me away into the world of hexes and conjures of centuries past, I wondered how a larger story could be created out of my mother's story; one that would be true to the magnitude of her humiliation and grief, and to the white woman's lack of sensitivity and compassion.

My third quandary was: How could I find out all I needed to know in order to write a story that used *authentic* black witchcraft?

Which brings me back, almost, to the day I became really interested in black women writers. I say "almost" because one other thing, from my childhood, made the choice of black magic a logical and irresistible one for my story. Aside from my mother's several stories about rootdoctors she had heard of or known, there was the story I had often heard about my crazy Walker aunt.

Many years ago, when my aunt was a meek and obedient girl growing up in a strict, conventionally religious house in the rural South, she had suddenly thrown off her meekness and had run away from home, escorted by a rogue of a man permanently attached elsewhere.

When she was returned home by her father she was declared quite "mad." In the backwoods South at the turn of the century, "madness" of this sort was cured, not by psychiatry, but by powders and by spells. (One may see Scott Joplin's *Treemonisha* to ascertain the role voodoo played among black people of that period.) My aunt's "madness" was treated by the community conjurer, who promised, and delivered, the desired results. His "treatment" was a bag of white powder, bought for fifty cents, and sprinkled on the ground around her house, with some of it sewed, I believe, into the bodice of her nightgown.

So when I sat down to write my story about voodoo, my crazy Walker aunt was definitely on my mind.

But she had experienced her temporary craziness so long ago that her story had all the excitement of a might-have-been. I needed, instead of family memories, some hard facts about the *craft* of voodoo, as practiced by Southern blacks in the 19th century. (It never once, fortunately, occurred to me that voodoo was not worthy of the interest I had in it, or was too ridiculous to seriously study.)

I began reading all I could find on the subject of "The Negro and His Folkways and Superstitions." There were Botkin and Puckett and others, all white, most racist. How was I to believe anything they wrote, since at least one of them, Puckett, was capable of wondering, in his book, if "The Negro" had a large enough brain? Who needed *him,* the racist turkey!

Well, I thought, where are the *black* collectors of folklore? Where is the *black* anthropologist? Where is the *black* person who took the time to travel the backroads of the South and collect the information I need: how to cure heart trouble, treat dropsy, hex somebody to death, lock bowels, cause joints to swell, eyes to fall out, and so on. Where was this black person?

And that is when I first saw, in a *footnote* to the white voices of authority, the name of Zora Neale Hurston.

Folklorist, novelist, anthropologist, serious student of voodoo, also all around black woman, with guts enough to take a slide rule and measure random black heads in Harlem; not to prove their inferiority, but to prove that whatever their size, shape, or present condition of servitude, those heads contained all the intelligence anyone could use to get through this world.

Zora Hurston, who went to Barnard to learn how to study what she really wanted to learn: the ways of her own people, and what ancient rituals, customs and beliefs had made them unique.

Zora, of the sandy-colored hair and the daredevil eyes, a girl who escaped poverty and parental neglect by hard work and a sharp eye for the main chance.

Zora, who left the South only to return to look at it again. Who went to rootdoctors from Florida to Louisiana and said, "Here I am. I want to learn your trade."

Zora, who had collected all the black folklore I could ever use.

That Zora.

And having found *that* Zora (like a golden key to a storehouse of varied treasure), I was hooked.

What I had discovered, of course, was a model. A model, who, as it happened, provided more than voodoo for my story, more than one of the greatest novels America had produced—though, being America, it did not realize this. She had provided, as if she knew someday I would come along wandering in the wilderness, a nearly complete record of her life. And though her life sprouted an occasional wart, I am eternally grateful for that life, warts and all.

It is not irrelevant, nor is it bragging (except perhaps to gloat a little on the happy relatedness of Zora, my mother, and me), to mention here that the story I wrote, called "The Revenge of Hannah Kemhuff," based on my mother's experiences during the Depression, and on Zora Hurston's folklore collection of the 1920s, and on my own response to both out of a contemporary existence, was immediately published and later selected, by a reputable collector of short stories, as one of the *Best Short Stories of 1974*.

I mention it because this story might never have been written, because the very bases of its structure, authentic black folklore, viewed from a black perspective, might have been lost.

Had it been lost, my mother's story would have had no historical underpinning, none I could trust, anyway. I would not have written the story, which I enjoyed writing as much as I've enjoyed writing anything in my life, had I not known that Zora had already done a thorough job of preparing the ground over which I was then moving.

In that story I gathered up the historical and psychological threads of the life my ancestors lived, and in the writing of it I felt joy and strength and my own continuity. I had that wonderful feeling writers get sometimes, not very often, of being *with* a great many people, ancient spirits, all very happy to see me consulting and acknowledging them, and eager to let me know, through the joy of their presence, that indeed, I am not alone.

To take Toni Morrison's statement further, if that is possible, in my own work I write not only what I want to read—understanding fully and indelibly that if I don't do it no one else is so vitally interested, or capable of doing it to my satisfaction—I write all the things I *should have read*.

Consulting, as belatedly discovered models, those writers—most of whom, not surprisingly, are women, who understood that their experience as ordinary human beings was also valuable, and in danger of being misrepresented, distorted, or lost:

Zora Hurston—novelist, essayist, anthropologist, autobiographer.

Jean Toomer—novelist, poet, philosopher, visionary, a man who cared what women felt.

Colette—whose crinkly hair enhances her French, part-black face: novelist, playwright, dancer, essayist, newspaper woman, lover of women, men, small dogs. Fortunate not to have been born in America.

Anais Nin, recorder of everything, no matter how minute.

Tillie Olsen, a writer of such generosity and honesty, she literally saves lives . . .

It is, in the end, the saving of lives that we writers are about. Whether we are "minority" writers or "majority." It is simply in our power to do this.

We do it because we care. We care that Vincent Van Gogh mutilated his ear. We care that behind a pile of manure in the yard he destroyed his life. We care that Scott Joplin's music *lives!* We care because we know this: *The life we save is our own.*

ZORA NEALE HURSTON

Born in Eatonville, Florida, around 1901, Zora Neale Hurston was a novelist, folklorist, and anthropologist, the first black person to go into the rural South and recognize the artistic and cultural dimensions of black life and expression. Her collection of folklore is entitled *Mules and Men* (1935). She also skillfully wove folklore into her fiction: *Jonah's Gourd Vine* (1934), *Their Eyes Were Watching God* (1937), *Tell My Horse* (1938), *Moses, Man of the Mountain* (1939), and *Seraph on the Suwanee* (1948). She published her autobiography, *Dust Tracks on a Road*, in 1942. Despite her contributions as a folklorist and her importance as a novelist and a literary figure during the flourishing twenties and thirties, Zora Neale Hurston died in 1960 in poverty and obscurity and was placed in an unmarked grave in a segregated cemetery in Fort Pierce, Florida. In 1973, Alice Walker placed a tombstone in the cemetery that reads:

Zora Neale Hurston
"A Genius of the South"
1901—1960
Novelist, Folklorist,
Anthropologist

INTRODUCTION TO MULES AND MEN

I was glad when somebody told me, "You may go and collect Negro folklore."

In a way it would not be a new experience for me. When I pitched head-foremost into the world I landed in the crib of negroism. From the earliest rocking of my cradle, I had known about the capers Brer Rabbit is apt to cut and what the Squinch Owl says from the house top. But it was fitting me like a tight chemise. I couldn't see it for wearing it. It was only when I was off in college, away from my native surroundings, that I could see myself like somebody else and stand off and look at my garment. Then I had to have the spy-glass of Anthropology to look through at that.

Dr. Boas asked me where I wanted to work and I said, "Florida," and gave, as my big reason, that "Florida is a place that draws people—white people from all over the world, and Negroes from every Southern state surely and some from the North and West." So I knew that it was possible for me to get a cross section of the Negro South in the one state. And then I realized that I was new myself, so it looked sensible for me to choose familiar ground.

First place I aimed to stop to collect material was Eatonville, Florida.

And now, I'm going to tell you why I decided to go to my native village first. I didn't go back there so that the home folks could make admiration over me because I had been up North to college and come back with a diploma and a Chevrolet. I knew they were not going to pay either one of these items too much mind. I was just Lucy Hurston's daughter, Zora, and even if I had—to use one of our down-home expressions—had a Kaiser baby,* and that's something that hasn't been done in this Country yet, I'd still be just Zora to the neighbors. If I had exalted myself to impress the town, somebody would have sent me word in a match-box that I had been up North there and had rubbed the hair off of my head against some college wall, and then come back there with a lot of form and fashion and outside show to the world. But they'd stand flat-footed and tell me that they didn't have me, neither my sham-polish, to study 'bout. And that would have been that.

I hurried back to Eatonville because I knew that the town was full of material and that I could get it without hurt, harm or danger. As early as I could remember it was the habit of the men folks particularly to gather on the store porch 'of evenings and swap stories. Even the women folks would stop and break a breath with them at times. As a child when I was sent down to Joe Clarke's store, I'd drag out my leaving as long as possible in order to hear more.

Folk-lore is not as easy to collect as it sounds. The best source is where there are the least outside influences and these people, being usually under-privileged, are the shyest. They are most reluctant at times to reveal that which the soul lives by. And the Negro, in spite of his open-faced laughter, his seeming acquiescence, is particularly evasive. You see we are a polite people and we do not say to our questioner, "Get out of here!" We smile and tell him or her something that satisfies the white person because, knowing so little about us, he doesn't know what he is missing. The Indian resists curiosity by a stony silence. The Negro offers a feather-bed resistance. That is, we let the probe enter, but it never comes out. It gets smothered under a lot of laughter and pleasantries.

The theory behind our tactics: "The white man is always trying to know into somebody else's business. All right, I'll set something outside the door of my mind for him to play with and handle. He can read my writing but he sho' can't read my mind. I'll put this play toy in his hand, and he will seize it and go away. Then I'll say my say and sing my song."

I knew that even *I* was going to have some hindrance among strangers. But here in Eatonville I knew everybody was going to help me. So below Palatka I began to feel eager to be there and I kicked the little Chevrolet right along.

I thought about the tales I had heard as a child. How even the Bible was

* Have a child by the Kaiser.

made over to suit our vivid imagination. How the devil always outsmarted God and how that over-noble hero Jack or John—not *John Henry*, who occupies the same place in Negro folk-lore that Casey Jones does in white lore and if anything is more recent—outsmarted the devil. Brer Fox, Brer Deer, Brer 'Gator, Brer Dawg, Brer Rabbit, Ole Massa and his wife were walking the earth like natural men way back in the days when God himself was on the ground and men could talk with him. Way back there before God weighed up the dirt to make the mountains. When I was rounding Lily Lake I was remembering how God had made the world and the elements and people. He made souls for people, but he didn't give them out because he said:

"Folks ain't ready for souls yet. De clay ain't dry. It's de strongest thing Ah ever made. Don't aim to waste none thru loose cracks. And then men got to grow strong enough to stand it. De way things is now, if Ah give it out it would tear them shackly bodies to pieces. Bimeby, Ah give it out."

So folks went round thousands of years without no souls. All de time de soul-piece, it was setting 'round covered up wid God's loose raiment. Every now and then de wind would blow and hist up de cover and then de elements would be full of lightning and de winds would talk. So people told one 'nother that God was talking in de mountains.

De white man passed by it way off and he looked but he wouldn't go close enough to touch. De Indian and de Negro, they tipped by cautious too, and all of 'em seen de light of diamonds when de winds shook de cover, and de wind dat passed over it sung songs. De Jew come past and heard de song from de soul-piece then he kept on passin' and all of a sudden he grabbed up de soul-piece and hid it under his clothes, and run off down de road. It burnt him and tore him and throwed him down and lifted him up and toted him across de mountain and he tried to break loose but he couldn't do it. He kept on hollerin' for help but de rest of 'em run hid 'way from him. Way after while they come out of holes and corners and picked up little chips and pieces that fell back on de ground. So God mixed it up wid feelings and give it out to 'em. 'Way after while when He ketch dat Jew, He's goin' to 'vide things up more ekal'.

So I rounded Park Lake and came speeding down the straight stretch into Eatonville, the city of five lakes, three croquet courts, three hundred brown skins, three hundred good swimmers, plenty guavas, two schools, and no jailhouse.

Before I enter the township, I wish to make acknowledgments to Mrs. R. Osgood Mason of New York City. She backed my falling in a hearty way, in a spiritual way, and in addition, financed the whole expedition in the manner of the Great Soul that she is. The world's most gallant woman.

VII

from *Mules and Men*

Kitty Brown is a well-known hoodoo doctor of New Orleans, and a Catholic. She liked to make marriages and put lovers together. She is squat, black and benign. Often when we had leisure, she told funny stories. Her herb garden was pretty full and we often supplied other doctors with plants. Very few raise things since the supply houses carry about everything that is needed. But sometimes a thing is wanted fresh from the ground. That's where Kitty's garden came in.

When the matter of my initiation came up she said, "In order for you to reach the spirit somebody has got to suffer. I'll suffer for you because I'm strong. It might be the death of you."

It was in October 1928, when I was a pupil of hers, that I shared in a hoodoo dance. This was not a pleasure dance, but ceremonial. In another generation African dances were held in Congo Square, now Beauregard Square. Those were held for social purposes and were of the same type as the fire dances and jumping dances of the present in the Bahamas. But the hoodoo dance is done for a specific purpose. It is always a case of death-to-the-enemy that calls forth a dance. They are very rare even in New Orleans now, even within the most inner circle, and no layman ever participates, nor has ever been allowed to witness such a ceremony.

This is how the dance came to be held. I sat with my teacher in her front room as the various cases were disposed of. It was my business to assist wherever possible, such as running errands for materials or verifying addresses, locating materials in the various drawers and cabinets, undressing and handling patients, writing out formulas as they were dictated, and finally making "hands." * At last, of course, I could do all of the work while she looked on and made corrections where necessary.

This particular day, a little before noon, came Rachael Roe. She was dry with anger, hate, outraged confidence and desire for revenge. John Doe had made violent love to her; had lain in her bed and bosom for the last three years; had received of Rachael everything material and emotional a woman can give. They had both worked and saved and had contributed to a joint savings account. Now, only the day before yesterday, he had married another. He had lured a young and pretty girl to his bed with Rachael's earnings, yes. Had set up housekeeping with Rachael's sweat and blood. She had gone to him and he had laughed at his former sweetheart, yes. The police could do nothing, no. The bank was sorry, but they could do nothing, no. So Rachael had come to Kitty.

Did she still love her John Doe? Perhaps; she didn't know. If he would return to her she should strive to forget, but she was certain he'd not return.

* Manufacturing certain luck charms.

How could he? But if he were dead she could smile again, yes—could go back to her work and save some more money, yes. Perhaps she might even meet a man who could restore her confidence in menfolk.

Kitty appraised her quickly. "A dance could be held for him that would carry him away right now, but they cost something."

"How much?"

"A whole lot. How much kin you bring me?"

"I got thirty-seven dollars."

"Dat ain't enough. Got to pay de dancers and set de table."

One hundred dollars was agreed upon. It was paid by seven o'clock that same night. We were kept very busy, for the dance was set from ten to one the next day, those being bad hours. I ran to certain addresses to assemble a sort of college of bishops to be present and participate. The table was set with cake, wine, roast duck and barbecued goat.

By nine-thirty the next morning the other five participants were there and had dressed for the dance. A dispute arose about me. Some felt I had not gone far enough to dance. I could wait upon the altar, but not take the floor. Finally I was allowed to dance, as a delegate for my master who had a troublesome case of neuritis. The food was being finished off in the kitchen.

Promptly on the stroke of ten Death mounted his black draped throne and assumed his regal crown, Death being represented by a rudely carved wooden statue, bust length. A box was draped in black sateen and Kitty placed him upon it and set his red crown on. She hobbled back to her seat. I had the petition and the name of the man written on seven slips of paper—one for each participant. I was told to stick them in Death's grinning mouth. I did so, so that the end of each slip protruded. At the command I up-ended nine black tapers that had been dressed by a bath in whiskey and bad vinegar, and bit off the butt end to light, calling upon Death to take notice. As I had been instructed, I said: "Spirit of Death, take notice I am fixing your candles for you. I want you to hear me." I said this three times and the assembly gave three snaps with the thumb and middle finger.

The candles were set upside down and lighted on the altar, three to the left of Death, three to the right, and three before him.

I resumed my seat, and everyone was silent until Kitty was possessed. The exaltation caught like fire. Then B. arose drunkenly and danced a few steps. The clapping began lightly. He circled the room, then prostrated himself before the altar, and, getting to his hands and knees, with his teeth pulled one of the slips from the jaws of Death. He turned a violent somersault and began the dance, not intricate, but violent and muscle-twitching.

We were to dance three hours, and the time was divided equally, so that the more participants the less time each was called upon to dance. There were six of us, since Kitty could not actively participate, so that we each had thirty minutes to dance. Plenty of liquor was provided so that when one appeared exhausted the bottle was pressed to his lips and he danced on. But the fury of the rhythm more than the stimulant kept the dancers going. The heel-patting was a perfect drum rhythm, and the hand clapping had various stimulating breaks. At any rate no one fell from exhaustion, though I know that even I, the youngest, could not have danced continuously on an ordinary dance floor unsupported by a partner for that length of time.

Nearly all ended on the moment in a twitchy collapse, and the next most inspired prostrated himself and began his dance with the characteristic somersault. Death was being continuously besought to follow the footsteps of John Doe. There was no regular formula. They all "talked to him" in their own way, the others calling out to the dancer to "talk to him." Some of the postures were obscene in the extreme. Some were grotesque, limping steps of old men and women. Some were mere agile leapings. But the faces! That is where the dedication lay.

When the fourth dancer had finished and lay upon the floor retching in every muscle, Kitty was taken. The call had come for her. I could not get upon the floor quickly enough for the others and was hurled before the altar. It got me there and I danced, I don't know how, but at any rate, when we sat about the table later, all agreed that Mother Kitty had done well to take me.

I have neglected to say that one or two of the dancers remained upon the floor "in the spirit" after their dance and had to be lifted up and revived at the end.

Death had some of all the food placed before him. An uncorked pint of good whiskey was right under his nose. He was paid fifteen cents and remained on his throne until one o'clock that night. Then all of the food before him was taken up with the tablecloth on which it rested and was thrown into the Mississippi River.

The person danced upon is not supposed to live more than nine days after the dance. I was very eager to see what would happen in this case. But five days after the dance John Doe deserted his bride for the comforting arms of Rachael and she hurried to Mother Kitty to have the spell removed. She said he complained of breast pains and she was fearfully afraid for him. So I was sent to get the beef heart out of the cemetery (which had been put there as a part of the routine), and John and Rachael made use of the new furniture bought for his bride. I think he feared that Rachael might have him fixed, so he probably fled to her as soon as the zest for a new wife had abated.

Kitty began by teaching me various ways of bringing back a man or woman who had left his or her mate. She had plenty to work on, too. In love cases the client is often told what to do at home. Minnie Foster was the best customer Kitty had. She wanted something for every little failing in her lover. Kitty said to her one day, "You must be skeered of yourself with that man of yours."

"No, Ma'am, I ain't. But I love him and I just want to make sure. Just you give me something to make his love more stronger."

"Alright, Minnie, I'll do it, but you ain't got no reason to be so unsettled with me behind you. Do like I say and you'll be alright.

"Use six red candles. Stick sixty pins in each candle—thirty on each side. Write the name of your sweetheart three times on a small square of paper and stick it underneath the candle. Burn one of these prepared candles each night for six nights. Make six slips of paper and write the name of the loved one once on each slip. Then put a pin in the paper on all four sides of the name. Each morning take up the sixty pins left from the burning of the candles, and save them. Then smoke the slip of paper with the four pins in it in incense smoke and bury it with the pins under your door step. The piece of paper with the name written on it three times, upon which each candle stands while burning, must be kept each day until the last candle is burned. Then bury it in the same hole with the rest. When you are sticking the pins in the candles, keep repeating: 'Tumba Walla, Bumba Walla, bring Gabe Staggers back to me.' "

Minnie paid her five dollars, thanked her loudly and hurried off to tighten the love-shackles on her Gabriel. But the following week she was back again.

"Ain't you got dat man to you wishes, yet, Minnie?" Kitty asked, half in fun and half in impatience.

"He love me, I b'lieve, but he gone off to Mobile with a construction gang and I got skeered he might not come back. Something might delay him on his trip."

"Oh, alright Minnie, go do like I say and he'll sure be back. Write the name of the absent party six times on paper. Put the paper in a water glass with two tablespoons full of quicksilver on it. Write his or her name three times each on six candles and burn one on a window sill in the daytime for six days."

Minnie paid and went home, but a week later she was back, washed down in tears. So Kitty gave her a stronger help.

"This is bound to bring him. Can't help it, Minnie. Now go home and stop fretting and do this:

"Write his name three times. Dig a hole in the ground. Get a left-foot soiled-sock from him secretly. His hatband may be used also. Put the paper with the name in the hole first. Then the sock or hatband. Then light a red candle on top of it all and burn it. Put a spray of Sweet Basil in a glass of water beside the candle. Light the candle at noon and burn until one. Light it again at six P.M. and burn till seven. (Always pinch out a candle—never blow it.) After the candle is lit, turn a barrel over the hole. When you get it in place, knock on it three times to call the spirit and say: 'Tumba Walla, Bumba Walla, bring Gabriel Staggers home to me.' "

We saw nothing of Minnie for six weeks, then she came in another storm of tears.

"Miss Kitty, Gabriel done got to de place I can't tell him his eye is black. What can I do to rule de man I love?"

"Do like I say, honey, and you can rule. Get his sock. Take one silver dime, some hair from his head or his hatband. Lay the sock out on a table, bottom up. Write his name three times and put it on the sock. Place the dime on the name and the hair or hatband on the dime. Put a piece of 'he' Lodestone* on top of the hair and sprinkle it with steel dust. As you do this, say, 'Feed the he, feed the she.' That is what you call feeding the Lodestone. Then fold the sock heel on the toe and roll it all up together, tight. Pin the bundle by crossing two needles. Then wet it with whiskey and set it up over a door. And don't 'low him to go off no more, do you going to lose all control.

"Now listen, honey, this is the way to change a man's mind about going away: Take the left shoe, set it up straight, then roll it one-half over first to the right, then to the left. Roll it to a coming-in door and point it straight in the door, and he can't leave. Hatband or sock can be made into a ball and rolled the same way: but it must be put under the sill or over the door."

Once Sis Cat got hongry and caught herself a rat and set herself down to eat 'im. Rat tried and tried to git loose but Sis Cat was too fast and strong. So jus' as de cat started to eat 'im he says, "Hol' on dere, Sis Cat! Ain't you got no manners atall? You going set up to de table and eat 'thout washing yo' face and hands?"

Sis Cat was mighty hongry but she hate for de rat to think she ain't got no manners, so she went to de water and washed her face and hands and when she got back de rat was gone.

So de cat caught herself a rat again and set down to eat. So de Rat said, "Where's yo' manners at, Sis Cat? You going to eat 'thout washing yo' face and hands?"

"Oh, Ah got plenty manners," de cat told 'im. "But Ah eats mah dinner and washes mah face and uses mah manners afterwards." So she et right on 'im and washed her face and hands. And cat's been washin' after eatin' ever since.

I'm sitting here like Sis Cat, washing my face and usin' my manners.

* Magnetic iron ore.

TONI MORRISON

Born in Ohio in 1931, Toni Morrison currently lives in New York City, where she is a senior editor at Random House. She has taught literature at Texas Southern University (1955–1957) and at Howard University (1957–1964). Most recently, she has been a guest lecturer in Afro-American literature at Yale University. Her published novels are *The Bluest Eye* (1971), *Sula* (1974), and *Song of Solomon* (1977).

"INTIMATE THINGS IN PLACE"
A Conversation with Toni Morrison

[*Stepto*]: *I want to start with something we've talked about before, and that is this extraordinary sense of place in your novels. By that I mean you create communities, the community that Pecola, Claudia and the rest live in, in* The Bluest Eye, *and of course, in* Sula, *the Bottom. The places are set in time; there are addresses—we know Sula's address, right down to the house number. Years are mentioned, seasons are mentioned, details are given, and I was struck by these features in two ways. First, by the extent to which you seem to be trying to create specific geographical landscapes, and second, by how landscape seems to perform different functions in the two novels.*

[Morrison]: I can't account for all aspects of it. I know that I never felt like an American or an Ohioan or even a Lorainite. I never felt like a citizen. But I felt very strongly—not much with the first book; more with the second; and very much with the one I'm working on now—I felt a very strong sense of place, not in terms of the country or the state, but in terms of the details, the feeling, the mood of the community, of the town. In the first book, I was clearly pulling straight out of what autobiographical information I had. I didn't create that town. It's clearer to me now in my memory of it than when I lived there—and I haven't really lived there since I was seventeen years old. Also, I think some of it is just a woman's strong sense of being in

This interview was conducted in Ms. Morrison's office at Random House Publishers in New York City on May 19, 1976. The interviewer is Robert B. Stepto.

a room, a place, or in a house. Sometimes my relationship to things in a house would be a little different from, say, my brother's or my father's or my sons'. I clean them and I move them and I do very intimate things "in place": I am sort of rooted in it, so that writing about being in a room looking out, or being in a world looking out, or living in a small definite place, is probably very common among most women anyway.

The other thing was that when I wrote *Sula* I was interested in making the town, the community, the neighborhood, as strong as a character as I could, without actually making it "The Town, they," because the most extraordinary thing about any group, and particularly our group, is the fantastic variety of people and things and behavior and so on. But nevertheless there was a cohesiveness there in my mind and it was true in my life. And though I live in New York, I don't relate easily to very, very large cities, because I have never lived in a huge city except this one. My tendency is to focus on neighborhoods and communities. And the community, the black community—I don't like to use that term because it came to mean something much different in the sixties and seventies, as though we had to forge one—but it had seemed to me that it was always there, only we called it the "neighborhood." And there was this life-giving, very, very strong sustenance that people got from the neighborhood. One lives, really, not so much in your house as you do outside of it, within the "compounds," within the village, or whatever it is. And legal responsibilities, all the responsibilities that agencies now have, were the responsibilities of the neighborhood. So that people were taken care of, or locked up or whatever. If they were sick, other people took care of them; if they needed something to eat, other people took care of them; if they were old, other people took care of them; if they were mad, other people provided a small space for them, or related to their madness or tried to find out the limits of their madness.

They also meddled in your lives a lot. They felt that you belonged to them. And every woman on the street could raise everybody's child, and tell you exactly what to do and you felt that connection with those people and they felt it with you. And when they punished us or hollered at us, it was, at the time, we thought, so inhibiting and so cruel, and it's only much later that you realize that they were interested in you. Interested in you—they cared about your behavior. And then I knew my mother as a Church woman, and a Club woman—and there was something special about when she said "Sister," and when all those other women said "Sister." They meant that in a very, very fundamental way. There were some interesting things going on inside people and they seemed to me the most extraordinary people in the world. But at the same time, there was this kind of circle around them—we lived within 23 blocks—which they could not break.

[S]: *From what you're telling me, it would seem that creating Medallion in* Sula *might have been a more difficult task than creating the neighborhood in* The Bluest Eye.

[M]: Oh, yes, Medallion was more difficult because it was wholly fabricated; but it was based on something my mother had said some time ago. When she first got married, she and my father went to live in Pittsburgh. And I remember her telling me that in those days all the black people lived in the hills of Pittsburgh, but now they lived amid the smoke and dirt in the heart of that city. It's clear up in those hills, and so I used that idea, but in a small river town in Ohio. Ohio is right on the Kentucky border, so there's not much difference between it and the "South." It's an interesting state from the point of view of black people because it is right there by the Ohio River, in the south, and at its northern tip is Canada. And there were these fantastic abolitionists there, and also the Ku Klux Klan lived there. And there is only really one large city. There are hundreds of small towns and that's where most black people live. You know, in most books, they're always in New York or some exotic place, but most of our lives are spent in little towns, little towns all throughout this country. And that's where, you know, we live. And that's where the juices came from and that's where we *made it,* not made it in terms of success but made who we are. So I loved writing about that because it was so wide open.

Sula was hard, for me; very difficult to make up that kind of character. Not difficult to think it up, but difficult to describe a woman who could be used as a classic type of evil force. Other people could use her that way. And at the same time, I didn't want to make her freakish or repulsive or unattractive. I was interested at that time in doing a very old, worn-out idea, which was to do something with good and evil, but putting it in different terms. And I wanted Nel to be a warm, conventional woman, one of those people you know are going to pay the gas bill and take care of the children. You don't have to ask about them. And they are magnificent, because they take these small tasks and they do them. And they do them without the fire and without the drama and without all of that. They get the world's work done somehow.

[S]: *How did Nel get to that point, given the background you provided her with? Why does her grandmother have those "questionable roots"? How does that lead to Nel?*

[M]: It has to do with Nel's attraction for Sula. To go back, a black woman at that time who didn't want to do the conventional thing, had only one other kind of thing to do. If she had talent she went into the theater. And if she had a little voice, she could sing, or she could go to a big town and she could pretend she was dancing or whatever. That was the only outlet if you chose not to get married and have children. That was it. Or you could walk the streets; although you might get there sort of accidentally; you might not choose to do that. So that Nel's grandmother just means that there's that kind of life from which Nel comes; that's another woman who was a hustler, that part is already in Nel and accounts for her attraction to Sula. And also those are the kinds of women there were. Here is this woman,

Nel, whose mother is just busy, busy, busy, reacting against her own mother, and goes to the far extreme of having this rather neat, rather organized, rather pompous life, forcing all of the creativity out of Nel. But Nel wants it anyway, which is what makes it possible for her to have a very close friend who is so different from her, in the way she looks at life. And I wanted to make all of that sort of reasonable. Because what was the attraction of Nel for Sula? Sula for Nel? Why would they become friends in the first place? You see? And so I wanted to say, as much as I could say it without being overbearing, that there was a little bit of both in each of those two women, and that if they had been one person, I suppose they would have been a rather marvelous person. But each one lacked something that the other one had.

[S]: *It's interesting you should mention this, because my students wanted to pursue the question of Sula and Nel being perhaps two sides of the same person, or two sides of one extraordinary character. But this character is nevertheless fractured into Sula and Nel.*

[M]: Precisely. They're right on target because that was really in my mind. It didn't come to me quite that way. I started out by thinking that one can never really define good and evil. Sometimes good looks like evil; sometimes evil looks like good—you never really know what it is. It depends on what uses you put it to. Evil is as useful as good is, although good is generally more interesting; it's more complicated. I mean, living a good life is more complicated than living an evil life, I think. And also, it wasn't hard to talk about that because everyone has something in mind when they think about what a good life is. So I put that in conventional terms, for a woman: someone who takes care of children and so on and is responsible and goes to church and so on. For the opposite kind of character, which is a woman who's an adventurer, who breaks rules, she can either be a criminal—which I wasn't interested in—or lead a kind of cabaret life—which I also wasn't interested in. But what about the woman who doesn't do any of that but is nevertheless a rule-breaker, a kind of law-breaker, a lawless woman? Not a law-abiding woman. Nel knows and believes in all the laws of that community. She *is* the community. She believes in its values. Sula does not. She does not believe in any of those laws and breaks them all. Or ignores them. So that she becomes more interesting—I think, particularly to younger girls—because of that quality of abandon.

But there's a fatal flaw in all of that, you know, in both of those things. Nel does not make that "leap"—she doesn't know about herself. Even at the end, she doesn't know. She's just beginning. She just barely grabs on at the end in those last lines. So that living totally by the law and surrendering completely to it without questioning anything sometimes makes it impossible to know anything about yourself. Nel doesn't even know what questions she's asking. When they come to touch one another in the bedroom, when Sula's sick—Nel doesn't even know why she's there. Sula, on the other hand, knows all there is to know about herself because she examines herself, she is experimental with herself, she's perfectly willing to think the unthinkable thing and so on. But she has trouble making a connection with other people and just feeling that lovely sense of accomplishment of being close in a very strong way. She felt that in a way, of course, with Nel, but then obviously they lost one another in friendship. She was able to retrieve it rather nicely with a man, which is lovely, except that in so many instances, with men, the very thing that would attract a man to a woman in the first place might be the one thing she would give over once she learned Nel's lesson, which is love as possession. You own somebody and then you begin to want them there all the time, which is a community law. Marriage, faithfulness, fidelity; the beloved belongs to one person and can't be shared with other people— that's a community value which Sula learned when she fell in love with Ajax, which he wasn't interested in learning.

[S]: *Richard Wright said in "How Bigger Was Born" that there were many Biggers that went into creating Bigger Thomas. Are there many Pecolas in Pecola? Or many Sulas in Sula?*

[M]: Oh, yes! Well, I think what I did is what every writer does—once you have an idea, then you try to find a character who can manifest the idea for you. And then you have to spend a long time trying to get to know who those people are, who that character is. So you take what there is from whomever you know. Sula—I think this was really part of the difficulty—I didn't know anyone like her. I never knew a woman like that at any rate. But I knew women who looked like that, who looked like they *could be* like that. And then you remember women who were a little bit different in the town, you know; there's always a little bit of gossip and there's always a little bit of something. There's a woman in our town now who is an absolute riot. She can do anything she wants to do. And it occurred to me about twenty years ago how depleted that town would be if she ever left. Everybody wanted her out, and she was a crook and she was mean and she had about twenty husbands—and she was just, you know, a huge embarrassment. Nevertheless, she really and truly was one of the reasons that they called each other on the telephone. They sort of used her excitement, her flavor, her carelessness, her restlessness, and so on. And that quality is what I used in Sula.

[S]: *What about Sula's mother and grandmother?*

[M]: Oh, Hannah, the mother—I tell you, I think I feel more affection for her than for anybody else in that book. I just loved her. What I was trying to do was to be very provocative without using all of the traditional devices of provocation. And I think—that's why I wrote so slowly—I think I know how to do it by simply relying an awful lot on what I believe the reader already knows. I wanted Sula to be missed by the reader. That's why she dies early. There's a lot of book after she dies, you know. I wanted them to miss her presence in that book as that town missed her presence. I also wanted them to dislike her a lot, and to be fascinated, perhaps, but also to feel that thing that the town might feel—that this is something askew. And I wanted for them to realize at some point—and I don't know if anybody ever realizes it—that she never does anything as bad as her grandmother or her mother did. However, they're alike; her grandmother kills her son, plays god, names people and, you know, puts her hand on a child. You know, she's god-like, she manipulates—all in the best interest. And she is very, very possessive about other people, that is, as a king is. She decided that her son was living a life that was not worth his time. She meant it was too painful for her; you know, the way you kill a dog when he breaks his leg because he can't stand the pain. He may very well be able to stand it, but you can't, so that's why you get rid of him. The mother, of course, was slack. She had no concept of love and possession. She liked to be laid, she liked to be touched, but she didn't want any confusion of relationships and so on. She's very free and open about that. Her relationship to her daughter is almost one of uninterest. She would do things for her, but she's not particularly interested in her.

[S]: *That conversation in her kitchen . . .*

[M]: That's right: "I love her, but I don't like her," which is an honest statement at any rate. And she'd sleep with anybody, you know, husbands. She just does it. But interestingly enough, the point was that the women in the town who knew that—they didn't like the fact—but at the same time *that* was something they could understand. Lust, sexual lust, and so on. So that when she dies, they will come to her aid. Now Sula might take their husbands, but she was making judgments. You see what it was—it wasn't about love. It wasn't about even lust. Nobody knows what that was about. And also, Sula did the one terrible thing for black people which was to put her grandmother in an old folks' home, which was outrageous, you know. You take care of people! So *that* would be her terrible thing. But at the same time, she is more strange, more formidable than either of those other two women because they were first of all within the confines of the community and their sensibilities were informed by it. Essentially, they were pacific in the sense of what they did do. They wanted to make things come together; you know, bring it together. Hannah didn't want to disturb anything. She did her work and she took care of people and so on; and Eva was generous, wide-spirited, and made some great sacrifices.

[S]: *I'm fascinated by all of the women in the two novels: your portraits are so rich. It's not just the main characters—you get that woman from Meridian, Geraldine, in* The Bluest Eye, *and of course Mrs. McTeer, who isn't always talked about, but she certainly is the kind of figure you were describing earlier as a mother to anybody and everybody who will take you in and knows how to raise everybody. With all of these various characters that you've created, certainly you must have some response to the feeling in certain literary circles that black women should be portrayed a certain way. I'm thinking now of the kinds of criticism that have been lodged against Gayl Jones.*

[M]: Do you mean black women as victims, that they should not be portrayed as victims?

[S]: *Either that or even—and I'm thinking more of Sula here—as emasculating.*

[M]: Oh yes. Well, in *The Bluest Eye,* I try to show a little girl as a total and complete victim of whatever was around her. But black women have held, have been given, you know, the cross. They don't walk near it. They're often on it. And they've borne that, I think, extremely well. I think everybody knows, deep down, that black men were emasculated by white men, period. And that black women didn't take any part in that. However, black women have had some enormous responsibilities, which in these days people call freedoms—in those days, they were called responsibilities—they lived, you know, working in other people's, white people's, houses and taking care of that and working in their own houses and so on and they have been on the labor market. And nobody paid them that much attention in terms of threats, and so on, so they had a certain amount of "freedom." But they did a very extraordinary job of just taking on that kind of responsibility and in so doing, they tell people what to do. Now I have to admit, however, that it's a new idea to me—the emasculating black woman. It really is new— that is, in the last few years. I can only go by my own experience, my own family, the black men I knew—the men I knew called the shots, whether they were employed or unemployed. And even in our classic set of stereotypes—Sapphire and Kingfish?—he did anything he was big enough to do! Anything! Talk 'bout free! And she bitched—that she was going to work and so on. But there is an incredible amount of magic and feistiness in black men that nobody has been able to wipe out. But everybody has tried.

Now, Sula—I don't regard her as a typical black woman at all. And the fact that the community responds to her that way means that she's unusual. So she's not the run-of-the-mill average black woman.

[S]: *If she weren't unusual, they'd know how to deal with her.*

[M]: That's right. There wouldn't have been that confusion about her. They did not know how to deal with her. So she's very atypical and perhaps she would be, you know, a kind of ball-breaker, in that sense. However, the one man who talked to her, and thought she was worthy of conversation, and who let her be, was the one man she could relate to on that level that would make her want something she had never been interested in before, which was a permanent relationship. He was a man who was not intimidated by her; he was interested in her. He treated her as a whole person, not as an extension of himself, not as a vessel, not as a symbol. Their sex was not one person killing the other—that's why I pictured her on top of him, you know, like a tree. He was secure enough and free enough and bright enough —he wasn't terrorized by her because she was odd. He was interested. I think there was a line in the book—he hadn't met an interesting woman since his mother, who was sitting out in the woods "making roots." When a man is whole himself, when he's touched the borders of his own life, and he's not proving something to somebody else—white men or other men and so on— then the threats of emasculation, the threats of castration, the threats of somebody taking over disappear. Ajax is strong enough. He's a terribly unemployed dude, who has interests of his own, whose mother neglected him, but nevertheless assumed all sorts of things about him that he lived up to like he knew he was doing. So he had a different kind of upbringing. Now that, I think, is interesting; that part of it interested me a lot, so that when he would see a woman like Sula, who had been somewhere and had some rather different views about life and so on, he was not intimidated at all. Whereas a man like Jude, who was doing a rather routine, macho thing, would split—you know, he was too threatened by all of that. Just the requirements of staying in the house and having to apologize to his wife were too much for him.

[S]: *Now you mention Jude, and that balance between Jude and Ajax is clear in the book. What about Ajax and Cholly Breedlove in* The Bluest Eye?

[M]: Exactly alike, in that sense. I don't mean that their backgrounds were alike. But in a way they sort of—through neglect of the fact that someone was not there—made up themselves. They allowed themselves to be whomever they were. Cholly, of course, lives a very tragic life, tragic in the sense that there was no reward, but he is the thing I keep calling a "free man," not free in the legal sense, but free in his head. You see, this was a free man who could do a lot of things; and I think it's a way of talking about what some people call the "bad nigger." Not in the sense of one who is so carousing, but that adjective "bad" meaning, you know, bad and good. This is a man who is stretching, you know, he's stretching, he's going all the way within his own mind and within whatever his outline might be. Now that's the tremendous possibility for masculinity among black men. And you see it a lot. Sometimes you see it when they do art things, sometimes just in personality and so on. And it's very, very deep and very, very complex and such men as they are not very busy. They may end up in sort of twentieth-century, contemporary terms being also unemployed. They may be in prison. They may be doing all sorts of things. But they are adventuresome in that regard.

And then when you draw a woman who is like that, which is unusual and uncivilized, within our context, then a man like that is interested in her. No, he doesn't want to get married, he doesn't want to do all those things, for all sorts of reasons, some of which are purely sociological. The other kind of man who is more like the Nel syndrome would be very, very preoccupied with it, and his masculinity is threatened all the time. But then you see a man who has had certain achievements—and I don't mean social achievements—but he's been able to manipulate crap games or, you know, just do things—because Cholly has done *everything*—in his life. So that by the time he met Pauline, he was able to do whatever his whims suggested and it's that kind of absence of control that I wanted—you know, obviously, that I'm interested in characters who are lawless in that regard. They make up their lives, or they find out who they are. So in that regard Cholly Breedlove is very much like Ajax.

[S]: *Is the progression from girlhood in* The Bluest Eye *to womanhood in* Sula *an intentional progression? Might we view the two novels in these terms?*

[M]: Yes. I think I was certainly interested in talking about black girlhood in *The Bluest Eye* and not so interested in it in *Sula*. I wanted to move it into the other part of their life. That is, what do the Claudias and Friedas, those feisty little girls, grow up to be? Precisely. No question about that.

The book that I'm writing now is about a man, and a lot of the things that I learned by writing about Cholly and Ajax and Jude are at least points of departure, leaping-off places, for the work that I'm doing now. The focus is on two men. One is very much like Ajax and Cholly in his youth, so stylish and adventuresome and, I don't know, I think he's truly masculine in the sense of going out too far where you're not supposed to go and running toward confrontations rather than away from them. And risks—taking risks. That quality. One of the men is very much like that. The other will learn to be a complete person, or at least have a notion of it, if I ever get him to the end of the book. When I wrote that section on Cholly in *The Bluest Eye*, I thought it would be very hard for me because I didn't know that as intimately as I knew Pauline. And I thought, well, let me get started on this 'cause I'm going to have a tough time trying to really feel that kind of thing. But it's the only time I've ever written anything in my life when it all came at once. I wrote it straight through. And it took me a long time, maybe eight or nine hours the first time, not stopping at all.

When I got to Pauline, whom I knew so well, I could not do it. I could not make it. I didn't know what to write or how. And I sort of copped out anyway in the book because I used two voices, hers and the author's. There were certain things she couldn't know that I had to come in. And then there were certain things the author would say that I wanted in her language—so that there were the two things, two voices, which I had regarded, at any rate, as a way in which to do something second-best. I couldn't do it straight out the way I did every other section. That was such a fascinating experience for me to perceive Cholly that way.

[S]: *Will these two men in the new book balance as Nel and Sula do?*

[M]: No. That is, they're friends and they're different from each other, but they're not incomplete the way Nel and Sula are. They are completely whoever they are and they don't need another man to give them that. They love each other—I mean, men love the company of other men—they're like that. And they enjoy the barber shop and the pool room and so on, and there's a lot of that because they aren't just interested in themselves. But their relationship is based on something quite different. And I think in the friendship between men there is, you know, something else operating. So the metaphors changed. I couldn't use the same kind of language at all. And it took a long time for the whole thing to fall together because men are different and they are thinking about different things. The language had to be different.

[S]: *Will neighborhood or a sense of neighborhood be just as important in this book?*

[M]: Yes. Well, I have one man who is a sort of middle-class black dude, whose mother was the daughter of the only black doctor. His father, who is a kind of self-taught man, owns a lot of shacks in the black part of the town and he loves things, you know, he's accumulating property and money and so on. And his son is the main character who makes friends with people in the kind of community that is described in *Sula*. You know, it's a different social class, there is a leap, but I don't think the class problems among black people are as great as the class problems among white people. I mean, there's just no real problems with that in terms of language and how men relate to one another—black men relate to one another whatever class they come from.

[S]: *Sort of like people living on the same block, going to the same barber shop . . .*

[M]: Yes, because whatever it is, you know, the little community is by itself. You go to the same barber shop and there you are. So this one has a little bit of money and that one doesn't but it doesn't make any difference because you're thrown into the same and you get your "stuff" from one another.

[S]: *Will there also be a character somewhat like Soaphead Church or Shadrack in this book? Tell me something about your two crazies.*

[M]: Well, in the first place, with Shadrack, I just needed, wanted, a form of madness that was clear and compact to bounce off of Sula's strangeness. And you know, he likes her and she goes to his house and he remembers her and so on. So there's a connection between the two of them. And I wanted the town to respond to him in one way and to her in another. They're both eccentrics, outside the law, except that Shadrack's madness is very organized. He has organized the world. He just wants all this to be done on one day. It's orderly, as madness is—isolation, total isolation and order. You know, it's trying to get order in what is perceived by the madman as a disordered world. So the town understands his own way of organizing chaos, once they find out what he's doing—you know, National Suicide Day.

With Soaphead, I wanted, needed someone to give the child her blue eyes. Now she was asking for something that was just awful—she wanted to have blue eyes and she wanted to be Shirley Temple, I mean, she wanted to do that white trip because of the society in which she lived and, very importantly, because of the black people who helped her want to be that. (The responsibilities are ours. It's our responsibility for helping her believe, helping her come to the point where she wanted that.) I had to have some-one—her mother, of course, made her want it in the first place—who would give her the blue eyes. And there had to be somebody who *could,* who had the means; that kind of figure who dealt with fortune-telling, dream-telling and so on, who would also believe that she was right, that it was preferable for her to have blue eyes. And that would be a person like Soaphead. In other words, he would be wholly convinced that if black people were more like white people they would be better off. And I tried to explain that in terms of his own West Indian background—a kind of English, colonial, Victorian thing drilled into his head which he could not escape. I needed someone to distill all of that, to say, "Yeah, you're right, you need them. Here, I'll give them to you," and really believe that he had done her a favor. Someone who would never question the request in the first place. That kind of black. It was very important in the story that the miracle happen, and she does get them, although I had to make it fairly logical in that only she can see them and that she's really flipped by that time.

[S]: *Does your job as an editor get in the way of your writing? I ask this partly because I remember so well having a creative writing teacher who told me once how his being an English major in college got in the way of his writing, so he became an anthropology major ...*

[M]: In order to free himself?

[S]: *Yes. A number of things can get in the way of writing; lots of teachers of literature would like to write, but perhaps their teaching gets in the way of writing. Now, you are a writer, and an editor, and a teacher—how do you do it?*

[M]: Well, I suspect that full-time teaching would get in the way of writing for me because you have to think a certain way about the literature you're teaching, and I think that would spill over into the way in which one has to think when writing. The critical stance—which is what teaching is—sometimes makes me feel, if I move right into my writing, too self-conscious. You're so aware of the theory and the effort and so on, that you become very self-conscious and maybe a little too tight about it. For me, it has to be very private and very unrelated. When I write, I can't read other people that I like. I have to read detective stories or things like that. I have to feel as if it's being done almost in a very separate womb of my own construction. Wholly free. And because it's the only activity at all that I engage in wholly for myself, it's the one place that I can't have any other interference of that sort.

The editing is no problem, because that is such a different way of thinking about things. I don't have to exercise the same skills or talent. I don't create as an editor, I simply do more of what one does in teaching, but in terms of someone who is creating—you see, that is my work, so I don't feel anything strong or deeply personal about it at all. What I want to do with an author is to get him into the position to do the best work he can, and then to try to publish it so it will receive the widest amount of attention, and look elegant, and be well-received. That's quite different. It's sort of like fishing—you catch fish, which is different from cooking them. You don't have to know one in order to do the other, and you can do one well and not do the other well. So that I don't find a conflict there. The problem, of course, is time, trying to find enough time for all of those things. And I like it all, you know, but probably the only one that I couldn't live without is the writing. I think that if all the publishers disappeared, I would write anyway, because that is a compulsion with me. To write, to think that way.

[S]: *How did the teaching go this term?*

[M]: Oh, I enjoyed it. I really did. I had a good time in both classes and in the "Black Women and Their Fiction" class, it was nice because I was able to discuss contemporary women and maybe introduce students to some women that they had never read before. And also, it was nice going into almost untrammeled territory with them. There isn't a lot of first-rate criticism about black women writers, so that in their papers I insisted that they make reference to the text that we had read in class. And I had given them outlines and general questions which we dealt with in class to get around to a decent topic for term papers. But they knew that they were very free to introduce ideas—in other words, there were not a lot of secondary sources to which they could go. I told them to feel free to draw their own conclusions. A couple of them did really first-rate work.

[S]: *You're quite right—there isn't very much good criticism of black literature and particularly of the literature by black women. What kinds of things do you feel, as a writer, a teacher, and as an editor, need to be pursued in this regard? Should criticism take a particular direction—do certain questions need to be asked more than others?*

[M]: Certain questions occur to me when I try to think of the body of black literature that there is in general and the body of black literature that women have produced. In the course, for example, I was very interested in how contemporary black women looked at the stereotype of black women. Did they accept that role? Did the writers believe, in the works we studied, that that was pretty much the way we were? Were there characters representative of the mammy, whore, whatever? show-girl, whatever? And emasculation and so on? How political were they? Were the writings very, very directed by new political awareness or were they distant from that, were they outside the so-called realm of politics? What were their perceptions about their role? How did they really see themselves? And even—if we could get a little bit deeper, if you could think in terms of not just characters but plot and tone and the attitude of the woman writer toward the world in which she lives—does she really feel burdened and harassed? Frequently, what I found so lacking in most black writing by men that seems to be present in a lot of black women's writing is a sense of joy, in addition to oppression and being women or black or whatever. With some exceptions. Gayl Jones is an exception to that. She never writes about joy. I think that's because she's young. But with others, there is a sense of comfort in being who one is, there's an expression of good times, not in the sense of "going out somewhere." There's a scene in *Sula* where the women are just having some fun, talking to one another. They enjoy that. That kind of woman. In Lucille Clifton's *Generations,* there's that sense of fun and joy. In Toni Cade, there's that sense of high-spiritedness. I don't mean comedy, and I don't mean jokes or anything. But part of this business of living in the world and triumphing over it has to do with a sense that there's some pleasure. And where do they get that pleasure from: How do they look at what we would call beauty in the world? What do they think it is? What pleases them? Just to see what the black woman's sensibilities are when she writes. What is she preoccupied with? What does she think are the crucial sorts of questions about existence, life, man-woman relationships? Are they seen the same way as the way in which the men have seen them?

[S]: *Most of the major male characters in black literature are in motion. They're frequently much more like Ajax—maybe not always as grand and high-spirited as Ajax—but mobile. I think of such books as* Invisible Man *and* Autobiography of an Ex-Colored Man, *where there's this movement and quite often, there's no name, in contrast to how women are named, how they are lovingly named. An exception to this might be Leon Forrest.*

[M]: But even there, he has that marvelous man, James Fishbond, you know, who is just a traveling man. Both of these things are very interesting to me. The name thing is a very, very strong theme in the book that I'm writing, the absence of a name given at all, the odd names and the slave names, the whole business, the feeling of anonymity, the feeling of orphanage. That's very important and became immediately clear to me in this new book. But the first thing you said about being in motion is also true, because I think that one of the major differences between black men's work— the major black characters—and black women's work is precisely that. The big scene is the traveling Ulysses scene, for black men. They are moving. Trains—you hear those men talk about trains like they were their first lover— the names of the trains, the times of the trains! And, boy, you know, they spread their seed all over the world. They are really moving! Perhaps it's because they don't have a land, they don't have dominion. You can trace that historically, and one never knows what would have been the case if we'd never been tampered with at all. But that going from town to town or place to place or looking out and over and beyond and changing and so on—that, it seems to me, is one of the monumental themes in black literature about men. That's what they do. It is the Ulysses theme, the leaving home. And then there's no one place that one settles. I mean, one travels. And I don't mean this in the sense of the Joycean character or even in the sense of just going off to find one's fortune in the classic sort of fairy tale, going off to see where the money is. But something else. Curiosity, what's around the corner, what's across the hill, what's in the valley, what's down the track. Go find out what that is, you know! And in the process of finding, they are also making themselves. Although in sociological terms that is described as a major failing of black men—they do not stay home and take care of their children, they are not there—that has always been to me one of the most attractive features about black male life. I guess I'm not suppose to say that. But the fact that they would split in a minute just delights me. It's part of that whole business of breaking ground, doing the other thing. They would leave, go someplace else. There was always that possibility. They were never—I don't say they were never, obviously there were exceptions to all of this—but they didn't just let it happen, just let it happen. That's part of that interesting magic I was talking about. And you know, the traveling musician, the theater group, those people who just stayed on the road, lived a different life. It's very beautiful, it's very interesting, and in that way, you know, they lived in the country, they lived here, they went all over it.

[S]: *It's interesting to compare that motif to what you did to* Sula, *in that she is in motion in a sense . . .*

[M]: Very much.

[S]: *. . . at the same time that she is most stationary and in those enclosures, like that bedroom where she dies.*

[M]: She is a masculine character in that sense. She will do the kinds of things that normally only men do, which is why she's so strange. She really behaves like a man. She picks up a man, drops a man, the same way a man picks up a woman, drops a woman. And that's her thing. She's masculine in that sense. She's adventuresome, she trusts herself, she's not scared, she really ain't scared. And she is curious and will leave and try anything. So that quality of masculinity—and I mean this in the pure sense—in a woman at that time is outrage, total outrage. She can't get away with that—unless she were in this sort of strange environment, this alien environment—for the normal—which would be the theater world, in which you realize, the people are living, even there, by laws. You know, somebody should do something interesting on that kind of show business woman—Billie Holiday, Bessie Smith—not just their art form, but their lives. It's incredible, that sense of adventure that those women had. And I think that's why they were there in the first place. They were outside of that little community value thing. It's more normal among men, but it's attractive, and with men, it seems to me to be one of the very interesting things to talk about when one is doing any criticism of black writing, rather than doing those books in which you do five hundred people and say a little bit about this one, a little bit about that one. If somebody could get one or two of the really major themes that are part and parcel of this canon. And there are some traceable, identifiable themes, and that's the kind of criticism that I would love to see. There may be some things that you could do with both men and women. But certainly this seems to me one of the major themes. And then there's the black woman as parent, not as a mother or father, but as a parent, as a sort of umbrella figure, culture-bearer, in that community with not just her children but all children, her relationship in that sense, how that is handled and treated and understood by writers, what that particular role is. We talk about all these things in terms of what her huge responsibilities have been, but a really penetrating analysis might be very helpful.

[S]: *You've just described, very well, some new directions for criticism. Can you say something about new directions in fiction?*

[M]: What I think is happening?

[S]: *Well, what you think is happening, what may happen in fiction by some of the writers we've been discussing, in this decade.*

[M]: Oh, I went to some meeting recently and there was a great deal of despair, it seemed to me, about what was happening in publishing and black fiction, the suggestion being that there was not much being published but that now it's not so popular anymore and that white publishers have decided that our age is over and that we are no longer fashionable as we were in the late sixties or early seventies. I think part of that's right—that is, we're no longer fashionable in that sense—all of which I am so grateful for, absolutely relieved to find, because some brilliant writers, I think, can surface now. Once you get off of the television screen, you can go home and do your work, because your responsibilities are different. Now I don't mean that there's any lessening of political awareness or political work, but I do think that one can be more fastidious, more discriminating. And it's open, it's just freer, that's all, and there's room, there's lots of room. People tend to think that the whole literary thing is a kind of pyramid, that somebody is on top, which is total anathema to me. There is enormous space! I think of it in terms of the one other art form in which black people have always excelled and that is music, an art form that opens doors, rather than closes them, where there are more possibilities, not fewer. But to continue to write the way somebody believes is the prescribed way is death. And if I know anything about black artists, I know they don't pay any attention to any prescriptions that anybody gives them at all!

It's harder perhaps in literature, because it has to be purchased by somebody in a publishing house, so that you're always under the eye of some other person. Nevertheless, it's exciting and it's new and it's marvelous and it's as though somebody pulled out the plug and we were left again to our own devices, not somebody else's, not the television's devices, not the *New York Times'* version of what we were supposed to do, but our own devices, which are the ones which we have to be left to. White writers, you know, write about us all the time. There are major black characters in Updike, in *Ragtime,* in all of them. That's where all the life is. That's where the life is. And the future of American literature is in that direction. I don't mean that's the only group, but that certainly is .one of the major groups. Obviously, lots of people are interested in it, not just for research purposes as you know, but in terms of the gem, the theme, the juice, of fiction. And we are certainly, obviously, interested; we have all sorts of philosophical attitudes about "the predicament." There's that incredible kind of movement which yields an artistic representation of something that one takes for granted in history. I think that accounts for the success of Gayl Jones's first book, where you have the weight of history working itself out in the life of one, two, three people; I mean a large idea, brought down small, and at home, which gives it a universality and a particularity which makes it extraordinary.

But there's so much that nobody ever, ever does. You know, I go sometimes and, just for sustenance, I read those slave narratives— there are sometimes three or four sentences or half a page, each one of which could be developed in an art form, marvelous. Just to figure out how to—you mean to tell me she beat the dogs and the man and pulled a stump out of the ground? Who is she, you know? Who is she? It's just incredible. And all of that will surface, it *will surface,* and my *huge* joy is thinking that I am in some way part of that when I sit here in this office and that somehow there must be those of us in white established publishers where a black author can feel that he's going to go and get some respect—he doesn't have to explain everything—somebody is going to understand what he's trying to do, in his terms, not in somebody else's, but in his. I'm not saying that only black editors can do it, but I'm certainly saying that it's important that we are here to participate, to contribute to "the shelf"—as Forrest likes to call it.

[S]: *I have one last question. What's the name of the new novel?*

[M]: At the moment, it's called *Milkman Dead.* [The novel was published as *Song of Solomon* in the fall of 1977.]

TRADITIONS, NARRATIVES, AND FICTION

ALICE WALKER

Born in 1944 in Georgia, Alice Walker is a contributing editor to *MS* Magazine. Her books include *The Third Life of Grange Copeland* (1970) and *Meridian* (1976), both   novels; *Once* (1968) and *Revolutionary Petunias and Other Poems* (1973), volumes of poetry; *In Love and Trouble* (1973), a collection of short stories; and *Langston Hughes, American Poet* (1974), a biography for children. Her essays and stories have appeared in numerous journals and magazines. She was awarded a Guggenheim in fiction for 1977–1978 and was the recipient of the Lillian Smith Award and a Creative Writing Award from the National Endowment for the Arts, among other fellowships. In 1974 *Revolutionary Petunias and Other Poems* was nominated for a National Book Award, and *In Love and Trouble* won the Rosenthal Award of the National Institute of Arts and Letters.

THE REVENGE OF HANNAH KEMHUFF

In grateful memory of Zora Neale Hurston

I

Two weeks after I became Tante Rosie's apprentice we were visited by a very old woman who was wrapped and contained, almost smothered, in a half-dozen skirts and shawls. Tante Rosie (pronounced Ro'*zee*) told the woman she could see her name, Hannah Kemhuff, written in the air. She told the woman further that she belonged to the Order of the Eastern Star.

The woman was amazed. (And I was, too! Though I learned later that Tante Rosie held extensive files on almost everybody in the county, which she kept in long cardboard boxes under her bed.) Mrs. Kemhuff quickly asked what else Tante Rosie could tell her.

Tante Rosie had a huge tank of water on a table in front of her, like an aquarium for fish, except there were no fish in it. There was nothing but water and I never was able to see anything in it. Tante Rosie, of course, could. While the woman waited Tante Rosie peered deep into the tank of water. Soon she said the water spoke to her and told her that although the woman looked old, she was not. Mrs. Kemhuff said that this was true, and wondered if Tante Rosie knew the reason she looked so old. Tante Rosie said she did not and asked if she would mind telling us about it. (At first Mrs. Kemhuff didn't seem to want me there, but Tante Rosie told her I was trying to learn the rootworking trade and she nodded that she understood and didn't mind. I scrooched down as small as I could at the corner of Tante Rosie's table, smiling at her so she wouldn't feel embarrassed or afraid.)

"It was during the Depression," she began, shifting in her seat and adjusting the shawls. She wore so many her back appeared to be humped!

"Of course," said Tante Rosie, "and you were young and pretty."

"How do you know that?" exclaimed Mrs. Kemhuff. "That is true. I had been married already five years and had four small children and a husband with a wandering eye. But since I married young—"

"Why, you were little more than a child," said Tante Rosie.

"Yes," said Mrs. Kemhuff. "I were not quite twenty years old. And it was hard times everywhere, all over the country and, I suspect, all over the world. Of course, no one had television in those days, so we didn't know. I don't even now know if it was invented. We had a radio before the Depression which my husband won in a poker game, but we sold it somewhere along the line to buy a meal. Anyway, we lived for as long as we could on the money I brought in as a cook in a sawmill. I cooked cabbage and cornpone for twenty men for two dollars a week. But then the mill closed down, and my husband had already been out of work for some time. We were on the point of starvation. We was so hungry, and the children were getting so weak, that after I had crapped off the last leaves from the collard stalks I couldn't wait for new leaves to grow back. I dug up the collards, roots and all. After we ate that there was nothing else.

"As I said, there was no way of knowing whether hard times was existing around the world because we did not then have a television set. And we had sold the radio. However, as it happened, hard times hit everybody we knew in Cherokee County. And for that reason the government sent food stamps which you could get if you could prove you were starving. With a few of them stamps you could go into town to a place they had and get so much and so much fat back, so much and so much of corn meal, and so much and so much of (I think it was) red beans. As I say, we was, by then, desperate. And my husband pervailed on me for us to go. I never wanted to do it, on account of I have always been proud. My father, you know, used to be one of the biggest colored peanut growers in Cherokee County and we never had to ask nobody for nothing.

"Well, what had happened in the meantime was this: My sister, Carrie Mae—"

"A tough girl, if I remember right," said Tante Rosie.

"Yes," said Mrs. Kemhuff, "bright, full of spunk. Well, she were at that time living in the North. In Chicago. And she were working for some good white people that give her they old clothes to send back down here. And I tell you they were good things. And I was glad to get them. So, as it was gitting to be real cold, I dressed myself and my husband and the children up in them clothes. For see, they was made up North to be worn up there where there's snow at and they were warm as toast."

"Wasn't Carrie Mae later killed by a gangster?" asked Tante Rosie.

"Yes, she were," said the woman, anxious to go on with her story. "He were her husband."

"Oh," said Tante Rosie quietly.

"Now, so I dresses us all up in our new finery and with our stomachs growling all together we goes marching off to ask for what the government said was due us as proud as ever we knew how to be. For even my husband, when he had on the right clothes, could show some pride, and me, whenever I remembered how fine my daddy's peanut crops had provided us, why there was nobody with stiffer backbone."

"I see a pale and evil shadow looming ahead of you in this journey," said Tante Rosie, looking into the water as if she'd lost a penny while we weren't looking.

"That shadow was sure pale and evil all right, said Mrs. Kemhuff. "When we got to the place there was a long line, and we saw all of our friends in this line. On one side of the big pile of food was the white line—and some rich peoples was in that line too—and on the other side there was the black line. I later heard, by the by, that the white folks in the white line got bacon and grits, as well as meal, but that is neither here nor there. What happened was this. As soon as our friends saw us all dressed up in our nice warm clothes, though used and castoff they were, they began saying how crazy we was to have worn them. And that's when I began to notice that all the people in the black line had dressed themselves in tatters. Even people what had good things at home, and I knew some of them did. What does this mean? I asked my husband. But he didn't know. He was too busy strutting about to even pay much attention. But I began to be terribly afraid. The baby had begun to cry and the other little ones, knowing I was nervous, commenced to whine and gag. I had a time with them.

"Now, at this time my husband had been looking around at other women and I was scared to death I was going to lose him. He already made fun of me and said I was arrogant and proud. I said that was the way to be and that he should try to be that way. The last thing I wanted to happen was for him to see me embarrassed and made small in front of a lot of people because I knew if that happened he would quit me.

"So I was standing there hoping that the white folks what give out the food wouldn't notice that I was dressed nice and that if they did they would see how hungry the babies was and how pitiful we all was. I could see my husband over talking to the woman he was going with on the sly. She was dressed like a flysweep! Not only was she raggedy, she was dirty! Filthy dirty, and with her filthy slip showing. She looked so awful she disgusted me. And yet there was my husband hanging over her while I stood in the line holding on to all four of our children. I guess he knew as well as I did what that woman had in the line of clothes at home. She was always much better dressed than me and much better dressed than many of the white peoples. That was because, they say she was a whore and took money. Seems like people want that and will pay for it even in a depression!"

There was a pause while Mrs. Kemhuff drew a deep breath. Then she continued.

"So soon I was next to get something from the young lady at the counter. All around her I could smell them red beans and my mouth was watering for a taste of fresh-water cornpone. I was proud, but I wasn't fancy. I just wanted something for me and the children. Well, there I was, with the children hanging to my dresstails, and I drew myself up as best I could and made the oldest boy stand up straight, for I had come to ask for what was mine, not to beg. So I wasn't going to be acting like a beggar. Well, I want you to know that that little slip of a woman, all big blue eyes and yellow hair, that little *girl,* took my stamps and then took one long look at me and my children and across at my husband—all of us dressed to kill I guess she thought—and she took my stamps in her hand and looked at them like they was dirty, and then she give them to an old gambler who was next in line behind me! 'You don't need nothing to eat from the way you all dressed up, Hannah Lou,' she said to me. 'But Miss Sadler,' I said, 'my children is hungry.' 'They don't look hungry,' she said to me. 'Move along now, somebody here may really need our help!' The whole line behind me began to laugh and snigger, and that little white moppet sort of grinned behind her hands. She give the old gambler double what he would have got otherwise. And there me and my children about to keel over from want.

"When my husband and his woman saw and heard what happened they commenced to laugh, too, and he reached down and got her stuff, piles and piles of it, it seemed to me then, and helped her put it in somebody's car and they drove off together. And that was about the last I seen of him. Or her."

"Weren't they swept off a bridge together in the flood that wiped out Tunica City?" asked Tante Rosie.

"Yes," said Mrs. Kemhuff. "Somebody like you might have helped me then, too, though looks like I didn't need it."

"So—"

"So after that looks like my spirit just wilted. Me and my children got a ride home with somebody and I tottered around like a drunken woman and put them to bed. They was sweet children and not much trouble, although they was about to go out of their minds with hunger."

Now a deep sadness crept into her face, which until she reached this point had been still and impassive.

"First one then the other of them took sick and died. Though the old gambler came by the house three or four days later and divided what he had left with us. He had been on his way to gambling it all away. The Lord called him to have pity on us and since he knew us and knew my husband had deserted me he said he were right glad to help out. But it was mighty late in the day when he thought about helping out and the children were far gone. Nothing could save them except the Lord and he seemed to have other things on his mind, like the wedding that spring of the mean little moppet."

Mrs. Kemhuff now spoke through clenched teeth.

"My spirit never recovered from that insult, just like my heart never recovered from my husband's desertion, just like my body never recovered from being almost starved to death. I started to wither in that winter and each year found me more hacked and worn down than the year before. Somewhere along them years my pride just up and left altogether and I worked for a time in a whorehouse just to make some money, just like my husband's woman. Then I took to drinking to forget what I was doing, and soon I just broke down and got old all at once, just like you see me now. And I started about five years ago to going to church. I was converted again, 'cause I felt the first time had done got worn off. But I am not restful. I dream and have nightmares still about the little moppet, and always I feel the moment when my spirit was trampled down within me while they all stood and laughed and she stood there grinning behind her hands."

"Well," said Tante Rosie. "There are ways that the spirit can be mended just as there are ways that the spirit can be broken. But one such as I am cannot do both. If I am to take away the burden of shame which is upon you I must in some way inflict it on someone else."

"I do not care to be cured," said Mrs. Kemhuff. "It is enough that I have endured my shame all these years and that my children and my husband were taken from me by one who knew nothing about us. I can survive as long as I need with the bitterness that has laid every day in my soul. But I could die easier if I knew something, after all these years, had been done to the little moppet. God cannot be let to make her happy all these years and me miserable. What kind of justice would that be? It would be monstrous!"

"Don't worry about it, my sister," said Tante Rosie with gentleness. "By the grace of the Man-God I have use of many powers. Powers given me by the Great One Herself. If you can no longer bear the eyes of the enemy that you see in your dreams the Man-God, who speaks to me from the Great Mother of Us All, will see that those eyes are eaten away. If the hands of your enemy have struck you they can be made useless." Tante Rosie held up a small piece of what was once lustrous pewter. Now it was pock-marked and blackened and deteriorating.

"Do you see this metal?" she asked.

"Yes, I see it," said Mrs. Kemhuff with interest. She took it in her hands and rubbed it.

"The part of the moppet you want destroyed will rot away in the same fashion."

Mrs. Kemhuff relinquished the piece of metal to Tante Rosie.

"You are a true sister," she said.

"Is it enough?" Tante Rosie asked.

"I would give anything to stop her grinning behind her hands," said the woman, drawing out a tattered billfold.

"Her hands or the grinning mouth?" asked Tante Rosie.

"The mouth grinned and the hands hit it," said Mrs. Kemhuff.

"Ten dollars for one area, twenty for two," said Tante Rosie.

"Make it the mouth," said Mrs. Kemhuff. "That is what I see most vividly in my dreams." She laid a ten-dollar bill in the lap of Tante Rosie.

"Let me explain what we will do," said Tante Rosie, coming near the woman and speaking softly to her, as a doctor would speak to a patient. "First we will make a potion that has a long history of use in our profession. It is a mixture of hair and nail parings of the person in question, a bit of their water and feces, a piece of their clothing heavy with their own scents, and I think in this case we might as well add a pinch of goober dust; that is, dust from the graveyard. This woman will not outlive you by more than six months."

I had thought the two women had forgotten about me, but now Tante Rosie turned to me and said, "You will have to go out to Mrs. Kemhuff's house. She will have to be instructed in the recitation of the curse-prayer. You will show her how to dress the black candles and how to pay Death for his interception in her behalf."

Then she moved over to the shelf that held her numerous supplies: oils of Bad and Good Luck Essence, dried herbs, creams, powders, and candles. She took two large black candles and placed them in Mrs. Kemhuff's hands. She also gave her a small bag of powder and told her to burn it on her table (as an altar) while she was praying the curse-prayer. I was to show Mrs. Kemhuff how to "dress" the candles in vinegar so they would be purified for her purpose.

She told Mrs. Kemhuff that each morning and evening for nine days she was to light the candles, burn the powder, recite the curse-prayer from her knees and concentrate all her powers on getting her message through to Death and the Man-God. As far as the Supreme Mother of Us All was concerned, She could only be moved by the pleas of the Man-God. Tante Rosie herself would recite the curse-prayer at the same time that Mrs. Kemhuff did, and together she thought the two prayers, prayed with respect, could not help but move the Man-God, who, in turn, would unchain Death, who would already be eager to come down on the little moppet. But her death would be slow in coming because first the Man-God had to hear all of the prayers.

"We will take those parts of herself that we collect, the feces, water, nail parings, et cetera, and plant them where they will bring for you the best results. Within a year's time the earth will be rid of the woman herself, even as almost immediately you will be rid of her grin. Do you want something else for only two dollars that will make you feel happy even today?" asked Tante Rosie.

But Mrs. Kemhuff shook her head. "I'm carefree enough already, knowing that her end will be before another year. As for happiness, it is something that deserts you once you know it can be bought and sold. I will not live to see the end result of your work, Tante Rosie, but my grave will fit nicer, having someone proud again who has righted a wrong and by so doing lies straight and proud throughout eternity."

And Mrs. Kemhuff turned and left, bearing herself grandly out of the room. It was as if she had regained her youth; her shawls were like a stately toga, her white hair seemed to sparkle.

II

To the Man-God: O great One, I have been sorely tried by my enemies and have been blasphemed and lied against. My good thoughts and my honest actions have been turned to bad actions and dishonest ideas. My home has been disrespected, my children have been cursed and ill-treated. My dear ones have been backbitten and their virtue questioned. O Man-God, I beg that this that I ask for my enemies shall come to pass:

That the South wind shall scorch their bodies and make them wither and shall not be tempered to them. That the North wind shall freeze their blood and numb their muscles and that it shall not be tempered to them. That the West wind shall blow away their life's breath and will not leave their hair grow, and that their fingernails shall fall off and their bones shall crumble. That the East wind shall make their minds grow dark, their sight shall fail and their seed dry up so that they shall not multiply.

I ask that their fathers and mothers from their furtherest generation will not intercede for them before the great throne, and the wombs of their women shall not bear fruit except for strangers, and that they shall become extinct. I pray that the children who may come shall be weak of mind and paralyzed of limb and that they themselves shall curse them in their turn for ever turning the breath of life into their bodies. I pray that disease and death shall be forever with them and that their worldly goods shall not prosper, and that their crops shall not multiply and that their cows, their sheep, and their hogs and all their living beasts shall die of starvation and thirst. I pray that their house shall be unroofed and that the rain, the thunder and lightning shall find the innermost recesses of their home and that the foundation shall crumble and the floods tear it asunder. I pray that the sun shall not shed its rays on them in benevolence, but instead it shall beat down on them and burn them and destroy them. I pray that the moon shall not give them peace, but instead shall deride them and decry them and cause their minds to shrivel. I pray that their friends shall betray them and cause them loss of power, of gold and of silver, and that their enemies shall smite them until they beg for mercy which shall not be given them. I pray that their tongues shall forget how to speak in sweet words, and that it shall be paralyzed and that all about them will be desolation, pestilence and death. O Man-God, I ask you for all these things because they have dragged me in the dust and destroyed my good name; broken my heart and caused me to curse the day that I was born. So be it.

This curse-prayer was regularly used and taught by rootworkers, but since I did not know it by heart, as Tante Rosie did, I recited it straight from Zora Neale Hurston's book, *Mules and Men,* and Mrs. Kemhuff and I learned it on our knees together. We were soon dressing the candles in vinegar, lighting them, kneeling and praying—intoning the words rhythmically—as if we had been doing it this way for years. I was moved by the fervor with which Mrs. Kemhuff prayed. Often she would clench her fists before her closed eyes and bite the insides of her wrists as the women do in Greece.

III

According to courthouse records Sarah Marie Sadler, "the little moppet," was born in 1910. She was in her early twenties during the Depression. In 1932 she married Ben Jonathan Holley, who later inherited a small chain of grocery stores and owned a plantation and an impressive stand of timber. In the spring of 1963, Mrs. Holley was fifty-three years old. She was the mother of three children, a boy and two girls; the boy a floundering clothes salesman, the girls married and oblivious, mothers themselves.

The elder Holleys lived six miles out in the country, their house was large, and Mrs. Holley's hobbies were shopping for antiques, gossiping with colored women, discussing her husband's health and her children's babies, and making spoon bread. I was able to glean this much from the drunken ramblings of the Holleys' cook, a malevolent nanny with gout, who had raised, in her prime, at least one tan Holley, a preacher whom the Holleys had sent to Morehouse.

"I bet I could get the nanny to give us all the information and nail parings we could ever use," I said to Tante Rosie. For the grumpy woman drank muscatel like a sow and clearly hated Mrs. Holley. However, it was hard to get her tipsy enough for truly revealing talk and we were quickly running out of funds.

"That's not the way," Tante Rosie said one evening as she sat in her car and watched me lead the nanny out of the dreary but secret-evoking recesses of the Six Forks Bar. We had already spent six dollars on muscatel.

"You can't trust gossips or drunks," said Tante Rosie. "You let the woman we are working on give you everything you need, and from her own lips."

"But that is the craziest thing I have ever heard," I said. "How can I talk to her about putting a fix on her without making her mad, or maybe even scaring her to death?"

Tante Rosie merely grunted.

"Rule number one. OBSERVATION OF SUBJECT. Write that down among your crumpled notes."

"In other words—?"

"Be direct, but not blunt."

On my way to the Holley plantation I came up with the idea of pretending to be searching for a fictitious person. Then I had an even better idea. I parked Tante Rosie's Bonneville at the edge of the spacious yard, which was dotted with mimosas and camellias. Tante Rosie had insisted I wear a brilliant orange robe and as I walked it swished and blew about my legs. Mrs. Holley was on the back patio steps, engaged in conversation with a young and beautiful black girl. They stared in amazement at the length and brilliance of my attire.

"Mrs. Holley, I think it's time for me to go," said the girl.

"Don't be silly," said the matronly Mrs. Holley. "She is probably just a light-skinned African who is on her way somewhere and got lost." She nudged the black girl in the ribs and they both broke into giggles.

"How do you do?" I asked.

"Just fine, how you?" said Mrs. Holley, while the black girl looked on askance. They had been talking with their heads close together and stood up together when I spoke.

"I am looking for a Josiah Henson"—a runaway slave and the original Uncle Tom in Harriet Beecher Stowe's novel, I might have added. "Could you tell me if he lives on your place?"

"That name sounds awful familiar," said the black girl.

"Are you *the* Mrs. Holley?" I asked gratuitously, while Mrs. Holley was distracted. She was sure she had never heard the name.

"Of course," she said, and smiled, pleating the side of her dress. She was a grayish blonde with an ashen untanned face, and her hands were five blunt and pampered fingers each. "And this is my . . . ah . . . my friend, Caroline Williams."

Caroline nodded curtly.

"Somebody told me ole Josiah might be out this way. . . ."

"Well, we hadn't seen him," said Mrs. Holley. "We were just here shelling some peas, enjoying this nice sunshine."

"Are you a light African?" asked Caroline.

"No," I said. "I work with Tante Rosie, the rootworker. I'm learning the profession."

"Whatever *for?*" asked Mrs. Holley. "I would have thought a nice-looking girl like yourself could find a better way to spend her time. I been hearing about Tante Rosie since I was a little bitty child, but everybody always said that rootworking was just a whole lot of n——, I mean colored foolishness. Of course we don't believe in that kind of thing, do we, Caroline?"

"Naw."

The younger woman put a hand on the older woman's arm, possessively, as if to say "You get away from here, bending my white folks' ear with your crazy mess!" From the kitchen window a dark remorseful face worked itself into various messages of "Go away!" It was the drunken nanny.

"I wonder if you would care to prove you do not believe in rootworking?"

"Prove?" said the white woman indignantly.

"Prove?" asked the black woman with scorn.

"That is the word," I said.

"Why, not that I'm afraid of any of this nigger magic!" said Mrs. Holley staunchly, placing a reassuring hand on Caroline's shoulder. *I* was the nigger, not she.

"In that case won't you show us how much you don't have fear of it." With the word *us* I placed Caroline in the same nigger category with me. Let her smolder! Now Mrs. Holley stood alone, the great white innovator and scientific scourge, forced to man the Christian fort against heathen nigger paganism.

"Of course, if you like," she said immediately, drawing herself up in the best English manner. Stiff upper lip, what? and all that. She had been grinning throughout. Now she covered her teeth with her scant two lips and her face became flat and resolute. Like so many white women in sections of the country where the race was still "pure" her mouth could have been formed by the minute slash of a thin sword.

"Do you know a Mrs. Hannah Lou Kemhuff?" I asked.

"No I do not."

"She is not white, Mrs. Holley, she is black."

"Hannah Lou, Hannah Lou . . . do we know a Hannah Lou?" she asked, turning to Caroline.

"No ma'am, we don't!" said Caroline.

"Well, she knows you. Says she met you on the bread lines during the Depression and that because she was dressed up you wouldn't give her any corn meal. Or red beans. Or something like that."

"Bread lines, Depression, dressed up, corn meal . . . ? I don't know what you're talking about!" No shaft of remembrance probed the depth of what she had done to colored people more than twenty years ago.

"It doesn't really matter, since you don't believe . . . but she says you did her wrong, and being a good Christian, she believes all wrongs are eventually righted in the Lord's good time. She came to us for help only when she began to feel the Lord's good time might be too far away. Because we do not deal in the work of unmerited destruction, Tante Rosie and I did not see how we could take the case." I said this humbly, with as much pious intonation as I could muster.

"Well, I'm glad," said Mrs. Holley, who had been running through the back years on her fingers.

"But," I said, "we told her what she could do to bring about restitution of peaceful spirit, which she claimed you robbed her of in a moment during which, as is now evident, you were not concerned. You were getting married the following spring."

"That was '32," said Mrs. Holley. "Hannah *Lou?*"

"The same."

"How black *was* she? Sometimes I can recall colored faces that way."

"That is not relevant," I said, "since you do not believe. . . ."

"Well of *course* I don't believe!" said Mrs. Holley.

"I am nothing in this feud between you," I said. "Neither is Tante Rosie. Neither of us had any idea until after Mrs. Kemhuff left that you were the woman she spoke of. We are familiar with the deep and sincere interest you take in the poor colored children at Christmastime each year. We know you have gone out of your way to hire needy people to work on your farm. We know you have been an example of Christian charity and a beacon force of brotherly love. And right before my eyes I can see it is true you have Negro friends."

"Just what is it you want?" asked Mrs. Holley.

"What *Mrs. Kemhuff* wants are some nail parings, not many, just a few, some hair (that from a comb will do), some water and some feces—and if you don't feel like doing either number one or number two, I will wait— and a bit of clothing, something that you have worn in the last year. Something with some of your odor on it."

"What!" Mrs. Holley screeched.

"They say this combination, with the right prayers, can eat away part of a person just like the disease that ruins so much fine antique pewter."

Mrs. Holley blanched. With a motherly fluttering of hands Caroline helped her into a patio chair.

"Go get my medicine," said Mrs. Holley, and Caroline started from the spot like a gazelle.

"Git away from here! Git away!"

I spun around just in time to save my head from a whack with a gigantic dust mop. It was the drunken nanny, drunk no more, flying to the defense of her mistress.

"She just a tramp and a phony!" she reassured Mrs. Holley, who was caught up in an authentic faint.

Not long after I saw Mrs. Holley, Hannah Kemhuff was buried. Tante Rosie and I followed the casket to the cemetery. Tante Rosie most elegant in black. Then we made our way through briers and grass to the highway. Mrs. Kemhuff rested in a tangly grove, off to herself, though reasonably near her husband and babies. Few people came to the funeral, which made the faces of Mrs. Holley's nanny and husband stand out all the more plainly. They had come to verify the fact that this dead person was indeed *the* Hannah Lou Kemhuff whom Mr. Holley had initiated a search for, having the entire county militia at his disposal.

Several months later we read in the paper that Sarah Marie Sadler Holley had also passed away. The paper spoke of her former beauty and vivacity, as a young woman, and of her concern for those less fortunate than herself as a married woman and pillar of the community and her church. It spoke briefly of her harsh and lengthy illness. It said all who knew her were sure her soul would find peace in heaven, just as her shrunken body had endured so much pain and heartache here on earth.

Caroline had kept us up to date on the decline of Mrs. Holley. After my visit, relations between them became strained and Mrs. Holley eventually became too frightened of Caroline's darkness to allow her close to her. A week after I'd talked to them Mrs. Holley began having her meals in her bedroom upstairs. Then she started doing everything else there as well. She collected stray hairs from her head and comb with the greatest attention and consistency, not to say desperation. She ate her fingernails. But the most bizarre of all was her response to Mrs. Kemhuff's petition for a specimen of feces and water. Not trusting any longer the earthen secrecy of the water mains, she no longer flushed. Together with the nanny Mrs. Holley preferred to store those relics of what she ate (which became almost nothing and then nothing, the nanny had told Caroline) and they kept it all in barrels and plastic bags in the upstairs closets. In a few weeks it became impossible for anyone to endure the smell of the house, even Mrs. Holley's husband, who loved her but during the weeks before her death slept in a spare room of the nanny's house.

The mouth that had grinned behind the hands grinned no more. The constant anxiety lest a stray strand of hair be lost and the foul odor of the house soon brought to the hands a constant seeking motion, to the eyes a glazed and vacant stare, and to the mouth a tightly puckered frown, one which only death might smooth.

TONI CADE BAMBARA

Toni Cade Bambara was born and raised in New York, where she lived in Harlem and Bedford-Stuyvesant. After graduating from Queens College in 1959 and receiving her MA from the City College of New York in 1963, she has worked as a community organizer, youth counselor, welfare investigator, and free-lance writer. Her publications include *The Black Woman* (1970), a collection of essays, poems, and stories; *Tales and Stories for Black Folks* (1971); and *Gorilla, My Love* (1972), a book of short stories. She took the name Bambara from a signature on a sketchbook she found in her great-grandmother's trunk.

MAGGIE OF THE GREEN BOTTLES

Maggie had not intended to get sucked in on this thing, sleeping straight through the christening, steering clear of the punch bowl, and refusing to dress for company. But when she glanced over my grandfather's shoulder and saw "Aspire, Enspire, Perspire" scrawled across the first page in that hardcore Protestant hand, and a grease stain from the fried chicken too, something snapped in her head. She snatched up the book and retired rapidly to her room, locked my mother out, and explained through the door that my mother was a fool to encourage a lot of misspelled nonsense from Mr. Tyler's kin, and an even bigger fool for having married the monster in the first place.

I imagine that Maggie sat at her great oak desk, rolled the lace cuffs gently back, and dipped her quill into the lavender ink pot with all the ceremony due the Emancipation Proclamation, which was, after all, exactly what she was drafting. Writing to me, she explained, was serious business, for she felt called upon to liberate me from all historical and genealogical connections except the most divine. In short, the family was a disgrace, degrading Maggie's and my capacity for wings, as they say. I can only say that Maggie was truly inspired. And she probably ruined my life from the get-go.

There is a photo of the two of us on the second page. There's Maggie in Minnie Mouse shoes and a long polka-dot affair with her stockings rolled up at the shins, looking like muffins. There's me with nothing much at all on, in her arms, and looking almost like a normal, mortal, everyday-type baby— raw, wrinkled, ugly. Except that it must be clearly understood straightaway that I sprang into the world full wise and invulnerable and gorgeous like a goddess. Behind us is the player piano with the spooky keys. And behind that, the window outlining Maggie's crosshatched face and looking out over the yard, overgrown even then, where later I lay lost in the high grass, never hoping to be found till Maggie picked me up into her hair and told me all about the earth's moons.

Once just a raggedy thing holding telegrams from well-wishers, the book was pleasant reading on those rainy days when I didn't risk rusting my skates, or maybe just wasn't up to trailing up and down the city streets with the kids, preferring to study Maggie's drawings and try to grab hold of the fearsome machinery which turned the planets and coursed the stars and told me in no uncertain terms that as an Aries babe I was obligated to carry on the work of other Aries greats from Alexander right on down to anyone you care to mention. I could go on to relate all the wise-alecky responses I gave to Maggie's document as an older child rummaging in the trunks among the canceled checks and old sheet music, looking for some suspicioned love letters or some small proof that my mother had once had romance in her life, and finding instead the raggedy little book I thought was just a raggedy little book. But it is much too easy to smile at one's ignorant youth just to flatter one's present wisdom, but I digress.

Because, on my birthday, Saturn was sitting on its ass and Mars was taken unawares, getting bumped by Jupiter's flunkies, I would not be into my own till well past twenty. But according to the cards, and my palm line bore it out, the hangman would spare me till well into my hundredth year. So all in all, the tea leaves having had their say and the coffee-ground patterns being what they were, I was destined for greatness. She assured me. And I was certain of my success, as I was certain that my parents were not my parents, that I was descended, anointed and ready to gobble up the world from urgent, noble Olympiads.

I am told by those who knew her, whose memories consist of something more substantial than a frantic gray lady who poured coffee into her saucer, that Margaret Cooper Williams wanted something she could not have. And it was the sorrow of her life that all her children and theirs and theirs were uncooperative—worse, squeamish. Too busy taking in laundry, buckling at the knees, putting their faith in Jesus, mute and sullen in their sorrow, too squeamish to band together and take the world by storm, make history, or even to appreciate the calling of Maggie the Ram, or the Aries that came after. Other things they told me too, things I put aside to learn later though I always knew, perhaps, but never quite wanted to, the way you hold your breath and steady yourself to the knowledge secretly, but never let yourself understand. They called her crazy.

It is to Maggie's guts that I bow forehead to the floor and kiss her hand, because she'd tackle the lot of them right there in the yard, blood kin or by marriage, and neighbors or no. And anybody who'd stand up to my father, gross Neanderthal that he was, simply had to be some kind of weird combination of David, Aries, and lunatic. It began with the cooking usually, especially the pots of things Maggie concocted. Witchcraft, he called it. Home cooking, she'd counter. Then he'd come over to the stove, lift a lid with an incredible face, and comment about cesspools and fertilizers. But she'd remind him of his favorite dish, chitlins, addressing the bread box, though. He'd turn up the radio and make some remark about good church music and her crazy voodoo records. Then she'd tell the curtains that some men, who put magic down with nothing to replace it and nothing much to recommend them in the first place but their magic wand, lived a runabout life, practicing black magic on other men's wives. Then he'd say something about freeloading relatives and dancing to the piper's tune. And she'd whisper to the kettles that there wasn't no sense in begging from a beggar. Depending on how large an audience they drew, this could go on for hours until my father would cock his head to the side, listening, and then try to make his getaway.

"Ain't nobody calling you, Mr. Tyler, cause don't nobody want you." And I'd feel kind of bad about my father like I do about the wolf man and the phantom of the opera. Monsters, you know, more than anybody else, need your pity cause they need beauty and love so bad.

One day, right about the time Maggie would say something painful that made him bring up freeloaders and piper's tunes, he began to sputter so bad it made me want to cry. But Maggie put the big wooden spoon down and whistled for Mister T—at least that's what Maggie and my grandmother, before she died, insisted on calling him. The dog, always hungry, came bounding through the screen door, stopped on a dime by the sink, and slinked over to Maggie's legs the way beat-up dogs can do, their tails all confused as to just what to do, their eyes unblinkingly watchful. Maggie offered him something from the pot. And when Mister T had finished, he licked Maggie's hand. She began to cackle. And then, before I could even put my milk down, up went Maggie's palm, and *bam,* Mister T went skidding across the linoleum and banged all the seltzer bottles down.

"Damn-fool mutt," said Maggie to her wooden spoon, "too dumb to even know you're supposed to bite the hand that feeds you."

My father threw his hand back and yelled for my mother to drop whatever she was doing, which was standing in the doorway shaking her head, and pack up the old lady's things posthaste. Maggie went right on laughing and talking to the spoon. And Mister T slinked over to the table so Baby Jason could pet him. And then it was name-calling time. And again I must genuflect and kiss her ring, because my father was no slouch when it came to names. He could malign your mother and work your father's lineage over in one short breath, describing in absolute detail all the incredible alliances made between your ancestors and all sorts of weird creatures. But Maggie had him beat there too, old lady in lace talking to spoons or no.

My mother came in weary and worn and gave me a nod. I slid my peanut-butter sandwich off the icebox, grabbed Baby Jason by his harness, and dragged him into our room, where I was supposed to read to him real loud. But I listened, I always listened to my mother's footfalls on the porch to the gravel path and down the hard mud road to the woodshed. Then I could give my attention to the kitchen, for "Goldilocks," keep in mind, never was enough to keep the brain alive. Then, right in the middle of some fierce curse or other, my father did this unbelievable thing. He stomped right into Maggie's room—that sanctuary of heaven charts and incense pots and dream books and magic stuffs. Only Jason, hiding from an August storm, had ever been allowed in there, and that was on his knees crawling. But in he stomped all big and bad like some terrible giant, this man whom Grandma Williams used to say was just the sort of size man put on this earth for the " 'spress purpose of clubbing us all to death." And he came out with these green bottles, one in each hand, snorting and laughing at the same time. And I figured, peeping into the kitchen, that these bottles were enchanted, for they had a strange effect on Maggie, she shut right up. They had a strange effect on me too, gleaming there up in the air, nearly touching the ceiling, glinting off the shots of sunshine, grasped in the giant's fist. I was awed.

Whenever I saw them piled in the garbage out back I was tempted to touch them and make a wish, knowing all the while that the charm was all used up and that that was why they were in the garbage in the first place. But there was no doubt that they were special. And whenever Baby Jason managed to drag one out from under the bed, there was much whispering and shuffling on my mother's part. And when Sweet Basil, the grocer's boy, delivered these green bottles to Maggie, it was all hush-hush and backdoor and in the corner dealings, slipping it in and out of innumerable paper bags, holding it up to the light, then off she'd run to her room and be gone for hours, days sometimes, and when she did appear, looking mysterious and in a trance, her face all full of shadows. And she'd sit at the sideboard with that famous cup from the World's Fair, pouring coffee into the saucer and blowing on it very carefully, nodding and humming and swirling the grinds. She called me over once to look at the grinds.

"What does this look like, Peaches?"

"Looks like a star with a piece out of it."

"Hmm," she mumbled, and swirled again. "And now?"

Me peering into the cup and lost for words. "Looks like a face that lost its eyes."

"Hmm," again, as she thrust the cup right under my nose, and me wishing it was a box of falling glass I could look at where I knew what was what instead of looking into the bottom of a fat yellow cup at what looked like nothing but coffee grinds.

"Looks like a mouth losing its breath, Great Granny."

"Let's not get too outrageous, Peaches. This is serious business."

"Yes ma'am." Peering again and trying to be worthy of Alexander and the Ram and all my other forebears. "What it really seems to be"—stalling for time and praying for inspiration—"is an upside-down bird, dead on its back with his heart chopped out and the hole bleeding."

She flicked my hand away when I tried to point the picture out which by now I was beginning to believe. "Go play somewhere, girl," she said. She was mad. "And quit calling me Granny."

"What happened here today?" my mother kept asking all evening thumping out the fragrant dough and wringing the dishtowel, which was supposed to help the dough rise, wringing it to pieces. I couldn't remember anything particular, following her gaze to Maggie's door. "Was Sweet Basil here this afternoon?" Couldn't remember that either, but tried to show I was her daughter by staring hard at the closed door too. "Was Great Granny up and around at all today?" My memory failed me there too. "You ain't got much memory to speak of at all, do you?" said my father. I hung onto my mother's apron and helped her wring the dishtowel to pieces.

They told me she was very sick, so I had to drag Baby Jason out to the high grass and play with him. It was a hot day and the smell of the kerosene soaking the weeds that were stubborn about dying made my eyes tear. I was face down in the grass just listening, waiting for the afternoon siren which last year I thought was Judgment Day because it blew so long to say that the war was over and that we didn't have to eat Spam any more and that there was a circus coming and a parade and Uncle Bubba too, but with only one leg to show for it all. Maggie came into the yard with her basket of vegetables. She sat down at the edge of the gravel path and began stringing the peppers, red and green, red and green. And, like always, she was humming one of those weird songs of hers which always made her seem holier and blacker than she could've been. I tied Baby Jason to a tree so he wouldn't crawl into her lap, which always annoyed her. Maggie didn't like baby boys, or any kind of boys I'm thinking, but especially baby boys born in Cancer and Pisces or anything but in Aries.

"Look here, Peaches," she called, working the twine through the peppers and dropping her voice real low. "I want you to do this thing for your Great Granny."

"What must I do?" I waited a long time till I almost thought she'd fallen asleep, her head rolling around on her chest and her hands fumbling with the slippery peppers, ripping them.

"I want you to go to my room and pull out the big pink box from under the bed." She looked around and woke up a bit. "This is a secret you-and-me thing now, Peaches." I nodded and waited some more. "Open the box and you'll see a green bottle. Wrap this apron around it and tuck it under your arm like so. Then grab up the mushrooms I left on the sideboard like that's what you came for in the first place. But get yourself back here right quick." I repeated the instructions, flopped a necklace of peppers around me, and dashed into the hot and dusty house. When I got back she dumped the mushrooms into her lap, tucked the bottle under her skirt, and smiled at the poor little peppers her nervous hands had strung. They hung wet and ruined off the twine like broken-necked little animals.

I was down in the bottoms playing with the state-farm kids when Uncle Bubba came sliding down the sand pile on his one good leg. Jason was already in the station wagon hanging onto my old doll. We stayed at Aunt Min's till my father came to get us in the pickup. Everybody was in the kitchen dividing up Maggie's things. The linen chest went to Aunt Thelma. And the souvenirs from Maggie's honeymoons went to the freckle-faced cousins from town. The clothes were packed for the church. And Reverend Elson was directing the pianist's carrying from the kitchen window. The scattered sopranos, who never ever seemed to get together on their high notes or on their visits like this, were making my mother drink tea and kept nodding at me, saying she was sitting in the mourner's seat, which was just like all the other chairs in the set; same as the amen corner was no better or any less dusty than the rest of the church and not even a corner. Then Reverend Elson turned to say that no matter how crazy she'd been, no matter how hateful she'd acted toward the church in general and him in particular, no matter how spiteful she'd behaved towards her neighbors and even her blood kin, and even though everyone was better off without her, seeing how she died as proof of her heathen character, and right there in the front yard too, with a bottle under her skirts, the sopranos joined in scattered as ever, despite all that, the Reverend Elson continued, God rest her soul, if He saw fit, that is.

The china darning egg went into Jason's overalls. And the desk went into my room. Bubba said he wanted the books for his children. And they all gave him such a look. My mother just sat in the kitchen chair called the mourner's seat and said nothing at all except that they were selling the house and moving to the city.

"Well, Peaches," my father said. "You were her special, what you want?"

"I'll take the bottles," I said.

"Let us pray," said the Reverend.

That night I sat at the desk and read the baby book for the first time. It sounded like Maggie for the world, holding me in her lap and spreading the charts on the kitchen table. I looked my new bottle collection over. There were purple bottles with glass stoppers and labels. There were squat blue bottles with squeeze tops but nothing in them. There were flat red bottles that could hold only one flower at a time. I had meant the green bottles. I was going to sell them and then I didn't. I was too small for so much enchantment anyway. I went to bed feeling much too small. And it seemed a shame that the hope of the Aries line should have to sleep with a light on still, and blame it on Jason and cry with balled fists in the eyes just like an ordinary, mortal, everyday-type baby.

ANN PETRY

Ann Petry was born in Old Saybrook, Connecticut, where she still resides. She attended the University of Connecticut College of Pharmacy, from which she received her Ph.G. She began writing in high school and has written for *The New York Times Book Review* and *The New Yorker*. Her first novel, *The Street* (1946), a story of life in Harlem, achieved wide acclaim and became a best seller. Her other books include *Country Place* (1947), *The Narrows* (1953), *Legends of the Saints* (1970), and *Miss Muriel and Other Stories* (1971).

DOBY'S GONE

When Doby first came into Sue Johnson's life her family were caretakers on a farm way up in New York State. And because Sue had no one else to play with, the Johnsons reluctantly accepted Doby as a member of the family.

The spring that Sue was six they moved to Wessex, Connecticut—a small New England town whose neat colonial houses cling to a group of hills overlooking the Connecticut River. All that summer Mrs. Johnson had hoped that Doby would vanish long before Sue entered school in the fall. He would only complicate things in school.

For Doby wasn't real. He existed only in Sue's mind. He had been created out of her need for a friend her own age—her own size. And he had gradually become an escape from the very real world that surrounded her. She first started talking about him when she was two and he had been with her ever since. He always sat beside her when she ate and played with her during the day. At night he slept in a chair near her bed so that they awoke at the same time in the morning. A place had to be set for him at mealtime. A seat had to be saved for him on trains and buses.

After they moved to Wessex, he was still her constant companion just as he had been when she was three and four and five.

On the morning that Sue was to start going to school she said, "Doby has a new pencil, too. And he's got a red plaid shirt just like my dress."

"Why can't Doby stay home?" Mrs. Johnson asked.

"Because he goes everywhere I go," Sue said in amazement. "Of course he's going to school. He's going to sit right by me."

Sue watched her mother get up from the breakfast table and then followed her upstairs to the big front bedroom. She saw with surprise that her mother was putting on her going-out clothes.

"You have to come with me, Mommy?" she asked anxiously. She had wanted to go with Doby. Just the two of them. She had planned every step of the way since the time her mother told her she would start school in the fall.

"No, I don't have to, but I'm coming just the same. I want to talk to your teacher." Mrs. Johnson fastened her coat and deftly patted a loose strand of hair in place.

Sue looked at her and wondered if the other children's mothers would come to school, too. She certainly hoped so because she wouldn't want to be the only one there who had a mother with her.

Then she started skipping around the room holding Doby by the hand. Her short black braids jumped as she skipped. The gingham dress she wore was starched so stiffly that the hemline formed a wide circular frame for her sturdy dark brown legs as she bounced up and down.

"Ooh," she said suddenly. "Doby pulled off one of my hair ribbons." She reached over and picked it up from the floor and came to stand in front of her mother while the red ribbon was retied into a crisp bow.

Then she was walking down the street hand in hand with her mother. She held Doby's hand on the other side. She decided it was good her mother had come. It was better that way. The street would have looked awfully long and awfully big if she and Doby had been by themselves, even though she did know exactly where the school was. Right down the street on this side. Past the post office and town hall that sat so far back with green lawn in front of them. Past the town pump and the old white house on the corner, past the big empty lot. And there was the school.

It had a walk that went straight down between the green grass and was all brown-yellow gravel stuff—coarser than sand. One day she had walked past there with her mother and stopped to finger the stuff the walk was made of, and her mother had said, "It's gravel."

She remembered how they'd talk about it. "What's gravel?" she asked.

"The stuff in your hand. It's like sand, only coarser. People use it for drive-ways and walks," her mother had said.

Gravel. She liked the sound of the word. It sounded like pebbles. Gravel. Pebble. She said the words over to herself. You gravel and pebble. Pebble said to gravel. She started making up a story. Gravel said to pebble, "You're a pebble." Pebble said back, "You're a gravel."

"Sue, throw it away. It's dirty and your hands are clean," her mother said.

She threw it down on the sidewalk. But she kept looking back at it as she walked along. It made a scattered yellow, brown color against the rich brown-black of the dirt-path.

She held on to Doby's hand a little more tightly. Now she was actually going to walk up that long gravel walk to the school. She and Doby would play there every day when school was out.

The school yard was full of children. Sue hung back a little looking at them. They were playing ball under the big maple trees near the back of the yard. Some small children were squatting near the school building, letting gravel trickle through their fingers.

"I want to play, too." She tried to free her hand from her mother's firm grip.

"We're going inside to see your teacher first." And her mother went on walking up the school steps holding on to Sue's hand.

Sue stared at the children on the steps. "Why are they looking so hard?" she asked.

"Probably because you're looking at them so hard. Now come on," and her mother pulled her through the door. The hall inside was dark and very long. A neat white sign over a door to the right said FIRST GRADE in bold black letters.

Sue peered inside the room while her mother knocked on the door. A pretty lady with curly yellow hair got up from a desk and invited them in. While the teacher and her mother talked grown-up talk, Sue looked around. She supposed she'd sit at one of those little desks. There were a lot of them and she wondered if there would be a child at each desk. If so then Doby would have to squeeze in beside her.

"Sue, you can go outside and play. When the bell rings you must come in," the teacher said.

"Yes, teacher," Sue started out the door in a hurry.

"My name is Miss Whittier," the teacher said, "You must call me that."

"Yes, Miss Whittier. Good-bye, Mommy," she said, and went quickly down the hall and out the door.

"Hold my hand, Doby," she said softly under her breath.

Now she and Doby would play in the gravel. Squeeze it between their fingers, pat it into shapes like those other children were doing. Her short starched skirt stood out around her legs as she skipped down the steps. She watched the children as long as she could without saying anything.

"Can we play, too?" she asked finally.

A boy with a freckled face and short stiff red hair looked up at her and frowned. He didn't answer but kept ostentatiously patting at a little mound of gravel.

Sue walked over a little closer, holding Doby tightly by the hand. The boy ignored her. A little girl in a blue and white checked dress stuck her tongue out.

"Your legs are black," she said suddenly. And then when the others looked up she added, "Why, look, she's black all over. Looky, she's black all over."

Sue retreated a step away from the building. The children got up and followed her. She took another backward step and they took two steps forward. The little girl who had stuck her tongue out began a chant, "Look, look. Her legs are black. Her legs are black."

The children were all saying it. They formed a ring around her and they were dancing up and down and screaming, "Her legs are black. Her legs are black."

She stood in the middle of the circle completely bewildered. She wanted to go home where it was safe and quiet and where her mother would hold her tight in her arms. She pulled Doby nearer to her. What did they mean her legs were black? Of course they were. Not black but dark brown. Just like these children were white some other children were dark like her. Her mother said so. But her mother hadn't said anyone would make her feel bad about being a different color. She didn't know what to do; so she just stood there watching them come closer and closer to her—their faces red with excitement, their voices hoarse with yelling.

Then the school bell rang. And the children suddenly plunged toward the building. She was left alone with Doby. When she walked into the school room she was crying.

"Don't you mind, Doby," she whispered. "Don't you mind. I won't let them hurt you."

Miss Whittier gave her a seat near the front of the room. Right near her desk. And she smiled at her. Sue smiled back and carefully wiped away the wet on her eyelashes with the back of her hand. She turned and looked around the room. There were no empty seats. Doby would have to stand up.

"You stand right close to me and if you get tired just sit on the edge of my seat," she said.

She didn't go out for recess. She stayed in and helped Miss Whittier draw on the blackboard with colored chalk—yellow and green and red and purple and brown. Miss Whittier drew the flowers and Sue colored them. She put a small piece of crayon out for Doby to use. And Miss Whittier noticed it. But she didn't say anything, she just smiled.

"I love her," Sue thought. "I love my teacher." And then again, "I love Miss Whittier, my teacher."

At noon the children followed her halfway home from school. They called after her and she ran so fast and so hard that the pounding in her ears cut off the sound of their voices.

"Go faster, Doby," she said. "You have to go faster." And she held his hand and ran until her legs ached.

"How was school, Sue?" asked her mother.

"It was all right," she said slowly. "I don't think Doby likes it very much. He likes Miss Whittier though."

"Do you like her?"

"Oh, yes," Sue let her breath come out with a sigh.

"Why are you panting like that?" her mother asked.

"I ran all the way home," she said.

Going back after lunch wasn't so bad. She went right in to Miss Whittier. She didn't stay put in the yard and wait for the bell.

When school was out, she decided she'd better hurry right home and maybe the children wouldn't see her. She walked down the gravel path taking quick little looks over her shoulder. No one paid any attention and she was so happy that she gave Doby's hand a squeeze.

And then she saw that they were waiting for her right by the vacant lot. She hurried along trying not to hear what they were saying.

"My mother says you're a little nigger girl," the boy with the red hair said.

And then they began to shout: "Her legs are black. Her legs are black."

It changed suddenly. "Run. Go ahead and run." She looked over her shoulder. A boy was coming toward her with a long switch in his hand. He raised it in a threatening gesture and she started running.

For two days she ran home from school like that. Ran until her short legs felt as though they couldn't move another step.

"Sue," her mother asked anxiously, watching her try to catch her breath on the front steps, "what makes you run home from school like this?"

"Doby doesn't like the other children very much," she said panting.

"Why?"

"I don't think they understand about him," she said thoughtfully. "But he loves Miss Whittier."

The next day the children waited for her right where the school's gravel walk ended. Sue didn't see them until she was close to them. She was coming slowly down the path hand in hand with Doby trying to see how many of the big pebbles they could step on without stepping on any of the finer, sandier gravel.

She was in the middle of the group of children before she realized it. They started off slowly at first. "How do you comb that kind of hair?" "Does that black color wash off?" And then the chant began and it came faster and faster: "Her legs are black. Her legs are black."

A little girl reached out and pulled one of Sue's braids. Sue tried to back away and the other children closed in around her. She rubbed the side of her head—it hurt where her hair had been pulled. Someone pushed her. Hard. In the middle of her back. She was suddenly outraged. She planted her feet firmly on the path. She started hitting out with her fists. Kicking. Pulling hair. Tearing at clothing. She reached down and picked up handfuls of gravel and aimed it at eyes and ears and noses.

While she was slapping and kicking at the small figures that encircled her she became aware that Doby had gone. For the first time in her life he had left her. He had gone when she started to fight.

She went on fighting—scratching and biting and kicking—with such passion and energy that the space around her slowly cleared. The children backed away. And she stood still. She was breathing fast as though she had been running.

The children ran off down the street—past the big empty lot, past the old white house with the green shutters. Sue watched them go. She didn't feel victorious. She didn't feel anything except an aching sense of loss. She stood there panting, wondering about Doby.

And then, "Doby," she called softly. Then louder, "Doby! Doby! Where are you?"

She listened—cocking her head on one side. He didn't answer. And she felt certain he would never be back because he had never left her before. He had gone for good. And she didn't know why. She decided it probably had something to do with growing up. And she looked down at her legs hoping to find they had grown as long as her father's. She saw instead that her dress was torn in three different places, her socks were down around her ankles, there were long angry scratches on her legs and on her arms. She felt for her hair—the red hair ribbons were gone and her braids were coming undone.

She started looking for the hair ribbons. And as she looked she saw that Daisy Bell, the little girl who had stuck her tongue out that first day of school, was leaning against the oak tree at the end of the path.

"Come on, let's walk home together," Daisy Bell said matter-of-factly.

"All right," Sue said.

As they started past the empty lot, she was conscious that someone was tagging along behind them. It was Jimmie Piebald, the boy with the stiff red hair. When she looked back he came up and walked on the other side of her.

They walked along in silence until they came to the town pump. They stopped and looked deep down into the well. And spent a long time hallooing down into it and listening delightedly to the hollow funny sound of their voices.

It was much later than usual when Sue got home. Daisy Bell and Jimmie walked up to the door with her. Her mother was standing on the front steps waiting for her.

"Sue," her mother said in a shocked voice. "What's the matter? What happened to you?"

Daisy Bell put her arm around Sue. Jimmie started kicking at some stones in the path.

Sue stared at her mother, trying to remember. There was something wrong but she couldn't think what it was. And then it came to her. "Oh," she wailed, "Doby's gone. I can't find him anywhere."

LUCILLE CLIFTON

Born in 1936 in Depew, New York, Lucille Clifton attended Howard University and Fredonia State Teachers' College. She is the author of children's books as well as three books of poetry: *Good Times* (1969), *Good News— About the Earth* (1972), and *An Ordinary Woman* (1974). She published her autobiographical narrative, *Generations,* in 1976.

LUCY

I

"Lucille Sale, called Lucy, was the daughter of Caroline Donald and Sam Louis Sale," my Daddy would say. "They called him Uncle Louis like they did back then. This man, Bob Donald, bought Mammy Ca'line and set her to work in the orchard. They was big fruit growers and Ca'line worked in the orchards from when she was a little girl. One day when she had got big she was in the field and a carriage come by and stopped. And two old men was in it. It was Uncle Louis Sale and he was a slave but he was too old to work in the field and so his job was to drive his master in the carriage. His master was Old Man John F. Sale and he was a old man too, Lue, and blind. Uncle Louis had been given to his family as a boy. He was a present to their family. He was somebody and he was a present, a wedding present, Lue. And he was driving this carriage, an old man driving another old man, and he saw Ca'line in the orchard. And he stopped the horses and asked Old Man John F. to buy her for him for his wife. And Old Man John F. did. She was a young lady by then, Lue, and Uncle Louis had been born in 1777 but she was bought and went off to the Sale place and Old Man John F. married them legal cause he was a lawyer and they always said he was a good man. She lived there on the Sale place and they trained her to be a midwife and Mammy Ca'line and Uncle Louis had seven or more children, Lue, and one of the first ones was a girl. They called her Lucy but her name was Lucille. Like my own sister. And like you.

"Oh slavery, slavery," my Daddy would say. "It ain't something in a book, Lue. Even the good parts was awful."

My father looked like stone in a box. Like an old stone man caught in a box. He looks good, don't he, Lue? my sisters begged. Don't he look real good?

The room was heavy with flowers. My sisters had taken me to view the body and we were surrounded by cards bearing the names of my uncles and aunts and strange Polish names from our old neighborhood. I looked at the thin hook-nosed man in the box. He was still handsome, straight and military as he always was when he slept. He sleeps like he was dead, we used to laugh. His hand was curved as if his cane was in it, but his body was slightly on its side so that his missing leg was almost hidden. They were hiding his missing leg. The place where there was no leg was hidden. They were hiding his nothing. Nothing was hidden. They were missing nothing. I thought I was going to laugh. They were hiding where there was nothing to hide. Nothing was missing. I walked out of the room.

My father was an old man. My father had become an old man and I didn't even know it. This old man in a box was my father. Daddy had been an old man.

My sisters stood behind me. Don't he look good, Lue? They kept saying it. No, I finally answered. He's dead. I walked away.

My mother bore two children, a boy and a girl. My father was the father of four. He had three daughters by three different women, his first wife who died when she was twenty-one years old, my mother who triumphed with a son, and my youngest sister's mother who had been my father's lover when my mother was a bride. Our mothers had all known each other, had been friends. We were friends. My sisters and I. And my Mama had raised us all.

When Mama died they said he wouldn't last long. He'll have a hard time without Thel, they whispered, he can't make it without Thel. Even the widows and old girlfriends that gathered like birds nodded to each other. He needed Thel, he'll be gone soon.

But he fooled them. He was a strong man, a rock, and he lived on for ten years in his house, making a life. He took one of Mama's friends for his girlfriend, just as easily as he had married Mama when Edna Bell, his first wife and my sister Jo's mother, had died at twenty-one. And Mama's friend took care of him just as Mama had done, cooking and cleaning and being hollered at so much that once my children had asked me Is that lady Papa's maid or what? And I had answered No, not really, she's like my Mama was.

He lived on ten years in that house after Mama died, but my Mama lingered there too. His friend said she could hear her in mornings early when it was time to get up and get his breakfast, and she would roll over and jump out of bed and run toward the kitchen, calling I'll get it, Thel, I'll get it. She was tough as a soldier, my father would say of my dead mother. She wasn't a Dahomey woman, but she was the Mama of one.

III

"When you was born we was going to name you Georgia," Daddy told me once. "Because my mother's name was Georgia and your Mama's mother was named Georgia too. But when I saw you there you was so pretty I told your Mama I wanted to name you Thelma for her. And she said she didn't like her name and for me to give you another name with the Thelma. So I looked at you and you looked just like one of us and I thought about what Mammy Ca'line used to say about Dahomey women and I thought this child is one of us and I named you Lucille with the Thelma. Just like my sister Lucille and just like my real Grandmother Lucy. Genie, my Daddy's mother. First Black woman legally hanged in the state of Virginia."

He said Black like that, back then. And he would be looking proud.

Fred and I slept in the room that had once been mine. We were going to find a motel, but my sisters cried and asked us to stay with them. Just one night, you'll just be one night, they said. You ought to stay. And I looked at them and knew that they were right. I ought to stay. My sisters had stood by my father's bed while his leg had been amputated and Jo had cursed the nurses and made them clean his mess in the hospital and my sister Punkin had held his hand and they had bought him his wheelchair. And you ought to stay, they said to Sammy and me.

Sammy grumbled and took his suitcase to his old room and went out to visit with his own children and to get drunk, and Fred took our bags up to my old room. I looked at the women who were my sisters, one seven years older than I, the other six months younger, and thought about the other death we had shared in this house. Mama. My Mama. Jo's mother had died in another town when Jo was a baby, and Punkin's mother was alive and cooking quietly at last in her lover's kitchen. Three women who had loved Daddy. Three daughters who had loved Daddy. I shook my head and walked up the stairs to my old room. These are my sisters, I whispered to myself.

Lue, Jo cried up the steps to me. We're scared. He's gonna haunt us.

No he won't. I tried to comfort.

He sure will haunt me, Jo was crying. I'm bad and he'll haunt me for sure.

Not you, Lue, Punkin whispered. He won't bother you. You always was his heart.

IV

"They named this daughter Lucille," my Daddy would say. "They say she was a tall skinny dark-skinned girl, look just like her mother. Mammy Ca'line. They say they couldn't get her to work as hard as the rest and she was quiet and thought she was better than the rest. Mammy Ca'line taught her that, they say, and I wouldn't be surprised if she did. They tell me she was mean. Lucy was mean always, I heard Aunt Margaret Brown say to Mammy Ca'line one time. And Mammy just said no she wasn't mean, she was strong. 'Strong women and weak men,' is what she said, 'sister, we be strong women and weak men.' And I run up to her and said Mammy, I ain't weak. And she just smiled at me and said 'Not you, mister, you won't be weak. You be a Sayle.'

"And Mammy was a midwife all through the war and her daughter Lucy worked with her sometime and after the war, after emancipation like they said, they just kept up delivering babies all around, white and Black. And the town just grew up, after the war, Lue, cause a lot of white folks come South to make money you know, off the South's trouble. And one of them was a carpetbagger from Connecticut. Named Harvey Nichols. The white man Lucy killed."

I waited all night for morning. Fred and I lay without sleeping in the room that had been my own and cried and talked about my Daddy. He had been a great storyteller. His life had been full of days and his days had been full of life.

V

My father was born in Bedford Virginia in 1902. His father Gene Sayle had died when he was a little boy and his mother had gone to work in the tobacco factory, leaving my father and his two brothers and one sister in the care of her dead husband's grandmother. My father's great-grandmother, who had been a slave. My father had left school in the second or third grade and could barely write more than his name, but he was an avid reader. He loved books. He had changed his name to Sayles (instead of Sayle) after finding a part of a textbook in which the plural was explained. There will be more than one of me, my father thought, and he added the *s* to his name. He had worked in coal mines and in laboring camps throughout the South, and had come North during a strike at a steel plant which hired him. He had married as a young man a girl named Edna Bell who died at twenty-one and he had then married her friend Thelma Moore, who died at forty-four. I won't get married again, he used to say, I'm a jinx, to young women.

He. and Edna Bell had had a daughter Josephine, called Jo. He and Thelma Moore had had a daughter Thelma Lucille and then a neighbor woman had borne him a daughter Elaine, called Punkin, six months later. Two years after, he and Thelma became the parents of a son. A son. He had no other children and he never slept with his wife again. He said he had seen his son ever since he was a little boy in Virginia and he had never wanted any other thing.

And now he was dead. Fred and I lay and listened to the house. My Daddy and Mama were dead and their house was full of them.

V I

"Harvey Nichols was a white man," my Daddy would say, "who come South after the war to make money. He brought his wife and family down and bought himself a house and everything. And it was close to the Sale place and all the slaves had stayed there after emancipation because they said the Sales was good people, but they had just changed their last name to Sayle so people would know the difference. And this Harvey Nichols saw Lucy and wanted her and I say she must have wanted him too because like I told you, Lue, she was mean and didn't do nothing she didn't want to do and nobody could force her because she was Mammy Ca'line's child and everybody round there respected Mammy Ca'line so much. And her daughter Lucy had this baby boy by this Connecticut Yankee named Harvey Nichols. They named the baby Gene Sayle. He was my Daddy, Lue. Your own grandfather and Mammy Ca'line's grandson. But oh, Lue, he was born with a withered arm.

"Yes, Lord, he was born with a withered arm and when he was still just a baby Lucy waited by the crossroad one night for Harvey Nichols to come to her and when he rode upon a white horse, she cocked up a rifle she had stole and shot him off his horse and killed him, Lue. And she didn't run away, she didn't run away, she waited right there by the body with the rifle in her hand till the horse coming back empty-saddled to the stable brought a mob to see what had become of Harvey Nichols. And when they got to the crossroad they found Lucy standing there with the rifle in her hand. And they didn't lynch her, Lue, cause she was Mammy Ca'line's child, and from Dahomey women. That's what I believe. Mammy Ca'line got one of the lawyer Sale family to defend her daughter, cause they was all lawyers and preachers in that family. They had a legal trial and Lucy was found guilty. And hanged. Mammy Ca'line took the baby boy Genie and raised him and never let him forget who he was. I used to ask her sometime, Mammy, was you scared back then bout Granma Lucy? And she would look right at me and say 'I'm scared for you, mister, that's all.' She always called me mister. She said I was Mister Sayle. And Lue, I always was."

And Lucy was hanged. Was hanged, the lady whose name they gave me like a gift had her neck pulled up by a rope until the neck broke and I can see Mammy Ca'line standing straight as a soldier in green Virginia apart from the crowd of silent Black folk and white folk watching them and not the wooden frame swinging her child. And their shame making distance between them and her a real thing. And I know she made no sound but her mind closed round the picture like a frame and I know that her child made no sound and I turn in my chair and arch my back and make this sound for my two mothers and for all Dahomey women.

Later I would ask my father for proof. Where are the records, Daddy? I would ask. The time may not be right and it may just be a family legend or something. Somebody somewhere knows, he would say. And I would be dissatisfied and fuss with Fred about fact and proof and history until he told me one day not to worry, that even the lies are true. In history, even the lies are true.

And there would be days when we young Sayles' would be trying to dance and sing in the house and Sammy would miss a step and not be able to keep up to the music and he would look over in the corner of the room and holler "Damn Harvey Nichols." And we would laugh.

PAULE MARSHALL

Paule Marshall was born in Brooklyn in 1929 of parents who had recently immigrated from Barbados. She lives in New York City, where she works full time on her writing, interrupting her schedule from time to time to lecture on black literature at universities across the country. Her published books include two novels: *Brown Girl, Brownstones* (1959) and *The Chosen Place, The Timeless People* (1969) and a collection of short stories, *Soul Clap Hands and Sing* (1961). She has been the recipient of a Guggenheim Fellowship (1961–1962), a Rosenthal Award from the National Institute of Arts and Letters (1962), a Ford Foundation Theater Award (1964–1965), and a National Endowment for the Arts Grant (1967).

BROOKLYN

A summer wind, soaring just before it died, blew the dusk and the first scattered lights of downtown Brooklyn against the shut windows of the classroom, but Professor Max Berman—B.A., 1919, M.A., 1921, New York; Docteur de l'Université, 1930, Paris—alone in the room, did not bother to open the windows to the cooling wind. The heat and airlessness of the room, the perspiration inching its way like an ant around his starched collar were discomforts he enjoyed; they obscured his larger discomfort: the anxiety which chafed his heart and tugged his left eyelid so that he seemed to be winking, roguishly, behind his glasses.

To steady his eye and ease his heart, to fill the time until his students arrived and his first class in years began, he reached for his cigarettes. As always he delayed lighting the cigarette so that his need for it would be greater and, thus, the relief and pleasure it would bring, fuller. For some time he fondled it, his fingers shaping soft, voluptuous gestures, his warped old man's hands looking strangely abandoned on the bare desk and limp as if the bones had been crushed, and so white—except for the tobacco burn on the index and third fingers—it seemed his blood no longer traveled that far.

He lit the cigarette finally and as the smoke swelled his lungs, his eyelid stilled and his lined face lifted, the plume of white hair wafting above his narrow brow; his body—short, blunt, the shoulders slightly bent as if in deference to his sixty-three years—settled back in the chair. Delicately Max Berman crossed his legs and, looking down, examined his shoes for dust.

(The shoes were of a very soft, fawn-colored leather and somewhat foppishly pointed at the toe. They had been custom made in France and were his one last indulgence. He wore them in memory of his first wife, a French Jewess from Alsace-Lorraine whom he had met in Paris while lingering over his doctorate and married to avoid returning home. She had been gay, mindless and very excitable— but at night, she had also been capable of a profound stillness as she lay in bed waiting for him to turn to her, and this had always awed and delighted him. She had been a gift—and her death in a car accident had been a judgment on him for never having loved her, for never, indeed, having even allowed her to matter.) Fastidiously Max Berman unbuttoned his jacket and straightened his vest, which had a stain two decades old on the pocket. Through the smoke his veined eyes contemplated other, more pleasurable scenes. With his neatly shod foot swinging and his cigarette at a rakish tilt, he might have been an old *boulevardier* taking the sun and an absinthe before the afternoon's assignation.

A young face, the forehead shiny with earnestness, hung at the half-opened door. "Is this French Lit, fifty-four? Camus and Sartre?"

Max Berman winced at the rawness of the voice and the flat "a" in Sartre and said formally, "This is Modern French Literature, number fifty-four, yes, but there is some question as to whether we will take up Messieurs Camus and Sartre this session. They might prove hot work for a summer-evening course. We will probably do Gide and Mauriac, who are considerably more temperate. But come in nonetheless. . . ."

He was the gallant, half rising to bow her to a seat. He knew that she would select the one in the front row directly opposite his desk. At the bell her pen would quiver above her blank notebook, ready to commit his first word—indeed, the clearing of his throat—to paper, and her thin buttocks would begin sidling toward the edge of her chair.

His eyelid twitched with solicitude. He wished that he could have drawn the lids over her fitful eyes and pressed a cool hand to her forehead. She reminded him of what he had been several lifetimes ago: a boy with a pale, plump face and harried eyes, running from the occasional taunts at his yamilke along the shrill streets of Brownsville in Brooklyn, impeded by the heavy satchel of books which he always carried as proof of his scholarship. He had been proud of his brilliance at school and the Yeshiva, but at the same time he had been secretly troubled by it and resentful, for he could never believe that he had come by it naturally or that it belonged to him alone. Rather, it was like a heavy medal his father had hung around his neck—the chain bruising his flesh—and constantly exhorted him to wear proudly and use well.

The girl gave him an eager and ingratiating smile and he looked away. During his thirty years of teaching, a face similar to hers had crowded his vision whenever he had looked up from a desk. Perhaps it was fitting, he thought, and lighted another cigarette from the first, that she should be present as he tried again at life, unaware that behind his rimless glasses and within his ancient suit, he had been gutted.

He thought of those who had taken the last of his substance—and smiled tolerantly. "The boys of summer," he called them, his inquisitors, who had flailed him with a single question: "Are you now or have you ever been a member of the Communist party?" Max Berman had never taken their question seriously—perhaps because he had never taken his membership in the party seriously—and he had refused to answer. What had disturbed him, though, even when the investigation was over, was the feeling that he had really been under investigation for some other offense which did matter and of which he was guilty; that behind their accusations and charges had lurked another which had not been political but personal. For had he been disloyal to the government? His denial was a short, hawking laugh. Simply, he had never ceased being religious. When his father's God had become useless and even a little embarrassing, he had sought others: his work for a time, then the party. But he had been middle-aged when he joined and his faith, which had been so full as a boy, had grown thin. He had come, by then, to distrust all pieties, so that when the purges in Russia during the thirties confirmed his distrust, he had withdrawn into a modest cynicism.

But he had been made to answer for that error. Ten years later his inquisitors had flushed him out from the small community college in upstate New York where he had taught his classes from the same neat pack of notes each semester and had led him bound by subpoena to New York and bandied his name at the hearings until he had been dismissed from his job.

He remembered looking back at the pyres of burning autumn leaves on the campus his last day and feeling that another lifetime had ended—for he had always thought of his life as divided into many small lives, each with its own beginning and end. Like a hired mute, he had been present at each dying and kept the wake and wept professionally as the bier was lowered into the ground. Because of this feeling, he told himself that his final death would be anticlimactic.

After his dismissal he had continued living in the small house he had built near the college, alone except for an occasional visit from a colleague, idle but for some tutoring in French, content with the income he received from the property his parents had left him in Brooklyn—until the visits and tutoring had tapered off and a silence had begun to choke the house, like weeds springing up around a deserted place. He had begun to wonder then if he were still alive. He would wake at night from the recurrent dream of the hearings, where he was being accused of an unstated crime, to listen for his heart, his hand fumbling among the bedclothes to press the place. During the day he would pass repeatedly in front of the mirror with the pretext that he might have forgotten to shave that morning or that something had blown into his eyes. Above all, he had begun to think of his inquisitors with affection and to long for the sound of their voices. They, at least, had assured him of being alive.

As if seeking them out, he had returned to Brooklyn and to the house in Brownsville where he had lived as a boy and had boldly applied for a teaching post without mentioning the investigation. He had finally been offered the class which would begin in five minutes. It wasn't much: a six-week course in the summer evening session of a college without a rating, where classes were held in a converted factory building, a college whose campus took in the bargain department stores, the five-and-dime emporiums and neon-spangled movie houses of downtown Brooklyn.

Through the smoke from his cigarette, Max Berman's eyes—a waning blue that never seemed to focus on any one thing—drifted over the students who had gathered meanwhile. Imbuing them with his own disinterest, he believed that even before the class began, most of them were longing for its end and already anticipating the soft drinks at the soda fountain downstairs and the synthetic dramas at the nearby movie.

They made him sad. He would have liked to lead them like a Pied Piper back to the safety of their childhoods—all of them: the loud girl with the formidable calves of an athlete who reminded him, uncomfortably, of his second wife (a party member who was always shouting political heresy from some picket line and who had promptly divorced him upon discovering his irreverence); the two sallow-faced young men leaning out the window as if searching for the wind that had died; the slender young woman with crimped black hair who sat very still and apart from the others, her face turned toward the night sky as if to a friend.

Her loneliness interested him. He sensed its depth and his eye paused. He saw then that she was a Negro, a very pale mulatto with skin the color of clear, polished amber and a thin, mild face. She was somewhat older than the others in the room—a schoolteacher from the South, probably, who came north each summer to take courses toward a graduate degree. He felt a fleeting discomfort and irritation: discomfort at the thought that although he had been sinned against as a Jew he still shared in the sin against her and suffered from the same vague guilt, irritation that she recalled his own humiliations: the large ones, such as the fact that despite his brilliance he had been unable to get into a medical school as a young man because of the quota on Jews (not that he had wanted to be a doctor; that had been his father's wish) and had changed his studies from medicine to French; the small ones which had worn him thin: an eye widening imperceptibly as he gave his name, the savage glance which sought the Jewishness in his nose, his chin, in the set of his shoulders, the jokes snuffed into silence at his appearance. . . .

Tired suddenly, his eyelid pulsing, he turned and stared out the window at the gaudy constellation of neon lights. He longed for a drink, a quiet place and then sleep. And to bear him gently into sleep, to stay the terror which bound his heart then reminding him of those oleographs of Christ with the thorns binding his exposed heart—fat drops of blood from one so bloodless—to usher him into sleep, some pleasantly erotic image: a nude in a boudoir scattered with her frilled garments and warmed by her frivolous laugh, with the sun like a voyeur at the half-closed shutters. But this time instead of the usual Rubens nude with thighs like twin portals and a belly like a huge alabaster bowl into which he poured himself, he chose Gauguin's Aita Parari, her languorous form in the straight-back chair, her dark, sloping breasts, her eyes like the sun under shadow.

With the image still on his inner eye, he turned to the Negro girl and appraised her through a blind of cigarette smoke. She was still gazing out at the night sky and something about her fixed stare, her hands stiffly arranged in her lap, the nerve fluttering within the curve of her throat, betrayed a vein of tension within the rock of her calm. It was as if she had fled long ago to a remote region within herself, taking with her all that was most valuable and most vulnerable about herself.

She stirred finally, her slight breasts lifting beneath her flowered summer dress as she breathed deeply—and Max Berman thought again of Gauguin's girl with the dark, sloping breasts. What would this girl with the amber-colored skin be like on a couch in a sunlit room, nude in a straight-back chair? And as the question echoed along each nerve and stilled his breathing, it seemed suddenly that life, which had scorned him for so long, held out her hand again—but still a little beyond his reach. Only the girl, he sensed, could bring him close enough to touch it. She alone was the bridge. So that even while he repeated to himself that he was being presumptuous (for she would surely refuse him) and ridiculous (for even if she did not, what could he do—his performance would be a mere scramble and twitch), he vowed at the same time to have her. The challenge eased the tightness around his heart suddenly; it soothed the damaged muscle of his eye and as the bell rang he rose and said briskly, "Ladies and gentlemen, may I have your attention, please. My name is Max Berman. The course is Modern French Literature, number fifty-four. May I suggest that you check your program cards to see whether you are in the right place at the right time."

Her essay on Gide's *The Immoralist* lay on his desk and the note from the administration informing him, first, that his past political activities had been brought to their attention and then dismissing him at the end of the session weighed the inside pocket of his jacket. The two, her paper and the note, were linked in his mind. Her paper reminded him that the vow he had taken was still an empty one, for the term was half over and he had never once spoken to her (as if she understood his intention she was always late and disappeared as soon as the closing bell rang, leaving him trapped in a clamorous circle of students around his desk), while the note which wrecked his small attempt to start anew suddenly made that vow more urgent. It gave him the edge of desperation he needed to act finally. So that as soon as the bell rang, he returned all the papers but hers, announced that all questions would have to wait until their next meeting and, waving off the students from his desk, called above their protests, "Miss Williams, if you have a moment, I'd like to speak with you briefly about your paper."

She approached his desk like a child who has been cautioned not to talk to strangers, her fingers touching the backs of the chair as if for support, her gaze following the departing students as though she longed to accompany them.

Her slight apprehensiveness pleased him. It suggested a submissiveness which gave him, as he rose uncertainly, a feeling of certainty and command. Her hesitancy was somehow in keeping with the color of her skin. She seemed to bring not only herself but the host of black women whose bodies had been despoiled to make her. He would not only possess her but them also, he thought (not really thought, for he scarcely allowed these thoughts to form before he snuffed them out). Through their collective suffering, which she contained, his own personal suffering would be eased; he would be pardoned for whatever sin it was he had committed against life.

"I hope you weren't unduly alarmed when I didn't return your paper along with the others," he said, and had to look up as she reached the desk. She was taller close up and her eyes, which he had thought were black, were a strong, flecked brown with very small pupils which seemed to shrink now from the sight of him. "But I found it so interesting I wanted to give it to you privately."

"I didn't know what to think," she said, and her voice—he heard it for the first time for she never recited or answered in class—was low, cautious, Southern.

"It was, to say the least, refreshing. It not only showed some original and mature thinking on your part, but it also proved that you've been listening in class—and after twenty-five years and more of teaching it's encouraging to find that some students do listen. If you have a little time I'd like to tell you, more specifically, what I liked about it. . . ."

Talking easily, reassuring her with his professional tone and a deft gesture with his cigarette, he led her from the room as the next class filed in, his hand cupped at her elbow but not touching it, his manner urbane, courtly, kind. They paused on the landing at the end of the long corridor with the stairs piled in steel tiers above and plunging below them. An intimate silence swept up the stairwell in a warm gust and Max Berman said, "I'm curious. Why did you choose *The Immoralist?*"

She started suspiciously, afraid, it seemed, that her answer might expose and endanger the self she guarded so closely within.

"Well," she said finally, her glance reaching down the stairs to the door marked EXIT at the bottom, "when you said we could use anything by Gide

I decided on *The Immoralist,* since it was the first book I read in the original French when I was in undergraduate school. I didn't understand it then because my French was so weak, I guess, so I always thought about it afterward for some odd reason. I was shocked by what I did understand, of course, but something else about it appealed to me, so when you made the assignment I thought I'd try reading it again. I understood it a little better this time. At least I think so. . . ."

"Your paper proves you did."

She smiled absently, intent on some other thought. Then she said cautiously, but with unexpected force, "You see, to me, the book seems to say that the only way you begin to know what you are and how much you are capable of is by daring to try something, by doing something which tests you. . . ."

"Something bold," he said.

"Yes."

"Even sinful."

She paused, questioning this, and then said reluctantly, "Yes, perhaps even sinful."

"The salutary effects of sin, you might say." He gave the little bow.

But she had not heard this; her mind had already leaped ahead. "The only trouble, at least with the character in Gide's book, is that what he finds out about himself is so terrible. He is so unhappy. . . ."

"But at least he knows, poor sinner." And his playful tone went unnoticed.

"Yes," she said with the same startling forcefulness. "And another thing, in finding out what he is, he destroys his wife. It was as if she had to die in order for him to live and know himself. Perhaps in order for a person to live and know himself somebody else must die. Maybe there's always a balancing out. . . . In a way"—and he had to lean close now to hear her—"I believe this."

Max Berman edged back as he glimpsed something move within her abstracted gaze. It was like a strong and restless seed that had taken root in the darkness there and was straining now toward the light. He had not expected so subtle and complex a force beneath her mild exterior and he found it disturbing and dangerous, but fascinating.

"Well, it's a most interesting interpretation," he said. "I don't know if M. Gide would have agreed, but then he's not around to give his opinion. Tell me, where did you do your undergraduate work?"

"At Howard University."

"And you majored in French?"

"Yes."

"Why, if I may ask?" he said gently.

"Well, my mother was from New Orleans and could still speak a little Creole and I got interested in learning how to speak French through her, I guess. I teach it now at a junior high school in Richmond. Only the beginner courses because I don't have my master's. You know, *je vais, tu vas, il va* and *Frère Jacques*. It's not very inspiring."

"You should do something about that then, my dear Miss Williams. Perhaps it's time for you, like our friend in Gide, to try something new and bold."

"I know," she said, and her pale hand sketched a vague, despairing gesture. "I thought maybe if I got my master's . . . that's why I decided to come north this summer and start taking some courses. . . ."

Max Berman quickly lighted a cigarette to still the flurry inside him, for the moment he had been awaiting had come. He flicked her paper, which he still held. "Well, you've got the makings of a master's thesis right here. If you like I will suggest some ways for you to expand it sometime. A few pointers from an old pro might help."

He had to turn from her astonished and grateful smile—it was like a child's. He said carefully, "The only problem will be to find a place where we can talk quietly. Regrettably, I don't rate an office. . . ."

"Perhaps we could use one of the empty classrooms," she said.

"That would be much too dismal a setting for a pleasant discussion."

He watched the disappointment wilt her smile and when he spoke he made certain that the same disappointment weighed his voice. "Another difficulty is that the term's half over, which gives us little or no time. But let's not give up. Perhaps we can arrange to meet and talk over a weekend. The only hitch there is that I spend weekends at my place in the country. Of course you're perfectly welcome to come up there. It's only about seventy miles from New York, in the heart of what's very appropriately called the Borsch Circuit, even though, thank God, my place is a good distance away from the borsch. That is, it's very quiet and there's never anybody around except with my permission."

She did not move, yet she seemed to start; she made no sound, yet he thought he heard a bewildered cry. And then she did a strange thing, standing there with the breath sucked into the hollow of her throat and her smile, that had opened to him with such trust, dying—her eyes, her hands faltering up begged him to declare himself.

"There's a lake near the house," he said, "so that when you get tired of talking—or better, listening to me talk—you can take a swim, if you like. I would very much enjoy that sight." And as the nerve tugged at his eyelid, he seemed to wink behind his rimless glasses.

Her sudden, blind step back was like a man groping his way through a strange room in the dark, and instinctively Max Berman reached out to break her fall. Her arms, bare to the shoulder because of the heat (he knew the feel of her skin without even touching it—it would be like a rich, fine-textured cloth which would soothe and hide him in its amber warmth), struck out once to drive him off and then fell limp at her side, and her eyes became vivid and convulsive in her numbed face. She strained toward the stairs and the exit door at the bottom, but she could not move. Nor could she speak. She did not even cry. Her eyes remained dry and dull with disbelief. Only her shoulders trembled as though she was silently weeping inside.

It was as though she had never learned the forms and expressions of anger. The outrage of a lifetime, of her history, was trapped inside her. And she stared at Max Berman with this mute, paralyzing rage. Not really at him but to his side, as if she caught sight of others behind him. And remembering how he had imagined a column of dark women trailing her to his desk, he sensed that she glimpsed a legion of old men with sere flesh and lonely eyes flanking him: "old lechers with a love on every wind . . ."

"I'm sorry, Miss Williams," he said, and would have welcomed her insults, for he would have been able, at least, to distill from them some passion and a kind of intimacy. It would have been, in a way, like touching her. "It was only that you are a very attractive young woman and although I'm no longer young"—and he gave the tragic little laugh which sought to dismiss that fact—"I can still appreciate and even desire an attractive woman. But I was wrong. . . ." His self-disgust, overwhelming him finally, choked off his voice. "And so very crude. Forgive me. I can offer no excuse for my behavior other than my approaching senility."

He could not even manage a little marionette bow this time. Quickly he shoved the paper on Gide into her lifeless hand, but it fell, the pages separating, and as he hurried past her downstairs and out the door, he heard the pages scattering like dead leaves on the steps.

She remained away until the night of the final examination, which was also the last meeting of the class. By that time Max Berman, believing that she would not return, had almost succeeded in forgetting her. He was no longer even certain of how she looked, for her face had been absorbed into the single, blurred, featureless face of all the women who had ever refused him. So that she startled him as much as a stranger would have when he entered the room that night and found her alone amid a maze of empty chairs, her face turned toward the window as on the first night and her hands serene in her lap. She turned at his footstep and it was as if she had also forgotten all that had passed between them. She waited until he said, "I'm glad you decided to take the examination. I'm sure you won't have any difficulty with it"; then she gave him a nod that was somehow reminiscent of his little bow and turned again to the window.

He was relieved yet puzzled by her composure. It was as if during her three-week absence she had waged and won a decisive contest with herself and was ready now to act. He was wary suddenly and all during the examination he tried to discover what lay behind her strange calm, studying her bent head amid the shifting heads of the other students, her slim hand guiding the pen across the page, her legs—the long bone visible, it seemed, beneath the flesh. Desire flared and quickly died.

"Excuse me, Professor Berman, will you take up Camus and Sartre next semester, maybe?" The girl who sat in front of his desk was standing over him with her earnest smile and finished examination folder.

"That might prove somewhat difficult, since I won't be here."

"No more?"

"No."

"I mean, not even next summer?"

"I doubt it."

"Gee, I'm sorry. I mean, I enjoyed the course and everything."

He bowed his thanks and held his head down until she left. Her compliment, so piteous somehow, brought on the despair he had forced to the dim rear of his mind. He could no longer flee the thought of the exile awaiting him when the class tonight ended. He could either remain in the house in Brooklyn, where the memory of his father's face above the radiance of the Sabbath candles haunted him from the shadows, reminding him of the certainty he had lost and never found again, where the mirrors in his father's room were still shrouded with sheets, as on the day he lay dying and moaning into his beard that his only son was a bad Jew; or he could return to the house in the country, to the silence shrill with loneliness.

The cigarette he was smoking burned his fingers, rousing him, and he saw over the pile of examination folders on his desk that the room was empty except for the Negro girl. She had finished—her pen lay aslant the closed folder on her desk—but she had remained in her seat and she was smiling across the room at him—a set, artificial smile that was both cold and threatening. It utterly denuded him and he was wildly angry suddenly that she had seen him give way to despair; he wanted to remind her (he could not stay the thought; it attacked him like an assailant from a dark turn in his mind) that she was only black after all. . . . His head dropped and he almost wept with shame.

The girl stiffened as if she had seen the thought and then the tiny muscles around her mouth quickly arranged the bland smile. She came up to his desk, placed her folder on top of the others and said pleasantly, her eyes like dark, shattered glass that spared Max Berman his reflection, "I've changed my mind. I think I'd like to spend a day at your place in the country if your invitation still holds."

He thought of refusing her, for her voice held neither promise nor passion, but he could not. Her presence, even if it was only for a day, would make his return easier. And there was still the possibility of passion despite her cold manner and the deliberate smile. He thought of how long it had been since he had had someone, of how badly he needed the sleep which followed love and of awakening certain, for the first time in years, of his existence.

PAULE MARSHALL
223

"Of course the invitation still holds. I'm driving up tonight."

"I won't be able to come until Sunday," she said firmly. "Is there a train then?"

"Yes, in the morning," he said, and gave her the schedule.

"You'll meet me at the station?"

"Of course. You can't miss my car. It's a very shabby but venerable Chevy."

She smiled stiffly and left, her heels awakening the silence of the empty corridor, the sound reaching back to tap like a warning finger on Max Berman's temple.

The pale sunlight slanting through the windshield lay like a cat on his knees, and the motor of his old Chevy, turning softly under him could have been the humming of its heart. A little distance from the car a log-cabin station house—the logs blackened by the seasons—stood alone against the hills, and the hills, in turn, lifted softly, still green although the summer was ending, into the vague autumn sky.

The morning mist and pale sun, the green that was still somehow new, made it seem that the season was stirring into life even as it died, and this contradiction pained Max Berman at the same time that it pleased him. For it was his own contradiction after all: his desires which remained those of a young man even as he was dying.

He had been parked for some time in the deserted station, yet his hands were still tensed on the steering wheel and his foot hovered near the accelerator. As soon as he had arrived in the station he had wanted to leave. But like the girl that night on the landing, he was too stiff with tension to move. He could only wait, his eyelid twitching with foreboding, regret, curiosity and hope.

Finally and with no warning the train charged through the fiery green, setting off a tremor underground. Max Berman imagined the girl seated at a window in the train, her hands arranged quietly in her lap and her gaze scanning the hills that were so familiar to him, and yet he could not believe that she was really there. Perhaps her plan had been to disappoint him. She might be in New York or on her way back to Richmond now, laughing at the trick she had played on him. He was convinced of this suddenly, so that even when he saw her walking toward him through the blown steam from under the train, he told himself that she was a mirage created by the steam. Only when she sat beside him in the car, bringing with her, it seemed, an essence she had distilled from the morning air and rubbed into her skin, was he certain of her reality.

"I brought my bathing suit but it's much too cold to swim," she said and gave him the deliberate smile.

He did not see it; he only heard her voice, its warm Southern lilt in the chill, its intimacy in the closed car—and an excitement swept him, cold first and then hot, as if the sun had burst in his blood.

"It's the morning air," he said. "By noon it should be like summer again."

"Is that a promise?"

"Yes."

By noon the cold morning mist had lifted above the hills and below, in the lake valley, the sunlight was a sheer gold net spread out on the grass as if to dry, draped on the trees and flung, glinting, over the lake. Max Berman felt it brush his shoulders gently as he sat by the lake waiting for the girl, who had gone up to the house to change into her swimsuit.

He had spent the morning showing her the fields and small wood near his house. During the long walk he had been careful to keep a little apart from her. He would extend a hand as they climbed a rise or when she stepped uncertainly over a rock, but he would not really touch her. He was afraid that at his touch, no matter how slight and casual, her scream would spiral into the morning calm, or worse, his touch would unleash the threatening thing he sensed behind her even smile.

He had talked of her paper and she had listened politely and occasionally even asked a question or made a comment. But all the while detached, distant, drawn within herself as she had been that first night in the classroom. And then halfway down a slope she had paused and, pointing to the canvas tops of her white sneakers, which had become wet and dark from the dew secreted in the grass, she had laughed. The sound, coming so abruptly in the midst of her tense quiet, joined her, it seemed, to the wood and wide fields, to the hills; she shared their simplicity and held within her the same strong current of life. Max Berman had felt privileged suddenly, and humble. He had stopped questioning her smile. He had told himself then that it would not matter even if she stopped and picking up a rock bludgeoned him from behind.

"There's a lake near my home, but it's not like this," the girl said, coming up behind him. "Yours is so dark and serious-looking."

He nodded and followed her gaze out to the lake, where the ripples were long, smooth welts raised by the wind, and across to the other bank, where a group of birches stepped delicately down to the lake and bending over touched the water with their branches as if testing it before they plunged.

The girl came and stood beside him now—and she was like a pale-gold naiad, the spirit of the lake, her eyes reflecting its somber autumnal tone and her body as supple as the birches. She walked slowly into the water, unaware, it seemed, of the sudden passion in his gaze, or perhaps uncaring; and as she walked she held out her arms in what seemed a gesture of invocation (and Max Berman remembered his father with the fringed shawl draped on his outstretched arms as he invoked their God each Sabbath with the same gesture); her head was bent as if she listened for a voice beneath the water's murmurous surface. When the ground gave way she still seemed to be walking and listening, her arms outstretched. The water reached her waist, her small breasts, her shoulders. She lifted her head once, breathed deeply and disappeared.

She stayed down for a long time and when her white cap finally broke the water some distance out, Max Berman felt strangely stranded and deprived. He understood suddenly the profound cleavage between them and the absurdity of his hope. The water between them became the years which separated them. Her white cap was the sign of her purity, while the silt darkening the lake was the flotsam of his failures. Above all, their color— her arms a pale, flashing gold in the sunlit water and his bled white and flaccid with the veins like angry blue penciling—marked the final barrier.

He was sad as they climbed toward the house late that afternoon and troubled. A crow cawed derisively in the bracken, heralding the dusk which would not only end their strange day but would also, he felt, unveil her smile, so that he would learn the reason for her coming. And because he was sad, he said wryly, "I think I should tell you that you've been spending the day with something of an outcast."

"Oh," she said and waited.

He told her of the dismissal, punctuating his words with the little hoarse, deprecating laugh and waving aside the pain with his cigarette. She listened, polite but neutral, and because she remained unmoved, he wanted to confess all the more. So that during dinner and afterward when they sat outside on the porch, he told her of the investigation.

"It was very funny once you saw it from the proper perspective, which I did, of course," he said. "I mean here they were accusing me of crimes I couldn't remember committing and asking me for the names of people with whom I had never associated. It was pure farce. But I made a mistake. I should have done something dramatic or something just as farcical. Bared my breast in the public market place or written a tome on my apostasy, naming names. It would have been a far different story then. Instead of my present ignominy I would have been offered a chairmanship at Yale.... No? Well, Brandeis then. I would have been draped in honorary degrees...."

"Well, why didn't you confess?" she said impatiently.

"I've often asked myself the same interesting question, but I haven't come up with a satisfactory answer yet. I suspect, though, that I said nothing because none of it really mattered that much."

"What did matter?" she asked sharply.

He sat back, waiting for the witty answer, but none came, because just then the frame upon which his organs were strung seemed to snap and he felt his heart, his lungs, his vital parts fall in a heap within him. Her question had dealt the severing blow, for it was the same question he understood suddenly that the vague forms in his dream asked repeatedly. It had been the plaintive undercurrent to his father's dying moan, the real accusation behind the charges of his inquisitors at the hearing.

For what had mattered? He gazed through his sudden shock at the night squatting on the porch steps, at the hills asleep like gentle beasts in the darkness, at the black screen of the sky where the events of his life passed in a mute, accusing review—and he saw nothing there to which he had given himself or in which he had truly believed since the belief and dedication of his boyhood.

"Did you hear my question?" she asked, and he was glad that he sat within the shadows clinging to the porch screen and could not be seen.

"Yes, I did," he said faintly, and his eyelid twitched. "But I'm afraid it's another one of those I can't answer satisfactorily." And then he struggled for the old flippancy. "You make an excellent examiner, you know. Far better than my inquisitors."

"What will you do now?" Her voice and cold smile did not spare him.

He shrugged and the motion, a slow, eloquent lifting of the shoulders, brought with it suddenly the weight and memory of his boyhood. It was the familiar gesture of the women hawkers in Belmont Market, of the men standing outside the temple on Saturday mornings, each of them reflecting his image of God in their forbidding black coats and with the black, tumbling beards in which he had always imagined he could hide as in a forest. All this had mattered, he called loudly to himself, and said aloud to the girl, "Let me see if I can answer this one at least. What *will* I do?" He paused and swung his leg so that his foot in the fastidious French shoe caught the light from the house. "Grow flowers and write my memoirs. How's that? That would be the proper way for a gentleman and scholar to retire. Or hire one of those hefty housekeepers who will bully me and when I die in my sleep draw the sheet over my face and call my lawyer. That's somewhat European, but how's that?"

When she said nothing for a long time, he added soberly, "But that's not a fair question for me any more. I leave all such considerations to the young. To you, for that matter. What will you do, my dear Miss Williams?"

It was as if she had been expecting the question and had been readying her answer all the time that he had been talking. She leaned forward eagerly and with her face and part of her body fully in the light, she said, "I will do something. I don't know what yet, but something."

Max Berman started back a little. The answer was so unlike her vague, resigned "I know" on the landing that night when he had admonished her to try something new.

He edged back into the darkness and she leaned further into the light, her eyes overwhelming her face and her mouth set in a thin, determined line. "I will do something," she said, bearing down on each word, "because for the first time in my life I feel almost brave."

He glimpsed this new bravery behind her hard gaze and sensed something vital and purposeful, precious, which she had found and guarded like a prize within her center. He wanted it. He would have liked to snatch it and run like a thief. He no longer desired her but it, and starting forward with a sudden envious cry, he caught her arm and drew her close, seeking it.

But he could not get to it. Although she did not pull away her arm, although she made no protest as his face wavered close to hers, he did not really touch her. She held herself and her prize out of his desperate reach and her smile was a knife she pressed to his throat. He saw himself for what he was in her clear, cold gaze: an old man with skin the color and texture of dough that had been kneaded by the years into tragic folds, with faded eyes adrift behind a pair of rimless glasses and the roughened flesh at his throat like a bird's wattles. And as the disgust which he read in her eyes swept him, his hand dropped from her arm. He started to murmur, "Forgive me . . ." when suddenly she caught hold of his wrist, pulling him close again, and he felt the strength which had borne her swiftly through the water earlier hold him now as she said quietly and without passion, "And do you know why, Dr. Berman, I feel almost brave today? Because ever since I can remember my parents were always telling me, 'Stay away from white folks. Just leave them alone. You mind your business and they'll mind theirs. Don't go near them.' And they made sure I didn't. My father, who was the principal of a colored grade school in Richmond, used to drive me to and from school every day. When I needed something from downtown my mother would take me and if the white saleslady asked me anything she would answer. . . .

"And my parents were always telling me, 'Stay away from niggers,' and that meant anybody darker than we were." She held out her arm in the light and Max Berman saw the skin almost as white as his but for the subtle amber shading. Staring at the arm she said tragically, "I was so confused I never really went near anybody. Even when I went away to college I kept to myself. I didn't marry the man I wanted to because he was dark and I knew my parents would disapprove. . . ." She paused, her wistful gaze searching the darkness for the face of the man she had refused, it seemed, and not finding it she went on sadly, "So after graduation I returned home and started teaching and I was just as confused and frightened and ashamed as always. When my parents died I went on the same way. And I would have gone on like that the rest of my life if it hadn't been for you, Dr. Berman"— and the sarcasm leaped behind her cold smile. "In a way you did me a favor. You let me know how you—and most of the people like you— see me."

"My dear Miss Williams, I assure you I was not attracted to you because you were colored. . . ." And he broke off, remembering just how acutely aware of her color he had been.

"I'm not interested in your reasons!" she said brutally. "What matters is what it meant to me. I thought about this these last three weeks and about my parents—how wrong they had been, how frightened, and the terrible thing they had done to me . . . And I wasn't confused any longer." Her head lifted, tremulous with her new assurance. "I can do something now! I can begin," she said with her head poised. "Look how I came all the way up here to tell you this to your face. Because how could you harm me? You're so old you're like a cup I could break in my hand." And her hand tightened on his wrist, wrenching the last of his frail life from him, it seemed. Through the quick pain he remembered her saying on the landing that night: "Maybe in order for a person to live someone else must die" and her quiet "I believe this" then. Now her sudden laugh, an infinitely cruel sound in the warm night, confirmed her belief.

Suddenly she was the one who seemed old, indeed ageless. Her touch became mortal and Max Berman saw the darkness that would end his life gathered in her eyes. But even as he sprang back, jerking his arm away, a part of him rushed forward to embrace that darkness, and his cry, wounding the night, held both ecstasy and terror.

"That's all I came for," she said, rising. "You can drive me to the station now."

They drove to the station in silence. Then, just as the girl started from the car, she turned with an ironic, pitiless smile and said, "You know, it's been a nice day, all things considered. It really turned summer again as you said it would. And even though your lake isn't anything like the one near my home, it's almost as nice."

Max Berman bowed to her for the last time, accepting with that gesture his responsibility for her rage, which went deeper than his, and for her anger, which would spur her finally to live. And not only for her, but for all those at last whom he had wronged through his indifference: his father lying in the room of shrouded mirrors, the wives he had never loved, his work which he had never believed in enough and, lastly (even though he knew it was too late and he would not be spared), himself.

Too weary to move, he watched the girl cross to the train which would bear her south, her head lifted as though she carried life as lightly there as if it were a hat made of tulle. When the train departed his numbed eyes followed it until its rear light was like a single firefly in the immense night or the last flickering of his life. Then he drove back through the darkness.

GAYL JONES

Born in Kentucky in 1949, Gayl Jones is presently an assistant professor of English at the University of Michigan. Her books include *Corregidora* (1975), *Eva's Man* (1976), and *White Rat* (1977). Her short stories have also appeared in *Panache, Essence, Black Scholar,* and *Amistad 11.*

THE ROUNDHOUSE

I didn't know what was wrong with him, even after I went to see him. I'd heard at work that he was sick, and asked if he had anybody to do for him. They said he had a room in Will Darcy's rooming house. He didn't have a family, and nobody knew anything about him, and there was no one to take care of him. I hadn't known him long, just three weeks, and we'd never really said more than "Hi." He was a quiet man. He was the kind you feel close to even though you've said no more than "Hi."

I was working at the roundhouse in Garrett, Indiana. Garrett, not Gary. Just after the war, the first one. The roundhouse was where the trains came in. It was our job to polish the parts, and keep the engines shining. I was hired during the war, when they were hiring women. I'd been working a year there, and my kids were going to school, when he came. He never said anything to anybody. He did his work. He did more work than he had to, and he didn't talk to anyone. He looked like a foreigner, reddish brown. Maybe he was a Negro, maybe he was Puerto Rican or something or maybe mixed. People said maybe he couldn't speak English. He never bothered anybody, and nobody bothered him. He came to work and he left work and he never talked. I don't even know if he stopped for lunch.

One day we'd been assigned to the same engine. He was there before I was, polishing away. He looked up when I came. "Hi," I said. He didn't smile. He looked back down. He wasn't being unfriendly. There are some people who just don't talk. I could tell he knew English though. I don't know how but I could tell. He didn't have the look of someone who didn't know the language.

We worked. At lunchtime I quit and started away but saw he was still working. I started to ask, "Aren't you going to have lunch?" but didn't. I thought maybe he wouldn't want me to.

I went and sat down on a bench, eating a sandwich. Some other people were there. Joe McDowell was there.

"Did he say anything to you?" he asked.

"He said 'Hi,'" I said.

"That's more than he said to me," McDowell said. "I worked with him a whole day. Funny thing, though. I didn't feel uncomfortable. Most people don't talk, you feel uncomfortable as hell. With him you don't."

"I know," I said. "It's nice."

"Nobody knows anything about him." McDowell said. "Henderson says he's taken a room over at Darcy's place. That's not far from where you live. I've heard of people that don't talk much. He don't talk at all."

"He probably does when he has to," I said.

"Ask for a job or a room," McDowell said, not sarcastically.

"Anyway, he seems very nice," I said.

McDowell nodded. It was time to start working again. Four more hours. The kids would be home from school.

When five o'clock came, he stopped work, and left. He was practically the first to be gone. It was summer and he didn't need to grab a coat. He rolled down his shirt-sleeves. Neither Darcy's nor where I lived was far from the station, so we both walked home, about a fifteen or twenty minute walk, a half hour on bad days. He walked fast. I didn't try to catch up with him. When I got to the street, he was a block ahead of me. I saw him turn into the rooming house. I passed where he lived and walked a block more up the street.

The next day we walked home the same way, he walking rapidly ahead again. He seemed always in a hurry, even when he worked. He worked hard and fast. It was a wonder the men hadn't got together and told him to slow down, he made the others look bad, but people liked him, though he didn't talk much. As I said, he was walking ahead and turned in at his gate, but when I passed the rooming house this time, he had not gone in the door, but was standing there, his hand on the doorknob, his head turned looking at me. He didn't say anything and went inside. I walked on. I felt funny.

"I knew a switchman I worked with," McDowell was saying then he stopped and looked up.

I looked up. *He* was standing there, looking down at me.

"I want to walk you home," he said to me.

"O-kay," I said, bewildered. Then he walked away. McDowell looked at me and grinned.

When I got outside, he was waiting for me. It had been cooler this morning and he had a jacket slung over his shoulder. He looked down and smiled. We started walking.

"How are you?" I asked.

"Okay," he said.

We walked on.

"I didn't know you came this way," he said, the first time he'd said more than a word or two. "We could have walked together before."

Now I didn't say anything.

"You live a block away from me," he said. I wondered how he knew. "In a house."

"I have two kids," I said.

"You're married?" he asked, as if I might not be.

"I was."

"How do you mean?"

"He died."

"In the war?"

"No."

I was waiting for him to ask how, like most people had, but he didn't. He seemed to feel if I wanted him to know I'd tell him. I wanted him to know. "From alcohol," I said.

"Oh," he said. I guess I hadn't really expected an "I'm sorry" from him either. The platitudes. I guess he didn't do things that way.

Then we were at the boarding house. I was stopping for him to turn in, but he didn't. He took my elbow slightly.

"I'll see you home," he said.

He saw me home, and then went back. I went inside.

"Who's he?" Jean asked. "He's handsome." Jean was my daughter, thirteen, with her hairs in plaits.

"His name's . . . I don't know his name. He works where I work."

"I haven't seen him before."

"He hasn't walked me home before. Where's Ben?"

"He's in the kitchen."

Ben was my son. He was fourteen. He was light, almost white. Jean was brown. My grandmother had been white. It was hard explaining to people. It was better in Indiana.

"How was school?" I asked.

"The same."

"Much homework?"

"Yes."

Ben came in and said "Hi." I started supper.

"Mama's got a beau," I heard Jean tell Ben.

"I have not," I called. "He works at the roundhouse."

"He walked her home," Jean said, triumphantly. "He's good-looking," she added. "You'll have to check him out."

I didn't hear Ben say anything. I was thinking Ben might like him.

The next day I didn't see him at all, not even after work, and the day after he was not there. I had lunch with McDowell.

"He's probably gone," McDowell said.

"Gone?" I asked.

"You know how it is with them. Come to one town. Hold down a job for a while. Have to keep moving."

"You don't mean he's running from the law?"

"Don't have to be the law."

"What then?"

"Himself. Somebody. How should I know?"

"I didn't know his name," I said.

"James Buchanan Jones, named for the President. Henderson says he calls himself Jake. Wants the people that know him to."

Lunchtime was over. I went back to work.

The next day, McDowell came over to where I was working.

"Henderson says Jake's sick."

"What's wrong?"

"Don't know."

Hasn't anybody been to see about him?"

"Don't think so. He didn't get close with people."

I frowned and put down the rag and started away. McDowell grabbed my arm.

"Where you going?" he asked.

"To see about him."

"The Man won't like it, stopping on the job."

"I don't care."

"You've got two kids."

"Tell him I got sick, Joe."

Joe shook his head slowly.

"It's an hour till lunch," he said.

"All right." I picked up the rag.

He started away.

"Thanks, Joe," I called. He nodded.

At lunchtime I went outside.

"What did the boss say when I didn't come back?" I asked McDowell, the first thing in the morning, before I even started.

"I told him you got sick," he said.

"Thank you."

"How is he?"

"Fever. Wouldn't let me call a doctor. I'm doing what I can. He didn't have any food."

"How are you going to work and take care of him and yourself and the kids?"

"I can manage," I said.

"If you need me you know where to reach me," he said.

"Sure, Joe," I said. I thanked him again. He tapped my arm and went to work. I thought I wouldn't know what to do without him. He had been awfully good to me and the kids.

That afternoon I stopped at the rooming house before going home. I had a bundle with me. A loaf of bread and some curtains. I put the bundle down and went over to him and placed my hand on his forehead. He hadn't been able to shave for about a week now.

"How do you feel?" I asked.

"Better, thanks to you," he said.

"You still have a fever," I said.

I went over to the bundle and started taking the curtains out.

"What are they for? I have curtains," he said.

"Your curtains are ugly," I said.

"They're not, if you don't look at them," he said.

"These you can look at," I said, and started putting the curtains up. The window was small and faced the street. There was only the bed in the room and a chest of drawers, a table and chair.

"Now you won't be able to tell I'm a bachelor," he said.

"I can tell," I said.

I sat down in the chair.

"I've got to go home and fix supper," I said. "I'll be back a little later and bring you something over."

I started up to go but he took one of my hands in both his and said thank you. I smiled and went home.

I went back with some chicken soup. He didn't eat much.

"Your fever's going down," I said. "You couldn't tell by the way you eat, though."

"I never eat much. You have to learn not to."

"Joe McDowell says you're the kind of person that never stays in one place."

"I guess that's right," he said.

"Where are you from?" I asked.

He didn't answer. I didn't press him to.

"You have kids," he said. "What are they like?"

"They're nice," I said.

"You know you live with people a long time and then when somebody asks you what they're like you say they're nice. I guess that's all you can say really." He wasn't being sarcastic.

"I have their pictures," I said. I took out a billfold from my purse and opened it and showed him their pictures.

"The boy's half white," he said.

"Is there a crime against having white blood?" I asked. I was jumpy on that subject.

"The same crime as having black," he said.

"My grandmother," I said.

"You don't have to explain," he said.

"I know," I said.

"They say my mother was a gypsy," he said. "If she showed anybody my picture they would have asked, 'What makes the boy so brown?' "

"You didn't know her?"

"I didn't know her or my father," he said. "I grew up in homes."

"I'm sorry."

He grew angry suddenly. "Don't say you're sorry."

"Okay, Jake." I was hurt.

He touched my hand.

"Don't take it wrong," he said.

"Okay."

I stood up. "I'd better go."

"You're not angry?"

"No, no."

"Promise?"

"I promise."

The next day I saw McDowell for lunch.

"How's he doing?" he asked.

"The fever's almost gone," I said. "I think it's just overwork. He doesn't take care of himself. He doesn't eat."

"He needs a wife," Joe said.

I didn't say anything.

In a couple of days, Jake was well but didn't come back to work again. He had done what McDowell said people like that did.

"You miss him don't you?" McDowell said. "You knew what he'd do. Men like that . . ."

"Yeah, I know about men like that," I said.

He touched my arm, "I'm sorry," he said.
"Don't be," I said.

When the war was over and the men had come home, the roundhouse had kept some of us on, mostly those who didn't have husbands. Now they were laying some of us off again or reducing our hours. My hours had been reduced, and what I was making now would hardly buy chicken feed, less more support two kids.

When somebody started paying my grocery bills and coal bills, the first person I thought of was McDowell.

"What are you doing?" I asked Joe. I explained. He said he wasn't doing anything. No, it couldn't be, I decided.

The mysterious bill payments went on for several months. I asked the store not to take any more money, but they said there was nothing they could do about it.

I was in the kitchen fixing supper when the doorbell rang. Jean went to answer it. She came back into the kitchen, smiling.

"Who is it?" I asked.

"Go see," she said.

I frowned and wiped my hands on my apron. I stopped in the doorway to the hall.

"Jake!" I exclaimed. I went over to him. "How are you?"

"Very well," he said. "You look well."

There was a bench in the hall.

"Let's sit down," I said.

He said he'd rather stand, and if things went well then we could sit down. I asked him what he was talking about.

He said he wanted to take care of me. He said I had taken care of him when he was sick, and now he was ready to take care of me.

I looked up at him. He wasn't smiling. He was waiting.

I sat down.

He sat down beside me.

TONI MORRISON

Born in Ohio in 1931, Toni Morrison currently lives in New York City, where she is a senior editor at Random House. She has taught literature at Texas Southern University (1955–1957) and at Howard University (1957–1964). Most recently, she has been a guest lecturer in Afro-American literature at Yale University. Her published novels are *The Bluest Eye* (1971), *Sula* (1974), and *Song of Solomon* (1977).

1 9 2 1

From *Sula*

Sula Peace lived in a house of many rooms that had been built over a period of five years to the specifications of its owner, who kept on adding things: more stairways—there were three sets to the second floor—more rooms, doors and stoops. There were rooms that had three doors, others that opened out on the porch only and were inaccessible from any other part of the house; others that you could get to only by going through somebody's bedroom. The creator and sovereign of this enormous house with the four sickle-pear trees in the front yard and the single elm in the back yard was Eva Peace, who sat in a wagon on the third floor directing the lives of her children, friends, strays, and a constant stream of boarders. Fewer than nine people in the town remembered when Eva had two legs, and her oldest child, Hannah, was not one of them. Unless Eva herself introduced the subject, no one ever spoke of her disability; they pretended to ignore it, unless, in some mood of fancy, she began some fearful story about it—generally to entertain children. How the leg got up by itself one day and walked on off. How she hobbled after it but it ran too fast. Or how she had a corn on her toe and it just grew and grew and grew until her whole foot was a corn and then it traveled on up her leg and wouldn't stop growing until she put a red tag at the top but by that time it was already at her knee.

Somebody said Eva stuck it under a train and made them pay off. Another said she sold it to a hospital for $10,000—at which Mr. Reed opened his eyes and asked, "Nigger gal legs goin' for $10,000 a *piece?*" as though he could understand $10,000 a *pair*—but for *one?*

Whatever the fate of her lost leg, the remaining one was magnificent. It was stockinged and shod at all times and in all weather. Once in a while she got a felt slipper for Christmas or her birthday, but they soon disappeared, for Eva always wore a black laced-up shoe that came well above her ankle. Nor did she wear overlong dresses to disguise the empty place on her left side. Her dresses were mid-calf so that her one glamorous leg was always in view as well as the long fall of space below her left thigh. One of her men friends had fashioned a kind of wheelchair for her: a rocking-chair top fitted into a large child's wagon. In this contraption she wheeled around the room, from bedside to dresser to the balcony that opened out the north side of her room or to the window that looked out on the back yard. The wagon was so low that children who spoke to her standing up were eye level with her, and adults, standing or sitting, had to look down at her. But they didn't know it. They all had the impression that they were looking up at her, up into the open distances of her eyes, up into the soft black of her nostrils and up at the crest of her chin.

Eva had married a man named BoyBoy and had three children: Hannah, the eldest, and Eva, whom she named after herself but called Pearl, and a son named Ralph, whom she called Plum.

After five years of a sad and disgruntled marriage BoyBoy took off. During the time they were together he was very much preoccupied with other women and not home much. He did whatever he could that he liked, and he liked womanizing best, drinking second, and abusing Eva third. When he left in November, Eva had $1.65, five eggs, three beets and no idea of what or how to feel. The children needed her; she needed money, and needed to get on with her life. But the demands of feeding her three children were so acute she had to postpone her anger for two years until she had both the time and energy for it. She was confused and desperately hungry. There were very few black families in those low hills then. The Suggs, who lived two hundred yards down the road, brought her a warm bowl of peas, as soon as they found out, and a plate of cold bread. She thanked them and asked if they had a little milk for the older ones. They said no, but Mrs. Jackson, they knew, had a cow still giving. Eva took a bucket over and Mrs. Jackson told her to come back and fill it up in the morning, because the evening milking had already been done. In this way, things went on until near December. People were very willing to help, but Eva felt she would soon run her welcome out; winters were hard and her neighbors were not that much better off. She would lie in bed with the baby boy, the two girls wrapped in quilts on the floor, thinking. The oldest child, Hannah, was five and too young to take care of the baby alone, and any housework Eva could find would keep her away from them from five-thirty or earlier in the morning until dark—way past eight.

The white people in the valley weren't rich enough then to want maids; they were small farmers and tradesmen and wanted hard-labor help if anything. She thought also of returning to some of her people in Virginia, but to come home dragging three young ones would have to be a step one rung before death for Eva. She would have to scrounge around and beg through the winter, until her baby was at least nine months old, then she could plant and maybe hire herself out to valley farms to weed or sow or feed stock until something steadier came along at harvest time. She thought she had probably been a fool to let BoyBoy haul her away from her people, but it had seemed so right at the time. He worked for a white carpenter and toolsmith who insisted on BoyBoy's accompanying him when he went West and set up in a squinchy little town called Medallion. BoyBoy brought his new wife and built them a one-room cabin sixty feet back from the road that wound up out of the valley, on up into the hills and was named for the man he worked for. They lived there a year before they had an outhouse.

Sometime before the middle of December, the baby, Plum, stopped having bowel movements. Eva massaged his stomach and gave him warm water. Something must be wrong with my milk, she thought. Mrs. Suggs gave her castor oil, but even that didn't work. He cried and fought so they couldn't get much down his throat anyway. He seemed in great pain and his shrieks were pitched high in outrage and suffering. At one point, maddened by his own crying, he gagged, choked and looked as though he was strangling to death. Eva rushed to him and kicked over the earthen slop jar, washing a small area of the floor with the child's urine. She managed to soothe him, but when he took up the cry again late that night, she resolved to end his misery once and for all. She wrapped him in blankets, ran her finger around the crevices and sides of the lard can and stumbled to the outhouse with him. Deep in its darkness and freezing stench she squatted down, turned the baby over on her knees, exposed his buttocks and shoved the last bit of food she had in the world (besides three beets) up his ass. Softening the insertion with the dab of lard, she probed with her middle finger to loosen his bowels. Her fingernail snagged what felt like a pebble; she pulled it out and others followed. Plum stopped crying as the black hard stools ricocheted onto the frozen ground. And now that it was over, Eva squatted there wondering why she had come all the way out there to free his stools, and what was she doing down on her haunches with her beloved baby boy warmed by her body in the almost total darkness, her shins and teeth freezing, her nostrils assailed. She shook her head as though to juggle her brains around, then said aloud, "Uh uh. Nooo." Thereupon she returned to the house and her bed. As the grateful Plum slept, the silence allowed her to think.

Two days later she left all of her children with Mrs. Suggs, saying she would be back the next day.

Eighteen months later she swept down from a wagon with two crutches, a new black pocketbook, and one leg. First she reclaimed her children, next she gave the surprised Mrs. Suggs a ten-dollar bill, later she started building a house on Carpenter's Road, sixty feet from BoyBoy's one-room cabin, which she rented out.

When Plum was three years old, BoyBoy came back to town and paid her a visit. When Eva got the word that he was on his way, she made some lemonade. She had no idea what she would do or feel during that encounter. Would she cry, cut his throat, beg him to make love to her? She couldn't imagine. So she just waited to see. She stirred lemonade in a green pitcher and waited.

BoyBoy danced up the steps and knocked on the door.

"Come on in," she hollered.

He opened the door and stood smiling, a picture of prosperity and good will. His shoes were a shiny orange, and he had on a citified straw hat, a light-blue shirt, and a cat's-head stickpin in his tie. Eva smiled and told him to sit himself down. He smiled too.

"How you been, girl?"

"Pretty fair. What you know good?" When she heard those words come out of her own mouth she knew that their conversation would start off polite. Although it remained to be seen whether she would still run the ice pick through the cat's-head pin.

"Have some lemonade."

"Don't mind if I do." He swept his hat off with a satisfied gesture. His nails were long and shiny. "Sho is hot, and I been runnin' around all day."

Eva looked out of the screen door and saw a woman in a pea-green dress leaning on the smallest pear tree. Glancing back at him, she was reminded of Plum's face when he managed to get the meat out of a walnut all by himself. Eva smiled again, and poured the lemonade.

Their conversation was easy: she catching him up on all the gossip, he asking about this one and that one, and like everybody else avoiding any reference to her leg. It was like talking to somebody's cousin who just stopped by to say howdy before getting on back to wherever he came from. BoyBoy didn't ask to see the children, and Eva didn't bring them into the conversation.

After a while he rose to go. Talking about his appointments and exuding an odor of new money and idleness, he danced down the steps and strutted toward the pea-green dress. Eva watched. She looked at the back of his neck and the set of his shoulders. Underneath all of that shine she saw defeat in the stalk of his neck and the curious tight way he held his shoulders. But still she was not sure what she felt. Then he leaned forward and whispered into the ear of the woman in the green dress. She was still for a moment and then threw back her head and laughed. A high-pitched big-city laugh that reminded Eva of Chicago. It hit her like a sledge hammer, and it was then that she knew what to feel. A liquid trail of hate flooded her chest.

Knowing that she would hate him long and well filled her with pleasant anticipation, like when you know you are going to fall in love with someone and you wait for the happy signs. Hating BoyBoy, she could get on with it, and have the safety, the thrill, the consistency of that hatred as long as she wanted or needed it to define and strengthen her or protect her from routine vulnerabilities. (Once when Hannah accused her of hating colored people, Eva said she only hated one, Hannah's father BoyBoy, and it was hating him that kept her alive and happy.)

Happy or not, after BoyBoy's visit she began her retreat to her bedroom, leaving the bottom of the house more and more to those who lived there: cousins who were passing through, stray folks, and the many, many newly married couples she let rooms to with housekeeping privileges, and after 1910 she didn't willingly set foot on the stairs but once and that was to light a fire, the smoke of which was in her hair for years.

Among the tenants in that big old house were the children Eva took in. Operating on a private scheme of preference and prejudice, she sent off for children she had seen from the balcony of her bedroom or whose circumstances she had heard about from the gossipy old men who came to play checkers or read the *Courier,* or write her number. In 1921, when her granddaughter Sula was eleven, Eva had three such children. They came with woolen caps and names given to them by their mothers, or grandmothers, or somebody's best friend. Eva snatched the caps off their heads and ignored their names. She looked at the first child closely, his wrists, the shape of his head and the temperament that showed in his eyes and said, "Well. Look at Dewey. My my mymymy." When later that same year she sent for a child who kept falling down off the porch across the street, she said the same thing. Somebody said, "But, Miss Eva, you calls the other one Dewey."

"So? This here's another one."

When the third one was brought and Eva said "Dewey" again, everybody thought she had simply run out of names or that her faculties had finally softened.

"How is anybody going to tell them apart?" Hannah asked her.

"What you need to tell them apart for? They's all deweys."

When Hannah asked the question it didn't sound very bright, because each dewey was markedly different from the other two. Dewey one was a deeply black boy with a beautiful head and the golden eyes of chronic jaundice. Dewey two was light-skinned with freckles everywhere and a head of tight red hair. Dewey three was half Mexican with chocolate skin and black bangs. Besides, they were one and two years apart in age. It was Eva saying things like, "Send one of them deweys out to get me some Garret, if they don't have Garret, get Buttercup," or, "Tell them deweys to cut out that noise," or, "Come here, you dewey you," and, "Send me a dewey," that gave Hannah's question its weight.

Slowly each boy came out of whatever cocoon he was in at the time his mother or somebody gave him away, and accepted Eva's view, becoming in fact as well as in name a dewey—joining with the other two to become a trinity with a plural name . . . inseparable, loving nothing and no one but themselves. When the handle from the icebox fell off, all the deweys got whipped, and in dry-eyed silence watched their own feet as they turned their behinds high up into the air for the stroke. When the golden-eyed dewey was ready for school he would not go without the others. He was seven, freckled dewey was five, and Mexican dewey was only four. Eva solved the problem by having them all sent off together. Mr. Buckland Reed said, "But one of them's only four."

"How you know? They all come here the same year," Eva said.

"But that one there was one year old when he came, and that was three years ago."

"You don't know how old he was when he come here and neither do the teacher. Send 'em."

The teacher was startled but not unbelieving, for she had long ago given up trying to fathom the ways of the colored people in town. So when Mr. Reed said that their names were Dewey King, that they were cousins, and all were six years old, the teacher gave only a tiny sigh and wrote them in the record book for the first grade. She too thought she would have no problem distinguishing among them, because they looked nothing alike, but like everyone else before her, she gradually found that she could not tell one from the other. The deweys would not allow it. They got all mixed up in her head, and finally she could not literally believe her eyes. They spoke with one voice, thought with one mind, and maintained an annoying privacy. Stouthearted, surly, and wholly unpredictable, the deweys remained a mystery not only during all of their lives in Medallion but after as well.

The deweys came in 1921, but the year before Eva had given a small room off the kitchen to Tar Baby, a beautiful, slight, quiet man who never spoke above a whisper. Most people said he was half white, but Eva said he was all white. That she knew blood when she saw it, and he didn't have none. When he first came to Medallion, the people called him Pretty Johnnie, but Eva looked at his milky skin and cornsilk hair and out of a mixture of fun and meanness called him Tar Baby. He was a mountain boy who stayed to himself, bothering no one, intent solely on drinking himself to death. At first he worked in a poultry market, and after wringing the necks of chickens all day, he came home and drank until he slept. Later he began to miss days at work and frequently did not have his rent money. When he lost his job altogether, he would go out in the morning, scrounge around for money doing odd jobs, bumming or whatever, and come home to drink. Because he was no bother, ate little, required nothing, and was a lover of cheap wine, no one found him a nuisance. Besides, he frequently went to Wednesday-night prayer meetings and sang with the sweetest hill voice imaginable "In the Sweet By-and-By."

He sent the deweys out for his liquor and spent most of his time in a heap on the floor or sitting in a chair staring at the wall.

Hannah worried about him a little, but only a very little. For it soon became clear that he simply wanted a place to die privately but not quite alone. No one thought of suggesting to him that he pull himself together or see a doctor or anything. Even the women at prayer meeting who cried when he sang "In the Sweet By-and-By" never tried to get him to participate in the church activities. They just listened to him sing, wept and thought very graphically of their own imminent deaths. The people either accepted his own evaluation of his life, or were indifferent to it. There was, however, a measure of contempt in their indifference, for they had little patience with people who took themselves that seriously. Seriously enough to try to die. And it was natural that he, after all, became the first one to join Shadrack— Tar Baby and the deweys—on National Suicide Day.

Under Eva's distant eye, and prey to her idiosyncrasies, her own children grew up stealthily: Pearl married at fourteen and moved to Flint, Michigan, from where she posted frail letters to her mother with two dollars folded into the writing paper. Sad little nonsense letters about minor troubles, her husband's job and who the children favored. Hannah married a laughing man named Rekus who died when their daughter Sula was about three years old, at which time Hannah moved back into her mother's big house prepared to take care of it and her mother forever.

With the exception of BoyBoy, those Peace women loved all men. It was manlove that Eva bequeathed to her daughters. Probably, people said, because there were no men in the house, no men to run it. But actually that was not true. The Peace women simply loved maleness, for its own sake. Eva, old as she was, and with one leg, had a regular flock of gentleman callers, and although she did not participate in the act of love, there was a good deal of teasing and pecking and laughter. The men wanted to see her lovely calf, that neat shoe, and watch the focusing that sometimes swept down out of the distances in her eyes. They wanted to see the joy in her face as they settled down to play checkers, knowing that even when she beat them, as she almost always did, somehow, in her presence, it was they who had won something. They would read the newspaper aloud to her and make observations on its content, and Eva would listen feeling no obligation to agree and, in fact, would take them to task about their interpretation of events. But she argued with them with such an absence of bile, such a concentration of manlove, that they felt their convictions solidified by her disagreement.

With other people's affairs Eva was equally prejudiced about men. She fussed interminably with the brides of the newly wed couples for not getting their men's supper ready on time; about how to launder shirts, press them, etc. "Yo' man be here direc'lin. Ain't it 'bout time you got busy?"

"Aw, Miss Eva. It'll be ready. We just having spaghetti."

"Again?" Eva's eyebrows fluted up and the newlywed pressed her lips together in shame.

Hannah simply refused to live without the attentions of a man, and after Rekus' death had a steady sequence of lovers, mostly the husbands of her friends and neighbors. Her flirting was sweet, low and guileless. Without ever a pat of the hair, a rush to change clothes or a quick application of paint, with no gesture whatsoever, barefoot in the summer, in the winter her feet in a man's leather slippers with the backs flattened under her heels, she made men aware of her behind, her slim ankles, the dew-smooth skin and the incredible length of neck. Then the smile-eyes, the turn of her head— all so welcoming, light and playful. Her voice trailed, dipped and bowed; she gave a chord to the simplest words. Nobody, but nobody, could say "hey sugar" like Hannah. When he heard it, the man tipped his hat down a little over his eyes, hoisted his trousers and thought about the hollow place at the base of her neck. And all this without the slightest confusion about work and responsibilities. While Eva tested and argued with her men, leaving them feeling as though they had been in combat with a worthy, if amiable, foe, Hannah rubbed no edges, made no demands, made the man feel as though he were complete and wonderful just as he was—he didn't need fixing—and so he relaxed and swooned in the Hannah-light that shone on him simply because he was. If the man entered and Hannah was carrying a coal scuttle up from the basement, she handled it in such a way that it became a gesture of love. He made no move to help her with it simply because he wanted to see how her thighs looked when she bent to put it down, knowing that she wanted him to see them too.

But since in that crowded house there were no places for private and spontaneous lovemaking, Hannah would take the man down into the cellar in the summer where it was cool back behind the coal bin and the newspapers, or in the winter they would step into the pantry and stand up against the shelves she had filled with canned goods, or lie on the flour sack just under the rows of tiny green peppers. When those places were not available, she would slip into the seldom-used parlor, or even up to her bedroom. She liked the last place least, not because Sula slept in the room with her but because her love mate's tendency was always to fall asleep afterward and Hannah was fastidious about whom she slept with. She would fuck practically anything, but sleeping with someone implied for her a measure of trust and a definite commitment. So she ended up a daylight lover, and it was only once actually that Sula came home from school and found her mother in the bed, curled spoon in the arms of a man.

Seeing her step so easily into the pantry and emerge looking precisely as she did when she entered, only happier, taught Sula that sex was pleasant and frequent, but otherwise unremarkable. Outside the house, where children giggled about underwear, the message was different. So she watched her mother's face and the faces of the men when they opened the pantry door and made up her own mind.

Hannah exasperated the women in the town—the "good" women, who said, "One thing I can't stand is a nasty woman"; the whores, who were hard put to find trade among black men anyway and who resented Hannah's generosity; the middling women, who had both husbands and affairs, because Hannah seemed too unlike them, having no passion attached to her relationships and being wholly incapable of jealousy. Hannah's friendships with women were, of course, seldom and short-lived, and the newly married couples whom her mother took in soon learned what a hazard she was. She could break up a marriage before it had even become one—she would make love to the new groom and wash his wife's dishes all in an afternoon. What she wanted, after Rekus died, and what she succeeded in having more often than not, was some touching every day.

The men, surprisingly, never gossiped about her. She was unquestionably a kind and generous woman and that, coupled with her extraordinary beauty and funky elegance of manner, made them defend her and protect her from any vitriol that newcomers or their wives might spill.

Eva's last child, Plum, to whom she hoped to bequeath everything, floated in a constant swaddle of love and affection, until 1917 when he went to war. He returned to the States in 1919 but did not get back to Medallion until 1920. He wrote letters from New York, Washington, D.C., and Chicago full of promises of homecomings, but there was obviously something wrong. Finally some two or three days after Christmas, he arrived with just the shadow of his old dip-down walk. His hair had been neither cut nor combed in months, his clothes were pointless and he had no socks. But he did have a black bag, a paper sack, and a sweet, sweet smile. Everybody welcomed him and gave him a warm room next to Tar Baby's and waited for him to tell them whatever it was he wanted them to know. They waited in vain for his telling but not long for the knowing. His habits were much like Tar Baby's but there were no bottles, and Plum was sometimes cheerful and animated. Hannah watched and Eva waited. Then he began to steal from them, take trips to Cincinnati and sleep for days in his room with the record player going. He got even thinner, since he ate only snatches of things at beginnings or endings of meals. It was Hannah who found the bent spoon black from steady cooking.

So late one night in 1921, Eva got up from her bed and put on her clothes. Hoisting herself up on her crutches, she was amazed to find that she could still manage them, although the pain in her armpits was severe. She practiced a few steps around the room, and then opened the door. Slowly, she manipulated herself down the long flights of stairs, two crutches under her left arm, the right hand grasping the banister. The sound of her foot booming in comparison to the delicate pat of the crutch tip. On each landing she stopped for breath. Annoyed at her physical condition, she closed her eyes and removed the crutches from under her arms to relieve the unaccustomed pressure. At the foot of the stairs she redistributed her weight between the crutches and swooped on through the front room, to the dining room, to the kitchen, swinging and swooping like a giant heron, so graceful sailing about in its own habitat but awkward and comical when it folded its wings and tried to walk. With a swing and a swoop she arrived at Plum's door and pushed it open with the tip of one crutch. He was lying in bed barely visible in the light coming from a single bulb. Eva swung over to the bed and propped her crutches at its foot. She sat down and gathered Plum into her arms. He woke, but only slightly.

"Hey, man. Hey. You holdin' me, Mamma?" His voice was drowsy and amused. He chuckled as though he had heard some private joke. Eva held him closer and began to rock. Back and forth she rocked him, her eyes wandering around his room. There in the corner was a half-eaten store-bought cherry pie. Balled-up candy wrappers and empty pop bottles peeped from under the dresser. On the floor by her foot was a glass of strawberry crush and a *Liberty* magazine. Rocking, rocking, listening to Plum's occasional chuckles, Eva let her memory spin, loop and fall. Plum in the tub that time as she leaned over him. He reached up and dripped water into her bosom and laughed. She was angry, but not too, and laughed with him.

"Mamma, you so purty. You so purty, Mamma."

Eva lifted her tongue to the edge of her lip to stop the tears from running into her mouth. Rocking, rocking. Later she laid him down and looked at him a long time. Suddenly she was thirsty and reached for the glass of strawberry crush. She put it to her lips and discovered it was blood-tainted water and threw it to the floor. Plum woke up and said, "Hey, Mamma, whyn't you go back to bed? I'm all right. Didn't I tell you? I'm all right. Go on, now."

"I'm going, Plum," she said. She shifted her weight and pulled her crutches toward her. Swinging and swooping, she left his room. She dragged herself to the kitchen and made grating noises.

Plum on the rim of a warm light sleep was still chuckling. Mamma. She sure was somethin'. He felt twilight. Now there seemed to be some kind of wet light traveling over his legs and stomach with a deeply attractive smell. It wound itself—this wet light—all about him, splashing and running into his skin. He opened his eyes and saw what he imagined was the great wing of an eagle pouring a wet lightness over him. Some kind of baptism, some kind of blessing, he thought. Everything is going to be all right, it said. Knowing that it was so he closed his eyes and sank back into the bright hole of sleep.

Eva stepped back from the bed and let the crutches rest under her arms. She rolled a bit of newspaper into a tight stick about six inches long, lit it and threw it onto the bed where the kerosene-soaked Plum lay in snug delight. Quickly, as the *whoosh* of flames engulfed him, she shut the door and made her slow painful journey back to the top of the house.

Just as she got to the third landing she could hear Hannah and some child's voice. She swung along, not even listening to the voices of alarm and the cries of the deweys. By the time she got to her bed someone was bounding up the stairs after her. Hannah opened the door. "Plum! Plum! He's burning, Mamma! We can't even open the door! Mamma!"

Eva looked into Hannah's eyes. "Is? My Baby? Burning?" The two women did not speak, for the eyes of each were enough for the other. Then Hannah closed hers and ran toward the voices of neighbors calling for water.

POETRY

MARGARET WALKER

Born in Alabama in 1915, Margaret Walker is a professor of English and the director of the Institute for the Study of History, Life and Culture of Black People at Jackson State College in Mississippi. In 1942 she published *For My People*, which won the Yale University Younger Poets Competition. Her novel, *Jubilee*, appeared in 1966 and received the Houghton Mifflin Literary Fellowship Award. More recently, she has published *Prophets for a New Day* (1970), *October Journey* (1973), and *A Poetic Equation: Conversations Between Nikki Giovanni and Margaret Walker* (1974).

I WANT TO WRITE

I want to write
I want to write the songs of my people.
I want to hear them singing melodies in the dark.
I want to catch the last floating strains from their sob-torn throats.
I want to frame their dreams into words; their souls into notes.
I want to catch their sunshine laughter in a bowl;
fling dark hands to a darker sky
and fill them full of stars
then crush and mix such lights till they become
a mirrored pool of brilliance in the dawn.

FOR GWEN—1969
(Gwendolyn Brooks)

The slender, shy, and sensitive young girl
is woman now,
her words a power in the Ebon land.
Outside her window on the street
a mass of life moves by.
Chicago is her city.
Her heart flowers with its flame—

old stock yards, new beaches
all the little store-front churches
and the bar on the corner.
Dreamer and seer of tales
She witnesses rebellion,
struggle and sweat.
The people are her heartbeat—
In their footsteps pulsate daily
all her black words of fire and blood.

GWENDOLYN BROOKS

Born in Kansas in 1917, Gwendolyn Brooks grew up in Chicago, where she presently lives. The first black to receive a Pulitzer Prize for poetry (in 1950 for *Annie Allen*), she has had a distinguished literary career and received numerous awards, including two Guggenheim fellowships (1946 and 1947) and the American Academy of Letters Award (1946). Her major publications include *A Street in Bronzeville* (1945); *Annie Allen* (1949); *Maud Martha* (1953), a novel; *The Bean Eaters* (1960); *Selected Poems* (1963); and *In the Mecca* (1968). Her autobiography, *Report from Part One,* was published in 1972. She is poet laureate of Illinois.

kitchenette building

We are things of dry hours and the involuntary plan,
Grayed in, and gray. "Dream" makes a giddy sound, not strong
Like "rent," "feeding a wife," "satisfying a man."

But could a dream send up through onion fumes
Its white and violet, fight with fried potatoes
And yesterday's garbage ripening in the hall,
Flutter, or sing an aria down these rooms

Even if we were willing to let it in,
Had time to warm it, keep it very clean,
Anticipate a message, let it begin?

We wonder. But not well! not for a minute!
Since Number Five is out of the bathroom now,
We think of lukewarm water, hope to get in it.

the old-marrieds

But in the crowding darkness not a word did they say.
Though the pretty-coated birds had piped so lightly all the day.
And he had seen the lovers in the little side-streets.

And she had heard the morning stories clogged with sweets.
It was quite a time for loving. It was midnight. It was May.
But in the crowding darkness not a word did they say.

WHAT SHALL I GIVE MY CHILDREN?

What shall I give my children? who are poor,
Who are adjudged the leastwise of the land,
Who are my sweetest lepers, who demand
No velvet and no velvety velour;
But who have begged me for a brisk contour,
Crying that they are quasi, contraband
Because unfinished, graven by a hand
Less than angelic, admirable or sure.
My hand is stuffed with mode, design, device.
But I lack access to my proper stone.
And plenitude of plan shall not suffice
Nor grief nor love shall be enough alone
To ratify my little halves who bear
Across an autumn freezing everywhere.

BRONZEVILLE WOMAN IN A RED HAT

Hires out to
Mrs. Miles

I

They had never had one in the house before.
    The strangeness of it all. Like unleashing
A lion, really. Poised
To pounce. A puma. A panther. A black
Bear.
There it stood in the door,
Under a red hat that was rash, but refreshing—
In a tasteless way, of course—across the dull dare,
The semi-assault of that extraordinary blackness.
The slackness
Of that light pink mouth told little. The eyes told of heavy care.
But that was neither here nor there.

And nothing to a wage-paying mistress as should
Be getting her due whether life had been good
For her slave, or bad.
There it stood
In the door. They had never had
One in the house before.

But the Irishwoman had left!
A message had come.
Something about a murder at home.
A daughter's husband—"berserk," that was the phrase:
The dear man had "gone berserk"
And short work—
With a hammer—had been made
Of this daughter and her nights and days.
The Irishwoman (underpaid,
Mrs. Miles remembered with smiles),
Who was a perfect jewel, a red-faced trump,
A good old sort, a baker
Of rum cake, a maker
Of Mustard, would never return.
Mrs. Miles had begged the bewitched woman
To finish, at least, the biscuit blending,
To tarry till the curry was done,
To show some concern
For the burning soup, to attend to the tending
Of the tossed salad. "Inhuman,"
Patsy Houlihan had called Mrs. Miles.
"Inhuman." And "a fool."
And "a cool
One."
The Alert Agency had leafed through its files—
On short notice could offer
Only this dusky duffer
That now made its way to her kitchen and sat on her kitchen stool.

I I

Her creamy child kissed by the black maid! square on the mouth!
World yelled, world writhed, world turned to light and rolled
Into her kitchen, nearly knocked her down.

Quotations, of course, from baby books were great
Ready armor; (but her animal distress

Wore, too and under, a subtler metal dress,
Inheritance of approximately hate).
Say baby shrieked to see his finger bleed,
Wished human humoring—there was a kind
Of unintimate love, a love more of the mind
To order the nebulousness of that need.
—This was the way to put it, this the relief.
This sprayed a honey upon marvelous grime.
This told it possible to postpone the reef.
Fashioned a huggable darling out of crime.
Made monster personable in personal sight
By cracking mirrors down the personal night.
Disgust crawled through her as she chased the theme.
She, quite supposing purity despoiled,
Committed to sourness, disordered, soiled,
Went in to pry the ordure from the cream.
Coming, "Come" (Come out of the cannibal wilderness,
Dirt, dark, into the sun and bloomful air.
Return to freshness of your right world, wear
Sweetness again. Be done with beast, duress.)

Child with continuing cling, issued his No in final fire,
     Kissed back the colored maid.
     Not wise enough to freeze or be afraid.
     Conscious of kindness, easy creature bond:
     Love had been handy and rapid to respond.

Heat at the hairline, heat between the bowels,
Examining seeming coarse unnatural scene,
She saw all things except herself serene:
Child, big black woman, pretty kitchen towels.

NAOMI LONG MADGETT

Born in 1923 in Norfolk, Virginia, Naomi Long Madgett currently lives in Detroit, where she is a professor of English at Eastern Michigan University. Her published collections of poetry include *Songs to a Phantom Nightingale* (1941), *One and the Many* (1956), *Star by Star* (1965, 1970), *Pink Ladies in the Afternoon* (1972), and *Exits and Entrances* (1978). Of her writing, she says, "I think that I am sensitive to the internal experiences of black people and women, in particular, but my poetry goes beyond the particular to the more general needs and impressions of a larger humanity that defies classification. I write primarily out of my own experience, whether it is first-hand, vicarious, or imagined. If I am honest as a poet, I feel that others will identify with these expressions without my being particularly concerned about my audience. The response will come if the expression is true."

OFFSPRING

I tried to tell her:
    This way the twig is bent.
    Born of my trunk and strengthened by my roots,
    You must stretch newgrown branches
    Closer to the sun
    Than I can reach.
I wanted to say:
    Extend my self to that far atmosphere
    Only my dreams allow.

But the twig broke,
And yesterday I saw her
Walking down an unfamiliar street,
    Feet confident,
    Face slanted upward toward a threatening sky,
And
    She was smiling
    And she was
    Her very free,
    Her very individual,
    Unpliable
    Own.

WRITING A POEM

Writing a poem is trying to catch a fluff of cloud
With open-fingered hands.
Slim ghosts of truths, ethereal in twilight's mist,
Glide and evade and dissipate into enormous air.
Making a poem is trying to capture gold-winged
                                        butterflies
With only a net of dreams.

BLACK WOMAN

My hair is springy like the forest grasses
That cushion the feet of squirrels—
Crinkled and blown in a south breeze
Like the small leaves of native bushes.

My black eyes are coals burning
Like a low, full jungle moon
Through the darkness of being.
In a clear pool I see my face,
Know my knowing.

My hands move pianissimo
Over the music of the night:
Gentle birds fluttering through leaves and grasses
They have not always loved,
Nesting, finding home.

Where are my lovers?
Where are my tall, my lovely princes
Dancing in slow grace
Toward knowledge of my beauty?
Where
Are my beautiful
Black men?

MAY MILLER

May Miller was born and now lives in Washington, D.C., where she frequently participates as a poet, panelist, reader, and teacher in seminars related to poetry and the arts. She has recorded her own poetry for the Library of Congress Collection of Poets Reading Their Own Work. Her books of poetry include *Into the Clearing* (1959), *Poems* (1962), *Lyrics of Three Women* (with Katie Lyle and Maud Rubin) (1964), *The Clearing and Beyond* (1974), and *Dust of Uncertain Journey* (1975). She is a member of the Commission on the Arts for the District of Columbia.

DEATH IS NOT MASTER

I cannot let you die.
I block factual death
And its memorial apology;
Within a secret self
I build a barricade
Against the dark,
There fix you shining
In a place of sun.
No soft rain of tears dwarfs you;
Straight and desperate you walk
The corridors as before
Eclipsing the minions of grief
In their naked hours,
Gathering about your head
Scorn for the grave
In which they say you lie
Until memory glows
In that astonished quarter
Burning the night white
That would bind you in sculpture.

PLACE IN THE MORNING

A silken transfer waking from sleep
To breaking light flushed
On the window sill.
Shadows separate one by one.
You go away
Beyond the spindrift neon sign
Lost in a blinding arc.
I call your name.
The wild and steely echoes
Out of where you've gone—
Wheels on concrete, grinding, shrieking—
Crisp my cries
Until the fog of the dream unwinds.
You seem returned through branches
That have shed the dark.
In the flute of the morning
You are mirrored in new sun
And I take my place there too.

THE SCREAM

I am a woman controlled.
Remember this: I never scream.
Yet I stood a form apart
Watching my other frenzied self
Beaten by words and wounds
Make in silence a mighty scream—
A scream that the wind took up
And thrust through the bars of night
Beyond all reason's final rim.

Out where the sea's last murmur dies
And the gull's cry has no sound,
Out where city voices fade,
Stilled in a lyric sleep
Where silence is its own design,
My scream hovered a ghost denied
Wanting the shape of lips.

MARI EVANS

Currently an assistant professor of English at Indiana University, Mari Evans has published two books of poetry: *Where Is All the Music?* (1968) and *I Am a Black Woman* (1970). She also writes children's books, stories, plays, and articles. Her poetry has been widely anthologized, and some of the poems have been included in television programs, filmstrips, and record albums. She comments, "The poems selected for inclusion in this anthology are early poems, and may not as clearly reflect my commitment to the belief that while Black writers have the prerogative to write as they choose, they will, hopefully, understand a responsibility to use the language and their crafts in a political way, and therefore choose to use their medium to express a political view of the society."

I AM A BLACK WOMAN

I am a black woman
the music of my song
some sweet arpeggio of tears
is written in a minor key
and I
can be heard humming in the night
Can be heard
              humming
in the night

I saw my mate leap screaming to the sea
and I/with these hands/cupped the lifebreath
from my issue in the canebreak
I lost Nat's swinging body in a rain of tears
and heard my son scream all the way from Anzio
for Peace he never knew. . . . I
learned Da Nang and Pork Chop Hill
in anguish
Now my nostrils know the gas
and these trigger tire/d fingers
seek the softness in my warrior's beard

I
am a black woman
tall as a cypress
strong
beyond all definition still
defying place
and time
and circumstance
   assailed
     impervious
       indestructible
Look
  on me and be
renewed

THE FRIDAY LADIES OF THE PAY ENVELOPE

they take
stations
in the broken doorways
the narrow alcoves
and the flaking
gray paint
the rainandsoot paint
clings
to their limpworn
sweaters clings
hair and limpworn souls they
wait
for the sullen
triumph
for the crumpled lifeblood
wet with reluctance
thrust
       at them
in the direction
of them
     of their reaching
of their drydamp
  limpworn hands

A GOOD ASSASSINATION SHOULD BE QUIET

he had
A Dream
e x p loded
down
his
th r o a t.

whereon
a million hard white eyes
swung impiously heavenward
to mourn
the gross indelicate demise

Such public death
transgresses
all known rules

A good assassination
should be quiet

and occupy the heart
four hundred
years

JUNE JORDAN

A prolific writer, June Jordan has written ten books. Her novel, *His Own Where* (1971), was selected by the *New York Times* as one of the outstanding books of the year in 1971 and nominated for the National Book Award in 1972. She has published poetry in numerous places, including *Black World, MS,* and *The New Republic.* Her most recent collection of poetry is *Things That I Do in the Dark* (1977). In addition to her work as contributing editor to *American Poetry Review* and *Chrysalis,* she has also taught at the City College of New York, Sarah Lawrence, and Yale University.

IF YOU SAW A NEGRO LADY

If you saw a Negro lady
sitting on a Tuesday
near the whirl-sludge doors of
Horn & Hardart on the main drag
of downtown Brooklyn

solitary and conspicuous as plain
and neat as walls impossible to
fresco and you watched her self-
conscious features shape about
a Horn & Hardart teaspoon
with a pucker from a cartoon

she would not understand
with spine as straight and solid
as her years of bending over floors
allowed

skin cleared of interest by a ruthless
soap   nails square and yellowclean
from metal files

sitting in a forty-year-old flush
of solitude and prickling
from the new white cotton blouse

concealing nothing she had ever noticed
even when she bathed and never
hummed a bathtub tune nor knew óne

If you saw her square
above the dirty
mopped-on antiseptic floors
before the rag-wiped table tops

little finger   broad and stiff
in heavy emulation of a cockney

mannerism

would you turn her treat
into surprise observing
happy birthday

IN MEMORIAM:
REV. MARTIN LUTHER KING, JR. (PART ONE)

honey people murder mercy U.S.A.
the milkland turn to monsters teach
to kill to violate pull down destroy
the weakly freedom growing fruit
from being born

America

tomorrow yesterday rip rape
exacerbate despoil disfigure
crazy running threat the
deadly thrall
appall belief dispel
the wildlife burn the breast
the onward tongue
the outward hand
deform the normal
rainy riot sunshine
shelter wreck of darkness
derogate delimit blank
explode deprive
assassinate and batten up
like bullets fatten up

the raving greed
reactivate a springtime
terrorizing
duplication death
by death by men by more
than you or I can
STOP

NIKKI GIOVANNI

A graduate of Fisk College, Nikki Giovanni has published several collections of poetry, including *Black Feeling, Black Folk/Black Judgement* (1970), *Re:Creation* (1970), *Spin a Soft Black Song* (1971), *My House* (1972), and *The Women and the Men* (1975). Her many honors include an Honorary Doctorate of Humanities from Wilberforce University.

THEY CLAPPED

they clapped when we landed
thinking africa was just an extension
of the black world
they smiled as we taxied home to be met
black to black face not understanding africans lack
color prejudice
they rushed to declare
cigarettes, money, allegiance to the mother land
not knowing despite having read fanon and davenport
hearing all of j.h. clarke's lectures, supporting
nkrumah in ghana and nigeria in the war that there was once
a tribe called afro-americans that populated the whole
of africa
they stopped running when they learned the packages
on the women's heads were heavy and that babies didn't
cry and disease is uncomfortable and that villages are fun
only because you knew the feel of good leather on good
pavement
they cried when they saw mercedes benz were as common
in lagos as volkswagens are in berlin
they shook their heads when they understood there was no
difference between the french and the english and the americans
and the afro-americans or the tribe next door or the country

across the border
they were exasperated when they heard sly and the family stone
in francophone africa and they finally smiled when little boys
who spoke no western tongue said "james brown" with reverence
they brought out their cameras and bought out africa's drums
when they finally realized they are strangers all over
and love is only and always about the lover not the beloved
they marveled at the beauty of the people and the richness
of the land knowing they could never possess either

they clapped when they took off
for home despite the dead
dream they saw a free future

[29 aug 71]

LEGACIES

her grandmother called her from the playground
    "yes, ma'am"
    "i want chu to learn how to make rolls," said the old
woman proudly
but the little girl didn't want
to learn how because she knew
even if she couldn't say it that
that would mean when the old one died she would be less
dependent on her spirit so
she said
    "i don't want to know how to make no rolls"
with her lips poked out
and the old woman wiped her hands on
her apron saying "lord
    these children"
and neither of them ever
said what they meant
and i guess nobody ever does

[27 jan 72]

COLLEEN McELROY

Born in St. Louis in 1935, Colleen McElroy presently lives in Seattle, where she is an assistant professor of English at the University of Washington. She has published *Speech and Language of the Preschool Child* (1972), *The Mules Done Long Since Gone* (1973), and *Music from Home: Selected Poems* (1976). In addition, her poetry has appeared in numerous journals, including *Poetry Northwest, South Dakota Review, Essence, Black Lines, Choice, Sunbury, Aphra, Black World,* and *Yardbird Reader.* She comments, "I believe that the world is rich and varied in meaning, that meaning itself grows and expands with each new instance of ethnic creativity. The black poet and writer preserves an experience of the world—a profile, a vision—possible only through the expression of black subjectivity. It is through this vision and voice that I share my sense of life with others." At present, she is working on a novel and two textbooks, *Continuity: A Basic Writing Course in English for Bilingual Asian Students* and *The Afro-American Voice: Art/Blues/Meter* (an introduction to poetry).

DEFINING IT FOR VANESSA

She is too young to eat
chocolates
they blossom on her black face
like peppercorns
she is 16 and dreams
of the alphabet stitched
to the winter wool
of teenage gladiators
in single capital letters
she leans across the table
and asks us older ladies
about love and the future
but we cannot see past
a few days at any time
we are pregnant
with memories
and move slowly
like Egyptian geese grazing

we tell her put Xmas
in your eyes
and keep your voice low
knowing this answer
as insane as any

will soothe her
while she dreams
wrapped like a mummy
inside her flowered sheets
she thinks we hold secrets
and watches us closely
as we shop for dried flowers
lovely center pieces
for the best china
we tell her smiling

later when we describe
our little aches and pains
she turns away
puzzled by the antidotes
of blues reds and greens
we tell her how the reds
stick like anger
or clock the tides of the moon
we tell her how she'll guard
her lovely eyes
how only in her blackness
will she grow
large as the moon
we tell her how women
with whiskey voices
will try to stop her
how men will strip her clean
of secrets
how the flesh hurts
how the world does not end
with the body
but the longing for it

DANCING WITH THE FIFTH HORSEMAN

If you drape 39 iron chains over your arms and do a dance,
the whole point of the dance will be to seem light and
effortless.

—Robert Francis

one day, you stepped
into my horoscope

bringing summer
and a view of the mountains
I had never known
you insisted on answers
I said for better or worse
not knowing your definition
of time and closing distance
in the singular sky
of my dreams
I tried to fly tandem
your wingtip to mine

last summer you left
my life quivering
like a battlefield
I wore headaches like garments
you cut me so thin
my lunar cycle was left
without a channel
I angrily snatched the next
egg from its bloody cradle
now, veins show
where I have no veins
and age hangs
flat against my face
still, I don't know
how to answer my anger

I tear myself dry
with memories
the sky fills
with your shadows
a rain heavy cloud
the feathered cry
of north bound geese
I hear Mama's complaints
louder than your vows
but I know you are there
I find your scribbled notes
you dreamed of brisk mountains
desert air and Ponce de Leon girls
I saw myself
in your lunar dreams
trapped in a strange language
under a muggy mooned sky

now I drape myself
in slammed doors, confused answers
and friends as definite
as the wind or shadows
my friends slice the moon
and sprinkle the night
around my ears
they cut me even thinner
I don't believe in them
but find little else I can trust
you practiced your dreams
running against traffic
racing home sweaty and happy
falling across the bed
like a surf pushing against
my excuses
of work, motherhood, blackness
and a world I know too well

I was thirty-nine today
and the air repeats
he is gone, he is gone
all day I swayed to its chant
but have not yet learned
to move with the rhythm
tonight I fell
into the pit of my pillow
fighting dreams rising around me
like clouds of perfume
I am caught in a symphony of years
my pulse racing as each crescendo
is followed by a slow dirge of pain
when exhaustion became
the silver bullet
plunging me into timeless sleep
I raced away from you
into the moon
laughing with relief
light headed with the pleasure
of definite speed

WHERE IGUANAS STILL LIVE

For Kevin

This is what is important
A first birthday picture
The rubber bathtub toy
Clutched in your fat fingers
You giggly and myopic
How important it was
When you locked all the doors
Three years old
And instant master of the house
Outside I danced to your amusement
A black Natasha snowbound
And twirling in a web
Of my own desperation
How fragile it seems when years
Cannot release us
The mystery of time
Is not important
One night you said Mama
I can hear the whistles blowing
Then still asleep
You walked away from me

You are out there now
A man walking quickly
To another shore
I am here where
Knights and their ladies still romp
Through your story books
You helped your sister
Learn the alphabet
Tracing the mystery of each letter
Now your posters of African kings
Curl like delicate petals
In the corner of the closet
They are still strong and willing
To hunt lions in the tall grass
It is here we keep time
The carefully measured ticking
Like watching buds grow

We planted corn seeds
Inside freezer bags
Experiments in temperature you said
Quietly proud and so serious
I enrolled you in a club
An animal a month delivered by mail
Fish lizards mice
Jelled dehydrated beheaded
Laced with ink from overdue bills
And letters from your grandmother
Later you stood on the abyss of my anger
While baby snakes nested warm
Inside half filled cosmetic jars
It is important that even now
Though you are not here
I remember how we groped
Hand in hand in the dark
Softly calling the iguana
Lost forever
Inside the pattern of the Persian rug.

YVONNE

Born in Pennsylvania, Yvonne currently lives and works in New York City, where she is a poetry editor for *Ms.* Magazine. She has published poetry in *Aphra* and *Ms.* and in such anthologies as *We Become New* (1975) and *Tangled Vines* (1978). Of her goals as a writer she says, "I want to reinstate, as an aesthetic priority, the older dimensions of poetry, that is, epic and narrative verse. Prose writers are *not* the only storytellers in this nation."

AUNT MARTHA: SEVERANCE PAY

Martha kept no box
under the board
no jar in the flour
nothing in the brim
of her bonnet
nothing in the hem
of her coat
but lint
in every corner
nothing but.

Once in a while a liberty dime
across a cracked
lineoleum.

He belched:
I got you in my hip pocket.
She didn't back off:
*Honey, I'm your hell
way overdue!*
She was the burn. A tax.
Though less than a penny.
He was a drip.
A trickle. Then
washout.

Now long before she stole Aunt Ida's man
Aunt Martha was warned about by their own mother:
When there's sour in the salt, it's too late to fry.
But Martha had a righteous hold
on Eva.

Eva, comfortable
in the clutter of her second marriage
(his dead mother's overstuffed settee, cigar smoke
at breakfast, store-bought teeth beside the bedroom
telephone, her own old pair of satin slippers)
yet poor
somewhat, somehow
wrote to Martha
who had never dared herself ten miles beyond home.
Eva wrote without intimacy like a telegram:
County auction. Some foreclosures. Not too
far from the town cesspit. Please come.
Eva thought a postscript: *Your Tenny can do better*
just like any normal colored man.
But she did not write it.

Martha squinted along the letter and then
sniffed the air: *Town cesspit?*
Evie's turnin' stout and hincty in Pennsylvania.
But Martha obeyed Eva
her only full-blooded sister

and left their mother's house in West Virginia
now empty of daughters, except Susquehanna
who was so bossy,
and came to live in Eastwick
with her Tenny and her girls.
And these were the names of Martha's daughters:

> *one bone china cup*
> *water blue with a stain in your crack*
> *too-much-sassafras-too-much-chicory*
> *delicate Wenonah*
>
> *stone colored cup*
> *everlasting as my black iron pot*
> *some call you pewter, call you Mary*
> *but I call you Iwilla*
>
> *white ironstone cup, my no-handle cup*
> *I use like a mother*

bowl of vengeance, bowl of spring
my Savannah

two red clay cups
one-eyed hawk flying upside down
Sierra, hold a bit of copper
bit of paper

for to buy me teeth
what can feed?
the other, Sequoyah,
hold my tongue

Martha had two sons also.
But they came later.
An afterthought.
A severance pay.
And in their naming
Martha never hoped
for much.

1 9 3 6

Puckering in a speckled porcelain
pot, Corinna's starch could have been
whipped white potatoes for her best
lady's prime cut steak.
She was no less careful and determined.
Martha, the younger, came visiting
to borrow praise and her curling iron.
"Your Mary's an alright girl," said Corinna.
"Never give me no back talk."
"Never give Spivey none before, but
good hustlin' needs good feedin' *on time.*"

Behind schedule, a fine Christian woman,
Corinna lifted her strength
from her sister's whining, more daily than
rheumatism and more like sin.
"You suppose that's *all* she done wrong?"
Martha stiffened and brayed.
"All them Spiveys is crazy!
Mae Reen's an epileptic!
And my Mary don't go nowhere!

(she spoke straight as a knife)
Don't have to work nobody's kitchen but her own!''

Lifting the wide-mouthed pot,
thick-lipped cornerstone
where the base of life
was a potbellied coal stove
where the flesh of life
is still hog maws, the blood
strong with sassafras tea;
lifting, setting the starch down
on the chipped drainboard to cool,
Corinna broke her peace,
"My best lady died on me this Friday."

"Ain't none of 'em *that* good.
What'd she die of?"
Corinna's mind centered: Jason's
clerical shirts piled dry as wrinkled
money. Soon they would hang
in that pale winter bathroom, in
that tumultuous bungalow, as
starched and stiff as plaster
wings for the dead.
"Old age took her.
Her eyes was flat and kind to the end."

Now Corinna wet each shirt
with a thick solid hand.
She bathed each shirt in cooked-down starch
with a grease-burnt hand.
She wrung each shirt
with a thorough hand.
She hung them on black wire hangers
wrapped with old waxed paper.
"Did she leave you what you said
she said she was gonna leave you?"
"She never said what."

Martha was quiet and looked around.
The lineoleum flecked black and white
turned grey
with Corinna's faithful scouring.
Wallpaper, thick with chicken fat, lard,
turned blank
with Corinna's righteous scouring.

Woodwork rough with gritty
cleanser, coal stove rough
with tough white cleanser.
The ceiling was out of reach.

"Ain't none of 'em that good.
What you doin' this Saturday evenin'?"
"Ironin'."
"Ironin'?
High price for your high yallah man."
"No, he's more than a redcap, now.
And I'm his wife.
And I'm no common-law arrangement."

AUDRE LORDE

Currently on a sabbatical from John Jay College of the City University of New York, where she is a professor of English, Audre Lorde lives on Staten Island with her two children. She has published numerous collections of poetry, including most recently *Coal* (1976) and *The Black Unicorn* (1978). Another book of poetry, *From a Land Where Other People Live* (1973), was nominated for the National Book Award in Poetry in 1974. Her works have also appeared in *Essence, Black World, Freedomways, Iowa Review, Ms., Aphra,* and *The Massachusetts Review,* among other places. Listed in *Who's Who in American Women International* and *Who's Who in Poetry—Contemporary Authors,* she has also been a recipient of a National Endowment for the Arts Fellowship in 1968 and has served as poetry editor of *Crysalis—A Magazine of Women's Culture.*

CONVERSATION IN CRISIS

I speak to you as a friend speaks
or a true lover
not out of friendship or love
but for a clear meeting
of self upon self
in sight of our hearth
but without fire.

I cherish your words that ring
like late summer thunders
to sing without octave
and fade, having spoken the season.
But I hear the false heat of this voice
as it dries up the sides of your words
coaxing melodies from your tongue
and this curled music is treason.

Must I die in your fever—
or, as the flames wax, take cover
in your heart's culverts
crouched like a stranger
under the scorched leaves of your other burnt loves
until the storm passes over?

PAPERWEIGHT

Paper is neither kind nor cruel
only white in its neutrality
and I have for reality now
the brown bar of my arm
moving in broken rhythms
across this dead place.

All the poems I have ever written
are historical reviews of a now absorbed country
a small judgement
hawking and coughing them up
I have ejected them not unlike children
now my throat is clear
perhaps I shall speak again.

All the poems I have ever written
make a small book
the shedding of my past in patched conceits
moulted like snake skin, a book of leavings
now
I can do anything I wish
I can love them or hate them
use them for comfort or warmth
tissues or decoration
dolls or japanese baskets
blankets or spells;
I can use them for magic
lanterns or music
advice or small council
for napkins or past-times or
disposable diapers
I can make fire from them
or kindling
songs or paper chains

Or fold them all into a paper fan
with which to cool my husband's dinner.

ROOMING HOUSES ARE OLD WOMEN

Rooming houses are old women
rocking dark windows into their whens
waiting incomplete circles
rocking
rent office to stoop to
community bathrooms to gas rings
and under-bed boxes of once useful garbage
city issued with a twice-a-month check
the young men next door with their loud midnight parties
and fishy rings left in the bathtub
no longer arouse them
from midnight to mealtime no stops inbetween
light breaking to pass through jumbled up windows
and who was it who married the widow that Buzzie's son messed with?

To Welfare and insult from the slow shuffle
from dayswork to shopping bags heavy with leftovers

Rooming houses
are old women waiting
searching
through their darkening windows
the end or beginning of agony
old women seen through half-ajar doors
hoping
they are not waiting
but being
an entrance to somewhere
unknown and desired
and not new.

NTOZAKE SHANGE

Born in New Jersey in 1948, Ntozake Shange has been an instructor of women's studies, Afro-American studies, and creative writing at Sonoma State College, Mills College, the University of California at Berkeley, City College of New York, and Medgar Evers Community College. Her work has been published in numerous small magazines, and she has won many awards, including Woman of the Year (*Mademoiselle*) and the Audelco Award for Best Playwright (Black Theatre Alliance). Her play, *For Colored Girls Who Have Considered Suicide/When the Rainbow Is Enuf*, was nominated for a Tony Award, and the book selected as the main feature for several literary guilds. She has also published *Sassafrass* (1976) and *Nappy Edges* (1978).

cypress

dancin is the movement of oceans/
the caress of many lovers in canyons
laced with poppies n coca leaves/
dancin is union of spirits layed
to rest among splinterin shells
n fires of adoration in the heat
of comets n volcanoes/ dancin
is how i love/ how i share carin/
how did mama say it/ is all i'm good for/
cypress didnt i tell you to come
straight home from school to help me
wid this cloth/ ya beeen standin
round that ballet class aint ya/
ballet is for white girls/ now
cant ya understand/ yr ass is too
big n yr legs too short/ n ya cant
afford all them shoes n special
clothes/ but if ya must be just
like my sistah/ n hanker after
classical movements n grace
i'ma send you up to new york/ effie
is workin wid some nigra woman
doin ballet/ i took care of her
long enough for her to take ya

for a while/ i'ma write her/ see
if all that white folks mess dont
fix yr hard-headed behind for a
minute/ cypress/ i dont wanna see
none of my children hangin round
no crackers to learn nothin/ if
ya wanna study dance ya gotta wait
til i can send ya to effie/ if ya
dont/ i'ma fix ya so ya wont be able
to move nothin at all/ not a muscle/
now get started on that tapestry for

sassafrass

down to the wharf/ there waz always
sailors/ shippers from all over the
world/ daddy waz a seaman/ a ships'
carpenter/ he waz always goin round
the world/ that's what mama said/ n
he died in the ocean offa zanzibar/
that's what mama said/ the ship just
caught fire/ n went on down to the
bottom of the ocean/ that's why she
n sassafrass n cypress n indigo/ wd
toss nickels n food n wine in the sea
down the coast/ so daddy wd have all
he needed to live a good life in the
other world/ sassafrass stayed by the
wharf whenever she cd/ after school she
watched the men tyin knots/ fixin nets
n she figures her daddy knew all that/
n he cd sing too like the sailors n
dance like the west indians/ who waz
crew on a lotta of the boats in the
seamy port of charleston/ sassafrass
wd sit on barrels wid the men n help
em straighten out their nets/ n listen
to the tales of other colored folks'
lives in the islands n as far off as
new guinea/ she tried to imagine what
they looked like if they werent tryin

to look like white folks/ what did the
languages sound like/ n the cloth n
the dance/ n who were their spirits/ did
they believe in jesus or were there
other gods/ n other heavens/ like there
were drums n special dances the bermu
dans n trinidadian sailors played in
the evenin/ n showed sassafrass what

    cypress

miz fitzhugh/ it's gotta be done by
spring fore ya leave for new york/
n i'll be damned if ya dont come
back some kinda ballerina/ all proper/

then they worked n cypress made a
secret promise to her mother/ to
dance as good as white folks n
to find out the truth abt colored
people's movements/ cuz she knew
dancin waz in her blood/ every step/

effie wore a lotta makeup n lived
6 flights up on the east side in
nyc near brooklyn sorta/ cypress
didnt go to school/ she wenta class
n rehearsal wid effie/ n she sweat
n arched n cried cuz she hurt/ n she
tried to learn french/ n the difference
tween modern n classical ballet/ n effie
waz impatient n mean abt dancin/ cuz it
gotta be right/ n cypress went on/ her
body tight/ her mind astounded by
dancin in new york/ n no fresh food/
n funny languages n old ukrainian
women lookin in garbage cans/ the
moon hidden by concrete offices/
effie entertainen dancers n singers
til the next rehearsal/ n always
more to learn/ more energy to find/
n no congratulations abt gettin

better/ n bein almost 16 n not knowin
nobody under twenty-five/ cypress
gave her life to dancin/ reducin
complex actions to the curve of her

      sassafrass

they called the 'jump-up'/ or the mambo/
sassafrass picked up a slight accent/
n put her hand on her hip the way the
men did when they were imitatin their
girls at home/ n sassafrass prayed
she cd live like that/ free in the
country/ surrounded by orange trees
n men makin drums n goin out to fish
n feasts for the different spirits/
sassafrass decided/ bein with the
colored sailors n dock workers/ that
she shd go everywhere there were dark
folks at/ all over the world where her
people lived/ n she wd write it all
down so other children wdnt feel lost
n think they waz stupid ninnies/ like
miz fitzhugh told her/ 'it's too bad
you a lil ninny, sassafrass or i'd
take you with me on this cruise'/
n to the surprise of the spry seafarers/
sassafrass announced/ 'i'ma be a cunjah'
they laughed incredulously/ sayin/
'you awready a geechee/ how much more
magic you want?'/

sassafrass wished on flowers/ the
flight pattern of birds/ the angle
of leaves fallin/ n swore to bring
the old ways back/ old spirits n their
children n any new-fandangled kinda
mystic aids that was demanded by cir-
cumstances/ sassafrass stopped hangin
by the wharf n started hangin round
the old folks at the church n bars in
skinny streets/ learnin how to fix up

cypress

wrist/ aerial moroe took her into
his troupe of The Kushites Returned
n immersed her in the ways of pre-
egyptian black nile culture/ n cypress
waz discoverin the movements of the
colored people that had been lost/
year after year ariel's company
nearly starved/ but they danced
9 hours a day/ n moved all over the
country playin audiences rallied
behind the sit-in movement n equal
opportunity for colored folks/ The
Kushites Returned/ played itsy bitsy
lil ol southern towns/ n introduced
factory workers n sharecroppers n
doctors n church-women to the brazen
mystical motions of black nile dance/

cypress took up wid some of the musicians
in the troupe/ n she wd listen n soar
towards indefinite heavens when they played/
n her dance took on the essence of the
struggle of colored americans to survive
their enslavement/ n grew scornful of her
years of clamorin for ballet/ n grew deep
into her difference/ her ass n her legs/
she used like a colored girl/ when she
danced/ she waz alive/ when she danced/
she waz free/ her people/ waz free

sassafrass

sick folks/ n spells that so n so's
granny usedta murder whoever/
n she layed up nights readin
histories of ancient civilizations
that were closer to her than all that
stuff abt england n the wars of the roses
she wrote songs of love n vindication
for all the african & indian deities

disgraced by the comin of the white
man n loss of land n cities reflectin
respect for livin things/

i am sassafrass/ my fingers behold you
i call upon you with my song you teach
in my sleep/ i am not a besieger of yr
fortress/ i am a crusader/ for you are
all my past/ i offer you my body to
make manifest yr will in this dungeon
of machines n carolian blues/ i wanna
sing yr joy/ n make present our beauty/
spirits/ black n brown/ find yr way
thru my tainted blood/ make me one of
yr own/ i am yr child in the new world/
i am yr fruit/ yet to be chosen for
a single battle in yr behalf/ come to
n thru me/ i am dazzled by yr beneficence
i shall create new altars/ new praises
& be ancient among you/

MAYA ANGELOU

Though she is perhaps best known for her best-selling works, *I Know Why the Caged Bird Sings* (1970) and *Gather Together in My Name* (1974), Maya Angelou has also authored several collections of poetry, including *Just Give Me a Cool Drink of Water 'fore i Diiie* (1973), *O Pray My Wings Are Gonna Fit Me Well* (1975), and *And Still I Rise* (1978). A member of the American Film Institute, she has also written several screenplays for her own works and written and produced a ten-part TV series on African traditions in American life. A recipient of honorary degrees from Smith, Mills, Lawrence University, and Wake Forest University, she was named Woman of the Year in Communications by the *Ladies Home Journal* in 1975.

PHENOMENAL WOMAN

Pretty women wonder where my secret lies.
I'm not cute or built to suit a fashion model's size
But when I start to tell them,
They think I'm telling lies.
I say,
It's in the reach of my arms,
The span of my hips,
The stride of my step,
The curl of my lips.
I'm a woman
Phenomenally.
Phenomenal woman,
That's me.

I walk into a room
Just as cool as you please,
And to a man,
The fellows stand or
Fall down on their knees.
Then they swarm around me,
A hive of honey bees.
I say,
It's the fire in my eyes,
And the flash of my teeth,

The swing in my waist,
And the joy in my feet.
I'm a woman
Phenomenally.
Phenomenal woman,
That's me.

Men themselves have wondered
What they see in me.
They try so much
But they can't touch
My inner mystery.
When I try to show them
They say they still can't see.
I say,
It's in the arch of my back,
The sun of my smile,
The ride of my breasts,
The grace of my style.
I'm a woman
Phenomenally.
Phenomenal woman,
That's me.

Now you understand
Just why my head's not bowed.
I don't shout or jump about
Or have to talk real loud.
When you see me passing
It ought to make you proud.
I say,
It's in the click of my heels,
The bend of my hair,
The palm of my hand,
The need for my care.
'Cause I'm a woman
Phenomenally.
Phenomenal woman,
That's me.

SHERLEY WILLIAMS

Sherley Williams lives in San Diego, where she is chairperson of the Department of Literature at the University of California, San Diego. She has worked at Federal City College and at Miles College. Her first book, *Give Birth to Brightness* (1972), contains essays in literary criticism on black literature. In 1975 she published her first collection of poems, *The Peacock Poems,* which was nominated for the National Book Award in Poetry in 1976. Her stories and poems have also been published in *The Massachusetts Review, New Letters, Change, Iowa Review, Partisan Review,* and *Essence.*

ANY WOMAN'S BLUES
every woman is a victim of the feel blues, too

Soft lamp shinin
       and me alone in the night.
Soft lamp is shinin
       and me alone in the night.
Can't take no one beside me
       need mo'n jest some man to set me right.

I left many peoples and places
       tryin not to be alone.
Left many a person and places
       I lived my life alone.
I need to get myself together.
       Yes, I need to make myself to home.

What's gone can be a window
       a circle in the eye of the sun.
What's gone can be a window
       a circle, well, in the eye of the sun.
Take the circle from the world, girl,
       you find the light have gone.

These is old blues
       and I sing em like any woman do.

These the old blues
        and I sing em, sing em, sing em. Just like any woman do.
My life ain't done yet.
        Naw. My song ain't through.

THE COLLATERAL ADJECTIVE

I sing my song in
a cycle a round
spiral up spiral
down the adjective
has little to do
with the noun

        The round
is showy and loud
proud like the noun it
designates person
place thing. To find *place*
call name (and thing is
a greased pole) So much
to gain and nothing
to lose: the noun has
all the lines and the
lines, they cover all
the pain.

        Spiral up
spiral down. Cycle
the round circle the
song. Without a drum
that sings soprano
the tongue's only a
wagging member in
the void of the mouth
speechless in the face
of what it has said.
I never never
thought to sing this song.
The adjective the
noun—This is not my
idea of a game.

SAY HELLO TO JOHN

I swear I ain't done what Richard
told me bout jumpin round and stuff.
And he knew I wouldn't do nothin to make the baby
come, just joke, say I'mo cough

this child up one day.
So in the night when I felt the water tween
my legs, I thought it was pee and I laid
there wonderin if maybe I was in a dream.

Then it come to me that my water broke and I went
in to tell Ru-ise. *You been havin pains?*
she ask. I hear her fumblin for the light.
Naw, I say. Don't think so. The veins

stand out along her temples. *What time
is it?* Goin on toward four o'clock.
*Nigga, I told you:
You ain't havin no babies, not*

*in the middle of the night.
Get yo ass back to bed.
That ain't nothin but pee.* And what
I know bout havin kids cept what she said?

Second time it happen, even she
got to admit this mo'n pee.
And the pain when it come, wa'n't bad
least no mo'n I eva expect to see

again. I remember the doctor smilin,
sayin, Shel, you got a son.
His bright black face above me
sayin, Say hello to John.

GENERATIONS:

Mamma
is a silent movie
I hear her voice in
honky tonk wonder
see her lips move in

speechless quiet on
the screen

This is the
season of sad singing
of fall out and love
in West Texas and
California
in a pick-up truck.

GENERATIONS:

Daddy
is a shadow on
the silver screen his
talk is in his walk
in the soundless
rhythm of his toed
out strut.

This is the
season of sad sad
singing of the present
and the last crop.

GENERATIONS: I

My mamma is a
silent movie my
daddy a quiet
shadow on the screen
they framed now in
Arvin; in someplace
where we picked hops; a
time up in Hillsborough
and past and present
stop.

This the season of
sad singing yo'all of
people can't tell no
one they name.

GENERATIONS: II

I live on a hill
in the city that
spread her lights like
diamonds and profile
in the waters of
the bay.

My mamma
is a movie she
shine on daddy's screen
this the season of
sad singing singing
singing unnamed.

ALICE WALKER

Born in 1944 in Georgia, Alice Walker is a contributing editor to *Ms.* magazine. Her books include *The Third Life of Grange Copeland* (1970) and *Meridian* (1976), both novels; *Once* (1968) and *Revolutionary Petunias* and *Other Poems* (1973), volumes of poetry; *In Love and Trouble* (1973), a collection of short stories; and *Langston Hughes, American Poet* (1974), a biography for children. Her essays and stories have appeared in numerous journals and magazines. She was awarded a Guggenheim in fiction for 1977–1978 and was the recipient of the Lillian Smith Award and a Creative Writing Award from the National Endowment for the Arts, among other fellowships. In 1974 *Revolutionary Petunias and Other Poems* was nominated for a National Book Award, and *In Love and Trouble* won the Rosenthal Award of the National Institute of Arts and Letters.

BURIAL

I

They have fenced in the dirt road
that once led to Wards Chapel
A.M.E. church,
and cows graze
among the stones that
mark my family's graves.
The massive oak is gone
from out the church yard,
but the giant space is left
unfilled;
despite the two-lane blacktop
that slides across
the old, unalterable
roots.

II

Today I bring my own child here;
to this place where my father's
grandmother rests undisturbed
beneath the Georgia sun,

above her the neatstepping hooves
of cattle.
Here the graves soon grow back into the land.
Have been known to sink. To drop open without
warning. To cover themselves with wild ivy,
blackberries. Bittersweet and sage.
No one knows why. No one asks.
When Burning Off Day comes, as it does
some years,
the graves are haphazardly cleared and snakes
hacked to death and burned sizzling
in the brush. . . . The odor of smoke, oak
leaves, honeysuckle.
Forgetful of geographic resolutions as birds,
the farflung young fly South to bury
the old dead.

III

The old women move quietly up
and touch Sis Rachel's face.
"Tell Jesus I'm coming," they say.
"Tell Him I ain't goin' to *be*
long."

My grandfather turns his creaking head
away from the lavender box.
He does not cry. But looks afraid.
For years he called her "Woman";
shortened over the decades to
" 'Oman."
On the cut stone for " 'Oman's" grave
he did not notice
they had misspelled her name.
(The stone reads *Racher Walker*—not "Rachel"
Loving Wife, Devoted Mother.)

IV

As a young woman, who had known her? Tripping
eagerly, "loving wife," to my grandfather's
bed. Not pretty, but serviceable. A hard
worker, with rough, moist hands. Her own two

babies dead before she came.
Came to seven children.
To aprons and sweat.
Came to quiltmaking.
Came to canning and vegetable gardens
big as fields.
Came to fields to plow.
Cotton to chop.
Potatoes to dig.
Came to multiple measles, chickenpox,
and croup.
Came to water from springs.
Came to leaning houses one story high.
Came to rivalries. Saturday night battles.
Came to straightened hair, Noxzema, and
feet washing at the Hardshell Baptist church.
Came to zinnias around the woodpile.
Came to grandchildren not of her blood
whom she taught to dip snuff without
sneezing.
Came to death blank, forgetful of it all.

When he called her " 'Oman" she no longer
listened. Or heard, or knew, or felt.

v

It is not until I see my first grade teacher
review her body that I cry.
Not for the dead, but for the gray in my
first grade teacher's hair. For memories
of before I was born, when teacher and
grandmother loved each other; and later
above the ducks made of soap and the orange-
legged chicks Miss Reynolds drew over
my own small hand
on paper with wide blue lines.

V I

Not for the dead, but for memories. None of
them sad. But seen from the angle of her
death.

WOMEN

They were women then
My mamma's generation
Husky of voice—Stout òf
Step
With fists as well as
Hands
How they battered down
Doors
And ironed
Starched white
Shirts
How they led
Armies
Headragged Generals
Across mined
Fields
Booby-trapped
Ditches
To discover books
Desks
A place for us
How they knew what we
Must know
Without knowing a page
Of it
Themselves.

ALICE WALKER

ADDITIONAL READINGS

Note: The following list is only a representative sample of anthologies, journals, periodicals, novels, and poetry collections by and about contemporary black women writers.

Anthologies

Bambara, Toni Cade, ed. *The Black Woman.* New York, New American Library, 1970. A collection of essays, poems, short stories.
————, ed. *Tales and Stories for Black Folks.* New York, Doubleday, 1971.
Barksdale, Richard, and Keneth Kinnamon, eds. *Black Writers of America.* New York, Macmillan, 1972. A comprehensive survey of black literature organized chronologically.
Bell, Roseann, Bettye Parker, and Beverly Sheftall, eds. *Sturdy Black Bridges: Visions of Black Women in Literature.* New York, Doubleday, 1978.
Bontemps, Arna, ed. *American Negro Poetry.* New York, Hill & Wang, 1963; revised ed., 1974. Includes a representative selection of early and modern women poets.
Brawley, Benjamin, ed. *Early Negro American Writers.* Chapel Hill, University of North Carolina Press, 1935.
Brooks, Gwendolyn, ed. *Jump Bad: A New Chicago Anthology.* Detroit, Broadside Press, 1971. This collection of poetry contains works by Ronda Davis, Linyatta (Doris Turner), Peggy Kenner, Carolyn Rodgers, and Sharon Scott.
Brown, Sterling A., Arthur P. Davis, and Ulysses Lee, eds. *The Negro Caravan.* New York, Dryden, 1941. A classic.
Chapman, Abraham, ed. *Black Voices.* New York, New American Library, 1968. Among the women writers included are Ann Petry, Paule Marshall, Diane Oliver, Gwendolyn Brooks, Naomi Long Madgett, and Mari Evans. Chapman provides a good introduction to the study of black literature.
————, ed. *New Black Voices.* New York, New American Library, 1971. An update.
Clarke, John H., ed. *American Negro Short Stories.* New York, Hill & Wang, 1966. Includes Zora Neale Hurston, Ann Petry, Paule Marshall, and Mary Elizabeth Vroman.
Davis, Arthur P., and Saunders Redding, eds. *Cavalcade: Negro American Writing from 1760 to the Present.* Boston, Houghton Mifflin, 1971. A comprehensive anthology organized by historical periods. Contains representative works by early black women writers.
Harper, Michael, and Robert B. Stepto, eds. *Chant of Saints.* Urbana, University of Illinois Press, 1979. A collection of essays, poems, interviews, short stories, and criticism. It originally appeared as Vol. 18, no. 3 and 4 of *The Massachusetts Review.*
Hayden, Robert, ed. *Kaleidoscope, Poems by American Negro Poets.* New York, Harcourt Brace and World, 1967.

Hayden, Robert, David Burrows, and Frederick Lapides, eds. *Afro-American Literature: An Introduction.* New York, Harcourt Brace Jovanovitch, 1971. Includes selections by Margaret Walker, Margaret Danner, Gwendolyn Brooks, Lucille Clifton, and Alice Walker.

Hughes, Langston, ed. *The Best Short Stories by Negro Writers.* Boston, Little, Brown & Co., 1967. Includes stories by Alice Walker, Alice Childress, Gwendolyn Brooks, Paule Marshall, and Zora Neale Hurston.

Hughes, Langston, and Arna Bontemps, eds. *The Book of Negro Folklore.* New York, Dodd, Mead, 1959.

———, eds. *The Poetry of the Negro,* 1746–1970. Garden City, New York, Doubleday, 1970. An update of their 1949 anthology. Includes a representative selection of the early women poets.

Iverson, Lucille and Kathryn Ruby. *We Become New—Poems by Contemporary American Women.* New York, Bantam, 1975. Includes a number of black women poets.

James, Charles L., ed. *From the Roots: Short Stories by Black Americans.* New York, Dodd, Mead, 1970. Includes selections by Zora Neale Hurston and Ann Petry.

Jordan, June, ed. *Soulscript: Afro-American Poetry.* Garden City, New York, Doubleday, 1970. Includes works by Vanessa Howard, Linda Curry, Julia Alvarez, Gayl Jones, Nikki Giovanni, Gwendolyn Brooks, June Jordan, Audre Lorde, Sonia Sanchez, Naomi Long Madgett, and Alice Walker.

Randall, Dudley, ed. *The Black Poets.* New York, Bantam, 1971. Divided into folk poetry, spirituals, and literary poetry, this anthology contains representative works by early and contemporary women poets.

Reed, Ishmael and Al Young, eds. *Yardbird Lives.* New York, Grove Press, 1978. Includes a number of selections by black women.

Turner, Darwin T., ed. *Black American Literature: Fiction.* Columbus, O., Merrill, 1969.

———, ed. *Black American Literature: Poetry.* Columbus, O., Merrill, 1962.

Washington, Mary Helen, ed. *Black-eyed Susans.* Garden City, N.Y., Doubleday, 1975. A collection of short stories by Jean Wheeler Smith, Toni Morrison, Gwendolyn Brooks, Louise Meriwether, Toni Cade Bambara, Alice Walker, and Paule Marshall.

Yellin, Jean Fagan. *Writings By and About Afro-American Women, 1800–1910.* Boston, G. K. Hall, 1980 expected publication.

Journals and Periodicals

The Black Scholar (San Francisco Black World Foundation)
Black World (formerly *Negro Digest*)
Callaloo (University of Kentucky)
College Language Association Journal (Morgan State University)
Essence
Iowa Review (Vol. 6, No. 2 (Spring 1975) is on black writing)
Journal of Black Poetry
Journal of Black Studies
Liberator (New York Afro-American Research Institute)
The Massachusetts Review (Vol. 18, Nos. 3 and 4)
Ms.
Negro American Literature Forum (Indiana State University)
Negro History Bulletin
Negro Quarterly
New Letters
Obsidian (New York State University College at Fredonia)
Phylon (Atlanta University)
Studies in Black Literature (Mary Washington College)
Yardbird Reader

Primary Sources

Angelou, Maya. *I Know Why the Caged Bird Sings.* New York, Random House, 1970. Autobiography.

———. *Just Give Me a Cool Drink of Water 'fore i Diiie.* New York, Bantam, 1973. Poetry.

———. *Oh Pray My Wings Are Gonna Fit Me Well.* New York, Random House, 1975. Poetry.

———. *Singin' & Swingin' & Gettin' Merry Like Christmas.* New York, Random House, 1976. Autobiography.

———. *And Still I Rise.* New York, Random House, 1978. Poetry.

Bambara, Toni Cade. *Gorilla, My Love.* New York, Random House, 1972. Short stories.

Brooks, Gwendolyn. *Annie Allen.* New York, Harper, 1949. Poetry.

———. *The Bean Eaters.* New York, Harper, 1960. Poetry.

———. *Bronzeville Boys and Girls.* New York, Harper, 1956. Poetry.

———. *Family Pictures.* Detroit, Broadside Press, 1970. Poetry.

———. *In the Mecca.* New York, Harper & Row, 1968. Poetry.

———. *Maud Martha.* New York, Harper, 1953. Fiction.

———. *Riot.* Detroit, Broadside Press, 1969. Poetry.

———. *Selected Poems.* New York, Harper, 1963. Poetry.

———. *A Street in Bronzeville.* New York, Harper, 1945. Poetry.

———. *The World of Gwendolyn Brooks.* New York, Harper & Row, 1971. Poetry.

Clifton, Lucille. *Generations: A Memoir.* New York, Random House, 1976.

———. *Good News about the Earth.* New York, Random House, 1972. Poetry.

———. *Good Times.* New York, Random House, 1969. Poetry.

———. *An Ordinary Woman.* New York, Random House, 1974. Poetry.

Evans, Mari. *I Am a Black Woman.* New York, William Morrow, 1970. Poetry.

———. *Where Is All the Music?* London, Breman, 1968. Poetry.

Giovanni, Nikki. *Black Feeling, Black Folk/Black Judgement.* New York, William Morrow, 1970. Poetry.

———. *My House.* New York, William Morrow, 1972. Poetry.

———. *Re: Creation.* Detroit, Broadside Press, 1970. Poetry.

———. *Spin a Soft Black Song.* New York, Hill & Wang, 1971. Poetry.

———. *The Women and the Men.* New York, William Morrow, 1975. Poetry.

Hurston, Zora Neale. *Dust Tracks on a Road.* Philadelphia, J. B. Lippincott, 1942; reprinted, 1971. Autobiography.

———. *Jonah's Gourd Vine.* Philadelphia, J. B. Lippincott, 1934; reprinted, 1971. Fiction.

———. *Moses, Man of the Mountain.* Philadelphia, J. B. Lippincott, 1939; reprinted by Chatham Bookseller, 1974. Fiction.

———. *Mules and Men.* Philadelphia, J. B. Lippincott, 1935; reprinted by Harper & Row, 1970. Folklore.

———. *Seraph on the Suwanee.* New York, Charles Scribner's Sons, 1948; reprinted by AMS Press, 1974. Fiction.

————. *Their Eyes Were Watching God.* Philadelphia, J. B. Lippincott, 1937; reprinted by the University of Illinois Press, 1978. Fiction.

Jones, Gayl. *Corregidora.* New York, Random House, 1975. Fiction.

————. *Eva's Man.* New York, Random House, 1976. Fiction.

————. *The White Rat.* New York, Random House, 1977. Short stories.

Jordan, June. *His Own Where.* New York, Crowell, 1971. Fiction.

————. *Some Changes.* New York, Dutton, 1971. Poetry.

————. *Who Look at Me.* New York, Crowell, 1969. Poetry.

Lorde, Audre. *The Black Unicorn.* New York, Norton, 1978. Poetry.

————. *From a Land Where Other People Live.* Detroit, Broadside Press, 1973. Poetry.

————. *New York Head Shop and Museum.* Detroit, Broadside Press, 1974. Poetry.

McElroy, Colleen. *Music from Home: Selected Poems.* Carbondale, Southern Illinois Press, 1976.

Madgett, H., Naomi Long. *Exits and Entrances.* Detroit, Lotus Press, 1978. Poetry.

————. *One and the Many.* New York, Exposition, 1961. Poetry.

————. *Pink Ladies in the Afternoon.* Detroit, Lotus Press, 1972. Poetry.

————. *Songs to a Phantom Nightingale.* New York, Fortuny's, 1941. Poetry.

————. *Star by Star.* Detroit, Harlo, 1965.

Marshall, Paule. *Brown Girl, Brownstones.* New York, Random House, 1959. Fiction.

————. *The Chosen Place, the Timeless People.* New York, Harcourt Brace & World, 1969. Fiction.

————. *Soul Clap Hands and Sing.* New York, Atheneum, 1961. Short stories.

Meriwether, Louise. *Daddy Was a Numbers Runner.* Englewood Cliffs, N.J., Prentice-Hall, 1970. Fiction.

Miller, May. *The Clearing and Beyond.* Washington, D.C., Charioteer Press, 1974. Poetry.

————. *Dust of Uncertain Journey.* Detroit, Lotus Press, 1975. Poetry.

————. *Into the Clearing.* Washington, D.C., Charioteer Press, 1959. Poetry.

Morrison, Toni. *The Bluest Eye.* New York, Holt, Rinehart, 1970. Fiction.

————. *Song of Solomon.* New York, Alfred A. Knopf, 1977. Fiction.

————. *Sula.* New York, Alfred A. Knopf, 1973. Fiction.

Petry, Ann. *Country Place.* Boston, Houghton Mifflin, 1947. Fiction.

————. *Miss Muriel and Other Stories.* Boston, Houghton Mifflin, 1971.

————. *The Narrows.* Boston, Houghton Mifflin, 1953. Fiction.

————. *The Street.* Boston, Houghton Mifflin, 1946. Fiction.

————. *Tituba of Salem Village.* New York, Crowell, 1964. Fiction.

Rodgers, Carolyn. *How i got ovah!* Garden City, N.Y., Anchor Press, 1975. Poetry.

————. *Now ain't that love.* Detroit, Broadside Press, 1970. Poetry.

————. *Songs of a Blackbird.* Chicago, Third World Press, 1969. Poetry.

Sanchez, Sonia. *Homecoming.* Detroit, Broadside Press, 1969. Poetry.

————. *We a Baddddd People.* Detroit, Broadside Press, 1970. Poetry.

Shange, Ntozake. *For Colored Girls Who Have Considered Suicide/When the Rainbow Is Enuf.* New York, Macmillan, 1978. Choreopoem.

————. *Nappy Edges.* New York, Macmillan, 1978. Poetry.

————. *Sassafrass.* Berkeley, Calif., Shameless Hussy Press, 1976.

Walker, Alice. *In Love and Trouble.* New York, Harcourt Brace Jovanovich, 1973. Short stories.

————. *Meridian.* New York, Harcourt Brace Jovanovich, 1976. Fiction.

————. *Once; Poems.* New York: Harcourt Brace Jovanovich, 1968.

————. *Revolutionary Petunias.* New York, Harcourt Brace Jovanovich, 1971. Poetry.

————. *The Third Life of Grange Copeland.* New York, Harcourt Brace Jovanovich, 1970. Fiction.

Walker, Margaret. *For My People.* New Haven, Yale University Press, 1942. Poetry.

————. *Jubilee.* Boston, Houghton Mifflin, 1966. Fiction.

————. *October Journey.* Detroit, Broadside Press, 1973. Poetry.

————. *Prophets for a New Day.* Detroit, Broadside Press, 1970. Poetry.

Williams, Sherley. *Give Birth to Brightness.* New York, Dial Press, 1972. Literary criticism.

————. *The Peacock Poems.* Middletown, Conn., Wesleyan University Press, 1975.

Wright, Sarah. *This Child's Gonna Live.* New York, Seymour Lawrence, 1969. Fiction.

HERITAGE

Heritage
I look for you all day in the streets of Oaxaca.
The children run to me, laughing,
spinning me blind and silly.
They call to me in words of another language.
My brown body searches the streets
for the dye that will color my thoughts.

But Mexico gags
"ESPUTA" *
on this bland pochaseed.†

I didn't ask to be brought up tonta! ‡
My name hangs about me like a loose tooth.
Old women know my secret,
*"Es la culpa de los antepasados" ***
Blame it on the old ones.
They give me a name
that fights me.

Lorna Dee Cervantes

* "spit"; *Es puta* also means "She is a prostitute." See Appendix D for a fuller discussion of this poem.
† Americanized Mexican
‡ As a fool
** "It's the fault of the ancestors"

CHICANA WRITERS

INTRODUCTION

HISTORICAL PERSPECTIVES

At the core of the Chicano literary imagination is a profound sense of heritage. Born of the forced union between the Indian mother and the European father, Chicanos are descendants of the Aztecs and offspring of the Spanish conquistadors, inheritors of the dichotomy between conditions of power and powerlessness. Inhabiting the landscape between two cultures, they are Mexican Americans, generally able to converse easily in Spanish and English, yet unable to identify totally with either Mexico or the United States. They seek through their literature to articulate the paradox of their past, to understand what Lorna Dee Cervantes has expressed as "a name/that fights me."

In seeking to carve out their particular identity, contemporary writers have chosen to call themselves Chicanos, a name that summons up their Indian past.[1] "Mexican" originally referred to those people of Nahua background who spoke the Nahuatl language. Of these, the Aztecs formed the largest group and were often called Mexicanos, which phonetically was pronounced "Mechicano."[2] For most writers, "Chicano" has a political and cultural resonance that comes closer to the truth of their experience than "Mexican American," "Hispanic," or "Latino." Individual writers, however, do vary in their preference and orientation. Some identify more with the Spanish language and similarities they might share with other Hispanic and Latin American writers, while others consider themselves authors of Mexican origin writing in America. The term "Chicano" reflects a recognition of and respect for an Indian heritage that is as important to the Chicano sensibility as are its Spanish roots.

Another name of importance to Chicanos is Aztlan, the legendary homeland of the Aztecs, which is said to have embraced the region that is today the American Southwest. Though migrations eventually carried the Aztecs south to the area where they would build their great civilization at Teotihuacán (on the periphery of Mexico City), Aztlan remains a mythical and spiritual symbol of their origins. For Chicanos, Aztlan symbolizes their struggle for liberation. In 1969 over three thousand Chicanos met in Denver to draft *El Plan Espiritual de Aztlan,* a series of resolutions leading to freedom from economic, social, and political oppression. Identifying themselves as members of the autonomous nation-state of Aztlan they declared:

> We, the Chicano inhabitants and civilizers of the northern land of
> Aztlan, from whence came our forefathers, reclaiming the land of their

birth and consecrating the determination of our people of the sun, declare that the call of our blood is our power, our responsibility, and our inevitable destiny. . . . We are a Nation, We are a Union of free pueblos, We are Aztlan.[3]

Aztlan symbolizes an indigenous nation-state; it is also a reminder of the politics of history. In 1848 Mexico signed the treaty of Guadalupe Hidalgo, ending the war between Mexico and the United States and giving over to the United States all of the territory that encompasses the present states of Arizona, Nevada, Utah, New Mexico, California, and part of Colorado. (Texas had already become an independent territory in the Revolution of 1836.) By the terms of the treaty, the Mexicans then living in that region could remain and become American citizens with the right to retain their language and culture. Many chose to return to Mexico but more stayed, and today the majority of the almost eight million Chicanos in America live in the Southwest. Their proximity to Mexico and the ease of two-way travel across the border has made it possible for Chicanos to remain fairly bilingual and bicultural. These factors of proximity and mobility between cultures, however, have also been the instruments of their isolation from the mainstream of American culture, and they have been forced economically and educationally into America's second largest minority group. Neither Mexico nor America claims the descendants of the original inhabitants of the Southwest. In spite of this marginal position between two cultures—or perhaps because of it— Chicanos have forged a distinct culture of their own and created a unique literature that fuses characteristics from their Indian, Spanish, and Anglo-American heritage. Their literature abounds with linguistic innovations; new sounds and rhythms are created by the juxtaposition of English with Spanish and even with Nahuatl. Myth informs symbolism, and folklore and legends influence genre and theme.

The cultural influences that spawned Chicano literature can be traced back to the early expeditions of the Spanish explorers in the sixteenth century. In their northward movement from Mexico into the Southwest, they left behind the Spanish language, songs, tales, legends. One of the first popular literary forms to emerge,. aside from the journals and diaries kept by the conquistadors, was the folk drama, anonymous plays designed to entertain the Spanish and educate the Indians. Priests were often the authors of these dramas, or *autos,* which were passed on through the oral tradition well into the nineteenth century.[4]

Through a process of cultural syncretism, the combining of different elements into a whole, legends began to appear in the sixteenth century that could be traced to both Spanish and indigenous origins. One of the most famous of these is *La Llorona,* the legend of the weeping woman. (Three variations of this legend are included in "Contexts.") Historically, La Llorona was a native woman betrayed by her husband. When she discovered his infidelity, she committed infanticide and was then condemned to wander through an infinity of nights sorrowing for her children. Native elements in the story link the legend to Aztec mythology.[5] La Llorona is the victim, the oppressed mother whose only defense against betrayal is to turn against her own flesh. While the violence of her act makes her a harbinger of danger, it also expresses the depth of her anguish. So central to the Chicano imagination is *La Llorona* that innumerable folktales about the weeping woman continue to be told all over Mexico and the Southwest. The legend is representative of an aura of fatalism that characterizes the Mexican sensibility and has carried over into Mexican American literature—the feeling that heritage has rendered inevitable the condition of living between two worlds in each of which the individual has little or no power.

Another influence on the development of a Mexican American literary tradition is the folk song. In the mid-nineteenth century, the Spanish ballad was transformed into the Mexican *corrido,* a narrative ballad that literally "runs." [6] The *corrido* is particularly important as one of the first examples of a new literary genre created by the indigenous Mexican population out of Spanish forms. Primarily oral, the *corrido* is the mode of expression for the common person, the means for musically recounting the struggles of romantic heroes, passing on personal and communal histories, and releasing repressed anger over border hostilities between Anglo-Americans and Mexican Americans.[7] Most importantly, the *corrido* transforms folklore into art, an influence that is still apparent in contemporary Chicano literature. As Raymund Paredes has suggested, folklore links Chicano writers to their heritage and is at the heart of their literary sensibility.

The Chicana writers included here, with a few exceptions, are products of the literary renaissance that occurred in the 1960s in conjunction with the civil rights movement and the farm workers' struggle led by Cesar Chavez. A further impetus to the Chicano literary movement came in 1967 with the establishment of Quinto Sol Publications in Berkeley, California, which offered publishing opportunities to Chicano writers who were not yet considered profitable by commercial publishers. In an effort to affirm the uniqueness of their perspective outside the mainstream of the American literary tradition, the Quinto Sol writers have turned to their Indian heritage and to a bilingual style to express their position between two cultures. Some of the women writers have sought expression in the literature of social protest; others have turned to the past and centered their narratives around folklore and legend. Still other Chicanas have looked to the writers of Latin America for new forms and symbols. All have been able to draw on a heritage rich and complex in its images of women.

Of these images, Tonantzin is, perhaps, the oldest and most enduring model of feminine energy. The Aztec goddess of fertility, she symbolizes the generative powers in the universe. She is the Indian earth mother, the indigenous brown goddess who protects the pregnant and watches over childbirth. In her province lie the cycles of reproduction, and to worship her is to celebrate the very rhythms of life. She is the archetype of woman as mother.[8] Through the impact of Spanish and Indian cultures, Tonantzin became identified with Guadalupe when the cult of the Virgin was introduced to Mexico by the Spaniards. According to Octavio Paz,

> The Catholic Virgin is also the Mother (some Indian pilgrims still call her Guadalupe/Tonantzin), but her principal attribute is not to watch over the fertility of the earth but to provide refuge for the unfortunate. The situation has changed; the worshipers do not try to make sure of their harvests but to find a mother's lap. The Virgin is the consolation of the poor, the shield of the weak, the help of the oppressed.[9]

In contrast to Guadalupe and Tonantzin, who are mother images of consolation and nourishment, is *La Malinche*, "the violated mother." The Indian consort of Cortés and mother of his illegitimate children, *La Malinche* (Doña Marina) is said to symbolize the Spanish conquest. Her rape opened the way physically and spiritually to the defeat of the Indians and the birth of the Mestizo race.[10]

CONTEXTS AND NARRATIVES

The context for Chicano literature is rich in history, folklore, and, inevitably, political conflict. If *La Llorona* symbolizes anguish and *La Malinche* betrayal, Tonantzin embodies primordial energy. Despair is countered by promise. Both impulses reverberate throughout Chicano literature, creating a tension of opposites that is grounded in folk tradition and expressed in linguistic diversity. In the three selections on La Llorona, this synthesis between folk elements and literary form is illustrated in the different ways the same story is told. Soledad Perez records two versions of *La Llorona* in a conversational style that is similar to that of oral storytellers. Carmen Toscano chooses the form of a dramatic dialogue to emphasize the tragic aspects of the tale, while Victoria Moreno tells the story in poetic form, suggesting that the plight of La Llorona may be part of the universal condition of woman. In her essay entitled "The Dilemma of the Modern Chicana Artist and Critic," Marcela Christine Lucero-Trujillo discusses the implications of these images of woman as earth mother, spiritual mother, and violated mother for contemporary Chicana writers. Her essay poses the question of what it means to be a writer and a Chicana.

In "The Women of New Mexico," Fabiola Cabeza de Baca, one of the first Mexican American women writers to recognize that the spirit of a people resides in its folk beliefs and expressions, explores the area of folk medicine in her colorful portrait of the *curandera,* or medical practitioner. The rigors of the frontier made it necessary for women to develop home remedies for various ailments, and the *curandera* soon became a familiar key figure in the community.

In "Traditions, Narratives, and Fiction," fiction replaces discourse, and heritage becomes the background pattern on which individual designs are woven. Josefina Niggli turns to folklore and legend for the theme of her short story "The Street of the Cañon." Set in Mexico, the story is a reworking of the familiar folktale of the devil disguising himself as a lover to court a pretty and innocent young woman. The story opens with a proverb that immediately signals the presence of tradition within the story and within the minds of the townspeople of Hidalgo. Indeed, Niggli gently but ironically points out the folly of blind adherence to tradition. As one of the earlier Mexican American writers, Niggli is particularly important because she captures the complexity and diversity of her culture, opening the door to a literary realism that becomes the launching pad for contemporary Chicano literature.

The tension between tradition and the tragic reality of one's life propels the narrative line in "Las Dos Hermanas" by Rosalie Otero Peralta. Here, the woman is victimized by her tenacious fidelity to the institution of marriage, even though that marriage has been nonexistent for years. Yielding finally to the oppression of emptiness and the sudden realization that her life has disintegrated, Aunt Marcelina returns to her sister's home to die. The narrator of the story is Aunt Marcelina's grandniece, whose innocence of the double standard in a male-dominated culture conveys her aunt's position even more poignantly.

In "The Burning," Estela Portillo Trambley examines the conflict between the Indian and Spanish heritage within the Mexican sensibility. The protagonist is an Indian woman whose powers to heal both fascinate and terrify the Catholic women of the village. In alienating this woman from their community, they are casting out a part of themselves that still resides in their collective unconscious. The failure to integrate the roots of one's being—in this case, the indigenous native side with the colonial Spanish side—inspires a fatalistic sense of the burden of heritage that runs through Chicano literature.

The last two stories in this section center on the struggle that women must make to substitute independence for empty ritual. "Recuerdo" by Guadalupe Valdés Fallis charts a mother's memory of her own youthful but vain attempt to be free as she negotiates the freedom of her daughter with a despicable man. And in "Pay the Criers," the protagonist is caught in a conflict between her attempts to respond to the irresponsible desires of her husband and a deathbed promise to her mother. The author exaggerates the rhythms of nature to punctuate the helplessness of the woman whose world is seemingly controlled by external and unseen forces.

Chicano literature has been called a literature of protest, and, in many ways, protest does characterize the poetry of the last section. Chicanas condemn the social inequities that breed problems of unemployment, discrimination, welfare, and poor housing, but they also decry the impotence of rhetoric in the face of oppression. The realities of feeding one's children demand more than words, as Lorna Dee Cervantes points out in "Para un Revolucionario," and in "1975," Ana Castillo says, "We are tired of talking." Among contemporary Chicana poets, there is a movement away from the rhetoric of dissent, with its clichés and empty slogans, to a poetry of protest—a poetry that is not confined to a given political moment but rather shapes experience and speaks individually of shared concerns. Those concerns range from the "pimping fringe benefits" of "Urban Life" catalogued by Xelina to the struggle of the grape pickers in "Napa, California" by Ana Castillo. Angela de Hoyos violently disapproves of the condition of powerlessness in "The Final Laugh" and ironically mocks those who would seek "a formula infallible/for painless living" in "The Missing Ingredient," while Inés Hernandez Tovar speaks out against the imposed values of the Madison Avenue advertising world that would "Glamour-us/out of existence."

The double standard that implies one set of rules for white America and another for minorities comes under attack in "No more cookies, please" by Marcela Christine Lucero-Trujillo, who also criticizes machismo and its manifest discrimination against women in "Machismo Is Part of Our Culture." Personal relationships also come under poetic scrutiny in the sharply honed lines of "Station" and "Chon" by Marina Rivera and in the softer lyrics of Victoria Moreno and Carmen Tafolla. The ultimate protest is against anonymity, as Judy Lucero ironically and tragically demonstrates in her poems from prison by signing them with her prison number. For some Chicanas, the very act of writing and publishing outside the mainstream of the literary establishment becomes a political statement.

But what perhaps most characterizes the element of political and verbal dissent in Chicano poetry is the experimentation with language, the breaking away from established models to create a new linguistic space. The poetry in this section represents the range of this linguistic innovation. By combining Spanish words and phrases with English, and vice versa, Chicana poets establish a continuum from the past to the present, affirming their heritage through their linguistic identity. As their experience is bilingual and bicultural, so is their poetry, and the result is an expansion of the possibilities for expression. The juxtaposition of Spanish to English stylistically has the effect of creating pause and emphasis; it also allows for new sounds and rhythms to enter the poetry that modulate the subtleties of meaning inherent in each language. Regional dialects and idiomatic expressions abound, adding texture and color to the poetry. Spanish may be used to intensify the emotion of a poem, or it may be the most authentic way to portray a particular voice or character. Margarita Cota Cárdenas, for example, writes many of her poems entirely in Spanish and then translates them into English to indicate the different shades of meaning that reside in each language. Two of her poems and their translations are included here. "Chicana Evolution" by Sylvia Alicia Gonzales runs the gamut of linguistic possibilities and illustrates that the promise of Chicano literature lies in the fluidity of its language. Finally, the bilingual nature of Chicano poetry reflects the cultural space inhabited by Chicanos. They move between two landscapes, and language is a way of fixing their experience in each.

NOTES

1. "Chicano" is the popular term for Mexican American. The feminine form is "Chicana." Another term frequently used is "La Raza," which literally means "the race" or "the people."
2. Jack D. Forbes, *Aztecas Del Norte—The Chicanos of Aztlan* (Greenwich, Conn.: Fawcett Publications, 1973), p. 18.
3. "El Plan Espiritual de Aztlan," in *Aztlan: An Anthology of Mexican American Literature,* eds. Luis Valdez and Stan Steiner (New York: Alfred A. Knopf–Vintage, 1972), pp. 402–403.
4. For a thorough discussion of the background of Chicano literature, see Raymund A. Paredes, "The Evolution of Chicano Literature," *Melus,* 5, No. 2 (Summer, 1978), 71–110, and Philip D. Ortego, "Backgrounds of Mexican American Literature" (Ph.D. dissertation, University of New Mexico, 1971).
5. See Robert A. Barakat, "Aztec Motifs in 'La Llorona,'" *Southern Folklore Quarterly,* 29 (1965), 288–296, and Bacil F. Kirtley, "La Llorona and Related Themes," *Western Folklore,* 19 (1960), 155–168.
6. The root of *corrido* is the verb *correr,* "to run."
7. For more information on the *corrido,* see Américo Paredes, *A Texas-Mexican Cancionero* (Urbana: University of Illinois Press, 1976) and *With His Pistol in His Hand* (Austin: University of Texas Press, 1958).
8. For background material on the Aztecs, see Miguel Leon-Portilla, *Aztec Thought and Culture* (Norman, University of Oklahoma Press, 1963), and Martha P. Cotera, *Diosa y Hembra The History and Heritage of Chicanas in the United States* (Austin: Information Systems Development, 1976).
9. *The Labyrinth of Solitude,* trans. Lysander Kemp (New York: Grove, 1961), p. 85.
10. Mestizo literally means of mixed blood; with Chicanos specifically it refers to their Indian and European mixture.

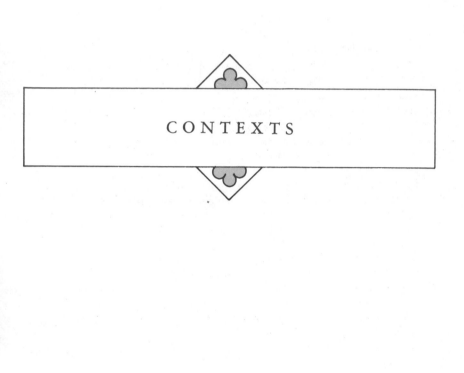

CONTEXTS

SOLEDAD PÉREZ

Biographical information about this author is unavailable.

THE WEEPING WOMAN

Do you know why La Llorona appears near the Colorado River? Well, La Llorona was a woman who lived here in Austin. She had two children, but she didn't love them. One day she took them to the river and drowned them. She never repented, and that is why she appears there and cries for her children.

My son, Rodolfo, was ten or eleven years old when he and some other boys decided to spend the night out near the river. They went in a little cart and took some blankets.

At night they spread the blankets out on the ground and went to sleep. He says that after midnight all of them woke up at the same time and saw a shadow flit across them. Then they heard the piercing wail of La Llorona. They got up and came home immediately. My son was very frightened when he got home.

THE WEEPING WOMAN

My brother had a very good friend who was a shoemaker. The two were heavy drinkers, and they liked to go out together to eat and drink.

Well, one night my brother went to see his friend about twelve-thirty and prevailed on him to go out to drink with him.

Shortly after the two had started out for their favorite saloon, they noticed

that a very attractive woman was walking just ahead of them. They decided
to follow her. The two followed for a long time, but they couldn't catch up with
her. When it seemed that they were coming up even with the woman, she
suddenly seemed to get about half a block ahead of them. Finally, my brother
and his friend decided to turn back, but as a parting gesture they said,
"Good-by, my dear!"

At the same time that the two said, "Good-by, my dear!" the attractive
woman whom they had followed turned around. She had the face of a horse,
her fingernails were shiny and tin-like, and she gave a long, piercing cry. It
was La Llorona.

My brother would have run, but his friend had fainted, and he had to
revive him. The two reformed after that encounter with La Llorona.

CARMEN TOSCANO

Carmen Toscano was born in Mexico City, Mexico, in 1910.

LA LLORONA

WHILE THE STAGE IS STILL DARK, A CLOCK BEGINS TO CHIME. IT STRIKES TWELVE O'CLOCK. WEIRD BACKGROUND MUSIC IS PLAYED. AFTERWARDS, ONE HEARS THE MOURNFUL WAILING OF LA LLORONA.

La Llorona   Ayyy . . . my sorrowful progeny . . . my poor dears . . . my unfortunate children . . .

THE CROSS IS ILLUMINATED, SEVERAL STARTLED WOMEN ADVANCE TOWARDS IT WITH MODERN DANCE MOVEMENTS.

First Woman   It's her.

Second Woman   May God protect us (SHE MAKES THE SIGN OF THE CROSS).

Third Woman   I almost felt her next to me the other day, as if she had brushed against my skin . . . a cold shiver invaded my body.

First Woman   They say one can see her at San Angel, and at the same time in El Portal and at La Quemada, at Mercaderes, and way over by Los Indios Verdes.

Fourth Woman   What merciless destiny drags her through the silent streets, and over the most hidden paths. Everywhere, her white spectre makes hearts tremble, everywhere one can hear her hideous lament.

Second Woman   What horrible sin could that condemned soul have committed?

First Woman   Her weeping has run through the fields, it has invaded the mountains, it spreads out over the valleys, her shadow often disappears among the waters, and the tenuous veils of her gown seem to float among the clouds.

Fourth Woman She crosses roads dappled in moonlight, and her voice filters among the tree branches in the woods, it reverberates against the rocks, weaves among the mountains.

Fifth Woman At nightfall, her long, shrill lament makes the hardiest person shudder. . . . I have seen the rosary fall from the hands of many frightened women as they hear her mournful wail.

Second Woman It's not a human cry, but it resounds in our consciousness, it invades the inner coils of our hearing.

First Woman It seems that she carries with her, inside of herself, the voices of many women.

Second Woman Far away, beyond time.

Fourth Woman To hear her is a bad omen.

First Woman They say that her most doleful cry is uttered when she gets to la Plaza Mayor. . . . That she kneels down there. . . . Turning towards the ancient temples of the Indians, she kisses the ground and wails in anguish and fills everything with sorrow.

Second Woman They say that she loved passionately.

Fourth Woman That she was abandoned . . .

Third Woman That she committed a horrible crime.

Fifth Woman That she spilled the blood of her loved ones.

First Woman One thing we know, she must have suffered greatly . . . poor woman. Why can't she find any rest?

VICTORIA MORENO

Born in Texas in 1957, Victoria Moreno is a faith healer. She comments, "I am a visionary. I live between the centuries—most frequently in the fifteenth. In former lives I was a seamstress, a *curandera* [medicine woman], a murderer, a tavern dancer, a maid, and a sculptor. I have fourteen children. My writing is full of these people. They cry out from within me. I am all of them and they are me. Each one adds the strength of their experiences. My poetry seeks to dance—my legs are paralyzed. I would like my writing to create, to sing, and especially, to dance."

LA LLORONA, CRYING LADY OF THE CREEKBEDS, 483 YEARS OLD, AND AGING

(—when we were children, we were told how La Llorona had lost her children, how one could hear her cry at night, searching for their dead lives, wailing, flying hair, and wild eyes. Different versions and different reasons, each to tell us a moral, to warn us. Once, we found out what her phone number was and used to dial and listen to her cry, passing around the phone from one to the next.

Years later, we learned that the myth predated the arrival of the Spaniards. The crying lady, a *malinche,* had bemoaned the fate of her own children, a fate she had been accomplice to. We knew she would be forever with us, forever in our memories, crying for her dead children and for her children yet unborn that were to die.

But creekbeds got scarce in the barrio, and so, La Llorona had to get a phone installed so we could reach her, so we could hear her, so she could let us know the truth.)

La Llorona
   they took away her children
      the welfare office came and stole away her children
      because she had no right, they said,
         to be a single parent, non-model American family

   they took away her children
         (all unborn)

because He was married and she was on the pill and
He didn't care to fool with divorces and didn't care to
have any bastard children and asked her
not to have his.

they took away her children
　　it was way-out-of-style to long for large families
　　and staying home with one's babies and breast-feeding truth
　　and love and all that rot, especially if you were a professional
　　and should know better, and one was only allowed to have two
　　anyway, and only if one let the day-care raise them.

they took away her children
　　"how are you *PROTECTING* yourself?" they always asked,
　　as if one could be *attacked* by pregnancy at any minute
　　and torn to shreds like the most horrible distortion

they took away her children
　　because there was no time
　　to build them a world, no time
　　in the battlefront, soldiers always needed
　　and she had to struggle just
　　to stay alive

they took away her children
　　and made decrees about all children-to-be
　　(too soon) and slipped anti-fertility chemicals into
　　the water, to insure a society that was *clean* and
　　scheduled and *sterile*, like the clinics designed to—
　　(well, don't worry about preserving health, just make sure to
　　FIGHT DISEASE!)

they took away her children

And the Aztec Lady crying down the creekbeds
ran into a concrete wall and, puzzled blank,
stopped her wailing for her children
and just stared, realizing that
　　　　　　　　hope was gone.
While I took up the dirge
and, screaming down the streets at night,
carried on the insane truth, the pain
knowing that

they took away her children.

FABIOLA CABEZA de BACA

Born in 1896, Fabiola Cabeza de Baca now lives in Santa Fé. She has written several pamphlets on food preparation, including *Historic Cookery*, which is currently published by La Galeria de los Artesanos in Las Vegas, New Mexico. Her memoirs of pioneer life in New Mexico, *We Fed Them Cactus*, were published in 1954. Of her background, she says, "My Spanish ancestors were here before the pilgrims arrived in the East. The Spanish settlers for centuries kept their culture, traditions, religion, language. I am including these notes so that you may realize that we may not have the problems encountered by persons who may not have had the background which we have kept here through the centuries."

THE WOMEN OF NEW MEXICO

The women on the Llano* and Ceja† played a great part in the history of the land. It was a difficult life for a woman, but she had made her choice when in the marriage ceremony she had promised to obey and to follow her husband. It may not have been her choice, since parents may have decided for her. It was the Spanish custom to make matches for the children. Whether through choice or tradition, the women had to be a hardy lot in order to survive the long trips by wagon or carriage and the separation from their families, if their families were not among those who were settling on the Llano.

The women had to be versed in the curative powers of plants and in midwifery, for there were no doctors within a radius of two hundred miles or more.

The knowledge of plant medicine is an inheritance from the Moors, and brought to New Mexico by the first Spanish colonizers. From childhood we are taught the names of herbs, weeds, and plants that have curative potency; even today, when we have doctors at our immediate call, we still have great faith in plant medicine. Certainly this knowledge of home remedies was a source of comfort to the women who went out to Llano, yet their faith in God helped more than anything in their survival.

Every village had its curandera‡ or médica, and the ranchers rode many

* Rolling plains country.
† Mountaintop.
‡ Medicine woman.

miles to bring the medicine woman or the midwife from a distant village or neighboring ranch.

Quite often the wife of the patrón* was well versed in plant medicine. I know that my grandmother, Doña Estéfana Delgado de Baca, although not given the name of médica, because it was not considered proper in her social class, was called every day by some family in the village, or by their empleados,† to treat a child or some other person in the family. In the fall of the year she went out to the hills and valleys to gather her supply of healing herbs. When she went to live in La Liendre, there were terrible outbreaks of smallpox and she had difficulty convincing the villagers that vaccination was a solution. Not until she had a godchild in every family was she able to control the dreaded disease. In Spanish tradition a godmother takes the responsibility of a real mother, and in that way grandmother conquered many superstitions which the people had. At least she had the power to decide what should be done for her godchildren.

From El Paso, Texas, she secured vaccines from her cousin Dr. Samaniego. She vaccinated her children, grandchildren, and godchildren against the disease. She vaccinated me when I was three years old, and the vaccination has passed many doctors' inspections.

As did my grandmother, so all the wives of the patrones held a very important place in the villages and ranches on the Llano. The patrón ruled the rancho, but his wife looked after the spiritual and physical welfare of the empleados and their families. She was the first one called when there was death, illness, misfortune, or good tidings in a family. She was a great social force in the community—more so than her husband. She held the purse strings, and thus she was able to do as she pleased in her charitable enterprises and to help those who might seek her assistance.

There may have been class distinction in the larger towns, but the families on the Llano had none; the empleados and their families were as much a part of the family of the patrón as his own children. It was a very democratic way of life.

The women in these isolated areas had to be resourceful in every way. They were their own doctors, dressmakers, tailors, and advisers.

The settlements were far apart and New Mexico was a poor territory trying to adapt itself to a new rule. The Llano people had no opportunity for public schools before statehood, but there were men and women who held classes for the children of the patrones in private homes. They taught reading in Spanish and sometimes in English. Those who had means sent their children to school in Las Vegas, Santa Fe, or Eastern states. If no teachers were available, the mothers taught their own children to read, and many of the wealthy

* Landlord.
† Employees.

ranchers had private teachers for their children until they were old enough to go away to boarding schools.

Doña Luisa Gallegos de Baca, who herself had been educated in a convent in the Middle West, served as teacher to many of the children on the Llano territory.

Without the guidance and comfort of the wives and mothers, life on the Llano would have been unbearable, and a great debt is owed to the brave pioneer women who ventured into the cruel life of the plains, far from contact with the outside world. Most of them have gone to their eternal rest, and God must have saved a very special place for them to recompense them for their contribution to colonization and religion in an almost savage country.

MARCELA CHRISTINE LUCERO-TRUJILLO

Born in Colorado, Marcela Christine Lucero-Trujillo currently lives in Minnesota, where she is an instructor in Chicano studies at the University of Minnesota. Her poetry has appeared in *Time to Greez!* (1975), *La Razon Mestiza* (1975), and *La Luz*. She includes the following poem to explain her position as a writer:

> My epitaph in poetry should read thusly . . .
> Lit major learned in "isms"
>   symbols and imagery,
> but if she ain't communicated
> with the barrio educated,
>   then this one here, ain't she.

THE DILEMMA OF THE MODERN
CHICANA ARTIST AND CRITIC

The literary rebirth of the Chicanos in the 60s coincided with certain simultaneous contemporary historical moments: (1) the passage of the Civil Rights Act of 1964, (2) identification with Cesar Chavez's farmworkers' struggle, (3) the inception of Chicano Studies departments, and (4) the initiation of the socio-economic political national Chicano movement.

Through unification and national mobilization, the Chicanos began to be aware of their history, previously obliterated in U.S. textbooks. The return to Mexican history, the emphasis on Mexican culture and traditions in order to seek self-affirmation and a positive self-identification, was almost in repudiation of this U.S. Anglo-European system which has held us in second-class citizenship status since 1846, denying us the rights and privileges afforded us in the Treaty of Guadalupe Hidalgo and agreed upon by the U.S. government at the close of the Mexican-American war.

As the Chicano movement began its evolution into unification, Chicanos were faced with the problem of diversity. Not all Chicanos were brown; not all were Catholic; not all were Spanish surnamed and not all were Spanish speaking. It therefore became necessary to invent or borrow symbols as common denominators around which all Chicanos could unite.

One of these was the symbol of the mestizaje, the tripartite face of the Indian mother, the Spanish father and their offspring, the mestizo. Another was the concept of a Chicano nation—Aztlan. Linguistically, there was an emergence of pachuquismos and regional dialects in the literature. The pachuco became an ideal Chicano type as the prototype of rebelling against the gringo-racist society at a time when American patriotism was at an all time high: the Second World War.

Like the Latin American, the Chicano also diminished the European psyche by establishing the Chicano Amerindia concept, which emphasized knowledge about the highly developed Aztec and Mayan civilizations as having been equal to, if not superior to, the Greek and Roman civilizations so predominant in all facets of Anglo-American education.

In the beginning, in the early 60s, the Chicanos were repeating the same concerns of the Latin American philosophers and writers of the late nineteenth and twentieth centuries, among them José Martí, José Vasconcelos, Leopoldo Zea, Samuel Ramos, Silva J. Herzog, Iturriaga and Octavio Paz, to name only a few. That dilemma of being an American of this continent, but imbued and dominated by European language, culture and customs called for ethnic self-introspection, which led to a recognition of autochthonous American elements.

Hence the popularity of Mexican writers and historians, especially Octavio Paz's *Labyrinth of Solitude,* which carried a compilation of his predecessors concerning Mexicanism, Mexican philosophy, psyche, thought and all the problematics of achieving economic independence.

Paz's popularity among Chicanos may have stemmed from the fact that he wrote about a Chicano type in his book: the pachuco, and thus, he brought to the present a social phenomenon that Chicanos were familiar with, through oral tradition, or the experience itself.

The questions that Mexicans were asking prior to the 1910 revolution in repudiation of Positivism, the philosophy of Scientism, were repeating themselves in the Chicano movement and the literature. The leitmotif "Yo soy Chicano/a" * predominated in much of the writings; however, as the militancy decreased, the self-affirmation diluted into an anguished question. Was this due to the fact that since the Chicano movement began ten years ago, Chicanos are now realizing that the Mexican identification has not been sufficient to provide us with solutions in order to survive within this capitalist racist oppressive society?

This is more acute for the Chicana than for the Chicano, as evidenced by the statistics that Chicanas place lowest on the financial and educational scale in comparison with any other ethnic group, male or female (Neomi Lorenzo, *De Colores,* p. 11).

The impetus of the woman's movement together with the Chicano movement contributed to the Chicana's latest potential and so she began to focus in on her particular feministic experience through the arts. The Chicanas took the symbols afforded them through the Chicano movement and transformed them according to their feminist perspective. Some Chicanas' poetry is a tra-

* I am a Chicano/a.

jectory of self-examination that terminates with a "cuestionamiento" * of all socio-economic and political factors that have taken their toll on their individualism.

Some Chicanas' literature has been a vehicle whereby they could escape into another temporal scene of our folklore, our legends and modus vivendi; of that particular past which seemed a safer and saner world, the world as it ought to be, albeit a very traditional romantic view.

Through the arts there is an attempt at liberation from the Anglo-European culture, that system of government that has conquered and colonized us in the same way it had Cuba and now Puerto Rico, the difference being that Chicanos are peripheral, marginal characters within the Metropolis, whereas the other colonized Latin American countries are controlled by foreign multinational corporations within their midst.

Literature has also provided an outlet for the frustrations of being a woman within the sexist microcosmic Chicano world of machismo, and the alienation of being a Chicano woman in the larger macrocosmic white male club that governs the United States.

In a quest for identity and an affirmation that brown is beautiful, the Chicana has sought refuge in the image of the indigenous mother. Some Chicanas view the Indian mother as Mother Earth; some identify with the bronze reality in religious themes of the Virgin of Guadalupe, the spiritual mother; and still others identify directly with the Mexican Eve, the historical mother, La Malinche. The latter will be explained in more detail.

La Malinche theme:

The fact that some Chicanas view Doña Marina in a sympathetic manner in contrast to the portrayal of Mexican authors may mean that her redefinition may be a Chicana phenomenon.

According to Octavio Paz's aforementioned book, Mexicans view La Malinche as the Mexican Eve, the one who betrayed the country, the one who opened up the country to foreign invaders. This opening up, paving the way for the Conquest, has sexual allusions of opening up her body to procreate the illegitimate sons of a rape called the Conquest. According to Paz, it was her treason, her betrayal, that caused the dual Mexican society of chingones vs. chingados,† with Cortés being the prototype of the "chingon," and Malinche being the highest exponent of the "chingado/a." Within this classification of Mexican types, the people who have power are the chingones, but the macho is the "gran chingon."

As the Chingada, according to Paz, Malinche is "the Mother." Not a mother of flesh and blood but a mythical figure. The *Chingada* is one of the Mexican representations of Maternity, like La Llorona or the "long-

* Questioning.
† Rapists versus the raped, or violators versus the violated.

suffering Mexican mother" who is celebrated on May 10th. The *Chingada* is the mother who has suffered—metaphorically or actually—the corrosive and defaming action implicit in the verb that gives her her name" (Paz, *Labyrinth,* p. 75).

Thus, Paz says, "hijos de la chingada" * is a true battle cry, charged with a peculiar electricity; it is a challenge and an affirmation, a shot fired against an imaginary enemy, and an explosion in the air." The Mexican denies La Malinche, and the anguish shows when he shouts "Viva Mexico, hijos de la chingada" (Ibid., p. 75).

It is no wonder, then, that the Mexicans wanted to transcend this mythical maternal image to find refuge in a Christian feminine deity, one who could replace the Mexican Eve, and so "La Virgen Morena"—the brown virgin. La Virgen de Guadalupe became the patron saint of Mexico who is often also called "the mother of orphans." She is also called Guadalupe-Tonantzin among some of the Indian population, and this latter concept reflects the Christian-Aztec mingling of religion and culture.

La Virgen de Guadalupe is the Christian virgin, symbolizing, perhaps, the Spanish 16th century concept of honor which considered virginity as the repository of the family honor, a concept deeply rooted in Catholic ideology.

Tonantzin, the Aztec goddess of fertility, is viewed as Mother Nature. In Chicana literature, the technique of pathetic fallacy merges with the symbol of the good mother, Guadalupe or Tonantzin, presenting a harmonious relationship of the universe in fusion with nature.

If Chicanas use the concept of the long-suffering mother, they revert to the identification of La Malinche. Thus, in deciphering the symbols of the historical and spiritual mothers, the word "madre" in Mexican Spanish is at once a prayer or a blasphemy, a word whose antonymical dichotomy is manifested in ambiguities, ambivalence or oscillation in Chicana literature.

In her poem "Chicana Evolution," Sylvia Gonzales sees La Malinche as the feminine Messiah who must return to redeem her forsaken daughters, born out of the violence of the Spanish and Aztec religions and cultures. She moves away from the cosmopolitan ambiance of Greenwich Village in New York to the nativistic world of the Aztecs to encounter Malinche.

In the closing stanza of the aforementioned poem, Sylvia is the collective Chicana, the spiritual sister of the Latin Americans, Mother Nature, mother, daughter, Malinche, the totality of womanhood: "todo seré . . . y hasta bastarda seré, antes de dejar de ser mujer." †

Chicanos see themselves as muy mejicanos‡ in the affinity of the woman and orphanhood concept, illegitimate sons and daughters of La Malinche. This concept, projected within the confines of the U.S. environment, rein-

---

* Sons of the violated one.
† I will be everything . . . I will even be illegitimate before forsaking my womanhood.
‡ Very Mexican.

forces the feeling of orphanhood, of alienation and marginalization to both U.S. and Mexican societies, in the prismatic view of Indian identity that pervades much of the Chicana's literature.

However, to blame one woman, Doña Marina, for the Conquest, is, in my opinion, a false historical conscience. One woman could not stand in the way of European expansion; one woman could not impede the alliance of native class interests with the foreign invader's economic interests. God, glory and gold, economic, political and religious reasons were one total objective since Church and State were not separated at the time of the Conquest. "Independence" is a misnomer in Latin America as one foreign power after another has influenced and dominated its economic sphere to perpetuate a cycle of dependency and neo-colonial status for its inhabitants.

In the case of the Chicanos, the gringo has replaced the Spaniards as the "gran chingon" by virtue of his having the positions of power. And those in positions of power oppress through racism, which has made Chicanos react and revert to the Indian mother to say, through her, that brown is beautiful. It is this contemporary society which has classified "brown" as inferior in the schematics of relative beauty. Thus, to refute the racism and the stereotypes, Chicanas have emphasized the bronze race which, ironically, in the past, has not appeared in the race classification. Under the present categories, only the black, white, red and yellow races are visible. And, perhaps, for that reason, Chicanos have been called the "Invisible" the "forgotten" or the "Silent Americans."

THE PROBLEMATICS OF THE MODERN CHICANA

Sylvia Gonzales in her poetry is first of all a woman, then a Chicana poetess with a mission. Maternal imagery permeates much of her poetry. She writes poetry to her future generations, and she ponders their fate as she weaves in and out of herself, from the first to the third person in the poem that begins "Yo soy la mujer poeta.*

"¿Como será la generación; criada con la inquietud de la mujer poeta?" † She expresses the anxieties of being a woman poet, not a poetisa, but a mujer poeta, who is faced with the sisyphus responsibility of advising and advising well to the future generation of Chicano readers. Her mission is to write, because she has many "consejos" ‡ to give.

In her personal Ars Poetica (De Colores, p. 15) she gives us her philosophy in declaring that "the artist must be true to her own soul and her own personal experiences, and in so doing, the message will be universal and eternal" (Ibid., p. 15).

* I am the woman poet.
† How will the generation be; fostered by the restlessness of the woman poet?
‡ "Advices."

Sylvia speaks collectively for the Chicana and for all women when she states that "we are all sisters under the flesh." In her poem "On an untitled theme," whose principal theme is machismo, she exacerbates the dilemma felt by every intellectual woman who wants to use her head, or who wants to be recognized for her intelligence, and not only for her body. She must convince her macho colleagues that her goal is not their bed. She would reject the finality of the Chicana's life of bearing sons for wars, of being alienated after the children grew up and left home. The choice of bearing sons for wars or as victims of a technological society whose recourse from pressures are drugs is an anxiety that every contemporary mother faces. The Chicana mother whose only life has been her children may have difficulties in her later years. She may seek refuge in the bottle or transform into a nagging wife or a "vieja chismosa." *

The sanctuary of the Chicano home then becomes a replica of the conflictive society. The modern Chicana faces a double conflict. On the one hand, she must overcome Chicano family overprotection, and on the other, she faces contempt from the outside world as she emerges into the professional world, only to find indifference as answers to her questions on reality and life. These are themes that women can relate to in Sylvia's poetry, but amidst these problems, Sylvia affirms her individualism in "Te acuerdas mujer." †

This assertion of intellectualism is indirect in the praises and eulogies to Sra. Juana Ines de la Cruz, the renowned genius of Mexican colonial times. Dorinda Moreno, among other poetesses, identifies with this victim of Catholic machismo who was made to give up her academic life and go out into the world, where she contracted the plague and died a premature death at the age of 45, a martyr to feminine intelligentsia.

The modern Chicana, in her literature, tries to synthesize the material and spiritual conflict of her essence. Her spirit is ingrained in the roots of Mexican culture and traditions, but her body is trying to survive in a hostile capitalistic environment, and she keenly feels the technological battle of scientism vs. humanism. In trying to resolve the two, her literature often shows the contradictions that exist between the two.

Sylvia Gonzales expresses this concern in her article in the following: "There are many Mexican cultural values that we can relate to, but are they reliable in our search for an identity within the Anglo American cultural tradition?" The answer, she says, is a link between science and the soul (Gonzales, De Colores, pp. 15–18).

An elaboration of that answer can be found in A. Sanchez-Vasquez's book, Art and Society. "Creative freedom and capitalist production are hostile to the artist. . . . Art representing denied humanity opposes an inhuman so-

* Shrewish old woman.
† Remember you are a woman.

ciety, and society opposes the artist insofar as he resists reification, insofar as he tries to express his humanity" (A.S.V., p. 116).

The dilemma of the Chicano/a artist is trying to create an art for people's sake, and not for art's sake or for commercialism. He/She is working in a hostile, scientific milieu whose marginalization is twofold: one, because the artist's creation is not scientific, but humanistic, for the enjoyment of humanity, with no utilitarian value, and second, because Chicanos' cultural values are not understood or appreciated by the dominant society. Yet, the Chicano artists and writers must continue to create and to communicate with the grass roots people, and in so doing, will reach the universal masses who identify with their contemporary situation whether in this or other countries, whether in this or another historical moment, for art has its own laws which transcend the artist, his/her time and even the ideology that brought forth his/her art.

Literature is a medium and a praxis whereby we can start to question our oppression, not by escapism into the mythical past in sentimental lyricism reminiscent of other literary ages, but in dealing with the everyday problems. The Chicana can question and confront the society which holds her in double jeopardy, of being a woman and a minority.

Every Chicana's life is a novel, yet we have not read a contemporary Chicana feminist novel. The Chicana has had to be a cultural schizophrenic in trying to please both the Chicano and Anglo publishers, not to mention pleasing the readers, who may neutralize her potential to create within her own framework of ideas.

We must examine closely the published works of Chicanas who have been selected for publication by male editors and publishers. We have to ask ourselves if we have been published because we have dealt with themes that reinforce the male ego. As urban professional Chicanas, we must reinterpret our pantheistic view of the world. Are we really the prototype of the long-suffering indigenous mother? Are we co-opting and neutralizing our emotions by writing what the publishers want to read?

I remind you that "macho" in classical Nahuatl means "image," "reflection of myself." Are we then only a narcissistic reflection, and consequently do we define ourselves as a reflection of the Chicano perspective, as a reaction, rather than action of that definition?

Then it becomes necessary to examine the totality of the Chicana's artistic expression, her motives for writing, the audience for whom it was intended, her biography as a product of all of her past experiences which are projected into her work, and lastly to understand why her particular content is important in this space and time. For in examining a work in this critical vein, we would also be examining ourselves, and could come to a collective conclusion of what direction we are taking within the feministic framework of the Chicano's socioeconomic and political status within the United States.

Therefore, it may be somewhat premature at this time to view the present literature of the Chicanas as a culmination of the Chicana experience. All of the literature has been positive in that it has provided a historical awareness, "una concientización," an inspiration to other Chicanas to affirm their literary talents, and those Chicanas who have been writing and publishing for some time now are progressing steadily on the incline of their own apogee.

BIBLIOGRAPHY

Chicana Poets. *Chicanas en la literatura y el arte,* Book I, Year VII, El Grito, Berkeley, California, 1973.

Chicanas in *De Colores,* Pajarito Publications, Albuquerque, N.M. Vol. 2, #3, 1975.

Chicanas in *Tejidos,* University of Texas, Austin, Vol. 1, #3, Julio, 1974.

Gonzales, Sylvia. "National Character vs. Universality in Chicano Poetry," *De Colores,* Vol. 1, #4, Pajarito Publications, Albuquerque, N.M., 1975.

————. Poetry, unpublished, n.d.

Lorenzo, Neomi. "La Chicana: Transcending the Old and Carving Out a New Life and Self Image," *De Colores,* Vol. 2, #3, Pajarito Publications, Albuquerque, N.M.

Mondragon, Maria. Poetry, unpublished, n.d.

Paz, Octavio. *Labyrinth of Solitude,* Grove Press, N.Y., 1958.

Sanchez-Vasquez, Adolfo. *Art and Society,* Monthly Review Press, New York and London, 1973.

Sartre, Jean Paul. *Search for a Method,* Random House, New York, 1968.

TRADITIONS, NARRATIVES, AND FICTION

JOSEFINA NIGGLI

Born in Monterey, Mexico, in 1910, Josefina Niggli currently lives in North Carolina. Until her recent retirement, she was an associate professor of speech and theater arts, as well as head of the theater, at Western Carolina University. She has also taught at the University of North Carolina and spent a year as a scriptwriter at Metro-Goldwyn-Mayer Studios in California (1951–1952). A recipient of a Rockefeller Fellowship to study in England in 1950, she later returned there as a guest professor of playwriting at Bristol University from 1955 to 1956. In 1946 she received the Mayflower Cup Award for *Mexican Village*. A prolific writer, she is the author of numerous plays and short stories, as well as television and film scripts. Her plays about Mexico, especially *Sunday Costs Five Pesos*, are frequently produced in the English-speaking world, particularly in England and Australia. Besides her two collections of plays and short stories respectively—*Mexican Folk Plays* (1938) and *Mexican Village* (1945)—she has published *Miracle for Mexico* (1964) and *New Pointers on Playwriting* (1967).

THE STREET OF THE CAÑON

To the best cook goes the whole tomato.
Mexican proverb

It was May, the flowering thorn was sweet in the air, and the village of San Juan Iglesias in the Valley of the Three Marys was celebrating. The long dark streets were empty because all of the people, from the lowest-paid cowboy to the mayor, were helping Don Roméo Calderón celebrate his daughter's eighteenth birthday.

On the other side of the town, where the Cañon Road led across the mountains to the Sabinas Valley, a tall slender man, a package clutched tightly against his side, slipped from shadow to shadow. Once a dog barked, and the man's black suit merged into the blackness of a wall. But no voice called out, and after a moment he slid into the narrow, dirt-packed street again.

The moonlight touched his shoulder and spilled across his narrow hips. He was young, no more than twenty-five, and his black curly head was bare. He walked swiftly along, heading always for the distant sound of guitar and flute. If he met anyone now, who could say from which direction he had come? He might be a trader from Monterrey, or a buyer of cows' milk from farther north in the Valley of the Three Marys. Who would guess that an Hidalgo man dared to walk alone in the moonlit streets of San Juan Iglesias?

Carefully adjusting his flat package so that it was not too prominent, he squared his shoulders and walked jauntily across the street to the laughter-filled house. Little boys packed in the doorway made way for him, smiling and nodding to him. The long, narrow room with the orchestra at one end was filled with whirling dancers. Rigid-backed chaperones were gossiping together, seated in their straight chairs against the plaster walls. Over the scene was the yellow glow of kerosene lanterns, and the air was hot with the too-sweet perfume of gardenias, tuberoses, and the pungent scent of close-packed humanity.

The man in the doorway, while trying to appear at ease, was carefully examining every smiling face. If just one person recognized him, the room would turn on him like a den of snarling mountain-cats, but so far all the laughter-dancing eyes were friendly.

Suddenly a plump, officious little man, his round cheeks glistening with perspiration, pushed his way through the crowd. His voice, many times too large for his small body, boomed at the man in the doorway. "Welcome, stranger, welcome to your house." Thrusting his arm through the stranger's, and almost dislodging the package, he started to lead the way through the maze of dancers. "Come and drink a toast to my daughter—to my beautiful Sarita. She is eighteen this night."

In the square patio the gentle breeze ruffled the pink and white oleander bushes. A long table set up on sawhorses held loaves of flaky crusted French bread, stacks of thin, delicate tortillas, plates of barbecued beef, and long red rolls of spicy sausages. But most of all there were cheeses, for the Three Marys was a cheese-eating valley. There were yellow cheese and white cheese and curded cheese from cows' milk. There was even a flat white cake of goat cheese from distant Linares, a delicacy too expensive for any but feast days.

To set off this feast were bottles of beer floating in ice-filled tin tubs, and another table was covered with bottles of mescal, of tequila, of maguey wine.

Don Roméo Calderón thrust a glass of tequila into the stranger's hand. "Drink, friend, to the prettiest girl in San Juan. As pretty as my fine fighting cocks, she is. On her wedding day she takes to her man, and by the Blessed Ribs may she find him soon, the best fighter in my flock. Drink deep, friend. Even the rivers flow with wine."

The Hidalgo man laughed and raised his glass high. "May the earth be always fertile beneath her feet."

Someone called to Don Roméo that more guests were arriving, and with a final delighted pat on the stranger's shoulder, the little man scurried away. As the young fellow smiled after his retreating host, his eyes caught and held another pair of eyes—laughing black eyes set in a young girl's face. The last time he had seen that face, it had been white and tense with rage, and the lips clenched tight to prevent an outgushing stream of angry words. That had been in February, and she had worn a white lace shawl over her hair. Now it was May, and a gardenia was a splash of white in the glossy dark braids. The moonlight had mottled his face that February night, and he knew that she did not recognize him. He grinned impudently back at her, and her eyes widened, then slid sideways to one of the chaperones. The fan in her small hand snapped shut. She tapped its parchment tip against her mouth and slipped away to join the dancing couples in the front room. The gestures of a fan translate into a coded language on the frontier. The stranger raised one eyebrow as he interpreted the signal.

But he did not move towards her at once. Instead, he inched slowly back against the table. No one was behind him, and his hands quickly unfastened the package he had been guarding so long. Then he nonchalantly walked into the front room.

The girl was sitting close to a chaperone. As he came up to her, he swerved slightly toward the bushy-browed old lady.

"Your servant, señora. I kiss your hands and feet."

The chaperone stared at him in astonishment. Such fine manners were not common to the town of San Juan Iglesias.

"Eh, you're a stranger," she said. "I thought so."

"But a stranger no longer, señora, now that I have met you." He bent over her, so close she could smell the faint fragrance of talcum on his freshly shaven cheek. "Will you dance the *parada* with me?"

This request startled her eyes into popping open beneath the heavy brows. "So, my young rooster, would you flirt with me, and I old enough to be your grandmother?"

"Can you show me a prettier woman to flirt with in the Valley of the Three Marys?" he asked audaciously.

She grinned at him and turned toward the girl at her side. "This young fool wants to meet you, my child."

The girl blushed to the roots of her hair and shyly lowered her white lids. The old woman laughed aloud.

"Go out and dance, the two of you. A man clever enough to pat the sheep has a right to play with the lamb."

The next moment they had joined the circle of dancers, and Sarita was trying to control her laughter.

"She is the worst dragon in San Juan. And how easily you won her!"

"What is a dragon," he asked imperiously, "when I longed to dance with you?"

"*Ay,*" she retorted, "you have a quick tongue. I think you are a dangerous man."

In answer he drew her closer to him and turned her towards the orchestra. As he reached the chief violinist, he called out, "Play the 'Virgencita,' 'The Shy Young Maiden.'"

The violinist's mouth opened in soundless surprise. The girl in his arms said sharply, "You heard him, the 'Borachita.' 'The Little Drunken Girl.'"

With a relieved grin, the violinist tapped his music stand with his bow, and the music swung into the sad farewell of a man to his sweetheart:

Farewell, my little drunken one,
I must go to the capital
To serve the master
Who makes me weep for my return.

The stranger frowned down at her. "Is this a joke, señorita?" he asked coldly.

"No," she whispered, looking about her quickly to see if the incident had been observed. "But the 'Virgencita' is the favorite song of Hidalgo, a village on the other side of the mountains in the next valley. The people of Hidalgo and San Juan Iglesias do not speak."

"That is a stupid thing," said the man from Hidalgo as he swung her around in a large turn. "Is not music free as air? Why should one town own the rights to a song?"

The girl shuddered slightly. "Those people from Hidalgo—they are wicked monsters. Can you guess what they did not six months since?"

The man started to point out that the space of time from February to May was three months, but he thought it better not to appear too wise. "Did these Hidalgo monsters frighten you, señorita? If they did, I personally will kill them all."

She moved closer against him and tilted her face until her mouth was close to his ear. "They attempted to steal the bones of Don Rómolo Balderas."

"Is it possible?" He made his eyes grow round and his lips purse up in disdain. "Surely not that! Why, all the world knows that Don Rómolo Balderas was the greatest historian in the entire Republic. Every school child reads his books. Wise men from Quintana Roo to the Río Bravo bow their heads in admiration to his name. What a wicked thing to do!" He hoped his virtuous tone was not too virtuous for plausibility, but she did not seem to notice.

"It is true! In the night they came. Three devils!"

"Young devils, I hope."

"Young or old, who cares? They were devils. The blacksmith surprised them even as they were opening the grave. He raised such a shout that all of San Juan rushed to his aid, for they were fighting, I can tell you. Especially one of them—their leader."

"And who was he?"

"You have heard of him, doubtless. A proper wild one named Pepe Gonzalez."

"And what happened to them?"

"They had horses and got away, but one, I think, was hurt."

The Hidalgo man twisted his mouth remembering how Rubén the candy-maker had ridden across the whitewashed line high on the cañon trail that marked the division between the Three Marys' and the Sabinas' sides of the mountains, and then had fallen in a faint from his saddle because his left arm was broken. There was no candy in Hidalgo for six weeks, and the entire Sabinas Valley resented that broken arm as fiercely as did Rubén.

The stranger tightened his arm in reflexed anger about Sarita's waist as she said, "All the world knows that the men of Hidalgo are sons of the mountain witches."

"But even devils are shy of disturbing the honored dead," he said gravely.

" 'Don Rómolo was born in our village,' Hidalgo says. 'His bones belong to us.' Well, anyone in the valley can tell you he died in San Juan Iglesias, and here his bones will stay! Is that not proper? Is that not right?"

To keep from answering, he guided her through an intricate dance pattern that led them past the patio door. Over her head he could see two men and a woman staring with amazement at the open package on the table.

His eyes on the patio, he asked blandly, "You say the leader was one Pepe Gonzalez? The name seems to have a familiar sound."

"But naturally. He has a talent." She tossed her head and stepped away from him as the music stopped. It was a dance of two *paradas*. He slipped his hand through her arm and guided her into place in the large oval of parading couples. Twice around the room and the orchestra would play again.

"A talent?" he prompted.

"For doing the impossible. When all the world says a thing cannot be done, he does it to prove the world wrong. Why, he climbed to the top of the Prow, and not even the long-vanished Joaquín Castillo had ever climbed that mountain before. And this same Pepe caught a mountain lion with nothing to aid him but a rope and his two bare hands."

"He doesn't sound such a bad friend," protested the stranger, slipping his arm around her waist as the music began to play the merry song of the soap bubbles:

> Pretty bubbles of a thousand colors
> That ride on the wind
> And break as swiftly
> As a lover's heart.

The events in the patio were claiming his attention. Little by little he edged her closer to the door. The group at the table had considerably enlarged. There was a low murmur of excitement from the crowd.

"What has happened?" asked Sarita, attracted by the noise.

"There seems to be something wrong at the table," he answered, while trying to peer over the heads of the people in front of him. Realizing that this might be the last moment of peace he would have that evening, he bent toward her.

"If I come back on Sunday, will you walk around the plaza with me?"

She was startled into exclaiming, "*Ay*, no!"

"Please. Just once around."

"And you think I'd walk more than once with you, señor, even if you were no stranger? In San Juan Iglesias, to walk around the plaza with a girl means a wedding."

"Ha, and you think that is common to San Juan alone? Even the devils of Hidalgo respect that law." He added hastily at her puzzled upward glance, "And so they do in all the villages." To cover his lapse he said softly, "I don't even know your name."

A mischievous grin crinkled the corners of her eyes. "Nor do I know yours, señor. Strangers do not often walk the streets of San Juan."

Before he could answer, the chattering in the patio swelled to louder proportions. Don Roméo's voice lay on top, like thick cream on milk. "I tell you it is a jewel of a cheese. Such flavor, such texture, such whiteness. It is a jewel of a cheese."

"What has happened?" Sarita asked of a woman at her elbow.

"A fine goat's cheese appeared as if by magic on the table. No one knows where it came from."

"Probably an extra one from Linares," snorted a fat bald man on the right.

"Linares never made such a cheese as this," said the woman decisively.

"Silence!" roared Don Roméo. "Old Tío Daniel would speak a word to us."

A great hand of silence closed down over the mouths of the people. The girl was standing on tiptoe trying vainly to see what was happening. She was hardly aware of the stranger's whispering voice, although she remembered the words that he said. "Sunday night—once around the plaza."

She did not realize that he had moved away, leaving a gap that was quickly filled by the blacksmith.

Old Tío Daniel's voice was a shrill squeak, and his thin, stringy neck jutted forth from his body like a turtle's from its shell. "This is no cheese from Linares," he said with authority, his mouth sucking in over his toothless gums between his sentences. "Years ago, when the great Don Rómolo Balderas was still alive, we had such cheese as this—*ay*, in those days we had it. But after he died and was buried in our own sainted ground, as was right and proper. . . ."

"Yes, yes," muttered voices in the crowd. He glared at the interruption. As soon as there was silence again, he continued, "After he died, we had it no more. Shall I tell you why?"

"Tell us, Tío Daniel," said the voices humbly.

"Because it is made in Hidalgo!"

The sound of a waterfall, the sound of a wind in a narrow cañon, and the sound of an angry crowd are much the same. There were no distinct words, but the sound was enough.

"Are you certain, Tío?" boomed Don Roméo.

"As certain as I am that a donkey has long ears. The people of Hidalgo have been famous for generations for making cheese like this—especially that wicked one, that owner of a cheese factory, Timotéo Gonzalez, father to Pepe, the wild one, whom we have good cause to remember."

"We do, we do," came the sigh of assurance.

"But on the whole northern frontier there are no vats like his to produce so fine a product. Ask the people of Chihuahua, of Sonora. Ask the man on the bridge at Laredo, or the man in his boat at Tampico, '*Hola,* friend, who makes the finest goat cheese?' And the answer will always be the same, 'Don Timotéo of Hidalgo.' "

It was the blacksmith who asked the great question. "Then where did that cheese come from, and we haters of Hidalgo these ten long years?"

No voice said, "The stranger," but with one fluid movement every head in the patio turned toward the girl in the doorway. She also turned, her eyes wide with something that she realized to her own amazement was more apprehension than anger.

But the stranger was not in the room. When the angry, muttering men pushed through to the street, the stranger was not on the plaza. He was not anywhere in sight. A few of the more religious crossed themselves for fear that the devil had walked in their midst. "Who was he?" one voice asked another. But Sarita, who was meekly listening to a lecture from Don Roméo on the propriety of dancing with strangers, did not have to ask. She had a strong suspicion that she had danced that night within the circling arm of Pepe Gonzalez.

ROSALIE OTERO PERALTA

Biographical information about this author is unavailable.

LAS DOS HERMANAS*

I watched my aunt Marcelina tie the traditional embultorio.† I couldn't remember a time that I hadn't carried cariños‡ from one sister to another. Poor
though they both were, they always shared the little they had ... a few
tortillas, fresh eggs, biscochitos or a prized can of golden peaches ... tied
up neatly in a bleached muslin dishcloth. But today Marcelina absently
brought the corners together in a neat knot. She was sadly quiet. I stood as
tall as my eight-year-old body would reach and tried to look big and responsible. I sensed that I mustn't add my share to her troubles.

I scrambled up the hill and straight home ... even the ditch didn't look
inviting. As soon as I entered Grandmother's kitchen, I breathlessly began,
"... Nina was so sad ... and ..."

Grandmother quickly dismissed me and the entire matter in her "children
should be seen and not heard" manner. It was little by little that I grew
to realize the importance of the decision, and awe at the love and faith of
the two sisters.

The following Sunday, catching sight of my aunt's blue hat, I skipped
down the dirt pathway to meet her. By the time we reached each other,
Grandmother was already shouting her welcomes from the doorway, "Cui-
dado con el gallo colorado,** Marcelina ... he's a mean rooster ... he'll

* The Two Sisters.
† Package.
‡ Small gifts of affection.
** Be careful of the red rooster.

run your nylons . . . look what he did to my leg yesterday . . . Margarita, shoo him away from your tía!" *

I grabbed a rock and pursued the old rooster clear to the hen house whereupon he turned with ruffled feathers . . . that was his territory . . . it was my turn to back off. A few minutes later when I reached the kitchen, Grandmother and Aunt Marcelina were still discussing the old gallo, but already the embultorio lay opened on the table. Nina had brought us apples, some golden-crusted home-made bread and a slab of bacon. I knelt on the chair leaning my elbows on the table and regarded each woman in turn as the conversation shifted.

My grandmother, Teresina, was the dominant one, her dark hair neatly intertwined into a braid that she wound into a chignon and pinned to the back of her head with large bone hairpins. Today, being Sunday, she had waved the sides of her hair with her old curling iron and donned her silver filigree earrings. As she talked, her penetrating hazel eyes would capture the minutest detail through green tinted wire-framed spectacles. She still wore the customary black dress of a widow, although Grandpa had been dead for five years. I watched her walk from the table to the cupboard clicking her heels. Grandma always wore black oxfords, size five, triple A . . . years later when sickness and old age had taken her weight and shrunk her size, Teresina still insisted on size five, AAA.

Marcelina was the younger. Grandmother said she was only fifty, but to me she looked much older. She had wispy hair much grayer than Grandmother's and she had more wrinkles, too. But sometimes when she was sitting near a window the sun would lighten every line and her face would appear smooth and beautiful. Her hands were rough and red and gnarled with rheumatism. Only last Sunday I had watched her slip on a pair of gloves in order to put on her sheer stockings.

"So that I don't run them, hijita," † she had explained. Now those hands were gently cleaning her rose-tinted eye-glasses.

I loved hearing them talk . . . Teresina's resounding vociferous tones mingling with Marcelina's almost gentle humming . . .

"That was Juanita Cruz, daughter of José and María from Vallecito."

"Cousin to Martina Padilla?"

"Yes, María and Pablita were sisters by Don Joaquin's first marriage."

"Oh, sí, and then he married his first cousin . . ."

"Yes, well, you know how people talk."

"No wonder she had to move away."

"Doña Francisca even told her she could no longer be a member of the Altar Society."

"Bah, as if she was so lily white with that illegitimate boy of hers."

---

* Aunt.
† My dear; literally, little daughter.

Their voices would rise and fall tracing geneaologies and sharing the latest gossip of the village.

But today Marcelina sat quietly listening to Teresina's chatter about the rooster and watched her bustle about the kitchen. Teresina brought out some tortillas and then put them away again. When she wrapped the bacon twice, I giggled. With a worried frown she handed me an apple. "Margarita, go play outside." Then, without noticing that I had shrunk into the pantry near the doorway, Teresina turned to Marcelina and half-whispered, "Marcelina, did you go see the Padre?"

"Speak to my right side, Tere, I didn't bring my hearing aid today." Marcelina dragged the chair closer to her sister.

"I don't see why you save it. That's the least he can do, buy you new batteries once a year." Teresina scolded with that outraged voice intended for the villain, not the victim. And again, "Did you see Father O'Shaw this morning?"

"Sí, he is such a holy man . . . but so very thin. He's coming to see me Wednesday. Maybe you can come to help me get ready for him."

"Sí, I'll go and take along the beautiful doilies Juanita sent me and my statue of the Sacred Heart."

"I don't know what to do. It's becoming so hard to dissimulate."

"Well, I warned you about marrying him. He was twice your age . . . viejo calbo, fiero* . . . and all those children. Everytime I think of your wasted youth with that sin verguenza† and how he repays you now, I could kick him."

I pictured my uncle Flavio, a tall ruddy-faced bald man surrounded by ten babies and standing beside a beautiful young bride. Grandmother set a jar of capulín jelly on the table with such vehemence that it startled me out of the imaginary wedding. Aunt Marcelina was weeping softly while Teresina continued her ranting.

"Vagamundo, ese tal! ‡ Someday he will realize what a good woman you are. He can never point an accusing finger at you. You have been an example of such loyalty and goodness all these years. What he wanted was a maid, not a wife . . . he'll rot in hell! And you, mi hermanita, will be rewarded by Our Father and His Blessed Mother."

I stopped chewing on the apple and remembered the day Grandma and I had stopped to see my aunt Marcelina after Mass. Uncle Flavio was there. He was usually at his brother's ranch in northern New Mexico or in Wyoming herding sheep. But that Sunday he was home.

"Teresina, cómo estas? ** Come in," he politely invited. Then he swooped

* A mean old bald man.
† Shameless one.
‡ That good-for-nothing!
** How are you?

me up by the waist. He reeked of the familiar smell of Beechnut chewing tobacco.

"Put her down!" the icy command from my grandmother interrupted my giggles. I was glad; any moment he would have rubbed his whiskered face against mine. I hated that!

Grandma hurried me into the bedroom, leaving Uncle Flavio standing there in his suspendered trousers and yellowed undershirt.

Aunt Marcelina had been crying . . . her eyes still red and swollen.

"What's the matter?" Grandmother began and as if she knew the answer continued, "When did he return?" indicating the kitchen with her head.

"Juana came home Friday so I knew he was due soon. Sure enough, he arrived last night about two."

I couldn't understand why Doña Juana, my aunt's next door neighbor, had anything to do with my uncle's coming home.

My aunt's whispered voice continued, ". . . began bragging about his good times in Wyoming . . ."

Uncle Flavio's entrance interrupted her. "Qué ya esta chuchando? * Already she's telling you her lies and suspicions?" It was a sarcastic loud voice that left "suspicions" echoing in the room.

My grandmother turned and faced him, her eyes flaming. Lines of anger were forming around her eyes and along her forehead. I shrunk into a corner.

"You coward . . . tormentor . . . haven't you done enough to this woman? She was a beautiful young woman and too naive to know what you were really like! You took advantage of her . . . now look at her. You never even gave the proper mourning period for your first wife . . . you needed an immediate maid for your ten children! And now you dare call her the LIAR!"

"Tere . . . Tere, stop . . ." a pitiful plea from my sobbing aunt.

I could feel my heart beating faster and terror tightening my throat. My uncle's almost purple neck and face bulged out hate-filled eyes, his jaws working, tightening and loosening and tobacco juice escaping from the sides of his twisted mouth. Then, pointing a large hairy arm and hand toward the kitchen door, he hissed, "Get out of my house!"

Grandmother stood her ground. "So that you can hit Marcelina like you know how to do so well?"

Uncle Flavio stood pointing for what seemed to me endless seconds. Then with one quick movement he grabbed his hat off the chair, spit a black tobacco cud at my grandmother's feet and lurched toward the kitchen door slamming it behind him.

"Why didn't you go?" He might have hit you!"

* What are you whispering about now?

Teresina embraced her sister, "If I had gone he might have killed you. Let's go home with me. You don't have any reason to remain. Before, you used the children as an excuse . . . now the children are all gone . . . you've done your duty . . . you don't have to stay on with that sin verguenza, vagamundo!" *

My aunt gathered some of her things and the three of us started up the hill. I carried the embultorio.

Aunt Marcelina stayed with us a few weeks. As soon as she heard that Uncle Flavio had returned to his brother's ranch, she went home. My grandmother wanted her to remain, but Aunt Marcelina explained, "What will people say, 'Tan buena Católica y divurciada,' " † mimicking the squeaking tones of Doña Francisca.

Doña Francisca was the president of the Altar Society. On Sundays she always was up front lighting and rearranging candles and thought it her duty to shush at the choir girls who sat in the first pew. Everytime she passed in front of the tabernacle, which was often, she would genuflect on her left knee and make three tiny crosses on her forehead, nose and throat followed by an enormous one from the top of her hat to both shoulders and ending with a loud clap between her large breasts.

The imaginary clap became a realistic whop as the pantry door hit the kitchen wall and Grandmother stood over me.

"Margarita, what are you doing in here? I said outside!" I dropped the browning apple core as she pulled me up and out by one arm.

Wednesday I went with Grandma to prepare for Padre O'Shaw. About two that afternoon, when Father was due, I was sent to the parlor for its final inspection.

". . . and when you see Father coming let us know," Grandmother commanded.

I liked my aunt's neat parlor although I wasn't allowed to be in there very often. Today I surveyed the white freshly calcimined walls, the picture of the Good Shepherd holding the stray lamb, a larger oval gold frame enclosing a wedding photograph and near the window, a replica of Our Lady of Guadalupe. Just below her painting stood my grandmother's Sacred Heart surrounded by fresh white and violet lilacs I had picked that morning. The strong fragrance of the lilacs made me aware of the blue and pink flower patterns on the carpet, worn into gray disfigured spots at the entrance and directly in front of the settee and the two maroon wing chairs. Using the pink roses as stepping stones I danced a criss-cross pattern in the room, stopping before the wedding picture. It was my aunt Marcelina and uncle Flavio. She looked so beautiful . . . her wedding veil and train draped over the chair

* That shameless vagabond!
† Such a good Catholic and now she's divorced!

in which she was sitting, her hands holding a small bouquet of pink-tinted flowers and a pearl rosary. It was like looking at a princess in silks and lace. He, too, looked beautiful ... so tall in his dark suit and white shirt and he had so much hair then!

Footsteps and a soft knock took me at a run to the kitchen ... "He's here ... he's here!" I ran back to the parlor door and stood there waiting for my aunt to open it. She moved slowly; her navy blue dress made soft swishing noises and barely noticeable was the colorless cord running from the right side of her neck and hiding behind her ear.

"Good afternoon Mrs. Trujillo ... Margaret! What are you doing here?" Father's clean-shaven face smiled at the both of us. I had never seen such blue eyes.

"Hello, Father. Come in ..."

Father sat leaning forward in one of the maroon wing chairs, his hands folded together. Aunt Marcelina sat primly on the brown settee, her small rough hands playing with the solid gold band on her left hand.

My grandmother's "Maaarrgaritaaaa!" interrupted my move to the rocker. Reluctantly I left the guest with his hostess.

Long after Father O'Shaw had gone, Marcelina sat in the parlor. I had crept back quietly, but the pathetic slight figure of my aunt bent over, her voice coming and going, disjointed, unclear, paralyzed me in the doorway.

"... the Church agrees to separation, no divorce ... But I loved him ... Why God? Why? The children ... Tere was right! Oh Tere! ... Mis hijos ... My home ... what punishment ... what evil did I commit? Aye Diós ... Now that I'm old ... where would I go if it weren't for Tere ... Oh, my God ... the scandal ... But I just can't live with him anymore ... I just can't go on pretending that nothing is the matter ... Oh my God! The scandal!" Her tears mingled with tears. Her handkerchief had long since drowned in a crumpled ball in her hand. I watched her walk slowly to her wedding photograph and take it down leaving the naked nail sticking out conspicuously.

Saturday I rose early, dressed and helped Grandmother with last minute errands. I was excited ... my aunt Marcelina was coming to live with us. Grandmother had promised it would be forever. I went to wait for her at the old apricot tree. It formed a natural bench. Grandma had told me that it had been split by lightning many many years ago.

I thought of my aunt. I understood she was leaving Uncle Flavio and that it had something to do with Doña Juana. I pictured her ... a large nose with a hairy mole on the left side, and squinty eyes underneath thick glasses. And she always wore a wide-brimmed red hat. I remember overhearing Doña Francisca whispering that Don Flavio had brought it for Doña Juana from Wyoming. I didn't understand. Perhaps he had brought it home and Marcelina had sold it to her or given it away because she didn't like it.

I spotted Aunt Marcelina through the apricot leaves, jumped down from the tree and ran at a gallop to meet her. I took the large white embultorio from her and we chattered our way to the house.

She no longer looked the small pitiful aunt we had left on Wednesday ... she looked resolute and determined. I thought this must have been the way she looked when she defied everyone to marry Uncle Flavio. I remember Grandmother's words, "We warned you against marrying that viejo ... but no ... you knew better ... you were determined to go with him despite his age and all those children ... AND our warnings!"

When I was almost twelve, Aunt Marcelina became very ill. We had to take her to the hospital, but even then the doctor gave us little hope. She had been with us almost four years.

That evening I asked my grandmother why Aunt Marcelina had come to live with us. "Did it have anything to do with Doña Juana?"

Grandmother's eyes moistened and her voice quivered. "Your aunt has had a hard life, hijita. Flavio had bad women everywhere. Yes, Doña Juana was one of them. At first he tried to hide it, but after your aunt found out, he'd even brag to her about them."

"When did my aunt know? How did she find out?"

Grandmother began to speak softly, occasionally wiping her glasses and eyes almost in simultaneous movement. Sometimes her voice would rise in angry tones and then fall to a soft pitying murmur. It was like she was delivering lines from a play she had been rehearsing a long time. "It was a terrible night. The snow had steadily fallen all that day. By six, Marcelina was frantic, your cousin María still wasn't home from school. Marcelina thought perhaps the bus had been held up by the storm. She decided to go next door and ask Doña Juana if Gilbert had come home. So she wrapped herself in her woolen shawl and went next door. She stood in the snow knocking for a long time. Finally Doña Juana opened the door and I imagine with a shocked expression asked Marcelina in. Marcelina began to explain her visit ... that María had not come home and she wondered if Gilbert had since they both rode the same bus. All of a sudden she noticed Flavio's denim jacket, boots and trousers on the chair next to the stove and became conscious of the strong tobacco smell. Marcelina said she doesn't remember what happened or how she got home. The next thing she remembered was the door crashing open. She found herself still wrapped in her shawl sitting near the fireless stove. Flavio had begun yelling at her ... things like, 'Why were you spying on me? ... What was the idea of busting into a lady's home ... like Mrs. Juanita?' Imagine the sin verguenza calling Juana a lady to your aunt! Marcelina tried to explain but he called her a liar. The fight went on for hours. He admitted to his women and threatened Marcelina. Pobrecita mi hermanita." *

"But why didn't she just come to stay with us then?"

* My poor little sister.

"Rosa, José and María were still living at home and she thought it was her duty to stay and take care of them. Anyway, he was gone much of the time."

"Well, I'm glad she finally did leave him!"

"Sí, although she was so worried about the scandal it would cause. But Father O'Shaw was good to her and between the two of us, we convinced her she no longer had obligations to Flavio."

I slept in snatches that night. My dreams were flooded with wide-brimmed red hats, huge cavernous mouths chewing tobacco, my aunt Marcelina and Teresina wrapped together in a black shawl in a field of snow.

When I awoke, Grandmother was already dressed and hurrying me.

We were going to the hospital. I dressed quickly. Then, taking a fresh muslin dishcloth, I wrapped up my favorite statue of the Immaculate Conception which I had received for perfect attendance at school, a pearl rosary I had saved for Grandmother's birthday . . . she wouldn't mind, and a small box of chocolates, my aunt's favorites.

We were only allowed to go in one at a time and the nurse had said we were to stay in there only one minute. I would be last. The dreams of the night still haunted me.

My turn. I walked slowly down the antiseptic white hall and into my aunt's room. She looked so small, so frail, her wispy hair smeared on the pillow. She smiled weakly. I kissed her and handed her the small embultorio.

ESTELA PORTILLO TRAMBLEY

Estela Portillo Trambley was born in 1936 in El Paso, where she currently lives and is director of theater arts at El Paso Community College. Her play, *The Days of the Swallows,* was published in 1972 and has appeared in several anthologies. In 1975 she published a collection of short stories, *Rain of Scorpions,* and she is currently working on a novel, *Woman of the Earth.* She has also edited *Mujeres en Arte y Literatura,* a 1973 Quinto Sol publication. She comments, "As a Chicana writer I am a composite of my people: *Chicana muy gringa* to an extent. I wish I could gather the essences, the organic of the pure Chicano. I can't in all honesty, for I am too American. But I think I have the feel, the earth-roots, the historical consciousness of the Mejicana, enough to re-create the authentic experience, enough to perceive outlooks on life and the magnificent tenacity in struggle."

THE BURNING

The women of the barrio, the ones pock-marked by life, sat in council. Existence in dark cubicles of wounds had withered the spirit. Now, all as one, had found a heath. One tired soul stood up to speak. "Many times I see the light she makes of darkness, and that light is a greater blackness, still."

There was some skepticism from the timid. "Are you sure?"

"In those caves outside the town, she lives for days away from everybody. At night, when she is in the caves, small blinking lights appear, like fireflies. Where do they come from? I say, the blackness of her drowns the life in me."

Another woman with a strange wildness in her eyes nodded her head in affirmation. "Yes, she drinks the bitterness of good and swallows, like the devil-wolf, the red honey milk of evil."

A cadaverous one looked up into a darkened sky. "I hear thunder; lightning is not far." In unison they agreed, "We could use some rain."

The oldest one among them, one with dirty claws, stood up with arms outstretched and stood menacingly against the first lightning bolt that cleaved the darkness. Her voice was harsh and came from ages past. "She must burn!"

The finality was a cloud, black and tortured. Each looked into another's eyes to find assent or protest. There was only frenzy, tight and straining. The thunder was riding the lightning now, directly over their heads. It was a blazing canopy that urged them on to deeds of fear. There was still no rain. They found blistering words to justify the deed to come. One woman, heavy with anger, crouched to pour out further accusations. "She is the devil's pawn. On nights like this, when the air is heavy like thick blood, she sings among the dead, preferring them to the living. You know why she does it . . . eh? I'll tell you! She chases the dead back to their graves."

"Yes, yes. She stays and stays when death comes. Never a whimper, nor a tear, but I sense she feels the death as life like one possessed. They say she catches the flitting souls of the dead and turns them into flies. That way the soul never finds heaven."

"Flies! Flies! She is a plague!"

A clap of thunder reaffirmed. The old one with nervous, clutching claws made the most grievous charge, the cause for this meeting of the judgment. She shaped with bony gestures the anger of the heart. "She is the enemy of God! She put obscenities on our doorsteps to make us her accomplices. Sacrilege against the holy church!"

There was a fervor now, rising like a tide. They were for her burning now. All the council howled that Lela must burn that night. The sentence belonged to night alone. The hurricane could feed in darkness. Fear could be disguised as outrage at night. There were currents now that wanted sacrifice. Sacrifice is the umbilical cord of superstition. It would devastate before finding a calm. Lela was the eye of the storm, the artery that must flow to make them whole when the earth turned to light. To catch an evil when it bounced as shadow in their lives, to find it trapped in human body, this was an effective stimulant to some; to others it was a natural depressant to cut the fear, the dam of frustration. This would be their method of revelation. The doubt of themselves would dissolve.

But women know mercy! Mercy? It was swallowed whole by chasms of desire and fear of the unknown. Tempests grow in narrow margins that want a freedom they don't understand. Slaves always punish the free.

But who was Lela? She had come across the mountain to their pueblo many years before. She had crossed la Barranca del Cobre alone. She had walked into the pueblo one day, a bloody, ragged, half-starved young girl. In an apron she carried some shining sand. She stood there, like a frightened fawn, at the edge of the village. As the people of the pueblo gathered around her strangeness, she smiled, putting out her hand for touch. They drew back and she fell to the ground in exhaustion.

They took her in, but she remained a stranger the rest of her life in the pueblo upon which she had stumbled. At the beginning, she seemed but a harmless child. But, as time passed and she resisted their pattern of life, she was left alone. The people knew she was a Tarahumara from Batopilas. Part of her strangeness was the rooted depth of her own religion. She did not convert to Christianity. People grew hostile and suspicious of her.

But she had also brought with her the miracle sand. It had strange curative powers. In no time, she began to cure those in the pueblo who suffered from skin disease, from sores, or open wounds.

"Is it the magic of her devil gods?" the people asked themselves. Still, they came for the miracle cure that was swift and clean. She became their *curandera* outside their Christian faith.

The people in her new home needed her, and she loved them in silence and from a distance. She forgave them for not accepting her strangeness and learned to find adventure in the Oneness of herself.

Many times she wanted to go back to Batopilas, but too many people needed her here. She learned the use of medicinal herbs and learned to set broken bones. This was what she was meant to do in life. This purpose would not let her return to Batopilas. Still, she did not convert to Christianity. The people, begrudgingly, believed in her curative powers, but did not believe in her. Many years had passed and Lela was now an old woman, and the council of women this night of impending storm had decided her fate.

Lela lay dying in her one room hut. There was a fire with teeth that consumed her body. She only knew that her time was near an end as she lay in her small cot. Above the bed was a long shelf she had built herself that held rows of clay figurines. These were painted in gay colors and the expression on the tiny faces measured the seasons of the heart. They were live little faces showing the full circle of human joy and pain, doubt and fear, humor and sobriety. In all expressions there was a fierceness for life.

Lela had molded them through the years, and now they stood over her head like guardians over their maker. . . . Clay figurines, an act of love learned early in her childhood of long ago. In Batopilas, each home had its own rural god. He was a friend and a comforter. The little rural gods were like any other people. They did not rule or demand allegiance. The little rural gods of river, sky, fire, seed, birds, all were chosen members of each family. Because they sanctified all human acts, they were the actions of the living, like an aura. They were a shrine to creation.

Lela's mother had taught the little girl to mold the clay figures that represented the rural gods. This was her work and that of Lela's in the village, to provide clay little gods for each home and for festive occasions. This is why Lela never gave them up in her new home. She had molded them with her hands, but they dwelled boundless in the center of her being. The little gods had always been very real, very important, in her reverence for life.

There had been in Batopilas a stone image of the greater god, Tecuat. He was an impressive god of power that commanded silence and obedience. People did not get close to Tecuat except in ritual. As a girl, Lela would tiptoe respectfully around the figure of Tecuat, then she would breathe a sigh of relief and run off to find the little gods.

This was her game, god-hunting. One day, she had walked too far towards the pines, too far towards a roar that spoke of rushing life. She followed a yellow butterfly that also heard a command of dreams. She followed the butterfly that flitted towards a lake. As she followed, she looked for little gods in the glint of the sun, and in the open branches that pierced the absoluteness of the sky. The soft breath of wind was the breath of little gods, and the crystal shine of rocks close to the lake was a winking language that spoke of peace and the wildness of all joy.

When she had reached the lake, she stepped into the water without hesitation. She felt the cool wet mud against her open toes. She walked into the water, touching the ripple of its broken surface with her finger tips. After a while, there was no more bottom. She began to cut the water with smooth, clean strokes, swimming out towards the pearl-green rocks that hid the roar. She floated for a while looking up at the light filtering through eternal trees. The silence spoke of something other than itself. It spoke in colors born of water and sun. She began to swim more rapidly towards the turn that led to the cradle of the roar, the waterfall. . . .

This is what Lela, the old Lela dying on her bed, was remembering . . . the waterfall. It helped to ease the pain that came in waves that broke against her soul and blackened the world. Then, there was the calm, the calm into which the experience machine brought back the yesterdays that were now soft, kind memories. She opened her eyes and looked up at the row of clay figures. She was not alone. "The waterfall . . ." she whispered to herself. She remembered the grotto behind the waterfall. It had been her hermitage of dreams, of wonder. Here her Oneness had knitted all the little gods unto herself until she felt the whole of earth—things within her being. Suddenly, the pain cut her body in two. She gripped the edge of the cot. There were blurs of throbbing white that whirled into black, and all her body trembled until another interval of peace returned for a little while.

There was no thought; there was no dream in the quiet body. She was a simple calm that would not last. The calm was a gift from the little gods. She slept. It was a fitful, brief sleep that ended with the next crash of pain. The pain found gradual absorption. She could feel the bed sheet clinging to her body, wet with perspiration. She asked herself in a half-moan, "When will the body give way?" Give way . . . give way, for so long, Lela had given way and had found ways to open herself and the world she understood. It had been a vital force in her. She could have been content in Batopilas. The simple truths of Nature might have fulfilled her to the end of her days if she had remained in Batopilas. But there was always that reach in her for a larger self. Nature was a greatness, but she felt a different hunger and a different thirst.

There was a world beyond Batopilas; there were people beyond Batopilas. She was no longer a child. It was easy to find little gods in Nature, but as she grew older, it became a child's game. There was time to be a child, but there was now time for something more. That is why, one day, she had walked away from Batopilas.

Beyond the desert, she would find another pueblo. She knew there were many pueblos and many deserts. There was nothing to fear because her little gods were with her. On the first day of her journey, she walked all day. The piercing sun beat down on her and the world, as she scanned the horizon for signs of a way. Something at a distance would be a hope, would be a way to something new, a way to the larger self. At dusk, she felt great hunger and great thirst. Her body ached and her skin felt parched and dry. The night wind felt cold, so she looked for a shelter against the wind. She found a clump of mesquite behind some giant sahuaros. This was not the greenness she knew so well, but a garden of stars in the night sky comforted her until she fell asleep.

At first light she awakened refreshed and quickly resumed her journey. She knew she must make the best out of the early hours before the sun rose. By late morning, the desert yielded a mountain at a distance. She reached the mountain in time to rest from the sun and the physical effort of her journey. When the sun began to fall, she started up a path made narrow by a blanket of desert brush. It tore the flesh of her feet and legs as she made her way up the path. In a little while, it was hard to find sure footing. The path had lost itself in a cleavage of rocks. Night had fallen. She was not afraid, for the night sky, again, was full of blinking little gods.

Then it happened. She lost her footing and fell down, down over a crevice between two huge boulders. As she fell, her lungs filled with air. Her body hit soft sand, but the edge of her foot felt the sharpness of a stone. She lay there stunned for a few minutes until she felt a sharp pain at the side of her foot. Somewhat dizzy, she sat up and noticed that the side of her foot was bleeding profusely. She sat there and watched the blood-flow that found its way into the soft sand. She looked up at the boulders that silently rebuked her helplessness; then she began to cry softly. She had to stanch the blood. She wiped away her tears with the side of her sleeve and tore off a piece of skirt to use as a bandage. As she looked down at the wound again, she noticed that the sand where she had fallen was extremely crystalline and loose. It shone against a rising moon. She scooped up a handful and looked at it with fascination. "The sand of little gods," she whispered to herself. She took some sand and rubbed it on the wound before she applied the bandage. By now, she felt a burning fever. She wrapped the strip of skirt around the wound now covered with the fine, shining sand. Then she slept. But it was a fitful sleep, for her body burned with fever. Half awake and half in a dream, she saw the sands take the shapes of happy, little gods. Then, at other times, the pain told her she was going to die. After a long time, her exhausted body slept until the dawn passed over her head.

When she finally awakened, she felt extremely well. Her body was rested and her temperature, to her great surprise, was normal. She looked down at the wound. The blood was caked on the bandage. She took it off to look at the wound. She could hardly believe her eyes. There was no longer any open wound. There was a healthy scab, and the area around the wound had no infection. It was a healing that normally would have taken weeks. She stood on her foot and felt no pain. "My little gods!" she thought. She fell down on her knees and kissed the shining sand. After a while, she removed her apron and filled it with the shining sand. She secured it carefully before she set off on her climb. As she made her way out of the crevice, she marked the path leading to the shining sand to find her way to it again. It was hard making marks with a sharp stone, and it seemed to take forever. At last, she reached the top of the crevice and noticed, to her great joy, that it led down to a pueblo at a distance. She made her way to strangers that day. Now, at the end of a lifetime, Lela felt the pain roll, roll, roll, roll itself into a blindness. She struggled through the blackness until she gasped back the beginning of the calm. With the new calm came a ringing memory from her childhood. She saw the kindly face of the goddess, Ta Te. She who was born of the union of clean rock, she who was eternal. Yes, Ta Te understood all the verdant things . . . the verdant things.

And who were these women who sat in council? They were one full sweep of hate; they were one full wave of fear. Now these village women were outlined against a greyish sky where a storm refused to break. Spider-like, apelike, toadlike was the ferocity of their deadness. These were creatures of the earth who mingled with mankind. But they were minions to torture because the twist of littleness bound them to condemn all things unknown, all things untried. The infernal army could not be stopped now. The scurry-ing creatures began to gather firewood in the gloom. With antlike obedience they hurried back and forth carrying wood to Lela's hut. They piled it in a circle around her little house. The rhythm of their feet sang, "We'll do! We'll do!"

"The circle of fire will drain her powers!" claimed the old one with claws.

"Show me! Show me! Show me!" Voices lost as one.

As the old one with claws ordered more wood, the parish priest came run-ning from his church. With raised arms he shouted as he ran, "Stop! Do you hear? Stop this madness!"

It can be argued that evil is not the reversal of good, but the vacuum of good. Thus, the emptiness is a standing still, a being dead, an infinite pain . . . like dead wood. No one listened to him.

"Burn! Burn! Burn!"

Life? The wood? The emptiness? The labor pains were that of something already lost, something left to the indefinite in life. The priest went from one woman to another begging, pleading, taking the wood from their hands.

"Burn! Burn! Burn!"

The old priest reasoned. "All is forgiven, my children. She only made some figurines of clay!"

There was a hush. The one woman with the claws approached the priest and spit out the condemnation, "She took our holy saints, Mary, Joseph, and many others and made them obscene. How can you defend the right hand of the devil? Drinking saints! Winking saints! Who can forgive the hideous suggestions of her clay devils? Who?"

The priest said simply, "You."

But if there is only darkness in a narrow belief, who can believe beyond the belief, or even understand the belief itself? The women could not forgive because they did not believe beyond a belief that did not go beyond symbol and law. Somehow, symbol and law, without love, leaves no opening. The clay figures in the church with sweet, painted faces lifted to heaven were much more than figures of clay to these women. Their still postures with praying hands were a security. Now, the priest who had blessed them with holy water said they were not a sanctuary of God. Why did he contradict himself?

The old one with the claws felt triumphant. "She has made our saints into pagan gods!"

The priest shook his head sadly. "It is not a sin, what she did!"

No one listened. The piling of wood continued until the match was lit. Happy . . . Happy fire . . . it would burn the sin and the sinner.

Something in Lela told her this was the last struggle now. She looked up at her clay figurines one last time. Her eyes had lost their focus. The little gods had melted into one another; all colors were mixed. They grew into silver strands of light that crossed and mingled and found new forms that pulled away from one center. In half consciousness, she whispered, "Yes, yes, pull away. Find other ways, other selves, grow. . . ."

She smiled; the last calm had taken her back to the caves outside the pueblo. The caves were not like the grotto behind the waterfall, but they were a place for Oneness, where one could look for the larger self. Here the solitude of the heart was a bird in space. Here, in the silence of aloneness, she had looked for the little gods in the townspeople. In her mind, she had molded their smiles, their tears, their embraces, their seeking, their *just being*. Her larger self told her that the miracle of the living act was supreme, the giving, the receiving, the stumbling, and the getting up.

In the caves she had sadly thought of how she had failed to reach them as a friend. Her silences and her strangeness had kept them apart. But, she would find a way of communicating, a way of letting them know that she loved them. "If I give shape and form to their beauty," she thought. "If I cannot tell them I love them with words. . . ."

The light of the moving, mixing little gods was becoming a darkness. Her body would give in now. Yet, she still wished for Batopilas and the old ways with her last breath, "If only . . . if only I could be buried in the tradition of my fathers . . . a clean burning for new life . . . but here, here, there is a dark hole for the dead body. . . . Oh, little gods, take me back to my fathers. . . ."

The little gods were racing to the waterfall.

GUADALUPE VALDÉS FALLIS

Though Guadalupe Valdés Fallis was born in El Paso in 1941, she lived in Chihuahua, Mexico, until 1961. She currently teaches Spanish at New Mexico State University in Las Cruces. She has worked and published extensively in the area of Spanish for Spanish-speakers and is the editor of a newsletter on the subject. Her articles have appeared in *Hispania, Colorado Quarterly, Revista Chicano-Riqueña,* and *Accent on ACTFL.*

RECUERDO*

It was noon. It was dusty. And the sun, blinding in its brightness, shone unmercifully on the narrow dirty street.

It was empty. And to Rosa, walking slowly past the bars and the shops and the curio stands, it seemed as if they all were peering out at her, curiously watching what she did.

She walked on . . . toward the river, toward the narrow, muddy strip of land that was the dry Rio Grande; and she wished suddenly that it were night and that the tourists had come across, making the street noisy and gay and full of life.

But it was noon. And there were no happy or laughing Americanos; no eager girls painted and perfumed and waiting for customers; no blaring horns or booming bongos . . . only here and there a hungry dog, a crippled beggar, or a drunk, thirsty and broke from the night before.

She was almost there. She could see the narrow door and the splintered wooden steps. And instinctively she stopped. Afraid suddenly, feeling the hollow emptiness again, and the tightness when she swallowed.

And yet, it was not as if she did not know why he had wanted her to come, why he had sent for her. It was not as though she were a child. Her reflection in a smudged and dirty window told her that she was no longer even a girl.

And still, it was not as if she were old, she told herself, it was only that her body was rounded and full, and her eyes in the dark smooth face were

* Remembrance.

hard and knowing, mirroring the pain and the disappointment and the tears of thirty-five years . . .

She walked to the narrow door slowly, and up the stairs . . . thumping softly on the creaking swollen wood. At the top, across a dingy hallway, she knocked softly at a door. It was ajar, and Rosa could see the worn chairs and the torn lineoleum and the paper-littered desk. But she did not go in. Not until the man came to the door and looked out at her impatiently.

He saw her feet first and the tattered sandals. Then her dress clean but faded, a best dress obviously, because it was not patched. Finally, after what seemed to Rosa an eternity, he looked at her face, at her dark black hair knotted neatly on top of her head; and at last, into her eyes.

"Come in, Rosa," he said slowly, "I am glad that you could come."

"Buenas tardes Don Lorenzo." * Rosa said meekly, looking up uneasily at the bulky smelly man. "I am sorry I am late."

"Yes," he said mockingly; and turning, he walked back into the small and dirty room.

Rosa followed him, studying him, while he could not see her, seeing the wrinkled trousers, the sweat stained shirt, and the overgrown greasy hair on the back of his pudgy neck.

He turned suddenly, his beady eyes surveying his domain smugly; then deliberately, he walked to the window and straightened the sign that said:

DIVORCES . . . LORENZO PEREZ SAUZA . . . ATTORNEY AT LAW

It was not as important as the neon blinking sign, of course, but sometimes people came from the side street, and it was good to be prepared.

"Well, Rosa," he said, looking at her again, "and where is Maruca?"

"She is sick, señor."

"Sick?"

"Yes, she has had headaches and she is not well . . . she . . ."

"Has she seen a doctor, Rosa?" The question was mocking again.

"No . . . she . . . it will pass, señor. . . . It's only that now . . . I do not think that she should come to work."

"Oh?" He was looking out of the window distractedly, ignoring her.

"I am sorry, I should have come before," she continued meekly . . .

"Maruca is very pretty, Rosa," Don Lorenzo said suddenly.

"Thank you, señor, you are very kind." She was calmer now . . .

"She will make a man very happy, someday," he continued.

"Yes."

"Do you think she will marry soon then?" he asked her, watching her closely.

"No," she hesitated, "that is, I don't know, she . . . there isn't anyone yet."

"Ah!" It was said quietly but somehow triumphantly . . .

* Good afternoon, Don Lorenzo.

And Rosa waited, wondering what he wanted, sensing something and suddenly suspicious.

"Do you think she likes me, Rosa," he asked her deliberately, baiting her.

And she remembered Maruca's face, tear-stained, embarrassed telling her: "I can't go back, Mama. He does not want me to help in his work. He touches me, Mother . . . and smiles. And today, he put his large sweaty hand on my breast, and held it, smiling, like a cow. Ugly!"

"Why, yes, Don Lorenzo," she lied quickly. "She thinks you are very nice." Her heart was racing now, hoping and yet not daring to—

"I am much of a man, Rosa," he went on slowly, "and the girl is pretty. . . . I would take care of her . . . if she let me."

"Take care of her?" Rosa was praying now, her fingers crossed behind her back.

"Yes, take care of her," he repeated. "I would be good to her, you would have money. And then, perhaps, if there is a child . . . she would need a house . . ."

"A house." Rosa repeated dully. A house for Maruca. That it might be. That it might be, really, was unbelievable. To think of the security, of the happy future frightened her suddenly, and she could only stare at the fat man, her eyes round and very black.

"Think about it, Rosita," he said smiling benevolently . . . "You know me . . ." And Rosa looked at him angrily, remembering, and suddenly feeling very much like being sick.

The walk home was long; and in the heat Rosa grew tired. She wished that she might come to a tree, so that she could sit in the shade and think. But the hills were bare and dry, and there were no trees. There were only shacks surrounded by hungry crying children.

And Rosa thought about her own, about the little ones. The ones that still depended on her even for something to eat. And she felt it again, the strange despair of wanting to cry out: "Don't, don't depend on me! I can hardly depend on myself."

But they had no one else; and until they could beg or steal a piece of bread and a bowl of beans, they would turn to her, only to her, not ever to Pablo.

And it wasn't because he was drunk and lazy, or even because only the last two children belonged to him. He was kind enough to all of them. It was, though, as if they sensed that he was only temporary.

And still it was not that Pablo was bad. He was better actually than the others. He did not beat her when he drank, or steal food from the children. He was not even too demanding. And it gave them a man, after all, a man to protect them. . . . It was enough, really.

True, he had begun to look at Maruca, and it had bothered Rosa. But perhaps it WAS really time for Maruca to leave. For the little ones, particularly. Because men are men, she said to herself, and if there is a temptation . . .

But she was not fooling anyone, and when at last she saw the tin and cardboard shack against the side of the hill, with its cluttered front and screaming children, she wanted to turn back.

Maruca saw her first.

"There's Mama," she told the others triumphantly, and at once they took up the shout: "Mama! Mama! Mama!"

The other girl, standing with Maruca, turned to leave as Rosa came closer.

"Buenas tardes," she said uncomfortably, sensing the dislike and wanting to hurry away.

"What did Petra want?" Rosa asked Maruca angrily, even before Petra was out of earshot.

"Mama, por favor, she'll hear you."

"I told you I did not want her in this house."

"We were only talking, Mama. She was telling me about her friends."

"Her friends!" Rosa cut in sharply, "as if we did not know that she goes with the first American that looks at her. Always by the river that one, with one soldier and another, her friends indeed!"

"But she says she has fun, Mama, and they take her to dance and buy her pretty things."

"Yes, yes, and tomorrow, they will give her a baby. . . . And where is the fun then . . . eh? She is in the streets . . . no?"

Rosa was shaking with anger. "Is that what you want? Do you?"

"No, Mama," Maruca said meekly, "I was just listening to her talk."

"Well, remember it," Rosa snapped furiously, but then seeing Maruca's face, she stopped suddenly. "There, there, it's alright," she said softly. "We will talk about it later."

And Rosa watched her, then, herding the children into the house gently, gracefully; slim and small, ·angular still, with something perhaps a little doltish in the way she held herself, impatient, and yet distrusting, not quite daring to go forward.

And she thought of Don Lorenzo, and for a moment, she wished that he were not so fat, or so ugly, and especially, so sweaty.

But it was an irrecoverable chance! Old men with money did not often come into their world, and never to stay.

To Rosa, they had been merely far away gods at whose houses she had worked as a maid or as a cook; faultless beings who were to be obeyed without question; powerful creatures who had commanded her to come when they needed variety or adventure . . .

But only that.

She had never been clever enough, or even pretty enough to make it be more.

But Maruca! Maruca could have the world.

No need for her to marry a poor young bum who could not even get a job. No need for her to have ten children all hungry and crying. No need for her to dread, even, that the bum might leave her. No need at all.

"Maruca," Rose said decidedly, turning to where she sat playing with the baby, "I went to see Don Lorenzo."

"Oh?" There was fear in the bright brown eyes.

"And he wants to take care of you," Rosa continued softly. "He thinks you're pretty, and he likes you."

"Take care of me?" It was more of a statement than a question.

"He wants to make an arrangement with you, Maruca." Rosa too was afraid now. "He would come to see you . . . and . . . well . . . if there is a baby, there might very well be a house."

"A baby?" The face was pale now, the eyes surprised and angry. "You want me to go to bed with Don Lorenzo? You want me to let him put his greasy hands all over me, and make love to me? You want that? Is that how much better I can do than Petra?"

"Don't you see, I want you to be happy, to be safe. I want you to have pretty things and not to be afraid. I want you to love your babies when you have them, to hear them laugh with full fat stomachs . . . I want you to love life, to be glad that you were born."

"To be happy?" Maruca repeated slowly, as if it had never occurred to her that she was not.

"Yes, to be happy."

"And sleeping with Don Lorenzo," Maruca asked uncertainly, "will that make me glad that I was born?"

And Rosa looked at her, saw her waiting for an answer, depending on it . . .

And she wanted to scream out. "No, no! You will hate it probably, and you will dread his touch on you and his breath smelling of garlic. But it isn't HE, that will make you happy. It's the rest of it. Don't you see, can't you understand how important HE is?"

But the brown eyes stared at her pleadingly, filling with tears, like a child's, and Rosa said quietly: "Yes, Maruca, it will make you happy."

But then suddenly, unexpectedly, she felt alone and very very tired.

"Go on to church now," she said slowly, "it's time for benediction and you have the novena to complete." And Rosa watched her go, prayer book clutched tightly in one hand, hopeful still, trusting still, and so very, very young still. And she wondered if she would change much, really, after Don Lorenzo, and the baby and the house. She wondered if she would still be gay and proud and impatient.

But then suddenly Maruca was out of sight, and Rosa turned to the others, kissing one, patting another's head, and hurrying to have the beans hot and the house tidy for the time that Pablo would come home.

ESTELA PORTILLO TRAMBLEY

Estela Portillo Trambley was born in 1936 in El Paso, where she currently lives and is director of theater arts at El Paso Community College. Her play, *The Days of the Swallows*, was published in 1972 and has appeared in several anthologies. In 1975 she published a collection of short stories, *Rain of Scorpions*, and she is currently working on a novel, *Woman of the Earth*. She has also edited *Mujeres en Arte y Literatura*, a 1973 Quinto Sol publication. She comments, "As a Chicana writer I am a composite of my people: *Chicana muy gringa* to an extent. I wish I could gather the essences, the organic of the pure Chicano. I can't in all honesty, for I am too American. But I think I have the feel, the earth-roots, the historical consciousness of the Mejicana, enough to re-create the authentic experience, enough to perceive outlooks on life and the magnificent tenacity in struggle."

PAY THE CRIERS

Rain knows the earth and loves it well, for rain is the passion of the earth. It is tears, joy, hope, melted into cool torrents that fall on the longing and the hunger of the earth in rigorous tenderness to give her life. How well it speaks of senses in its cool excitement. The beginning of passion is a burst of flame. Its culmination speaks of an open door unto light, a lucidity of life, more life, forever life.

The giver, rain, comforts, forgives, understands, as it tells of mountains, oceans, skies, and a breathing consciousness of all things. Earth and rain become dark moisture that finds its brightness of a womb. The first beginning was in rain. After copulation . . . there is a silence. It is similar to the silence that follows love. Like love, it confirms the truth of immortality. Like love, it has the vastness of acceptance. This glorious silence is that open door into a clean, free clarity.

Chucho listened to the silence and watched the water on mud puddles circling for an open way. The smell of rain is rich with life. He, too, was full of the same silence. He stood looking out the door leading to the backyard. The desert had welcomed the rain as Juana had welcomed love. He could hear her soft breathing from the bed. He looked up to see the sky, a cloudless blue. The sun had found its throne again. Juana had gotten up from the bed and was now behind him. The silence was part of her too. His glance now fell upon the jarros full of rain water outside the doorway. The water played with light like singing senses. The rain had given.

Chucho felt Juana's small hands caressing his body. The smell of the clay from the jarros increased the pleasure. The aftermath of love and set earth became the same affirmation. Juana's cheek felt warm and soft on his bare back . . . now her half-opened lips pressed hard, tenacious in their love. The lips held a reverence and a claim. Outside the door there was a newness in the world as if all the ills that fester with droughts had been swept away.

"Will you stay, Chucho?"

"I have things to do."

"You must keep your promise, Chucho."

He shrugged his shoulders indifferently. Droughts lengthen out into interminable desperations for Juana. A time and a place had defined her among the vanquished. This is why inquietude existed within the well-being of love, why melancholy sought a claim. It was now that Chucho became aware of his dead mother-in-law, hidden in the darkness of the room. This was the focus now, the presence of a dead woman who had been a part of them. This was also the reason for Juana's misery.

His thoughts returned to the early afternoon when he had come home after a long absence. Chucho had found Juana, grief-stricken, over the dead body of her mother. The old woman's long drawn-out battle was over. She had given in to death. Juana was clutching the old purse stuffed with bills and coins that the mother had entrusted to her with her last breath. Juana had promised to use the money for a grand funeral. When life left the body, Juana, lost in her despair, let it fall to the floor. She clung to the dead mother with a lostness.

A clap of thunder and lightning broke the heaviness of death. It was at this moment that Chucho had arrived as if he had brought the welcomed rain. She now turned from the dead mother to the live haven of his arms. He gave comfort simply and silently. Waiting for Chucho to come home had been long and frugal for Juana. Now in the realness of his compassion, Juana felt the body hunger, tormented and bursting into flame.

As he made love to Juana, his glance fell upon the purse fallen to the floor. He knew what it contained. For many years, he had fought with his mother-in-law and with his wife over the use of this money. The old mother, Refugio, had worked hard for it. She had saved it religiously for her funeral for a long time. "A waste!" Chucho had screamed. Refugio was their only means of support. She meted out the necessary money for frugal survival. The purse had grown fat with time. "I wonder how much?" Chucho asked himself as he caressed his weeping wife.

"Oh, Chucho, it was a bad time . . . I've been so alone."

"Hush, don't cry; I'm back."

Another clap of thunder brought Juana closer to him. The natural shocks of the body found their end. It was enough. Chucho whispered in Juana's ear, "I will take care of everything. I'll see about the funeral." He felt the sudden tenseness of her body. She held her breath. She knew too well her husband's ways. The fear, however, was secondary to her husband's arms. He was here; he could do as he wished. The gentle rain soon became heavy storm; with it, ascended the heartbeats of the living, a symphony of open doors, the light of life, more life, forever life.

In the shadows of the room, the old cot with the body of the dead woman served as a counterpoint, now lost, as Juana and Chucho swam the colors of the struggle. At one time, the now dead woman had known a struggle too. When youth had passed, the colors of struggle became greys in black descents of tragic things. The colors, the greys, even the black descent had ended for Refugio. Was there some kind of open door in death?

In life, Refugio had been a lusty warrior full of battle cry. The ready passion, the ready appetite, the way out of things, all had been her banner. Her crude grasp had been bloody and her blow heavy. This was her kind of grandeur. In the midst of her poor, monotonous greys, the armed savage had many times touched, harshly and with numbness, the consequence of rainbow spectrums so delicate they had made her fear a shattering of spirit. Perhaps this was why she had scorned impracticality, dream, illusion. But she had walked stoutly across the actuality of things. Her vision had small radius outside the slavish ways in the life struggle. The focus had always been to keep fighting, to keep abreast. If there was rest she reached for greys, for her eyes were now unaccustomed to the colors of the youthful dream or hope. She was earth with its tenacity, its instinctual freedom, and its voracity. The roughness of Refugio gave way only to a simple faith, a childish belief in the ritual wonders of her church. Its pageantry made her one with God, the master in the center of the ring. She had wanted a warrior's funeral when her time came with all its mummery and the jugglers of immortal hope. A fiery skyrocket must streak the heavens with her names for one last time to make up for shackles and for colors lost. A feast in her honor where tears would be wept in ceremonious grace. This had been the wish of the dead woman on the cot.

This was the woman that Chucho and Juana had forgotten when the flame had burst the glory—affirmation of the seed denying death in the dark corner. Now in the silence and the calm, her deadness became real to those well satisfied with love. Juana could not stand the thought of what she had done. Anxiety, too, suffocated her with doubt.

"You must take the money into town and pay the criers, Chucho." Now Chucho stood looking out the door. His wife's anxiety had made him rise impatiently from her side to seek a cleaner refuge with the rain. He reached down and picked up the old worn purse full of money. He put it in the pocket of the coat lying on a chair and returned to watch the rain. Suddenly, he turned and began to dress.

Juana sensed herself alone again. She looked towards the cot apprehensively and shivered with guilt. A horror began to grow. She had proved herself faithless to her mother. The money was now in Chucho's hands, easily taken. When she had come up behind him at the door, she was still warm with love, but guilt was taking hold. Chucho sensed it. Now that the rain had stopped, the jolt of life sounds from the barrio made his blood race. He must go. He walked away from the door to finish dressing. Juana's hold on him had been broken without ceremony. Juana felt the consequence of her stupidity. "Oh, God . . . I wish I could trust him . . . I wish I could erase the fears." But there had been so many times before when he had used her for his ends. The money is for the funeral; he must use it for that . . . he must. Her voice was thick with anxiety.

"You must pay the criers." He dared not look her in the face.

"Yes, yes . . . now leave me alone." He finished dressing hurriedly. He was alone in his pride and his plans. The shadows grew and made her cringe against her own weakness. This was the stamp long ago given to her by her dead mother and a disgusted husband when they had shared the wine. This creature well accepted condemnation as the measure of her life. The pain of loss found pulse again. "My mother's dead . . . my mother's dead . . . what can I do?" The weakness was a falling . . . a fearful falling. . . .

The dark hysteria grew. There will be no funeral. He will spend the money. In sudden desperation, she reached for Chucho's coat before he picked it up and fumbled through the pockets. He was beside her with a curse. He hit her and the blow erased the world for a second as she fell backwards against a chair. Again, she had done the wrong thing. He would leave her now. In desperate defeat, she had tried and failed.

"You must keep your promise, Chucho."

No! He was gone. The money was gone; her mother was gone. Her sobs came slow at first; soon they were hard and painful. Instinct took its course. The blind child from the womb went to her mother. She dragged herself across the floor to the cot where her dead mother lay. Her arms reached out to touch a stiffness; it was little comfort. "Mamacita . . . que voy a hacer? * What is there without you? Without him?" She laid her head on the bosom of a dead woman, cradling her non-existing safeness, a nipple of security with no nourishment but touch. . . . Where? How?

Chucho walked out of the two room hut he had helped Refugio build. The old bitch was dead! He touched the pocket of his coat where the money was. He had got the best of her after all.

He quickened his steps when he reached the bottom of the hill. The smell of food for evening meals mixed strangely with the fragrance of wet earth. Yes . . . the first thing he would buy would be a good supper for his best friend Chapo and himself. The best in the house . . . he could afford it. The anticipation made him rather light-headed. He felt joy rising to the throat, escaping into a shout of joy. All the things that would be his in the next

* Mama, what am I going to do?

few hours! The lighting of lamps in the houses that he passed reminded him of the people of the world! They had all the meaning for the time he touched them, talked to them, shared with them. He would treat everyone tonight. It was a beautiful thought. He would be the giver . . . he, Chucho! Never before could he give so much. He was always broke. Tonight he had much money. The glory of the feeling filled him.

He would tell Chapo about the money and then he would buy a full tank of gas for Chapo's old car. Tonight he would try his luck at the gambling table. Tonight he would visit Adela's girls . . . yes, this would be a night to remember. He reached the bottom of the hill and turned towards Chapo's house. Chapo washed cars all day long with a trance-like vigor. This was the pattern of his day. Soap, mop, hose, car after car. Chapo was a machine, numb to the soul, grateful for the pittance to buy existence for another day. He had to close his eyes against himself as a man to give his life away for a few centavos. He had lost the freedom, poor Chapo! Chucho knew deep down in himself he would never give up the freedom. He was condemned by everyone as shiftless, worthless, no-account, but he would never give up the freedom.

The old dead bitch had been the worst one. He remembered her wild roars and accusations. Why tell him what he already knew? He drank too much and played the fool too often. The old woman's venom had been a fearsome thing. But, then, he curiously remembered times when they had laughed together. There was always relief in the eyes of his simple wife when he was friends with his mother-in-law. It meant peace for a little while. But the old woman had never understood his need for the freedom . . . perhaps because she had never had it herself.

One time he had seen some ice-skaters in the city. He had watched their graceful, skillful skating with great wonderment. Such a difficult thing looked so easy, so effortless. That was beauty. Somehow he felt it had something to do with the freedom he loved so well, but he could not explain it. The skaters must work hard for that beauty . . . very hard. The easy, swift, graceful gliding was the work conquered and transformed into a freedom now a part of them. Yes, yes . . . that was it . . . ease came with becoming a some-thing in action. That is what he wanted to do in life . . . find an ease of action. Now, he was only a spectator of a great number of confusions and fears. But he was also a spectator and he shared the freedom with others.

There were glimpses of many kinds of beauties that went beyond the traps of every day. Each man must be involved in his destiny, but first he must recognize the part he plays, and the ease behind the play. Otherwise, the skill that brought the freedom would never be found. He remembered watching the skaters and remarking to Chapo:

"I want a skill like that, Chapo."

"You want to be a skater?" Chapo was never too surprised at Chucho's remarks.

"I want a skill for life, a smooth running to a freedom to make people see that I can see."

"Oh, you have a skill for life, Chucho. You can drink more, fight harder . . . you have been in jail more often than anyone I know . . . why I remember . . ."

"Never mind, Chapo, I mean . . . never mind."

"I know what you mean, Chucho, it doesn't buy you any bread. What do you care? You have a mother-in-law with a good job."

"Oh, shut up, Chapo!"

"You play with many blows for the freedom, Chucho, but at least you still have the freedom. Look at me! That bastard without balls pays me like a slave because I need the money for food for my little ones. I would like to spit in his face . . . but I don't think about it. I just wash cars until they shine. Pretty soon, I get my centavos and I go home . . . we eat one more day."

"I find a skill . . . a good skill . . . then I will skate through life like a god." Chucho reached Chapo's shack. Next to it stood Chapo's bright green car like a sentinel against total decay. The oil lamps were lit. Chapo must be sitting down to supper.

Chucho let out a shrill whistle; then, he called out, "Chapo!" The door opened and Chapo came out hurriedly, closing the door behind him. Chucho was not welcomed at Chapo's house. All the neighborhood women considered him a bad influence.

"Hey, Chapo . . . let's fill the car tank with gas . . . and maybe you would like some new tires?"

"You joking?"

"The old woman died today. I got the money."

"May she rest in peace . . . all the money?"

"All the money . . ."

"Ah . . . jaaaaaaaa!" Chapo grabbed Chucho and happily began to wrestle like a bear. They fell to the ground with much laughter and rolled around in happy jest. Finally they lay there looking up at the first stars of evening.

"It's going to be quite a night, eh, Chapo?"

"Hey, let's get going." Chapo jumped to his feet and kicked Chucho, who was still looking at the stars.

"You see something special, you old dog?"

"A bigness . . ."

"Let's go!"

A moment later the old green car was rattling off towards town where city lights spoke of temporary lightning dreams.

"I am waiting for Chucho," Juana's voice was tired. She sat in her neighbor's kitchen. She had waited for Chucho to come back two nights now, waited with the growing stench of death. It did not change the indecisions in her life. She just waited for Chucho until the neighbor found her. It was now two days since the afternoon of life and death. The days had divided themselves in Juana's mind into convulsive terrors, where the chasms with no anchors whirled into a darkness. Memories were a surer stronghold. Then, the neighbor had come to warn her.

"Someone told the authorities about your mother. They're coming today to take her to the crematory if she is not buried right away."

Juana began to cry softly. "I can do nothing until Chucho comes."

"He will not come. He is passed out somewhere. Why wait for the scoundrel?"

"But what can I do? I have no money. No one can help."

"They are going to take her to the crematory today, just wait and see."

"When he feels guilty, he always comes back; he spent all my mother's money, so he will be back."

"Chucho . . . feel guilty? The devil he does!"

"Not guilty . . . it is more of a remorse, after he drinks too much . . . there is always the remorse." Juana remembered well her mother and her husband in the aftermath of drink. The tears for tears' sake, open memories like wet catacombs of sorrows that echoed a burning. Yes, there would be remorse when Chucho came back.

"The crematory will test its new efficiency if your mother is not buried by this afternoon."

"No . . . it is against our religion. My mother's body cannot be burned."

"If there is no money to bury her, she will be burned."

Juana began to weep again. "Mamacita . . . forgive me . . . what did I do to you?" It was a piteous crying of self-accusation. The neighbor stroked the disheveled head of the poor girl in sympathy. Such a soft, helpless thing. That brute of a Chucho should be flogged!

They both heard the car stop at the bottom of the hill. The voices of Chucho and Chapo were heavy with happy memories.

"Oh, Chucho, thank you for the beautiful tires. You are a good friend. Was that a good time or was that a good time?"

There was a short silence as they heard the men go into the house. Suddenly, a long, drawn-out bellow filled the air. Both women ran outside. Chucho was standing at the door looking like a wild man. He shook his head in disbelief and let out another bellow like a wounded animal. He fell to his knees and began to pound the wooden planks of the porch. Chapo stood by helpless and greatly distressed by Chucho's agony.

Chucho moaned, "She's still here. Oh, God . . . the rot! the rot!"

"We'll do something, Chucho." Chapo clumsily reassured, walking nervously around Chucho's kneeling body.

"It's not fair! It's not fair! Life should not rot!" Again he hit his fists against the planked floor.

Juana had run across to him to comfort. He needed her. She went on her knees to take his head in her hands and kiss his forehead as if to stop the suffering. She knew the heights and depths of her husband as she knew the old surface freedoms of his ways. She must tell him right away. "Chucho, the authorities are coming to take her away because there is no money to bury her."

Chucho looked into her face in bewilderment. "I cannot believe the stench . . . but her face, it is the young face of a virgin . . . God forgive me!"

"They will burn her body, Chucho."

He put his arms around her body as if to ask for forgiveness. "I won't let them, Juana."

"You have some money left?" There was a ray of hope in Juana's voice. Chucho shook his head in utter despair, not because of the money, but because he could not imagine the body being burned. It was against God . . . never! never!

He raised himself to his feet and picked up his clinging wife. He turned to Chapo.

"She must not be burned, Chapo."

"What can we do?"

"Get some money somehow."

"Let's take the tires back, Chucho." Juana looked from one to the other, hoping.

Chucho said nothing for he was thinking hard. "The money from the tires will not be enough. We must go to our friends, to our many friends. We can take the body with us, so the authorities will not find it. We can tie it to the trunk of the car." He turned to Juana. "Get some saffron."

The neighbor shook her head in disapproval. Juana stood by helplessly and asked blankly, "Saffron?"

"Yes . . . it will stop the smell. Get as much as you can."

She seemed unable to move. She had no certainties in her experience bank. The neighbor took Juana's arm gently. "Come, I'll go with you." As she led the girl away, she turned to the two men. "You're a couple of fools if you think they are going to let you drive around with a dead body that should have been buried a long time ago."

"They'll have to catch us first . . . go . . . get the stuff."

Half an hour later a mummy-like body was being carried from the house into the trunk of the car. The saffron had been found; sheets had been used to wrap the body carefully. Chucho and Chapo then tied the body to the trunk securely. Juana and the neighbor watched in quiet disbelief. The trunk door remained half-way open when the job was done. It could not be helped. Chapo seemed skeptical.

"You sure it will work, Chucho?"

"Of course I'm not sure, but something has to be done. I'm not going to leave her for the authorities to burn. She was a very brave woman."

"You hated her guts, Chucho."

Chucho did not answer. He got into the car and turned on the ignition. "Get in." Chapo jumped in beside Chucho murmuring, "¡Que Dios nos bendiga!" * As the car started off, Chucho called out of the window, "Don't tell the authorities anything. You know nothing." The car rattled down the road in a cloud of dust.

When the car had disappeared, the neighbor turned to Juana, "Stay with me if you want."

"No . . . thank you. I have many things to do before Chucho comes back. He will come back soon."

The neighbor walked away shaking her head. Juana sat down on the porch steps to watch the dying afternoon glorious in color. All traces of the rain were gone. The land had settled down to wait for the long drought. Gravely, her eyes looked out to the familiar desert, waiting too. She imagined an apricot tree fully in bloom. She never had seen one; she looked out into the glare of the sun and her mind's eye saw the apricot tree. There was no mother now, no weekly ritual of expectation, no stories from her mother so full of the outside world. The apricot tree grew in beauty with the mounting loneliness. What was she to do? Tears came to her eyes. She opened the palm of her hand to catch the tears. They glistened in the reflection on the sun. Colors could be found in slight whispers. She looked for a jewel in the wetness. Soon . . . she lost the world around.

Chapo's face was fiercely red. He shook his fists in the air, "Thieves . . . they would not even give me a part of the price we paid for them. We can twist the tires around their necks . . . we have to take the money."

Chucho shrugged his shoulders. "Never mind . . . that small amount won't help . . . and we need the tires to get around."

"Where you wanna go now?"

"Let's try La Sevilla. The sun has set; our night friends will be there." La Sevilla was the favorite bar among the poor, for the owner Mando would many times forget an old bill. Here Chucho had spent money two nights before. Chucho was right; there were many people as Chucho and Chapo went in. Here were the faces of night friends wiped free of fear, this was the place to grapple with the honest fear and the honest hope. Eyes were the full story, here, past the neon lights. The nuances and puppet strings simply did not belong where eyes spoke truth. How well loneliness speaks; it has no cotton mouth or twisted word; tried lies have no place where men go to seek themselves.

Outside, the red neon cast a fierceness on the exposed dead body in the trunk of the car. On and off . . . on and off; the vigil yet was young, a reversion of destiny where one dead woman waited for the living to find

* May God bless us!

life. Inside, the place was filled with tourists and Mando worked feverishly for a "good" night, wiping clean the altar full with communal warmth. The welcomes, too, were warm for Chucho and Chapo. The current carried them towards the usual rectitude that built, slowing to a common human victory.

"Have a drink, Chucho. This is for you, Chapo."

"Listen, the gypsy is still here, Chucho, the one that found the spirit of the mountain in you the other night. Hey, Gitano, look who just came in."

The gypsy saw Chucho and rushed to him with arms outstretched. "You have come back . . . to share the spirit . . . ah! what a night it was! My music and you, the bull, in the arena."

"Not tonight, Gitano . . . I have a mission."

"We all have a mission . . . there will be tears and joy this night." He began a lament on his guitar that extended itself to find the sad waiting in all who heard. Waiting for what? No one really knew. Chucho gulped his drink and slammed his glass upon the bar. "There is something much sadder than your music . . . it is a sadness of the world. If you only knew!"

Chucho put his head down on the bar feeling the weight of Refugio's death. "I did a terrible thing, muchachos . . . a terrible thing."

"What's the matter with him, Chapo?"

"He did a terrible thing."

Chucho raised his head and wiped his eyes with his sleeve unashamedly. "All that money I spent the other night . . . it was the money to pay for a fine funeral for my mother-in-law. Now the authorities will cremate her if we don't find the money to bury her."

"We need the money for the living, Chucho; the dead don't care about their funeral."

Gitano's wailing song rose to torture in sound. Chucho's voice was earnest: "You don't understand. This was no ordinary woman. She was a beautiful fighter. She spat on misfortune and dug her heels for a fight because life was a grand thing to her. There are a few women like her."

"Is that the mother-in-law that had you thrown in jail so often . . . eh, Chucho . . . here have another drink; you can't think straight."

"The fights . . . it was because we cared as human beings, muchachos. Listen, this is no joke. I will not let the authorities cremate her." Gitano's song began to gather wisps of growing frenzy. It was a happy frenzy that well belonged to the snapping of fingers and the flame tapping of feet.

"Hey, Chucho . . . toro! toro!" The boys began to jostle him. "Dance . . . fight the bull as you did the other night . . . come on, Chucho . . . Olé!"

Chucho was determined to convince them of his plight; Chapo, on the other hand, had been caught up with the music and the mood. Refugio was a far-away thought when someone put another drink in his hand. Chucho screamed "She deserves a burial . . . you understand . . . she deserves it!"

The boys laughed and continued their chant: "Ola . . . toro! Dance for her, Chucho ... she would like for you to dance for her. ... Dance for her ... dance for her. ..."

Chucho looked into their faces in half-denial. "But she is. ..." Suddenly he jumped up on the table next to Gitano. "I dance for her!" He exclaimed to the world. "I dance for Refugio! You understand, I dance for Refugio." The frenzy grew as Chucho dared life and pain and fear with his feet and the furious movements of his body. "She felt life like this!" The dance became hard and unrelenting until both Gitano and Chucho were spent. There was no clapping. Only a silence. The toro now sat as clown upon the table to make things tolerable.

"That was a good thing to do for her, Chucho ... a good thing." Voices rose in agreement. Chucho looked at them like a prince of sadness and confided, "You know what? She liked autumns best because it was a time of realness when the fruits were gathered and the flowers had given of their bloom to all. She used to say dreams were cruel because the waiting sometimes has no end. But autumn ... ah! It gives men heart, the golden things that are ... you think I'm crazy ... eh?"

"You talk as if you loved her ... who loves his mother-in-law?"

"One who remembers long after ... long after the things of heart ... that's who!"

Chucho took another drink from an outstretched hand and gulped it down. Then he took another and another. "Hey, look at Chucho go ... more! more! more!"

Chucho fell back upon the table like one dead; his eyes were closed. Everybody stared in silence. He spoke slowly and deliberately. "We have the body tied to the back of the car. Just go out the door and see for yourselves; she is waiting ... how can I go to her without help ... she is waiting." The crowd mumbled disbelief, but almost all of them hurried out to see. The commotion grew; so did the crowd until Mando went out himself to look. He ran back into the bar and shouted at Chucho, "You crazy fool. You have a dead body outside my place. You know what the authorities will do to me? I'll lose my license. Get her out of here ... do you hear?" Chucho, still lying on the table, sat up and saw his friends too lost in the circus of things. He knew he could ask no more. He spotted Chapo looking anxiously at the crowd. "Hey, Chapo ... let's go!"

Outside the neon lights still claimed the body. Chucho and Chapo got into the car without a word. They drove off with the crowd still looking on. They drove down the street drowned in the neon promises of desires, eerie in their brightness. After a while, Chapo asked, "Where to?"

"Adela's place." Chucho leaned back thinking of the woman in the trunk.

"Chucho, she's stinking terrible. Did you see the dogs sniff and run?"

"Shut up. Let's find some money."

"They were right back there. You talk as if you love her."

"I loved her. That is why I hated her so much. But when she bought wine . . . those were very warm times. She used to tell me about her man. He was shot mysteriously. She never found out who did it; she had to bury him by herself. She lost four children in the epidemic. She survived everything. When we drank too much wine we understood things without saying."

"What did you understand, Chucho?"

"Life . . . and each other."

"That's a lot."

"That way we could hold on tight."

"She used to call you a coward."

"She called me everything. She had a big mouth. She was just jealous of my freedom. She worked hard; she had a right to resent me, I suppose."

"Remember when she cracked your skull?"

"What's the matter with you? You bring up all the bad things. Drive and don't talk." The silence was brief for they soon arrived at Adela's. Her place was a dilapidated two story building that seemed almost deserted except for lamp-light and shadows that escaped through drawn shades. Most of the windows were dark. The place did not wear a sign. In earlier days, Adela had catered to the best clientele. The police commissioner had been her confidant and protector. But all good things had come to an end. Both Adela and the establishment had resigned themselves to second-rate flurries.

Chapo parked the car as Chucho hurried to the door of the establishment. Chapo soon caught up with him. One of the girls opened the door, then silently disappeared. They entered a small foyer dimly lighted and filled with artificial palms weighed down with dust. Beyond was the sitting room. Behind an old, flowered, satin sofa was a beaded curtain, covering the stairway leading to the rooms. As usual, Adela came into the room with her greeting for customers. Chucho and Chapo had been there a few nights ago. They had been most splendid and companionable. They seemed to be sober tonight.

She gave Chucho a hug. "Still sporting?" She then kissed him fondly.

"Not tonight, Adela. We have a mission."

The middle-aged madam took his arm and led him to the sofa. "A mission?"

Chapo followed doggedly behind. Chucho asked right out, "Adela, we need some money."

Instinctively, Adela straightened her back and her tone became business-like. "You came to ask me for money?"

"It is to bury my mother-in-law. It was her money I spent the other night. If I don't raise the money, the authorities will burn her."

"You get your wish then. You were always damning her to hell." She was both amused and cautious.

"You and your girls . . . everybody says you have the biggest hearts."

"No!"

"No," echoed Chapo.

"NO!" repeated the madam. She stood up and looked at them. Then she began to pace the floor up and down as she explained. "You say this is a good cause. Every time an old customer asks for help, they all have good causes. Believe me, we have heard stories of real distress. But, if I am not around, my poor girls are fleeced. They give all . . . foolish, foolish creatures! They cannot afford the luxury of helping everybody who asks. They have next to nothing. Only I stand between them and the world. I sympathize with you. I like you, but they are little sheep . . . little sheep."

"This one exception, Adela."

"If I make one exception, I will have to make many. That is the way. I cannot do it. However, I shall make a small personal contribution." She lifted her skirt and pulled out some money from the fold of her garter. "Here . . . I know it is not much, but I hope it helps." Chucho took the money, graciously accepting her generosity. He thanked her and kissed her before departing. Adela begged him to come back again. Out in the street, Chucho put up the collar of his old, worn coat. The wind was now raw. Chapo followed behind him. They got into the car without saying a word. They drove around a while and then decided to go to Kiko's. There would be winners there tonight. When they came to Kiko's place, they found it in total darkness. Chucho jumped out of the car and went to inquire next door. In a little while he was back.

"The place was raided. Everybody's in jail." They both stared out into the darkness.

"There will be no criers, Chucho. You cannot pay the criers."

"To hell with the criers, those wailing banshees, fakes!" Laughter spilled from opened doorways. Far off in the distance, the howl of a coyote could be heard. They continued staring into the darkness. "The criers are not good enough, Chapo."

"What are we going to do with the body, Chucho. We are going to land in jail."

"We are going to bury her ourselves, Chapo, out there where the coyote cries."

"You are crazy. We are going to dig a grave in this freezing weather? With what shovel?"

"We shall go to the undertaker and borrow a shovel."

"He's asleep."

"We'll borrow it anyway. It's justice since he refused to bury her just because we had no money."

"Now, Chucho?"

"Yes . . . but first we buy a couple of bottles with Adela's money. It will keep us warm."

It was well past midnight when they got to the outskirts of the city. The climb up the hill and the biting wind had been torturous. The weight of the body and the overpowering stench made the bitter wind welcome. The heat of over-exertion mixed in with the smell of rotting flesh would have been intolerable if it had not been for the cold. Nevertheless, their fingers and faces were half-frozen. Chucho climbed the hill first, carrying the greater part of the weight. Chapo held the lower part of the body. Around his waist he had tied a rope that dragged the shovel after him. Twice they stopped to rest, but not for long, for too many stops meant wasted effort.

When they finally reached the top, they did not know how much time had passed, but the lights of the city still blinked back in reassurance. Distant and much smaller, they had lost their glaring vulgarity. They were now clear lights in sympathy with the night. The men began to feel the cold.

"Let us build a fire, Chapo."

They began to gather sagebrush and dead pieces of wood. It was hard to start the fire without protection from the wind. In time, they managed to start one behind a huge boulder that broke the wind. Soon it was blazing bright.

"I think I am freezing to death, Chucho."

Chucho began to scan the area for the proper burial ground. He finally pointed to a high spot next to a dead clump of trees. The spot was close to the edge of the hill with a full view of the town . . . her town, thought Chucho. He walked over to the spot and dug his foot on the soft earth. "We'll dig the grave here." They took turns with the shovel. Every so often, Chucho would take out a bottle and drink, then he would hand it to Chapo, who did the same. In the midst of the warm glow, they looked down into the town that spoke of lifetimes. Then, one would resume the digging while the other scooped the earth out of the shallow grave. They had laid the body next to the boulder where they had built the fire. It was hardly discernible from where they were digging. Finally, the grave was ready. Chucho went back to where Refugio's body lay. "Come, help me carry it to the grave. Careful! Be gentle!" Chapo did as he was told. When they reached the grave Chucho laid it down close to the edge of the grave almost reverently. "Now we wait."

"Wait?"

"For the sunrise. I want her to see it one more time." Chapo did not answer. He took out the bottle in his pocket and offered it to Chucho. They drank in silence. Chucho asked Chapo for his knife.

"What are you going to do, Chucho?" It was something crazy; Chapo was sure. Chucho took the knife that Chapo offered him and sat down on the ground next to the body. He picked up its head and held it on his lap. Then, he carefully cut into the cloth that covered the face of the dead woman. He stopped when the face was fully exposed. "There, she will be able to see."

They watched the lights from the town gradually disappear as they waited for the sunrise. The fire, too, was dying. Chapo decided to look for more firewood. Chucho sat watching with the head of the dead woman still on his lap. From time to time, he would look down at the face as if trying to understand something on the other side of life . . . past death.

"Do you suppose, Chucho, that where she is now there are city lights?" Chapo was now warming himself in the replenished fire. The town was now in almost total darkness. The friends of night had given up the quest.

The first light rose in the East. It took the darkness gently like a lover. The city did not have long to sleep. The mingling of lives with chance would have another day to try. Chucho was holding the head of the dead woman high as they faced the East. "Look at the sunrise, Refugio. It is like the sunrise already in your face. Chapo, look . . . what beautiful peace, look! All the strength of life is in her face. Are all faces beautiful in death?"

Chapo left the fire and looked at the face. "She was a fine looking woman." Chucho felt the stiff, dead weight in his arms. As he watched the coming of the morning, tears filled his eyes. "Refugio, I didn't give you fancy criers. I, the poor fool, found my own way. I hope it is good enough. You deserved a grand funeral."

"She cannot hear you, Chucho."

"But I am listening now, Chapo, to all the sounds she left, good and bad. You are clear to me now, Refugio." He bent his head and kissed her fully on the lips.

"I love you, Refugio, for having lived." With care, he laid the body down on the ground. Then he jumped into the shallow grave. He took off his coat and made a pillow for Refugio's head.

"That is your only coat, Chucho."

"Here, help me lower the body." With great effort they lowered it until Refugio's head rested on Chucho's coat. Chucho scuttled out of the grave. Both men, dirty, tired, and half-frozen, looked down at the body, and suddenly became very conscious of death. The silence of the two men expected something more than finality. There was the morning and the sunrise unexplained, like the life of days; then, there was the still, white form deep in the earth. Both spoke of something more . . . but what?

Chucho found his way out of the mystery. The grave had to be covered. Then there were the coyotes.

"Let's fill the grave . . . then, we must find the rocks to cover it." They took different paths to find the rocks. Each one would come back with some and he would put them beside the grave. It was a long, tedious job, but the rocks were gathered. The sun was high when they finally filled the grave and then sat down to fit the rocks into the mound.

In the atmosphere that diffuses light, there is celestial song of currents and a higher mathematics. There is the push and flux of life that finds its way to man. Man tastes it as a freedom, a way of depths, a way of new life. If the skill lies in the freedom, thought Chucho, then it belongs to death as well as life. The sunrise became part of the "not enough." Refugio has sufficed. Clowns must be because the world sometimes does not see. The task was done; the moment of somber thought passed. They were filled with a great relief and a great joy. They began to laugh. Then, they clapped each other on the back. There was an intensity in their horseplay; there was a realness in their jest. Chucho took out his bottle and peered into it. "Look . . . there is still some left." He took two gulps and handed the bottle to Chapo. A thought came to Chucho, "A plain cross with two good pieces of wood and her name on it. It would please her."

They found the wood. They sat down near the grave again to make a cross, sharing the rest of the drink.

POETRY

LORNA DEE CERVANTES

Born in 1954 in San Francisco, Lorna Dee Cervantes currently lives in San Jose, where she is editor, publisher, and printer of *Mango Publications*. Her poetry has appeared in *Revista Chicano-Riqueña, Tin-Tan, Samisdat,* and *Latin American Review*. In 1978 she received a Creative Writing Fellowship from the National Endowment for the Arts. She says, "I feel a deep sense of commitment and dedication toward my work as a poet. I choose poetry as a way of life."

BENEATH THE SHADOW OF THE FREEWAY

I

Across the street—the freeway,
blind worm, wrapping the valley up
from Los Altos to Sal Si Puedes.
I watched it from my porch
unwinding. Every day at dusk
as Grandma watered geraniums
the shadow of the freeway lengthened.

II

We were a woman family:
Grandma, our innocent Queen;
Mama, the Swift Knight, Fearless Warrior.
Mama wanted to be Princess instead.
I know that. Even now she dreams of taffeta
and foot-high tiaras.

Myself—I could never decide.
So I turned to books, those staunch, upright men.
I became Scribe, Translator of Foreign Mail,
interpreting letters from the government, notices

of dissolved marriages and welfare stipulations.
I paid the bills, did light man-work, fixed faucets,
insured everything
against all leaks.

III

Before rain I notice seagulls.
They walk in flocks,
cautious across lawns:
splayed toes, indecisive beaks.
Grandma says seagulls mean a storm.

In California in the summer
mockingbirds sing all night.
Grandma says they are singing for their mates
who are nesting.

> "Mockingbirds sing for their wives,
>   don't leave their families
>   'borrachando.' " *

She likes the ways of birds,
respects how they show themselves
in exchange for toast and a whistle.

She believes in myths and birds
and trusts only what she has built
with her own hands.

IV

The fireplace in the backyard,
cocky, disheveled masonry,
she built it out of old bricks.
Before that she lived for twenty-five years
with a man who tried to kill her.

Grandma from the hills of Santa Barbara,
I would open my eyes to see her stir mush
in the morning, hair in loose braids,
tucked close around her head
with a yellow scarf.

* Becoming intoxicated.

Mama said, "It's her own fault,
getting screwed by a man for that long.
Sure as shit wasn't hard."
soft she was
soft . . .

v

in the night I would hear it
glass bottles shattering on the street
words cracking into shrill screams
inside my throat a cold fear
as it entered the house in hard
unsteady steps stopping at my door
my name   bathrobe   slippers
outside a 3am mist heavy
as a breath full of whiskey
stop it   go home   come inside
mama if he comes here again
I'll call the police

inside
a grey kitten   a touchstone
purring beneath grandma's
hand-sewn quilts   the singing
of mockingbirds

v i

"You're too soft . . . always were.
You'll get nothing but shit.
Baby, don't count on nobody . . ."

—a mother's wisdom.
The lines on her face are beginning to show.
The bitter years are all so visible now
as she spends her hours
washing down the bile.
Soft. I haven't changed, grown
more silent somehow, cynical
on the outside.

"O Mama, with what's inside of me
I could wash that all away . . . I could."

"But Mama, if you're good to them
they'll be good to you back . . ."

Back. The freeway is across the street.
It's summer now. Every night I sleep with a gentle man
to the hymn of mockingbirds,

and in time, I will plant geraniums.
I will tie up my hair into loose braids,
and trust only
what I have built
with my own hands.

REFUGEE SHIP

like wet cornstarch
I slide past *mi abuelita's** eyes
bible placed by her side
she removes her glasses
the pudding thickens

mamá raised me with no language
I am an orphan to my spanish name
the words are foreign, stumbling on my tongue
I stare at my reflection in the mirror
brown skin, black hair

I feel I am a captive
aboard the refugee ship
a ship that will never dock
a ship that will never dock

PARA UN REVOLUCIONARIO†

You speak of art
and your soul is like snow,

* My grandmother's.
† For a Revolutionary.

LORNA DEE CERVANTES
381

a soft powder raining from your
mouth,
covering my breasts and hair.
You speak of your love of mountains,
freedom,
and your love for a sun
whose warmth is like *una liberación**
pouring down upon brown bodies.
Your books are of the souls of men,
carnales† with a spirit
that no army, pig or *ciudad* ‡
could ever conquer.
You speak of a new way,
a new life.

When you speak like this
I could listen forever.

Pero your voice is lost to me, *carnal,***
in the wail of *tus hijos,*††
in the clatter of dishes
and the pucker of beans upon the stove.
Your conversations come to me
de la sala‡‡ where you sit,
spreading your dream to brothers,
where you spread that dream like damp clover
for them to trod upon,
when I stand here reaching
para ti con manos bronces*** that spring
from *mi espíritu*†††
(for I to am Raza).

Pero,‡‡‡ it seems I can only touch you
with my body.
You lie with me
and my body *es la hamaca**
that spans the void between us.

* A liberation.
† Bodies.
‡ City.
** But . . . brother.
†† Your children.
‡‡ From the room.
*** For you with brown hands.
††† My soul.
‡‡‡ But.
* Is the hammock.

Hermano Raza,*
I am afraid that you will lie with me
and awaken too late
to find that you have fallen
and my hands will be left groping
for you and your dream
in the midst of *la revolución.*†

    * Blood brother.
    † The revolution.

XELINA

Born in San Antonio in 1954, Xelina currently lives in La Jolla, California, where she is chief editor of *Maize,* a literary journal. Her poems have been published in *Caracol* and *Trece Aliens.*

URBAN LIFE

city blues pay tribute to:
   massage parlors
   sauna rooms
   peep shows
   and
   cheap thrills
   lesbians
   homosexuals
   hustlers
   playgirls
   and
   playboys
   pseudo-marxists
   nazis
   hare krishnas
   drug centers
   A.A. centers
   and
   H.E.L.P. centers:
   all avant garde
pimping fringe benefits

WITNESSES

abode pueblos
woven of white sun tierra
painted skies
whispering new moon spells
ancestral sons
upon nipples of mountains
suckle
witnesses of the flowering tree

NIGHTMARE

bailando por pesetas*
sylvia earns to quench
her beer stenched bloated belly
closed eyes
to what moves outside
society's swinging doors
spinning head
chancleando†
conjunto‡ music
thumping along
with her high blood pressure
"hey, sylvia,
ese viejo es el de anoche,
no te dejes!" **

* Dancing for quarters.
† Joking.
‡ At one with the music.
** That old man is the one from last night.
   Don't let him use you!

ANA CASTILLO

Ana Castillo was born in Chicago, where she currently lives and works full time on her writing. Her poems have been published in a variety of bilingual literary magazines, including *Revista Chicano-Riqueña* and *Maize*. Her books of poetry include *Otro Canto* (1978) and *A Melody for Dancing When Legs Intertwine* (1979), a collection of erotica.

NAPA, CALIFORNIA

Dedicado al Sr. Chávez, Sept. 1975

We pick
     the bittersweet grapes
     at harvest
     one
       by
         one
     with leather worn hands
As they pick
     at our dignity
     and wipe our pride
     away
     like the sweat we wipe
     from our sun beaten brows
     at mid day
In fields
     so vast
     that our youth seems
     to pass before us
     and we have grown
     very
       very
         old
           by dark . . .

(bueno pues ¿qué vamos hacer, Ambrosio?
bueno pues, ¡seguirle, compadre, seguirle!
¡Ay, Mamá!
Sí pues ¿qué vamos hacer, compadre?
¡Seguirle, Ambrosio, seguirle!) *

We pick
     with a desire
     that only survival
     inspires
While the end
     of each day only brings
     a tired night
     that waits for the sun
     and the land
     that in turn waits
     for us . . .

1975

talking proletariat talks
over instant coffee
and nicotine.
in better times
there is tea
to ease the mind.
talking proletariat talks
during laid-off hours
cussing and cussing
complaining of unpaid bills
and bigoted unions
that refuse to let us in.
talking proletariat talks
of pregnant wives
and shoeless kids.
no-turkey-thanksgivings.
bare x-mas tree this year.
santa claus is on strike

   * Well, what are we going to do, Ambrosio?
    Well, follow him, old friend, follow him!
    Oh, boy!
    Yes, but what are we going to do, my friend?
    Follow him, Ambrosio, follow him!

again.
talking proletariat talks
with proletariat friends
and relations who need
a few bucks til the end
of the week
waiting
for compensation checks.
talking proletariat talks
of plants closing down
and deportations.
tight immigration
busting our brothers again.
talking proletariat talks
of next spring or some
unforeseen vacation
to leave all this behind
to forget the winter
in unheated flats
turned off gas and
'ma bell' who serves
the people
took the phone away
when we were out
looking for a gig.
talking proletariat talks
of next presidential elections
the emperor of chicago
who lives off the fat of the land
and only feeds his sty of pigs.
talking proletariat talks
over rum and schlitz
of lottery tickets
on bingo nights at St. Sebastian's.
talking proletariat talks
climbing crime, defenseless
women, unsafe parks, and
congested highways.
talking proletariat talks
of higher rent two months
behind, landlords who live
on lake shore drive or over
where the grass *is* greener.
talking proletariat talks

talking proletariat talks
talking proletariat talks
until one long
awaited day—
we are tired
of talking.

A CHRISTMAS CAROL: c. 1976

Today i went downtown and signed away
another dream. i watched the other women
frown, the other women scream
with bitter sadness sign away their dreams;
as they became statistics for the
legal aid divorce division, new numbers
for the welfare line, eligible recipients
for social security benefits . . .
as they signed away.

Today i sat among them, with the
stoned face dignity necessary for one
who wears a borrowed coat for the winter cold;
and counts her change for the clark st. bus
while x-mas shoppers push and shove.
among paperback readers/ public sleepers:
i tuck away my dream into some distant past/
i tuck away a love that couldn't last,
but has. i stare at the appointment cards:
the court date/ the job i hope to have.
but the only hope left is that winter won't last
forever/ that winter won't last . . .
after all, nothing ever does:

A little girl held her mother's hand
with wide eyed fascination watched
the holiday decorations on state street/
the parade went by/ santa claus with a crooked
cotton beard would wave/ and mamá'd say:
"¿Ya vez? Portate bien y haber que te trae." *
and i wondered how santa claus would arrive
at a second floor flat in the back where even

* You see? Be good and let's see what he brings you.

those who lived on the block wouldn't go out
at night. but mamá went out each morning at
5 a.m. and on christmas day, a doll with pink
ribbons in its yellow hair and smelling of new
plastic, would always be there. 'cause after
all, i had been a good girl/ i had always been good.

Today i went downtown and walked
among the hurrying crowd, but no one
held my hand this time/ no one smiled/
no one wished a merry x-mas to anyone.
but i thought how nice it would be to buy
her something special this year/ to send him
a greeting card/ and how much nicer it would
be, to be a little girl again:

when dreams get tucked away in future spaces
instead. and my signature got nothing more
than a star in penmanship to take home and
paste proudly on a paint chipped wall:
"¿Ya vez bien? ¡Haber que te trae Santa Claus,
haber que te trae!" * and that would be all.

OUR TONGUE WAS NAHUATL

You.
We have never met
yet
we know each other
well.
I recognized
your high
            set
                  cheekbones,
slightly rounded
                  nose,
the deep brownness
of your hardened face—
soft full lips.

Your near-slanted eyes
follow me—

* See how good you are. Let's see what Santa Claus brings you. Let's see what
comes.

sending flashback memories
to your so-called
primitive mind.
And I know
you remember . . .

It was a time
of turquoise blue-greenness,
sky-topped mountains,
god-suns/
wind-swept rains;
oceanic deities
naked children running
in the humid air.

I ground corn
upon a slab of stone,
while you bargained
at the market
dried skins
and other things
that were our own.

I would watch
our small sons
chase behind your bare legs
when you came home those days.
We would sit—
              eat;
Give thanks to our
                rich golden
                      Earth.
Our tongue was Nahuatl.

We were content—
With the generosity
of our gods
           and our kins;
knowing nothing
         of a world
across the bitter waters—
Until they came . . .

White foreign strangers
riding high
           on four-legged
               creatures;

that made us bow to them.
In our ignorance to the
                              unknown
they made us bow.

They made us bow—
until our skin became
the color of caramel
and nothing anymore
was our own.

Raped of ourselves—
Our civilization—
Even our gods turned away
from us in shame . . .

Yet we bowed,
                    as we do now—
On buses
          going to factories
where "No-Help Wanted" signs
laugh at our faces,
stare at our hungry eyes.

Yet we bow . . .
                    WE BOW!

But I remember you
                    still—
It was a time
much different
                    than now . . .

ANGELA DE HOYOS

Born in Mexico, Angela de Hoyos currently lives in San Antonio, where she works as coeditor of M&A Editions and as a proofreader for *Caracol Journal.* Her books of poetry include *Selecciones* (1976), poems in Spanish translation; *Arise Chicano & Other Poems* (1976), bilingual poems; and *Chicano Poems: For the Barrio* (1977). Her works have also appeared in *Caracol, Tejidos, Fuego de Aztlan,* and *Revista Chicano-Riqueña,* among other places. As a writer, she says, "I consider myself a 'peoples' poet, not only because most of my work falls in the socially conscious and/or protest category, but because I employ a simple, uncluttered and natural language, certainly appropriate to my themes and easily understood by all."

THE FINAL LAUGH

On an empty stomach,
with the pang of mendicant yesterdays,
I greet my reflection
in the dark mirror of dusk.

What do the entrails know
about the necessity of being white
—the advisability of mail-order parents?

Or this wearing in mock defiance
the thin rag of ethnic pride,
saying to shivering flesh and grumbling belly:
Patience, O companions of my dignity?

Perhaps someday I shall accustom myself
to this: my hand held out
in eternal supplication, being content
with the left-overs of a greedy establishment.

Or—who knows?—perhaps tomorrow
I shall burst these shackles
and rising to my natural full height
fling the final parting laugh
O gluttonous omnipotent alien white world.

BELOW ZERO

No se puede traducir
el aullido del viento:*
     you can only feel it
     piercing your skinny bones
     through last year's coat
       papel-de-China

walking to work
from deep in the barrio
una mañana de tantas.
     bajo cero.†

THE MISSING INGREDIENT

Geared to the sterility
of machine-made symbols,
out of his element he was
—victim of a daily trauma.

Become maladroit
at calling his own cards
robot-like, he was seeking

(lost in a ticker-tape mountain
of mundane ideas:
       love-thine-enemy policies
       hypocritical handshakes
       social-science amenities
       and e pluribus unum)

a formula infallible
for painless living.

When before him there appeared
the guardian-ghost of alchemy
who—surveying the situation—
transmuted life's baser metals,
extracting the gold of Wisdom
from the heap.

  * The fierce howling of the wind cannot be translated.
  † One of so many mornings when it's below zero.

JUDY LUCERO

The following statement is taken from *De Colores:* "Judy was twenty-eight when she died. Her life had not been a void. She was introduced to drugs when she was eleven by one of her stepfathers. She lost two children as a result of beatings, she was an ex-con and a 'tecata' [heroine addict]. At the end, she was on methadone and was known as a soft touch who went into debt to lend her friends money. . . . She signed all her work with her prison identification number."

JAIL-LIFE WALK

Walk in the day . . . Walk in the night
Count off the time . . . One to Ten
Then you'll be free. . . . Free again

Walk without pain . . . Walk without care . .

Walk til you see. . . . See the sign
Look at the sign. . . . Walk in Line!

Then walk in hate
Walk without the world
Walk in fear . . .
See the anger
In their eye
just walking by . . .

The only thing free
is your mind
Free to count
As U walk in Line

21918

I SPEAK IN AN ILLUSION

I speak but only in an illusion
For I see and I don't

It's me and it's not
I hear and I don't

These illusions belong to me—
I stole them from another

Care to spend a day in my House of Death?
Look at my garden . . . are U amazed?
No trees, no flowers, no grass . . . no gardens . . .

I love and I don't
I hate and I don't
I sing and I don't
I live and I don't

For I'm in a room of clouded smoke
And a perfumed odor

Nowhere can I go and break these bonds
Which have me in an illusion

But the bonds are real

21918

VICTORIA MORENO

Born in Texas in 1957, Victoria Moreno is a faith healer. She comments, "I am a visionary. I live between the centuries—most frequently in the fifteenth. In former lives I was a seamstress, a *curandera,* a murderer, a tavern dancer, a maid, and a sculptor. I have fourteen children. My writing is full of these people. They cry out from within me. I am all of them and they are me. Each one adds the strength of their experiences. My poetry seeks to dance—my legs are paralyzed. I would like my writing to create, to sing, and especially, to dance."

en público*

Making love with fingertips and eyelashes
           across a crowded room.
       Waves over my honeymilk
          of red ebony
       You cut stone figurines out of mountains
          and carve my soul
               with your eyes.
       I wrap your crystal-voiced silence
          in my breath.

The world plays chess
     at the Olympics
   while we whisper a scrawled note
     under two conversation circles
          facing different directions.

* In public.

MARGARITA COTA-CÁRDENAS

Born in California in 1941, Margarita Cota-Cárdenas currently lives in Tucson, where she is an editor at Scorpion Press. In 1976 she published her first book of poetry, *Noches Despertando Inconciencias*. Her poems have also appeared in *Revista Chicano-Riqueña, Caracol, Hojas Poeticas,* and *Noticiero Chicano,* among other places. She describes her poetry as "laced with irony and humor" and says, "I strive for a minimum of powerful, connotative words to convey the maximum effect."

SPELLING OUT THE COSMOS

letters of the alphabet
     we are
sisters   we
      germinate man
      conjugate his all
before there was
     a bull
      a stone
       a myth
     and n
        o
         t
          h
           i
            n
             g

DELETREANDO AL COSMOS

letras del alfabeto
    somos
hermanas   nosotras
   al hombre
       le germinamos
         le conjuntamos su todo
   antes
     un toro
       una piedra
          un mito
   y un n
     a
       d
        a

GULLIBLE

how patiently
    how lonely
      you weave your tapestries
   Penelope
he's over there Circeing himself
   taking his sweet time
   you're working so prettily
   a symbol now of patience
     slowly   slowly   slowly
   for so many years   a lovely example
    weaving   unweaving
    frustrated years
      or
he satisfied you through egotistical telepathy
      or
    you had a lover

CREIDISIMAS

qué paciente
        qué insólita
                tejes tus paisajes
      Penélope
él allá circeándose
        tomándose la buena gana
      tú trabajando tan bonito
      símbolo ahora de la paciencia
          despacito   despacito   despacito
   por tantos años   muy lindo ejemplo
       haciendo   deshaciendo
         años frustrados
             o
te saciaba por egoística telepatía
             o
      tú tenías   amante

MARCELA CHRISTINE LUCERO-TRUJILLO

Born in Colorado, Marcela Christine Lucero-Trujillo currently lives in Minnesota, where she is an instructor in Chicano studies at the University of Minnesota. Her poetry has appeared in *Time to Greez* (1975), *La Razon Mestiza* (1975), and *La Luz*. She includes the following poem to explain her position as a writer:

> My epitaph in poetry should read thusly...
> Lit major learned in "isms"
>   symbols and imagery,
> but if she ain't communicated
> with the barrio educated,
>   then this one here, ain't she.

"MACHISMO* IS PART OF OUR CULTURE"
For Jesse

Hey Chicano bossman
don't tell me that
machismo is part of our culture
if you sleep
and marry W.A.S.P.
>   You constantly remind me,
>   me, your Chicana employee
that machi-machi-machismo
is part of our culture.
>   I'm conditioned, you say,
to bearing machismo
which you only learned
day before yesterday.
>   At home you're no patron,†
>   your liberated gabacha‡
>   has gotcha where
>   she wants ya,
>   y a mi me ves cara**
>   de steppin' stone.

* Exaggerated masculinity.
† Boss.
‡ Anglo woman.
** To you, I must look like a steppin' stone.

Your culture emanates
      from Raza posters on your walls
      from bulletin boards in the halls
      and from the batos* who hang out at the barrio bar.
Chicanismo through osmosis
acquired in good doses
remind you
to remind me
that machi-machi-machismo
is part of our culture.

NO MORE COOKIES, PLEASE

WASP liberationist
you invited me
token minority
but your abortion idealogy
failed to integrate me.
Over cookies and tea,
you sidled up to me
and said,
"Sisterhood is powerful"
I said
"Bullshit and allmotherful"
The right to choose, you say,
Then, can you choose,
Can you guarantee,
the Chicana in Aztlan will see
all of her children
survive malnutrition
to arrive into adulthood?
Genocide culture
of uterine cords
and Rockefeller propaganda—
"It is cheaper to kill a guerrilla in the womb
than in the mountains."
Yet, what of our bachelors
and spinsters, never married
never bore children

    * Dudes.

zero population, i.e. none
yet they stagnate in poverty
in the barrios of Aztlan.
I didn't hear you say
"more brown babies now"
so the minority
can be the majority.

"No more cookies, please."
We bequeath our brown babies
heirlooms of future generations
to remind you
that an "ism" by any other name
is still racism.

"No more cookies, please."
You differentiate between the two,
but can you really separate
your sex from your color
No? Then see, it won't do.
And, by the way
have you offered the campesina*
a piece of the American pie?
Did I hear you say?—
"She can be the baker
in this 'land of opportunity.' "
See?—Only the rich are free—
free to dictate the right
of their to be
and our not to be
in this, quote, land of liberty.
See?

"No more cookies, please."

ROSEVILLE, MINN., U.S.A.

In Roseville, one notices
      a speck on a white wall
      a moustache on a brown face
and listens to right wing dilemmas
      of another race.

   * Peasant.

MARCELA CHRISTINE LUCERO-TRUJILLO

403

Turn that corrido* record down,
    walk softly in ponchos,
Speak Spanish in whispers
    or they'll approach you to say,
    "I've been to Spain too, ¡Ole!"
    (even if you never have),
In Roseville, U.S.A.

Start the stove fan,
    close the windows on a summer day,
    'cause the neighbors might say,
    "Do they eat beans everyday, even on Sundays?"
In Roseville, U.S.A.

At the sign of the first snowflake
    Inquiring eyes will pursue you,
    asking why you haven't returned with the migrant stream
    that went back in June, or even in September,
In Roseville, U.S.A.

My abuela† would turn in her grave
    to think that the culmination
    of her cultural perpetuation
    is Marcela at Target's food section
    searching desperately for flour tortillas,
No way—I live in ROSEVILLE, U.S.A.
My modus vivendi
of New Mexico piñon and green chili
and my Colorado Southwest mentality
are another reality
in ROSEVILLE, U.S.A.

THE MUSICOS FROM CAPULÍN

MANY SUMMER MOUNTAIN NIGHTS AGO.
    LOS VIEJITOS‡ WITH SQUEAKY VIOLINS,
CAME TO THE VALLEY FOR WEDDING DANCES,
    THOSE WERE THE MUSICOS ** FROM CAPULÍN.

* Border folksong.
† Grandmother.
‡ The little old men.
** Musicians.

THEY PLAYED AND COMPOSED ORIGINAL VERSES
    TO ALL LA RAZA* PRESENT.
THEY TRACED THE LINEAGE OF FAMILY TREES
    AND TIED OUR BLOOD TO GREAT DESCENDANTS.
THE RAZA TAPPED THEIR FEET
          TO THE REPETITIOUS BEAT
AND THE GENERATIONS PRESENT,
            GRATEFULLY THREW MONEY AT THEIR FEET.
THEIR "VERSOS"† WERE CUSTOMS OF ANOTHER AGE,
LEARNED BY ORAL TRADITION, OR SO THEY SAY.
    A MOUNTAIN SOUL IN VIOLIN STRINGS,
    SYNCHRONIZED TO A MOUNTAIN SPRING.

THEY'RE GONE NOW, THESE OLD MEN,
AND YOU CAN'T FIND OTHERS LIKE THEM IN CAPULÍN,
OR MONTE VISTA OR EVEN SAN LUIS,
    IT PASSED INTO OBLIVION,
    THIS CULTURAL RITE
    OF ANOTHER AGE
    MANY MOUNTAIN NIGHTS.

THE ADVENT OF MY DEATH

The Curandera‡ arrived too late
One Santa Fe Day in 1848.
That winter day of my obituary,
my parched lips asking for some tea
of the heart flower, the yoloxochitl,
to cure and heal my heart condition,
aggravated by the Anglo Occupation
and the advent of
The American Cancer Society.
          Black shawled prayers,
          beads in bony hands,
          Sighed "Dios Mío" between "Ave,"
          or "Sea por Dios" or "¿Quién sabe?" **

* The people of one heritage.
† Verses.
‡ Medicine woman.
** My God . . . Ay . . . It's God's will . . . Who knows?

The Curandera knew the cure
of my broken heart, spirit and soul,
but she arrived too late,
That Santa Fe Day in 1848.

I was born in the Valley in 1933
And all the vecinas* came to see
La niña bonita—iqué blanquita!—
Parece americana;—parece gringuita—†

And my heart/soul murmured once more
for the yoloxochitl flower,
and the Curandera who never came
That Santa Fe Day back in 1848.

* Neighbors.
† The pretty little girl—how white she is! She looks like an American;—like a little white girl.

MARINA RIVERA

Born in 1942 in Arizona, Marina Rivera teaches high school in Tucson. Her two chapbooks of poetry, *Sobra* and *Mestiza,* were published in 1977. Other poetry has appeared in *The Face of Poetry* (1976) and *Southwest: A Contemporary Anthology* (1977). She comments, "I am a binge writer, writing a great deal between dry spells. Full-time teaching in the public schools drains off a certain kind of energy needed for good poetry. But I try to write what I can. I give all my profits from poetry to a group which gives scholarships to talented Chicano youth who otherwise would not have funds to continue in school."

STATION

He is leaving
the front end
of the calendar,
green moss in his mouth.
He is cold!
She is leaving the back
end of the calendar
for the station,
hot coals in her eyes.
Dead leaves, dreams of
dead leaves in fitful
sleeps all the way.
He sees her through
the sweating window!
Which branch has pinned him?
Why are the aisles slick
with melting snow?
Somewhere in Phoenix
their metaphors cross,
no room among the numerals
for hot moss or coal crystals.
Every window she opened
he would close.

Every switch she touched
he changed back.
Alone in Flagstaff
her heart a warm ruby
in an ice-cough chest,
tight hot room there snow.

EVEN

You look for her
someone you could crack
down the noseline
between the breasts
and lower see
brown organs, brown blood
brown bone even

these words you want
are a game and those of us
who have learned the game
have triangular hearts
which spin, gyrate
toward white, toward brown
toward ourselves most often

our way; to gather
edges like dry wood
make a bed, a bridge
lie on it

our lives are mouths
no matter how
the jaw placed
the teeth don't seal
they buckle here
we point them out
so when you point
at our lives
you get it straight.

Running through the house, out the gate
you chased me, tortilla in hand, you a
long-legged wolf, me the moppet but fleet.
How would you have done it, Uncle?
How open my mouth of sharp, strong teeth
how stuff it down, since my nails were long
and my soles could have struck you in a fine spot.

We'd feast on ice cream but you'd wait longer,
knew how to sit, pretending to grey, to wizen
with the sun's setting that you might frighten
me with stories till the long, low dragging began.
The Indians going home, street dusty, pot-holed,
darkening, figures morose, hunchbacked
in the wagons. You saying how they'd come
for me soon, stuff me in their gunny sacks,
the roar of the wagons growing. I could not
see the mules' ribs but sensed them,
the wagons dragging, not rolling.
Later you would marry, have children,
come to axe our two pet ducks that you
might feast, careful to persuade in my absence,
cautious to gobble yours at home, the ducks
I loved to feed, hear, watch bathe
glistening at us in segments no one ate,
parts too unlike friends to bury.

Returning the tent, you hid the gash.
I can see you shivering,
determined to chop wood in the tent at night,
your strokes fiercer till you brought in
darkness through the wet smile in the canvas.

It was always your flaw:
That you would warm yourself through force.
And always the darkness falling on your head.
Immensely tired, going grey, the nose longer,
face thinner—I know I ought to forgive you.
The hatred of the small, brown child
is the hardest kind to change, Chon.

CARMEN TAFOLLA

Carmen Tafolla was born in San Antonio in 1951. At present, she lives in Austin and is a doctoral student in bilingual education and the coordinator of Multimedia Parent Training Packages for the Southwest Educational Development Laboratory. Her poetry has appeared in *Get Your Tortillas Together* (1976) and *El Quetzal Emplumece* (1977). Of her writing, she says, "My poetry is portrait and voice. It is folk narrative and the voices within it are reflections of my barrio. I like to melt the lines between categories and voyage from poetry to drama to folk legend."

BAILAR...*

The cominot† morning sits down on the dawn
and breaks its desayuno con su taza de café.‡
Y yo,** trapped between night and day,
Struggling to breathe my eyes open
Into a mind heating up with the sunlight
Mientras baila mi alma en cool sueños descansos de tí.††

El mundo tiembla y renace por sus ojos,‡‡
Child and mother and father and seed, y luz.***
Y tú, tan lejos que resfrías la casa,
Tan cerquita que te toco adentro de mis dedos.
En vuelos de música nocturna, juntos, locos, libres,
Bailo, abrasándote adentro de la almohada.†††

* To dance.
† Cumin seed.
‡ Breakfast with its cup of coffee.
** And I.
†† While my soul dances in cool dreams, relaxations of you.
‡‡ The world trembles and is reborn through its eyes.
*** And light.
††† And you, so distant that you chill the house, ·
   So near that I touch you inside my fingers.
   In flights of night music, together, crazy, free,
   I dance, embracing you inside my pillow.

The sunshine peeks under the leaves of my eyes
Y se hincha‡‡‡ into armor, as I wrestle with a heavyweight daylight.
Gana. ¡Que pesado estar aquí sola sin tí! ****
Dogs singing at the moon now squint and curl to sleep,
I stagger out of bed, caddycorner to the floor.
The comino morning sighs, gets up, and goes to work.

...REPEATING CHORUS...

melting out my emerald spring
I stretch a lazy butterfly-bloom
that sails gradual turns with the air
soaking Midmorning's again.
Curling into suncorners,
spilling onto peace,
I dance my fingers through crisp-toasted tunes,
knowing they smile easy like old friends.
As I leave and breathe,
greening full new veins,
my branches stretch to start again.
love is reborn with the sun.
love is reborn with the sun.

ALLÍ POR LA CALLE SAN LUÍS*

West Side—corn tortillas for a penny each
    Made by an aged woman
       and her mother.
       Cooked on the homeblack of a flat stove,
       Flipped to slap the birth awake.
       Wrapped by corn hands.
Toasted morning light and dancing history—
       earth gives birth to corn gives birth to man
       gives birth to earth.
Corn tortillas—penny each.
    No tax.

‡‡‡ And it swells.
**** How sickening it is to be here alone, without you!
* Over there on San Luis Street.

SAN ANTONIO

San Antonio,
    They called you lazy.
They saw your silent, subtle, screaming eyes,
    And called you lazy.
They saw your lean bronzed workmaid's arms,
    And called you lazy.
They saw your centuries-secret sweet-night song,
    And called you lazy.

San Antonio,
    They saw your skybirth and sunaltar,
    Your corn-dirt soul and mute bell-toll,
    Your river-ripple heart, soft with life,
    Your ancient shawl of sigh on strife,
        And didn't see.
San Antonio,
    They called you lazy.

INÉS HERNANDEZ TOVAR

Born in Texas in 1947, Inés Tovar is an assistant professor of English and Chicano studies at the University of Texas in Austin. She has published *Con Razon, Corazon: Poetry* (1977) and is editor of *Hembra*, a publication of the Center for Mexican American Studies at UT Austin. She says, "Because I accept no limitations or rules regarding poetry, I am able to experiment with language, dialects, sounds, rhythm to an extent that I cannot in formal writing. I believe my poetry mirrors an awareness of myself as an individual and as a member of a collective voice (of which the Chicano-Chicana voice is only a part) which is seeking a more humanistic society."

PARA UN VIEJITO DESCONOCIDO
QUE AUN CONOZCO*

Old man walking into Mi Tierra,†
Famous Chicano restaurant in San Anto,
Old man, with the worn and gleaming pants,
the softly faded shirt, the thin belt
Old man, old man
Why, when you enter, do you walk so cautiously?
Why do you barely whisper to your compadre? ‡
Why do you wish to go unnoticed?
Your own people would not belittle you because you're poor
They would not cast sly, demeaning glances at you
They would not turn you away—
Or would they?
This is "Mi Tierra"—nuestra tierra, no? **
As I watch you and your compadre
As I count the lines and see the ravages, the suffering you have known
And sense deep within me what courage you have shown each day
I smile at you and nod
Hoping you will know

* For an unknown old man whom even I know.
† My Country.
‡ Companion; literally, godfather.
** Our country.

That my heart reaches out to you
And my soul embraces you.

PARA TERESA*

A tí-Teresa Compean
Te dedico las palabras estás
que explotan de mi corazón†

That day during lunch hour
at Alamo which-had-to-be-its-name
Elementary
my dear raza
That day in the bathroom
Door guarded
Myself cornered
I was accused by you, Teresa
Tú y las demas de tus amigas
Pachucas todas
Eran Uds. cinco.‡

Me gritaban que porque me creía tan grande**
What was I trying to do, you growled
Show you up?
Make the teachers like me, pet me,
Tell me what a credit to my people I was?
I was playing right into their hands, you challenged
And you would have none of it.
I was to stop.

I was to be like you
I was to play your game of deadly defiance
Arrogance, refusal to submit.
The game in which the winner takes nothing
Asks for nothing
Never lets his weaknesses show.

But I didn't understand.
My fear salted with confusion

* For Teresa.
† To you, Teresa Compean, I dedicate these words that explode from my heart.
‡ You and the rest of your friends, all Pachucas, there were five of you.
** You were screaming at me, asking me why I thought I was so hot.

Charged me to explain to you
I did nothing *for the teachers.*
I studied for my parents and for my grandparents
Who cut out honor roll lists
Whenever their nietos' * names appeared
For my shy mother who mastered her terror
to demand her place in mother's clubs
For my carpenter-father who helped me patiently with my math.
For my abuelos que me regalaron lápices en la Navidad †
And for myself.

Porque reconocí en aquel entonces
una verdad tremenda
que me hizo a mi un rebelde
Aunque tú no te habías dadocuenta.‡
We were not inferior
You and I, y las demás de tus amigas
Y los demás de nuestra gente**
I knew it the way I know I was alive
We were good, honorable, brave
Genuine, loyal, strong

And smart.
Mine was a deadly game of defiance, also.
My contest was to prove
· beyond any doubt
that we were not only equal but superior to them.
That was why I studied.
If I could do it, we all could.

You let me go then,
Your friends unblocked the way
I who-did-not-know-how-to-fight
was not made to engage with you-who-grew-up-fighting
Tu y yo, Teresa††
We went in different directions
Pero fuimos juntas.‡‡

In sixth grade we did not understand
Uds. with the teased, dyed-black-but-reddening hair,

* Grandchildren's.
† Grandparents who gave me gifts of pencils at Christmas.
‡ Because I recognized a great truth then that made me a rebel, even though you didn't realize it.
** And the rest of your friends / And the rest of our people.
†† You and I.
‡‡ But we were together.

Full petticoats, red lipsticks
and sweaters with the sleeves
pushed up
Y yo conformándome con lo que deseaba mi mamá*
Certainly never allowed to dye, to tease, to paint myself
I did not accept your way of anger,
Your judgements
You did not accept mine.

But now in 1975, when I am twenty-eight
Teresa Compean
I remember you.
Y sabes—
Te comprendo,
Es más, te respeto.
Y, si me permites,
Te nombro—"hermana." †

TO OTHER WOMEN WHO WERE UGLY ONCE

Do you remember how we used to panic
when Cosmo, Vogue and Mademoiselle
      ladies
         would Glamour-us
         out of existence
                  so ultra bright
                  would be their smile
                  so lovely their
                  complexion
      their confianza‡ based on
      someone else's fashion
      and their mascara'd mascaras**
            hiding the cascaras††
            that hide their ser? ‡‡

* And I conforming to my mother's wishes.
† And do you know what, I understand you. Even more, I respect you. And, if you
permit me, I name you my sister.
‡ Confidence.
** Masks.
†† Shells.
‡‡ Being.

I would always become cold inside
                    mata*onda** to compete
            to need
            to dress right
            speak right
            laugh in just the
            right places
            dance in just
            the right way

My resistance to this type of
        existence
        grows stronger every day
Y al cabo ahora se
        que se vale
        preferir natural luz†

                to neon.

* Dampener; *onda* is a "trip" in the positive sense—to *matar onda* is to kill, to frustrate the "trip"—to dishearten.
    † And now anyway I know that it is worthy to prefer natural light.

SYLVIA ALICIA GONZALES

Born in Arizona in 1943, Sylvia Gonzales has written on Chicano literature, the women's movement, the position of Chicanos in society, and many other subjects. Her work has been published in various places, including *De Colores, La Luz* Magazine, *The Los Angeles Times, The Social Science Journal, Caracol,* and the *Civil Service Journal*. Commenting on her poetry, she says, "My poetry seeks not to be defined as I now find pride in not being defined. A definition will come only when we no longer need a voice. And as literature is the mirror of humankind so thus literature will continue to voice the needs of humankind. In this evolutionary process, then, my woman's voice surpasses my Chicano voice."

CHICANA EVOLUTION

PART I—GENESIS AND THE ORIGINAL SIN

I am Chicana
Something inside revolts.
The words surface with difficulty.
I am Chicana
By pronouncing this statement,
do I give authenticity to the trivia
which makes this statement me?

Last night I had visions
of New York and Greenwich Village
where artists gather.
I am Chicana
And I have convulsions.
My head throbs.
Is that reality
or romanticized lies
I read somewhere?
I am Chicana
I'll never know.

My friends tell me I waste energies
on bohemian fantasies

because I've read books
about Paris and Pernod,
sidewalk cafes and cappuccino.
I am Chicana
Who taught me to read?
I see yesterday's heroine
climb a lonely staircase
to a naked flat
where Van Gogh has
sliced off an ear.
I am Chicana
Not far from the reality
of nakedness and slashed faces.

I entered your pages
Muses of wisdom,
where your words protected
my frail spirit.
I am Chicana
Who dares to write the letters
given to me by a generous nun
while promising to enjoy hell on earth
for fewer days in purgatory.
I am Chicana
And the words tire me.
What value has my verse?
I am Chicana
I am oblivion,
an appendage to the universe,
a poverty statistic in life's data bank.

I am Chicana
Why, muses, did I taste your sweetness?
Why did your pages excite me,
with the pain of literacy?
I am Chicana
Is ignorance sublime?
Would I be a problem
if I did not learn of problems?
I am Chicana
A creation of actions
as well as words.

I am Chicana
All of you reincarnated

into the bastard child.
I am Chicana
And you are the women who sinned
by stripping yourselves of passivity
and with your pens,
gave virgin births.
I am Chicana
And I too have sinned
by stripping myself of guilt.
I am Chicana
And the only guilt I claim
is desiring your legacy.

I am Chicana
I am your creation.
I stand in wait of your baptism.
I was conceived the moment
you put pen to paper.
I am Chicana
Born in the shadows
of your creative orgasms.
I am Chicana
Now, Madison Avenue woman,
give me my birthright.

I am Chicana
Baptize my soul,
give breath to my lungs,
mothers of the universe,
wherever you are.
I am Chicana
In my claim to legitimacy
I cry with despair.
I am Chicana
Bastard child of the universe
because you make me so.
I am Chicana
But I know my mother,
while you sleep with your fathers.

I am Chicana
I have not sinned,
nor lied.
Your sins are my necessity.
I am Chicana

Because you say I am.
I am Chicana
And my body shakes in anger
for wanting to be,
what I cannot be,
and not to be.
But what is the question,
if I am Chicana.

PART II—IN SEARCH OF THE MESSIAHS OF NATIVISM

I am Chicana
And I turn to you,
my sisters of the flesh.
I cry to your cities,
Buenos Aires, Caracas, Bogota,
Lima, Mejico, Rio and Montevideo.
I am Chicana
Our seed was the same,
born of an Indian womb
victims of the rape.

I am Chicana
But while you developed
in the womb,
I was raped again.
I am Chicana
In a holocaust of sperm,
bitter fragments of fertilization.
Mankind's victim,
humankind's burden.

I am Chicana
Daughter of Malinche,
hija de la chingada madre*
of Cautemoc's vengeance.
I am Chicana
A blistering Indian sun
waiting to be sacrificed.
A pale Catholic virgin,
waiting to be baptized.
Each awaiting the paradise of purpose.

* Daughter of the violated mother.

SYLVIA ALICIA GONZALES
421

I am Chicana
Who knows that in either case,
death does not discriminate.

I am Chicana
Abandoned child of Cortés,
mistress of Huitzilopochtli
who conceive and abandon mine.
I am Chicana
Latina, hispana americana,
does not your blood
flow with the original sin
of Montezuma's shame
and the Church's penance
for a taste of Christian flesh.
I am Chicana
And I know my sisters.
I see you in Catholic confessionals
reciting the same
mia culpa, mia culpa, mia culpa.

I am Chicana
Waiting for the return
of la Malinche,
to negate her guilt,
and cleanse her flesh
of a confused Mexican wrath
which seeks reason
to the displaced power of Indian deities.
I am Chicana
Waiting for the coming of a Malinche
to sacrifice herself
on an Aztec altar
and Catholic cross
in redemption of all her forsaken daughters.

PART III—RENACIMIENTO SEGUN
EL NUEVO TESTAMENTO*

Luna que vas bajando por las sierras
Ve y avisa a mis hermanas del sur

* Translation follows.

que ya estoy aquí revivida.
Yo soy la Chicana
La hermana abandonada.
Madre, tu que siempre has sido generosa
¿porqué abandonastes una de las tuyas?
Yo soy la Chicana
Y mis hermanas no eschuchan mi queja.
Me abortan cada instante.
A veces me abrazan.
A veces niegan mi existencia.
De día me abrazan;
De noche me esconden.
¿Tan misteriosa como la noche seré yo,
para prohibirme hospicio
en sus corazones?

Yo soy la Chicana
Sé de curanderas y brujerías,
tanto como de Cervantes y la Academia Real,
el lumfardo y el caló.
Yo soy la Chicana
Y se llorar y cantar.
Se del café y el vino
y la buena conversación.
"No soy de aquí,
ni soy de allá,
no tengo edad, ni porvenir,
y ser feliz es mi color
de identidad."

Yo soy la Chicana
Se de Atalhuapa Yupanqui
Corrientes y Santa Fe,
Copacabana y Jorge Amado.
Yo soy la Chicana
Y se cantar del llano
y los versos de Chabuca Grande.
Fina estampa también tengo yo
por el orgullo de ser raza
de alma y corazón.

Yo soy la Chicana
He visto mis hermanas de corazón y piel
celebrando ambientes extranjeros
enfrentando al nuevo Cortez

con un escosés en la mano.
Tal vez tengan un recuerdo lejano
de la chicha y el vino
Yo soy la Chicana
Y no lo comparten conmigo.
Niegan mi existencia
para no ser negadas
del hospicio del enemigo.
Yo soy la Chicana
Y tú, Malinche revivida.

Yo soy la Chicana
Tu Colombiana, Argentina, Peruana.
Yo soy tierra, agua y fuego
y la madre,
que ha dado luz al mundo.
Yo soy la Chicana
Yo soy tu madre.
Y tú, mi hija serás.
La misma cosa somos,
tú y yo.
Si madre no quieres ser,
yo tu bastarda no seré.
Yo soy la Chicana
Malinche, madre e hija
y hasta bastarda, seré.
Pero nunca dejaré de ser
MUJER.

PART III—REBIRTH ACCORDING TO THE
NEW TESTAMENT

Moon, as you pass through the night
Go and tell my sisters of the South*
that I stand here revived.
I am the Chicana
the abandoned sister.
Mother, you who have always been so kind
why have you left me behind?
I am the Chicana
and my sisters do not hear my plea,

* South America.

They reject me constantly.
Sometimes they embrace me,
Yet other times, they deny me.
Am I to stay in the shadows of the night,
without feeling the warm sunlight
of their hearts?

I am the Chicana
who knows of folk medicine and witchcraft.
I know of Cervantes and the Spanish Language Academy
as well as of Argentine dialects
and Mexican slang.
I am the Chicana
I sing and sometimes I cry.
I savor coffee and wine
and linger over good conversation.
"I am not from here,
nor there,
I am timeless, yet have no future.
To be happy is my quest for identity."

I am the Chicana
I know of Atalhupa Yupanqui
Corrientes and Santa Fe.
Copacabana and Jorge Amado.
I am the Chicana
I can sing the songs of the plains
and the verses of Chabuca Grande.
I am refined in the ways of the culture,
and my pride binds me and you.

We are Raza, one in spirit and soul,
I am the Chicana
I have seen my spiritual and racial sisters
celebrating in distant lands
a different way of life
with a whiskey in their hands.
Perhaps a fleeting memory
of chicha† and wine
glimmers in their eyes.
as they confront the new Cortés.
I am the Chicana
These sisters do not share

† South American corn liquor.

SYLVIA ALICIA GONZALES

their fate with me.
They deny my existence
in order to affirm theirs
in the eyes of the enemy.
I am the Chicana
And you, Malinche, born again.

I am the Chicana
You women, from Colombia, Argentina and Peru
Know that I am the earth, the water and the fire,
I have the natural elements
to give birth to the world
I am the Chicana
I am your mother
and you, my daughter, will be
like me
you and me
are we.
If you do not want to be my mother,
I cannot be your illegitimate child.
I am the Chicana
Malinche, both mother and daughter,
And even, bastard child.
But above all,
I AM WOMAN.

Translated by Marcela Christine Lucero-Trujillo

Note: For a comprehensive bibliography of Chicano literature, see Francisco A. Lomelí and Donaldo W. Urioste, eds. *Chicano Perspectives in Literature: A Critical and Annotated Bibliography.* Albuquerque, Pajarito Publications, 1976.

Anthologies

Alurista, et al., eds. *Festival de Flor y Canto: An Anthology of Chicano Literature.* Los Angeles, University of Southern California Press, 1976. An anthology of previously unpublished material by representative Chicano writers.

Dwyer, Carlota Cárdenas de, ed. *Chicano Voices.* Boston, Houghton Mifflin, 1975. This collection is divided into five areas: *la raza,* the barrio, the Chicana woman, life, and *la causa.*

First Chicano Literary Prize, Irvine 1974–1975. Bogotá, Colombia, Ediciones El Dorado, 1975. Presents the results of a literary contest sponsored by the Spanish and Portuguese departments at the University of California at Irvine.

Garza, Roberto J., ed. *Contemporary Chicano Theatre.* Notre Dame, Ind., University of Notre Dame Press, 1976. A good introduction to Chicano drama. Includes work by Estela Portillo Trambley.

Harth, Dorothy E., and Lewis M. Baldwin, eds. *Voices of Aztlan: Chicano Literature of Today.* New York, New American Library, 1974. Geared to an English-speaking audience, this collection contains fiction, poetry, and drama.

Mirikitani, Janice, et al., eds. *Time to Greez—Incantations from the Third World.* San Francisco, Glide Publications, 1975. Includes work by Nina Serrano, Dorinda Moreno, and Marcela Christine Lucero-Trujillo.

Ortega, Philip D., ed. *We Are Chicanos: An Anthology of Mexican-American Literature.* New York, Washington Square Press, 1973. A representative collection of all genres in Chicano literature, including essays and folklore. "The Day of the Swallows," a drama by Estela Portillo Trambley, is one of the selections.

Paredes, Américo, and Raymundo Paredes, eds. *Mexican-American Authors.* Boston, Houghton Mifflin, 1972. This collection is particularly valuable for its inclusion of Chicano literature before World War II. It contains works by Josefina Niggli, as well as folk ballads and *dichos,* short stories and poetry by twelve authors.

Romano-V., Octavio I., and Herminio Ríos C., eds. *El Espejo/The Mirror: Selected Chicano Literature.* Berkeley, Quinto Sol Publications, 1969. The first anthology of Chicano literature, this book contains representative works, including poetry by Georgia Cobos and drama by Raquel Moreno and Estela Portillo Trambley.

Salinas, Luis Omar, and Lillian Faderman, eds. *From the Barrio: A Chicano Anthology.* San Francisco, Canfield Press, 1973. Includes poetry, short fiction, essays, drama, and excerpts from novels. The selections are geared toward the exploration of "chicanismo."

Shular, Antonia Castañeda, Tomás Ybarra-Frausto, and Joseph Sommers, eds. *Literatura Chicana: Texto y Contexto/Chicano Literature: Text and Context.* Englewood Cliffs, N.J., Prentice-Hall, 1972. Provides a historical framework for the emergence of Chicano literature. Emphasis is on Mexican origins and links with South American culture.

Siete Poetas. Tucson, Scorpion Press, 1978. Contains poetry by Margarita Cota-Cárdenas and Inés Hernandez Tovar.

Valdez, Luis, and El Teatro Campesino. *Actos.* San Juan Bautista, Calif., Cucaracha Publications, 1971. A collection of nine plays produced by the Teatro Campesino.

Valdez, Luis, and Stan Steiner, eds. *Aztlán: An Anthology of Mexican American Literature.* New York, Alfred A. Knopf, 1972. The selections range from pre-Conquest to contemporary Chicano literature. The works are viewed within their historical and sociological framework.

Journals and Periodicals

Aztlán: Chicano Journal of the Social Sciences and the Arts (Chicano Studies Center, UCLA)

Bilingual Review (Jamaica, N.Y., York College)

Caracol (San Antonio, Christopher Press)

De Colores: Journal of Emerging Raza Philosophies (Albuquerque, Pajarito Publications), Vol. 3, No. 3 of *De Colores, La Cosecha—Literatura y la Mujer Chicana* (1977), is devoted exclusively to Chicana writers.

Fomento Literario (Washington, D.C., El Congreso Nacional de Asuntos Colegiales)

El Grito—Journal of Contemporary Mexican American Thought (Berkeley, Quinto Sol Publications)

Grito del Sol: A Chicano Quarterly (Berkeley, Tonatiuh International)

Hembra (Center for Mexican American Studies, University of Texas at Austin)

Maize (San Diego)

Revista Chicano-Riqueña (Bloomington, Indiana University Northwest)

Tejidos (Austin, University of Texas)

Primary Sources

Baca, Fabiola Cabeza de. *We Fed Them Cactus.* Albuquerque, University of New Mexico Press, 1954. Autobiographical and historical narrative.

Castillo, Ana. *A Melody for Dancing (When Legs Intertwine).* Chicago, Playboy Foundation, 1979. Poetry.

————. *Otro Canto.* Chicago, Alternative Publications, 1978. Poetry.

Cota-Cárdenas, Margarita. *Noches despertando inconciencias.* Tucson, Scorpion Press, 1975. Poetry.

Gaitan, Marcela Trujillo. *Chicana Themes: Manita Poetry.* Minneapolis, Chicano Studies, University of Minnesota, 1975.

Gonzales, Sylvia Alicia. *La Chicana Piensa.* San Jose, 1974. Poetry.

Hoyos, Angela de. *Arise, Chicano.* Bloomington, Ind., Backstage Books, 1975. Poetry.

———. *Chicano Poems for the Barrio.* Bloomington, Ind., Backstage Books, 1975.

———. *Selecciones.* Mireya Robles, trans. Xalapa, Veracruz, Universidad Veracruzana, 1976. Poetry.

Moreno, Dorinda. *La mujer es la tierra: La tierra de vida.* Berkeley, Casa Editorial, 1975. Poetry and sketches.

Niggli, Josefina. *Mexican Folk Plays.* Chapel Hill, University of North Carolina Press, 1938.

———. *Mexican Village.* Chapel Hill: University of North Carolina Press, 1945. Short stories.

———. "Mexico: The Red Velvet Coat," in Samuel Selden, ed. *International Folk Plays.* Chapel Hill, University of North Carolina Press, 1949.

———. *Soldadera [Soldier-Woman]: A One-Act Play of the Mexican Revolution.* New York, French, 1936.

———. *Step down, elder brother.* New York, Rinehart, 1947. Fiction.

———. "Sunday Costs Five Pesos," in *One-Act Play Magazine,* Vol. 1, pp. 786-802, New York, 1938.

———. "This Bull Ate Nutmeg; A Mexican Folk Comedy," in William Kozlenko, ed. *Contemporary One-Act Plays.* New York, Charles Scribner's, 1938.

———. "This Is Villa," in *One-Act Play Magazine,* Vol. 1, pp. 611–630, New York, 1939.

———. *Tooth or Shave; A One-Act Mexican Folk Comedy.* New York, French, 1937.

Rivera, Marina. *Sobra.* San Francisco, Casa Editorial, 1977. Poetry.

———. *Mestiza.* Tucson, Grilled Flowers, 1977. Poetry.

Tovar, Inés Hernandez. *Con Razon, Corazon: Poetry.* San Antonio, Caracol Publications, 1977.

Trambley, Estela Portillo. *Rain of Scorpions.* Berkeley, Tonatiuh International, 1975. Short stories.

Trujillo, Marcela Christine Lucero-. *See* Marcela Trujillo Gaitan.

Zamora, Bernice. *Restless Serpents.* Menlo Park, Calif., Diseños Literarios, 1976. Poetry.

ALLEGORY

From the photograph the child
(Dutch-boy bob, cross-stitched yoke,
Sitting on one leg in a pavilion)
Looks out
At the monolithic spread of my view
Over the capital of the Empire State,

And at someone old enough to be her mother,
Who is also the child's child,
Since it is a portrait of myself as I posed
Five-years-old, in Peiping, in quite another story.

The child is translated into our native genre:
American, I am here to attest
To that child I was, misplaced
And found again.

How she remembers all that was to come
Is strange, incredible,
Past my understanding

Though her smile is worldly.
Mine, thirty years later, is skeptical.

From time to time our glances meet:
You are certainly outrageous, I inform her,
While she softly declares tall tales are everywhere.

Diana Chang

ASIAN AMERICAN
WOMEN WRITERS

INTRODUCTION

HISTORICAL PERSPECTIVES

In "Allegory," Diana Chang touches on a recurrent theme in Asian American literature—the ever-present urge to relocate the self. As a child, she is "translated" from one culture into another, "misplaced and found again." She becomes American with memories of a distant Chinese past. With each relocation, another dimension of experience is added, and another story finds its way into the arsenal of memory. The result is a bifocal vision that fuses both an Asian and an American sensibility into an integrated whole. This tension between echoes of one's racial past and the present reality of often being linguistically and culturally divorced from that past contributes to the complexity of the Asian American imagination and to the range of expression present in one of the "newest" branches of American literature.

As one of America's smallest minorities—less than 1 percent of the population—Asian Americans have been part of the history of America for 140 years. But their history has been one of struggle and political relocation and has hardly provided a context, until recently, for the development of a literary movement. The first Asians to immigrate to the United States were the Chinese. In the wake of a severe drought that destroyed the crops in the Canton province in 1847 to 1850, many Chinese came over to work on the Central Pacific Railroad, trying to earn enough money to return home to buy land. Since they intended eventually to return to China, and in light of the enormous expense of the trip, most men did not bring wives or families with them. The results were long, arduous separations that often threatened the family unit and made life painfully difficult on both sides of the Pacific. Women were left behind in small villages with barely enough resources to survive and the responsibility of caring for their families alone. Those few who were able to break tradition encountered an even bleaker life of poverty and hard work in the United States. In many instances, single women venturing the long voyage alone to join their husbands were kidnaped and sold into prostitution. The Chinese Exclusion Act of 1882, which prohibited immigration by laborers, increased the difficulties for women because, as wives of laborers, they were denied entry to the United States. By 1890 Chinese women in the United States numbered only 3,868 in comparison to 103,620 men. It was not until 1943 that the Exclusion Act was repealed, and many Chinese wives and their children were permitted to enter the United States. Reversing its previous policy and now intent on "promoting family unity," the government also passed the Amended War Brides Act in 1947, which allowed more Chinese wives to immigrate.[1]

For Japanese women, the pattern of immigration was somewhat different. Although women did not come in the first waves of immigration in the 1880s and 1890s, they did begin to immigrate in fairly large numbers in the early decades of the twentieth century. This in part was due to the "picture bride" practice. Prospective brides and bridegrooms would exchange pictures across the Pacific and would arrange marriages by proxy, a practice that was an extension of the Japanese custom of *omiai-kekkon,* whereby families arranged marriages for their offspring and handled all negotiations through an intermediary. Since there were few Japanese women in the United States, it was natural and culturally acceptable for Japanese men to select their wives in this fashion. As a result of this practice, the Issei (first generation),[2] unlike the early Chinese immigrants, were able to keep the family unit intact and to become permanent residents of the United States much more quickly.

But what unimaginable cultural differences awaited those first picture brides. With mixed emotions of anxiety and anticipation, the women endured the slow journey to meet husbands they had never seen. One woman describes her thoughts as she waited:

> On the way from Kobe to Yokohama, gazing upon the rising majestic Mount Fuji in a cloudless sky aboard the ship, I made a resolve. For a woman who was going to a strange society and relying upon an unknown husband whom she had married through photographs, my heart had to be as beautiful as Mount Fuji. I resolved that the heart of a Japanese woman had to be sublime, like that soaring majestic figure, eternally constant through wind and rain, heat and cold. Thereafter, I never forgot that resolve on the ship, enabling me to overcome sadness and suffering.[3]

Those resolutions were tested again and again as the picture brides confronted one strange custom after another. The most immediate change that had to be made was in mode of dress. Eager to have their new wives "fit in," husbands insisted that corsets replace kimonos. According to one woman,

> I was immediately outfitted with Western clothing. . . . Because I had to wear a tight corset around my chest, I could not bend forward. I had to have my husband tie my shoe laces. There were some women who fainted because it was too tight. There are stories of women being carried to the hotel rooms by their husbands who hurriedly untied the corset strings which were no joking matters. In my case, I wore a large hat, a high-necked blouse, a long skirt, a buckled belt around my waist, highlaced shoes, and, of course for the first time in my life, a brassiere and hip pads.[4]

But clothing proved to be the least of the problems. The romantic visions of flourishing farms and large homes soon faded into days and nights marked by the numbing sameness of hard work, poverty, and disillusionment. One woman recounts her experiences:

> At the beginning, I worked with my husband picking potatoes or onions and putting them in sacks. Working with rough and tumble men, I became weary to the bones; waking up in the mornings I could not bend over the wash basin. Sunlight came out about 4:00 A.M. during the summer in the Yakima Valley. I arose at 4:30. After cooking breakfast, I went out to the fields. There was no electric stove or gas like now. It took over one hour to cook, burning kindling wood. As soon as I came home, I first put on the fire, took off my hat, and then I washed my hands. After cooking both breakfast and lunch, I went to the fields.[5]

In short, America's streets were not golden, and opportunities were meager in a country that continued to discriminate against Orientals: In 1913 the Alien Land Law Act was passed, which prevented Asians from owning land in California, and in 1924 the Asian Exclusion Act, which prohibited intermarriage between Asians and whites and denied citizenship rights to Chinese and Japanese, became law.

Unfortunately, this pattern of legislation is only too familiar to America's minority groups, but what distinguishes the Asian American experience is the horror of relocation during World War II. Within four months of the attack on Pearl Harbor, over 110,000 Japanese living in the United States were forced to leave behind homes, businesses, and farms and were moved to internment camps in the West. At the root of this devastating action was the implication of guilt by association. *All* Japanese Americans were assumed to be conspiring against America, despite overwhelming evidence to the contrary. Even more tragically, Asians were pitted against Asians in an attempt to "uncover" conspiracy plans. Chinese Americans became allies of the United States and spied on Japanese Americans. Without question, the damage to the psyches of both groups during this period of physical relocation and psychological dislocation was enormous, and the legal repercussions were even more devastating, for it was not until ten years later, in 1952, that Japanese Americans were finally afforded the right of citizenship.

Given this tumultuous history of constant struggle, it is small wonder that it has only been since World War II that an Asian American literary movement has begun to emerge in full force. Asian American women have been an integral part of that movement from the beginning, seeking through their literature to define an Asian American sensibility. Sui Sin Far (1867–1914) is one of the first women to write about the Chinese American experience, publishing autobiographical sketches and short stories in *Ladies Home Journal*, *Good Housekeeping*, and *The Independent*. In 1912, she published a collection of short stories entitled *Mrs. Spring Fragrance.* Also known as Edith Eaton (her father was Edward Eaton, a landscape architect), she writes of the difficulties of being a Eurasian in America. The following excerpt is taken from "Mental Portfolio of an Eurasian" published in *The Independent,* January 21, 1909:

> I am only ten years old. And all the while the question of nationality perplexes my little brain. Why are we what we are? I and my brothers and sisters. Why did God make us to be hooted and stared at? Papa is English, mamma is Chinese. Why couldn't we have been either one thing or the other? Why is my mother's race despised? I look into the faces of my father and mother. Is she not every bit as dear and good as he? ... I do not confide in my father and mother. They would not understand. How could they? He is English, she is Chinese. I am different to both of them—a stranger, tho their own child (127–128).

In 1945 Jade Snow Wong published her autobiographical novel *Fifth Chinese Daughter,* which dealt with her adaptation to life between two cultures. And in 1946 Miné Okubo published *Citizen 13660,* a collection of drawings and observations based on life in the relocation camps. Monica Sone's reflections on the impact of World War II and the internment camps on traditional life appeared in *Nisei Daughter* in 1953, and in 1956 Diana Chang published *Frontiers of Love,* the first novel to explore in depth the internal psychological conflicts of being Eurasian that Sui Sin Far had described more than forty years earlier. She has since published five more novels on a variety of subjects.

The 1960s marked a period of increased literary activity among Asian Americans, particularly the women writers, in part as a response to the women's movement and civil rights legislation, and in part because an audience eager to listen to "minority" voices was beginning to emerge. Suddenly, there was a place to publish and someone to read the literature. Notably, *The Greenfield Review, Yardbird Reader, Amerasia Journal,* and *Bridge* all devoted issues to Asian American writers. Centers at UCLA and the University of California at Berkeley began developing their Asian American studies programs and producing collections such as *Roots: An Asian American Reader* and, more recently, *Counterpoint* (both UCLA publications). In addition, several anthologies have been published recently, indicating that there is, indeed, a substantial body of literature by Asian Americans that merits critical attention. For example, in 1972 Kai-Yu Hsu and Helen Palubinskas edited *Asian American Authors.* Two years later, David Hsin-Fu Wand brought out *Asian American Heritage: An Anthology of Prose and Poetry,* and in 1975 Frank Chin, Jeffery Paul Chan, Lawson Fusao Inada, and Shawn Wong published *Aiiieeeee: An Anthology of Asian American Writers.*

One question raised by all of these anthologies is that of identity. What is an Asian American and what is distinctive about the Asian American sensibility? Do Asian Americans, for example, identify more with their Asian roots or with their American experience? Or does their literature express a new voice that is *more* than Asian and American? Like "Native American," "Asian American" is a term that embraces a plurality of cultures—Chinese, Japanese, Filipino, Hawaiian, Korean, Malaysian, and so on—and as diverse as these backgrounds are, so are the voices in Asian American literature. What is shared by all is an urge toward self-definition, a working out in literary terms of what it means to be Asian American. At this point, among Asian American writers, the Chinese, Japanese, and Filipino Americans tend to dominate the literature, perhaps because they have a longer history here. What is clear is that the best of Asian American literature is, by and large, contemporary because, it would seem, the passage of time has allowed younger writers the distance to view the complexity of their experience within a cultural and historical context.

The women in this section include writers removed from their Asian origins by as much as six generations as well as recent immigrants. Some are conscious of Oriental literary forms; others write out of an Anglo-American literary tradition and, in some cases, are influenced by the blues tradition and linguistic diversity of black speech. Though Asian American women write on many subjects that may be seen in either "ethnic" or "universal" terms, all share in common a movement toward a working out of consciousness, whether it be through the personal narrative, poetry, essays, or fiction.

CONTEXTS AND NARRATIVES

The first section includes three essays that provide different perspectives on "context." In the opening essay, Joanne Harumi Sechi discusses issues of dual consciousness, assimilation, and self-identity. Though she is speaking specifically about her experience as a Japanese American, she creates a "context of identity," raising the question of how one defines an Asian American sensibility. Gail Miyasaki creates a "context of heritage" in her sensitive description of her grandmother. And in the third selection, Diana Chang discusses her personal exploration of the creative process of writing, establishing a "context of purpose" since, first and foremost, the women in this section are writers, conscious of developing and refining their literary craft at the same time they are carving out a literary tradition.

The writers of the second section, "Traditions, Narratives, and Fiction," have in common a concern with the process of language. Of *The Woman Warrior* by Maxine Hong Kingston (from which a selection is included here), Suzi Wong comments that it reflects a "consciousness which seems particularly Asian American because it is borne out of the struggle between speech and demon silence." [6] This statement can be made about all of the narratives that follow. The characters struggle to find their own voices and consequently their identities. But there are certain limitations imposed by language and culture. In Kingston's "No Name Woman" the limitation is convention. Her aunt has dared to live a life that is private, outside the mores of the village, and in the process has offended a system of values that keeps order within the social organization. Cast out and punished by the villagers for committing adultery and giving birth to an illegitimate child, she drowns herself and the baby. In the imaginative retelling of this story, Maxine Hong Kingston not only flaunts tradition by ignoring her mother's warning in the first line—"You must not tell anyone"—but also reveals how difficult it is for the Asian American woman to find her own voice when the values of the two cultures she shares are in opposition.

This conflict of values is particularly clear in "Seventeen Syllables" by Hisaye Yamamoto, which is the story of one woman's attempt to fill a gaping void in her life by writing haiku. A traditional Japanese poetic form, the haiku represents all that the woman yearns for in her past; the irony lies in trying to express the pain of emptiness in only seventeen syllables. Hisaye Yamamoto's other story, "Las Vegas Charley," explores the problem of communication on another level. Here the narrative centers on an immigrant who suffers from a literal language barrier and, through a series of inevitable historical events, becomes more and more locked within his own silence until he dies. The language of death is difficult to render in any culture, but Wakako Yamauchi captures beautifully the consciousness behind silence in "The Boatmen on Toneh River." From behind the mask of a coma, a dying woman tells her own story of a slow death. The demon silence has indeed taken over here because she cannot break the barrier of physical communication; yet, her perception of consciousness is acute, and she yearns for a real moment of truth with her husband.

In the excerpt from *Intimate Friends,* Diana Chang employs a type of stream of consciousness to explore questions of loneliness and sexuality. Defining a feeling becomes a way to order and contain it and finally to possess it. By turning a sensitive ear to the subtle modulations of language in her characters, Diana Chang reveals their psychological complexities. The last selection, "The Bath" by Karen Yamashita, is an exercise in the process of storytelling and a demonstration of the integral connection between language and culture. The bath is a metaphor for the communication of tradition and is the central unifying element in the stories told about the characters.

POETRY

All of the narratives are shaped at some level by a consciousness of tradition, whether it is the tradition of superstition and ghost stories in "No Name

Woman" or the tradition of the Japanese bath in the last story. But the traditions are filtered through a particular Asian American sensibility, and in the process a new voice is heard that blends elements from both cultures. The subtle modulations of that voice are particularly clear in the language of the poetry in the third section. Jessica Tarahata Hagedorn, for example, writes out of the black experience and a commonly shared blues tradition. Her riff on Lady Day employs jazz rhythms and repetitions—"the fire still," "the walk you have"—which become improvisations of impressions in which the collapsed code of language suggests the "blues" feeling. Her song for her father, on the other hand, has a different tone. It is a lament, a longing to recapture a relationship that has been altered by time and distance.

Geraldine Kudaka's abbreviated language is also reminiscent of a blues mode. Her poems combine words and symbols from two cultures, producing a sense of duality that informs her vision of the world. Through her hybrid style, she delves into what it means to write Asian American poetry. Janice Mirikitani experiments with form and language in still another way in her poetry. Intensely aware of political struggle, she writes searing poems like "Attack the Water" that juxtapose images of World War II relocation camps with horrors from the recent Vietnam war. Yet, her voice can also be soft in a minor key, as in her love poem to her daughter.

Love takes its place quietly in the poetry of Mei-Mei Berssenbrugge, whose lyrics are like subtle pen and ink drawings. For Shirley Geok-Lin Lim, a recent immigrant from Malaysia, looking back to her country of birth occasions mixed emotions and moments of deep nostalgia. "Christmas in Exile" and "Modern Secrets" both express a sense of dislocation of self that is put in clear relief by differences in custom.

Translating oneself into understandable terms is a major preoccupation of most of the authors in this section, a preoccupation that is symbolized by the literal problem of speaking another language—again, the dilemma of being caught between speech and demon silence. Laureen Mar expresses this tension of opposites in her poignant poems to her mother whose "words do not end with consonants/ They tilt upwards, cling to the air like leaves." In her Chinatown series, she depicts other barriers to "translation" that exist in cultural differences between generations. Though the generations might be separated, there is still a deep respect for ancestors, relatives, parents. In "Enigma," for example, Helen Kaneko wonders what history stirs behind the immobile demeanor of an aged woman. The form of her poem is as spare as the woman's slight movements.

Form is a major concern for poets and, particularly, for Diana Chang. As an artist, she has a visual commitment to imagery that she succeeds in translating into verbal form. "Rhythms" and "What Matisse Is After" are poems about art and perception, while in "Still Life," art becomes an inverted metaphor for lovemaking. Her use of understatement lends an element of surprise to her poetry as well as a resonance that goes beyond the subject.

Surprise also operates in the poetry of Ai, but here the effect is one of shock. Her poems are strong, harsh statements that go right to the core of womanhood and love. Using earth and animal imagery, she strips off the layers of formality that encase our illusions about birth, love, and marriage, exposing raw nerves that lie just beneath the surface.

Though diversity characterizes the literature of Asian American women, what begins to reveal itself is a self-conscious commitment to establishing a literary tradition that will communicate the special tensions that hyphenate the Asian and American worlds. Asian American women writers are growing in numbers and in quiet excellence. They sing in many keys, yet their song is uniquely Asian American.

NOTES

1. For more information on Chinese immigration and women, see Betty Jung's article, "Chinese Immigrants," which appears in *Asian Women* (Berkeley: Asian Women's Journal Workgroup, 1971). This book has recently gone through its third printing and can be obtained through the Asian American Studies Center at UCLA. Another book on the history of Chinese immigration, particularly before the nineteenth century, is *Fusang: The Chinese Who Built America* by Stan Steiner (New York: Harper & Row, 1979).
2. "Nisei" signifies second-generation Japanese American, and "Sansei" means third generation.
3. Emma Gee, "Issei: The First Women," *Asian Women* (Berkeley: Asian Women's Journal Workgroup, 1971), p. 11. The original source is Kazuo Ito, *Hokubei Hyakunen Sakura,* Yuji Ichioka, trans. (Seattle: 1969).
4. Ibid., p. 12.
5. Ibid., p. 13.
6. In her review of *The Woman Warrior,* which appeared in *Amerasia Journal,* 4, No. 1 (1977), 165–167.

CONTEXTS

JOANNE HARUMI SECHI

Biographical information about this author is unavailable.

BEING JAPANESE-AMERICAN DOESN'T MEAN "MADE IN JAPAN"

... the Eastern world of the Ivy League was certainly a dazzling one for a West Coast Nisei whose only social contact with thoroughbreds had been at the Santa Anita stables. In the midst of this white, intellectual and, in some senses, social elite I felt rather like a rooster in a peacock's nest. (Daniel I. Okimoto, *American in Disguise,* '76)

Many people have spoken for me. They have said that my life is only one tale of the more encompassing Japanese-American success legend. They have said that my acceptance in the United States has been complete but that I must appease my discomfort with my dark hair, epicanthic fold of my eyes, and my yellow skin with the cultural laurels of Japan. While some tell me that "white is right," and I therefore can never "make it," others would have me believe that a syncopated rhythm of being Japanese and then American is an easy lifestyle.

To all these people, I have questioned, "Are you sure this is the solution to being an Asian-American woman in a predominantly white society?" I have doubted and even smothered my repulsion with all of these ideas. I have rejected each of them in turn, for I have refused to accept anything less than what I can comfortably and proudly describe as my ethnic experience.

Despite what one might believe, writers of the 70's like Daniel I. Okimoto have also failed to describe the Japanese-American experience accurately. *American in Disguise* is acclaimed as the first and, therefore, significantly important work of the post-war generation of Japanese-Americans. Unfortunately, his resolution to his identity problem is a renewed belief in dual personality and white racist love. Okimoto would have me believe that I must develop a cultural pride in Japan so that I need not feel apologetic for my ethnic history. Unlike Okimoto, however, I reject white society's expectations that I sensitively interpret Japan, let alone understand her. The Japanese nation is not the same as the fragmented development of a culture in a slightly hospitable country, handed down five generations: a condition resulting in the evolution of a distinctly Japanese-American culture.

For me, the life and spirit of Japanese America is sustained through its culture. It is not, as Daniel Okimoto believes, a fashionable tale easily concocted by anyone but the Japanese:

> ... it appears unlikely that literary figures of comparable stature to those minorities like the Jews and Blacks will emerge to articulate the Nisei soul. Japanese-Americans will be forced to borrow the voices of James Michener, Jerome Charyn, and other sympathetic novelists to distill their own experience. Even if a Nisei of Bernard Malamud's or James Baldwin's talents did appear, he would no doubt have little to say that John O'Hara has not already said (p. 150).

Rather, the Japanese-American experience is a human story recorded by these people in their own language, void of the stereotypes and over-used images white writers have imposed on ethnic minorities. Japanese-American writers don't speak a contemptible, humiliating American dialect. They speak a familiar language, a crazy, mixed-up combination of English and Japanese, that soothes and reassures me that I'm not a freak, an abnormal creature or, at best, a spectacle. Japanese-American writers have had the guts to establish their own criteria by which they wish to be judged; and having done that, they alone can effectively capture the familiar sounds, smells, feelings and idiosyncracies of Japanese America.

The literature itself evolved as people individually recorded on paper their stories of day-to-day incidents and tales of immigration. Though much of it was written in the years preceding World War II, it was not until the 1940's that a collection of literary works could be said to be available. The internment period turned out to be more than just a war-time security measure or a racist action for it brought together all those people who had believed themselves to be alone in their artistic pursuits. The cohesive and strengthened Japanese-American voice which developed was revealed in literary camp journals such as *Trek* and *All Aboard* which are bountiful packages of Japanese-American stories, poems and commentaries.

A Nisei, for example, assumed the pen name Globularious Schraubi to write with wit and humor about the intermixing of things Japanese and American that Okimoto claims the Japanese do not have. James Yamada writes stories with ethnic sensitivity. In "Guadeamus Igitur ...," he relates an Issei's experiences with his son at his graduation from U.C. Berkeley.

Through his story, he reflects the generation gap of the Issei's never-ending hope in and "shi kata ga nai" attitude toward life and the more apprehensive, questioning nature of the Nisei as he feels caught between two worlds. Toyo Suyemoto's poetry throbs with hope for better times, despite the windblown, uprooted life he's lived.

While these journals have sensitized me to the compassionate aspects of the relocation, the substance or lack of substance of sociological and historical studies, TV specials and publications only vaguely hint at the human indignities such an injustice involved. TV programs such as NBC's "Guilty by Reason of Race" stress the involvement of little girls and pregnant women in the internment. There is virtually no discussion concerning the effects upon the Japanese-American male, the obliteration of his style of manhood. Once again, his manhood has been made obsolete. As Jeffery Chan and Frank Chin write in "Racist Love" (*Seeing Through Shuck*), "At our worst we are contemptible because we are womanly, effeminate, devoid of all the traditionally masculine qualities of originality, daring, physical courage, creativity."

When I listened to Ernest Uno, a returning 442nd veteran, describe his homecoming, I couldn't disregard the humiliation and the indignation he conveyed. He and his family were reunited in the visiting quarters of a relocation camp while a white American sentry stood in the background, acting the role of overseer. Chaplain Roy Sano was then a young boy. He now often tells with incredulity of the times his dad would take him hunting for rats to supplement the camp rationings of meat. He vividly remembers the weeks just prior to relocation as well. His family would hang heavy wool blankets over the windows at night to stop the speed of any bullets shot at their house.

My dad doesn't talk about the years of the 1940's. He tries to but he can't. I do not even know where he was interned after Santa Anita and before he was drafted into the United States Army. He can't understand why Sansei activists must delve into those years. Although he knows that I too have questions to ask, defensiveness prevents me from asking them, let alone him answering. I'm really sorry that my dad can't accept the fact that we've inherited the scars of the psychological wounds he suffered. We've inherited the need to win back the love of a host-adopting country at almost any expense to ourselves. As I grew up, I was made to feel thankful that once again white folks would give me a chance to satisfy their expectations and to meet their standards. My early childhood world was secure because most of my closer friends were Japanese-American, but I inherited a consciousness of expectations and a cultural burden when we moved to West Covina, California.

That secure world of Japanese things and people revolved for me, as a child, around tomo ame, arare, dried cuttlefish, origami, udon at a mochi tsuki, fragile paper balloons with confetti inside them. My child world of Japan was equivalent to ba-chan (Grandma) and all that we shared. When I now read Toshio Mori's *Yokohama, California,* I can experience again the times we cooked tempura together, played with homemade beanbags, and walked to Tokyo Foods Market every Saturday. My Japanese-American childhood was losing a tooth and stuffing it under my pillow for the good fairy to take, only to learn the next morning that ba-chan didn't know about fairies who left nickels and dimes in exchange for a tooth.

The unquestionable naturalness of speaking a crazy Japanese-English language and of growing up Japanese-American comes alive again whenever I read Toshio Mori's stories. They are simple tales about the hopes, dreams, fears and personal conflicts of three generations of the Japanese. When his ba-chan tells her grandchildren about her immigration to the United States in "Tomorrow Will Come, Children," I feel the warmth and never-ending patience of ba-chan teaching me things. When Mori's characters speak, I can hear their pauses, feel their thoughtfulness over word selection, and relish their halting Japanese-American language. His love, compassion and human understanding envelop me in a secure time when I didn't feel I had to justify who I was. Indeed, his stories assure me that others had childhoods like mine, and my anxiety that I will always have to qualify the differences of my Japanese-American childhood to others disappears. It wasn't a time of what I didn't have but a time of all the treasures I did have.

When we moved from Pasadena to West Covina, I left my secure world of Japanese-America and learned to move to a frenzied and unpredictable rhythm of being both Japanese and American. That which was natural—being Japanese-American—was put on trial. My ethnic identity became an unending list of Japanese do's and do not's for we had to be good representatives of the Japanese people as the only Japanese kids in the school. My mother said that people would judge all that we did as characteristic of the Japanese in general. We had to do well and bring no shame to the family name; and although I followed her code of behavior for a long time, I don't think I was ever really convinced that it was correct or comfortable. It was simply easier to do than frustratingly to question why.

I'll never forget the "ching, chong Chinaman" phrases we heard or the etchings of slant-eyed Oriental faces on the walk in front of a Chinese home. If they had to call me names, I thought they could at least call me by the right name. I was made to feel different, if not weird; I learned to despise that element in me which would induce those taunting words. To resolve my discomfort over "sticking out like a sore thumb," I was determined to be the "best." I had to prove to myself that I was just as good as, if not better than, the white kids. I was determined not to let them laugh at me, make fun of me, or call me stupid; and by being "best," I wouldn't have to fear the guilt that would befall if I disgraced the family name.

Playing the duality role didn't really satisfy my questions about who I was when I tried to believe in it and to live it. I felt that I had to be expert on things Japanese. I had to know the proper Japanese names for objects, the correct origins of ceremonies. I always tried to present "my" culture to others on a silver platter before they could attack it. When the little awareness I did have about Japanese culture led to questions I couldn't answer, I felt ashamed and guilty. I had internalized the greater society's expectations to be culturally aware of a country I'd never lived in, let alone wanted to be responsible for. I was made to feel that cultural pride would justify and make good my difference in skin color while it was a constant reminder that I was different. I don't know why or when I started to do it, but I did question the relevance a culture "over there" had to do with my experiences "over here." For some reason, it just didn't jibe.

I too had accepted the brainwashing of white racist love—the belief that white standards of beauty, objectivity, behavior and achievement are morally absolute. I over-achieved in efforts to prove my capabilities to myself. I had to wash myself of feelings of deviancy. That was the time I didn't feel Japanesey when with Japanese; I saw myself more as white but not totally white. I was rejected by the Japanese community in part because they were jealous over my success at playing white, at beating them at their own game "to make it" in this society. I never denied that I was Japanese-American; I was only too aware of hating that element in me. When the white kids at school used to tell bad jokes about blacks, I wanted to scream at them, "Why not substitute Japanese for black? I'm not white either; we've only been sweet talked into thinking so." The bitter self-contempt which motivated me to excel and to accomplish many things only estranged me from my people. My mother was wrong; Japanese are not necessarily good to other Japanese or happy and proud of other Japanese successes. They're too busy trying to beat each other out and trying to prove they're not Japanese.

It was that rejection by my "own people" that unconsciously convinced me. I still couldn't verbalize it—that duality wasn't right. I had learned that I needed to seek the approval of both Japanese and whites when I was with one or the other of the groups. It's also why I hated to think of having dinner with the parents of most Japanese-American guys. I believed that they had a criterion of whiteness and a criterion of Japaneseness I was expected to fit. Most Nisei parents would want to know that I could easily fit into the company of either group. Yet, somehow, the stereotyped quiet, obedient, conforming modes of Japanese behavior clashed with white expectations of being a motivated, independent, ambitious thinker. When I was with whites, I worried about talking loud enough; when I was with Japanese, I worried about talking too loud. I refused to be hassled into trying to display the right quality at the right time so I skirted the issue entirely.

My childhood was not as quiet and graceful as a flower arrangement. It was fast—baseball, kick-the-can, war games in acres of strawberry farms, and occasional time-outs for asthma attacks. My actions and stance sometimes still reflect the shortstop, play-ball position of my baseball childhood. I resent and refuse to live up to James Michener's stereotype of pattering mama-san whose sole pleasure is serving her man for I refuse to be bossed or intimidated by men. I have had to be terribly self-sufficient and given the opportunity, I'll run other people. Having run our family for many years, I naturally take over when a group flounders and gets nowhere. I think I understand some of the problems Sansei guys try to deal with; I can often empathize with them. Yet, I think I destroy their egos more than help build them. I'm too independent, too impatient, and have too much desire to win an argument or be right. I know that I still have stereotyped images of them as they do of me but I try to destroy them. Then, too, because I talk so much, I can easily intimidate quieter guys and too often I'll order them around.

In part, my rejection of duality was due to my knowing that my childhood did not allow for the proper Japanese roles that white writers tell me I've experienced. Maybe it was because I knew I couldn't pull it off, let alone want to, that I turned my back on all of it. Yet, with that decision, I was left alone, with questions I couldn't really phrase but only feel, with no one I could really discuss these issues, and with a shaky conviction that I was right, but what exactly was I right about?

Japanese-American literature hasn't resolved all of my questions or problems but it's given me jargon and experiences to define rather than to deprive me of my own sensibility. It has confirmed that I am unique and that I don't have to be a split personality. It has solidified my convictions that my life wasn't weird because only a few people I knew had similar experiences. It was as it should have been—no changes, no deletions.

Writers like Lawson Inada and John Okada describe specific incidents, stories and feelings in their works; and through them, they expose the subtlest forms of white racism, and require one to come to grips with oneself and thereby accept oneself. They refuse to pretend that something doesn't exist, thinking that it will soon dissolve itself anyway. They hit ideas head on.

In Lawson Inada's book of poetry, *Before the War,* the camp experience, self-contempt and social comments are much of what hits home with me. While he implies hope through his musical style, he attacks racism, dual personality and self-contempt through his words. His railroad images express insider/outsider hostilities and suppression of racial interaction. He attacks the media's racism in language by using the same words and giving them different meanings. While the repeated phrase, "on the sly" reflects the sneaky Jap image of the media, "eju-kei-shung, eju-kei-shung" reflects the Issei pronunciation of English. "Their tongues were yellow with 'r's' and 'l's' " reflects a self-contempt in speaking English with a distinct Japanese accent. When Inada writes "I used to be Japanese" and "Don't marry no Chinese" at the end of his poems "Japs" and "Chinks," I can sense his ultimate contempt in proper names Japanese and Chinese.

In the novel *No-No Boy,* John Okada's hero Ichiro is a Japanese-American looking for his identity. Kenji is all-American while Ma is pro-Japan. Ichiro cannot merely intermarry to resolve his personal conflicts as Kenji suggests in his dream: "Go someplace where there isn't another Jap within a thousand miles. Marry a white girl or a Negro or an Italian or even a Chinese. Anything but a Japanese. After a few generations of that, you've got the thing beat" (p. 208).

He cannot, as does his mother, live with the delusion that Japan won the war. He wants and needs to be able to accept himself and to be worthy of himself even though Emi says that being Japanese and being American sometimes don't mix.

Through his usage of language, Okada reflects his cultural environment. "Not sick someplace for sure" is a crazy combination of words; and, yet, it has more ethnic quality than if Pa had merely asked, "Do you feel sick?" Funny, idiosyncratic changes in language reflect the telegraphic quality with which Issei attempt to speak English concisely and precisely. Likewise, Okada's description that Pa drinks tea with a "slup, slup" sound more effectively captures the old man's noisy intake of Japanese tea than would the words "slurp, slurp" which more comfortably accompany eating American soup.

Moreover, the characters of these writers are real; they are their own ethnic experience. They are not merely fabrications of white American culture made respectable by Margaret Mead and Pearl Buck. They have their personal problems to solve; and each battle is individual and unique. They are respectable and admirable in their own rights.

Writers such as Toshio Mori, Monica Sone, John Okada and Lawson Inada have helped me to more clearly define my perspective and my sensibility of who I am. I have always told myself that I was glad that I had two cultures for it gave me a varied awareness and double sensitivity to any event. The more pervasive discomfort of trying to live one and then the other, however, trapped me bad enough to convince me that double sensitivity was merely a weak compensating rationalization. I know now that it's not a matter of trying to live a culture. My identity is a matter of accepting myself with dignity, a self which is the result of the two cultural forces acting upon me. I am jolted when the good-looking Asian-American dude wins the pingpong match but loses the exotic Asian-American chick to a blonde, blue-eyed stud on the Command Dry and Natural Hair Spray commercial. I feel uncomfortable when I watch the movie *If Tomorrow Comes.* . . . Then I realize why: the hero, though Asian, fits white standards of attractiveness quite well. His cousin who is more "foreign looking" dies by the hands of the white man he hates because he retaliates, he gets mad, he fights back. He has guts. He refuses to be silent. The docile stereotype of Asian men persists for only they survive; the indignant and the belligerent are silenced.

To be Japanese-American used to mean writing my legal name as Joanne H. Sechi. The humiliation and embarrassment I experienced whenever white people massacred the pronunciation of my last name was enough for me to refuse to admit my middle name. First, it was a matter of self-contempt; having two Japanese names was too much to deal with. Moreover, I felt stupid because I didn't know what Harumi meant in a literal English translation.

Then it was a matter of protection; a refusal to subject it to the unimaginative tongues of white people. I used to think they were stupid because the only pronunciation they knew was English. If a foreign word or name sounded funny, I felt it was because the word was "foreign," and at fault— not because they did not have the ability to handle anything other than their own language. Those were the days when kids would jokingly ask if the H in my name was for "hara-kiri" which they pronounced "harry karry." Now when I tell people my middle name, I anticipate with impatient boredom their inquiry about its cultural significance. But if they can't deal with it, I know it's their problem, not mine.

Japanese-American writers have basically always had hope: in America, in music, in themselves. I likewise have hope that in time people will change and thereby be able to deal with others as people, to destroy racism and really to live with compassion and love. I still have hope but now I also believe more in myself as I am able to accept myself with dignity. I refuse to seek acceptance as anything that I am not—white American or Japanese. I am proudly Japanese-American.

GAIL Y. MIYASAKI

Gail Y. Miyasaki was born in 1949 in Hawaii, where she still lives and works as a publications editor and promotions assistant for Hawaii Public Television. She comments, "I am a third-generation Japanese-American (Sansei). My grandparents immigrated from rice-farming villages in rural Japan near the turn of the century.... I have taught ethnic studies (Japanese in Hawaii) at the University of Hawaii and Windward Community College in Hawaii; worked as a newspaper reporter and feature writer for the *Hawaii Hochi* and *Hawaii Herald,* bilingual newspapers (Japanese/English) in Honolulu; and have done various free-lance projects—most notable is the research and script writing for a multimedia presentation celebrating the eighty-fifth anniversary of the Honpa Hongwanji Mission (Buddhist) in Hawaii." Her publications include *Asian Women* (1971), *A Legacy of Diversity* (1975), *Montage: An Ethnic History of Women in Hawaii* (1977).

OBĀCHAN*

Her hands are now rough and gnarled from working in the canefields. But they are still quick and lively as she sews the "futon" cover. And she would sit like that for hours Japanese-style with legs under her, on the floor steadily sewing.

She came to Hawaii as a "picture bride." In one of her rare self-reflecting moments, she told me in her broken English-Japanese that her mother had told her that the streets of Honolulu in Hawaii were paved with gold coins, and so encouraged her to go to Hawaii to marry a strange man she had never seen. Shaking her head slowly in amazement, she smiled as she recalled her shocked reaction on seeing "Ojitchan's" (grandfather's) ill-kept room with only lauhala mats as bedding. She grew silent after that, and her eyes had a faraway look.

She took her place, along with the other picture brides from Japan, beside her husband on the plantation's canefields along the Hamakua coast on the island of Hawaii. The Hawaiian sun had tanned her deep brown. But the sun had been cruel too. It helped age her. Deep wrinkles lined her face and made her skin look tough, dry, and leathery. Her bright eyes peered out from narrow slits, as if she were constantly squinting into the sun. Her brown arms, though, were strong and firm, like those of a much younger woman, and so different from the soft, white, and plump-dangling arms of so many old teachers I had had. And those arms of hers were always moving—scrub-

* Grandmother.

bing clothes on a wooden washboard with neat even strokes, cutting vegetables with the big knife I was never supposed to touch, or pulling the minute weeds of her garden.

I remember her best in her working days, coming home from the canefields at "pauhana" time. She wore a pair of faded blue jeans and an equally faded navy-blue and white checked work shirt. A Japanese towel was wrapped carefully around her head, and a large straw "papale" or hat covered that. Her sickle and other tools, and her "bento-bako" or lunch-box, were carried in a khaki bag she had made on her back.

I would be sitting, waiting for her, on the back steps of her plantation-owned home, with my elbows on my knees. Upon seeing me, she would smile and say, "Tadaima" (I come home). And I would smile and say in return, "Okaeri" (Welcome home). Somehow I always felt as if she waited for that. Then I would watch her in silent fascination as she scraped the thick red dirt off her heavy black rubber boots. Once, when no one was around, I had put those boots on, and deliberately flopped around in a mud puddle, just so I could scrape off the mud on the back steps too.

Having retired from the plantation, she now wore only dresses. She called them "makule-men doresu," Hawaiian for old person's dress. They were always gray or navy-blue with buttons down the front and a belt at the waistline. Her hair, which once must have been long and black like mine, was now streaked with grey and cut short and permanent-waved.

The only time she wore a kimono was for the "Bon" * dance. She looked so much older in a kimono and almost foreign. It seemed as if she were going somewhere, all dressed up. I often felt very far away from her when we all walked together to the Bon dance, even if I too was wearing a kimono. She seemed almost a stranger to me, with her bent figure and her short pigeon-toed steps. She appeared so distantly Japanese. All of a sudden, I would notice her age; there seemed something so old in being Japanese.

She once surprised me by sending a beautiful "yūkata" or summer kimono for me to wear to represent the Japanese in our school's annual May Day festival. My mother had taken pictures of me that day to send to her. I have often wondered, whenever I look at that kimono, whether she had ever worn it when she was a young girl. I have wondered too what she was thinking when she looked at those pictures of me.

My mother was the oldest daughter and the second child of the six children Obāchan bore, two boys and four girls. One of her daughters, given the name of Mary by one of her school teachers, had been disowned by her for marrying a "haole" or Caucasian. Mary was different from the others, my mother once told me, much more rebellious and independent. She had refused to attend Honokaa and Hilo High Schools on the Big Island of Hawaii, but chose instead to go to Honolulu to attend McKinley High School. She

* The Lantern Festival, the Buddhist's All Soul's Day.

smoked cigarettes and drove a car, shocking her sisters with such unheard of behavior. And then, after graduation, instead of returning home, Mary took a job in Honolulu. Then she met a haole sailor. Mary wrote home, telling of her love for this man. She was met with harsh admonishings from her mother.

"You go with haole, you no come home!" was her mother's ultimatum.

Then Mary wrote back, saying that the sailor had gone home to America, and would send her money to join him, and get married. Mary said she was going to go.

"Soon he leave you alone. He no care," she told her independent daughter. Her other daughters, hearing her say this, turned against her, accusing her of narrow-minded, prejudiced thinking. She could not understand the words that her children had learned in the American schools; all she knew was what she felt. She must have been so terribly alone then.

So Mary left, leaving a silent, unwavering old woman behind. Who could tell if her old heart was broken? It certainly was enough of a shock that Honolulu did not have gold-paved streets. Then, as now, the emotionless face bore no sign of the grief she must have felt.

But the haole man did not leave Mary. They got married and had three children. Mary often sends pictures of them to her. Watching her study the picture of Mary's daughter, her other daughters know she sees the likeness to Mary. The years and the pictures have softened the emotionless face. She was wrong about this man. She was wrong. But how can she tell herself so, when in her heart, she only feels what is right?

"I was one of the first to condemn her for her treatment of Mary," my mother told me, "I was one of the first to question how she could be so prejudiced and narrow-minded." My mother looked at me sadly and turned away.

"But now, being a mother myself, and being a Japanese mother above all, I *know* how she must have felt. I just don't know how to say I'm sorry for those things I said to her."

Whenever I see an old Oriental woman bent with age and walking with short steps, whenever I hear a child being talked to in broken English-Japanese, I think of her. She is my grand-mother. I call her "Obāchan."

DIANA CHANG

A prolific writer, Diana Chang has published poetry in numerous journals and magazines and written six novels: *The Frontiers of Love* (1956), *A Woman of Thirty* (1959), *A Passion for Life* (1961), *The Only Game in Town* (1963), *Eye to Eye* (1974), and *A Perfect Love* (1978). Though she was born in New York, she spent her childhood in China reared by her Eurasian mother. Of herself, she says, "I feel I'm an American writer whose background is Chinese. The source of my first and fourth novels was Chinese, but exoticism can stand in the way of the universal I strive for in my themes. Therefore, since I write fiction in English and am living my life in the USA, I've often subsumed aspects of my background in the interest of other truths and recognitions. . . . I believe an abiding interest in character and emotion informs all my work—not only because the relationships, situations, and problems I write about arise out of the characters of my protagonists, out of their personalities, but also because I seem preoccupied a lot with identity or selfness. Being or becoming seems to be an underlying denominator of my work, at least so far. . . . My poems have been described as lyrical and concise, perhaps even too condensed. I hope to be economical and not dwell too lovingly on my own words. One owes it to everyone not to be boring."

WOOLGATHERING, VENTRILOQUISM AND THE DOUBLE LIFE

People who happen to write novels are nervous. I think one can make this statement without risking storms of controversy. And their nervousness is fully justified, it seems to me. I say "who happen to write novels," meaning to put it just that way, for I really think no one can *will* a novel into existence, and that deep down everyone who attempts to write one recognizes this with his heart in his mouth.

A great deal of writing comes from voluntary, though often dreaded, effort steadily applied, but what makes its whole form alive and breathing is a lucky happening. It is this very accidentalness, of course, which makes the would-be novelist so anxious. He knows his powers (or that synthesis of a set of necessary powers) are in the hands of arbitrary laws of chance. One can and must encourage and invite that chance with discipline, study and experience, but no one is ever absolutely certain of it. I don't think Lloyds of London would risk insuring it. Those born beautiful, who therefore have more than a normal fear of losing their perfection in a car crash, or those who can only hope against hope they will not be picked off by stray shrapnel in a war zone understand the precariousness all writers experience. Reality is disinterested, not giving a tinker's damn at all who you are.

There are many writers who have not died, but who are no longer writing. Some are leading full lives, relieved of literary ambitions, but they are no longer counted as writers simply because they are not onto their next work. Every book extant has an author, but the writer, to justify the name, must write. The moment a work is completed, he is again a would-be writer, a hopeful, naive, star-struck aspirant. For the next novel may never come right. Consequently, I personally only admit to writing at all when I'm *actually* in the process of putting something down on paper. And only if I'm specifically asked. Then I admit it in a mutter which I hope is inaudible and will not be held against me later, "Well, yes and no. I'm sort of thinking about something, maybe." Thinking, you notice. Not writing. There are other hedges (I've heard them with my own ears), but everyone is welcome to paraphrase mine.

After all, can I promise to have a particular dream next Tuesday night? In the theater I'm speaking of, there are no such things as command performances. Perhaps I won't be able to dream anything at all that I can remember. Maybe I won't have anything at all to write two hours from now on this very same afternoon. So how can I blatantly claim to be writing or to be a writer? Other people can declare, "I'm a nurse." Or, "I'm an architect specializing in motels." I don't notice them touching wood every time they're introduced as such, either. Yet, they would probably think it great to be Evan S. O'Connell, Jr. at a cocktail party, if they've heard of him. But he could be envying them, the characters he has peopled his books with or the people his characters will free into meaningfulness. And be hoping against hope he, The Writer, will be overlooked as he sips his drink while, at the same time, he's preparing his face not to look crestfallen if he's ignored.

Other people have occasionally referred to me as a writer. I realize they mean well. But it agitates me, gives me mixed feelings. They are feelings of sheepishness, dislocation (Me? All I really did yesterday was market and clean out a couple of closets.), and jeopardy. I would much rather they said, "She wrote a book I read last year. I forget the title." That's factual. I myself talk freely enough about books I've written, the longer ago the freer I am. I never discuss what I'm working on at the moment. And I've never called myself a writer. I'm too scared to. Anyhow, I'm a housewife more of the time.

From day to day, I'm only a person trying to live my life and possibly, with luck, get in the path of another idea. Trying to catch a beep, tune into a channel, all ears. But years could go by, with nothing going on up there in my particular language. It can make one feel deaf.

"How do you get an idea for a novel? Do you make up your characters out of whole cloth or do you keep specific friends in mind? A composite? Of people you know really well?" These are not impossible questions. They can be answered, more or less. But one suspects the questioner isn't going to be satisfied with the answers, and that's enervating from the outset. So the interviewee's face begins to look up against it while he sits down hard on his despair.

One doesn't "get" an "idea" for a novel. The "idea" more or less "gets" you. It uses you as a kind of culture, the way a pearl uses an oyster. One makes up characters in order to reveal, embody that-which-one-wants-to-say-through-that-story. Hopefully, they also and at the same time seem like real people. But story (or vehicle), characters, setting, theme exist for themselves and also for their relationship to, with, for, in and out of all the other ingredients. The shape of a Modigliani hand must satisfy the viewer as a hand, but its shape and placement on the canvas is also dependent on and determines all the other parts of the painting. Everything depends on everything else and is invented in relation to everything else. And must seem quite accidentally right. Every aspect of a novel has a secondary reason for being. That's probably what makes that ingredient feel so necessary, so rooted, so given, so inevitable. Maybe that's why people call writing creative. What is created exists like a hill. A hill is a rising form in itself. But it also brings out the opposite, makes valleys exist. And valleys give rise to hills. You can't see the one without the other. Each provides its contrast. What you are reading is contrasts. What you are moved by is relating, is relationship itself. A paragraph, a single page lifted out of a novel, has no magnetism, does no work.

It appears irrefutable to me that the life of one's imagination does not belong to one, you belong to it. You are seized by your imagination to dream out a particular story. Lawrence Durrell never promised to write any other species of novel. He is writing *his* novels, like them or not. They are writing themselves through Lawrence Durrell, which is why he lends his name to them, that twinkle in his eyes possibly one of disbelief.

I have learned there's no point starting a novel until one has an intuitive grasp of the whole. One can, of course, take notes, feel things out for a chapter or two. But it is the total form—the knowledge of the whole—which determines what one ought to invent for the parts. Intuitions about the total form cause one to feel very fertile about creating that which will manifest the form.

I'd begun a novel in which there were seven characters. At first, I tried telling it from one person's point of view, with all the others known only through his consciousness. I abandoned this and decided the story was better seen by each one of the seven, alternately. I had a plot, even all the chapters worked out on file cards and, of course, a theme. By theme, I mean a main preoccupation, the meaning of the thing, say, identity, or manhood, or the fear of dying. I had everything in hand, and also the desire to write it. But it would not jell. Finally, I put it aside. Perhaps someday it will occur to me how to tell this story. Or I will see it doesn't beg to be told at all. By me. Plenty of other people are doing an excellent job of not letting literature down, so I need not feel I've shirked the job.

But the book I've just finished writing came differently. Differently enough from my usual pattern (except for one other exception) to make me want to record it.

On and off for over a year I've had the temptation to figure out a novel to be entitled "Separate Checks." ("To figure out" accurately describes my drive, how I felt toward this possible project.) It was to be the story of two young women on a lunch date, two girls who knew each other well. At the end of the lunch, they ask for separate checks, which would also be a metaphor for the theme as their conversation would reveal it while they discuss their husbands or lovers. Each one is in her way separate, isolated, alone, as are the men they try to make relationships with. The girls are communicative with one another, but their relationships are oddly sterile, as are some of their friends'.

This idea recurred to me from time to time, but with no sense of urgency. I was simply toying with something. Besides, I couldn't quite commit myself to the alienated tone of this idea. I knew what one of the two young women had to be like: alluring, clued in, articulate but inextricably and disastrously hung up on impossible, emotionally crippled men. Her presence—the intimations I had about her personality—haunted me. It was almost as if she was in the room sometimes, lounging about while I read in my corner. But I knew her presence was not enough to make a story. I did not know in what way it was inadequate. However, now and then I daydreamed about this girl.

During this time I was also thinking about what it is that a woman is, what it means to be a woman. A woman today. What *is* gender, drive, sexuality, the ability to relate to one other person fully? I use the word thinking, but it is not apropos here. I was bothered, is more to the point. I was recurrently irked. It bugged me. I had disjointed, amorphous little dialogues with myself about Woman. But I would not have been able to say *what* it was I thought about the subject. I couldn't have produced a coherent magazine article on it. I wouldn't even have stated *that* I was interested in the subject.

But one day, a Thursday, I realized consciously I was indeed preoccupied about Women. Two days later I was walking on Madison Avenue with my husband. It was a brilliant New York afternoon, one of those Saturdays when the avenue seems festooned like a world's fair pavilion. We'd spent the day in and out of galleries, having a bite at a Soup Burg, talking about summer plans.

Suddenly, out of the blue, I felt . . . onto it. To the novel. Suddenly, I knew how the book *had* to be. The whole thing. My alluring hung-up girl would be the Other character, sitting across the table from the main character, the Narrator. In that instant, I realized exactly what the Narrator *had* to be like, so that their stories and personalities and life-styles would counterpoint the other, bring it out, as light makes shadow visible.

I knew too how they had to be involved, in a way the narrator herself does not suspect until the end. The narrator is a positive person but with a specific conflict, and the girls' regard for one another is profound and affectionate. The novel had a new title, "Girl Friends" (which I later changed to "Intimate Friends"), and the tone was one of engagement and not alienation.

The story possessed me, and I couldn't wait to get home and jot down an indication or two, quick, quick. I was like a needle recording a seismic tremor. I felt electrified, plugged in.

I felt in terror lest the story get lost. As if it were a river running along beside my life, and if I didn't dip my net in it right away, the fish I needed would be downstream and out of reach. I realize my similies are mixed, but I want to describe it in all the ways it felt like to me.

Once I started, which was the very next day, I did almost nothing else but write it. Or to be more exact, it wrote itself through me. I was driven and I drove the story onward, until I wrote the last sentence thirty-two days later. *As* I wrote the story (and not before I started), I invented two ex-husbands, a present husband, a lover, a couple who are good friends of both girls, and the scenes these people had roles in and at the same time made certain that each of the four men was distinctly different from the others and represented, if you like, complementary types as one might find them at large in New York. The couple provided a needed standard and contrast to the others, and the wife was necessary to bring the ending about. I brought in several neighborhoods of the city, and the general context of life in America now so that my two young women had a real world to live in.

I bring up all of the above only in order to make the point that I handled a lot of material, and I don't believe I am capable of it—that I could have managed it—consciously in so short a span of time. A violinist has to create notes with his left hand as he bows with the right. But I improvised and orchestrated a small band of people as I at the same time let the story unreel. I couldn't quite believe what was happening as it was happening. Scenes I invented—keeping the end firmly in mind—worked and foreshadowed what was needed relevantly and economically. There was no waste at all.

My terror and excitement and obsessiveness were practically unbearable. I was in a state. Exhausted by a day's work, I still begrudged myself half-an-hour's reading or relaxation lest—lest what? Lest what was afoot hurtle past me. I wanted to catch whatever was coming and plant it in the right place in the composition. I wanted to be all there to make those split-second decisions. In any case, I couldn't read. There was no room in me for new information; I was all taken up with this other life.

Each time I had to put my work aside to shop or cook or teach or chat with anyone, I felt I was being wrenched from a precious, necessary dream. But was I sleepwalking while writing? Or was I sleepwalking on the bus on the way to the dentist? I am inclined to believe I was awake as I was organizing the book at the typewriter. More awake than normally. Awake and anxious and viscerally engaged, and high.

I went through the motions of my regular life only half-invested in it, though I don't think anyone noticed, since my lips were sealed about the whole project. (I'm afraid my husband felt like a fifth wheel that month, but I kept his hopes up by telling him it was coming so fast it couldn't take very long in its entirety.) I walked around like someone who had done a tremendously long column of addition and was carrying a complicated six-digit figure in her head to add to the next column. I "protected" myself and held that figure away from the world, so that when I sat down again in my room, it was there and ready to be added to the next column while I invented *its* numbers.

I was truly living a double life, the way a pregnant woman does, or a secret agent. Things I was not aware I knew, my narrator was quite on top of. As soon as I found her voice, the writing of the novel was no problem at all. In fact, that Saturday afternoon it was her voice which started speaking through me. We'd made contact with each other, and that was why I felt onto it. Without that voice, the novel would never have come into being. I feel *she* wrote the novel. She knows what it means to have once been an actress, not I. The imagery is the way it is because she's an actress and therefore sees things a certain way. I've never been an actress. From the four quarters of myself, the information I needed arrived, bidden and also unbidden. If I had decided she had to be a market researcher, she would have supplied me with a different set of insights.

After those thirty-two days, she let me go, and I, the writer, got down to business. It took me three weeks simply to reread what I had. I cut practically nothing. But I added paragraphs, sentences, phrases, words to sharpen or to improve the cadence. Then I started the laborious, tedious, exacting, boring, irritating job of retyping it. Even if I'd wished it then, no one else could have done this first round of retyping. The manuscript was a mess and only I could have deciphered it. This retyping took me almost another four weeks. Every so often, while brushing my teeth or walking down the street, a correction or improvement came to mind, and I'd jot down or memorize the phrase and look for where it belonged in the manuscript. Until a couple of weeks after I finished the retyping, I was still listening, still aware of something asking to be heard. Then I felt returned from outer space. Or perhaps I should say inner space.

I had read almost nothing else during those two and a half months. An immense pile of magazines and parts of the *Times* I'd saved was waiting for me. This was the day I had longed for all those weeks. The day I'd be free again, not compelled, obsessed, in the throes of something I hadn't really invited. Again I was me, a single personality, both less and more autonomous.

Yet, now I also feel like a dancer who is condemned to walking only, and already I am like a has-been who doubts (and I'm not being disingenuous) she'll ever experience this kind of happening again. I am safe enough, landed back in one body, and grateful for having traveled. But I know what it's like and what I'm in danger of never achieving again. It's spellbinding and chancy, this business of being at the mercy of one's waking dreams.

TRADITIONS, NARRATIVES, AND FICTION

MAXINE HONG KINGSTON

Born in California in 1940, Maxine Hong Kingston currently lives in Hawaii. She has written numerous articles, book reviews, and poems that have appeared in journals and popular periodicals. Her book *The Woman Warrior* won the National Book Critics' Circle Award in 1976 and was listed as one of the best books of 1976 by *The New York Review of Books*. Of her writing, she says, "What I write is what I think, whether or not there is an audience. If others want to call my work fiction or nonfiction or ethnic or feminist, that's the way it goes. I do hope someday that readers will remember my work as human, transcending categories."

NO NAME WOMAN
From The Woman Warrior

"You must not tell anyone," my mother said, "what I am about to tell you. In China your father had a sister who killed herself. She jumped into the family well. We say that your father has all brothers because it is as if she had never been born.

"In 1924 just a few days after our village celebrated seventeen hurry-up weddings—to make sure that every young man who went 'out on the road' would responsibly come home—your father and his brothers and your grandfather and his brothers and your aunt's new husband sailed for America, the Gold Mountain. It was your grandfather's last trip. Those lucky enough to get contracts waved good-bye from the decks. They fed and guarded the stowaways and helped them off in Cuba, New York, Bali, Hawaii. 'We'll meet in California next year,' they said. All of them sent money home.

"I remember looking at your aunt one day when she and I were dressing; I had not noticed before that she had such a protruding melon of a stomach. But I did not think, 'She's pregnant,' until she began to look like other pregnant women, her shirt pulling and the white tops of her black pants showing. She could not have been pregnant, you see, because her husband had been gone for years. No one said anything. We did not discuss it. In early summer she was ready to have the child, long after the time when it could have been possible.

"The village had also been counting. On the night the baby was to be born the villagers raided our house. Some were crying. Like a great saw, teeth strung with lights, files of people walked zigzag across our land, tearing the rice. Their lanterns doubled in the disturbed black water, which drained away through the broken bunds. As the villagers closed in, we could see that some of them, probably men and women we knew well, wore white masks. The people with long hair hung it over their faces. Women with short hair made it stand up on end. Some had tied white bands around their foreheads, arms, and legs.

"At first they threw mud and rocks at the house. Then they threw eggs and began slaughtering our stock. We could hear the animals scream their deaths —the roosters, the pigs, a last great roar from the ox. Familiar wild heads flared in our night windows; the villagers encircled us. Some of the faces stopped to peer at us, their eyes rushing like searchlights. The hands flattened against the panes, framed heads, and left red prints.

"The villagers broke in the front and the back doors at the same time, even though we had not locked the doors against them. Their knives dripped with the blood of our animals. They smeared blood on the doors and walls. One woman swung a chicken, whose throat she had slit, splattering blood in red arcs about her. We stood together in the middle of the house, in the family hall with the pictures and tables of the ancestors around us, and looked straight ahead.

"At that time the house had only two wings. When the men came back, we would build two more to enclose our courtyard and a third one to begin a second courtyard. The villagers pushed through both wings, even your grandparents' rooms, to find your aunt's, which was also mine until the men returned. From this room a new wing for one of the younger families would grow. They ripped up her clothes and shoes and broke her combs, grinding them underfoot. They tore her work from the loom. They scattered the cooking fire and rolled the new weaving into it. We could hear them in the kitchen breaking our bowls and banging the pots. They overturned the great waist-high earthenware jugs; duck eggs, pickled fruits, vegetables burst out and mixed in acrid torrents. The old woman from the next field swept a broom through the air and loosed the spirits-of-the-broom over our heads. 'Pig.' 'Ghost.' 'Pig,' they sobbed and scolded while they ruined our house.

"When they left, they took sugar and oranges to bless themselves. They cut pieces from the dead animals. Some of them took bowls that were not broken and clothes that were not torn. Afterward we swept up the rice and sewed it back up into sacks. But the smells from the spilled preserves lasted. Your aunt gave birth in the pigsty that night. The next morning when I went for the water, I found her and the baby plugging up the family well.

"Don't let your father know that I told you. He denies her. Now that you have started to menstruate, what happened to her could happen to you. Don't humiliate us. You wouldn't like to be forgotten as if you had never been born. The villagers are watchful."

Whenever she had to warn us about life, my mother told stories that ran like this one, a story to grow up on. She tested our strength to establish realities. Those in the emigrant generations who could not reassert brute survival died young and far from home. Those of us in the first American generations have had to figure out how the invisible world the emigrants built around our childhoods fit in solid America.

The emigrants confused the gods by diverting their curses, misleading them with crooked streets and false names. They must try to confuse their offspring as well, who, I suppose, threaten them in similar ways—always trying to get things straight, always trying to name the unspeakable. The Chinese I know hide their names; sojourners take new names when their lives change and guard their real names with silence.

Chinese-Americans, when you try to understand what things in you are Chinese, how do you separate what is peculiar to childhood, to poverty, insanities, one family, your mother who marked your growing with stories, from what is Chinese? What is Chinese tradition and what is the movies?

If I want to learn what clothes my aunt wore, whether flashy or ordinary, I would have to begin, "Remember Father's drowned-in-the-well sister?" I cannot ask that. My mother has told me once and for all the useful parts. She will add nothing unless powered by Necessity, a riverbank that guides her life. She plants vegetable gardens rather than lawns; she carries the odd-shaped tomatoes home from the fields and eats food left for the gods.

Whenever we did frivolous things, we used up energy; we flew high kites. We children came up off the ground over the melting cones our parents brought home from work and the American movie on New Year's Day— *Oh, You Beautiful Doll* with Betty Grable one year, and *She Wore a Yellow Ribbon* with John Wayne another year. After the one carnival ride each, we paid in guilt; our tired father counted his change on the dark walk home.

Adultery is extravagance. Could people who hatch their own chicks and eat the embryos and the heads for delicacies and boil the feet in vinegar for party food, leaving only the gravel, eating even the gizzard lining—could such people engender a prodigal aunt? To be a woman, to have a daughter in starvation time was a waste enough. My aunt could not have been the lone romantic who gave up everything for sex. Women in the old China did not choose. Some man had commanded her to lie with him and be his secret evil. I wonder whether he masked himself when he joined the raid on the family.

Perhaps she encountered him in the fields or on the mountain where the daughters-in-law collected fuel. Or perhaps he first noticed her in the marketplace. He was not a stranger because the village housed no strangers. She had to have dealings with him other than sex. Perhaps he worked an adjoining field, or he sold her the cloth for the dress she sewed and wore. His demand must have surprised, then terrified her. She obeyed him; she always did as she was told.

When the family found a young man in the next village to be her husband, she stood tractably beside the best rooster, his proxy, and promised before they met that she would be his forever. She was lucky that he was her age and she would be the first wife, an advantage secure now. The night she first saw him, he had sex with her. Then he left for America. She had almost forgotten what he looked like. When she tried to envision him, she only saw the black and white face in the group photograph the men had had taken before leaving.

The other man was not, after all, much different from her husband. They both gave orders: she followed. "If you tell your family, I'll beat you. I'll kill you. Be here again next week." No one talked sex, ever. And she might have separated the rapes from the rest of living if only she did not have to buy her oil from him or gather wood in the same forest. I want her fear to have lasted just as long as rape lasted so that the fear could have been contained. No drawn-out fear. But women at sex hazarded birth and hence lifetimes. The fear did not stop but permeated everywhere. She told the man, "I think I'm pregnant." He organized the raid against her.

On nights when my mother and father talked about their life back home, sometimes they mentioned an "outcast table" whose business they still seemed to be settling, their voices tight. In a commensal tradition, where food is precious, the powerful older people made wrongdoers eat alone. Instead of letting them start separate new lives like the Japanese, who could become samurais and geishas, the Chinese family, faces averted but eyes glowering sideways, hung on to the offenders and fed them leftovers. My aunt must have lived in the same house as my parents and eaten at an outcast table. My mother spoke about the raid as if she had seen it, when she and my aunt, a daughter-in-law to a different household, should not have been living together at all. Daughters-in-law lived with their husbands' parents, not their own; a synonym for marriage in Chinese is "taking a daughter-in-law." Her husband's parents could have sold her, mortgaged her, stoned her. But they had sent her back to her own mother and father, a mysterious act hinting at disgraces not told me. Perhaps they had thrown her out to deflect the avengers.

She was the only daughter; her four brothers went with her father, husband, and uncles "out on the road" and for some years became western men. When the goods were divided among the family, three of the brothers took land, and the youngest, my father, chose an education. After my grandparents gave their daughter away to her husband's family, they had dispensed all the adventure and all the property. They expected her alone to keep the traditional ways, which her brothers, now among the barbarians, could fumble without detection. The heavy, deep-rooted women were to maintain the past against the flood, safe for returning. But the rare urge west had fixed upon our family, and so my aunt crossed boundaries not delineated in space.

The work of preservation demands that the feelings playing about in one's guts not be turned into action. Just watch their passing like cherry blossoms.

But perhaps my aunt, my forerunner, caught in a slow life, let dreams grow and fade and after some months or years went toward what persisted. Fear at the enormities of the forbidden kept her desires delicate, wire and bone. She looked at a man because she liked the way the hair was tucked behind his ears, or she liked the question-mark line of a long torso curving at the shoulder and straight at the hip. For warm eyes or a soft voice or a slow walk—that's all—a few hairs, a line, a brightness, a sound, a pace, she gave up family. She offered us up for a charm that vanished with tiredness, a pigtail that didn't toss when the wind died. Why, the wrong lighting could erase the dearest thing about him.

It could very well have been, however, that my aunt did not take subtle enjoyment of her friend, but, a wild woman, kept rollicking company. Imagining her free with sex doesn't fit, though. I don't know any woman like that, or men either. Unless I see her life branching into mine, she gives me no ancestral help.

To sustain her being in love, she often worked at herself in the mirror, guessing at the colors and shapes that would interest him, changing them frequently in order to hit on the right combination. She wanted him to look back.

On a farm near the sea, a woman who tended her appearance reaped a reputation for eccentricity. All the married women blunt-cut their hair in flaps about their ears or pulled it back in tight buns. No nonsense. Neither style blew easily into heart-catching tangles. And at their weddings they displayed themselves in their long hair for the last time. "It brushed the backs of my knees," my mother tells me. "It was braided, and even so, it brushed the backs of my knees."

At the mirror my aunt combed individuality into her bob. A bun could have been contrived to escape into black streamers blowing in the wind or in quiet wisps about her face, but only the older women in our picture album wear buns. She brushed her hair back from her forehead, tucking the flaps behind her ears. She looped a piece of thread, knotted into a circle between her index fingers and thumbs, and ran the double strand across her forehead. When she closed her fingers as if she were making a pair of shadow geese bite, the string twisted together catching the little hairs. Then she pulled the thread away from her skin, ripping the hairs out neatly, her eyes watering from the needles of pain. Opening her fingers, she cleaned the thread, then rolled it along her hairline and the tops of her eyebrows. My mother did the same to me and my sisters and herself. I used to believe that the expression "caught by the short hairs" meant a captive held with a depilatory string. It especially hurt at the temples, but my mother said we were lucky we didn't have to have our feet bound when we were seven. Sisters used to sit on their beds and cry together, she said, as their mothers or their slaves removed the bandages for a few minutes each night and let the blood gush back into their veins. I hope that the man my aunt loved appreciated a smooth brow, that he wasn't just a tits-and-ass man.

Once my aunt found a freckle on her chin, at a spot that the almanac said predestined her for unhappiness. She dug it out with a hot needle and washed the wound with peroxide.

More attention to her looks than these pulling of hairs and pickings at spots would have caused gossip among the villagers. They owned work clothes and good clothes, and they wore good clothes for feasting the new seasons. But since a woman combing her hair hexes beginnings, my aunt rarely found an occasion to look her best. Women looked like great sea snails—the corded wood, babies, and laundry they carried were the whorls on their backs. The Chinese did not admire a bent back; goddesses and warriors stood straight. Still there must have been a marvelous freeing of beauty when a worker laid down her burden and stretched and arched.

Such commonplace loveliness, however, was not enough for my aunt. She dreamed of a lover for the fifteen days of New Year's, the time for families to exchange visits, money, and food. She plied her secret comb. And sure enough she cursed the year, the family, the village, and herself.

Even as her hair lured her imminent lover, many other men looked at her. Uncles, cousins, nephews, brothers would have looked, too, had they been home between journeys. Perhaps they had already been restraining their curiosity, and they left, fearful that their glances, like a field of nesting birds, might be startled and caught. Poverty hurt, and that was their first reason for leaving. But another, final reason for leaving the crowded house was the never-said.

She may have been unusually beloved, the precious only daughter, spoiled and mirror gazing because of the affection the family lavished on her. When her husband left, they welcomed the chance to take her back from the in-laws; she could live like the little daughter for just a while longer. There are stories that my grandfather was different from other people, "crazy ever since the little Jap bayoneted him in the head." He used to put his naked penis on the dinner table, laughing. And one day he brought home a baby girl, wrapped up inside his brown western-style greatcoat. He had traded one of his sons, probably my father, the youngest, for her. My grandmother made him trade back. When he finally got a daughter of his own, he doted on her. They must have all loved her, except perhaps my father, the only brother who never went back to China, having once been traded for a girl.

Brothers and sisters, newly men and women, had to efface their sexual color and present plain miens. Disturbing hair and eyes, a smile like no other threatened the ideal of five generations living under one roof. To focus blurs, people shouted face to face and yelled from room to room. The immigrants I know have loud voices, unmodulated to American tones even after years away from the village where they called their friendships out across the fields. I have not been able to stop my mother's screams in public libraries or over telephones. Walking erect (knees straight, toes pointed forward, not pigeon-toed, which is Chinese-feminine) and speaking in an inaudible voice, I have tried to turn myself American-feminine. Chinese communication was loud, public. Only sick people had to whisper. But at the dinner table, where the family members came nearest one another, no one could talk, not the outcasts nor any eaters. Every word that falls from the mouth is a coin lost. Silently they gave and accepted food with both hands. A preoccupied child who took his bowl with one hand got a sideways glare. A complete moment of total attention is due everyone alike. Children and lovers have no singularity here, but my aunt used a secret voice, a separate attentiveness.

She kept the man's name to herself throughout her labor and dying; she did not accuse him that he be punished with her. To save her inseminator's name she gave silent birth.

He may have been somebody in her own household, but intercourse with a man outside the family would have been no less abhorrent. All the village were kinsmen, and the titles shouted in loud country voices never let kinship be forgotten. Any man within visiting distance would have been neutralized as a lover—"brother," "younger brother," "older brother"—one hundred and fifteen relationship titles. Parents researched birth charts probably not so much to assure good fortune as to circumvent incest in a population that has but one hundred surnames. Everybody has eight million relatives. How useless then sexual mannerisms, how dangerous.

As if it came from an atavism deeper than fear, I used to add "brother" silently to boys' names. It hexed the boys, who would or would not ask me to dance, and made them less scary and as familiar and deserving of benevolence as girls.

But, of course, I hexed myself also—no dates. I should have stood up, both arms waving, and shouted out across libraries, "Hey, you! Love me back." I had no idea, though, how to make attraction selective, how to control its direction and magnitude. If I made myself American-pretty so that the five or six Chinese boys in the class fell in love with me, everyone else—the Caucasian, Negro, and Japanese boys—would too. Sisterliness, dignified and honorable, made much more sense.

Attraction eludes control so stubbornly that whole societies designed to organize relationships among people cannot keep order, not even when they bind people to one another from childhood and raise them together. Among the very poor and the wealthy, brothers married their adopted sisters, like doves. Our family allowed some romance, paying adult brides' prices and providing dowries so that their sons and daughters could marry strangers. Marriage promises to turn strangers into friendly relatives—a nation of siblings.

In the village structure, spirits shimmered among the live creatures, balanced and held in equilibrium by time and land. But one human being flaring up into violence could open up a black hole, a maelstrom that pulled in the sky. The frightened villagers, who depended on one another to maintain the real, went to my aunt to show her a personal, physical representation of the break she had made in the "roundness." Misallying couples snapped off the future, which was to be embodied in true offspring. The villagers punished her for acting as if she could have a private life, secret and apart from them.

If my aunt had betrayed the family at a time of large grain yields and peace, when many boys were born, and wings were being built on many houses, perhaps she might have escaped such severe punishment. But the men—hungry, greedy, tired of planting in dry soil, cuckolded—had had to leave the village in order to send food-money home. There were ghost plagues, bandit plagues, wars with the Japanese, floods. My Chinese brother and sister had died of an unknown sickness. Adultery, perhaps only a mistake during good times, became a crime when the village needed food.

The round moon cakes and round doorways, the round tables of graduated size that fit one roundness inside another, round windows and rice bowls—these talismen had lost their power to warn this family of the law: a family must be whole, faithfully keeping the descent line by having sons to feed the old and the dead, who in turn look after the family. The villagers came to show my aunt and her lover-in-hiding a broken house. The villagers were speeding up the circling of events because she was too shortsighted to see that her infidelity had already harmed the village, that waves of consequences would return unpredictably, sometimes in disguise, as now, to hurt her. This roundness had to be made coin-sized so that she would see its circumference: punish her at the birth of her baby. Awaken her to the inexorable. People who refused fatalism because they could invent small resources insisted on culpability. Deny accidents and wrest fault from the stars.

After the villagers left, their lanterns now scattering in various directions toward home, the family broke their silence and cursed her. "Aiaa, we're going to die. Death is coming. Death is coming. Look what you've done. You've killed us. Ghost! Dead ghost! Ghost! You've never been born." She ran out into the fields, far enough from the house so that she could no longer hear their voices, and pressed herself against the earth, her own land no more. When she felt the birth coming, she thought that she had been hurt. Her body seized together. "They've hurt me too much," she thought. "This is gall, and it will kill me." Her forehead and knees against the earth, her body convulsed and then released her onto her back. The black well of sky and stars went out and out and out forever; her body and her complexity seemed to disappear. She was one of the stars, a bright dot in blackness, without home, without a companion, in eternal cold and silence. An agoraphobia rose in her, speeding higher and higher, bigger and bigger; she would not be able to contain it; there would be no end to fear.

Flayed, unprotected against space, she felt pain return, focusing her body.

This pain chilled her—a cold, steady kind of surface pain. Inside, spasmodically, the other pain, the pain of the child, heated her. For hours she lay on the ground, alternately body and space. Sometimes a vision of normal comfort obliterated reality: she saw the family in the evening gambling at the dinner table, the young people massaging their elders' backs. She saw them congratulating one another, high joy on the mornings the rice shoots came up. When these pictures burst, the stars drew yet further apart. Black space opened.

She got to her feet to fight better and remembered that old-fashioned women gave birth in their pigsties to fool the jealous, pain-dealing gods, who do not snatch piglets. Before the next spasms could stop her, she ran to the pigsty, each step a rushing out into emptiness. She climbed over the fence and knelt in the dirt. It was good to have a fence enclosing her, a tribal person alone.

Laboring, this woman who had carried her child as a foreign growth that sickened her every day, expelled it at last. She reached down to touch the hot, wet, moving mass, surely smaller than anything human, and could feel that it was human after all—fingers, toes, nails, nose. She pulled it up on to her belly, and it lay curled there, butt in the air, feet precisely tucked one under the other. She opened her loose shirt and buttoned the child inside. After resting, it squirmed and thrashed and she pushed it up to her breast. It turned its head this way and that until it found her nipple. There, it made little snuffling noises. She clenched her teeth at its preciousness, lovely as a young calf, a piglet, a little dog.

She may have gone to the pigsty as a last act of responsibility: she would protect this child as she had protected its father. It would look after her soul, leaving supplies on her grave. But how would this tiny child without family find her grave when there would be no marker for her anywhere, neither in the earth nor the family hall? No one would give her a family hall name. She had taken the child with her into the wastes. At its birth the two of them had felt the same raw pain of separation, a wound that only the family pressing tight could close. A child with no descent line would not soften her life but only trail after her, ghostlike, begging her to give it purpose. At dawn the villagers on their way to the fields would stand around the fence and look.

Full of milk, the little ghost slept. When it awoke, she hardened her breasts against the milk that crying loosens. Toward morning she picked up the baby and walked to the well.

Carrying the baby to the well shows loving. Otherwise abandon it. Turn its face into the mud. Mothers who love their children take them along. It was probably a girl; there is some hope of forgiveness for boys.

"Don't tell anyone you had an aunt. Your father does not want to hear her name. She has never been born." I have believed that sex was unspeakable and words so strong and fathers so frail that "aunt" would do my father mysterious harm. I have thought that my family, having settled among immigrants who had also been their neighbors in the ancestral land, needed to clean their name, and a wrong word would incite the kinspeople even here. But there is more to this silence: they want me to participate in her punishment. And I have.

In the twenty years since I heard this story I have not asked for details nor said my aunt's name; I do not know it. People who can comfort the dead can also chase after them to hurt them further—a reverse ancestor worship. The real punishment was not the raid swiftly inflicted by the villagers, but the family's deliberately forgetting her. Her betrayal so maddened them, they saw to it that she would suffer forever, even after death. Always hungry, always needing, she would have to beg food from other ghosts, snatch and steal it from those whose living descendants give them gifts. She would have to fight the ghosts massed at crossroads for the buns a few thoughtful citizens leave to decoy her away from village and home so that the ancestral spirits could feast unharassed. At peace, they could act like gods, not ghosts, their descent lines providing them with paper suits and dresses, spirit money, paper houses, paper automobiles, chicken, meat, and rice into eternity—essences delivered up in smoke and flames, steam and incense rising from each rice bowl. In an attempt to make the Chinese care for people outside the family, Chairman Mao encourages us now to give our paper replicas to the spirits of outstanding soldiers and workers, no matter whose ancestors they may be. My aunt remains forever hungry. Goods are not distributed evenly among the dead.

My aunt haunts me—her ghost drawn to me because now, after fifty years of neglect, I alone devote pages of paper to her, though not origamied into houses and clothes. I do not think she always means me well. I am telling on her, and she was a spite suicide, drowning herself in the drinking water. The Chinese are always very frightened of the drowned one, whose weeping ghost, wet hair hanging and skin bloated, waits silently by the water to pull down a substitute.

HISAYE YAMAMOTO

Hisaye Yamamoto was born in California in 1921. Her short stories have been widely published in such magazines and journals as *Partisan Review, Kenyon Review, Furioso, Arizona Quarterly,* and *Amerasia Journal,* and have also appeared in *Asian American Authors* (1972), *Asian American Heritage* (1974), *Aiiieeeee: An Anthology of Asian American Writers* (1975), and *Counterpoint* (1976).

LAS VEGAS CHARLEY

There are very few Japanese residing in Las Vegas proper, that glittering city which represents, probably, the ultimate rebellion against the Puritan origins of this singular country. A few Japanese families farm on the outskirts, but I can't imagine what they grow there in that arid land where, as far as the eye can see from a Greyhound bus (and a Scenicruiser it was, at that), there are only sand, bare mountains, sagebrush, and more sand. Sometimes the families come into town for shopping; sometimes they come for a feast of Chinese food, because the Japanese regard Chinese cuisine as the height of gourmandism, to be partaken of on special occasions, as after a wedding or a funeral.

But there are a handful of Japanese who live in the city itself, and they do so because they cannot tear themselves away. They are victims of Las Vegas fever, that practically incurable disease, and while they usually make their living as waiters or dishwashers, their principal occupation, day after hopeful day, is to try their luck at feeding those insatiable mechanical monsters which swallow up large coins as though they were mere Necco wafers, or at blotting out, on those small rectangular slips of paper imprinted with Chinese characters, the few black words which may justify their whole existence.

The old Japanese that everyone knew as Charley (he did not mind being called that—it was as good a name as any and certainly easier to pronounce than Kazuyuki Matsumoto) was a dishwasher in a Chinese restaurant. His employer, a most prosperous man named Dick Chew, owned several cafés in the city, staffed by white waitresses and by relatives he had somehow arranged—his money was a sharp pair of scissors that snipped rapidly through tangles of red tape—to bring over from China. Mr. Chew dwelt, with his wife and children, in a fabulous stucco house which was a showplace (even the mayor had come to the housewarming). He left most of the business in the hands of relatives and went on many vacations. One year he had even gone as far as England, to see London and the charms of the English countryside.

As for Charley, he worked ten hours a night, in five-hour shifts. He slept a few hours during the day, in a dormitory with the Chinese kitchen employees; the rest of his free time was spent in places called the Boulder Club, the California Club, the Pioneer Club, or some such name meant to evoke the derring-do of the Old West. He belonged to the local culinary union, so his wages were quite satisfactory. His needs were few; sometimes he bought a new shirt or a set of underwear. But it never failed: at the end of each month, he was quite penniless.

Not that life was bleak for Charley, not at all. Each day was exciting, fraught with the promise of sudden wealth. Why, one Japanese man who claimed to be eighty-five years old had won $25,000 on a keno ticket! And he had been there only a day or two, on a short holiday from Los Angeles. The Oriental octogenarian's beaming face (Charley decided the man had lied about his age; he looked to be more his own age—sixty-two or so) had been pictured on the front page of the *Las Vegas Sun,* and Charley had saved the whole newspaper, to take out and study now and then, in envy and hope.

And all the waitresses were nice to Charley, not only because Charley was a conscientious dishwasher (better than those sloppy Chinese, they confided), but because he was usually good for the loan of a few dollars when their luck had been bad. The bartender was also very good to him; when he came off shift at six o'clock in the morning, tired to the bone, there was always waiting for him a free jigger or two of whiskey, which would ease his body and warm his spirit, reminding him sometimes of the small glass of *sake* he had been wont to sip, with an appetizer of pickled greens, just before supper, after a day's toil out in the fields. (But it seemed as though it had been another man, and not himself, who had once had a farm in Santa Maria, California, and a young wife to share his work and his bed.)

Then there had been the somewhat fearful time when the Army had conducted those atom bomb tests in the Nevada desert. Everyone had talked about it; the whole town had been shaken by intermittent earthquakes, each accompanied by a weird flash of light that hovered over the whole town for a ghastly instant. It was during this time that Charley had been disconcerted by a tipsy soldier, who, after their first encounter, had searched out Charley time and again. Although Charley's command of pidgin English was not sufficient to take in every meaning of the soldier's message, he had understood that the man was most unhappy over having been chosen to push the button that had dropped the atomic bomb over Hiroshima.

Indeed, once, tears streaming down his cheeks, the soldier had grabbed Charley by the shoulders and apologized for the heinous thing he had done to Charley's people. Then he had turned back to his drink, pounded the counter with one tight fist, and muttered, "But it was them or us, you understand, it was them or us!"

Charley had not said a word then. What was there to say? He could have said he was not from Hiroshima, but from Kumamoto, that province whose natives are described as among the most amiable in all Japan, unless aroused, and then they are considered the most dangerous. He could have said that the people of Kumamoto-*ken* had always regarded the people of Hiroshima-*ken* as being rather too parsimonious. But his English was not up to imparting such small talk, and he doubted, too, that information of this kind would have been of much interest to such a deeply troubled man.

So Charley was doubly relieved when the Army finally went away. The soldier had revived a couple of memories which Charley had pushed far back in his mind. There had been that time, just after the war, when he had been a janitor in Los Angeles' Little Tokyo, and he had been walking down the sidewalk, just minding his own business. This white man had come out of nowhere, suddenly shoved Charley against a wall, and placed an open penknife against his stomach. "Are you Japanese or Chinese?" the man had demanded, and Charley had seen then that the man, middle-aged, red-faced, had been drinking. Charley had not said a word. What was there to say at such a startling time? "If you're Chinese, that's okay, but if you're Japanese . . . !" The man had moved the point of the penknife a little closer to Charley's stomach. Charley had remained silent, tense against the brick wall of the building. Then, after a few moments, possibly because he obtained no satisfaction, no argument, the man had closed his penknife and gone unsteadily on his way.

There had been a similar incident not long after, but Charley had talked his way out of that one. Charley had just gotten off the streetcar when he bumped into a Mexican man about his own age. This man, who had also reeked of liquor, had grabbed his arm tightly and cursed him. "My boy, my Angel, he die in the war! You keel him! Only nineteen years old, and you Japs keel him! I'm going to keel you!" But somehow a Mexican had not been as intimidating as a white man; hadn't he hired Mexicans once upon a time, been their boss, each summer when he and his wife had needed help with the harvesting of the vegetables?

"Mexicans, Japanese, long time good friends," Charley had answered. "My boy die in the war, too. In Italy. I no hate Germans. No use."

Wonderingly, the Mexican had released his grip on Charley's arm. "Oh, yeah?" he had asked, tilting his head.

The magic word had come to Charley's tongue. *"Verdad,"* he had said, *"Verdad."* *

So this man, too, had turned away and gone, staggering a bit from side to side.

It was not long after that Charley, dismissed from his janitorial duties for spending too much time in the pool hall down in the basement, had been sent by the Japanese employment agency to Las Vegas, where dishwashers were in great demand.

It was like Paradise: the heavy silver dollars that were as common as pennies; the daily anticipation of getting rich overnight; the rejoicing when a fellow worker had a streak of luck and shared his good fortune with one and all, buying presents all around (the suitcase under Charley's bed became full of expensive neckties which were never used) and treating everyone to the drink of his choice.

It was a far cry from Tomochi-machi, that small village of his birth in the thirtieth year of the reign of the Emperor Meiji. The place had been known in those days as Hara-machi, meaning wilderness, and it had been a lonely backwoods, in a sector called Aza-Kashiwagawa, or Oakstream. Above his father's tiny house had risen the peaks of Azame-yama and Karamata-dake; beyond that mountains higher still. Below was Midori-kawa, Emerald Lake, where abounded the troutlike fish called *ayu*. The mountains about were thick with trees, the larger of them pine and redwood, and he had, as a small boy, been regularly sent to bring down bundles of wood.

He still wore a deep purple scar on his leg from those days, and there was a bitterness he could not help when he remembered why. A nail had lodged deep in his leg, too deep to remove; the leg had swollen to a frightening size and finally the nail had burst out with the pus. He could not forget that when he was in agony from the pain and unable to walk, his mother (that good, quiet woman) had asked, "Will you bring down one more load of wood from the mountain?"

He had attended school for two or three years, but he was not much for studying, so he had hired out as a babysitter, going about his chores with some damp baby strapped to his back. Older, he had worked on farms.

When he was twenty, he had ridden the *basha*, the horse-drawn carriage, to the town of Kumamoto, from thence taken the train to Nagasaki, where he had boarded the *Shunryo-Maru* as a steerage passenger bound for America, that far land where, it was said, people had green hair and red eyes, and where the streets were paved with gold.

In Santa Maria, friends who had preceded him there from his village had helped him lease a small farm (Japanese were not allowed to buy property, they told him—it was part of something called a Gentleman's Agreement

* Truth.

between Japan and the United States). A couple of years later, his picture bride, Haru, had joined him, and she had been a joy as refreshing as the meaning of her name (Spring), hard-working, docile, eager to attend to his least wants. Within the first year, she had presented him with a boy-child, whom they had named Isamu, because he was the first.

What New Year celebrations they had held in this new land! Preparations had begun about Christmastime, with relatives and friends gathering for the day-long making of rice cakes. Pounds and pounds of a special glutinous rice, soaked overnight in earthen vats, would be steamed in square wooden boxes, two or three piled one atop the other, over an outside fire. The men would all tie handkerchiefs or towels about their heads, to absorb the sweat, then commence to clean out the huge wooden mortar, the tree trunk with a basin carved out at the top. One box of the steaming rice would be dumped into the basin; then the rhythmic pounding of the rice would begin, the men grunting exaggeratedly as they wielded the long-handled wooden mallets. Usually two men at a time would work on the rice, while one woman stood by with a pan of cold water. It was the woman's job to quickly dab water at the rice dough so it would not stick to the mortar or mallets, while the men did not once pause in their steady, alternate pounding.

The rest of the aproned women would be waiting at a long table spread with befloured newspapers, and when the rice had become a soft lump of hot dough, it was thrown onto the table, where each woman would wring off a handful to pat into shape before placing it on a floured wooden tray. Some of the cakes would be plain, some filled with a sweet mealy jam made of an interminable boiling together of tiny, maroon Indian beans and sugar. There were not only white cakes; there were pink ones, made so during the pounding with a touch of vegetable coloring; green ones, made so during the steaming with the addition of dried seaweed; and yellow ones, which were green ones dusted with orangish bean flour.

But the main purpose of the work was to make the larger unsweetened cakes which in tiers two or three high, one tier for each member of the family, topped with choice tangerines with the leafy stems left on, decorated the *hotoke-sama,* the miniature temple representing the Buddha which occupies a special corner in every Buddhist household. On New Year's morning, the cakes would be joined, reverently placed, by miniature bowls of rice and miniature cups of *sake.*

Sometimes, enough *mochi* was made to last almost throughout the whole year, either preserved in water periodically changed, or cut into strips and dried. The sweet cakes would be eaten early, toasted on an asbestos pad over the tin winter stove (when done, the dark filling would burst out in a bubble); the soaked rice would be boiled and eaten plain with soy sauce or sugared bean flour, or made into dumplings with meat and vegetables. The dried flinty strips would be fried in deep oil until they became crisp, puffy confections which were sprinkled with sugar.

How rosy the men had grown during the cake-making, not only from their exertions but from frequently repairing to the house for a taste of fresh *mochi* and a sip of *sake*. There would be impromptu singing above the sound of the slapping mallets; women chasing men with threatening, floury hands; and continuous shouted jokes with earthy references more often than not.

Then, on New Year's Eve, Haru would prepare the last meal of the year, to be eaten just before midnight. This was *somen,* the very thin, gray, brown-flecked noodles, served with *tororo,* the slippery brown sauce of grated raw yams. At the stroke of midnight, Kazuyuki Matsumoto (he was not Charley then) went outside with his shotgun and used up several shells, to bid appropriate farewell to the passing year.

On New Year's morning, dressed in brand-new clothing, Kazuyuki and Haru would, following tradition, eat that first breakfast of the New Year, the thick soup of fresh *mochi* dumplings, vegetables, tender strips of dried cuttlefish. It was also necessary to take, from tiny cups, token sips of hot mulled *sake,* poured from a small porcelain decanter shaped like a rosebud vase.

Then it was open house everywhere, for almost the whole week, and it was an insult not to accept token sips of hot *sake* at each house visited. Sometimes Kazuyuki Matsumoto was so polite that when they somehow arrived home, in that old topless Ford, Haru had to unlace his shoes, undress him, and tuck him in bed.

And the ritual was the same with each friend seen for the first time in the year, each solemn, prescribed greeting accompanied by deep, deep bows:

"Akema-shite omedeto gozai-masu." (The old year has ended and the new begun—congratulations!)

"Sakunen wa iro-iro o-sewa ni nari-mashite, arigato gozai-masu." (Thank you for the many favors of the past year.)

"Konnen mo onegai itashi-masu." (Again this year, I give myself unto your care.)

What a mountain of food Haru had prepared on New Year's Eve, cooking till almost morning: bamboo shoots, stalks of pale green bog rhubarb, both taken from cans with Japanese labels; red and white fish galantines, fish rolls with burdock root centers, both of these delicacies purchased ready-made from the Japanese market; fried shrimp; fried chicken; thin slices of raw fish; gelatinous red and white agar-agar cakes, tasting faintly of peppermint; sweet Indian-bean cakes; dried herring roe soaked in soy sauce; vinegared rice rolls covered with thin sheets of dried seaweed and containing in the center thin strips of fried egg, canned eel, long strings of dried gourd, mushrooms, carrots, and burdock root—neatly sliced; triangles of fried bean curd filled with vinegared rice and chopped vegetables; sliced lotus root stems, which when bitten would stretch shimmering, cobwebby filaments from the piece in your mouth to the remnant between your chopsticks. The center-piece was usually a huge red lobster, all appendages intact, or a red-gold sea-bream, resting on a bed of parsley on the largest and best platter in the house.

But that had been long, long ago. The young Japanese, the *nisei*, were so Americanized now. While most of them still liked to eat their boiled rice, raw fish, and pickled vegetables, they usually spent New Year's Eve in some nightclub. Charley knew this because many of them came to Las Vegas, from as far away as San Francisco and Los Angeles, to inaugurate the New Year.

Then, abruptly, Haru, giving birth to the second boy, had died. He had been a huge baby, almost ten pounds, and the midwife said Haru, teeth clenched, had held with all her might to the metal bed rods behind her head; and at long last, when the infant gargantua had emerged, she had asked, "Boy or girl?" The midwife had said, "It's a boy, a giant of a boy!" And Haru, answering, "Good . . . ," had closed her eyes and died.

Kazuyuki Matsumoto had sent his two small sons over to a cousin of Haru's, but this woman, with five older children of her own, had eventually, embarrassedly, confessed that her husband was complaining that the addi-tional burden was too much, that the babies did not allow her enough time in the fields. So Kazuyuki had taken his sons to Japan, to Tomochi-machi, where his own mother had reluctantly accepted them.

Returning to California, Kazuyuki had stopped farming on his own and worked for friends, for twenty cents an hour with room and board. Frugal, he sent most of his wages to Japan, where, at the favorable rate of exchange, his mother and father had been able to build a larger house and otherwise raise their standard of living, as well as their prestige in the sector.

For several years, Kazuyuki had kept to this unvaried but rewarding way of life. Friends had shaken their heads over his truly self-sacrificing ways; he was admired as an exceptional fellow.

But Kazuyuki, living in bunkhouses with the other seasonal workers, who were usually bachelors, gradually came to love the game of *hana-fuda*, flower cards, which relaxed him of evenings, giving him a more immediate pleasure to look forward to than taking a hot bath and going to bed. So the money orders to Japan became fewer and farther between before they had finally stopped. By that time, Kazuyuki had wandered the length of California, picking grapes in Fresno, peaches in Stockton, strawberries in Watsonville, flowers in San Fernando, cantaloupe in Imperial Valley, always ending his day and filling his Saturdays off with the shuffling and dealing of flower cards.

His mother had written once in a while, in her unpunctuated *katakana*,*

* The straight-lined or square Japanese syllabary.

unacknowledged (he was not one for writing letters) messages which nevertheless moved him to the core, saying that his sons were fine and bright, but that both she and his father were getting older and that they would like to see him once more before they died. When was he coming to visit them? Finally, his father had died during the New Year holidays; they had found him drunk, lying helplessly there on the steep path home after visiting friends in the village below. Since this had become a common event, they had merely carried him home and put him to bed. But this, as it happened, was the sleep from which he never awoke.

Learning of this news, Kazuyuki had secretly wept. Like father, like son, the saying went, and it was true, it was true. He was as worthless, as *tsumaranai*, as his father had in the end become.

The shock had the effect of reforming him; he gave up flower cards and, within a couple of diligent years, had saved enough money to send for his boys. The wages had risen to fifty cents per hour with room and board; the rate of exchange had become even more favorable, so his few hundred American dollars had amounted to a considerable pile of yen.

With his sons by his side to assist him, he leased again a small farm, this time in Orange County, but somehow things did not go well. They tried things like tomatoes and Italian squash. The vegetables flourished, but it seemed that since the man called Rusuberuto had been elected President of the United States, there had come into being a system called prorating, in which one had to go into town and get coupons which limited the number of boxes one could pick and send to market. This was intended to keep the prices up, to help the farmer. The smaller the farm, the fewer the coupons it was allotted, so it was a struggle. They lived on tomato soup and sliced Italian squash fried in batter—this was quite tasty, with soy sauce —and, of course, boiled rice, although the cost of a hundred-pound sack of Blue Rose had become amazing. During the winter, the fare was usually the thick yellow soup made by adding water to soy bean paste, and pickled vegetables.

At first, too, the relationship with his sons had been a source of distress. They had expected wondrous things of America, not this drudgery, this poverty. Alien, too, to their father, they had done his bidding as though he were some lord and master who expected them to wash his feet. This had annoyed him and he had treated them sternly, too sternly. And both of them had been resentful of the fact that their contemporaries here, the *nisei,* looked down upon them as *kibei,* for lacking English, as though there were rice hulls sticking to their hair.

As he had come to know them better, however, he saw that the two were as different as gray and white. Isamu, now nineteen, was quick to pick up colloquial English, eager to learn how to drive the old pickup truck, fascinated with the American movies which now and then they were able to afford, and his father perceived that he was ambitious, perhaps too ambitious, restless for the day when he could own a shining automobile and go on his way. Noriyuki, two years younger, was more like Haru, quiet, amiable, content to listen to the Japanese popular songs which he played over and over on the Victrola (he sang a nice baritone himself as he worked out in the fields), and he spoke nostalgically of his grandmother, the blue-green coolness of Midori-kawa, the green loveliness of the fields of rape and barley in the spring.

Then, after only a little more than a year together, had come the incredible war, and the trio, along with all the other Japanese on the West Coast, had been notified that they would be sent to concentration camps. How uneasy they had been in those days, with government men coming in unannounced, on three occasions, to inspect the small wooden house for evidence of sabotage. In their panic, they had burned all their Japanese magazines and records, hidden the *hotoke-sama,* buried the *judo* outfits and the *happi* coats the boys had brought with them from Japan. They had had to turn in their little Kodak (it had never been retrieved), lest they be tempted to photograph American military installations and transmit them secretly to Japan.

But the Arizona concentration camp, once they became accustomed to the heat and dust and mudstorms, was not too unbearable. In fact, Noriyuki, with his repertoire of current Japanese songs, became quite popular with even the *nisei* girls, and he was in great demand for the amateur talent shows which helped illuminate that drab incarceration. Kazuyuki Matsumoto settled for a job as cook in one of the mess halls; Isamu immediately got a job driving one of the covered surplus Army trucks which brought supplies to these mess halls; and Noriyuki went to work with the men and women who were making adobe bricks for the school buildings which the government planned to build amidst the black tarpapered barracks.

One day, a white officer, accompanied by a *nisei* in uniform, came to recruit soldiers for the United States Army, and Isamu was among the few who unhesitatingly volunteered. He was sent to Mississippi, where an all-Japanese group from Hawaii and the mainland was being given basic training, and his regular letters to his father and brother indicated that he was, despite some reservations, satisfied with his decision. Once he was able to come on a furlough, and they saw that he was a new man, all (visible) trace of boy gone, with a certain burliness, a self-confidence that was willing to take on all comers. Then, after a silence, came small envelopes called V-Mail, which gave no indication of his whereabouts. Finally, he was able to tell them that he was in Italy, and he sent them sepia postcards of the ancient ruins of Rome. Almost on the heels of this packet, the telegram had come, informing them of the death in action of Pfc. Isamu Matsumoto; a later letter from his sergeant had filled in the details—it had occurred near a town called Grosseto; it had been an 88-millimeter shell; death had been (if it would comfort) instantaneous.

Kazuyuki Matsumoto continued to cook in the mess hall and Noriyuki went on making adobe bricks. After the school buildings were completed— they turned out quite nicely—Noriyuki decided to attend classes in them. As he was intelligent and it was mostly a matter of translating his solid Japanese schooling into English, he skipped rapidly from one grade to the next, and although he never lost the accent which marked him as a *kibei*, he was graduated from the camp high school with honors.

By this time, Kazuyuki Matsumoto was on the road that would lead, inexorably, to Las Vegas. At first, in that all-Japanese milieu, he had taken courage and tried courting a *nisei* spinster who worked as a waitress in the same mess hall. Once he had even dared to take her a gift of a bag of apples, bought at the camp canteen; but the woman already had her eye on a fellow-waiter several years her junior. She refused the apples and proceeded to ensnare the younger man with a desperation which he was simply not equipped to combat. After this rejection, Kazuyuki Matsumoto had returned to his passion for flower cards. What else was there to do? He had tried passing the time, as some of the other men did, by making polished canes of mesquite and ironwood, by carving and enameling little birds and fish to be used as brooches, but he was not truly cut out for such artistic therapy. Flower cards were what beguiled—that occasional unbeatable combination of the four cards: the pink cherry blossoms in full, festive bloom; the black pines with the stork standing in between; the white moon rising in a red sky over the black hill; and the red-and-black crest symbolizing the paulownia tree in flower.

Then had come the day of decision. The government announced that all Japanese wanting to return to Japan (with their American-born children) would be sent to another camp in northern California, to await the sailings of the Swedish *Gripsholm*. The removal was also mandatory for all young men of draft age who did not wish to serve in the United States Army and chose to renounce their American citizenship. Kazuyuki Matsumoto, busy with the cooking and absorbed in flower cards, was not too surprised when Noriyuki decided in favor of Japan. At least, there would not be another son dead in Europe; the boy would be a comfort to his grandmother in her old age. As for himself, he would be quite content to remain in this camp the rest of his life—free food, free housing, friends, flower cards; what more could life offer? It was true that he had partially lost his hearing in one ear, from standing by those hot stoves on days of unbearable heat, but that was a small complaint. The camp hospital had provided free treatment, free medicines, free cottonballs to stuff in his bad ear. Kazuyuki Matsumoto was far from agreeing with one angry man who had one day, annoyed with a severe duststorm, shouted, "America is going to pay for every bit of this suffering! Taking away my farm and sending me to this hell! Japan will win the war, and then we'll see who puts who where!"

So Noriyuki was among those departing for Tule Lake, where, for a time, he thoroughly enjoyed the pro-Japanese atmosphere, the freedom of shouting a *banzai* or two whenever he felt like it. Then, despite himself, he kept remembering a *nisei* girl in that Arizona camp he thought he had been glad to leave behind. She had wept a little when he left. He recalled the habit she had of saying something amusing and then sticking out her tongue to lick a corner of her lip. He began to dream of her almost nightly. Once, he wired together and enameled with delicate colors a fragile corsage, fashioned of those tiny white seashells which one could harvest by the basketful in that region. This he sent on to her with a tender message. One morning his dormitory mates teased him, saying he had cried out in his sleep, clear as a bell, "Alice, Alice, don't leave me!" In English, too, they said. So, one day, Noriyuki, as Isamu had before him, volunteered for service in the Army of the United States. He spent most of his hitch in Colorado, as an instructor in the Japanese language, and ended up as a technical sergeant. Alice joined him there, and they were married in Denver one fine day in June.

Since the war had ended in the meantime, Noriyuki and Alice went to live in Los Angeles, where most of their camp friends had already settled, and Kazuyuki Matsumoto, already in Las Vegas, already Charley, received a monthly long-distance call from them, usually about six in the morning, because, as they said, they wanted to make sure he was still alive and kicking.

Noriyuki was doing well as an assistant in the office of a landscape architect; Alice had first a baby girl, then another. Each birth was announced to Charley by telephone, and while he rejoiced, he was also made to feel worthless, because he was financially unable to send even a token gift of felicitations.

But he would make up for it, he knew. One day his time would come, and he would return in triumph to Los Angeles, laden with gifts for Noriyuki (a wristwatch, probably), for Alice (she might like an ornate necklace, such as he had seen some of these rich women wear), and an armload of toys for the babies.

But Charley began having trouble with his teeth, and he decided to take a short leave of absence in order to obtain the services of a good Japanese dentist in Los Angeles. He had to stay with Noriyuki and his family, and they, with no room for a houseguest, allowed him the use of the couch in the front room which could be converted into a bed at night. Charley, paid at the end of each month, had brought some money with him, so, at first, the reunion went quite well. After his visits to the dentist, who decided to remove first all the upper teeth, then all the lower, and then to fit him with plates, he remembered to bring back a giftbox of either the rice cakes and bean confections of all shapes and colors known as *manju,* or of *o-sushi,* containing a miscellany of vinegared rice dolls and squares. He bought a musical jack-in-the-box for the older child, and a multicolored rubber ball for the baby. After a while, the dentist asked for a hundred dollars as part payment, and Charley gave it to him, although this was about all he had left, except for the return bus ticket to Las Vegas.

About the middle of his month in Los Angeles, Charley felt unwelcome, but there was no help for it. The dentist was not through with him. He could hear, from the sofa bed, the almost nightly reproaches, sometimes accompanied with weeping, that Noriyuki had to listen to. Since his hearing was not too good, he could not make out all that Alice said, but it seemed there was the problem of his napping on the couch and thus preventing her from having friends over during the day, of his turning on the television (and so loud) just when she wanted the children to take their nap, and just how long did that father of his intend to stay? Forever?

Charley was crushed; it had never been his intention to hurt anyone, never once during his lifetime. The dentist, however, took his time; a month was up before he finally got around to inserting both plates, and he still wanted Charley to return for three appointments, in order to insure the proper fit. But Charley ignored him and returned to Las Vegas, posthaste, to free Noriyuki and Alice from their burden.

Some days before he left, Alice, who was not at heart unkind, but irritable from the daily care of two active youngsters and the requirement of having to prepare three separate meals (one for the babies, one for herself and husband, and a bland, soft diet for toothless Charley), had a heart-to-heart talk with her father-in-law. Noriyuki, patient, easygoing, had never mentioned the sorrows of his wife.

In halting Japanese, interspersed with the simplest English she could think of, Alice begged Charley to mend his ways.

"You're not getting any younger," she told him. "What of the future, when you're unable to work any longer? You're making a good salary; if you saved most of it, you wouldn't have to worry about who would take care of you in your old age. This *bakuchi* [gambling] is getting you nowhere. Why, you still owe the dentist two hundred dollars!"

Charley was ashamed. Every word she spoke was the truth. "You have been so good to me," he said, "when I have been so *tsumara-nai.* I know I have been a lot of trouble to you."

There and then, they made a pact. Charley would send Alice at least a hundred dollars a month; she would put it in the bank for him. When he retired, at sixty-five, he would be a man of substance. With his Social Security, he could visit Japan and see his mother again before she died. He might even stay on in Japan; at the rate of exchange, which was now about three thousand yen for ten American dollars, he could lead a most comfortable, even luxurious life.

But once in Las Vegas again, Charley could not keep to the pact. His compulsion was more than he could deny; and Noriyuki, dunned by the dentist, felt obliged to pay the two hundred dollars which Charley owed. Alice was furious.

Then Charley's mother died, and Charley was filled with grief and guilt. Those letters pleading for one more visit from her only son, her only child, of whom she had been so proud; those letters which he had not once answered. But he would somehow atone. When he struck it rich, he would go to Japan and buy a fine headstone for the spot under which her urn was buried. He would buy chrysanthemums (she had loved chrysanthemums) by the dozens to decorate the monument. It would make a lovely sight, to make the villagers sit up and take notice.

Charley's new teeth, handsome as they were (the waitresses were admiring, saying they made him look ten years younger), were troublesome, too. Much too loose, they did not allow the consumption of solids. He had to subsist on rice smothered with gravy, soft-boiled eggs, soups. But at least he did not have to give up that morning pickup that the bartender still remembered him with. That whiskey was a marvel, warming his insides (especially welcome on chilly winter mornings), giving him a glow that made him surer than ever that one day he, too, would hit the jackpot of jackpots.

But Charley's health began to fail. His feet would swell and sometimes he had to lean against the sink for support, in order to wash the endless platters, plates, dishes, saucers, cups, glasses, knives, forks, spoons, pots, and pans. Once, twice, he got so dizzy climbing the stairs to the dormitory that he almost blacked out, and, hearing him cry out, his Chinese roommates had to carry him the rest of the way to his bed.

One day Mr. Chew, coming to inspect, looked at Charley and said with some concern, "What's the matter? You look bad." And Charley admitted that he had not been feeling up to snuff of late.

Mr. Chew then insisted that he go home to his son in Los Angeles, for a short rest. That was what he probably needed.

By that time Charley was glad for the advice. He was so tired, so tired. One of the waitresses called Noriyuki on the telephone and asked him to come after his father. Charley was pretty sick, she said; he could probably use a good vacation.

So Noriyuki, in his gleaming station wagon, which was only partly paid for, sped to Las Vegas to fetch his father. Charley slept on and off during most of the long trip back.

The young Japanese doctor in Los Angeles shook his head when Charley listed his symptoms. Charley thought it was his stomach; there was a sharp pain there sometimes, right between the ribs.

The young Japanese doctor said to Noriyuki, "When an *issei* starts complaining about his stomach, it's usually pretty serious." He meant there was the possibility of cancer. For some reason, possibly because of the eating of raw fish, Japanese are more prone to stomach cancer than other races.

But the pain in Charley's stomach turned out to be an ulcer. That was not too bad. As for the swollen feet, that was probably an indication of hepatitis, serious but curable in time. Then, in the process of studying the routine X-rays, the doctor came upon a dismaying discovery. There was definite evidence of advanced cirrhosis of the liver.

"Cirrhosis of the liver?" said Noriyuki. "Doesn't that come from drinking? My father gambled, but he didn't drink. He's no drunkard."

"Usually it comes from drinking. Your father says he did drink some whiskey every day. And if his loose plates kept him from eating a good diet, that could do it, that could do it."

So Charley went to stay at the Japanese Hospital, where the excess fluid in his abdomen could be drained periodically. He was put on a low-sodium diet, and the dietitian was in a quandary. A salt-free diet for a man who could not eat solids; there was very little she could plan for him, hardly any variety.

Subsequent X-rays showed up some dark spots on the lungs. The young Japanese doctor shook his head again.

"It's hopeless," he said to Noriyuki. "That means cancer of the liver, spreading to the lungs. He doesn't have much time left."

Noriyuki told Alice, who, relieved that the culinary union had provided for insurance which would take care of the hospital bills, tried to console him. "Who can understand these things?" she said. "Look at your mother— dead at twenty-four, with so much to live for . . ."

Biting her lips, she stopped. She had said the wrong thing. Noriyuki, all his life, under his surface serenity, had known guilt that his birth had been the cause of his mother's death.

Thus Charley died, leaving a son, a daughter-in-law, two grandchildren. Toward the end, his mind had wandered, because the medication for the cirrhosis had drained him of potassium, and the pills prescribed to make up the lack had not sufficed. There was a huge stack of sympathy cards from Las Vegas, from the kitchen employees, the waitresses, the cashier, the sweet, elderly lady-bookkeeper who had always helped Charley file his income tax statements, a cab driver, and a few others who had come to accept Charley as part of the Las Vegas scene. They even chipped in to wire him an enormous floral offering.

The young Japanese doctor would not take his fee (the union insurance had not provided for his services). "The worst mistake I made in my life was becoming a doctor," he confided to Noriyuki. "Life is hell, nothing but hell."

"But you help people when they need help the most," Noriyuki tried to tell him. "What could be more satisfying than that?"

"Yeah, and you see people die right in front of you, and there isn't a

damn thing you can do about it! Well, at least your father had a good time—
he drank, he gambled, he smoked. I don't do any of those things; all I do
is work, work, work. At least he enjoyed himself while he was alive."

And Noriyuki—who, without one sour word, had lived through a succes-
sion of conflicting emotions about his father—hate for rejecting him as a
child; disgust and exasperation over that weak moral fiber; embarrassment
when people asked what his father did for a living; and finally, something
akin to compassion, when he came to understand that his father was not an
evil man, but only an inadequate one with the most shining intentions, only
one man among so many who lived from day to day as best as they could,
limited, restricted, by the meager gifts Fate or God had doled out to them—
could not quite agree.

HISAYE YAMAMOTO

Hisaye Yamamoto was born in California in 1921. Her short stories have been widely published in such magazines and journals as *Partisan Review, Kenyon Review, Furioso, Arizona Quarterly,* and *Amerasia Journal,* and have also appeared in *Asian American Authors* (1972), *Asian American Heritage* (1974), *Aiiieeeee: An Anthology of Asian American Writers* (1975), and *Counterpoint* (1976).

SEVENTEEN SYLLABLES

The first Rosie knew that her mother had taken to writing poems was one evening when she finished one and read it aloud for her daughter's approval. It was about cats, and Rosie pretended to understand it thoroughly and appreciate it no end, partly because she hesitated to disillusion her mother about the quantity and quality of Japanese she had learned in all the years now that she had been going to Japanese school every Saturday (and Wednesday, too, in the Summer). Even so, her mother must have been skeptical about the depth of Rosie's understanding, because she explained afterwards about the kind of poem she was trying to write.

See, Rosie, she said, it was a *haiku,* a poem in which she must pack all her meaning into seventeen syllables only, which were divided into three lines of five, seven, and five syllables. In the one she had just read, she had tried to capture the charm of a kitten, as well as comment on the superstition that owning a cat of three colors meant good luck.

"Yes, yes, I understand. How utterly lovely," Rosie said, and her mother, either satisfied or seeing through the deception and resigned, went back to composing.

The truth was that Rosie was lazy; English lay ready on the tongue but Japanese had to be searched for and examined, and even then put forth tentatively (probably to meet with laughter). It was so much easier to say yes, yes, even when one meant no, no. Besides, this was what was in her mind to say: I was looking through one of your magazines from Japan last night, Mother, and towards the back I found some *haiku* in English that delighted me. There was one that made me giggle off and on until I fell asleep—

> It is morning, and lo!
> I lie awake, comme il faut,
> sighing for some dough.

Now, how to reach her mother, how to communicate the melancholy song? Rosie knew formal Japanese by fits and starts, her mother had even less English, no French. It was much more possible to say yes, yes.

It developed that her mother was writing the *haiku* for a daily newspaper, the *Mainichi Shinbun,* that was published in San Francisco. Los Angeles, to be sure, was closer to the farming community in which the Hayashi family lived and several Japanese vernaculars were printed there, but Rosie's parents said they preferred the tone of the northern paper. Once a week, the *Mainichi* would have a section devoted to *haiku,* and her mother became an extravagant contributor, taking for herself the blossoming pen name, Ume Hanazono.

So Rosie and her father lived for awhile with two women, her mother and Ume Hanazono. Her mother (Tome Hayashi by name) kept house, cooked, washed, and, along with her husband and the Carrascos, the Mexican family hired for the harvest, did her ample share of picking tomatoes out in the sweltering fields and boxing them in tidy strata in the cool packing shed. Ume Hanazono, who came to life after the dinner dishes were done, was an earnest, muttering stranger who often neglected speaking when spoken to and stayed busy at the parlor table as late as midnight scribbling with pencil on scratch paper or carefully copying characters on good paper with her fat, pale green Parker.

The new interest had some repercussions on the household routine. Before, Rosie had been accustomed to her parents and herself taking their hot baths early and going to bed almost immediately afterwards, unless her parents challenged each other to a game of flower cards or unless company dropped in. Now, if her father wanted to play cards, he had to resort to solitaire (at which he always cheated fearlessly), and if a group of friends came over, it was bound to contain someone who was also writing *haiku,* and the small assemblage would be split in two, her father entertaining the non-literary members and her mother comparing ecstatic notes with the visiting poet.

If they went out, it was more of the same thing. But Ume Hanazono's life span, even for a poet's, was very brief—perhaps three months at most.

One night they went over to see the Hayano family in the neighboring town to the west, an adventure both painful and attractive to Rosie. It was attractive because there were four Hayano girls, all lovely and each one named after a season of the year (Haru, Natsu, Aki, Fuyu), painful because something had been wrong with Mrs. Hayano ever since the birth of her first child. Rosie would sometimes watch Mrs. Hayano, reputed to have been the belle of her native village, making her way about a room, stooped, slowly shuffling, violently trembling (*always* trembling), and she would be reminded that this woman, in this same condition, had carried and given issue to three babies. She would look wonderingly at Mr. Hayano, handsome, tall, and strong, and she would look at her four pretty friends. But it was not a matter she could come to any decision about.

On this visit, however, Mrs. Hayano sat all evening in the rocker, as motionless and unobtrusive as it was possible for her to be, and Rosie found the greater part of the evening practically anaesthetic. Too, Rosie spent most of it in the girls' room, because Haru, the garrulous one, said almost as soon as the bows and other greetings were over, "Oh, you must see my new coat!"

It was a pale plaid of grey, sand, and blue, with an enormous collar, and Rosie, seeing nothing special in it, said, "Gee, how nice."

"Nice?" said Haru, indignantly. "Is that all you can say about it? It's gorgeous! And so cheap, too. Only seventeen-ninety-eight, because it was a sale. The saleslady said it was twenty-five dollars regular."

"Gee," said Rosie. Natsu, who never said much and when she said anything said it shyly, fingered the coat covetously and Haru pulled it away.

"Mine," she said, putting it on. She minced in the aisle between two large beds and smiled happily. "Let's see how your mother likes it."

She broke into the front room and the adult conversation, and went to stand in front of Rosie's mother, while the rest watched from the door. Rosie's mother was properly envious. "May I inherit it when you're through with it?"

Haru, pleased, giggled and said yes, she could, but Natsu reminded gravely from the door, "You promised me, Haru."

Everyone laughed but Natsu, who shamefacedly retreated into the bedroom. Haru came in laughing, taking off the coat. "We were only kidding, Natsu," she said. "Here, you try it on now."

After Natsu buttoned herself into the coat, inspected herself solemnly in the bureau mirror, and reluctantly shed it, Rosie, Aki, and Fuyu got their turns, and Fuyu, who was eight, drowned in it while her sisters and Rosie doubled up in amusement. They all went into the front room later, because Haru's mother quaveringly called to her to fix the tea and rice cakes and open a can of sliced peaches for everybody. Rosie noticed that her mother and Mr. Hayano were talking together at the little table—they were discussing a *haiku* that Mr. Hayano was planning to send to the *Mainichi*, while her father was sitting at one end of the sofa looking through a copy of *Life*, the new picture magazine. Occasionally, her father would comment on a photograph, holding it toward Mrs. Hayano and speaking to her as he always did—loudly, as though he thought someone such as she must surely be at least a trifle deaf also.

The five girls had their refreshments at the kitchen table, and it was while Rosie was showing the sisters her trick of swallowing peach slices without chewing (she chased each slippery crescent down with a swig of tea) that her father brought his empty teacup and untouched saucer to the sink and said, "Come on, Rosie, we're going home now."

"Already?" asked Rosie.

"Work tomorrow," he said.

He sounded irritated, and Rosie, puzzled, gulped one last yellow slice and stood up to go, while the sisters began protesting, as was their wont. "We have to get up at five-thirty," he told them, going into the front room quickly, so that they did not have their usual chance to hang onto his hands and plead for an extension of time.

Rosie, following, saw that her mother and Mr. Hayano were sipping tea and still talking together, while Mrs. Hayano concentrated, quivering, on raising the handleless Japanese cup to her lips with both her hands and lowering it back to her lap. Her father, saying nothing, went out the door, onto the bright porch, and down the steps. Her mother looked up and asked, "Where is he going?"

"Where is he going?" Rosie said. "He said we were going home now."

"Going home?" Her mother looked with embarrassment at Mr. Hayano and his absorbed wife and then forced a smile. "He must be tired," she said.

Haru was not giving up yet. "May Rosie stay overnight?" she asked, and Natsu, Aki, and Fuyu came to reinforce their sister's plea by helping her make a circle around Rosie's mother. Rosie, for once, having no desire to stay, was relieved when her mother, apologizing to the perturbed Mr. and Mrs. Hayano for her father's abruptness at the same time, managed to shake her head no at the quartet, kindly but adamant, so that they broke their circle to let her go.

Rosie's father looked ahead into the windshield as the two joined him. "I'm sorry," her mother said. "You must be tired." Her father, stepping on the starter, said nothing. "You know how I get when it's *haiku*," she continued, "I forget what time it is." He only grunted.

As they rode homeward, silently, Rosie sitting between, felt a rush of hate for both, for her mother for begging, for her father for denying her mother. I wish this old Ford would crash, right now, she thought, then immediately, no, no, I wish my father would laugh, but it was too late: already the vision had passed through her mind of the green pick-up crumpled in the dark against one of the mighty eucalyptus trees they were just riding past, of the three contorted, bleeding bodies, one of them hers.

Rosie ran between two patches of tomatoes, her heart working more rambunctiously than she had ever known it to. How lucky it was that Aunt Taka and Uncle Gimpachi had come tonight, though, how very lucky. Otherwise, she might not have really kept her half-promise to meet Jesus Carrasco. Jesus, who was going to be a senior in September at the same school she went to, and his parents were the ones helping with the tomatoes this year. She and Jesus, who hardly remembered seeing each other at Cleveland High, where there were so many other people and two whole grades between them, had become great friends this Summer—he always had a joke for her when he periodically drove the loaded pick-up up from the fields to the shed where she was usually sorting while her mother and father did the packing, and they laughed a great deal together over infinitesimal repartee during the afternoon break for chilled watermelon or ice cream in the shade of the shed.

What she enjoyed most was racing him to see which could finish picking a double row first. He, who could work faster, would tease her by slowing down until she thought she would surely pass him this time, then speeding up furiously to leave her several sprawling vines behind. Once he had made her screech hideously by crossing over, while her back was turned, to place atop the tomatoes in her green-stained bucket a truly monstrous, pale green worm (it had looked more like an infant snake). And it was when they had finished a contest this morning, after she had pantingly pointed a green finger at the immature tomatoes evident in the lugs at the end of his row and he had returned the accusation (with justice), that he had startlingly brought up the matter of their possibly meeting outside the range of both their parents' dubious eyes.

"What for?" she had asked.

"I've got a secret I want to tell you," he said.

"Tell me now," she demanded.

"It won't be ready till tonight," he said.

She laughed. "Tell me tomorrow then."

"It'll be gone tomorrow," he threatened.

"Well, for seven hakes, what is it?" she had asked, more than twice, and when he had suggested that the packing shed would be an appropriate place to find out, she had cautiously answered maybe. She had not been certain she was going to keep the appointment until the arrival of her mother's sister and her husband. Their coming seemed a sort of signal of permission, of grace, and she had definitely made up her mind to lie and leave as she was bowing them welcome.

So, as soon as everyone appeared settled back for the evening, she announced loudly that she was going to the privy outside. "I'm going to the *benjo!*" and slipped out the door. And now that she was actually on her way, her heart pumped in such an undisciplined way that she could hear it with her ears. It's because I'm running, she told herself, slowing to a walk. The shed was up ahead, one more patch away, in the middle of the fields. Its bulk, looming in the dimness, took on a sinisterness that was funny when Rosie reminded herself that it was only a wooden frame with a canvas roof and three canvas walls that made a slapping noise on breezy days.

Jesus was sitting on the narrow plank that was the sorting platform and she went around to the other side and jumped backwards to seat herself on the rim of a packing stand. "Well, tell me," she said, without greeting, thinking her voice sounded reassuringly familiar.

"I saw you coming out the door," Jesus said. "I heard you running part of the way, too."

"Uh-huh," Rosie said, "Now tell me the secret."

"I was afraid you wouldn't come," he said.

Rosie delved around on the chicken-wire bottom of the stall for number two tomatoes, ripe, which she was sitting beside, and came up with a left-over that felt edible. She bit into it and began sucking out the pulp and seeds. "I'm here," she pointed out.

"Rosie, are you sorry you came?"

"Sorry? What for?" she said. "You said you were going to tell me something."

"I will, I will," Jesus said, but his voice contained disappointment, and Rosie, fleetingly, felt the older of the two, realizing a brand-new power which vanished without category under her recognition.

"I have to go back in a minute," she said. "My aunt and uncle are here from Wintersburg. I told them I was going to the privy."

Jesus laughed. "You funny thing," he said. "You slay me!"

"Just because you have a bathroom *inside*," Rosie said. "Come on, tell me."

Chuckling, Jesus came around to lean on the stand facing her. They still could not see each other very clearly, but Rosie noticed that Jesus became very sober again as he took the hollow tomato from her hand and dropped it back into the stall. When he took hold of her empty hand, she could find no words to protest; her vocabulary had become distressingly constricted and she thought desperately that all that remained intact now was yes and no and oh, and even these few sounds would not easily out. Thus, kissed by Jesus, Rosie fell, for the first time, entirely victim to a helplessness delectable beyond speech. But the terrible, beautiful sensation lasted no more than a second, and the reality of Jesus' lips and tongue and teeth and hands made her pull away with such strength that she nearly tumbled.

Rosie stopped running as she approached the lights from the windows of home. How long since she had left? She could not guess, but gasping yet, she went to the privy in back and locked herself in. Her own breathing deafened her in the dark, close space, and she sat and waited until she could hear at last the nightly calling of the frogs and crickets. Even then, all she could think to say was oh, my, and the pressure of Jesus' face against her face would not leave.

No one had missed her in the parlor, however, and Rosie walked in and through quickly, announcing that she was next going to take a bath. "Your father's in the bathhouse," her mother said, and Rosie, in her room, recalled that she had not seen him when she entered. There had been only Aunt Taka and Uncle Gimpachi with her mother at the table, drinking tea. She got her robe and straw sandals and crossed the parlor again to go outside. Her mother was telling them about the *haiku* competition in the *Mainichi* and the poem she had entered.

Rosie met her father coming out of the bathhouse. "Are you through, Father?" she asked. "I was going to ask you to scrub my back."

"Scrub your own back," he said shortly, going toward the main house.

"What have I done now?" she yelled after him. She suddenly felt like doing a lot of yelling. But he did not answer, and she went into the bathhouse. Turning on the dangling light, she removed her denims and T-shirt and threw them in the big carton for dirty clothes standing next to the washing machine. Her other things she took with her into the bath compartment to wash after her bath. After she had scooped a basin of hot water from the square wooden tub, she sat on the grey cement of the floor and soaped herself at exaggerated leisure, singing "Red Sails in the Sunset" at the top of her voice and using da-da-da where she suspected her words. Then, standing, still singing, for she was possessed by the notion that any attempt now to analyze would result in spoilage and she believed that the larger her volume the less she would be able to hear herself think, she obtained more hot water and poured it on until she was free of lather. Only then did she allow herself to step into the steaming vat, one leg first, then the remainder of her body inch by inch until the water no longer stung and she could move around at will.

She took a long time soaking, afterwards remembering to go around outside to stoke the embers of the tin-lined fireplace beneath the tub and to throw on a few more sticks so that the water might keep its heat for her mother, and when she finally returned to the parlor, she found her mother still talking *haiku* with her aunt and uncle, the three of them on another round of tea. Her father was nowhere in sight.

At Japanese school the next day (Wednesday, it was), Rosie was grave and giddy by turns. Preoccupied at her desk in the row for students on Book Eight, she made up for it at recess by performing wild mimicry for the benefit of her friend Chizuko. She held her nose and whined a witticism or two in what she considered was the manner of Fred Allen; she assumed intoxication and a British accent to go over the climax of the Rudy Vallee recording of the pub conversation about William Ewart Gladstone; she was the child Shirley

Temple piping "On the Good Ship Lollipop"; she was the gentleman soprano of the Four Inkspots trilling "If I Didn't Care." And she felt reasonably satisfied when Chizuko wept and gasped, "Oh, Rosie, you ought to be in the movies!"

Her father came after her at noon, bringing her sandwiches of minced ham and two nectarines to eat while she rode, so that she could pitch right into the sorting when they got home. The lugs were piling up, he said, and the ripe tomatoes in them would probably have to be taken to the cannery tomorrow if they were not ready for the produce haulers tonight. "This heat's not doing them any good. And we've got no time for a break today."

It *was* hot, probably the hottest day of the year, and Rosie's blouse stuck damply to her back even under the protection of the canvas. But she worked as efficiently as a flawless machine and kept the stalls heaped, with one part of her mind listening in to the parental murmuring about the heat and the tomatoes and with another part planning the exact words she would say to Jesus when he drove up with the first load of the afternoon. But when at last she saw that the pick-up was coming, her hands went berserk and the tomatoes started falling in the wrong stalls, and her father said, "Hey, hey! Rosie, watch what you're doing!"

"Well, I have to go to the *benjo*," she said, hiding panic.

"Go in the weeds over there," he said, only half-joking.

"Oh, Father!" she protested.

"Oh, go on home," her mother said. "We'll make out for awhile."

In the privy, Rosie peered through a knothole toward the fields, watching as much as she could of Jesus. Happily she thought she saw him look in the direction of the house from time to time before he finished unloading and went back toward the patch where his mother and father worked. As she was heading for the shed, a very presentable black car purred up the dirt driveway to the house and its driver motioned to her. Was this the Hayashi home, he wanted to know. She nodded. Was she a Hayashi? Yes, she said, thinking that he was a good-looking man. He got out of the car with a huge, flat package and she saw that he warmly wore a business suit. "I have something here for your mother then," he said, in a more elegant Japanese than she was used to.

She told him where her mother was and he came along with her, patting his face with an immaculate white handkerchief and saying something about the coolness of San Francisco. To her surprised mother and father, he bowed and introduced himself as, among other things, the *haiku* editor of the *Mainichi Shinbun,* saying that since he had been coming as far as Los Angeles anyway, he had decided to bring her the first prize she had won in the recent contest.

"First prize?" her mother echoed, believing and not believing, pleased and overwhelmed. Handed the package with a bow, she bobbed her head up and down numerous times to express her utter gratitude.

"It is nothing much," he added, "but I hope it will serve as a token of our great appreciation for your contributions and our great admiration of your considerable talent."

"I am not worthy," she said, falling easily into his style. "It is I who should make some sign of my humble thanks for being permitted to contribute."

"No, no, to the contrary," he said, bowing again.

But Rosie's mother insisted, and then saying that she knew she was being unorthodox, she asked if she might open the package because her curiosity was so great. Certainly she might. In fact, he would like her reaction to it, for personally, it was one of his favorite *Hiroshiges*.*

Rosie thought it was a pleasant picture, which looked to have been sketched with delicate quickness. There were pink clouds, containing some graceful calligraphy, and a sea that was a pale blue except at the edges, containing four sampans with indications of people in them. Pines edged the water and on the far-off beach there was a cluster of thatched huts towered over by pine-dotted mountains of grey and blue. The frame was scalloped and gilt.

After Rosie's mother pronounced it without peer and somewhat prodded her father into nodding agreement, she said Mr. Kuroda must at least have a cup of tea, after coming all this way, and although Mr. Kuroda did not want to impose, he soon agreed that a cup of tea would be refreshing and went along with her to the house, carrying the picture for her.

"Ha, your mother's crazy!" Rosie's father said, and Rosie laughed uneasily as she resumed judgment on the tomatoes. She had emptied six lugs when he broke into an imaginary conversation with Jesus to tell her to go and remind her mother of the tomatoes, and she went slowly.

Mr. Kuroda was in his shirtsleeves expounding some *haiku* theory as he munched a rice cake, and her mother was rapt. Abashed in the great man's presence, Rosie stood next to her mother's chair until her mother looked up inquiringly, and then she started to whisper the message, but her mother pushed her gently away and reproached, "You are not being very polite to our guest."

"Father says the tomatoes . . ." Rosie said aloud, smiling foolishly.

"Tell him I shall only be a minute," her mother said, speaking the language of Mr. Kuroda.

When Rosie carried the reply to her father, he did not seem to hear and she said again, "Mother says she'll be back in a minute."

"All right, all right," he nodded, and they worked again in silence. But suddenly, her father uttered an incredible noise, exactly like the cork of a bottle popping, and the next Rosie knew, he was stalking angrily toward the house, almost running, in fact, and she chased after him crying, "Father! Father! What are you going to do?"

He stopped long enough to order her back to the shed. "Never mind!" he shouted. "Get on with the sorting!"

And from the place in the fields where she stood, frightened and vacillating,

* Japanese artist (1797–1858).

Rosie saw her father enter the house. Soon Mr. Kuroda came out alone, putting on his coat. Mr. Kuroda got into his car and backed out down the driveway, onto the highway. Next her father emerged, also alone, something in his arms (it was the picture, she realized), and, going over to the bathhouse woodpile, he threw the picture on the ground and picked up the axe. Smashing the picture, glass and all (she heard the explosion faintly), he reached over the kerosene that was used to encourage the bath fire and poured it over the wreckage. I am dreaming, Rosie said to herself, I am dreaming, but her father, having made sure that his act of cremation was irrevocable, was even then returning to the fields.

Rosie ran past him and toward the house. What had become of her mother? She burst into the parlor and found her mother at the back window, watching the dying fire. They watched together until there remained only a feeble smoke under the blazing sun. Her mother was very calm.

"Do you know why I married your father?" she said, without turning.

"No," said Rosie. It was the most frightening question she had ever been called upon to answer. Don't tell me now, she wanted to say, tell me tomorrow, tell me next week, don't tell me today. But she knew she would be told now, that the telling would combine with the other violence of the hot afternoon to level her life, her world (so various, so beautiful, so new?) to the very ground.

It was like a story out of the magazines, illustrated in sepia, which she had consumed so greedily for a period until the information had somehow reached her that those wretchedly unhappy autobiographies, offered to her as the testimonials of living men and women, were largely inventions: Her mother, at nineteen, had come to America and married her father as an alternative to suicide.

At eighteen, she had been in love with the first son of one of the well-to-do families in her village. The two had met whenever and wherever they could, secretly, because it would not have done for his family to see him favor her— her father had no money; he was a drunkard and a gambler besides. She had learned she was with child; an excellent match had already been arranged for her lover. Despised by her family, she had given premature birth to a stillborn son, who would be seventeen now. Her family did not turn her out, but she could no longer project herself in any direction without refreshing in them the memory of her indiscretion. She wrote to Aunt Taka, her favorite sister, in America, threatening to kill herself if Aunt Taka would not send for her. Aunt Taka hastily arranged a marriage with a young man, but lately arrived from Japan, of whom she knew, a young man of simple mind, it was said, but of kindly heart. The young man was never told why his unseen betrothed was so eager to hasten the day of meeting.

The story was told perfectly, with neither groping for words nor untoward passion. It was as though her mother had memorized it by heart, reciting it to herself so many times over that its nagging vileness had long since gone.

"I had a brother then?" Rosie asked, for this was what seemed to matter now; she would think about the other later, she assured herself, pushing back the illumination which threatened all that darkness that had hitherto been merely mysterious or even glamorous. "A half-brother?"

"Yes."

"I would have liked a brother," she said.

Suddenly, her mother knelt on the floor and took her by the wrists. "Rosie," she said urgently, "promise me you will never marry!" Shocked more by the request than the revelation, Rosie stared at her mother's face. Jesus, Jesus, she called silently, not certain whether she was invoking the help of the son of the Carrascos or of God, until there returned sweetly the memory of Jesus' hand, how it had touched her and where. Still her mother waited for an answer, holding her wrists so tightly that her hands were going numb. She tried to pull free. "Promise," her mother whispered fiercely, "promise." "Yes, yes, I promise," Rosie said. But for an instant she turned away, and her mother, hearing the familiar glib agreement, released her, Oh, you, you, you, her eyes and twisted mouth said, you fool. Rosie, covering her face, began at last to cry, and the embrace and consoling hand came much later than she expected.

WAKAKO YAMAUCHI

Born in 1924 in California, where she now lives, Wakako Yamauchi works as a free-lance writer. Her stories have appeared in *Aiiieeeee: An Anthology of Asian American Writers* (1975), *Counterpoint* (1976), *Southwest* (1977), *Ayumi: The Japanese American Anthology* (1979), as well as in *Yardbird Reader* and *Amerasia Journal*. She has recently adapted "And the Soul Shall Dance" into a play that has been performed on public television by the East-West Players.

THE BOATMEN ON TONEH RIVER

Kimi Sumida knew the end was near. The bed she'd lived in for many months now ceased to resist the bony protuberances of her body and prolonged attitudes of discomfort reached a stage of stone-like numbness. The cancer that ate at her lungs had no more on which to feed.

Where once the long day steadily, slowly, inexorably moved into night, now darkness descended without warning—dark and light, dark and light, and dreams, always dreams. Sometimes daylight and reality seemed just beyond a door of pain—now near, now distant—on the other side of pain. "Mari, do I have to remind a 7-year-old every day to brush her teeth? What will your teacher say?" "Give me time, Daddy, you never give me enough time." "Shshsh. Not so loud." "Mommy still sleeping?" "Shshsh . . ." Like a stone at the bottom of the sea, Kimi lay on the ocean floor and the tide flowed over her. "Ryo! Mari! Me: wife and mother! Do you not need me?" Did she cry out?

The door opened and a thin light poured into the room with Ryo. A warped sandwich on the night-stand indicated to Kimi it was still day—late afternoon.

"How do you feel now, dear?"

Did I feel worse before? How long before? His mien is one of enormous cheer: he has on his cheer face. What happened to your other face, Ryo, the one that mirrors your heart? Did you discard it along with hope for my recovery? Honor me with a little honesty, the reality of my disease. Despair a little; feel free to despair a little with me. This is the time to be yourself. I hear the things you tell Mari: that I am going away; that we will all meet again some day; that this is not the time of sorrow; that flowers are sometimes broken in the bud, or plucked in bloom, or sometimes mature to seed and fruition and seed again. Are these words to take the edge off the rawness of death, or do you really believe, or do you only wish to believe? But you haven't known this desperate reluctance to leave life—you don't know the terror of the things I face. You don't even see me any more; you turn your back while the doctor presses, turns, and probes me like a vegetable, and mutters, "Comatose; can't see what keeps her here."

Once you looked at me with eyes soft and tender; eyes dull with desire. Now only this cheer. You won't acknowledge me. I'm the woman who moved you through those many dark streets hurrying, rushing to meet me; the woman who brought words and unspoken dreams from your lips; I'm the woman who brought the fire to your loins. I'm the one! Wasted now; my hair is too black against the fearful pallor of my skin. Do I frighten you? Do you drop your cheerful mask in alarm when you close my door? Do you keep my Mari from me to protect her from the horror of seeing me? Are you afraid I will sear the color from her warm lips, sow seeds of my disease in her tender body? But she's mine. Mine. And I have the right to insist she share my experience, just as, yes, just as my mother had shared hers with me. And she will no doubt travel the lonely channels I've charted; paths like the narrow canals on my cracked ceiling that angle off here, stop abruptly there, by-ways I've come to know as well as I know the palm of my hand. I'm at one of those dead ends now.

The door closed but the light remained and turned blood-red with pain. Slowly the red tide subsided and throbbing with the beat of her pulse, Kimi heard her own mother's voice call: "Kimi, Kimi . . ." Warm, a mother's voice. She opened her eyes.

This is the country kitchen of my childhood: furniture of raw unfinished wood, bare floors, sweaters on pegs, grey dishcloths drying on the sink rim, cosmic dust slowly sifting. And beyond the windows, the stretch of desert, broken nearby with rows of furrowed earth. All there. Am I mother or am I the child; am I the caller or the called?

"Kimi, go fix the bath for Father. He'll be back from the fields and will want his bath."

"Not now, Mother, I'll be back soon, and I will do it then."

"Now. Now. Every evening you go off when I need you. What's in this compulsion to commune with this nothing land. I need your help here; do you think this wild desert changes a whit for your walking through a piece of it? Stay here and use the strength God gave you where it'd do some good. Make the bath."

My Kimi, where do you go; what do you dream? Fancy clothes? Glittering lights? Love? There're none of these here. I was seventeen, the caress of my mother's fingers still warm in my hair, when they married me to a stranger from the next province. He must have a young healthy woman to help him in America, they said; and soon I would return, a rich, proud, honored lady. I looked forward to this promise in dewy-eyed innocence—unaware of even the conjugal night that lay before me. The years have devoured me with work and poverty and anxieties: early frost, fluctuating market, price of rice—what chance had love? They told me with this black mole on my ear lobe, I couldn't fail, a black mole on the ear lobe is a sure sign of fame and fortune, they said. I waited for this fortune; worked and waited and when finally my time was up, I counted my fortune. Fifty years of living and what was there to show? Ten thousand nights I lay there remembering my Japan; clear lakes, lonely shrines, the lyric of flowering cherry trees, street vendors' calls, plaintive and sweet as a mother's lullabyes, the sound of a flute on a summer evening. I spent a lifetime waiting to return to these. I thought my happiness was bound to these. I reached too far for what was always here, in the dust, in the sunrise, in the sunset, in you.

"Kimi, make the bath."

"Yes, I'll do it now."

I'm going now to heat the bath with sage that you and I gathered and spread out to dry in early summer. It will shoot up in crackling flames and tiny sparks and I'll think of your fireflies in Japan. Though you may not believe it, I've found something here in this arid desert that is gentle and sweet too. I want to ask you about it, but to put it to words or to your critical eye may be to profane it. And now the tall summer reeds bend in the wind, cicadas hum, shadows lengthen, cottonwood leaves catch the last flutter of sunlight, and the lad who peddles down the warm dusty road each evening at this time is passing by, and I am not there. I shall not see the wind move through his black hair, and touch his smooth brown cheeks and fill his blouse with air. I want to be as close to him as that wind. Where he comes from, where he peddles to, I don't know; but when I watch him, I see west winds in the sage, I see tumbleweeds lope across the prairie, and primrose petals fall, and I am moved. From my hiding place in the reeds, I watch him scan the horizon, and I wonder if he looks for me. Does he watch for me? Does he yearn for me?

Kimi, how extravagantly you dream; what disenchantment you court. What loneliness you will know.

The room was dark and cold. Night had come; the sandwich on the nightstand had been removed and a covered tray replaced it. This is Ryo's acknowledgement of me, Kimi thought; ashes of dreams he prepares for me. I am still here.

"Still here! Kimi, drat it! I tell you, put the dog out. He's still here!"

Three days of steady rain now; one more day and the tiny seedlings that last week pushed their tender shoots from the over-worked earth will rot. The kitchen is dank and murky with smoke from Bull Durhams and the smell of *sake* warming on the coal-oil stove. The patriarch sits at the table with Mr. Nagata, one of a legion of shifting rootless men who follows crops along the length of California. They sip the warm rice wine and talk, tugging exaggeratedly at one another's sleeve. They laugh; they sing half-remembered songs.

"Kimi, I tell you, put the dog out! If there's anything that annoys me, it's the smell of a wet dog. I've got troubles enough without that. The stench comes from the floor like something stepped on in the dark. Eh, Nagata-*kun?* Heh, heh. What a life, eh? Heh, heh."

Yah, those seedlings. A month's work destroyed. You sow one more row before sundown, pull one more weed before nightfall, for what? Rain, more seeding, more weeding. Don't look at me like that, Kimi; I didn't order this rain. I didn't ask for this kind of life. What would you have me do? Run out and stop the rain with my bare hands? I can't change the shape of fate. I know. I tried. I left my native shore to tread these "gold-paved" streets, heh, heh; to live and die, unseen, among aliens. And I've found when it rains there's nothing to do but jump into bed and pull the covers over your head, or find a friend and drink a little wine, sing a few songs, and explore those feelings you've forgotten you'd had; so remote, so beautiful, so fragile they are. And then you can pull out your *koto* (chin-chiri-rin) and close your eyes and leave this soggy life-style. Heh, heh. What would you have me do?

The smell of a wet dog isn't bad. There's hardly any smell sadder than the smell of *sake* and rain together. I read in school books where fathers return from work and kiss their wives and toss their children in the air, their pockets bulging with candies and balloons, and the smell of supper cooking on the range permeates the air. I'd like that. Warm smells and good sounds. Here rain drums on the tar-paper roof, and you and your crony sit and drink and you close your eyes and with this expression of tender sorrow, you pluck your imaginary *koto,* brown hands moving on the air; thick fingers touching phantom strings (chin-chiri-rin).

> I am a dying reed by the river bed
> As thou, a drying dying reed
> Alas, our lives together lie,
> Blossomless, on the river bed.
>
> Whether we live, or whether die
> Tides will ebb and flow
> Come then, thou with me, to dwell
> As boatmen on Toneh River.

Now you come to me. You come to haunt me as I had never permitted you to do when I was stronger. Sly old man. You waited until there was only a membrane between you and me. Is there still unfinished business? What do you want to tell me? That you are me and I am you and today is the same as yesterday, and tomorrow will be the same as today? I thought I could change the pattern of my life; I thought I could deny your existence, deny our lonely past together, but alas, I had preserved it carefully and when all the frills and furbelows are stripped away, you are here, the backbone of my life, the bleached hull of my shipwreck. And here between yesterday and today, I sing the same lonely song as you. I should not have denied you; I should have woven my life within the framework of our past. I should have loved you. Now my guilt comes home to me.

It's all right, Kimi. The pattern doesn't change, and the guilt doesn't change. It's too late now; too late for might-have-been and would-have-liked. Give yourself to the tide, give yourself to the river; the sun is setting, the desert is cooling. . . .

Kimi.

A nebulous anticipation filled Kimi's bowels as she drifted to a cold dimension. She surrendered to the chill that enveloped her, her lips twisted in a pain akin to joy as she moved with a wind that carried her out, back to the country road, and against the smooth brown cheeks of a lad on a bicycle, and into the blouse that billowed behind him.

DIANA CHANG

A prolific writer, Diana Chang has published poetry in numerous journals and magazines and written six novels: *The Frontiers of Love* (1956), *A Woman of Thirty* (1959), *A Passion for Life* (1961), *The Only Game in Town* (1963), *Eye to Eye* (1974), and *A Perfect Love* (1978). Though she was born in New York, she spent her childhood in China reared by her Eurasian mother. Of herself, she says, "I feel I'm an American writer whose background is Chinese. The source of my first and fourth novels was Chinese, but exoticism can stand in the way of the universal I strive for in my themes. Therefore, since I write fiction in English and am living my life in the USA, I've often subsumed aspects of my background in the interest of other truths and recognitions. . . . I believe an abiding interest in character and emotion informs all my work—not only because the relationships, situations, and problems I write about arise out of the characters of my protagonists, out of their personalities, but also because I seem preoccupied a lot with identity or selfness. Being or becoming seems to be an underlying denominator of my work, at least so far. . . . My poems have been described as lyrical and concise, perhaps even too condensed. I hope to be economical and not dwell too lovingly on my own words. One owes it to everyone not to be boring."

from INTIMATE FRIENDS*

At eleven the next morning Paul called me. And so it began. It was a Sunday and we went for a walk in the eerie quiet after the storm and had supper somewhere and came back to my place for a bourbon and water. On Thursday he took me to a buffet party. On Saturday, a week after the dinner at the Woods, I felt I had never *not* known Paul Grannis.

He said, "After the movie, I'd like you to come to my place. But only because it's larger."

"All right."

"I like your place, the way you've done it. It's like you exactly. It's just that my place is larger."

I smiled because he wanted to make things so clear to me. I know for a fact that Kenneth Kluback took for granted that Liza would go to his apartment. He never sees her home; if she's not spending the night at his place, she takes a cab home alone after their date. I've always thought all that talk about Jessie being in the way at Liza's is rationalizing. He simply wants to be on his own ground, and Liza swallows his reasons whole. Jessica has her own room and the housekeeper is around to take her off their hands any time Liza wants.

* As-yet-unpublished manuscript.

At his place later, Paul said when we were kissing, "I've been looking forward to this." He is very wiry and strong and moves with the minimum of wasted motion. I felt as though I was beginning a perfectly coordinated trip. I had no conflicts, qualifications, doubts. I would simply let what happened happen. And I wanted it to happen whenever it did.

He said, "You see, my bed is larger too. I want to make love to you properly."

It's true, my bed on Jane Street was quite narrow. He had seen that.

Then he did something which made me feel unmoored, loosened in my very bones, dissolving. He kissed me within my mouth, as though I were a flower and he a kind of humming bird. Love is not always blinding. And sex is not always compelling—I mean, always so overwhelmingly instinctive. It takes both physical attraction and a kind of trusting communication to effect the perfect giving of oneself in pleasure, a giving in which one also extracts gifts in return.

Spontaneously we started to undress; went into his bedroom. He drew the curtains quickly, left the lamp on. Paul likes to make love seeing.

I found I was not at all shy with him. I thought then, here, here, here.

I had been divorced four years by then. I might live in a cell-like apartment but I had not led a monastic life in the great big city. I'd been pretty close to falling in love a couple of times, once with a friend of Henry Perkins, a burly guy who did something or other on *Sports Illustrated*. I suspect he dropped me, but was nice enough to arrange it to seem as if things petered out. A year and a half later, he tried to date me again, but I was seeing someone else more or less exclusively, at least for six months. This someone else's name was Charles St. Roget, a French press agent with their consulate. I was very taken with him but it turned out, after *six mois de transport de joie,* that his family was very authoritarian and pressured him into returning to Lyons to be broken into the family factory there. I was quite angry that he knuckled under, but Charles had always betrayed that he would—even by his witticisms in which his father was always needled—so I can't say it took me by surprise. I owe Charles my French *vocabulaire,* such as it is.

I hoped there was someone somewhere on this earth for me. Sometimes I doubted it. Other times I knew it had to be. Yes. There had to be someone. But where? W . . h . . e . . r . . e . . ?

Sometimes I thought I couldn't bear it. Where? Where? Where? It is against all the rules of our culture to keen. But sometimes one does feel like keening.

W . . H . . E . . R . . E . . ?

Paul parted me as a canoe rides into water—lightly, efficiently, masterfully. He answered my where. Here, of course. Here, of course, I said to myself.

Sensation can be sensational. It's one of the marvels of nature that she should have thought of combining pleasure and procreation. (Nature herself is feminine and so wise.) To guarantee the latter, of course. But it has worked well. (Perhaps too well in most parts of the world.)

Paul said suddenly, having lost his senses briefly, "Should I do something? You know?"

"This time, yes." But actually, I didn't care. I noted that I didn't care about being careful at all.

He withdrew, got up and went to the bathroom. I watched him, my eyes wide and happy. It's a good thing men don't know how comical they look erect and nodding.

"Hi," I said, when he got back.

"Hi, and how is life treating you today?" he asked.

"So-so."

"Just so-so! We'll have to improve the situation," and proceeded to do so.

With Joe Weyman everything had been fraught, totally fraught. Tragedy had lurked behind the arras. He fixed it into my gaze with those screw-driver eyes of his . . . doom and direness and sex as conquest, sex as trophy, sex as a kind of grail. He absolutely lacked the light touch. When I married him I didn't know this, but I realized it even before Paul and I made love that first time. With Paul sex is sexual and love is lovely, and often they are the same thing. Or love is sexual and sex is lovely.

"Do you think you can?" Paul asked. It was like being partnered by a very good dancer who now wanted to know if the lady might or would or could let come (let go?) what may.

"Let's see," I said.

Riding a horse or a seesaw or rising so high on a swing you think you might be flung head over heels across the iron bar instead of swinging down properly—are not the same thing. It is not exactly a strenuousness which reaching an untenable pitch then collapses. It is not simply tension breaking. It is ineffable—like a letting.

The dictionary is full of treasures waiting to be mined. I looked it up. The dictionary read: *Let.*—syn. 1. See *allow.* 1,5. *suffer, grant.*

How interesting, I said to myself. Suffer. Yes, intercourse is like a kind of suffering *of.* You have to suffer and suffer. And suffer and suffer some more. And then comes the granting part. It's well worth it.

The suffering part, paradoxically, is voluntary. Paul and I worked at it very willingly. The granting part, strange to say, is involuntary. It's a kind of happening your body stages. A kind of surprise party ricocheting with light works. The blare of rock bands jars like an electrocution.

I looked up the word *come.* This word has lots of meanings, usages, etc. It means *to approach* and *arrive,* as in "Christmas comes but once a year." Or *to occur,* as in "A terrific idea came to me in the middle of the night." Or *to arrive* and *appear* as a result, as in "This comes of your awful wickedness."

Or *to be brought into* a specified state or condition, as in "The four-letter word came into popular use."

Or *to be born:* "The baby came at dawn."

Or *to become:* "My dress came undone under his eager hands."

I could go on, but won't.

We approached, occurred; were brought to, born and became undone again before we fell asleep together.

KAREN TEI YAMASHITA

"I am a Japanese-American Sansei born and raised in California. I spent over a year studying and traveling in Japan and graduated from Carleton College in Northfield, Minnesota, in 1973. After Carleton, I received a Thomas J. Watson Fellowship to study Japanese immigration to Brazil. In Brazil, I began to write in earnest—poetry, short stories, and a play. For the past three years I have been researching the history of the Japanese in Brazil and working on a novel based on that story." Married to a Brazilian architect, Karen Tei Yamashita divides her time between California and Brazil. In 1977 she was the Rockefeller Playwright-in-Residence at East-West Players' Theater in Los Angeles, where her play, *Omen: An American Kabuki*, opened in December 1977. She has published poetry and short stories in *Amerasia Journal, Rafu Shimpo, Ayumi: The Japanese American Anthology* (1979), and *In Heaven and Earth* (forthcoming).

THE BATH

I

In their house they have often said that mother has a special fascination for the bath. Father pointed this out many years ago. Perhaps it was only in answer to mother's suggestion that father might take a bath more frequently. Remembering, father seemed to take baths once a week on Saturday nights. Father bragged of his once a week bath but only in relation to mother's nightly affair. Over the years, it seems mother has taken to early morning baths as well, so father's comments on mother and the bath continue with an added flourish. He seems to believe that certain of mother's habits have come together to conspire against him by beginning all at once in the morning.

Mother is not one to deny such things. She laughs at herself in an embarrassed manner, pressing her lips together and looking around at the floor. Father's banter is an old and recurring one, and mother is not without her usual reply. She defends herself on two accounts, saying that a hot bath is the most relaxing thing. Her other retort is a more defensive stance on the necessity to be clean. "You perspire, and isn't it nice to have a clean body? You feel so much better." "After all," she will finally say, "the bath is my only luxury."

These are statements typical of mother. They suggest perhaps a certain simplicity. This is not to say mother is simple-minded. Not at all. Rather it is to suggest a sensibility that respects necessities for what they are, a practical sense that finds contentment, sometimes even luxury, in the simple duties to necessity. Mother is simple in that she does not carry around anything in excess be it pretension, desire, or fashionable decoration. As father says, "She is what she is." Mother's simplicity is finally honest. It is clean and naked in a hot bath tub.

It has been sometimes suggested that the bath is a return to the womb, to a foetal state. Mother freely admits that this must be a part of its pleasure. Nakedness is not something mother is shy about. Birth and bodies, it is all very natural and beautiful. However they have had some difficulty extracting from mother explanations as to processes, action, causes in the matter of birth and naked bodies. It is all very much a mystery. Mother's standard answer in these cases is, "What do you have that others haven't got?" That has somehow had to suffice for everything, that which is natural and that, mysterious.

Speaking of the bath, one has in mind the bathroom in the old house where they first lived as a family. It seems that this bathroom was painted all over in pink enamel. The built-in wood drawers and the large wood medicine cabinet behind the mirror: these too were painted in pink enamel. But the amazing thing was the tub itself, an old curving tub standing on four legs like a huge white iron pig in the middle of peeling linoleum.

In those days, the three of them, mother and the twins, took baths in this tub together. Mother would squat at the front of the tub adjusting cold and hot water while her two naked daughters stood leaning into her shoulders, splashing and floating rubber toys and bars of ivory soap. Mother would take a wash cloth and soap and scrub herself and the two children, rinse, and send them out before the *aka* or tub scum could gather much. Mother did this generally and quickly in a way they called *ikagen. Ikagen* is "just so" or "to suit your taste" or "just enough." *Ikagen* is a word mother used to describe what her mother had said about how much salt or *shōyu* to use in this or that recipe. If it was *ikagen,* it was an amount of common sense or taste. *Ikagen* is descriptive of a general approach mother maintains toward household duties, secretarial filing, letter writing, reading, and washing children.

But if mother washed *ikagen,* shampooing was sometimes a different matter. Not that the general style was not *ikagen,* a quick scrubbing on four sides of the scalp, it was that every once in a while, she would bring to bath three eggs. The eggs were cold out of the refrigerator. The twins leaned against the white curve of the old tub as she cracked the cold shells gently on the tops of wet heads. She let the yellow lump fall and the cool slime ooze, dribbling down the backs of ears and over the forehead around eyebrows, tongues reaching for taste. Then, *ikagen,* mother massaged the scalp, scrambling yellow eggs and black hair. She said, "When I was little, my mother always washed my hair with an egg. It gets it clean and shiny."

After a time, the twins took baths together without mother. And without mother's *ikagen* technique, they were free to develop an entire and gradually complicated ritual surrounding bathtime. It probably began with two tiny bodies at opposite ends of that steaming pink enamel bathroom scudding about with protruding stomachs and ramming into each other, laughing hysterically.

"My pompom's bigger! Yes it is."

"Lookit your belly button. It's all itchy."

"Don' touchit!"

Later applying the fruits of elementary school education, mother would find them performing the entire sequence of "You Do the Hokey-Pokey" from "You put your left foot in" to the final "whole self." In those days, baths were apt to be rather lukewarm. But after mother had them draw their own water for the bath, their ritual accommodated by creating a system of fore and aft as in "two men in a tub—." That is, one sat up front weathering the hot water and adding the cold and yelling at appropriate intervals, "Row! Row left!" while the other twin in the aft paddled, stirring up the incoming hot or cold. Sometimes they were able to coordinate several rounds of "Row Row Your Boat," changing directions at new verses. By the end of these songs, they were in a virtual whirlpool, water spilling over the sides of the tub, warping the linoleum.

The bubble bath was a new challenge to bathtime, calling for exceptionally delicate rowing technique in order to get the water stirred with the greatest and deepest amount of bubbles. They sat fore and aft in a white tub of white bubbles hardly daring to move or breathe. These were almost silent baths. They moved slowly, whispering like cloud people, listening to the soft snapping fizzle of dying bubbles. These were often lengthy bathtimes waiting silently for the bubbles to pass before getting to the business of washing the body, which was by now quite a minor portion of the main preoccupation of bathtime fantasy.

Emerging finally flushed and wrinkled skinny bodies, the twins watched the grey *aka* accumulate in a wide scummy ring, and the water finally disappearing in a tiny rushing whirl, the old tub sending up a long sucking noise beyond the dark rusting drain, its navel.

Now they came often to watch mother at her bath alone. They would usually find her lying deep in the tub, her head and shoulders propped up in a curve against the slope of the tub, a square wash cloth floating over her soft mound of stomach and hair. She would say, "Come in and close the door. It's cold air."

They leaned over the edge of the tub, talking. "Mommy you have a scar on your tummy? So isn't that where when I was a baby I came out of?"

"No, that's when I had my appendix taken out."

"See, I told you."

Watching mother was never much entertainment. She never used much soap but scrubbed her skin generally. It was in the usual manner of *ikagen*, the soaking horizontally being the thing.

It was quite a different thing to watch father's weekly productions which were extravagant in soap and water and flourish. He sat at the edge of the tub with a bar of soap, rubbing it into a thick white lather all over his body. He seemed to be very hairy. And then there was his bad leg and the wound in his right hip; a scarred hole, it seemed as big as one's small hand.

"Daddy you hurt your leg in the war?"

"No, I was a bad boy and fell off a fence."

"Oh."

The best part of his bath was to watch him plunge a hairy lather man into the deep white water, all the grey foam rising in waves, splashing about with water up to his chin. And when he rose, the water surged beneath him, and the tub echoed the din and squeak of his body and flat feet beating and rubbing against iron, and there was that wonderful and unbeatable amount of grey *aka*. It never occurred to them then, but the reason why father washed with the soap bar always melting it to half its size was probably because the washcloth somehow remained draped between his legs throughout the bath.

It was perhaps grandmother who had an ultimate flair for bathtime ritual, and when she came to visit, they followed her around the house watching to see what she would do next. It was not simply the bath, it was everything that led up to and continued after. Grandmother was a proud and somewhat stern woman, but they were able to talk with her through her broken English. She said so herself, "I bery broken Engurish."

She was a plump woman, fat at the middle, and she had long grey hair braided up in a longish bun at the back. They came to her like two young pages volunteering for buttons and zippers, but mostly they were fascinated with her heavy under-armor, a stiff thick pink corset with metal catches and a crisscross of lacing up the middle. The twins, each taking an end of lace, tugged and unhooked step by step, attached to grandmother by corset strings that slowly stretched across the room.

Grandmother always went to bathe with a long strip of cotton cloth, a *tenugui* for washing decorated by Japanese writing and design. In the tub, the thin cloth adhered to the fat folds of her old body, Japanese characters and woven ends trailing off in the clear hot water. Around her stomach, they saw the tight crisscross and wrinkles embedded by the confining corset swell and disappear.

She would begin by washing her face, working down over the entire surface of her body to her toes and using the cloth *tenugui* in a variety of ways, expressing a versatility remarkable in a thing so simple. The *tenugui* grasped at both ends across her back scoured every inch of skin in a seesaw fashion. The *tenugui* could bunch up in a soft round sponge with a smooth woven surface. She rubbed in circular motions over and under the loose layers of freckled flesh and sagging breasts. Finally, the *tenugui* squeezed within a breath of being dry served to soak up and even dry her entire body. Now she stood outside the tub steamy and damp, mopping the perspiration at her forehead. Grandmother and her *tenugui* in the tub seemed simply self-sufficient.

After came creaming the face and brushing and braiding her long grey hair. Then they would join her in pajamas on the large double bed for a session in group exercises. These were motions that ranged from rolling the head in circles and hunching up the shoulders to bicycling upside-down while lying in bed. These things the three did simultaneously while grandmother expounded on their obvious virtues, "The bery good for regs. Now you do. Old be much bettah."

It was not until many years later in Japan that they were to see such as grandmother's *tenugui*. In fact, it would be many years before they should again see an aging body naked at bath. It was not that one missed seeing grandmother in her bathing but that in rediscovering the bath in Japan, there was a vibrant sense of an old intimacy that seemed to radiate through the steam and crouching jostle at the public bath. It was great aunt Yae on mother's side who first introduced one of the twins to the public bath, the *sentō*.

II

She came in February to Kyoto, cold with a barren sense of an old winter. She had just become twenty-one and had been studying Japanese in Tokyo since the fall. She had never been so far from home before.

Great aunt Yae and her husband Chihiro lived retired in an old house, a small house of old polished wood and deteriorating paper and mats, a house perhaps over one or two hundred years old with the wear and darkness of time passing, passing through the war when Chihiro had been an officer in the Imperial Army, passing with the birth of children now married and gone, passing through the bitterness of war and the poverty after.

But of this past, she knew little, and it seemed then that she had passed into an old folktale beginning, *"Mukashi mukashi,"* long long ago there lived an old man and old woman in a little house at the bottom of a hill. They were poor. They lived alone. They had no children. Everyday the old man went out to chop wood to sell, carrying his heavy bundle on his back, trudging through the snow. This is the simple beginning of a recurring story; it seemed to convey the sad gracious charm of an old couple whose lives are simple and resigned.

Her old uncle was hard of hearing, and Yae was continually yelling into his ear, repeating words her niece had said or reminding him of various details he had forgotten. Yae, on the other hand, was rather blind; squinting behind thick wire spectacles, she read newspapers and letters two and three inches from her nose. Sometimes her niece found her washing dishes, inspecting bowls and cups a few inches from her face, shifting her spectacles and poking at cracks and spots.

Yae said that she and *ojisan* could not live without each other. She said, laughing, that they were sometimes like characters in a cartoon. One day she had heard rain on the roof above and announced to her husband that it was raining. Chihiro looked up from his newspapers and said, "That can't be. I don't hear anything. . . . Look, no rain today. *Omae,* you're wrong."

Yae went to the door and slid it aside. Looking out she saw nothing and came back to confirm that it was not raining after all.

Yae disappeared into the kitchen, but the old man's curiosity drew him to the door. Looking out he saw the falling rain and called his wife to the door, tugging at her hand and pushing it into the rain. They stood at the door looking out to the garden and the pouring rain, laughing.

At the door, Yae put her niece in a pair of her old wooden *geta.* They were so worn down at the outer toe side that she was forced to walk awkwardly, imitating Yae's pigeon-toed trot. Yae handed her a small plastic basin in which she had placed a folded *tenugui* along with soap, shampoo and combs. They stepped out. A light snow was falling, disappearing into the gravel about their *geta.* Nodding over her basin to curious neighbors, Yae led her to the *sentō.*

There she saw the layers of *kimono* fall away and Yae's thin aged body plump and wrinkled at the stomach. Yae stood naked slightly stooped in those thick wire spectacles, scrutinizing her belongings and folding everything into a small pile.

They enter the bathroom gripping their plastic basins, swimming through the warm steam that billows as the glass door slides aside. Rows of squatting women and children wash before running faucets. Yae leads her between the rows and echoing commotion of spilling water. Women flushed and dripping emerge from the deep pools. Others meditate silently, squatting low in the great tubs, hot water caressing their hunching shoulders; black wisps of fallen hair cling pasted to cheek and neck. Finding two free places, Yae goes off to steep herself in the hot tub.

Women of every age and shape scrub their bodies with the *tenugui,* busy at wash, vigorous and skillful in their movements. Women kneel and squat, never sitting on the tile, filling their basins and sending cascades of water over an area almost confined to their bodies. All stretching and standing returns to a compact crouch before the faucet or in the tub.

Under the bright shiny lights of the bath, their skin is a beautiful clear white, smooth rich flesh, full at the thighs and hips and small and round at the breasts. She watches a woman with her back turned, following the curving back to the nape of the neck and the fullness of the shoulders slop-ing forward over breasts and skin, shaking. Turning to draw the *tenugui* over her own back, she blushes to see her own shoulder.

The woman next to her kneels with her baby. She washes the baby gently. Leaning forward, the child rests in the curve of her two arms, its head supported in her hands. Her breasts hang swollen with milk. The baby's stubby arms and legs flap and kick.

Yae is now at her place, squatting and scrubbing vigorously. She and other elderly women kneel and squat easily without strain, without the brittle quality that would seem to signify age. Old women small and folded scrub their skin, rich lustre lost to a worn toughness, thin loose folds now useless, once fat and swollen.

A young woman rises from the water, her steaming flushing body waddles forward full and round with child.

Yae crouches behind her niece and offers to wash her back. She scrubs with a vigor the girl has not felt since her mother had done so. Finally spreading the damp *tenugui* over a well-polished back, Yae sends hot water in a smooth stream that, penetrating the cloth, clings. Yae peels the *tenugui* carefully up from the bottom edge to the shoulders; old skin falls away.

She turns to wash Yae's back. She is embarrassed, not being able to wash Yae in the same way. Yae turns squinting and laughing, saying that it does not matter, taking the *tenugui* from her niece and turning to continue her own washing. Yae is brusque in a way that does not care to indulge in matters that cannot change or sentimentality that forfeits honesty or pride. She is brusque but with a wry humor that cannot make one take offense but to know a sparse quality that is honest.

There are children in the bath. There is a beautiful girl child, her feet paddling across the wet tile from the tub to her mother and then to another woman who must be her grandmother. One follows her small protruding stomach and thin shoulders and dark eyes.

Before arriving in Kyoto to see Yae and Chihiro, she had been to Ise, alone, carrying a small blue backpack with all the necessities needed for a month and a half of travel. The days on the Ise peninsula were cold and crisp and the sky a deep blue. She found herself traveling in silence, listening to the noises and conversations of her surroundings, attempting to remain an observer unnoticed, another Japanese youth fading into the background and comfort of nondescription. In her attempt to melt into scenic obscurity, she found herself a sensitive observer as to whether or not others were in-deed aware of her and what they might have to say about it. She wanted to be alone and an observer and yet felt constantly the paranoia of her situa-tion: acting the part of a traveling Japanese student and yet beset by an anxious desire to know if she had succeeded in her disguise and angry at any evidence of failure. So she came on pilgrimage alone to the great Shinto shrines of Ise, walking in silence through the ancient woods of *hinoki* cedar, pausing as others to wash in the clear waters of the Isuzu.

Leaving the shrines, she found a small Buddhist temple that had opened recently its rooms for traveling youth. She was the only one to stop there that evening.

Two small children, a boy and a girl, beautiful with dark eyes, leaned into her window. They scuttled around by the back way and stood shyly, leaning against the edge of the door. Slowly their voices began to ease into her room, filling silent travels with a warmth she had forgotten. They watched her unpack with curiosity, standing or sitting, leaning elbows and faces against the low table.

"Are you really from America? Really?"

"No, you don't look like one."

"No, it's a lie. Really?"

"Teach us English, please. My other sister learns English in school."

"Hurry, teach us English!"

"Say something."

Then as if some other curiosity had aroused their attention, the two children were drawn away. She heard them running with excited voices.

She sat a long time in the doorway like a cat warming herself under the last rays of evening sun. Below her balcony, a young pregnant woman was hanging clothes to dry, sliding the damp pieces along a bamboo pole, reaching to expose her full blooming bag. The woman was the proprietress of the hostel. She said the two children were not her own but a neighbor's. She scolded the children gently for bothering her guest.

But when the woman left, they came again, this time with a friend and more aggressively, stepping inside the room to examine any recent changes.

"Are you really from America? Really?"

"Speak English! Hurry hurry. Teach us English. Hurry!"

The young woman's voice called from a distance. Only the girl child stayed lingering at the door. The child had been munching from a small bag of potato chips. "These are potato chips," the child informed her and leaving her with the small bag, ran off calling after the others.

She sat in the doorway a while longer, eating the remaining chips, and the cold air and shadows came slowly. Distant in America, grandmother was dying. Mother had written, "Granma wakes every morning and says, '*Mada ikite iru no.*'" (Still living.)

The proprietress slid open the paper door passing through from the hallway. Her face shone clean like a wet peach. The warmth of the bath seemed to radiate from her body and the wetness of her hair. Her stomach was round like a balloon, the weight of a child beneath her knitted dress. She said, "You may take your bath now."

Naked, Yae trots toward the steaming glass doors and steps out. A billow of steam follows her, and so does she.

At a wayside inn, a young man slipped into a small bathroom. Clothed or unclothed, in Japan he was a *gaijin,* blue-eyed with brown hair and bristled moustache beneath a longish nose. A *sansei* woman was already there bathing. She ignored him momentarily, washing in one corner with her back turned to him. She handed him a basin and soap, and he squatted in another corner. Soon he was a mass of lather and hair, spilling water from the basin over his head, sputtering. He removed the wooden boards from the steaming tub and stepped in. Only his head bobbed there above the tub; droplets dribbling down his forehead and from his moustache, he squinted. He said, "You know I used to think you were like Audrey Hepburn. You know what I mean? I mean not the way she looks but, you know what I mean? I mean Hepburn is simple and what you might call innocent, but she's not stupid. Hell, she's pretty darn intelligent. I don't know if you understand but, well, I'm not so sure anymore. Now I think you're more of a coquette than she is. In fact, you'd make a pretty fair Japanese hostess."

The woman looked up at him from shampoo suds spilling about. He smiled curiously. He looked blind without his glasses. She rinsed her hair and sent water splashing about the room. He rose from the tub and dried himself with the *tenugui,* slouched out.

The woman stayed to continue her bathing. They had come traveling together for a weekend. He had wanted to fish in one of the lakes surrounding Fuji-san, but it had been raining continuously since their arrival. Instead they had played cards and read inside the six mat room at the inn. When sun seemed promised, they had stepped out for walks and returned together muddy and soaked, or they had sat at one of the two cafes on the lake among the rubber-clad fishermen of the area, sipping tea. Most of the people served and ignored them politely, but the innkeeper had seemed rather curt. Sometimes shopkeepers would address her first, expecting her to translate. He had tried not to be annoyed, and she had tried never to answer for him.

The woman stepped in the tub. He had continued throughout to elaborate on his various and evolving impressions of her. He had discovered in her mysteries and attractions which he continued to muddle over. Over the weekend he had at various times become moody and confused. Simply, he was in love but did not want to admit it, knowing she was not. There was something threatening and cynical beneath her affections.

One could not be sure of the reasons people came to foreign countries, perhaps to search out exotic peoples or beautiful visions of the distant past. Maybe he had come to Japan to find Audrey Hepburn, something respectable, innocent and elegant. It was not fair to make fun of him, for the woman too had come for similar reasons, and it was pleasing to think that another might perceive in her these same traits. He had created an illusion that she longed to step into, but finding his elaborations ultimately trite, she could not trust his observations nor his sensitivity. Even the simplicity which she felt natural to herself cast snide glances at his innocent world.

He had bought her a small white clay cat, a four inch replica of the larger *maneki-neko* that beckons customers into shops and restaurants in Japan. The white cat sat on its haunches with wide eyes and one beckoning paw. It had a red string collar with a small bell. He put the cat on the *tokonoma*.* He had bought the white cat because it reminded him of her.

She slipped her damp body into the *yukata* robe provided by the inn. In the room he seemed asleep. She turned the lights out and slipped beneath the quilts near the floor. There was a stirring. He went out to brush his teeth.

Suddenly, she was under a mass of quilts muzzled, trapped by the heavy darkness and his body that hugged and enfolded. Laughing, she squirmed, groping to find the surface, to find air beyond the tossing quilts; they rolled. Her hand reached for the dry scrap of matting, and elbows squeezed and pushed away the billowing robes. Escaped, she knelt on the matting, watching. He threw the pile of quilts, dumping it over her, "I used to do that to my little sister."

He stood shaking the quilts and fanning them out over the bedding. "You know when I saw you in the bath, sitting there with your back to me and your hair wrapped up over your head, you know what you looked like? You looked like an *ukiyo-e* print, like an *ukiyo-e* woman in the bath—"

IV

In late September, the twins were together again in Japan. After a year, one was about to leave, and the other had just arrived for a year of study and travel.

She came downstairs to the bath with her sister, initiating her to the various buckets and faucets that had by now become quite commonplace. A long time since childhood baths together, they found themselves in the warmth of the small bath, talking.

Her sister, shaped more as mother, was full-breasted and thin-legged. Seeing her reminded one of how beautiful mother's figure must have been. And too, her sister and mother were alike in their realism or practicality of outlook. They moved forward with an eye on the minimal expectation, her sister with a saucy flamboyance defying, mother with a stark energy accepting, the time and the people and the circumstances that came to change their lives. They seemed to experience the events surrounding them more immediately, more honestly because their peripheral vision was wider, more encompassing. Their reactions whether silent or expressed were as they were

* An alcove in which pictures are hung.

at the moment, not afterthoughts screened through the mire of sensibilities and possibilities thought of in the past-tense.

To meet again after a year was to meet themselves at a new juncture. She saw herself in her twin at some former time, although she could not fully see what the time or change had come to. Now perhaps she could say that she had gone to Japan in search of something uncomplicated even as her own sensitivity and those around her were complicated in a way she had not reckoned and could not so easily abandon or disregard. Then too, she had thought of coming to Japan as a ritual to be performed and observed in its symbolic nuances, a return to the past, not simply as a time in life to be lived. In part, she had wanted to recapture a sensibility about life that her grandmothers had known.

She told her sister of a young man she had met while traveling in Nara. His name was Moto, and he had a car and had offered to drive them to Karuizawa for a weekend.

Arriving in Nara by train after solitary wandering on the Ise peninsula, she had stood in front of the station with backpack on back and a pink scarf bag in hand, trying to decipher the map. A swaggering skinny Kubo Moto threw his pack down at her feet and, assuming her to be a lost young sixteen year old, proceeded to give directions and to handle telephone reservations with a brusque self-assertion. She was disgusted and yet resigned to his aid. Besides he did not guess her identity, and this game pleased her. Likewise, she assumed him to be an eighteen year old high school traveler with a small knowledge of English which he bandied about when he seemed to have discovered her inadequacy at Japanese.

A state of confused identities continued for a portion of the day until they finally decided to abandon a game of bantering for confessions that were more startling than the game itself. Moto was a twenty-four year old college graduate who had spent the previous year traveling in Europe and had returned ready to enter the business world, the company.

To explain herself was difficult and finally unconvincing for all the suggestions implied in their game. It was not simply that she was American born. She had yet to concede to herself that her general dress and appearance were indeed quite young. Sacrificing style for practicality and any conspicuous foreign quality for nondescription, she had also succeeded to become by some standards rather childish, devoid of any sophisticated flair or manner. Sophistication of a sort in Japan would have called for cutting her long hair and wearing make-up and that she found repugnant. There was a need to preserve a basic philosophy about being natural. But moreover there was a curious pressing need to be the same. When that sameness was seemingly recognized, she felt the comfort of acceptance and for the time being escaped the humiliation of being thought of as a Chinese or Korean, a child of mixed blood or a copier after American tastes. It should not have been humiliating except for the crude manner and exploitative attitudes that often accompanied these assumptions.

Interestingly enough, a disguise had come about by a discarding of Americanisms, styles and manners that meant nothing to the Japanese. Americans and their pretensions to being more experienced looked silly in Japan. A *sansei* divested of these American manifestations would seem to become simply another Japanese. Yet it was necessary to take on another set of manners, and her manner had become one of a young Japanese girl with sufficient touches of innocence and certainly reticence, mostly due to difficulties with the language. At least it was a surface manner that others found approachable or, negligible. Even if it were an imitation or cover, there was a kind of comfort that exceeded pretensions or dishonesty.

Yae had explained the meaning of *"daikon no hana"*: the *daikon* flower is really, she said, a *"nani mo nai,"* nothing much flower, a tiny flower seen in a tuft of green leaves. But beneath the earth hidden from sight is the great white root, the *daikon.* One knew the *daikon,* a giant white radish that, grated, garnished fish, *ikagen,* with a clean pungent quality like lemon but not as sour—something more mellow. Yae said, "Long ago we used to call some girls '*daikon no hana,*' but nowadays there are no such girls. No, *daikon no hana* have disappeared."

She knew that Yae was such a flower, but as for herself, she was probably not what Yae had had in mind.

At first, she had toyed playfully, experimenting with various expressions in the language of the Japanese woman. Gradually these expressions and manners became natural to most communications, and the possibility of performing successfully roles in two different cultures became a sign of advancement in knowledge of both. There was, too, the secret delight of perceiving more about one's surroundings than one's image might suggest, of knowing that one knew what was what, in other words of being, after all, more experienced.

Therefore, she herself, unconvincing, put aside suspicions about Moto's maturity, confirmed by age, to see again what might come of it. His forward display of self-assertion seemed to allow for this maturity. In any case, they accepted each other's company for a three-day tour of Nara.

During the same week in Nara, a small cottage in the resort area of Karuizawa was under seige by hundreds of armed policemen. Inside the hillside cottage, members of the Red Guard, a small Marxist band, were holding a woman hostage while police sent torrents of water by firehose to batter down the cottage. It was a small war waged on a snowy hillside, police crouching behind fire tanks with rifles, and the husband of the hostage wailing through microphones echoing down the valley, "Please, my wife is a sick woman. Please take me, and let her go!"

Moto sympathized with the youth in the cottage. He said that they had no choice but to wait and to fight. He could not explain why these events had happened, but he said that the youth had no choice but to die. They would be killed by the police or in the courts.

After a long week, the police finally broke in, killing several youth, capturing others and saving the woman. Later stories revealed a bizarre tale that had begun in mountain cottages elsewhere where members of the guard fought among themselves in a game of power that led to private trials and the systematic execution and burial of their own people, one by one. A woman with child had barely escaped death. Her brothers were dead. Their bodies had been dismembered, buried over the mountain side. A young woman had led the group. Her plain harsh face stared from newspapers everywhere. Some said it was the woman's plain face that had made her bitter and angry.

Karuizawa was after all a resort area, and Moto's family had built a small cottage there. The long five-hour drive over winding highways was tedious, exhausting. Her sister refused to sit in the front seat and finally said, "That guy doesn't know how to drive. Shit, I know—He can't even shift gears smoothly. He's going to get us into an accident. Where did you pick up this guy anyway?"

Her twin had come a long way to disturb her perspective, but something inside her jumped, an old sense of strength, even of hostility, and she began to know that she had met and accepted Moto because of a game of sorts, a deception, and urge to imitation. Even if she had tried to suspend judgment or to allow another set of values or rules to decide, she was not now sure. She did not know who this Moto was.

The cottage was one of many, isolated among the trees far up on a hill. It seemed wedged into the side of the hill overlooking a dirt road below. What she had imagined would be an extravagant two-story cabin was rather a two-room kitchenette, compact and convenient. They scrounged around for supplies, and she was pleased to cook putting foods together, *ikagen,* out of a wide range of novel possibilities. She was pleased with her own ingenuity and the camplike self-sufficiency of the arrangement.

The twins talked constantly together. They began to leave Moto out. In fact they began to wish that he might disappear. Moto had at first confused one twin for the other. The initial humor of these confusions long past, he had continued, either by the growing schizophrenia of his perceptions or a need to release nervous energy, to recreate confusions and ensuing jokes. Her sister was not one to conceal boredom or disgust, and Moto could not conceal his now obvious immaturity. The swaggering self-confidence had dissipated into an insipid amiability and jokes that had been amusing once only because the Japanese had been simple enough to understand.

A typhoon was reported. There was a possibility of its heading their way. The resort season had virtually closed down. They seemed to be the only people in the area. There seemed to be nothing to do, and the rain threatened to trap them inside the cottage. They made preparations for the long stormy night, setting boards up over the windows.

She cooked, and her twin slept. Moto prepared a bath. Turning from the sink, she heard a huge BOOM! and Moto's body flew backwards out of the bathroom. He was stunned and wide-eyed, babbling about fire, about gas. He had lit leaking gas. The burnt ends of surface hair crinkled down his face. Fortunately his arms had been covered. He was not hurt, but she was becoming nervous at this enterprise, and the rain was coming steadily.

The twins stepped into that same bath together. Her sister talked constantly and animatedly on all subjects seemingly without awareness of the steady and increasing sound of the rain. The wind blew fiercely outside the boarded windows of the bathroom. Rain pounded intermittently against the thin walls, clanging madly at the tin shielding. Inside that closet of steam and hot water, they splashed soap and bubbles about. Her twin bent over her squatting back and scrubbed, entertaining her with the stories and events of the year past, and she could hear the increasing scream of the storm against their steaming closet and the violent chaos that was becoming her own fears. She thought of the precarious wedging of the cottage against the hill and of the slippage of land and mud and trees; she thought of the deluge and the mass of land ⁺hat might bury two naked soapy bodies.

Her sister said of Moto, "Where did you pick him up? You're always getting screwed. He's just like all those other immature Japanese dudes who think they're such hot shit. What a baby. And since I got in that car accident, I'm paranoid about cars, and he can't drive a stick shift. It's murder to try to drive with someone like that."

She turned her twin around, crouching behind, and poured water over her back, peeling the *tenugui* to her shoulders, trying as Yae had done. She admitted that Moto must be a fool, and foolishly wanted to hear her sister's voice echoing forcibly against the tile and wood, harsh or tender, but louder than the raging storm. Yet she saw in her mind the crushing weight of a mud wall bursting through that closet and the wild treachery and insipid irony of that disgusting death.

As she emerged from the steam closet, Moto looked up and said, "The typhoon will pass very near. Perhaps it will swerve off, but then, we may be at the center." He drew the standard shape of Japan on a small scratch pad, marking where they were, where the typhoon was, where it would or would not pass, and at what time, with all the authority of a radio broadcast. Then he looked at her; his face looked comically severe and then, just comical.

"Maybe this house will fall down the hill. . . . No, the house is probably stronger than that. What I'm more worried about is the car at the bottom. If it slipped off, we would never be able to leave." He smiled wild-eyed. "Perhaps we will die!"

She looked at him in disgust.

He continued, "But, in any case, I'll be happy. It will be like dying with you in a double suicide."

v

She received a letter today from her sister, who is still in Japan. Now she too is traveling alone. She writes that she has found a small beach in Kyushu called Ibusuki and that she has tried the sand baths there. When the tide recedes, old women come to bury her in sand. Deep deep from secret sources beneath the sand, the warm springs rise.

And mother went out early this morning to weed the garden and came in hot and muddy. She retired to the thing that gives her the most pleasure, her bath. Now she stands in her towel with wet hair adjusting her glasses.

"Oh," she says. "A letter from your sister. Now what does she say?"

POETRY

LAUREEN MAR

Laureen Mar, a Chinese American born in 1953 in Seattle, is presently pursuing an MFA in the Creative Writing Program at Columbia University. She has published poems in *Greenfield Review, Mademoiselle, Northwest Review,* and *Intro 7.* She says, "How I would characterize myself as a writer is beginning. I've been made painfully aware of the synonymity of language and attitude. I see where I haven't always succeeded in the truth I want for my poems, but I'm learning."

MY MOTHER, WHO CAME FROM CHINA, WHERE SHE NEVER SAW SNOW

In the huge, rectangular room, the ceiling
a machinery of pipes and fluorescent lights,
ten rows of women hunch over machines,
their knees pressing against pedals
and hands pushing the shiny fabric thick as tongues
through metal and thread.
My mother bends her head to one of these machines.
Her hair is coarse and wiry, black as burnt scrub.
She wears glasses to shield her intense eyes.
A cone of orange thread spins. Around her,
talk flutters harshly in Toisan wah.
Chemical stings. She pushes cloth
through a pounding needle, under, around, and out,
breaks thread with a snap against fingerbone, tooth.
Sleeve after sleeve, sleeve.
It is easy. The same piece.
For eight or nine hours, sixteen bundles maybe,
250 sleeves to ski coats, all the same.
It is easy, only once she's run the needle
through her hand. She earns money
by each piece, on a good day,
thirty dollars. Twenty-four years.

It is frightening how fast she works. _
She and the women who were taught sewing
terms in English as Second Language.
Dull thunder passes through their fingers.

CHINATOWN 1
Seattle, Washington

She boards the bus at Chinatown,
holding the brown paper shopping bag
with twine handles that comes from
San Francisco or Vancouver.
It is worn thin with creases.
An oil spot darkens one side
where juice dripped from warm
roast duck, another shopping trip.
Today there is fresh bok choy
wrapped in Chinese newspapers.
Grasping the rail with her right hand,
she climbs the steps carefully,
smiling at the driver, looking down
to check her footing, glancing
at him again. She sways down the aisle
as if she still carried wood buckets
on a bamboo pole through the village,
from the well to her house.
Her gray silk pajamas are loose,
better than "pantsuits."
Sometimes there are two or three women,
chattering with the quick, sharp tongue
of the wren: dried mushrooms too
expensive, thirteen dollars a pound now.
She sits down and sets the bag between her knees.
Her shoulder is close to mine.
I want to touch it, tell her I can understand
Chinese. Instead, I stare at the silver
bar crossing her back, and hope she knows
this is an Express; it does not stop before Genesee.

CHINATOWN 2

Photograph of Eight Chinese-American Children,
Ages 1½ to 10. Seattle, Washington, 1926.

For my father, Ling Kim

On the 19th and Jefferson block,
the trees are evenly spaced.
Sunlight falls in triangles
as regular as the trunks.
Eight Chinese children sit
as if they had just fallen
out of the tree they lean against,
and landed there in two neat rows,
their legs brushing the grass.
Their hair is cut like rice bowls;
a fringe of bangs runs high across
their foreheads, leaving eyebrows
below to umbrella somber eyes.
Dick Kim stares at shoes that overwhelm
his feet; sleeves end haphazardly
between Ling Kim's wrists and elbows.
Maye Kim does not like her corduroy pants.
There is one dress and one pair of suspenders.

Looking through the lens
of the heavy, borrowed camera,
Grandpa remembers the butterfly
resting on a stem, its thin
paper wings folding slowly together.
He had to prod himself to do more
than gawk at the bright stillness.
Pressing the button, he feels
the urgent beating between his fingers.
Not knowing they are the show,
his children watch the heavy, black box,
waiting for two white doves
to flap awkwardly into the sky,
or a brown jackrabbit to flop
on the lawn, the brown jackrabbit
my father chased for me around the dry
wheatgrass and periwinkle blue flowers.
Grandpa clucks his tongue to shoo them off.
They are only disappointed until they see

the neighbor's red trike waiting outside
the right corner, where sunlight
coming from the direction of the house
floods and fades the edge.

CHINATOWN 4

Each evening I watch my mother fight
the meaning of words without pictures.

She groups them like birds in a tree.
When she speaks, they careen in the wind.

She believes I dreamed. I dream. I will dream.
But does not understand the verb "could."

She thinks we were taught to say "l's" in school,
where to place our tongue, how to move our lips.

Her words do not end with consonants.
They tilt upwards, cling to the air like leaves.

DIANA CHANG

A prolific writer, Diana Chang has published poetry in numerous journals and magazines and written six novels: *The Frontiers of Love* (1956), *A Woman of Thirty* (1959), *A Passion for Life* (1961), *The Only Game in Town* (1963), *Eye to Eye* (1974), and *A Perfect Love* (1978). Though she was born in New York, she spent her childhood in China reared by her Eurasian mother. Of herself, she says, "I feel I'm an American writer whose background is Chinese. The source of my first and fourth novels was Chinese, but exoticism can stand in the way of the universal I strive for in my themes. Therefore, since I write fiction in English and am living my life in the USA, I've often subsumed aspects of my background in the interest of other truths and recognitions. . . . I believe an abiding interest in character and emotion informs all my work—not only because the relationships, situations, and problems I write about arise out of the characters of my protagonists, out of their personalities, but also because I seem preoccupied a lot with identity or selfness. Being or becoming seems to be an underlying denominator of my work, at least so far. . . . My poems have been described as lyrical and concise, perhaps even too condensed. I hope to be economical and not dwell too lovingly on my own words. One owes it to everyone not to be boring."

RHYTHMS

The landscape comes apart
in birds

A horse
detaches himself

from a fence
A criminal of love

breaks away
The child drops out of a tree

A ship uncouples
from the street

The canal, unhinged,
proceeds

Cars are pieces of the world
tearing away

But the crows
collect

in heaps
And stone

and sky
poised with being

grow steep
before

they faint
into the wind

and things
fly

again

WHAT MATISSE IS AFTER

The straight in a curve
is what Matisse is after

two lines
one veering in,

an invitation to
the rest of space,
the other

a long gourd
swelling
out of bone

an arm sings
that its reach

rounds
into a heave
of loving

the line of a thigh
on its departure
toward returning

in the teeth
of our dying

what elegant
flying

He exhales paint we need

to
breathe

STILL LIFE

We stare and shout—
Smash together,

Particles of you,
Straining to become

Before they are born,
Stampede my womb.

Bodies stunned,
Rich as clay,

We hope to be dumb
And try to bear.

Then the moon begets
Some intelligence . . .

It is the night
Thinks hard.

Elan of matter .
Aches for breath.

Life feels for us,
Reaches an end.

Flesh into words,
We begin to mind.

Again we complain
And die, awake.

CANNIBALISM

When I put myself out on a saucer
   in the sun
      or moonlight
         of the back stoop
cats
in
the form of
images
come feeding

PAULA YUP

Born in Arizona in 1957, Paula Yup, a Chinese American, completed her studies at Occidental College and spent two years studying Japanese at Waseda University in Japan. She has published poetry in *California Quarterly, Contemporary Quarterly, Occidental Community Review,* and *Southwest Anthology* (1977). Describing herself as an "expressive and spontaneous writer," she also translates poetry from Japanese into English.

UNTITLED

pounce the cat
   chatterbox jerry
      catches tom
 or is it tom masticates jerry
those lovable friends
     able to eat
        and reeat each other
in carnivore conservation.

PEACE

I spy butterfly
In quietly still waters
living for today.

OPAQUE

The scene is nature
in painted colors
and
   I touch
      the essence
through
     shades of grey.

TERU KANAZAWA

Born in New York City in 1950, Teru Kanazawa is a staff member of the Asian American Resource Center of the Basement Workshop and an editor of *AARchives,* the resource center publication. She says, "Having lived in New York all my life, writing at various times is a pastime, a survival tool; sustenance for such activity derives largely from the Asian American movement."

THE LOOK OF SUCCESS

The air is cold here.

Stones mark the limits of my stride
front door lit, not to
welcome strangers
wizened babies rehearse
rites of territorial impulse
in cluttered carriers
pushed
through
Stud
malls.

Suburbs strut
wearing their reputation
like a graduation tassel.

The 5 o'clock stubble of America

> Dreams gained,
> nothing to wish for.

DUMB PATRONAGE

Halloween has passed
for you, dear friends,
but I remain
behind a smile (angry)
laughing (sad)
drunk (sober) and finally
glaring (scared)
at all of you who take me
for what I feign.

My face is different
so you mistake
my yellow skin for parchment,
my broad, flat face for glee,
my aborted pupils for simplicity.
It has been said,
"You can tell so much from
appearance,"
        and so,
        it is so easy to hide.

SHIRLEY GEOK-LIN LIM

Shirley Geok-Lin Lim was born in Malaysia in 1944 and came to the United States to do her doctoral work at Brandeis. She currently lives near New York City and is an assistant professor of English at Westchester Community College. She has published poems and fiction in *Tengarra: A Journal of South-East Asian Writing, A Private Landscape* (1967), *Poetry Singapore* (1968), *Twenty-Two Malaysian Stories* (1968), and *Westerly* (1976), among other journals and anthologies. She characterizes herself as "a closet writer, a cowardly writer; an always-wanted-to-be-one writer. Needing time, which is money and more than money. Needing other writers—where are they? Believing in discipline and needing freedom. Working on craft but not crafty enough. Searching for a voice—there are too many. In circumstances one-of-a-kind, and uncomfortable about it. Having broken many promises, still promising for the future."

MODERN SECRETS

Last night I dreamt in Chinese.
Eating Yankee shredded wheat,
I told it in English terms
To a friend who spoke
In monosyllables,
All of which I understood:
The dream shrunk
To its fiction.
I knew its end
Many years ago.
The sallow child
Eating from a rice-bowl
Hides in the cupboard
With the tea-leaves and china.

CHRISTMAS IN EXILE

Christmas is coming and I think of home:
a colonial Christmas and second-hand nostalgia
as simple as home-made cottonwool snow,
paste holly and a cheap plastic conifer.
Where Christ is born in odd conditions,

to customary churches and celebration.
O silent and holy night, we sing, beneath
the clear hot equatorial sky.
Where, as everywhere, even to the hour of birth,
soldiers keep watch; and frivolity
is circumscribed by birth but especially by death.

POTIONS

Bitter tea,
Hot or cold,
Equally good
For chest pains,
Loose bowels,
Chills, fevers,
Sore throats,
Coughs in the night,
And other body ailments.
He drank thermos-flasks
But did not recover.

Ginger-root
Awakens hunger,
overcomes langour,
Combats age,
Heats the blood,
And revitalizes
Its motions.
He ate ginger
But lost weight;
Haloed with pain;
Grew light like a child.

Morphine pills,
Take one a day.
Take one when needed
Or every so often.
Like yellow wax
Dissolving,
He sheds hope
For his life.
His children meet
To bless his bones.

I WOULD LIKE

I would like to be happy as a servant:
Serve on committees, serve the community,
Serve the people, a government servant.
I would like to serve a family:
Clean house, polish flatware, arrange
Flowers, and fold away laundry,
Fluffed, lemon-scented, symmetry.

Pure home-maker, hand-maiden, I,
A foot-stool, would serve you hand and foot.
Then would it be no effort to lie:
Sycophant, flatterer, lady,
Efficient at this as in the others.
My mouth would gape, sing arias,
Tongue, and burn like widow's soot.

JESSICA TARAHATA HAGEDORN

Jessica Tarahata Hagedorn, a Filipino American, was born in the Philippines in 1949. Her work has appeared in *Four Young Women* (1973), *Third World Women* (1973), *Time to Greez* (1975), and *Yardbird Reader,* among other places. She has also published *Dangerous Music* (1975) and has a novel forthcoming. She says, "I see my writing going further and further out in the direction of music and theater, stand-up comedy, and the movies.... I hope to continue my work with my band, the Gangster Choir, in achieving these ends."

SOMETIMES YOU LOOK LIKE LADY DAY

I

sometimes you look like lady day
the way your eyes are colorless with pain
when you smile   & i tell you
how melancholy   the walk you have
kinda brave when you swing yr hips
the way you speak of men
sometimes when i hear the bitterness
i see the love
the walk you have
your beauty is timeless
no space can really hold you
& i tell you sadness
the walk you have
kinda brave when you swing yr hips
sometimes serenity in your mouth
the way you speak of men

II

sometimes you look like lady day
the way you hang yr head
in the afternoon
shadows across yr face
the weariness there
we drink the blood of rubies
in our teacups
and twist the solar cord
in our bellies
the afternoon sun waning
shadows across yr face
the weariness there
you wear hibiscus in yr hair
drunkenly dancing
in los angeles palace poolrooms
nibbling lettuce necklaces
off whimsical young men's shoulders
& i tell you sadness
the walk you have
sometimes serenity in yr eyes
and the music . . .

III

sometimes you look like lady day
the smokiness of yr silence
yr hand holding shreds of poetry,
old photographs; and broken hearts
are painted on yr cheeks as valentines
the beauty marks that have become scars
yr mother's smell
in the perfume you dab
on young men's wrists
the fire still
the fire still
the fire still
& i tell you sometimes
serenity in yr madness
& the love
always

SONG FOR MY FATHER

i arrive
in the unbearable heat
the sun's stillness
stretching across
the land's silence
people staring out
from airport cages
thousands of miles later
and i have not yet understood
my obsession to return

and twelve years
is fast
inside my brain
exploding like tears.

i could show you
but you already know.

you greet me
and i see
it is you
you all the time
pulling me back
towards this space

letters are the memory
i carry with me
the unspoken name
of you,
my father

in new york
they ask me
if i'm puerto rican
and do i live in queens?
i listen to pop stations chant
to iemaja
convinced i'm really brazilian
and you
a riverboat gambler
shooting dice in macao
during the war

roaches fly around us
like bats in twilight
and barry white grunts
in fashionable discotheques
setting the pace
for guerillas to grind

the president's wife
has a fondness
for concert pianists
and gossip is integral to conversation

if you eat enough papaya
your sex drive diminishes
lorenza paints my nails blue
and we giggle at the dinner table
aunts and whores
brothers and homosexuals
a contessa with chinese eyes
and an uncle cranky with loneliness
he carries an american passport
like me

and here we are,
cathedrals in our thighs
banana trees for breasts
and history all mixed up
saxophones in our voices
when we scream
the love of rhythms
inherent
when we dance

they can latin here
and shoot you
for the wrong glance
eyes that kill
eyes that kill

dope dealers are executed
in public
and senators go mad
in prison camps
the nightclubs are burning
with indifference
curfew drawing near

soldiers lurk in jeeps
of dawn war zones
as the president's daughter
boogies nostalgically
under the gaze
of sixteen smooth bodyguards
and decay is forever
even in the rage
of humorless revolutionaries

in hotel lobbies
we drink rum
testing each other's wit
snakes sometimes crawl
in our beds
but what can you do
in the heat
the laziness makes you love
so easily

you smile like buddha
urging me to swim with you
the water is clear
with corpses of dragonflies
and mosquitoes

i'm writing different poems now
my dreams have become reptilian
and green
everything green, green
and hot
eyes that kill
eyes that kill

women slither
in and out of barroom doorways
their tongues massage
the terror from your nightmares
the lizard hissing nervously
as he watches you breathe

i am trapped
by overripe mangoes
i am trapped
by the beautiful sadness of women
i am trapped

by priests and nuns
whispering my name in confession boxes
i am trapped
by antiques
and the music of the future

and leaving you
again and again
for america,
the loneliest of countries

my words change . . .
sometimes
i even forget english.

JANICE MIRIKITANI

Janice Mirikitani lives and works in San Francisco. She has published in and coedited *Third World Women* (1973), *Time to Greez* (1975), and *Ayumi: The Japanese American Anthology* (1979). She says, "Words from the Third World are like food. Universal, essential, procreative, freeing, connective, satisfying."

SING WITH YOUR BODY
To my daughter, Tianne Tsukiko

We love with great difficulty
spinning in one place
afraid to create
      spaces
            new/rhythm

the beat of a child
dangled by her own inner ear
takes Aretha with her
      upstairs,   somewhere.

go quickly, Tsukiko,
      into your circled dance
go quickly
      before your steps are
      halted by who you are not

go quickly
      to learn the mixed
      rhythm of your tongue,

go quickly
        to who you are

        before

            your mother swallows
            what she has lost.

ATTACK THE WATER

My first flash
on the newsprint/face
she could have been
obachan
back then/just after
the camps
when the land/dried/up
no water for months.
In town,
they would not sell
to japs.
we had to eat what
we could grow
that's only natural
when there is nothing
else
nothing
      else.
we ate rice with roots & rooster legs.

        Vietnamese woman
        her face etched old
        by newsprint/war
        mother/grandmother
        she has borne them all
        (have they all died?)
            flash!!

"they are bombing the waterways

"this new offensive
which has previously/been/avoided/
for humanitarian/reasons/
will/seriously/jeopardize/
their/food/situation."

Obachan
sitting
breathing heavily
in the sun
watching her pet rabbits
(she loved them like children)
which one/
tonight?
i still remember her eyes
drawing the blood
like water.
And the rice—
there were maggots
in the rice.
no water
to flush/them/out.

> Up river
> bodies floated in My Chanh
> eyes eaten by crabs
> flushed onto the land—
> fly food.
> "They are attacking the water.
> when all else fails
> attack the water."

Obachan
would chew
the food first/spit
out maggots.
Grandchildren
ate the spit-flushed rice.

> when all else fails
> attack the water.

AI (PELORHANKHE OGAWA)

Born in 1947 in Texas, Ai is currently an assistant professor of English at Wayne State University in Detroit. She has published *Cruelty* (1973) and *Killing Floor* (1979); and her poems have appeared in *Antaeus, Choice, American Poetry Review,* and *The American Poetry Anthology,* among other places. She comments, "I am above all things, a poet. I do not write about race, social comment, etc., but about people, life, suffering, and am now trying to bring about the transfiguration of men and women in my poetry. This transfiguration, of course, comes from the word, and both the word (my poetry) and I are (borrowing from T. E. Lawrence) of God, from God, and toward God. Although I appear in the Asian American section of this book (by my choice), I would like to add that I am mixed. My father was Japanese and my mother is black, Choctaw Indian, and Irish with some German coming from somewhere."

TWENTY-YEAR MARRIAGE

You keep me waiting in a truck
with its one good wheel stuck in the ditch,
while you piss against the south side of a tree.
Hurry. I've got nothing on under my skirt tonight.
That still excites you, but this pickup has no windows
and the seat, one fake leather thigh,
pressed close to mine is cold.
I'm the same size, shape, make as twenty years ago,
but get inside me, start the engine;
you'll have the strength, the will to move.
I'll push, you push, we'll tear each other in half.
Come on, baby, lay me down on my back.
Pretend you don't owe me a thing
and maybe we'll roll out of here,
leaving the past stacked up behind us;
old newspapers nobody's ever got to read again.

THE ANNIVERSARY

You raise the ax,
the block of wood screams in half,
while I lift the sack of flour
and carry it into the house.
I'm not afraid of the blade
you've just pointed at my head.
If I were dead, you could take the boy,
hunt, kiss gnats, instead of my moist lips.
Take it easy, squabs are roasting,
corn, still in husks, crackles,
as the boy dances around the table:
old guest at a wedding party for two sad-faced clowns,
who together, never won a round of anything but hard times.
Come in, sheets are clean,
fall down on me for one more year
and we can blast another hole in ourselves without a sound.

THE COUNTRY MIDWIFE: A DAY

I bend over the woman.
This is the third time between abortions.
I dip a towel into a bucket of hot water
and catch the first bit of blood,
as the blue-pink dome of a head breaks through.
A scraggy, red child comes out of her into my hands
like warehouse ice sliding down the chute.

It's done, the stink of birth, Old Grizzly
rears up on his hind legs in front of me
and I want to go outside,
but the air smells the same there too.
The woman's left eye twitches
and beneath her, a stain as orange as sunrise
spreads over the sheet.
I lift my short, blunt fingers to my face
and I let her bleed, Lord, I let her bleed.

GERALDINE KUDAKA

Geraldine Kudaka was born in Hawaii in 1951, the daughter of a plantation hand and a maid from Okinawa. She has worked as a free-lance photographer and writer, a poet-teacher for Poetry in the Schools, and an editor. She is presently living in San Francisco, working on a film script, editing a magazine, *Beyond Rice,* and writing both fiction and poetry. Her works have appeared in *Third World Women* (1973), *Time to Greez* (1975), *Greenfield Review,* and *Yardbird Reader.*

ON WRITING ASIAN-AMERICAN POETRY

Takamura Kotaro*
speaks
of fireplaces
ancient magpie homes
where
Chieko† lived

> my mixed up
> poems
> are hybrid races:
> an american birth

Takahashi Mutsuo‡
knows
of minos, pungent sex,
male tongues,
and sturdy legs

> under a terrible
> sunrise
> my grandparents
> came to america

* A contemporary Japanese poet.
† Chieko is the wife of Kotaro, whose story has been immortalized in *Portrait of Chieko,* a popular Japanese film.
‡ A contemporary Japanese poet.

Shiraishi Kazuko**
swirls cocks
and shadows
into statuesque carvings

>   we ate rice
>   and langendorf bread
>   plates of
>   *padded bras, blondes,*
>   *John Wayne, pigs n tofu*

shinkansen†† trains rush by
transporting kimono bodies
in suits and ties

>   we said the pledge
>   of allegiance
>   and learned english
>   as a 2nd language

outside new york
there is a
blizzard blazing

i invited you over
& fed you tea
behind coy hands you
snickered

>   *Ne chotto suifu-san*
>   *Umi kara agatta bakari no*‡‡

you took my poems
you took my soul
your hands rusty hangers
aborting my child

>   we learned racism
>   & believed
>   blondes had more fun

** A contemporary Japanese poet.
†† Special high-speed trains.
‡‡ This is a translation by Asakawa Maki of the first two lines from "Port Town"
by Langston Hughes:

>   Hello, sailor boy,
>   In from the sea!

you became the judge
and i condemned
your lily white suburbs
and i ghetto splattered

> my tempura-kim chi* menu
> spilled on tatami mat
> my black hair black eyes
> scan your proper stance

Asakawa Maki†
jazz priestess of
japaaan
wails Langston Hughes

> *Ne chotto suifu-san*
> *Umi kara agatta bakari no*

in america
did the vastness
of camps
feed
myopic vision?

i s h o u l d a   t o l d   y o u

last nite
i shoulda told you
you're not my friend
anymore

i shoulda said
something like/   are you
one of them
eternal children
them momma cooks n cleans
them turn out
saccharin sweet

i shoulda told you
'bout ladies & them
wouldbesaxmen

* Names of food dishes.
† One of the foremost jazz singers in Japan.

who can't understand
a word of poetry

i could catch
myself
hanging rumours
out to dry,
trying to objectify
bass clefs
& syncopated sounds

& 'stead of going
crazy,
i'd pick up a stethoscope &
in fine print
the by-lines glare
Everybody's Got a Melody

his receiver works
intermittently
& is sooo cooool
wrapped up in tapedeck
spools
& spinnin' on
six feet down

someone shoulda told you
when a man
does what he loves best,
he's never angry or
bitter or phony or cruel

& sometimes
even Viva Ricado
goes off
the brink
'cause it's hard to be cool
& contented
every day of the week

&, oh yeah,
i didn't tell you
three hours
before
i was cookin' his food
& feelin' kinda blue

i can't be bottling up
like good vintage wine

& feelin' kinda blue
i started to cry
& his screaming words
slammed thru the air
& it was cold cold
                    cold

i shoulda told you
i can sing the blues

FAY CHIANG

Born in New York City in 1952 of Chinese American parents, Fay Chiang is currently completing a degree in art at Hunter College of the City University of New York and doing volunteer work at the Basement Workshop with writers' workshops and performing groups. In addition to giving numerous poetry readings at prisons, college campuses, and women's centers in the Northeast, she has also coedited *Ordinary Women* (forthcoming) with Sarah Miles, Patricia Jones, and Sandra Esteves. Her poetry has appeared in *Bridge* and the *Sunbury Poetry Magazine,* and she has written a book of poems, *In the City of Contradictions* (1979). The thrust of her work, she says, centers on the experience of being an Asian American woman in New York City.

it was as if

it was as if there were not enough chances or places
    or spaces set aside
  a mood or something separate to chat
        and get to know you inside out
        or whatnot, you know
    without further dividing the boxes and shadows
        i dance to
    and cornered rooms and locked up doors:
      do not enter the sign read
      this inner region of my head
      move along instead
      so the living like some dead

you can walk for miles and miles and miles for blocks of time
  in new york city   on a winter's day
    not saying a single word or phrase
        getting lost in the daze
          i did that today:

catatonic to reality
confused and confounded
torn and profounded by a profusion of mystics and priests on
                    the streets
  screaming for jesus, hare krishna,

hailing mary on 42nd street and om to god and all
                    human beings:
    I AM BLIND. PLEASE HELP ME. THANK YOU.
    THIS IS THE ONLY WAY I MAKE MY LIVING.
    BLESS YOU.
    LOVE AND PEACE ON SALE TODAY. RADICAL
    IS CHIC.
    AND LEVI STRAUSS MAKES A BUNDLE. YES.
    ONLY GOD KNOWS. HE. IS. THE. TRUTH.
    WHILE WE THE FLOCK (METAPHYSICS LIVES)
                    GATHER.

and on the library steps at night, the lions roar. the
cleaning ladies say so, and children on streets and bums on
the bowery scream for dreams of sugar plum fairies and
elves . . . take it light, bro. or your mind's gonna blow.

headlines:
woman jumps off brooklyn bridge clutching her raggedy ann
    doll.
son kills mom and dad in outer suburbia in fit of rage.
miss america crowned in fairbanks alaska.
more than half the world population dying of starvation.
the unemployed masses marched toward the sea on both
coasts of the nation in the formation of lemmings. asked
one participating in this remarkable sight (by this
reporter) the reasoning behind such an exodus, he replied:
for lack of something better to do. unquote.
teenaged youngsters rampaged through the national parks in
their annual outburst of destruction, while our elderly
continue contemplating the nutritional value of bird seeds.
purina's warehouses have since been depleted of dog and
cat food.
heads of state gathered on the white house lawn in search
of easter eggs carefully camouflaged in the bushes;
united nations members continued playing monopoly far
into the night: this is the six o'clock news.

strolling along central park
    the shafts of light and beams of sunfilled air
ignited an atmosphere on the shortness of spectrums of
lifetimes of trees and old age; children's voices shifted, then
echoed and i picked up the stillness of one's universe
                    in the crumbling of a dried leaf in the
                            palm of my hand.

FAY CHIANG
551

the shortness, the smallness
the grumbling, the stumbling, the hitting, the shouting,
the screaming, and crying, the moaning and droning,
the laughter,
makes it all
makes it all even more smaller
    at times to the point where the scope and the hope
      of every day living dries up to a crisp
        like a teardrop on the desert's floor.

catatonic to reality
    lost in space about the feelings and needs of others/
                myself
                    alienated
      neurotic depressions reeling
          circular in 3-d spirals
     lower and lower, higher, higher
  manic suicidal masochistic mechanisms
         cutting—CAPITALISM CRIPPLES!
    fall back. internalize. so slowly crawl in the
      nauseam; HELP ME. I AM BLIND.
   shrill lights pierce screams unheard/careens in
   the corners of my aching mind, throbbing incessant,
   incessantly. silence:
        i am vulnerable
        a babe in the woodlands
      of creation and humanity
        dancing lightly, reaching with much trust
          for myself/others

dialogue:
I'm sorry about what happened.   (Is that what one says?)
—It was expected.   (What traditions to be
Can I be of any help. Please let   borne)
me.   (Is this what one does?)
—No, it's all right. There is
nothing.   (Support comes only in
I insist. I must help you.   crisis)
—No. it's all right, really.   (Why is my help being
nothing to be done. thank you.   refused?)
I want to do something!   (Where are you every day?)
—Oh, please then, sit with me.   (Maybe I shouldn't have
Well, uh, then, . . . how's the   come)
weather?   (I'm getting tired of this)

wanting change, caught in the midst of old values
lacking support and strength, refusing/ not
knowing how to give/to take, internalizing old
and new hesitations, wanting to help, not knowing
how, feeling clumsy, inept, cautious in action
and deed—in the end, nothing being done
except alot of silences and pain from those who
need to receive and those who need to give.

break loose and fight old ghosts and shadows. fall down.
get up, but fight with MIND AND HEART AND SOUL.

AND THE MASSES OF PEOPLE ARE MOVING
A POETRY IN THE SENSES OF FINENESS INHERENT
BURIED BENEATH LAYERS OFTIMES
CONDITIONED NOT TO NOTICE THE
SPIRITUALITY OF IT ALL
BURSTING FORTH, STRIVING AND PUSHING TO BE
SENSATE:
THERE IS A RHYTHM
THERE MUST BE WORK
AND THERE WILL BE A TIME.

HELEN AOKI KANEKO

Helen Aoki Kaneko was born in California in 1919. She lives and writes in Los Angeles.

ENIGMA

What do you think, old woman,
Who neither smiles nor uncurls her fingers
From her cane?

Are the years crushed in your hands
Too heavy to remove? Bitterness
Mars your eyes, has made the lips
Immobile.

And yet the pearl gray cat
Mews fondly at your step,
Curls softly at your feet.

WIND

Wind
Gives speech
To trees.

UPON SEEING AN ETCHING

A line in ebony starkness curved on the white page,
Turned right and left and shivered a while
Until it flushed a blur
Of fur and little feet.
The wandering line threw out a branch
And there was a monkey up a tree.

LAURA TOKUNAGA

Born in Hawaii in 1950, Laura Tokunaga currently lives in Los Angeles, where she works as a phototypesetter. Her poems have appeared in *Bridge, New Worlds,* and *Counterpoint* (1976).

BEHIND LOCKED DOORS

I hear a footstep on the walk outside.

> (you know, a sound
> is not necessarily a portent,
> a singular occurrence could be
> much less than a sign
> but the wind is an ocean
> black and deep)

I know.
I see red waves breaking between sunset and sky,
caravans of fog floating past cities
whose populations have retired to a raw intransigence
which allows neither
vision nor reflection.

while within these walls a garden is dying:
turning withered and black,
leaves dropping from stems
as constellations of albino insects gather
in the gaps in my attention.

I barely seem to care
I care just enough.
> (you know just

enough is rarely
good enough)

I hear a footstep on the walk outside.
the world making a final song
grinding shut under the weight
of the wind and
        (I feel
        what
        I want)
this wind will take me in
        (do I hear a hand on the door?)

GEOGRAPHY

it doesn't matter
what I hear inside
    that ocean sound
    is traffic.

when I close my eyes
I see dinosaurs
feathered serpents
burning in the air.
they scorch my ribcage black
    bones crumbling
    into ash
and I feel no pain.
smoke twists round my heart
floating in darkness
mingles
    white dust
    the moon
giant lizards.

here inside
that traffic sound
could be the ocean.

when I open my eyes
I see all the things
our hands have made
and unmade.

                buildings with mirror faces
                and windows you can't open
                or close
                broken bottles
                kicked into dry weeds
                around parking meters
                shining like dinosaur eyes
                in the sun.
the sky is blue
it's always noon

I can see we're held together
with telephone wire
and postage stamps.
impossible to pretend no distance
between inside and outside
much less
inside and inside.

stretch out your arms
                try to trace blue rivers
                from source to finish.
if you can
you do better than
        I
                never could say
                where they begin or end
                where they meet as one.

TIGER YEAR

new moon,
        you lie
in shadow—
traveling over the face
of silent water

as planets circle in the gathering dark
like pale insects
around the opened throats of flowers.

see how the stars are blossoming
one by one:
as if merely to breathe.

they blossom for you,
defining your way
through the clear night air
with hands as pure and bright as clouds.

will you hurry to my season?
it is time:
you bring the light.

MEI-MEI BERSSENBRUGGE

Mei-Mei Berssenbrugge was born in Peking in 1947. She currently lives in New Mexico, where she works full time on her writing. Her books of poetry include *Fish Souls* (1971), *Summits Move with the Tide* (1974), and *Random Possession* (1979). In addition, she has published poetry in numerous anthologies and journals, including *Partisan Review*, *Yardbird Reader*, *Pequod*, and *New Mexico Magazine*.

GHOST

When the Indian steps
across old rock
and his spirit sheds form
and cleaves the earth
an instant
and he settles his dry hand
across our valley

his terror is decayed with age
he sighs to his brother
Aua, Igliluk Eskimo whose food
consisted
entirely of souls

the rocks
the bent oak trees
the cranes feeding in the river.

OLD MAN LET'S GO FISHING
IN THE YELLOW REEDS OF THE BAY

Our flat bottomed boat
glides through the reeds of the bay.

Seagulls fly up like huge raucous princes.
Ducks turn their bottoms up in the mire.

The litter of clamshells and horsecrab
on the sand proves them better fishermen,
but we fish the whole afternoon.
The sun on its own line pulls slowly down.
. Red tomatoes on our bait-can turn gold.

I've made drawings
of grass streaming in the wind,
and you, straw hat, full suspenders,
eyes lost in thick spectacles listening to birds.

I would draw you now
if my two dreaming hands
were not caught happily in yours.

CHRONICLE

I was born the year of the loon
in a great commotion. My mother—
who used to pack $500 cash
in the shoulders of her fur gambling coat,
who had always considered herself
the family's "First Son"—
took one look at me
and lit out again
for a vacation to Sumatra.
Her brother purchased my baby clothes;
I've seen them, little clown suits
of silk and color.

Each day
my Chinese grandmother bathed me
with elaboration in an iron tub;
amahs waiting in lines
with sterilized water and towels
clucked and smiled
and rushed about the tall stone room
in tiny slippers.

After my grandfather
accustomed himself

to this betrayal by First Son,
he would take me in his arms,
walk with me
by the plum trees, cherries, persimmons;
he showed me the stiff robes
of my ancestors and their drafty hall,
the long beards of his learned old friends,
and his crickets.

Grandfather talked to me, taught me.
. At two months, my mother tells me,
I could sniff for flowers,
stab my small hand upwards to moon.
Even today I get proud
when I remember
this all took place in Chinese.

ADDITIONAL READINGS

Anthologies

Asian Women. Berkeley, *Asian Women's Journal Workshop,* 1971. This book may be obtained through the Asian American Studies Center at UCLA. It includes essays on the history of Asian women in America, as well as some literature.

Chiang, Fay, et al., eds. *American and Foreign Born.* New York, Sunbury Poetry Magazine, issues 7 and 8, 1979. Poetry.

————. *The Ordinary Women.* New York, Ordinary Women, Inc., P.O. Box 664, Old Chelsea Station, New York, N.Y. 10011. Poetry.

Chin, Frank, et al., eds. *Aiiieeeee: An Anthology of Asian American Writers.* Garden City, N.Y., Doubleday, 1975. Originally published by Howard University Press. Includes selections by Diana Chang, Momoko Iko, Hisaye Yamamoto, and Wakako Yamauchi. There is a long introduction that covers historical background and presents the editors' definition of Asian American literature.

Faderman, Lillian, and Barbara Bradshaw, eds. *Speaking for Ourselves.* Glenview, Ill., Scott, Foresman, 1975. The Asian American section includes literature by Ferris Takahashi, Hisaye Yamamoto, Diana Chang, and Pam Koo.

Gee, Emma, ed. *Counterpoint.* Los Angeles, University of California Asian American Studies Center, 1976. A collection of contemporary essays, poems, and short stories by Asian Americans.

Hsu, Kai-yu, and Helen Palubinskas, eds. *Asian-American Authors.* Boston, Houghton Mifflin, 1972. Provides a brief historical overview for each of the groups included: Chinese American, Japanese American, and Filipino American. Contains selections by Jade Snow Wong, Virginia Lee, Diana Chang, and Hisaye Yamamoto.

Kopp, Janet and Karl, eds. *Southwest: A Contemporary Anthology.* Albuquerque, Red Earth Press, 1977. Includes Asian American women writers.

Liwanag—Literary and Graphic Expression by Filipinos in America. San Francisco, Liwanag Publications, 1975. Includes selections by Jessica Tarahata Hagedorn, Cyn Zarco, Emy Cachapero, Virginia Cerenio, and Joselyn Ignacio.

Mirikitani, Janice, ed. *Ayumi: The Japanese American Anthology.* San Francisco, The Japanese American Anthology Committee, 1979. Distributed by New Glide Publications.

————. *Third World Women.* San Francisco, Third World Communications Press, 1973. Literature by minority women.

————. *Time to Greez! Incantations from the Third World.* San Francisco, Glide Publications, 1975. Contains works by Janice Mirikitani, Brenda Paik Sunoo, Jessica Tarahata Hagedorn, Geraldine Kudaka, Cyn Zarco, Emily Cachapero, and Dolores Feria.

Reed, Ishmael and Al Young, eds. *Yardbird Lives.* New York, Grove Press, 1978. Includes works by Asian American Women.

Wand, David Hsin-Fu, ed. *Asian-American Heritage*. New York, Washington Square Press, 1974. A collection of stories, poems, essays, novel excerpts, and oral poetry with commentary for each section. Includes selections by Hisaye Yamamoto, Diana Chang, and Janice Mirikitani.

Journals and Periodicals

Amerasia Journal (Yale and UCLA)
Bridge Magazine (Basement Workshop, New York)
Greenfield Review, Vols. 3 (1974) and 4 (1975)
Journal of Ethnic Studies (Western Washington State College)
Rafu Shimpo (Los Angeles)
Yardbird Reader, Vols. 5 (1976) and 6 (1977)

Primary Sources

Ai. *Cruelty*. Boston, Houghton Mifflin, 1973. Poetry.
———. *Killing Floor*. Boston, Houghton Mifflin, 1979. Poetry.
Berssenbrugge, Mei-Mei. *Random Possession*. New York, I. Reed Books, 1979. Poetry.
———. *Summits Move with the Tide*. Greenfield, N.Y., Greenfield Review Press, 1974. Poetry.
Chang, Diana. *Eye to Eye*. New York, Harper & Row, 1974. Fiction.
———. *The Frontiers of Love*. New York, Random House, 1956. Fiction.
———. *The Only Game in Town*. New York, New American Library, 1963. Fiction.
———. *A Passion for Life*. New York, Random House, 1961. Fiction.
———. *A Perfect Love*. New York, Jove Books, 1978. Fiction.
———. *A Woman of Thirty*. New York, Random House, 1959. Fiction.
Chiang, Fay. *In the City of Contradictions*. New York, Sunbury Poetry Magazine, 1979. Poetry.
Far, Sui Sin. *Mrs. Spring Fragrance*. Chicago, A. C. McClury & Co., 1912.
Hagedorn, Jessica Tarahata. *Dangerous Music: The Poetry and Prose of Jessica Hagedorn*. San Francisco, Momo's Press, 1975.
Kingston, Maxine Hong. *The Woman Warrior*. New York, Alfred A. Knopf, 1977. Fiction.
Lee, Virginia. *The House That Tai Ming Built*. New York, Macmillan, 1963. Fiction.
Mirikitani, Janice. *Awake in the River*. San Francisco, Isthmus Press, 1978. Poetry.
Miyasaki, Gail. *Montage: An Ethnic History of Women in Hawaii*. Honolulu, University of Hawaii Press, 1977. The recording of women's history by women.

Okubo, Miné. *Citizen 13660*. New York, Columbia University Press, 1946. A collection of drawings and thoughts about World War II relocation camps.

Sone, Monica. *Nisei Daughter*. Boston, Little, Brown, 1953. Autobiographical novel.

Wong, Jade Snow. *Fifth Chinese Daughter*. New York, Harper & Row, 1945. Autobiography.

Wong, Nellie. *Dreams in Harrison Railroad Park.* Berkeley, Kelsey St. Press, 1977.

Yamada, Mitsuye. *Camp Notes and Other Poems*. San Francisco, Shameless Hussy Press, 1976.

APPENDICES

APPENDIX A

FOLKLORE AND LITERATURE

Folklore is the artistic process by which the collective traditions of a group are communicated, transformed, and integrated into a particular and unique perspective. As the creative expression of a community, folklore includes such concrete forms as rug designs, recipes, customs, and architectural forms, as well as the verbal forms of folktales, sayings, proverbs, ballads, and toasts. For folklore to exist, the group must exist and must be united by common experience and shared knowledge. A group may be defined by culture, region, social class, or any combination thereof, so that one might refer to the folklore of such groups as urban northern blacks, Appalachian whites, or Harvard lawyers. In each case, the particular forms of expression that evolve as traditions within the group yield insights into the life and spirit of that group.

Folklore events, whether they be Navaho coyote tales or hoodoo hexes, occur in a specific cultural context, and knowledge of that context is essential to our understanding of the forms of folklore. What is communicated by a folktale or a saying, for example, will often depend on the dynamic between the speaker and the audience. Tales are told, songs are sung, the dozens* are played according to the ritual imperatives of both tradition and the performance context. While the content of a tale may remain constant, the oral performance of the story will be determined by the audience and the moral, philosophical, and aesthetic needs to be fulfilled by the communication of tradition.

As a communication process, folklore is fertile ground for writers who seek to perpetuate the traditions of their group and to suggest new perspectives on timeless human concerns. Minority writers, in particular, draw substantially on the oral traditions of their cultures, perhaps because they are more intimately connected with their groups than "mainstream" writers and more intent on countering the effects of assimilation by asserting what is uniquely theirs. Whatever the reason, the importance of folklore and the oral tradition to minority literature is paramount. In black literature, for example,

> the folk ballad, the blues, the prayer, the sermon, the hoodoo curse, the "dozens" are basic structural and tonal reference points for Black poetry, reflective to militant. Black folk tales naturally work their way into short stories and sometimes novels. The Black folk sermon further influences Black political rhetoric. And there is an evolution in Black narratives from church testimonials to slave narratives to autobiographies and, in some cases, into novels.[1]

---

* A form of verbal exchange among blacks in which insults are traded back and forth. The "winner" usually comes up with the most imaginative remarks.

Native American authors often incorporate familiar figures from the oral tradition, such as Coyote, into their literature, or, in some instances, structure their poems around the repetitive rhythms of traditional prayers. *La Llorona* and the *corridos* are folkloric elements that have been transformed into literary devices in Chicano literature. Transformation is the key word, because, as Robert Hemenway states, "an author does not *use* folklore. Consciously or unconsciously, an author represents, adapts, or transforms phenomena which existed as folklore during a prior communication event. What one studies is folklore *and* literature; the location of the analysis is the interface between the two." [2]

That interface exists on many different levels, as the literature of the women in this anthology affirms. In the selections from *Mules and Men*, for example, Zora Neale Hurston transcribes examples of folklore she has recorded in southern black communities. At least, so it appears on first reading. A second glance reveals the power of folklore to affect behavior in groups, which is conveyed by Hurston's own intimate involvement in the rituals of hoodoo. Folklore becomes the means for her as an outsider to communicate with the group. This is Hurston's success as an anthropologist. She treats folklore not as artifact to be collected, catalogued, and shelved but rather as a focus for evolving creative expression. Folklore operates in another way in "The Revenge of Hannah Kemhuff" by Alice Walker. Here, the material has been transformed into an integral part of the plot. Hannah Kemhuff relies on the power of the hex against Mrs. Holley to relieve her of the burden of anger she has carried for so many years. Again, the message is the same. Folklore is a means of communicating shared experience and affecting behavior within the group.

The minority women writers included here clearly are acutely aware of the rich linguistic and thematic possibilities afforded their literature by folklore and the oral tradition. Understanding the relationship between folklore and literature can be enormously important to appreciating the complexity of their literature.

NOTES

1. Clyde Taylor, "Black Folk Spirit and the Shape of Black Literature," *Black World*, 21 (August 1972), 35.
2. Robert Hemenway, "Are You a Flying Lark or a Setting Dove," *Afro-American Literature: The Reconstruction of Instruction,* eds. Dexter Fisher and Robert Stepto (New York: Modern Language Association, 1978), p. 130.

1. The coyote is a universal trickster figure in Native American societies. He is also the enabler, opening up possibilities for human endeavors and interaction. How does this duality operate in "The Great Spirit Names the Animal People" by Mourning Dove, "Toe'osh: A Laguna Coyote Story" by Leslie Marmon Silko, and "Black-Coat Meets Coyote" by Judith Ivaloo Volborth? For additional readings, see Paul Radin, *The Trickster: A Study in American Indian Mythology* (New York: Philosophical Library, 1956); Barre Toelken, "The 'Pretty Languages' of Yellowman: Genre, Mode, and Texture in Navaho Coyote Narratives" in *Folklore Genres,* ed. Dan Ben-Amos (Austin: University of Texas Press, 1976); Lawrence Evers, "Further Survivals of Coyote," *Western Literature,* 10 (1975), 233–236; and Hamilton A. Tyler, *Pueblo Animals and Myths* (Norman: University of Oklahoma Press, 1975).

2. Compare the ways in which Maxine Hong Kingston in "No Name Woman" and Karen Tei Yamashita in "The Bath" structure their narratives around folk beliefs and traditions. What is the relationship between folklore and behavior in the two stories?

3. In "The Revenge of Hannah Kemhuff," how does Alice Walker transform the folklore of hexes described in the selections from Zora Neale Hurston's *Mules and Men* into an integral component of the narrative structure?

4. Proverbs and sayings are also part of the folklore of a group. Explain the meaning of the proverb in "The Street of the Cañon" by Josefina Niggli and describe its importance to the action of the story.

5. Compare and contrast the three variations on the folk legend of *La Llorona* in the Chicana section. What new aspects of character are revealed in each selection?

6. Though folklore generally refers to secular experiences as opposed to mythology, which also includes religious beliefs, creation stories belong to both folklore and mythology. In the American Indian section, there are two versions of the Navaho creation story of Changing Woman. What is the point of view in each version? Read "World View" and "The Origin of Man" in *Navaho Religion* by Gladys A. Reichard (Princeton: Princeton University Press, Bollingen Paperback Edition, 1974) and discuss the symbolism of Changing Woman. How does this creation story differ from the Judeo-Christian story in Genesis?

7. In "The Blues Roots of Contemporary Afro-American Poetry," Sherley Williams says, "Blues is essentially an oral form meant to be heard rather

than read. . . . Blues is viewed here as a verbal—as distinct from musical—genre which developed out of the statement (or call) and response patterns of collective work groups." How does Williams transform the blues into poetic devices in her poetry? Discuss rhythm, tone, and diction. Compare her use of the blues to that of Jessica Tarahata Hagedorn in "Sometimes You Look Like Lady Day." See Williams's essay in *Massachusetts Review,* 18, No. 3 (Autumn 1977), 542–554; see also Harry Oster, "The Blues as a Genre" in *Folklore Genres,* ed. Dan Ben-Amos (Austin: University of Texas, 1976), pp. 59–75.

8. In Mexico and Mexican-American communities, the *curandera* has traditionally been the folk doctor, combining folk wisdom with practical knowledge to effect cures. Fabiola Cabeza de Baca describes the role of the *curandera* in "The Women of New Mexico." What is the difference between her description and Estela Portillo Trambley's portrayal of the *curandera* in "The Burning"? Discuss the symbol of the *curandera* in Trambley's story.

9. The form of communication often reveals as much about a people as the content of their communication, particularly in the area of folklore and folk speech, where oral transmission is essential. Gayl Jones has said of her own writing, "I have a tendency to trust a lot of my oral influences more than my literary ones, with some exceptions. . . . Hearing has to be essential. You have to be able to hear other people's voices and you have to be able to hear your own voice." Discuss the voices that are "heard" in "Maggie of the Green Bottles" by Toni Cade Bambara and "Lucy" by Lucille Clifton. What elements of folk speech are represented? Consider the "dozens," toasts, and sermonic elements. See Jones's interview in *Massachusetts Review,* 18, No. 4 (Autumn 1977), 692–715. The quote appears on p. 694.

10. Using "No Name Woman" by Maxine Hong Kingston and "Pay the Criers" by Estela Portillo Trambley, discuss the relationship between folklore and literature. How does context determine what is communicated?

TOPICS FOR WRITING

1. Discuss the significance of context in the poems by Wendy Rose.

2. What is the role of the *curandera* in "The Advent of My Death" by Marcela Christine Lucero-Trujillo? What does her presence add to the poem?

3. Compare and contrast the symbol of the bear in "she-bear" by Nia Francisco, "Shaman/Bear" by Anita Endrezze-Danielson, and "Storyteller" by Leslie Marmon Silko.

4. Discuss the importance of ritual as a communication process, using "Marriage" by Helen Sekaquaptewa as an example.

5. Animal stories are universal in the folklore of cultures. Read several examples from *The Book of Negro Folklore* (Langston Hughes and Arna Bontemps, eds. New York: Dodd, Mead, 1959) and compare them to the coyote stories included here. What general characteristics can be ascribed to animal folktales and what do they communicate?

APPENDIX B

TEXTS AND CONTEXTS

Literary texts—whether they be poems, novels, personal narratives, or short stories—occur in a context that may be defined as the cultural, temporal, linguistic, and aesthetic landscape that informs the vision of a writer. To "contextualize" a given work of literature is to read it in terms of the relationships within the text among the imaginative, personal, historical, and/or symbolic dimensions, and, thereby, to discover the particular literary space the work inhabits.

At the most fundamental level, context refers to the time and place in which an author writes and includes social and historical conditions as well as cultural and literary influences. This is the generating context, the environment in which the creative process takes place. The literature generated may or may not directly reflect external conditions, but it is important to place authors within a historical framework, if only to understand how they might depart from the conventions of the period. The danger in relying solely on a sociohistorical approach to context is that extraliterary concerns may take precedence over the work of literature. For example, the conditions under which authors write, while yielding important insights into their motivations for writing and, perhaps, into the thematic and stylistic thrust of their work, do not substitute for the literature itself. To read a piece of literature exclusively in terms of its political significance or chronological place in literary history is to miss its linguistic complexity. Too often, minority literature has been read and evaluated on the basis of its political impact rather than for its intrinsic literary quality, which does an injustice to the literature.

Another dimension of context is performance. Under what conditions, for example, is a given story told or a poem recited, and what is the dynamic between the teller (or author) and the audience (or reader)? The performance context is particularly relevant to Native American literature because many of the contemporary literary forms are extensions of their oral counterparts, especially in the area of storytelling. As we've already seen in the introduction to American Indian women writers, there are many dimensions to the oral telling of a story—voice intonations, gestures, facial expressions, and verbal embellishments. What happens to these elements of performance when oral storytelling is transformed to a written mode? How does Leslie Marmon Silko, for example, make her readers "hear" her stories and participate in them? In what way does the oral tradition inform the poetry of Wendy Rose or Marnie Walsh? Or, in black literature, how does Sherley Williams render poetically a verbal equivalent of the sung blues? Has the performance context influenced the variations of *La Llorona* in Chicano literature? The dynamic between the performance of a text and its reception is central to many of the works included here.

Context may also include intertextuality, which is the way texts of literature relate to one another and extend the metaphors of culture. The relationship between Alice Walker's short story "The Revenge of Hannah Kemhuff" and Zora Neale Hurston's *Mules and Men* is a good example of how intertextuality creates context. Walker draws her folklore sources directly from Hurston, citing her indebtedness to Hurston in the dedication and within the story. In so doing, despite the thirty years that separate *Mules and Men* from "The Revenge," Walker places her story in the context of the black folk tradition, thereby celebrating the artistic qualities of folklore and affirming the complex relationship between black literature and its oral roots.

But she does more than this. She also shapes a context for demonstrating the force and energy of language. Ultimately, "The Revenge" is about the power of the word. It is verbal suggestion, the intimation of the curse, that brings about the demise of Mrs. Holley. Through a series of clever but direct verbal maneuvers by Tante Rosie's apprentice, Mrs. Holley is manipulated into a position of fear that becomes so severe she literally victimizes herself. If, as Robert Stepto maintains, the pregeneric myth underlying black literature is the quest for freedom and literacy, then Walker surely extends that tradition by giving a voice to the powerless and asserting the liberating possibilities within individual expression. By acknowledging her relationship to Hurston, Walker has placed herself within the black literary tradition that is central to an understanding of the story. Yet, a full appreciation of the unique qualities of Walker's angle of vision comes only from a careful reading of the text and an analysis of the linguistic relationships within the text. Ultimately, it is the literary text itself, through its linguistic and metaphorical structures, that reveals the context in which its meaning resonates.

SUGGESTIONS FOR DISCUSSION

1. Describe the performance context of the excerpt from *Then Badger Said This* by Elizabeth Cook-Lynn. What is the relationship in this piece between the performance context and the sociohistorical context?

2. In their interviews, Leslie Marmon Silko and Toni Morrison both discuss the importance of place in creating a context for their literature. What are their concepts of place, and how do they compare and/or differ?

3. The generating context is a subject of the essays by Alice Walker and Diana Chang; each discusses the various aspects of creating a work of literature. Compare and contrast their views on creativity. How would you define the generating context based on these two essays?

4. Examine the three versions of *La Llorona* in the Chicana section and discuss how each text creates the context in which the folktale is to be read. Which version do you think is the most "authentic"?

5. Elizabeth Sullivan and Helen Sekaquaptewa both place their selections within a sociohistorical framework. How do the pieces differ? Consider the interrelationship between objective description and personal interpretation of events. How does language reflect their points of view?

6. In her essay, Alice Walker talks about the importance of models to writers who seek to contextualize their work within traditions that have been established in the past. This is an important concept to many of the minority women writers here, and they look to their grandmothers and ancestors for inspiration in order to place their personal histories within a larger framework. Discuss "Obāchan" by Gail Miyasaki, "Lucy" by Lucille Clifton, and "Grandmother" by Paula Gunn Allen in terms of the traditions each represents. Consider narrative structure, point of view, and figurative language.

7. In "Zuma Chowt's Cave" by Opal Lee Popkes and "The Burning" by Estela Portillo Trambley, both the protagonists are outsiders. Compare and contrast the way in which the texts of each story create the context of alienation. What sociohistorical information do you need to understand the two stories?

8. In what way do you think the tone of "The Great Spirit Names the Animal People" by Mourning Dove would change if it were performed orally? How does writing change the content of the oral tradition?

9. One aspect of the dilemma of the Chicana writer, according to Marcela Christine Lucero-Trujillo, is that she cannot identify completely with the images of women portrayed by her culture's history. How does Sylvia Gonzales address this problem in "Chicana Evolution"? Discuss the images of women that emerge from her poem.

10. Discuss how Ntozake Shange, Sherley Williams, Nia Francisco, and Inés Hernandez Tovar use language to "contextualize" the subjects of their poetry.

TOPICS FOR WRITING

1. It has been said that a characteristic of Asian American literature is the tension between speech and "Demon Silence." Discuss this tension in "The Boatmen on Toneh River" by Wakako Yamauchi. How does her use of language generate an aura of death?

2. Art inspires the imagery in the two poems entitled "Still Life" by Anita Endrezze-Danielson and Diana Chang. Compare the metaphorical relationship between art and life in each poem. What is the real subject of each?

3. How does the exterior world reflect the interior landscape of the characters in "Storyteller" by Leslie Marmon Silko?

4. Discuss the different uses of language to create images of sexuality in the poetry of Ai and in "Intimate Friends" by Diana Chang.

5. What is the relationship between ethnicity and context?

APPENDIX C

STORYTELLING AND NARRATIVES

Of storytelling, Gayl Jones says:

> When you tell a story, you automatically talk about traditions, but they're never separate from the people, the human implications. You're talking about language, you're talking about politics and morality and economics and culture, and you never have to come out and say you're talking about these things—you don't have to isolate them and therefore freeze them—but you're still talking about them. You're talking about all your connections as a human being.[1]

Storytelling *is* the art of making connections, of establishing relationships with people and the creative process, with nature, feelings, and the self, with one's heritage and progeny. Storytelling generates continuity, linking the past to the future and "contextualizing" individual histories within the framework of tradition. Storytelling may be oral or written. It may be a means of recording history for future generations, or it may be a fictional interpretation of experience. It is a narrative process of selection that reveals much about the values of the storyteller and the cultural landscape he or she inhabits.

Leslie Marmon Silko has said that storytelling is a natural resource for Indians because it is so much a part of the individual's experience from infancy to death. This is true for any culture whose existence is firmly rooted in a vital oral tradition. Whether the form is a folktale, autobiography, or imaginative narrative, the urge to narrate events and to transform the phenomena of the universe into metaphors for existence is a timeless art. That minority women especially identify with this narrative urge is evident in their commitment to perpetuate and revitalize their own cultural histories and traditions. "The chain of culture is the chain of women linking the past with the future" says the *Iroquois Great Law of Peace,* and this seems to characterize the role that minority women as mothers and as writers continue to fulfill. They have found in the narrative process the means of expressing and authenticating their individual and collective experience.

The purpose of this appendix is to raise certain questions about the narrative process of storytelling. For example, what is the relationship between history and storytelling? What does the form of a story tell us about the way history is recorded? How does the oral tradition influence the process of storytelling? Are contemporary stories written versions of their oral counterparts? What is the point of view of the narrator, and how does point of view influence the narrative flow of the action? If the narrator of a story is unspecified, is it possible to tell if it is female? Is there a feminine point of view? Similarly, is there a minority feminine voice? If storytelling is the "art of making connections," what are the connections that dominate the interest of minority women writers? What does storytelling communicate about tradition and culture? And, finally, what is the dialectic between narrative and language?

The narratives and stories included in this volume range from objective descriptions of tribal ceremonies to imaginative fiction. What is common is that each occurs in a context and can be analyzed in the following terms: (1) The conflict or tension that emerges from the interplay of two opposing forces in the narrative action: the protagonist versus the antagonist, the individual versus nature or society, or the person in conflict with the self. Conflict may also be expressed in terms of ideas such as reality versus illusion, or alienation versus conformity. It is through conflict that authors establish their area of focus in the story and, at the same time, create viable motivation for their characters. (2) Point of view: that is, who is telling the story, to whom, and for what? What is the relationship of the author to the narrator and to the material? (3) Narrative action or sequence of events: that is, what happens and what significance is conveyed by the flow of events? What values does the author communicate by presenting her story in a given way?

The following suggestions for discussion and topics for writing explore in more specific ways the art of storytelling.

NOTE

1. "Gayl Jones: An Interview," *Massachusetts Review,* 18, No. 4 (Autumn 1977), 693.

SUGGESTIONS FOR DISCUSSION

1. Discuss the difference between Helen Sekaquaptewa's recounting of the Hopi marriage ceremony and Elizabeth Sullivan's memory of the Legend of the Trail of Tears. What is the point of view in each and how does that influence the narrative action? What is the conflict in each piece?

2. Yvonne has said that "prose writers are not the only storytellers." Her two poems included here are from a much longer narrative poem on the black woman. What is the "story" that she tells? What are the relationships she explores in the piece?

3. The following stories are told from the point of view of the child: "Legend of the Trail of Tears" by Elizabeth Sullivan, "Maggie of the Green Bottles" by Toni Cade Bambara, and "Las Dos Hermanas" by Rosalie Otero Peralta. Compare and contrast the impact of the point of view in each story. Consider the relationship between point of view and irony, understatement, and paradox. Are these "growing up" stories?

4. Storytelling is a way of recording history and passing it on from one generation to the next. Analyze the narratives of Elizabeth Cook-Lynn, Mourning Dove, Zora Neale Hurston, and Lucille Clifton and discuss the relationship between form and content. That is, what kind of history is each author recording? How does context influence the narrative? Who is the audience?

5. Define the conflict in "Seventeen Syllables" by Hisaye Yamamoto and "Intimate Friends" by Diana Chang. What establishes the feminine voice in each selection? Is the point of view in each Asian American?

6. A common theme in the literature of minority women is the conflict of opposing values or ways of life. This may take the form of racial tension (white versus black), the individual caught between two worlds, or traditions versus a changing world. Discuss the conflict in "Zuma Chowt's Cave" by Opal Lee Popkes, "Brooklyn" by Paule Marshall, and "Pay the Criers" by Estela Portillo Trambley. How is the conflict resolved in each story? What is communicated by that resolution?

7. Compare and contrast the sense of place (landscape) in "Storyteller" by Leslie Marmon Silko and "1921" by Toni Morrison. Discuss the symbolism of the geography and how it affects the flow of the action in each story. What image of the woman emerges from each piece?

8. Kinship is another common theme in the literature of minority women. Kinship connects the individual to her history and illuminates the values and traditions by which she lives. Discuss the values communicated by the kinship system in "No Name Woman" by Maxine Hong Kingston, "Lucy" by Lucille Clifton, and "1921" by Toni Morrison.

9. Discuss the thematic and cultural implications of naming and names in "No Name Woman" by Maxine Hong Kingston, "The Changing Woman Story" by Kay Bennett, and "The Bath" by Karen Tei Yamashita.

10. Leslie Marmon Silko has said that a good story has to be accessible. What makes a story accessible?

1. Discuss the reality of illusion in "Doby's Gone" by Ann Petry.

2. Compare and contrast the mother-child relationship in "Gallup, New Mexico—Indian Capital of the World" by Leslie Marmon Silko and "Recuerdo" by Guadalupe Valdés Fallis. What is the point of view in each story?

3. If storytelling generates the continuity of tradition within the community, what are the traditions passed on in "The Street of the Cañon" by Josefina Niggli and "Las Vegas Charley" by Hisaye Yamamoto?

4. Discuss the function of humor in "Maggie of the Green Bottles" by Toni Cade Bambara and "The Bath" by Karen Tei Yamashita. How does humor link us to the past?

5. Mourning Dove and Zora Neale Hurston both record the folklore of their cultures. Compare and contrast the two narrative styles. What is the point of view in each, and how does it determine the way the narrative unfolds?

APPENDIX D

POETRY

I am the eye
without a lid
looking at you.

Marnie Walsh

The poet is the keen observer of life who renders, through rhythmic and coded language, the essence of human experience, eliciting from the reader an intense emotional recognition of the truth of what has been said. A complex verbal art, poetry has been defined variously as "musical thought," "a record of the best and happiest moments of the best and happiest minds," and "the rhythmic, inevitably narrative, movement from an overclothed blindness to a naked vision." [1] While an exact definition of poetry may elude us, poetry itself *is* an exact and imaginative linguistic art form whose components of imagery, diction, syntax, rhythm, and tone communicate a heightened perception of reality.

All language is a type of code that stands for the object or idea described, but poetry particularly challenges our abilities to decode because it is language compressed into an intricate network of images, symbols, and metaphors. *Imagery* may be defined as the figurative language of a poem. On the most basic level, "an image is any concrete representation of a sense impression or an idea." [2] An image may conjure up a visual picture of something, such as these lines from "Watching Crow, Looking South Towards the Manzano Mountains" by Joy Harjo:

crow floats in winter sun
a black sliver
in a white ocean of sky

Images may also appeal to our senses of touch, smell, hearing, and taste, as well as to our feelings. On a more complex level, images operate by comparison and analogy. Similes, for example, explicitly state the relationship between two objects, as in "My hair is springy like the forest grasses." In metaphors, on the other hand, the comparison is implied, as in "rooming houses are old women." By imaginatively comparing one object to another, poets share with us their acute powers of observation, stripping away the clichés of conventional verbal expression to offer fresh perspectives on experience and to intensify our capacity for emotional response.

Images may be analyzed in terms of the patterns or clusters they form in the poem that reveal the various levels of meaning. They are also part of the poet's *diction,* or overall choice of words. We all vary our language according to the situation that we are in; for example, the language we use for a job interview will be different from a conversation with a friend. It is the same with poetry, and poets may employ formal, informal, or colloquial diction depending on their subject. Analyzing a poem's diction is one way to see how well the poem "works." It is also a means of studying the linguistic innovations of poets, which becomes particularly pertinent in reading the poetry of minority women, because images and vocabulary are central to understanding their particular cultural metaphors and symbols. A great deal of poetry by Chicanas, for example, is bilingual. By juxtaposing Spanish with English, Chicana poets create emphasis and generate new poetic rhythms, increasing, at the same time, the thematic resonances of their poetry. In the following lines from "Heritage," Lorna Dee Cervantes skillfully interposes Spanish with English:

> But Mexico gags
> "ESPUTA"
> on this bland pochaseed.

"Esputa" is a resounding word that carries the weight of repugnance more fully than its English equivalent of "spit." It can be elongated vocally—ES PU TA—to sound almost like the spray of spittle. But in emphasizing the word, another meaning is revealed. *Es puta* means "she is a prostitute." The narrator of the poem feels that she is a "compromised" woman, caught between two cultures, treated like a *tonta* (fool) because she cannot participate fully in either. The interpolation of Spanish in this poem lends it a depth and richness that authenticates the author's experience and reflects a uniquely Chicana diction.

In black poetry, the blues poem exemplifies one aspect of a black poetic diction. In fact, the blues poem is a new genre within poetry that has come into the language through the black oral tradition. In the following excerpts from "Any Woman's Blues" by Sherley Williams, the choice of words constitutes a personal dialect of suffering:

> Soft lamp shinin
>   and me alone in the night.
> Soft lamp is shinin
>   and me alone in the night.
> Can't take no one beside me
>   need mo'n jest some man to set me right.
>   . . . .
> These is old blues
>   and I sing em like any woman do.
> These the old blues
>   and I sing em, sing em, sing em. Just like any woman do.
> My life ain't done yet.
>   Naw. My song ain't through.

While the informal diction is appropriate to convey the narrator's voice, what makes this a blues poem is the *syntax*, "the way in which the phrases, sentences and larger units of a poem are organized grammatically. By defining the relationship of statement and images, syntax helps to underline the meanings in a poem and to provide emphasis." [3] The "soft lamp shinin" punctuates the woman's loneliness by its contrast to the enveloping blackness of the night. But besides the image, there is the repetition of the lines that sets up the throb of feeling. By varying the same line with a word or phrase, Williams imitates the improvisatory nature of the sung blues, creating the overall sensation of a mournful lyric.

We can visually "hear" the sounds in "Any Woman's Blues," but to truly experience its mood, we should read the poem aloud. All poetry, in fact, should be read aloud and explored for emphasis, rhythm, rhyme, and *tone*. Tone refers to the attitude of the poem's narrator to the subject matter; it also includes the general mood of the poem, which may range from playful to serious, satirical to bitter, or joyful to melancholy. Another dimension of tone is the musical quality of the words in combination with each other, which deepens the sense of the poem in the same way that color adds depth to a drawing. While "tone coloration" is probably easier to feel than to analyze verbally, it is the quality that links sound with sense, yielding the "meaning" of a poem.

The poetry of minority women ranges from predominantly oral modes to metaphysical meditations. Its forms include poetic narratives, sonnets, elegies, ballads, blues, lyrics, and traditional prayers. And its subjects run the gamut from nostalgic reminiscences of the past to social protest. Firmly rooted in the oral tradition of their culture, minority women have transformed the voices and sounds of their culture into a linguistically rich and innovative poetry.

NOTES

1. Carlyle, Shelley, and Dylan Thomas, respectively, are the authors of the definitions of poetry, which are taken from William Flint Thrall and Addison Hibbard, *A Handbook to Literature,* revised and enlarged by C. Hugh Holman (New York: Odyssey Press, 1960), pp. 365–366.
2. Frank Brady and Martin Price, *Poetry—Past and Present* (New York: Harcourt Brace Jovanovich, 1974), p. 5. This volume provides an excellent introduction to the study of poetry.
3. Ibid., p. 12.

1. What makes "Sometimes You Look Like Lady Day" by Jessica Tarahata Hagedorn and "i shoulda told you" by Geraldine Kudaka blues poems? Compare them to "Any Woman's Blues" by Sherley Williams in terms of diction and syntax. See Sherley Williams, "The Blues Roots of Contemporary Afro-American Poetry," *Massachusetts Review,* 18, No. 3 (Autumn 1977), 542–554, for background material.

2. What is the effect of dialect in "cypress-sassafras" by Ntozake Shange and "Aunt Martha: Severance Pay" by Yvonne?

3. Analyze the diction of May Miller's poems and compare them to "What shall I give my children?" by Gwendolyn Brooks. Is the diction appropriate to the subject? Are these "universal" poems?

4. Nature imagery is predominant in the poetry of Leslie Marmon Silko and Nia Francisco. Identify the images and discuss their relationship to the theme of each poem.

5. Discuss the relationship between form and content in Diana Chang's poetry. What is the influence of art on her work? Compare "Still Life" and "What Matisse is After" to "Upon Seeing an Etching" by Helen Aoki Kaneko and "Still Life" by Anita Endrezze-Danielson.

6. Wendy Rose, Marnie Walsh, June Jordan, Nikki Giovanni, Ana Castillo, and Janice Mirikitani could all be called "protest poets." What are they protesting against? Do you see any similarities among the poets. Discuss the appropriateness of their choice of imagery to the subjects of their individual poems.

7. Carmen Tafolla and Inés Hernandez Tovar both write bilingual poetry. Compare and contrast the effectiveness of the combination of Spanish and English. Do you think the same meaning could be communicated by poems all in English or all in Spanish? Consider the four poems by Margarita Cota-Cárdenas in your discussion. (The Spanish versions are translations of the English.)

8. Compare and contrast the images of women in the following poems: "Keeping Hair" by Ramona C. Wilson, "Vickie Loans-Arrow 1972" by Marnie Walsh, "Leap in the Dark" by Roberta Hill, "Grandmother" by Paula Gunn Allen, "I Am a Black Woman," by Mari Evans, "If you saw a Negro lady" by June Jordan, "Phenomenal Woman" by Maya Angelou, "Rooming houses are old women" by Audre Lorde, "Women" by Alice

Walker, and "My Mother, Who Came from China, Where She Never Saw Snow" by Laureen Mar. Does a feminine poetic diction emerge?

9. Describe the tone of the following poems on mother-child relationships: "Where Iguanas Still Live" by Colleen McElroy, "Aaron Nicholas, Almost Ten" by Janet Campbell, "What shall I give my children?" by Gwendolyn Brooks, and "Sing with Your Body" by Janice Mirikitani. What attitude does the narrator take toward her subject?

10. Are the following poems love poems? Why or why not? "Are You Still There" by Joy Harjo, "Making Adjustments" by Anita Endrezze-Danielson, "the old-marrieds" by Gwendolyn Brooks, "Dancing with the Fifth Horseman" by Colleen McElroy, "Our Tongue Was Nahuatl" by Ana Castillo, "Twenty-Year Marriage" by Ai, and "Old Man Let's Go Fishing in the Yellow Reeds of the Bay" by Mei-Mei Berssenbrugge.

TOPICS FOR WRITING

1. Analyze "Moonshot: 1969" by Paula Gunn Allen and discuss what the moon means to "white" society and to Native American society.

2. "Paperweight" by Audre Lorde, "Poets/Poems" by Marnie Walsh, and "On Writing Asian-American Poetry" by Geraldine Kudaka all address the subject of what it means to be a writer. Compare and contrast the tone and the theme of the three poems.

3. Death is the subject of "The Advent of My Death" by Marcela Christine Lucero-Trujillo, "Burial" by Alice Walker, and "Death Is Not Master" by May Miller. Discuss the effectiveness of the diction in each poem. What is the attitude of the narrator to the subject in each?

4. Compare the two narrative poems about Coyote by Leslie Marmon Silko and Judith Ivaloo Volborth in terms of imagery, tone, and theme.

5. What are the "voices and sounds" of culture captured in "cypress-sassafras" by Ntozake Shange and "Para Teresa" by Inés Hernandez Tovar?

ABOUT DEXTER FISHER

Dexter Fisher serves on the staff of the Modern Language Association as director of English Programs and director of the Association of Departments of English (ADE), an organization for college and university English chairmen. In this position, she edits the quarterly *ADE Bulletin* and directs the meetings and conferences, publications, and information services of ADE, as well as the various projects, studies, and surveys that fall under English programs. Fisher received her B.A. and M.A. from San Diego State University and her Ph.D. from the Graduate Center of the City University of New York. She has taught English at San Diego State University and at Hostos Community College (CUNY), where she was director of Freshman English from 1970 to 1974. During 1974–1977, she was MIA program coordinator for an NEH grant to develop a national program of seminars and conferences designed to encourage the study and teaching of minority literature. Fisher is the editor of *Minority Language and Literature: Retrospective and Perspective* (New York: Modern Language Association, 1977) and co-editor, with Robert B. Stepto, of *Afro-American Literature: The Reconstruction of Instruction* (New York: Modern Language Association, 1979). In addition, she has published numerous articles on literary and professional topics.

3626